PSYCHOBIOLOGY OF PHYSICAL ACTIVITY

Edmund O. Acevedo, PhD, FACSM
University of Mississippi

Panteleimon Ekkekakis, PhD, FACSM
Iowa State University

EDITORS

Human Kinetics

Library of Congress Cataloging-in-Publication Data

Psychobiology of physical activity / [edited by] Edmund O. Acevedo, Panteleimon Ekkekakis.
    p.; cm.
  Includes bibliographical references and index.
  ISBN 0-7360-5536-3 (hard cover)
  1. Exercise--Physiological aspects. 2. Exercise--Psychological aspects. 3. Sports--Physiological aspects. 4. Sports--Psychological aspects. 5. Cognitive psychology. 6. Psychobiology.

  [DNLM: 1. Motor Activity. 2. Brain--physiology. 3. Exercise. WE 103 P974 2006] I. Acevedo, Edmund O. II. Ekkekakis, Panteleimon, 1968-

  QP301.P79 2006
  612'.044--dc22

                              2005024460

  ISBN-10: 0-7360-5536-3
  ISBN-13: 978-0-7360-5536-9

The Web addresses cited in this text were current as of July 1, 2005, unless otherwise noted.

Acquisitions Editor: Michael S. Bahrke, PhD; **Developmental Editor:** Judy Park; **Assistant Editors:** Kim Thoren, Sandra Merz Bott, and Kevin Matz; **Copyeditor:** Joyce Sexton; **Proofreader:** Anne Rogers; **Indexer:** Bobbi Swanson; **Permission Manager:** Carly Breeding; **Graphic Designer:** Fred Starbird; **Graphic Artist:** Dawn Sills; **Photo Manager:** Sarah Ritz; **Cover Designer:** Keri Evans; **Art Manager:** Kelly Hendren; **Illustrator:** Mic Greenberg; **Printer:** Sheridan Books

Printed in the United States of America   10 9 8 7 6 5 4 3 2 1

Human Kinetics
Web site: www.HumanKinetics.com

United States: Human Kinetics
P.O. Box 5076
Champaign, IL 61825-5076
800-747-4457
e-mail: humank@hkusa.com

Canada: Human Kinetics
475 Devonshire Road Unit 100
Windsor, ON N8Y 2L5
800-465-7301 (in Canada only)
e-mail: orders@hkcanada.com

Europe: Human Kinetics
107 Bradford Road
Stanningley
Leeds LS28 6AT, United Kingdom
+44 (0) 113 255 5665
e-mail: hk@hkeurope.com

Australia: Human Kinetics
57A Price Avenue
Lower Mitcham, South Australia 5062
08 8277 1555
e-mail: liaw@hkaustralia.com

New Zealand: Human Kinetics
Division of Sports Distributors NZ Ltd.
P.O. Box 300 226 Albany
North Shore City
Auckland
0064 9 448 1207
e-mail: info@humankinetics.co.nz

Contents

CHAPTER 7 Affective Responses to Acute Exercise: Toward a Psychobiological Dose–Response Model 91

Panteleimon Ekkekakis   •   Edmund O. Acevedo

CHAPTER 8 Physical Activity, Affect, and Electroencephalogram Studies 111

Steven J. Petruzzello   •   Panteleimon Ekkekakis   •   Eric E. Hall

CHAPTER 9 Physical Activity and Neurotransmitter Release . . 129

Romain Meeusen

Contributors

Edmund O. Acevedo, PhD

Department of Health, Exercise Science and Recreation Management
University of Mississippi
University, Mississippi, USA

Panteleimon Ekkekakis, PhD, FACSM, Editor

Department of Health and Human Performance
Iowa State University
Ames, Iowa, USA

Stephen H. Boutcher, PhD

School of Medical Sciences
University of New South Wales
Sydney, Australia

Michel Cabanac, MD

Department of Anatomy and Physiology
Laval University
Québec, Canada

David Collins, PhD

United Kingdom Athletics
Solihull, West Midlands, England, United Kingdom

Dane B. Cook, PhD

Department of Kinesiology
University of Wisconsin-Madison
Madison, Wisconsin, USA

A.D. (Bud) Craig, PhD

Atkinson Pain Research Laboratory
Barrow Neurological Institute
Phoenix, Arizona, USA

Eric E. Hall, PhD

Department of Health and Human Performance
Elon University
Elon, North Carolina, USA

Mark Hamer, PhD

Department of Epidemiology and Public Health
University College London
London, England, United Kingdom

Gregory A. Hand, PhD, MPH

Department of Exercise Science
University of South Carolina
Columbia, South Carolina, USA

Bradley D. Hatfield, PhD

Department of Kinesiology
University of Maryland
College Park, Maryland, USA

Amy J. Haufler, PhD

Department of Kinesiology
University of Maryland
College Park, Maryland, USA

Charles H. Hillman, PhD

Department of Kinesiology and Community Health
University of Illinois at Urbana-Champaign
Urbana, Illinois, USA

Paul S. Holmes, PhD

Department of Exercise and Sport Science
Manchester Metropolitan University
Alsager, Stoke-on-Trent, England, United Kingdom

Suzi Hong, PhD

Department of Psychiatry and Behavioral
Medicine
University of California San Diego
San Diego, California, USA

Arthur F. Kramer, PhD

Beckman Institute for Advanced Science and
Technology
University of Illinois at Urbana-Champaign
Urbana, Illinois, USA

Alan McPherson, PhD

Department of Physical Education, Sport and
Leisure Studies
University of Edinburgh
Edinburgh, Scotland, United Kingdom

Romain Meeusen, PhD

Department of Human Physiology and Sport
Medicine
Vrije Universiteit Brussel
Brussels, Belgium

Paul J. Mills, PhD

Department of Psychiatry and Behavioral
Medicine
University of California San Diego
San Diego, California, USA

Steven J. Petruzzello, PhD

Department of Kinesiology and Community
Health
University of Illinois at Urbana-Champaign
Urbana, Illinois, USA

Kenneth D. Phillips, PhD, RN

Center for Health Promotion and Risk
Reduction in Special Populations
University of South Carolina
Columbia, South Carolina, USA

Mark S. Sothmann, PhD

School of Health and Rehabilitation Sciences
Indiana University
Indianapolis, Indiana, USA

Thomas W. Spalding, PhD

Department of Kinesiology and Health
Promotion
California State Polytechnic University
Pomona, California, USA

Henriette van Praag, PhD

Laboratory of Genetics
The Salk Institute for Biological Studies
La Jolla, California, USA

Jon W. Williamson, PhD

College of Education
University of North Texas
Denton, Texas, USA

Marlene A. Wilson, PhD

University of South Carolina School of
Medicine
Columbia, South Carolina, USA

Preface

Physical activity inherently involves the body. However, the dominant theoretical paradigms within exercise and sport psychology, having been adopted primarily from cognitive and social psychology, typically give minimal attention to the body as a physical and biological entity. This constitutes a paradoxical phenomenon that impedes the advancement of knowledge within the fields of exercise and sport psychology. It is clear that an adequate understanding of physical activity cannot emerge if the scope of the investigation is limited to cognitive and social factors and the role of the physical body is dismissed. Recognizing the paradox and its disruptive impact, numerous authors over the years have called for an integrative analysis of behavior in exercise and sport settings (see chapter 1 in this volume). However, until now, such calls have not had the paradigm-shifting effect that those authors had hoped. It is reasonable to suggest that, at least to some extent, this might have been due to a failure to adequately educate researchers in the intricacies of the integrative psychobiologic approach. Remarkably, the scientific literature did not contain even a single volume encapsulating the significant contributions that psychobiological methods of inquiry had made to the study of behavior within the domain of physical activity.

The present volume, the first of its kind, fills this void. In 17 chapters, a group of leading scholars from five countries (United States, Canada, United Kingdom, Belgium, Australia) provide state-of-the-art reviews on a broad range of topics pertaining to health and performance. In each case, they illustrate not only the significant advances that have already been made but also the tremendous potential of the psychobiological approach. The hope of the editors is that this volume will help educate and motivate a new generation of researchers and, in turn, this human capital will help shape the future of the *psychobiology of physical activity*.

—The Editors

Acknowledgments

This volume would not have been possible without the commitment, time, and effort of the contributing authors. We thank each of you, with deep appreciation, for the excellent work that you have done. Your support has made possible our effort to foster the integrative study of the psychobiology of physical activity.

E.O.A. and P.E.

To my wife, Tracy, for her constant support and understanding, and to my children, Elena and Eddie. They are my inspiration.

E.O.A.

To the most important people in my life, George, Marietta, Liza, and my dear Aurelie, for enabling me to continue searching for my Ithaca.

P.E.

I

Introduction

This part of the book contains three chapters. The first chapter, co-authored by the editors, Ed Acevedo and Panteleimon Ekkekakis, serves as the introduction to the book, as well as a synopsis of the history of psychobiological inquiry within the fields of exercise and sport psychology, including both its successes and failures. The two subsequent chapters are unique in the scientific literature and provide the foundation for the rest of this book. Chapter 2 by Bud Craig describes, for the first time in a comprehensive manner, the path that exercise-induced peripheral physiological stimuli follow as they ascend the levels of the neuraxis, from the level of the primary afferent neurons to the cortex. Chapter 3 by Jon Williamson reviews, also for the first time, a series of human brain imaging studies that provide insights about the brain areas that are activated in response to exercise and exercise-related stimuli. Each chapter answers the question of "what happens" in the brain during exercise but does so from a different level of analysis. Chapter 2 focuses on animal research using the tools of basic neuroscience. Chapter 3 focuses on human research using brain-imaging technology. Together, the two chapters clearly illustrate the wealth of information that is currently available on this topic and shed the myth of the brain as a "black box," the workings of which in response to exercise are beyond our understanding.

To fully appreciate the contributions in these two foundational chapters, readers should have a fairly good grasp of the neuroanatomy and neurophysiology of interoception, the perception of the physiological condition of the body (Adám, 1998; Cameron, 2002). This includes (a) the types and threshold properties of the primary afferent neurons involved in detecting peripheral mechanical and chemical stimuli produced by exercise, such as muscle contractions or drops in pH (Belmonte & Cervero, 1996); (b) the spinal pathways that transmit the interoceptive information from the periphery to the brain (Willis & Coggeshall, 1991); (c) lower brainstem termination sites of the spinal projections (Blessing, 1997); (d) limbic (e.g., amygdala, hypothalamus) and thalamic areas involved in autonomic regulation and affective responding (Gloor, 1997; Lowey & Spyer, 1990); and (e) higher cortical processing areas, such as the insula, cingulate, somatosensory, and frontal cortices (Besson, Guilbaud, & Ollat, 1995; Nelson, 2001). A neuroanatomy text (e.g., Paxinos & Mai, 2003) with high-resolution images will also be a good companion, not only for these chapters but also for the remainder of this book. Some understanding of neurotransmitter function and neuropharmacology (Cooper, Bloom, & Roth, 2003; Feldman, Meyer, & Quenzer, 1997) would also be desirable. Finally, for readers interested in the technical aspects of the investigative techniques upon which the research described in these chapters is based, reference texts on contemporary methods of neuroscience (Windhorst & Johansson, 1999) and neuroimaging (Toga & Mazziotta, 2002) would be necessary.

Suggested Background Readings

Adám, G. (1998). *Visceral perception: Understanding internal cognition.* New York: Plenum Press.

Belmonte, C., & Cervero, F. (Eds.) (1996). *Neurobiology of nociceptors.* New York: Oxford University Press.

Besson, J.M., Guilbaud, G., & Ollat, H. (Eds.) (1995). *Forebrain areas involved in pain processing.* Paris: John Libbey Eurotext.

Blessing, W.W. (1997). *The lower brainstem and bodily homeostasis.* New York: Oxford University Press.

Cameron, A.G. (2002). *Visceral sensory neuroscience: Interoception.* New York: Oxford University Press.

Cooper, J.R., Bloom, F.E., & Roth, R.H. (2003). *The biochemical basis of neuropharmacology* (8th ed.). New York: Oxford University Press.

Feldman, R.S., Meyer, J.S., & Quenzer, L.F. (1997). *Principles of neuropsychopharmacology.* Sunderland, MA: Sinauer Associates.

Gloor, P. (1997). *The temporal lobe and limbic system.* New York: Oxford University Press.

Lowey, A.D., & Spyer, K.M. (Eds.) (1990). *Central regulation of autonomic functions.* New York: Oxford University Press.

Nelson, R.J. (Ed.) (2001). *The somatosensory system: Deciphering the brain's own body image.* Boca Raton, FL: CRC Press.

Paxinos, G., & Mai, J.K. (2003). *The human nervous system* (2nd ed.). San Diego: Elsevier Science.

Toga, A.W., & Mazziotta, J.C. (2002). *Brain mapping: The methods* (2nd ed.). San Diego: Academic Press.

Willis, W.D., & Coggeshall, R.E. (1991). *Sensory mechanisms of the spinal cord* (2nd ed.). New York: Plenum Press.

Windhorst, U., & Johansson, H. (1999). *Modern techniques in neuroscience research.* New York: Springer-Verlag.

Psychobiology of Physical Activity: Integration at Last!

Edmund O. Acevedo, PhD

Panteleimon Ekkekakis, PhD, FACSM, Editor

Psychobiology is defined here as the integrative study of behavior from the social, cognitive, and biological levels of analysis. This is a broad scientific field that encompasses psychophysiology, psychoneuroendocrinology, psychoneuroimmunology, physiological psychology, behavioral genetics, and several areas of neuroscience.

The struggle for integration between mind-focused and body-focused approaches within all branches of psychology has been long and arduous. It could be argued that, when examined from a historical perspective, the integrative psychobiological approach has enjoyed modest popularity within psychology and exercise science and has not yet lived up to its full potential for informational yield. This appears to be the result of an interesting paradox, with considerably more researchers seemingly willing to extol the wondrous advantages of integrative research than to undertake truly integrative and systematic psychobiological research.

In his presidential address, delivered during the first meeting of the Society for Psychophysiological Research on September 5, 1961, and later published in the inaugural issue of the journal *Psychophysiology,* Chester Darrow (1964) acknowledged that psychophysiology had not had the impact that the psychophysiologists themselves had envisioned. Nevertheless, he expressed the hope that, one day, "psychophysiology will be able to define so-called 'mental mechanisms' in psychoneurophysiological terms" (p. 7). He continued by stating that "then no longer as in decades past, will indulgent 'pure' psychologists supercil-iously inquire 'what has neurology or physiology revealed of importance regarding the working of the mind?'" (p. 7). In the same issue and along similar lines, Albert Ax (1964) admitted that "few of the physiological referents for psychological concepts are known in detail" (p. 9). Expressing a similar sentiment a few years later, in his presidential address to the American Psychosomatic Society on March 21, 1970, John Mason (1970) stated that "realistically, we must face the fact that the psychosomatic approach has not as yet had the sweeping, revolutionary impact on medicine of which it appears capable" (p. 427).

In contrast to these earlier views, however, contemporary assessments seem to reflect the substantial progress that has taken place in the interim. Taking stock of the achievements of modern psychophysiology, for example, Cacioppo, Tassinary, and Berntson (2000) noted that, although "there are undoubtedly psychological, social, and cultural phenomena whose secrets are not yet amenable to physiological analyses" (p. 4), "psychophysiological research has provided insights into almost every facet of human nature" (p. 5).

Arguably, progress also has been made in the integrative psychobiological study of human functioning within the contexts of exercise and sport. In the first comprehensive proposal for a psychophysiological orientation in sport psychology, Hatfield and Landers (1983) noted that "very few problem areas within sport and motor behavior have seen . . . psychophysiological approaches systematically applied" (p. 243). More than a decade later, Dishman (1994) similarly noted that "there has been very little use of biological psychology traditions and methods in exercise science" (p. 52). The present volume, the first of its kind and the product of a gestation phase that lasted for decades, is a reflection of the progress that has taken place.

The Progress of Scientific Investigations

Overall, and despite the progress that has been made in the last 35 years or so, the study of physical activity from a psychobiological perspective, relative to research from other perspectives, has had a limited impact on exercise science. Psychobiological studies make up only a small fraction of the articles published in exercise science journals. For example, only 3.9% of the articles published in *Medicine and Science in Sports and Exercise,* the official journal of the American College of Sports Medicine, between 1969 and 1993 could be classified in the area of psychobiology (Morgan, 1994a). Moreover, of these, the majority represented a single topic, namely perceptions of exertion. Similarly, training in psychobiological theories and procedures is provided in only a very small number of graduate programs in the exercise sciences (Sachs, Burke, & Schrader, 2000).

Likewise, psychobiology has been only a small area within the subdisciplines of sport and exercise psychology, typically given little space in journals and, at times, treated as a "fringe" area in conference programs. Sport and exercise psychology grew as scientific fields primarily under the dominant influence of the social-cognitive "revolution" in general psychology (Gardner, 1987; Johnson & Erneling, 1997). Still today, these areas of research continue to be influenced heavily by the social constructionist metatheory (Gergen, 1985) and associated self-report and qualitative methods of data collection.

Examples of the lack of appreciation for the psychobiological approach by proponents of social cognition and social constructivism are commonplace in the literature. With regard to research on emotion, for example, commenting on a model of emotional responding proposed by LeDoux (1986), which focused on the amygdala as a key structure, Lazarus (1986) stated that "neurophysiological concepts are generally inadequate templates for psychological concepts" (p.

245). Within this general context, psychobiology has been discarded by some as either irrelevant (i.e., not having anything substantive to contribute within the social constructionist framework) or having a low potential of informational yield, especially when considered in relation to its complexity and requisite investigative effort.

This disposition is puzzling, especially when the object of scientific study is *physical* activity. Exercise and sport inherently involve the body and mainly center around the physical nature of the body. Therefore, it is clear to us that an adequate understanding of *physical activity* cannot emerge if we limit the scope of the investigation to cognitive and social factors and dismiss the role of the body and the brain. We hold this position to be self-evident. From a truly integrative psychobiological standpoint, there is no conflict or mutually exclusive relationship between different levels of analysis. Although psychobiology does attribute ultimate causation to the brain and nervous system, it also accepts that all methods, including those of the biological, physiological, neuroscientific, and social-psychological traditions, have their place. This is nicely exemplified in the following excerpt by Cacioppo and colleagues (2004):

> "All human behavior, at some level, is biological but this is not to say that biological reductionism yields a simple, singular, or satisfactory explanation for complex behaviors, or that molecular forms of representation provide the only or best level of analysis for understanding human behavior. Molar constructs such as those developed by the social sciences provide a means of understanding highly complex activity without needing to specify each individual action of the simplest components, thereby providing an efficient means of describing the behavior of a complex system." (p. 399)

It has been said, and we agree, that unless psychology and cognitive theories of the mind are consistent with neuroanatomy and neurophysiology, they can degenerate into an "empty boxology" (Lang, 1994, p. 219), an assortment of boxes and arrows lacking in credibility and validity as models of cognition and behavior. Conversely, a psychobiological approach does not automatically bestow upon a psychological study objectivity or instant scientific value. Good psychobiology must have solid, well-informed psychological principles and hypotheses at its core (see Ursin, 1998, for an example in psychoneuroendocrinology). As John Mason (1970) reminded the members of the American Psychosomatic Society,

> *"although the physiologic approaches . . . may offer some important strategic assets, I hope it is clear that these research approaches can accomplish very little by themselves. It cannot be overemphasized that the principal task before psychosomatic research remains, first and foremost, the analysis of psychologic processes. The physiologic approaches should be viewed as mere adjuncts by comparison." (p. 435)*

Secondary Ignorance and Dualism

As noted earlier, this volume was literally decades in the making, as the psychobiology of exercise and sport grew to its current critical mass. One may wonder why the long delay in appreciating the value of psychobiological approaches and why the slow rate of progress. The reasons are many, and they are not necessarily obvious or unanimously agreed upon. Here we concentrate on two that we deem particularly critical. However, as we enter this discussion, we must make clear that searching for factors that might have prevented a higher rate of progress implies no criticism toward the field and its hard-working investigators. Inhibitory forces are a typical and essentially unavoidable part of the evolution of any field, and they are certainly not the making of a particular individual, group, or school of thought.

First, we focus on the absence of an appropriate educational infrastructure and, specifically, graduate programs and courses with an emphasis on the psychobiology of physical activity. This has resulted in psychobiological approaches that seem to reflect what Dishman (1990) astutely characterized "secondary ignorance," namely the notion that the right answer, theoretical concept or measurement approach, is out there in the literature but the fields of exercise and sport psychology are not aware of it. This has resulted in research attempts that have been unsystematic and ineffectively designed, thus often leading to dead ends. Eventually, the absence of meaningful findings has led to disappointment and the abandonment of the research question. Both sport and exercise psychology have seen several examples of this phenomenon.

In sport psychology, Hatfield and Landers (1983, 1987) commented on the widely held yet clearly erroneous assumption of an undifferentiated and unidirectional arousal response, which had resulted in an "overly simplistic perception of psychophysiological measurement" (1983, p. 245). Several studies in sport psychology in the 1970s and 1980s examined the correlations between various electrophysiological indices of arousal and self-reports of anxiety. Not finding a significant relationship, researchers were quick to reject the psychophysiological measures as uninformative. For example, expressing the general sentiment at the time, Martens (1987) stated that "certainly, physiological and biochemical measures have not been the answer, not for a lack of trying to make them work" (p. 47). Perhaps such measures did not "work" because, as Hatfield and Landers noted, researchers in sport psychology had not fully appreciated some fundamental principles of psychophysiological responses, such as the law of initial values, and individual and situational response specificity (Lacey, 1956), despite the fact that these had been fairly well established in the literature by that time.

In exercise psychology, a similar frustration and eventual abandonment of a line of research occurred with the widely publicized endorphin hypothesis for the exercise-induced "feel-better" effect (Hoffmann, 1997; La Forge, 1995; Morgan, 1985). In their simplest form, studies attempting to test the hypothesis that the "feel-better" effect was mediated by endogenous opioids did so by correlating the levels of circulating beta-endorphin with absolute scores or changes in scores on various self-report measures of mood. It is perhaps not surprising that these studies did not yield significant relationships, as most seem to have ignored highly important findings from neuroanatomy and neurophysiology—for example, that peripheral levels of beta-endorphin do not necessarily reflect (or influence) the dynamics of central opioids. Even the generally more sophisticated studies that attempted to manipulate central opioids by administering blocker agents (naloxone or naltrexone) had several problems, again due to an apparent lack of critical input from psychopharmacology. For example, the dosages of blockers and the timing of their administration (preexercise, postexercise, or intravenous drip during exercise) appear to have been selected arbitrarily. Once again, the failure to arrive at consistent and unambiguous findings has led investigators to the premature discontinuation of this line of research. Nevertheless, despite these problems, an author not only concluded that the endorphin hypothesis was a "myth" but also felt that the evidence was strong enough to justify the sweeping generalization that "physiological explanations for an improved mood after exercise do not fit any longer" (Stoll, 1997, p. 119).

The second problem is encapsulated in one distressing yet familiar term: dualism. As Dishman (1994) noted, the absence of systematic psychobiological research is "consistent with a dualistic view of mind and body adopted by exercise scientists. . . . Segregation of biological and behavioral methods cannot advance our knowledge . . . and must end" (p. 52). Dualism is perhaps the single most elusive, potent, and persistent adversary of progress. Over the years, there has been a seemingly endless stream of passionate quotes from leading figures in sport and exercise psychology condemning the evils of dualism. And yet, dualism evidently remains alive and well, not just in sport and exercise psychology but also in general psychology and neuroscience.

One particular variant of dualism, which the philosopher Drew Leder (1990) called "ontovaluational dualism," appears to be especially prevalent within sport and exercise psychology. This term is meant to convey that in this type of dualism, besides the familiar ontological notion of mind and body as distinct entities, there is an implicit or explicit valuation such that either the mind or the body is assumed to have primacy or a commanding role over the other. Consider, for example, the role of physiological processes in social-cognitive theory. According to Bandura (1997, p. 107), physiological processes within the body only acquire meaning for the individual once they are cognitively evaluated within the mind. As Lee (1995) put it, by not only separating the mind from the body but also placing the two in an antagonistic relationship with the mind in a commanding role, Bandura essentially seems to have reduced the individual to "a collection of subjective experiences, with a body more or less tacked on as a way of getting around" (pp. 261-262).

In sport and exercise psychology, one often has to read between the lines to uncover the subtle but unmistakable signs of dualism, veiled under a rich antidualism and prointegration rhetoric. Both varieties of ontovaluational dualism are present, one ascribing primacy to the mind and one to the body. At the risk of oversimplifying, one could say that the vision of integration that seems to emerge from many writings is not one in which the two sides meet somewhere in the middle, taking advantage of their collective theoretical treasure and methodological arsenal, but one in which it is suggested that proponents of the "other side" should abandon their views and methods and accept "ours." Although such exhortations are undoubtedly well intentioned, a skeptic might argue that they are also not the most effective way to achieve integration. As an example, no one could argue with the consensus-building potential of the following statements that reject dualism: (a) "A psychobiologic approach usually will be more fruitful than either a biologic or a psychologic model alone" (Morgan, 1983, p. 46) and (b) "It seems judicious to encourage the study of both biological and social cognitive variables simultaneously" (Rejeski & Thompson, 1993, p. 12) since "social cognition and human biological responses are reciprocal systems that cannot be studied in isolation—not if we are to reject dualistic thinking" (Rejeski & Thompson, 1993, p. 28).

This consensus is weakened, however, when such statements are accompanied by others that seem to move away from the direction of integration, reflecting one of the two varieties of ontovaluational dualism. As an example, with no criticism intended, a researcher approaching the study of behavior in the context of sport and exercise from a social-cognitive perspective might interpret statements such as the following as questioning the importance of the perspective that he or she represents: "Especially those who rely exclusively on cognitive psychology, seem to believe that the head does not have a body" and "If one waits a little while, a dump truck will surely back up with cognitive psychology scattered throughout its hold, along with numerous self-efficacy and self-appraisal measures" (Morgan, 1989, p. 100). Conversely, a researcher with a biological perspective might feel alienated or confused after reading that "[a model proposing that] the origin of all subjective experience [is] rooted in physiological substrata" is "*unfortunately* . . . reductionistic" (Rejeski & Thompson, 1993, p. 18, italics added). Reductionism seems to have acquired some negative connotations. Yet reductionism really means believing that "complex phenomena are best understood by a componential analysis which breaks down the phenomena into their fundamental, elementary aspects" (Reber, 1985, p. 622). Somehow this is often interpreted as an assumption that psychological phenomena should be reduced to the study of physiology (Brustad, 2002; Dzewaltowski, 1997). Thus, perhaps not unexpectedly, this causes a strong negative reaction among the proponents of the social-cognitive and constructivist approach. We believe that a truly integrative psychobiology can be founded only on genuine respect for the unique insights accessible from each of the multiple levels of analysis (Cacioppo & Berntson, 1992). Arguably, calls for integration juxtaposed with positions that could be viewed as rejecting the value of other viewpoints or levels of analysis are bound to be ineffective and ultimately work against the common goal of advancing the science. As Cacioppo and colleagues (2000) put it, "The abyss between biological and social levels of organization is a human construction, however, one that must be bridged to achieve a complete understanding of human behavior" (p. 830).

To summarize, sport and exercise psychology have not been immune to the problems that have delayed and hindered the application of psychobiology in other areas of psychology. But perhaps due to the limited size of the field, the delays have been prolonged and the internal tensions regarding ways to overcome dualism have resisted efforts toward mutual understanding and compromise. As we noted, the unsophisticated early attempts at psychophysiological investigations of arousal and anxiety and the various manifestations of ontovaluational dualism are not unusual phenomena or unique to sport and exercise psychology. Viewed from a historical perspective, they are par for the course, frustrating yet unsurprising obstacles on the way toward an evolved and mature science. The present volume represents a clear demonstration of the progress that the field has made.

Sport Psychology

A comprehensive review of the psychobiological investigations conducted in sport and exercise psychology in the previous 35 years is beyond the scope of this introductory chapter. However, we do wish to provide a context in which the cutting-edge research presented within this text can be appreciated. We limit our coverage to six themes in sport psychology and six themes in exercise psychology. The original studies and literature reviews that we chose to cite are meant as representative examples and certainly not as an exhaustive list.

In sport psychology, the key outcome of interest is athletic performance. Therefore, the main themes relate, directly or indirectly, to the optimization of performance. A first prevalent theme refers to the study of various electrophysiological

(e.g., electromyography, skin conductivity, heart rate, blood pressure) and neuroendocrine (e.g., catecholamines) responses associated with stress and anxiety. The main questions that have been examined include whether such variables relate to self-reports of state anxiety and whether they relate to or are predictive of performance in motor or athletic skills (e.g., Karteroliotis & Gill, 1987; Smith, Burwitz, & Jakeman, 1988; Weinberg & Hunt, 1976). As noted earlier, many of the studies in this early line of research were plagued by hypotheses that failed to take into account fundamental principles of psychophysiology, such as the law of initial values and response specificity. This research has been essentially discontinued in recent years, leaving behind more open questions than unequivocal answers. Unfortunately, the lack of consistent relationships between physiological measures and either self-reports of anxiety or indices of performance has left many in sport psychology with the impression that physiological measures entail too much effort for little eventual gain.

A second theme is reflected in studies with an applied orientation that examined the effectiveness of biofeedback techniques (typically involving heart rate, blood pressure, electromyography, skin conductance, and brain wave activity) for regulating competitive anxiety and enhancing performance (e.g., Daniels & Landers, 1981; see reviews by Petruzzello, Landers, & Salazar, 1991; Sandweiss & Wolf, 1985; Zaichkowsky & Fuchs, 1988). This research, which continues, albeit at a slower pace (e.g., Bar-Eli et al., 2002), has shown positive effects and has allowed the development of standardized intervention protocols (e.g., Blumenstein, Bar-Eli, & Tenenbaum, 1997).

A third theme focuses on the psychobiological manifestations of overtraining (O'Connor, 1997). This line of research has combined assessments of mood states and stress hormones, primarily cortisol, and has provided evidence of significant relationships between self-reports and hormonal assays (O'Connor et al., 1989). Recent studies have begun to extend this research to include the impact of overtraining and the associated psychological problems, such as depression, on immune parameters (Armstrong & Van Heest, 2002).

A fourth theme involves the examination of electrocortical activity as an index of attention and allocation of cognitive resources (e.g., Bird, 1987; Hatfield, Landers, & Ray, 1984; Konttinen & Lyytinen, 1992). This research, which is based on quantitative analyses of real-time electroencephalographic (EEG) data, has provided valuable insights into skilled performance that would have been impossible to obtain through a self-report methodology. Over two decades of research (e.g., Deeny et al., 2003; Haufler et al., 2000; Hillman et al., 2000) have led to the formulation of a conceptual model based on the efficient use of cognitive resources in skilled performers (Hatfield & Hillman, 2001).

A fifth theme is conveyed in studies focusing on the association between psychological factors (e.g., anxiety or mood states) and either physiological (e.g., oxygen uptake) or biomechanical (e.g., movement kinematics) parameters (e.g., Beuter & Duda, 1985; Beuter, Duda, & Widule, 1989), including those associated with running economy (e.g., Crews, 1992; Martin, Craib, & Mitchell, 1995; Williams, Krahenbuhl, & Morgan, 1991). This research has uncovered some relatively reliable associations, and in turn these findings have prompted studies examining the effectiveness of intervention strategies, such as biofeedback or relaxation, designed to improve movement patterns, the metabolic efficiency, and ultimately performance (e.g., Caird, McKenzie, & Sleivert, 1999).

A sixth theme focuses on imagery. Based mainly on Lang's (1979) bioinformational theory, studies have examined the efferent signals and peripheral physiological changes associated with imagery (e.g., Gallego et al., 1996; Wang & Morgan, 1992). More recently, there has been an effort to integrate this research with emerging neuroscientific evidence in order to understand the brain mechanisms involved (Keil et al., 2000).

Exercise Psychology

In exercise psychology, which focuses on health and well-being, perhaps due to the historical associations of this field with such areas as psychosomatic and behavioral medicine, psychophysiology, and psychophysics, the impact of psychobiological approaches has been deeper and wider than in sport psychology. A first prevalent theme is the study of perceived exertion. Starting with the introduction of Borg's Rating of Perceived Exertion (RPE) scale in the United States in the early 1970s (Borg, 1973; Borg & Noble, 1974), this topic has become one of the most prolific areas of research within exercise science (Borg, 2001). Likewise, following the endorsement by the American College of Sports Medicine of RPE as a basic method of prescribing and monitoring the intensity of exercise, this scale has become one of the most commonly used measures in clinical practice. According to Morgan (1994b), "From the very beginning of Borg's pioneering efforts . . . the rating of perceived exertion . . . has been conceptualized as a psychophysiological phenomenon; and there is now an extensive research literature supporting the theoretical proposition that effort sense is best viewed within a mind-body context" (p. 1072). Substantial portions of the variability in ratings of perceived exertion can be accounted for by physiological variables indicative of the intensity of exercise (e.g., heart rate, ventilation, oxygen uptake, lactate; see Chen, Fan, & Moe, 2002). However, it is clear that both dispositional (e.g., personality traits) and situational (e.g., perceived social evaluation) psychological variables also play an important role (e.g., Morgan, 1973, 1981, 1983, 1994b). According to an integrative conceptual model, cognitive factors are expected to be particularly influential when the intensity of exercise is submaximal, whereas peripheral physiological cues are expected to dominate the perception of exertion at near-maximal intensity (Rejeski, 1981, 1985).

A second theme comes from numerous studies that have been conducted to test the psychobiological hypotheses proposed by Morgan (Morgan, 1985; Morgan & O'Connor, 1988) and Hatfield (1991) to explain the "feel-better" effects of both acute and chronic exercise. These include the monoamine hypothesis, the endorphin hypothesis, the thermogenic hypothesis, and the cardiac influence model (see reviews by Hatfield, 1991; Hoffmann, 1997; Chaouloff, 1997; Dishman, 1997; Koltyn, 1997; La Forge, 1995). Although the thermogenic hypothesis seems untenable and research on the endorphin and cardiac influence hypotheses appears to be on a hiatus, research on the monoamine hypothesis, focusing mainly on norepinephrine and serotonin, is ongoing and is producing promising results (Meeusen & De Meirleir, 1995; Meeusen, Piacentini, & De Meirleir, 2001). The emerging challenge is the integration of the various mechanisms into a meaningful model (La Forge, 1995).

A third theme focuses on the influence of aerobic fitness and aerobic conditioning on the psychophysiological reactivity to "psychosocial" or "mental" stressors (e.g., the Stroop task, mental arithmetic, public speaking). Based on the assumption that a higher level of stress reactivity would increase the risk for cardiovascular disease, numerous studies have been conducted to test the hypothesis that aerobically fit or aerobically trained participants would exhibit a blunted stress response. Although some reviews indicated a modest effect in this direction (e.g., Crews & Landers, 1987; Sothmann et al., 1996), others have been critical of the methods and skeptical about the consistency of this effect (e.g., Dishman, 1994; van Doornen, de Geus, & Orlebeke, 1988). It has also been proposed that the nature (i.e., the familiarity, intensity, or controllability) of the stressor might play an important role, as fitness might increase, rather than decrease, the response to certain novel, intense, or particularly threatening stimuli (Dienstbier, 1989, 1991). Recent efforts have turned to an investigation of the central regulatory mechanisms of the stress response using animal models (Dishman, 1994; Dishman & Jackson, 2000).

A fourth theme involves examination of the effects of aerobic fitness and conditioning on cognitive performance. This research is of particular relevance to the aging population, as the ability to deal with cognitive challenges declines with age. Although the initial stages of this line of research involved behavioral measures, such as reaction time (see review by Etnier et al., 1997), psychobiological approaches, starting mainly with a series of oft-cited studies by Dustman and colleagues (Dustman et al., 1984, 1990), have been very influential. Following a seminal publication in *Nature* (Kramer et al., 1999) and a meta-analysis (Colcombe & Kramer, 2003) showing that the beneficial effect of exercise is selective, specifically affecting the tasks that involve a substantial executive control component, this line of research has seen a recent surge of activity, with hypothesis-driven studies that involve event-related potentials (Colcombe et al., 2004; Hillman et al., 2002) and brain imaging (Colcombe et al., 2003). At the same time, basic research is being conducted on the fascinating phenomena of exercise-induced neurogenesis (e.g., van Praag et al., 1999; van Praag, Kempermann, & Gage, 1999) and the action of brain growth factors (Cotman & Berchtold, 2002), processes that may underlie exercise-associated improvements in learning, memory, and problem solving.

A fifth theme involves the study of the phenomenon of exercise-induced analgesia and its underlying mechanisms. Shortly following the discovery of endogenous opioid peptides and the fact that their levels are elevated with vigorous exercise, researchers found evidence, in both rats (e.g., Shyu, Andersson, & Thorén, 1982) and humans (e.g., Janal et al., 1984), of a naloxone-reversible (i.e., opioid mediated) postexercise analgesic effect. Subsequent studies, treating exercise-induced analgesia as a case of the broader phenomenon of stress-induced analgesia and using forced swimming (e.g., Mogil et al., 1996) and forced walking (e.g., Nakagawasai et al., 1999) as stressors, showed both an opioid-mediated and a nonopioid-mediated type of analgesia, depending largely on the intensity and duration of exercise.

A sixth theme relates to the psychoneuroendocrinology of exercise, particularly acute exercise. Discussing the results of one of the first studies in this area, Marianne Frankenhaeuser commented that "it appears likely that the adrenaline [i.e., epinephrine] increase was at least partly associated with the subjective emotional reaction accompanying heavy physical work, rather than being elicited by the work itself" (Frankenhaeuser et al., 1969, p. 348). Likewise, a few years later, John Mason wrote: "It appears that it may be very difficult experimentally to separate the role of psychological versus physiological stimuli to cortisol secretion during relatively severe or prolonged muscular exertion. . . . Subjective reactions at different levels of exercise should be carefully evaluated in future work in this field in an effort to separate hormonal responses to muscular work per se from attendant psychological reactions" (Mason et al., 1976, pp. 160-161). Although the objective of separating the contribution of "muscular work per se" and the "attendant psychological reactions" to the secretion of stress hormones during and following exercise remains elusive, several studies have examined these factors, producing correlational evidence of an association between hormonal responses and both perceptions of exertion (e.g., Skrinar, Ingram, & Pandolf, 1983) and affective responses to exercise (e.g., Perna et al., 1998; Rudolph & McAuley, 1998).

In addition to the six themes that we chose to highlight, the literature contains several other cases in which the study of exercise behavior and its effects has been served well by psychobiological approaches. These include, for example, studies on the effects of exercise training on personality and related hormonal indices (e.g., Ismail & Young, 1977; Sothmann, Ismail, & Chodepko-Zajiko, 1984); the interrelations between exercise, self-reports of stress and well-being, and immune parameters (e.g., La Perriere et al., 1990); the effects of acute and chronic exercise on sleep (e.g., Youngstedt, 2000); and the association between asymmetries in frontal hemispheric activity, assessed via EEG, and affective responses to exercise (e.g., Petruzzello, Hall, & Ekkekakis, 2001). In the postgenomic era, it is also not surprising that one of the most prevalent and arguably most promising emerging trends is the appearance of the first animal (e.g., Rhodes, Garland, & Gammie, 2003) and human (e.g., Simonen et al., 2003) studies using methods of behavioral genetics to understand variations in exercise behavior.

Looking at the topics we have enumerated, one must reach the conclusion that psychobiology has had a meaningful impact on the efforts to better understand human behavior within sport and exercise settings. The breadth of scope and the diversity of topics are impressive and warrant considerable optimism for the future. To paraphrase Cacioppo and colleagues (2000), psychobiological research has provided insights into almost every facet of sport and exercise behavior. However, as we noted earlier, we see the potential as far greater.

The Present Volume

In an editorial in the *Journal of Sport and Exercise Psychology* in 2001, Steve Petruzzello wrote: "My sense is that we are at a crossroads as a field of inquiry. We can continue with our 'boxology' and draw boxes and arrows and ignore the body in which these boxes must reside. Or we can utilize the ever-expanding knowledge base, including the physiological along with the psychological and the social, and undoubtedly gain a far greater understanding of human behavior" (p. 266). We agree with this statement, and this volume is an effort to help further instigate and provide direction for integrative study. As we stated previously, we view the lack of education and the pervasive influence of dualistic thinking as the two primary hindrances to the integrative study of human behavior in the contexts of sport and exercise. The content of this volume was planned specifically with these two obstacles in mind.

First, we assembled a group of authors comprising some of the leading scholars from around the world who have developed truly integrative, systematic lines of inquiry into important aspects of the psychobiology of physical activity. These authors come from a variety of areas, including kinesiology, psychology, physiology, and neuroscience. But, despite this diversity, the common characteristic of the chapters in this book is that they represent exemplars of research that broke through the dualistic barrier by starting with a psychological or behavioral question and utilizing a psychobiological method or combination of methods to extend our understanding to a level otherwise unreachable. This is a particularly important point that we, as editors, hope will be abundantly clear in every chapter—utilizing the psychobiological approach is not scientism, science for the sake of science, but rather a way to understand a phenomenon more deeply or more fully than would be possible with a single level of analysis. Importantly, what we also hope will be evident is the absence of false dichotomies and dilemmas, pitting the body against the mind or psychobiological methods against the traditional "psychological" methods of behavioral observation and self-report. In fact, in many cases, readers will recognize excellent examples of multilevel analysis, in which the data gathered from the behavioral observation or the self-report inform and complement those gathered from the psychobiological method of inquiry and vice versa.

Second, we believe that a central mission of this volume is to help inspire and educate not only the next generation of exercise and sport psychobiologists but also the broader fields of exercise and sport psychology. Therefore, we instructed the authors to balance their desire to provide state of the science reviews in their areas of expertise with their role as educators. Specifically, we asked them to provide short descriptions of the methodologies involved in their research, from brain imaging to microdialysis to event-related potentials, and to organize their chapters in the following sections: (a) an introduction, outlining the relevance of the topic to the study of behavior in exercise and sport; (b) a description of the main questions addressed in the literature; (c) an identification of the limitations of the literature, both conceptual and methodological; and (d) directions for future investigations.

Arguably, a volume that does not have a unifying *thematic* focus such as motivation or anxiety or development, but is rather based on an epistemic philosophy and a diverse set of methodological approaches, may not be perfectly cohesive. Furthermore, as this volume could not encompass all areas of investigation, we made the decision to focus primarily, although not exclusively, on issues pertaining to exercise rather than sport performance, as this reflects the current balance in the research literature (a trend supported by the funding that is currently available for investigations targeting health and well-being).

The 17 chapters are organized in five sections, covering (a) foundational information on psychobiology, the brain, and the body (three chapters, including the present one), (b) the effects of exercise on cognition (two chapters), (c) the effects of exercise on emotion (four chapters), (d) the effects of exercise on psychosomatic health (five chapters), and (e) applications of psychobiology in human performance (three chapters). Finally, we offer some concluding comments and reflections in an epilogue.

In the two remaining chapters in this opening section, the authors open the "black box" to reveal the workings of the brain in response to exercise. **Bud Craig** describes what is presently known about the peripheral receptors, afferent spinal pathways, and brain centers that collect and process information about the physiological condition of the body. The information on the path that exercise-induced interoceptive cues follow as they ascend the levels of the neuraxis is usually scattered in journal sources from neuroanatomy and neurophysiology to neurology and has not been reviewed previously. This is also the first time that the coverage extends beyond the lower levels of the brain (such as the medulla), involved in basic life-preserving functions like cardiovascular regulation, to include areas relevant to cognition and emotion (such as the amygdala, the insula, the cingulate, and the prefrontal cortex). **Jon Williamson**'s chapter is also a "first"—it is the first to review imaging studies examining the patterns of activity in the human brain in response to exercise. The susceptibility of brain imaging technology to movement artifacts presents a persistent challenge that researchers are trying to address using various creative methodological approaches.

In the section on the effects of exercise on cognition, **Art Kramer** and **Chuck Hillman** review evidence, based on event-related potentials and brain imaging, in support of the selective beneficial effect of exercise on cognitive tasks that involve executive control. Their chapter places particular emphasis on the implications of this research for the prevention of cognitive decline in the elderly. **Henriette van Praag** focuses on basic research that addresses one of the possible reasons for the beneficial effects of exercise on cognitive performance. Specifically, she reviews the results of a series of animal studies demonstrating that wheel running is associated with neurogenesis, the development of new neurons, particularly in the hippocampus, an area of the brain involved in learning and memory. Importantly, the results, based on brain immunohistochemistry, are also accompanied by corroborating behavioral measures of learning.

In the section on the effects of exercise on emotion, **Michel Cabanac** discusses possible evolutionary explanations linking exercise to pleasure. The chapter also frames the hedonic responses to exercise within the context of consciousness and explains Cabanac's seminal idea of alliesthesia as it relates to sensations derived from exercise. **Panteleimon Ekkekakis** and **Ed Acevedo** examine new data on the dose–response relationship between the intensity of exercise and affective responses, with particular emphasis on the implications for the prescription of exercise and exercise adherence. **Steve Petruzzello, Panteleimon Ekkekakis,** and **Eric Hall** review theory-driven research connecting asymmetric patterns of electrocortical activity in the human brain, assessed through EEG, to affective responses to exercise. **Romain Meeusen** presents an overview of research on the effects of exercise training on brain neurotransmitters that are linked to depression and anxiety, including serotonin, norepinephrine, and dopamine. Of particular interest are the studies using microdialysis to study neurotransmitter changes in awake and moving animals.

In the section on the effects of exercise on psychosomatic health, **Mark Sothmann** presents the current evidence pertaining to the cross-stressor adaptation hypothesis. This hypothesis proposes that central and peripheral changes take place in response to exercise training, in both the cardiovascular and neuroendocrine systems and their central regulators, and that these changes then manifest themselves as an altered, more adaptive response to psychosocial or mental stress. **Steve Boutcher** and **Mark Hamer** focus specifically on exercise-induced adaptations in the cardiovascular system. This has been an area characterized by equivocal findings for decades. The authors attempt to resolve the controversy by presenting a multifactorial model of cardiovascular reactivity and delineating the individual-difference factors that may account for some of the variability in cardiovascular responses to stress and exercise adaptations. **Suzi Hong** and **Paul Mills** explore the fascinating area of psychoneuroimmunology, the interactions between exercise, stress, and the neuroendocrine and immune systems. **Greg Hand, Ken Phillips,** and **Marlene Wilson** present a chapter that exemplifies the shift from studying the peripheral manifestations of exercise-associated changes in stress reactivity to studying the central regulatory mechanisms, including limbic and hypothalamic areas. **Dane Cook** presents a review of the complex relationship between exercise and pain, including a description of the neurobiology of pain and modulatory mechanisms.

In the section on applications of psychobiology in human performance, **Brad Hatfield, Amy Haufler,** and **Tom Spalding** provide a summary of over 20 years of research using a cognitive psychophysiology and neuroscience paradigm to understand the bases of superior sport performance. The concept of efficiency—the recruitment of the appropriate amount of cognitive resources for the effective execution of a task—is the central theme of their chapter. **Dave Collins** and **Alan McPherson** review what is presently known about the application of various modalities of biofeedback in the domain of sport. Given that this is a line of inquiry and application with a fairly long history in sport psychology, the chapter importantly and appropriately places emphasis on the limitations of many of the extant studies and proposes ways to overcome them. **Paul Holmes** reviews the research on the psychophysiology of imagery. He proposes a neuroscientific approach to the study of imagery in sport, combining the new information emerging from neuroscience on image generation with lessons from motor control.

As editors, we are delighted to have had this opportunity to serve the research community investigating the psychobiology of physical activity with the publication of this text. As we noted previously, for decades researchers have conducted investigations in psychobiology without a foundational text to facilitate this direction of inquiry. We hold two major visions for the impact of this text. First, we are optimistic that the leaders in the field, who built the foundation of psychobiological inquiry within the domain of physical activity, will view this text as the gratifying culmination of a long developmental phase. Second, we hope that students pursuing study in the fields of exercise and sport psychology, exercise science, psychology, neuroscience, physiology, and genetics will be intrigued and inspired by the cutting-edge research presented in this volume.

References

Armstrong, L.E., & Van Heest, J.L. (2002). The unknown mechanism of the overtraining syndrome: Clues from depression and psychoneuroimmunology. *Sports Medicine, 32,* 185-209.

Ax, A.F. (1964). Goals and methods of psychophysiology. *Psychophysiology, 1,* 8-25.

Bandura, A. (1997). *Self-efficacy: The exercise of control.* New York: Freeman.

Bar-Eli, M., Dreshnan, R., Blumenstain, B., & Weinstein, Y. (2002). The effect of mental training with biofeedback on the performance of young swimmers. *Applied Psychology, 51,* 567-581.

Beuter, A., & Duda, J.L. (1985). Analysis of the arousal/motor performance relationship in children using movement kinematics. *Journal of Sport Psychology, 7,* 229-243.

Beuter, A., Duda, J.L., & Widule, C.J. (1989). The effect of arousal on joint kinematics and kinetics in children. *Research Quarterly for Exercise and Sport, 60,* 109-116.

Bird, E.I. (1987). Psychophysiological processes during rifle shooting. *International Journal of Sport Psychology, 18,* 9-18.

Blumenstein, B., Bar-Eli, M., & Tenenbaum, G. (1997). A five-step approach to mental training incorporating biofeedback. *Sport Psychologist, 11,* 440-453.

Borg, G.A.V. (1973). Psychophysical bases of perceived exertion. *Medicine and Science in Sports and Exercise, 14,* 377-381.

Borg, G. (2001). Borg's range model and scales. *International Journal of Sport Psychology, 32,* 110-126.

Borg, G.A.V., & Noble, B.J. (1974). Perceived exertion. *Exercise and Sport Sciences Reviews, 2,* 131-153.

Brustad, R. (2002). A critical analysis of knowledge construction in sport psychology. In T.S. Horn (Ed.), *Advances in sport psychology* (2nd ed., pp. 21-37). Champaign, IL: Human Kinetics.

Cacioppo, J.T., & Berntson, G.G. (1992). Social psychological contributions to the decade of the brain: Doctrine of multilevel analysis. *American Psychologist, 47,* 1019-1028.

Cacioppo, J.T., Berntson, G.G., Sheridan, J.F., & McClintock, M.K. (2000). Multilevel integrative analyses of human behavior: Social neuroscience and the complementing nature of social and biological approaches. *Psychological Bulletin, 126,* 829-843.

Cacioppo, J.T., Lorig, T.S., Nusbaum, H.C., & Berntson, G.G. (2004). Social neuroscience: Bridging social and biological systems. In C. Sansone, C.C. Morf, & A.T. Panter (Eds.), *The SAGE handbook of methods in social psychology* (pp. 383-404). Thousand Oaks, CA: Sage.

Cacioppo, J.T., Tassinary, L.G., & Berntson, G.G. (2000). Psychophysiological science. In J.T. Cacioppo, L.G. Tassinary, & G.G. Berntson (Eds.), *Handbook of psychophysiology* (2nd ed., pp. 3-23). New York: Cambridge University Press.

Caird, S.J., McKenzie, A.D., & Sleivert, G.G. (1999). Biofeedback and relaxation techniques improve running economy in sub-elite long distance runners. *Medicine and Science in Sports and Exercise, 31,* 717-722.

Chaouloff, F. (1997). The serotonin hypothesis. In W.P. Morgan (Ed.), *Physical activity and mental health* (pp. 179-198). Washington, DC: Taylor and Francis.

Chen, M.J., Fan, X., & Moe, S.T. (2002). Criterion-related validity of the Borg ratings of perceived exertion scale in healthy individuals: A meta-analysis. *Journal of Sports Sciences, 20,* 873-899.

Colcombe, S.J., Erickson, K.I., Raz, N., Webb, A.G., Cohen, N.J., McAuley, E., & Kramer, A.F. (2003). Aerobic fitness reduces brain tissue loss in aging humans. *Journal of Gerontology, 58,* M176-M180.

Colcombe, S., & Kramer, A.F. (2003). Fitness effects on the cognitive function of older adults: A meta-analytic study. *Psychological Science, 14,* 125-130.

Colcombe, S.J., Kramer, A.F., Erickson, K.I., Scalf, P., McAuley, E., Cohen, N.J., Webb, A., Jerome, G.J., Marquez, D.X., & Elavsky, S. (2004). Cardiovascular fitness, cortical plasticity, and aging. *Proceedings of the National Academy of Sciences, 101,* 3316-3321.

Cotman, C.W., & Berchtold, N.C. (2002). Exercise: A behavioral intervention to enhance brain health and plasticity. *Trends in Neurosciences, 25,* 295-301.

Crews, D.J. (1992). Psychological state and running economy. *Medicine and Science in Sports and Exercise, 24,* 475-482.

Crews, D.J., & Landers, D.M. (1987). A meta-analytic review of aerobic fitness and reactivity to psychosocial stressors. *Medicine and Science in Sports and Exercise, 19,* S114-S120.

Daniels, F.S., & Landers, D.M. (1981). Biofeedback and shooting performance: A test of dysregulation and systems theory. *Journal of Sport Psychology, 4,* 271-282.

Darrow, C.W. (1964). Psychophysiology, yesterday, today, and tomorrow. *Psychophysiology, 1,* 4-7.

Deeny, S.P., Hillman, C.H., Janelle, C.M., & Hatfield, B.D. (2003). Cortico-cortical communication and superior performance in skilled marksmen: An EEG coherence analysis. *Journal of Sport and Exercise Psychology, 25,* 188-204.

Dienstbier, R.A. (1989). Arousal and physiological toughness: Implications for mental and physical health. *Psychological Review, 96,* 84-100.

Dienstbier, R.A. (1991). Behavioral correlates of sympathoadrenal reactivity: The toughness model. *Medicine and Science in Sports and Exercise, 23,* 846-852.

Dishman, R.K. (1990). The failure of sport psychology in the exercise and sport sciences. *American Academy of Physical Education Papers, 24,* 39-47.

Dishman, R.K. (1994). Biological psychology, exercise, and stress. *Quest, 46,* 28-59.

Dishman, R.K. (1997). The norepinephrine hypothesis. In W.P. Morgan (Ed.), *Physical activity and mental health* (pp. 199-212). Washington, DC: Taylor and Francis.

Dishman, R.K., & Jackson, E.M. (2000). Exercise, fitness, and stress. *International Journal of Sport Psychology, 31,* 175-203.

Dustman, R.E., Emmerson, R.Y., Ruhling, R.O., Shearer, D.E., Steinhaus, L.A., Johnson, S.C., Bonekat, H.W., & Shigeoka, J.W. (1990). Age and fitness effects on EEG, ERPs, visual sensitivity, and cognition. *Neurobiology of Aging, 11,* 193-200.

Dustman, R.E., Ruhling, R.O., Russell, E.M., Shearer, D.E., Bonekat, H.W., Shigeoka, J.W., Wood, J.S., & Bradford, D.C. (1984). Aerobic exercise training and improved neuropsychological function of older adults. *Neurobiology of Aging, 5,* 35-42.

Dzewaltowski, D.A. (1997). The ecology of physical activity and sport: Merging science and practice. *Journal of Applied Sport Psychology, 9,* 154-176.

Etnier, J.L., Salazar, W., Landers, D.M., Petruzzello, S.J., Han, M., & Nowell, P. (1997). The influence of physical fitness and exercise upon cognitive functioning: A meta-analysis. *Journal of Sport and Exercise Psychology, 19,* 249-277.

Frankenhaeuser, M., Post, B., Nordheden, B., & Sjoberg, H. (1969). Physiological and subjective reactions to different physical work loads. *Perceptual and Motor Skills, 28,* 343-349.

Gallego, J., Denot-LeDunois, S., Vardon, G., & Perruchet, P. (1996). Ventilatory responses to imagined exercise. *Psychophysiology, 33,* 711-719.

Gardner, H. (1987). *The mind's new science: A history of the cognitive revolution.* New York: Basic Books.

Gergen, K.J. (1985). The social constructionist movement in modern psychology. *American Psychologist, 40,* 266-275.

Hatfield, B.D. (1991). Exercise and mental health: The mechanisms of exercise-induced psychological states. In L. Diamant (Ed.), *Psychology of sports, exercise, and fitness: Social and personal issues* (pp. 17-49). New York: Hemisphere.

Hatfield, B.D., & Hillman, C.H. (2001). The psychophysiology of sport: A mechanistic understanding of the psychology of superior performance. In R.N. Singer, H.A. Hausenblaus, & C.M. Janelle (Eds.), *Handbook of research on sport psychology* (2nd ed., pp. 362-388). New York: Wiley.

Hatfield, B.D., & Landers, D.M. (1983). Psychophysiology: A new direction for sport psychology. *Journal of Sport Psychology, 5,* 243-259.

Hatfield, B.D., & Landers, D.M. (1987). Psychophysiology in exercise and sport research: An overview. *Exercise and Sport Sciences Reviews, 15,* 351-387.

Hatfield, B.D., Landers, D.M., & Ray, W.J. (1984). Cognitive processes during self-paced motor performance: An electroencephalographic profile of skilled marksmen. *Journal of Sport Psychology, 6,* 42-59.

Haufler, A.J., Spalding, T.W., Santa Maria, D.L., & Hatfield, B.D. (2000). Neuro-cognitive activity during a self-paced visuospatial task: Comparative EEG profiles in marksmen and novice shooters. *Biological Psychology, 53,* 131-160.

Hillman, C.H., Apparies, R.J., Janelle, C.M., & Hatfield, B.D. (2000). An electrocortical comparison of executed and rejected shots in skilled marksmen. *Biological Psychology, 52,* 71-83.

Hillman, C.H., Weiss, E.P., Hagberg, J.M., & Hatfield, B.D. (2002). The relationship of age and cardiovascular fitness to cognitive and motor processes. *Psychophysiology, 39,* 303-312.

Hoffmann, P. (1997). The endorphin hypothesis. In W.P. Morgan (Ed.), *Physical activity and mental health* (pp. 163-177). Washington, DC: Taylor and Francis.

Ismail, A.H., & Young, R.J. (1977). Effect of chronic exercise on the multivariate relationships between selected biochemical and personality variables. *Journal of Multivariate Behavioral Research, 12,* 49-67.

Janal, M.N., Colt, E.W.D., Clark, W.C., & Glusman, M. (1984). Pain sensitivity, mood and plasma endocrine levels in man following long-distance running: Effects of naloxone. *Pain, 19,* 13-25.

Johnson, D.M., & Erneling, C.E. (Eds.) (1997). *The future of the cognitive revolution.* New York: Oxford University Press.

Karteroliotis, C., & Gill, D.L. (1987). Temporal changes in psychological and physiological components of state anxiety. *Journal of Sport Psychology, 9,* 261-274.

Keil, D., Holmes, P., Bennett, S., Davids, K., & Smith, N. (2000). Theory and practice in sport psychology and motor behaviour needs to be constrained by integrative modelling of brain and behaviour. *Journal of Sports Sciences, 18,* 433-443.

Koltyn, K.F. (1997). The thermogenic hypothesis. In W.P. Morgan (Ed.), *Physical activity and mental health* (pp. 213-226). Washington, DC: Taylor and Francis.

Konttinen, N., & Lyytinen, H. (1992). Physiology of preparation: Brain slow waves, heart rate, and respiration preceding triggering in rifle shooting. *International Journal of Sport Psychology, 23,* 110-127.

Kramer, A.F., Hahn, S., Cohen, N.J., Banich, M.T., McAuley, E., Harrison, C.R., Chason, J., Vakil, E., Bardell, L., Boileau, R.A., & Colcombe, A. (1999). Ageing, fitness and neurocognitive function. *Nature, 400,* 418-419.

Lacey, J.I. (1956). The evaluation of autonomic responses: Toward a general solution. *Annals of the New York Academy of Sciences, 67,* 125-163.

La Forge, R. (1995). Exercise-associated mood alterations: A review of interactive neurobiologic mechanisms. *Medicine in Exercise, Nutrition, and Health, 4,* 17-32.

Lang, P.J. (1979). A bio-informational theory of emotional imagery. *Psychophysiology, 16,* 495-512.

Lang, P.J. (1994). The varieties of emotional experience: A meditation on James-Lange theory. *Psychological Review, 101,* 211-221.

La Perriere, A.R., Antoni, M.H., Schneiderman, N., Ironson, G., Klimas, N., Caralis, P., & Fletcher, M.A. (1990). Exercise intervention attenuates emotional distress and natural killer cell decrements following notification of positive serologic status for HIV-1. *Biofeedback and Self-Regulation, 15,* 229-242.

Lazarus, R.S. (1986). Commentary. *Integrative Psychiatry, 4,* 245-247.

Leder, D. (1990). *The absent body.* Chicago: University of Chicago Press.

LeDoux, J.E. (1986). Sensory systems and emotion: A model of affective processing. *Integrative Psychiatry, 4,* 237-248.

Lee, C. (1995). Comparing the incommensurable: Where science and politics collide. *Journal of Behavior Therapy and Experimental Psychiatry, 26,* 259-263.

Martens, R. (1987). Science, knowledge, and sport psychology. *Sport Psychologist, 1,* 29-55.

Martin, J.J., Craib, M., & Mitchell, V. (1995). The relationships of anxiety to running economy in competitive male distance runners. *Journal of Sports Sciences, 13,* 371-376.

Mason, J.W. (1970). Strategy in psychosomatic research. *Psychosomatic Medicine, 32,* 427-439.

Mason, J.W., Maher, J.T., Hartley, L.H., Mougey, E.H., Perlow, M.J., & Jones, L.G. (1976). Selectivity of corticosteroid and catecholamine responses to various natural stimuli. In G. Serban (Ed.), *Psychopathology of human adaptation* (pp. 147-171). New York: Plenum Press.

Meeusen, R., & De Meirleir, K. (1995). Exercise and brain neurotransmission. *Sports Medicine, 20,* 160-188.

Meeusen, R., Piacentini, M.F., & De Meirleir, K. (2001). Brain microdialysis in exercise research. *Sports Medicine, 31,* 965-983.

Mogil, J.S., Sternberg, W.F., Balian, H., Liebeskind, J.C., & Sadowski, B. (1996). Opioid and nonopioid swim stress-induced analgesia: A parametric analysis in mice. *Physiology and Behavior, 59,* 123-132.

Morgan, W.P. (1973). Psychological factors influencing perceived exertion. *Medicine and Science in Sports, 5,* 97-103.

Morgan, W.P. (1981). Psychophysiology of self-awareness during vigorous physical activity. *Research Quarterly for Exercise and Sport, 52,* 385-427.

Morgan, W.P. (1983). Efficacy of psychobiologic inquiry in the exercise and sport sciences. *Quest, 20,* 39-46.

Morgan, W.P. (1985). Affective beneficence of vigorous physical activity. *Medicine and Science in Sports and Exercise, 17,* 94-100.

Morgan, W.P. (1989). Sport psychology in its own context: A recommendation for the future. In J.S. Skinner & C.B. Corbin (Eds.), *Future directions in exercise and sport science research* (pp. 97-110). Champaign, IL: Human Kinetics.

Morgan, W.P. (1994a). Forty years of progress: Sport psychology in exercise science and sports medicine. In

Anonymous (Ed.), *American College of Sports Medicine 40th anniversary lectures* (pp. 81-92). Indianapolis: American College of Sports Medicine.

Morgan, W.P. (1994b). Psychological components of effort sense. *Medicine and Science in Sports and Exercise, 26,* 1071-1077.

Morgan, W.P., & O'Connor, P.J. (1988). Exercise and mental health. In R.K. Dishman (Ed.), *Exercise adherence: Its impact on public health* (pp. 91-121). Champaign, IL: Human Kinetics.

Nakagawasai, O., Tadano, T., Tan-No, K., Niijima, F., Sakurada, S., Endo, Y., & Kisara, K. (1999). Changes in b-endorphin and stress-induced analgesia in mice after exposure to forced walking stress. *Methods and Findings in Experimental and Clinical Pharmacology, 21,* 471-476.

O'Connor, P.J. (1997). Overtraining and staleness. In W.P. Morgan (Ed.), *Physical activity and mental health* (pp. 145-160). Washington, DC: Taylor and Francis.

O'Connor, P.J., Morgan, W.P., Raglin, J.S., Barksdale, C.M., & Kalin, N.H. (1989). Mood state and salivary cortisol levels following overtraining in female swimmers. *Psychoneuroendocrinology, 14,* 303-310.

Perna, F.M., Antoni, M.H., Kumar, M., Cruess, D.G., & Schneiderman, N. (1998). Cognitive-behavioral intervention effects on mood and cortisol during exercise training. *Annals of Behavioral Medicine, 20,* 92-98.

Petruzzello, S.J. (2001). Reflecting, recognizing, and reintegrating. *Journal of Sport and Exercise Psychology, 23,* 265-267.

Petruzzello, S.J., Hall, E.E., & Ekkekakis, P. (2001). Regional brain activation as a biological marker of affective responsivity to acute exercise: Influence of fitness. *Psychophysiology, 38,* 99-106.

Petruzzello, S.J., Landers, D.M., & Salazar, W. (1991). Biofeedback and sport/exercise performance: Applications and limitations. *Behavior Therapy, 22,* 379-392.

Reber, A.S. (1985). *The Penguin dictionary of psychology.* New York: Penguin.

Rejeski, W.J. (1981). The perception of exertion: A social psychophysiological integration. *Journal of Sport Psychology, 4,* 305-320.

Rejeski, W.J. (1985). Perceived exertion: An active or passive process. *Journal of Sport Psychology, 7,* 371-378.

Rejeski, W.J., & Thompson, A. (1993). Historical and conceptual roots of exercise psychology. In P. Seraganian (Ed.), *Exercise psychology: The influence of physical exercise on psychological processes* (pp. 3-35). New York: Wiley.

Rhodes, J.S., Garland, T., & Gammie, S.C. (2003). Patterns of brain activity associated with variation in voluntary wheel running behavior. *Behavioral Neuroscience, 117,* 1243-1256.

Rudolph, D.L., & McAuley, E. (1998). Cortisol and affective responses to exercise. *Journal of Sports Sciences, 16,* 121-128.

Sachs, M.L., Burke, K.L., & Schrader, D.C. (Eds.) (2000). *Directory of graduate programs in applied sport psychology* (6th ed.). Morgantown, WV: Fitness Information Technology.

Sandweiss, J.H., & Wolf, S.L. (Eds.) (1985). *Biofeedback and sports science.* New York: Plenum Press.

Shyu, B.C., Andersson, S.A., & Thorén, P. (1982). Endorphin mediated decrease in pain threshold induced by long-lasting exercise in rats. *Life Sciences, 30,* 833-840.

Simonen, R.L., Rankinen, T., Pérusse, L., Leon, A.S., Skinner, J.S., Wilmore, J.H., Rao, D.C., & Bouchard, C. (2003). A dopamine D2 receptor gene polymorphism and physical activity in two family studies. *Physiology and Behavior, 78,* 751-757.

Skrinar, G.S., Ingram, S.P., & Pandolf, K.B. (1983). Effect of endurance training on perceived exertion and stress hormones in women. *Perceptual and Motor Skills, 57,* 1239-1250.

Smith, N.C., Burwitz, L., & Jakeman, P. (1988). Precompetitive anxiety and motor performance: A psychophysiological examination. *Journal of Sports Sciences, 6,* 115-130.

Sothmann, M.S., Buckworth, J., Claytor, R.P., White-Welkley, J.E., & Dishman, R.K. (1996). Exercise training and the cross-stressor adaptation hypothesis. *Exercise and Sport Sciences Reviews, 24,* 267-287.

Sothmann, M.S., Ismail, A.H., & Chodepko-Zajiko, W. (1984). Influence of catecholamine activity on the hierarchical relationships among physical fitness condition and selected personality characteristics. *Journal of Clinical Psychology, 40,* 1308-1317.

Stoll, O. (1997). Endorphine, laufsucht und runner's high: Aufstieg und niedergang eines mythos [in German]. *Leipziger Sportwissenschaftliche Beiträge, 38,* 102-121.

Ursin, H. (1998). The psychology in psychoneuroendocrinology. *Psychoneuroendocrinology, 23,* 555-570.

van Doornen, L.J., de Geus, E.J., & Orlebeke, J.F. (1988). Aerobic fitness and the physiological stress response: A critical evaluation. *Social Science and Medicine, 26,* 303-307.

van Praag, H., Christie, B.R., Sejnowski, T.J., & Gage, F.H. (1999). Running enhances neurogenesis, learning, and long-term potentiation in mice. *Proceedings of the National Academy of Sciences, 96,* 13427-13431.

van Praag, H., Kempermann, G., & Gage, F.H. (1999). Running increases cell proliferation and neurogenesis in the adult mouse dentate gyrus. *Nature Neuroscience, 2,* 266-270.

Wang, Y., & Morgan, W.P. (1992). The effect of perspectives on the psychophysiological responses to imagined exercise. *Behavior and Brain Research, 52,* 167-174.

Weinberg, R.S., & Hunt, V.V. (1976). The interrelationships between anxiety, motor performance and electromyography. *Journal of Motor Behavior, 8,* 219-224.

Williams, T.J., Krahenbuhl, G.S., & Morgan, D.W. (1991). Mood state and running economy in moderately trained male runners. *Medicine and Science in Sports and Exercise, 23,* 727-731.

Youngstedt, S.D. (2000). The exercise-sleep mystery. *International Journal of Sport Psychology, 31,* 241-255.

Zaichkowsky, L.D., & Fuchs, C.Z. (1988). Biofeedback applications in exercise and athletic performance. *Exercise and Sport Sciences Reviews, 16,* 381-421.

Physical Activity and the Neurobiology of Interoception

A.D. (Bud) Craig, PhD

Physical activity in humans and other mammals is under the constant control of the central nervous system, that is, the peripheral nerves, spinal cord, brainstem, and forebrain. The neural control mechanisms include not only the coordinated motor commands that drive the skeletal muscles and cause movement, but also autonomic control mechanisms that maintain adaptive physiological conditions within the tissues and organs of the body as needed to support the various modes of physical activity. The peripheral and central components of the autonomic nervous system control many aspects of the physiological condition (or health) of the body, for example cardiorespiratory, endocrine, thermoregulatory, and metabolic (energy) activities, and thereby levels of oxygen, CO_2, salt and water, and even immune function and pain sensitivity. Significantly, the central autonomic system also controls the affective (emotional) components that motivate goal-directed behaviors. Autonomic control mechanisms for individual physiological parameters are often studied separately, in isolation, in a reductionist manner. However, they all have the common goal of maintaining "homeostasis," the dynamic, interactive, ongoing process that achieves an optimal balance across all aspects of the physiological condition of the body for the purpose of survival (Cannon, 1939). The neural control mechanisms for these conditions are integrated within a common hierarchical homeostatic control network. Changes in a particular condition usually affect several aspects, and they elicit a combination of homeostatic responses that serve to restore an optimal balance of conditions.

Homeostasis in mammals depends on autonomic, endocrine, and behavioral mechanisms (Loewy & Spyer, 1990; Appenzeller & Oribe, 1997; Gisolfi & Mora, 2000; Swanson, 2000; Saper, 2002). Several chapters in this volume address critical aspects of the homeostatic control of the physiological condition of the body during exercise, focusing on such issues as emotion (chapter 8), cardiovascular function (chapter 11), immune function (chapter 12), and stress (chapter 13).

Mammalian homeostatic control mechanisms require ongoing sensory feedback on the state of the body in order to maintain moment-to-moment, adaptive balance of the body's physiological needs. The afferent sensory feedback provides information relating many aspects of the local and regional physiological conditions of the tissues of the body, such as temperature, physical stress, local hormonal and metabolic conditions, and so on; and this information is integrated centrally in the hierarchical homeostatic control networks. The central integration of afferent sensory feedback has been evolutionarily shaped in order to support different types of physical activity that have different goals, contexts, time courses, and exertion levels, each of which requires the body's physiological needs to be balanced differently. For example, the hormonal, thermoregulatory, and metabolic needs of long-distance running are obviously very different from those of sprint swimming or of sexual behavior; so behaviorally specific, context-dependent integration of all varieties of homeostatic afferent feedback must occur in order to balance present and future tissue needs appropriately. Context-dependent, adaptive integration requires accurate modality-selective afferent information in order for an appropriate balance to be achieved. The present chapter addresses the neuroanatomy and neurophysiology of the central integration of sensory feedback from the body in relation to the homeostatic maintenance of the body's physiological condition during physical activity. More detailed reviews of these topics are available elsewhere (Craig, 1996, 2002, 2003a, 2003b). Related psychophysical information on exercise and pain is presented in chapter 14.

In the following I describe first the basic techniques used to study the neuroanatomy and neurophysiology of homeostatic sensory processing, then the characteristics of afferent sensory input from muscle and other tissues of the body during exercise, followed by a description of the central ascending projection system and an overview of the central neural network that represents the sense of the physiological condition of the body (redefined as interoception) in the human brain. Finally, the limitations of our present knowledge and the possible directions for future work are highlighted.

Research Methods in the Neurobiology of Interoception

The neural connections from the peripheral nerves to the spinal cord or from neurons in one region of the central nervous system to other regions are elucidated in modern neuroanatomical tracing studies. Such studies use methods that rely on the transport of chemical markers in the forward (anterograde) direction or backward (retrograde) direction along the fibers (axons) that neurons send out to connect to the next region of integration. Anterograde markers that are injected near the cell bodies define the projections up the chain of processing or down the control sequence, and retrograde markers that are injected in the region of terminations define the cells of origin of projections to that region. By combining such tracing methods with immunohistochemical and cytoarchitectonic delineation of the anatomical structures of interest, as well as with precise physiological characterization of the injection sites and the terminal regions, researchers can construct anatomical maps that show the connections between regions and between particular types of neurons involved in processing different functions. Although neural connections and properties naturally display biological variance between individuals (just like faces and physiques), and can be affected by environmental conditions during development or by training, the basic neurobiological systems that are important for homeostasis are evolutionarily specified and reproducibly well organized.

Such anatomical maps are complemented by single-unit physiological studies of the functional characteristics of the neurons in each processing region. The activity of single afferent sensory nerve fibers that innervate particular peripheral tissues, such as muscle, joint, or skin, can be recorded with wire electrodes; and the activity of single neurons in the spinal cord or brain can be recorded with insulated microelectrodes. In each case, the frequency and pattern of action potentials (electrical impulses that are conveyed by the axons) revealed by such recordings afford a valid measure of the information carried by that neuronal element to the next level of processing. Thus, through use of quantitatively varied or qualitatively discriminating stimuli to test the sensitivity of such neurons, the response characteristics of the entire population of sensory elements can be identified and the integrative properties of the network estimated. For example, in this manner the neurophysiological effects of muscle activity at different levels of the neuraxis can be directly recorded and the homeostatic response channels identified.

Finally, the neuroanatomical and neurophysiological characteristics of central ascending sensory pathways gleaned from studies in experimental animals can be compared with the results of appropriately designed functional imaging experiments in awake humans. Through use of positron emission tomography (PET) with bolus injections of radioactive water or functional magnetic resonance imaging (fMRI) of oxygenated hemoglobin at appropriate time points during a behavioral task, a three-dimensional map of cerebral blood flow can be obtained that is representative of summated regional brain activation (see chapter 3 in this book by J.W. Williamson). By comparing exercise-related activation maps with other task-specific maps, and with the underlying functional anatomical results in experimental animals, one can study the properties of the neuronal networks associated with physical activity and with the sense and control of the physiological condition of the body in humans.

Primary Afferent Sensory Fibers From Muscle and Joint

Muscles and joints are innervated by several types of sensory nerve fibers. Large-diameter Group I or A fibers provide exquisite mechanical sensitivity to length, stretch, and tension and play an important role in the neural control of movement. More slowly conducting, small-diameter Group III and IV (Aδ and C) fibers provide sensory feedback on the physiological condition of the tissues. In general, the Aδ fibers from muscle are mechanically sensitive to muscle contractile state, and the C fibers are sensitive to metabolic conditions; but some in each category are sensitive to the other type of stimulus as well (Kaufman et al., 2002). In contrast to the large-diameter muscle afferents, these fibers do not represent muscle length and only few are directly sensitive to total tension. However, many Group III/IV fibers are activated in a graded manner by both static (steady, or tetanic) and dynamic (repetitive or oscillating) contractions, so they provide feedback mechanosensory inflow representative of muscular work during all types of movement (Sinoway et al., 1993; Pickar, Hill, & Kaufman, 1994). A metabolic representation of muscular work is directly provided by fibers that are sensitive to lactic acid accumulation during muscle activity. Many such muscle Aδ and C fibers are also more highly active during ischemic work, when lactic acid accumulation is accompanied by increases in pCO_2 and other (yet unidentified) metabolites under anaerobic conditions (Adreani et al., 1997; Adreani & Kaufman, 1998). Some fibers are very sensitive to distension along the intramuscular venules, suggesting that they supply mechanosensory information on the perfusion status of the vascular bed (Haouzi et al., 1999). Some are sensitive to noxious mechanical squeeze or to intra-arterial injections of bradykinin or potassium salts, consistent with a role in muscle fatigue, ache, and burning and cramping pain (Mense & Meyer, 1985; Simone et al., 1994).

These properties are consistent with the general characteristics of the small-diameter primary afferent fibers that innervate all tissues of the body, which are sensitive to any change in the mechanical, thermal, or chemical condition of the tissues. Considered as a whole, they convey slow activity sensitive to changes in a wide variety of physiological conditions—temperature, mechanical stress or damage, local metabolism (acidic pH, hypoxia, hypercapnia, hypoglycemia, hypo-osmolarity, lactic acid), cell rupture (adenosine triphosphate, glutamate), cutaneous parasite penetration (histamine, proteinases), mast cell activation (serotonin, bradykinin, eicosanoids), and immune and hormonal activity (cytokines, somatostatin). Aδ and C fibers have been heuristically classified in many studies as thermoreceptors (sensitive to temperature), nociceptors (sensitive to noxious stimulation), osmoreceptors (sensitive to osmotic pressure), C-tactile receptors (responsive to "sensual touch"), and metaboreceptors (sensitive to pH or other metabolic conditions); but many (particularly the C fibers) are in fact polymodal, in that they respond to some degree to several different modalities of stimuli. Thus, they can be viewed globally as signaling a generalized need for greater tissue perfusion, in order to bring more oxygen, nutrients, or warmth, or to remove toxic waste and metabolic by-products, or to deliver immunocytes and systemic hormones in response to local tissue damage. From this perspective, the small-diameter afferent fibers that innervate all tissues of the body, including those from muscle and joint tissue, can be viewed as homeostatic sensory receptors (Prechtl & Powley, 1990; Craig, 2002).

The individual modalities of small-diameter afferent fibers each elicit a characteristic pattern of somatoautonomic or visceroautonomic reflex responses that signify particular homeostatic effector mechanisms (Sato & Schmidt, 1973). The small-diameter afferents from muscle elicit the so-called exercise pressor reflex, that is, sympathetic activation that produces increased heart rate, blood pressure, and respiration (Mitchell & Schmidt, 1984; Wilson & Hand, 1997). The exercise pressor reflex is also partly initiated by the central motor commands. Nevertheless, the Aδ and C fibers from muscle are activated in a graded manner by muscular work, and not merely by extreme exercise, so they drive homeostatic response mechanisms continuously.

Second-Order Neurons in Lamina I

The small-diameter Aδ and C fibers that innervate all peripheral tissues have their cell bodies in the dorsal root ganglia and project their central terminals into the superficial dorsal horn of the spinal cord, where they monosynaptically contact neurons in lamina I and lamina II. The ontogeny (anatomical development) of the small-diameter afferent fibers and the laminae I-II neurons is temporally and genetically coordinated (Prechtl & Powley, 1990; Altman & Bayer, 1984). Thus, the small-diameter afferents originate from a second ("B") wave of small dorsal root ganglion cells that emerge subsequent to the large ("A") cells, which generate mechanoreceptors and proprioceptors and project to the center of the emerging dorsal horn. Simultaneously, laminae I-II neurons originate from the progenitors of autonomic interneurons in the lateral horn (the sympathetic cell column), and they migrate dorsolaterally into the top of the dorsal horn during a ventromedial rotation of the entire dorsal horn, arriving at precisely the right time to meet the ingrowth of the small-diameter fibers. This developmental relationship indicates that the small-diameter afferent fibers and lamina I neurons together form a cohesive homeostatic afferent system that subserves the parallel efferent sympathetic nervous system. This inference is confirmed by the observation that lamina I neurons, which constitute the source of output of the superficial dorsal horn, project directly and selectively to the autonomic preganglionic regions in the spinal cord and to the autonomic integration and premotor regions in the brainstem that hierarchically control homeostasis (Craig, 1996). The small-diameter afferents in cranial parasympathetic nerves (vagus and glossopharyngeal) that innervate visceral organs terminate similarly in the medullary nucleus of the solitary tract, which has similar projections to the homeostatic center.

The lamina I projections in the brainstem converge with afferent activity relayed by the solitary tract nucleus in regions that are heavily interconnected with the hypothalamus and amygdala (specifically, ventrolateral medulla, catecholamine cell groups A1-2 and A5-7, parabrachial nucleus, periaqueductal gray [Craig, 1996]). Lamina I terminations in the brainstem monosynaptically contact the catecholamine cells that identify autonomic premotor regions. Thus, the spinal and bulbar lamina I projections substantialize (provide the anatomic substrates for) the hierarchical somatoautonomic reflexes activated by small-diameter afferents (including visceroceptive activity), which are critical for cardiorespiratory and other homeostatic adjustments to physical activity (Potts, 2001). Notably, these reflex pathways are not simply emergency mechanisms; rather, they provide continuous homeostatic feedback. For example, respiration is linearly modulated by graded changes in innocuous thermosensory activity that is uniquely carried by thermoreceptive-specific lamina I neurons (Diesel, Tucker, & Robertshaw, 1990). This anatomical circuitry is complemented by the descending modulation that lamina I receives directly from brainstem preautonomic sources (A5, A7, raphe). The hierarchical integration of this homeostatic network is strikingly revealed by the observation that the only spinal regions that receive descending controls directly from the hypothalamic paraventricular nucleus, the main diencephalic autonomic control center, are the autonomic motor nuclei and lamina I (Holstege, 1988).

Physiological Characteristics of Lamina I Neurons

The physiological evidence complements these anatomical findings and indicates that lamina I projection neurons relate many aspects of the ongoing physiological status of the tissues of the body. They comprise several distinct, modality-selective classes of neurons that receive input from specific subsets of small-diameter fibers (Craig, 2003b). These classes can be regarded as virtual "labeled lines" (although their activity must be integrated in the forebrain; see later) because they differ morphologically, physiologically, and biochemically and because each class corresponds with a distinct "feeling" from the body, such as sharp pain, burning pain, cool, warm, itch, sensual touch, muscle ache, and cramp. For example, on the basis of cutaneous stimulation, two distinct classes of lamina I neurons can be recognized that, respectively, selectively receive input primarily from Aδ-nociceptors and polymodal C-nociceptors and signal sharp ("first") pain and burning ("second") pain. In addition, there are two types of thermoreceptive-specific lamina I cells that respond selectively to cooling or to warming, and there are distinct types of chemoreceptive cells that respond selectively to histamine or to noxious chemicals, as well as cells that respond selectively to mechanical "slow brush" (sensual touch). The role of lamina I projection neurons in sensation is convincingly highlighted by the subpopulation of histamine-selective cells that receive input only from C fibers with ultraslow conduction velocities and that have a response profile corresponding uniquely with the sensation of itch (Andrew & Craig, 2001). Visceroceptive-specific lamina I cells probably exist, too, although few such cells have so far been identified, apparently for technical reasons (most visceral cells reported to date had convergent cutaneous input and may have been sensitized by the preparation).

The class of lamina I neurons that generates burning pain sensation can be directly related to homeostasis (Craig & Andrew, 2002; Craig, 2003b). These polymodal nociceptive neurons receive predominantly monosynaptic C-nociceptor input; they have multipolar cell bodies that are endowed with receptors for substance P and have myelinated axons, and they respond to noxious heat, pinch, and noxious cold (hence, they are called HPC cells). Their association with burning pain sensation is indicated by three phenomena. First, during a pressure block of A fiber conduction in a peripheral nerve, heat, pinch, and cool (up to 24° C) all evoke a burning sensation, which only HPC lamina I cells can readily explain. Second, the distinct sensation of ice-like burning pain that is elicited by the so-called thermal grill illusion (in which mildly warm and cool bars are interlaced) is quantitatively and uniquely explained by HPC cell activity. Third, only HPC cells correspond with the augmenting sensation of burning pain that is selectively elicited by repeated brief-contact heat stimuli. In this test, a very hot thermode is used that causes only a perception of warmth when placed on the skin very briefly (~0.7 sec); but if such contact is repeated at intervals (<3 sec), then it evokes a strongly augmenting, burning pain sensation, with only a weak sensation of sharp (first) pain. Strikingly, if even one brief contact in a train of contacts is omitted, the sensation will "reset" and begin to augment again from baseline (indicating that the augmentation is a central phenomenon, unrelated to skin temperature, that is probably due to disinhibition). Only HPC lamina I projection cells respond in this way.

The association of polymodal nociceptive HPC lamina I cell activity with homeostasis is revealed by two features. First, ongoing activity of these cells is directly related to the strength of their afferent C fiber input, consistent with the hypothesis that their activity continuously relates tissue metabolic needs. Second, their activity is integrated with other thermosensory activity before generating the sensation of burning pain, which indicates that such pain is a thermoregulatory signal. Thus, their sensitivity to cold includes a dynamic response to temperatures just below normal skin temperature (~34° C) and a static response that begins below a median threshold of ~24° C (~75° F)—that is, they are increasingly active below a thermoneutral (comfortable) ambient temperature. The discomfort that humans increasingly feel below this temperature reflects the homeostatic motivation to thermoregulate behaviorally, though we don't normally interpret that feeling as pain. Cold generates a burning (aching) pain sensation below ~15° C; and at that temperature, HPC responses accelerate and the cooling-related activity in thermoreceptive-specific lamina I cells plateaus. This functional relationship is consistent with the inference that cold becomes noxious when HPC activity exceeds innocuous cooling activity, which is dramatically confirmed by the observation that an artificial reduction of activity in cooling-sensitive neurons (by a peripheral nerve block of cooling-sensitive Aδ fibers or by simultaneous warming in the thermal grill illusion of pain) allows normally innocuous cool temperatures (up to 24° C) to produce burning pain. Thus, the feeling of burning, aching pain (i.e., thermal distress) is normally inhibited by innocuous cooling activity (as all physical trainers and athletes know!). It depends on the integration of these two lamina I sensory channels in the forebrain (and also on core temperature), which directly indicates that the percept of burning pain, and the HPC cell activity that underlies it, signals a homeostatic (thermoregulatory) motivation (Craig, 2003a).

Selective Response of Lamina I Neurons

The role of lamina I in homeostasis is most clearly revealed by the neurons that respond selectively to Aδ and C fiber input from muscle (Wilson, Andrew, & Craig, 2002). By obtaining stable microelectrode recordings from single lamina I neurons in a preparation in which tonic muscle contraction could be elicited without interrupting the muscle's afferent fibers, we identified a class of lamina I spinobulbar neurons that respond selectively during or after (or both during and after) muscle contraction (figure 2.1). As noted earlier, some of the muscle Aδ and C fibers that activate these lamina I cells are sensitive to contraction; others, sensitive to lactic acid and other metabolites released during muscular exercise, can be viewed as metaboreceptors (or "ergoreceptors") that continuously drive a variety of regional and whole-body homeostatic adjustments to muscular

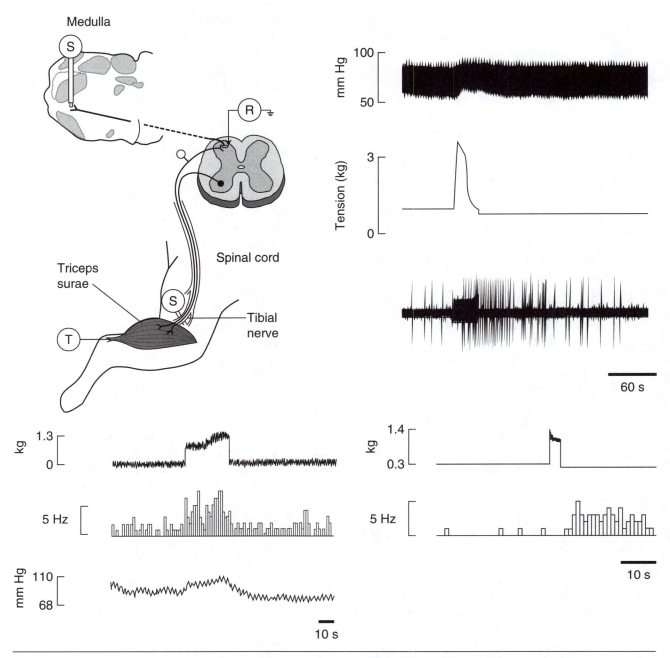

Figure 2.1 S: Stimulus site, R: Recording site, T: Tension measurement. Three representative examples of the responses of lamina I spinobulbar neurons to static contraction of the gastrocnemius-soleus muscle in the cat. The separate traces indicate the evoked blood pressure increase, the analog record of muscle tension, and the evoked neuronal activity (shown as the raw spike record or a histogram). The diagram in the upper left shows the experimental paradigm, in which single units were recorded in lamina I of the spinal cord. The units were antidromically identified as spinobulbar neurons using electrical stimulation in the ipsilateral caudal ventrolateral medulla. Contraction of the muscle was elicited by electrical stimulation of the intact nerve using brief electrical pulses that activated only the efferent tibial nerve fibers, not the afferent fibers.

Composed from data illustrated in Wilson et al., 2002.

work. Accordingly, some of the lamina I neurons we identified responded only during the contraction, with activity that paralleled the increase in mean arterial pressure recorded during the contraction. Other lamina I cells responded mainly or only after the contraction, consistent with a selective input from C fiber metaboreceptors. Because we identified these neurons physiologically as spinobulbar projection neurons by antidromic activation from the medulla (that is, by electrically activating their axon terminals in the brainstem to send retrograde impulses up the axon to the cell body, where the recording microelectrode was located), it seems likely that these neurons provide a substrate for the "exercise pressor reflex" by directly activating homeostatic (cardiorespiratory) integration centers in the brainstem. We have recorded similar (spinothalamic) lamina I neurons that were selectively responsive to small-diameter input from muscle or joint and projected to the forebrain, and these neurons could similarly generate muscle sensations (Craig & Kniffki, 1985). It is important to recognize that such muscle-sensitive lamina I neurons can subserve ongoing homeostatic adjustments to muscular work but can also be associated with muscle burn and pain. Large increases in muscle small-diameter afferent activity can cause the familiar aching or burning sensation from muscles, and synchronous activation causes a painful cramping sensation (Simone et al., 1994). Yet the activity elicited continuously by muscle contraction normally produces homeostatic adjustments without the conscious perception of a behaviorally motivating "feeling."

Lamina I has been viewed by many as having a role in "pain and temperature" sensations. However, these muscle-selective lamina I neurons clearly confirm the broader view that lamina I has a role in ongoing homeostasis, consonant with the anatomical findings. These neurons substantiate the fundamental concept that lamina I projections provide the ascending modality-selective afferent sensory activity that informs the nervous system about the current physiological condition of all tissues of the body (Craig, 2003b).

Forebrain Projections of Lamina I Neurons

Ascending lamina I activity is integrated in subprimates mainly in several sites in the brainstem, in particular the A1 cell group in the caudal ventrolateral medulla, the parabrachial nucleus (PB), and the periaqueductal gray (PAG). These regions integrate "sympathetic" afferent input from lamina I (i.e., afferent input that parallels the sympathetic autonomic output) and "parasympathetic" afferent input from the nucleus of the solitary tract (i.e., afferent input that parallels parasympathetic output) for the purpose of homeostatic control. By way of descending projections to the autonomic preganglionic cell columns in the spinal cord, they provide autonomic premotor control; and in a hierarchical fashion, they drive integrated homeostatic behavior by way of projections to the hypothalamus, which is the primary diencephalic autonomic motor center for goal-directed autonomic activity, and to the midline thalamus, which in turn projects to cingulate cortex, the limbic behavioral motor cortex (for references, see Craig, 2003b). The PB also projects to the central nucleus of the amygdala, which has a critical role in associative autonomic (cardiovascular) emotional responses to physical challenges as well as in fear conditioning and opiatergic mechanisms of analgesia.

Lamina I projections to the thalamus in subprimates basically seem to provide a medial pathway important for autonomic integration, indirectly by way of the brainstem and directly by way of the thalamic submedial nucleus (which projects to orbitofrontal cortex), and a lateral pathway important for visceromotor control of skeletal actions by way of inputs to the sensorimotor nuclei of the thalamus (Craig, 2002, 2004). In primates, however, there are two phylogenetically novel extensions of the lamina I afferent homeostatic pathway. Briefly, lamina I spinothalamic neurons activate a limbic sensory cortical field in the insula, by way of a specific thalamocortical relay nucleus (i.e., the posterior part of the ventral medial nucleus, VMpo), and they also activate a limbic behavioral motor cortical field in the anterior cingulate by way of a relay in the medial thalamus (i.e., the ventral caudal part of the medial dorsal nucleus, MDvc). These two projections correlate with the sensory and the motivational aspects of feelings from the body in humans, respectively. Both are strongly interconnected with amygdala, hypothalamus, orbitofrontal cortex, and brainstem homeostatic regions. Consonant with this view, a lesion of the spinal cord in humans interrupts contralateral temperature, pain, itch, sensual touch, and visceral sensations if made at the location of ascending lamina I axons in the lateral spinothalamic tract; in contrast, a lesion of dorsal posterior insula in humans disrupts the ability to localize and discriminate pain and temperature sensations, while a lesion of the anterior cingulate can block the affective (unpleasant) or aversive behavioral aspect of pain.

The lamina I spinothalamic projection to the dedicated thalamocortical relay nucleus in the posterolateral thalamus, the VMpo, is topographic and modality-selective (Craig, 2002, 2004). The VMpo is diminutive in the macaque monkey thalamus and is only primordially represented in subprimates, if at all, but it is proportionately greatly enlarged and well developed in the human thalamus. The VMpo projects topographically to a discrete portion of dorsal posterior insular cortex. This interoceptive cortex contains a modality-selective representation of all "sympathetic" afferent activity from lamina I that is contiguous anteriorly with a representation of all "parasympathetic" afferent activity from the solitary nucleus (by way of the adjacent basal part of the ventral medial nucleus, VMb). Although the dorsal posterior insular cortex that receives input from VMpo is often misidentified as "S2," or the second somatosensory cortex (which actually lies more lateral in the parietal operculum), many functional imaging studies in humans provide convergent data confirming the role of the dorsal posterior insula in pain, temperature, itch, muscle sensation, sensual touch, cardiorespiratory activity, taste, hunger, thirst, and so on.

The VMpo also activates cortical area 3a, a portion of the sensorimotor cortex that is intercalated between the primary somatosensory and primary motor areas. Vestibular and vagal afferents similarly activate area 3a (Ito & Craig, 2003), indicating that activation of area 3a should not simply be considered "exteroceptive," or related to external stimuli. Rather, this region may be involved in sensorimotor cortical control associated with interoceptive feelings (such as pain)—that is, viscerosomatic reflex activity—although a role in perception is also possible (see Perl, 1984). The VMpo projection to area 3a is probably responsible for the activation often ascribed to "S1," or the primary somatosensory cortex, in some functional imaging studies of pain (Bushnell et al., 1999; Craig, 2003b).

The direct relay of lamina I spinothalamic tract (STT) activity in primates and humans to the anterior cingulate cortex (ACC) by way of MDvc contrasts with the indirect pathway in subprimates that conveys lamina I activity to medial thalamus and the ACC after integration with other homeostatic afferent inputs in the brainstem PB. Whereas the insula can be regarded as limbic sensory cortex because of its association with homeostatic afferent activity, the ACC can be regarded as limbic motor cortex based on its association with homeostatic motor activity. Many functional imaging studies have documented the role of the human ACC in behavioral drive and volition (for references, see Craig, 2002). The ACC is activated in all imaging studies of pain. For example, functional imaging studies of the thermal grill illusion of pain and of hypnotically modulated pain unpleasantness demonstrate that this pathway engenders the affect and motivation that render pain a homeostatic emotional drive.

Interoception in Humans

Thus, in primates the lamina I spinothalamic projection activates a limbic sensory cortical field in the insula and also a limbic behavioral motor cortical field in the anterior cingulate. These two projections correlate, respectively, with the sensory and the motivational aspects of feelings from the body in humans; and because all emotions can be characterized as the combination of a feeling and a motivation, this supports the new view of feelings from the body as homeostatic emotions that drive survival behaviors (Craig, 2003a). So, if the body is too warm (hyperthermic), then a cool glass of water feels pleasant, reflecting thermoregulatory motivation; but if the body is too cool (hypothermic), then the same cool temperature feels gnawingly unpleasant (Mower, 1976). Similarly, if the body needs salt, then salt tastes good until a sufficient amount is ingested, and then it becomes unpleasant (so-called stimulus-specific satiety). The same perspective applies to muscle ache, hunger, thirst, pain, and other feelings from the body, which reflect different physiological (homeostatic) conditions and motivate appropriate homeostatic behaviors. Notably, the structural absence of the modality-selective interoceptive representation in the insula and the direct motivational pathway to cingulate in subprimates imply that they cannot experience feelings from the body in the same way that humans do.

The accumulating functional imaging data in humans indicate that homeostatic afferent activity is uniquely represented in the dorsal posterior insula and, for modalities such as thermal sensation and hunger, does not activate parietal somatosensory cortices at all (Craig et al., 2000). The same is true for muscle feelings associated with dynamic and isometric exercise. This validates the neuroanatomical distinction of interoceptive modalities, important for homeostasis and autonomic activity, from the exteroceptive modalities of touch and limb position, which are important for somatic motor control. The primordial role of the insular cortex seems to be modulation of brainstem homeostatic integration, because its main descending projections are to PB, PAG, amygdala, hypothalamus, and lamina I (Yasui et al., 1991). These considerations support the view that the interoceptive cortical image that provides the sense of the physiological condition of the body in humans emerged evolutionarily from the hierarchy of the homeostatic system. In other words, the sensory channels that produce sensations of muscle ache, temperature, pain, itch, and sensual touch evolved within this pathway because the primary role of such activity is homeostasis. In fact, the importance of the dorsal posterior insular cortex for physical well-being is underscored by its clear delimitation in the monkey by in situ hybridization labeling (that is, histological labeling for messenger RNA) for receptors for corticotropin releasing factors, which are thought by many to be definitive indicators of an association with homeostatic regulation (Sanchez et al., 1999). Of particular importance for studies of physical activity and exercise, the dorsal posterior insular cortex is selectively activated by both isometric and dynamic exercise, like the lamina I neurons that respond selectively during and after muscle contraction (Williamson et al., 1999; see chapter 3). Notably, these observations also provide a substantive neuroanatomical basis for interactions between these different homeostatic afferent modalities.

The most striking feature of the recent findings on the forebrain representation of homeostatic afferent activity is the indication that, in humans, the cortical rerepresentation of the interoceptive image of the body's condition provides a basis for the subjective awareness of all emotions (Craig, 2002, 2003a). The data indicate that the primary cortical homeostatic sensory representation in interoceptive cortex is successively rerepresented in a series of areas, first anteriorly in the middle insula and then in lateralized representations in the right (nondominant) anterior insula. These successive rerepresentations are not present in monkeys and seem to be unique to humans. Functional imaging data from PET and fMRI studies show that the right anterior insula is associated with subjective awareness of many emotions, including not only the homeostatic emotions of pain, temperature, sexual arousal, hunger, and thirst, but also primary emotions such as anger, disgust, sadness, happiness, and trust. This convergence fits with the notion that human emotions are based in part on feelings from the body, which is the essence of the James-Lange theory of emotion (James, 1890).

The meta-representation of the state of the body in the right anterior insula seems to differentiate inner from outer conditions and to provide a subjective mental image of the material self as a feeling (sentient) entity that is utilized during all emotional states—in other words, it seems to provide the anatomical basis for emotional awareness. This fits with the anatomical features of the so-called somatic marker hypothesis of consciousness proposed by Damasio (1993). Importantly, these neuroanatomical data indicate that the cortical image of subjective feelings is built upon the homeostatic (interoceptive) hierarchy. Thus, viewing pain, temperature, and muscle ache as homeostatic emotions enables ready explanations of the interactions between these homeostatic functions and emotional state. This neuroanatomical model also provides a ready explanation for psychosomatic illness, provides a mechanistic explanation for placebo analgesia (in which the anterior cingulate, the behavioral agent, directly modulates the subjective feeling state in the anterior insula), and provides a substantive proposal for understanding the conjoint activation of anterior insula and anterior cingulate during higher emotions, such as during the empathic registration of the feelings of others.

Finally, this conceptual framework has strong implications for clinical therapy and exercise science. The neural representation of all aspects of the physiological condition of the body in an integrated system that is responsible for homeostasis, and that is associated with stress, provides a solid, scientific epistemological foundation for using integrated, whole-body approaches to the treatment of pain and other physical disorders. For example, awareness of bodily feelings is correlated with emotionality, clearly suggesting that alterations in salt balance or oxygen availability can affect not only physical distress but also emotional distress, such as panic (Craig, 2002, 2003a; Richerson, 2004). It remains to be seen how endogenous homeostatic mechanisms provide integrated control of the activity that produces pain and muscle ache, and how these might be engaged by therapeutic intervention. The additional finding that sensual touch and sexual arousal are incorporated within the same interoceptive system that represents hunger, pain, and muscle ache has strong implications for the neurobiological and health effects of conspecific contact, particularly on pain and emotional state (Olausson et al., 2002). Lastly, the observation that the neuroanatomical substrates for subjective awareness and emotion in humans are based on a meta-representation of the physiological state of the body clearly emphasizes the role of the body's health in human consciousness and social behavior.

Weaknesses and Limitations in the Literature

There are four main issues to consider in evaluation of the literature: the limitations of neurobiological methods, the limited knowledge of neural substrates, species differences, and the limitations of functional imaging methods.

Neurobiological Methods

The single-unit analyses obtained in neurophysiological studies provide critical functional information that can be compared with human psychophysical responses. For example, the response properties of lamina I itch-selective neurons or lamina I thermoreceptive-specific (cooling) neurons match almost exactly the available psychophysical data on the sensitivity of human perception with comparable stimuli (Andrew & Craig, 2001). However, such experimental neurophysiological single-unit studies are almost always performed in animals under surgical anesthesia, by necessity, and the anesthetic must affect the response properties and integrative characteristics of such neurons. Furthermore, in the intact brain, entire populations of different types of neurons are activated even by the simplest stimuli, such as a thermal cooling ramp or muscle contraction; and their interactions and integration can be elucidated completely only through examination of whole populations of neurons in

ensemble recordings. Such studies are technically extremely difficult and are only just beginning to appear in the literature.

Distinctions in the Neural Substrates

Our knowledge of the central neurons that provide the afferent and efferent pathways for homeostasis is certainly inadequate, and future studies will of course identify subtle distinctions and resolve additional categories that will illuminate the homeostatic control of the physiological condition of the body. For example, recent retrograde anatomical findings indicate that lamina I spinobulbar neurons and lamina I spinothalamic neurons are two distinct subpopulations (Andrew, Krout, & Craig, 2003). This is quite surprising, because reviewers have often assumed that spinobulbar terminations are collaterals of spinothalamic projections. Nevertheless, the finding is consistent with single-unit physiological evidence that lamina I spinobulbar neurons receive muscle C fiber input, whereas spinothalamic lamina I neurons receive only Aδ muscle afferent input (Craig & Kniffki, 1985; Wilson, Andrew, & Craig, 2002). Although the functional significance of the latter distinction is not known, at a systems level, the separation of these two subpopulations means not only that different information is provided to the homeostatic control mechanisms in the brainstem and to the forebrain behavioral control systems, but also that the central neural homeostatic control systems can modulate the activity of these two sensory channels differentially by way of descending control pathways. At a behavioral level, this implies, for instance, that methods for biofeedback control of homeostatic integration may be separable from the psychological control of "feelings."

Neurobiological Species Differences

The lamina I homeostatic afferent pathway is an evolutionarily ancient neuroanatomical substrate that provides sensory feedback for control of integrative autonomic function in mammals; so, homeostatic integration can be aptly studied at the spinal and brainstem levels in experimental animals, such as rats and cats. Although there are naturally some differences in the homeostatic needs of humans, rats, and cats, there is a strong likelihood that similar mechanisms are in place at these levels in their central nervous systems. Similarly, the "parasympathetic" afferents that relay in the nucleus of the solitary tract are probably similarly integrated in the brainstems of all homeothermic mammals.

However, the neuroanatomical findings indicate that the forebrain connections in primates are phylogenetically novel, and the evolutionary enlargement of the lamina I spinothalamic projections in the human is certainly unique. Indeed, the meta-representations of the interoceptive cortical image in the right anterior insula of humans apparently are not present in monkeys at all (Craig, 2002, 2003a). A parallel neuroanatomical finding has been reported in that a unique type of cortical neuron (the so-called spindle cell) has been observed in the right anterior insula and ACC of humanoid primates (in decreasing frequency in aged humans, children, the gorilla, orangutan, bonobo, and pygmy chimp), but not in subhumanoid primates (macaque monkeys) (Allman et al., 2004). These are trenchant observations, because they also parallel the results of the mirror test for self-awareness (or consciousness; Macphail, 1998). These neurobiological levels can be studied therefore only in humans and humanoid primates.

Thus, psychophysical interactions between homeostatic conditions and emotional states during physical activity can be studied in subprimates only with the strong caveat that, whereas such animals display emotional behaviors that resemble ours (because of the common evolutionary heritage), they do not have the neuroanatomical substrates present in the human brain that provide the basis for self-awareness, sentience, and "feelings." Studies that seek insights into the interactions between physical state and experienced emotions are best performed in humans. For example, studies of the effects of physical activity on hormone levels in rats should be interpreted only in terms of brainstem and hypothalamic mechanisms of homeostatic integration, rather than in terms of effects on emotions and "feelings."

Functional Imaging

The advent of the functional imaging methods has afforded the ability to analyze forebrain mechanisms of psychophysiological phenomena in awake humans, which is a truly exciting advance. However, these methods have important limitations. They are all indirect indicators of neuronal activity, because they are actually measures of regional cerebral blood flow. These methods at present all have very limited sensitivity and spatial/temporal resolution. The technical burdens (e.g., shimming of magnetic field inhomogeneities) are enormous, and analysis methods vary between groups. So, similar experiments performed at different facilities often produce different results.

In order to avoid the vagueness of "blob-ology," functional imaging studies must be carefully interpreted. Negative findings have limited power, except where a double dissociation can be demonstrated in a two-factorial paradigm. Regression analyses that can be related directly to psychophysical response functions are most powerful. Congruence with functional anatomical results from primates or humans provides the strongest evidence of a functional association. On the other hand, comparing human functional imaging results with the neuroanatomical forebrain connections in rats would be rather weak.

Directions for Future Investigation

The most important future studies will bring together the different perspectives of what have been, to date, the different disciplines of neurobiology, psychophysiology, and exercise science. Enthusiasm for this timely conjunction is, of course, the impetus for this volume. A deeper examination of the sense of fatigue could provide such a focus, for example. The phenomenon of fatigue has received considerable attention in the fields of motor neurophysiology and exercise science, but fatigue-related sensory activity in lamina I neurons has not been examined yet with neurophysiological methods. The long-duration muscle activity that produces fatigue must be associated with changes in the activity of the lamina I neurons that represent $A\delta$ and C fiber inputs from muscle and joint. Blockade of muscle afferent activity has been used to examine cardiovascular integration during exercise (Smith et al., 2003) and could be used to examine fatigue as well. An examination of such changes could be combined with microneurographic studies of $A\delta$ and C muscle fiber activity in humans and with psychophysical studies of the interactions of fatigue with other homeostatic variables in humans or, further, with analyses of the interactions of fatigue with emotional drive.

Another example of an underappreciated issue is the very intriguing observation that the descending hypothalamic terminations in lamina I contain many peptides, such as oxytocin, vasopressin, and hypocretin, all of which are well known to be involved in homeostatic responses to metabolic and emotional conditions (e.g., van den Pol, 1999). The role of these peptides in modulating lamina I activity is unknown. For example, their actions could be significant for the pharmacological modulation of fatigue-related activity at the first central synapse, and such knowledge could have profound therapeutic significance. There are virtually no neurobiological findings that address the effects of hypothalamic modulation on the sense of the physiological condition of the body during physical activity.

Of course, there are many possible central integration sites at which pharmacological intervention might have therapeutic importance. As a final example, recent findings indicate that insulin-related growth factor-1 (IGF-1) released during exercise crosses the blood–brain barrier and affects neural activity in several central sites, including the cerebellum (Carro et al., 2000). Other substances released during exercise can affect feelings and emotions; for example, phenylethanolamine, with its effects on depression, can be related directly to the neural pathways described in this chapter. The observation that the human sense of emotional well-being is based on the representation of the physiological condition of the body emphasizes the importance of further knowledge on the biochemical bases of homeostasis and the effects of physical activity on the neurobiology of emotion and health. The use of rapidly evolving functional imaging methods to characterize the neural substrates for human homeostatic emotions can be expected to have enormous impact in this regard. These new methods include MR morphometry as well (Critchley et al., 2004).

References

Adreani, C.M., Hill, J.M., & Kaufman, M.P. (1997). Responses of group III and IV muscle afferents to dynamic exercise. *Journal of Applied Physiology, 82,* 1811-1817.

Adreani, C.M., & Kaufman, M.P. (1998). Effect of arterial occlusion on responses of group III and IV afferents to dynamic exercise. *Journal of Applied Physiology, 84,* 1827-1833.

Allman, J., Hakeem, A., Tetreault, N., & Semendeferi, K. (2004). The spindle neurons of frontoinsular cortex (area FI) are unique to humans and african apes. *Society for Neuroscience Abstracts Online 725.5.*

Altman, J., & Bayer, S.A. (1984). The development of the rat spinal cord. *Advances in Anatomy, Embryology and Cell Biology, 85,* 1-164.

Andrew, D., & Craig, A.D. (2001). Spinothalamic lamina I neurons selectively sensitive to histamine: A central neural pathway for itch. *Nature Neuroscience, 4,* 72-77.

Andrew, D., Krout, K.E., & Craig, A.D. (2003). Differentiation of lamina I spinomedullary and spinothalamic neurons in the cat. *Journal of Comparative Neurology, 458,* 257-271.

Appenzeller, O., & Oribe, E. (1997). *The autonomic nervous system: An introduction to basic and clinical concepts* (5th ed.). Amsterdam: Elsevier.

Bushnell, M.C., Duncan, G.H., Hofbauer, R.K., Ha, B., Chen, J.I., & Carrier, B. (1999). Pain perception: Is there a role for primary somatosensory cortex? *Proceedings of the National Academy of Sciences, 96,* 7705-7709.

Cannon, W.B. (1939). *The wisdom of the body.* New York: Norton.

Carro, E., Nunez, A., Busiguina, S., & Torres-Aleman, I. (2000). Circulating insulin-like growth factor I mediates effects of exercise on the brain. *Journal of Neuroscience, 20,* 2926-2933.

Craig, A.D. (1996). An ascending general homeostatic afferent pathway originating in lamina I. In G. Holstege, R. Bandler, & C.B. Saper (Eds.), *The emotional motor system* (pp. 225-242). Amsterdam: Elsevier.

Craig, A.D. (2002). How do you feel? Interoception: The sense of the physiological condition of the body. *Nature Reviews: Neuroscience, 3,* 655-666.

Craig, A.D. (2003a). A new view of pain as a homeostatic emotion. *Trends in Neuroscience, 26,* 303-307.

Craig, A.D. (2003b). Pain mechanisms: Labeled lines versus convergence in central processing. *Annual Review of Neuroscience, 26,* 1-30.

Craig, A.D. (2004). Distribution of trigeminothalamic and spinothalamic lamina I terminations in the macaque monkey. *Journal of Comparative Neurology, 477,* 119-148.

Craig, A.D., & Andrew, D. (2002). Responses of spinothalamic lamina I neurons to repeated brief contact heat stimulation in the cat. *Journal of Neurophysiology, 87,* 1902-1914.

Craig, A.D., Bushnell, M.C., Zhang, E.-T., & Blomqvist, A. (1994). A thalamic nucleus specific for pain and temperature sensation. *Nature, 372,* 770-773.

Craig, A.D., Chen, K., Bandy, D., & Reiman, E.M. (2000). Thermosensory activation of insular cortex. *Nature Neuroscience, 3,* 184-190.

Craig, A.D., & Kniffki, K.-D. (1985). Spinothalamic lumbo-sacral lamina I cells responsive to skin and muscle stimulation in the cat. *Journal of Physiology (London)*, *365*, 197-221.

Critchley, H.D., Wiens, S., Rotshtein, P., Ohman, A., & Dolan, R.J. (2004). Neural systems supporting interoceptive awareness. *Nature Neuroscience, 7*, 189-195.

Damasio, A.R. (1993). *Descartes' error: Emotion, reason, and the human brain.* New York: Putnam.

Diesel, D.A., Tucker, A., & Robertshaw, D. (1990). Cold-induced changes in breathing pattern as a strategy to reduce respiratory heat loss. *Journal of Applied Physiology, 69*, 1946-1952.

Gisolfi, C.V., & Mora, F. (2000). *The hot brain.* Cambridge, MA: MIT Press.

Haouzi, P., Hill, J.M., Lewis, B.K., & Kaufman, M.P. (1999). Responses of group III and IV muscle afferents to distension of the peripheral vascular bed. *Journal of Applied Physiology, 87*, 545-553.

Holstege, G. (1988). Direct and indirect pathways to lamina I in the medulla oblongata and spinal cord of the cat. In H.L. Fields & J.M. Besson. (Eds.), *Progress in brain research, vol. 77* (pp. 47-94). Amsterdam: Elsevier.

Ito, S.I., & Craig, A.D. (2003). Vagal input to lateral area 3a in cat cortex. *Journal of Neurophysiology, 90*, 143-154.

James, W. (1890). The Principles of Psychology. http://psychclassics.yorku.ca/James/Principles/index.htm (accessed July 13, 2005).

Kaufman, M.P., Hayes, S.G., Adreani, C.M., & Pickar, J.G. (2002). Discharge properties of group III and IV muscle afferents. *Advances in Experimental Medicine and Biology, 508*, 25-32.

Loewy, A.D., & Spyer, K.M. (1990). *Central regulation of autonomic functions.* New York: Oxford.

Macphail, E.M. (1998). *The evolution of consciousness.* Oxford: Oxford University Press.

Mense, S., & Meyer, H. (1985). Different types of slowly conducting afferent units in cat skeletal muscle and tendon. *Journal of Physiology (London), 363*, 403-417.

Mitchell, J.H., & Schmidt, R.F. (1984). Cardiovascular reflex control by afferent fibers from skeletal muscle receptors. In J.T. Shepard & F.M. Abboud (Eds.), *Handbook of physiology, sec. 2, The cardiovascular system, vol. 3* (pp. 623-658). Bethesda, MD: American Physiological Society.

Mower, G. (1976). Perceived intensity of peripheral thermal stimuli is independent of internal body temperature. *Journal of Comparative Physiological Psychology, 90*, 1152-1155.

Olausson, H., Lamarre, Y., Backlund, H., Morin, C., Wallin, B.G., Starck, G., Ekholm, S., Strigo, I., Worsley, K.,

Vallbo, A.B., & Bushnell, M.C. (2002). Unmyelinated tactile afferents signal touch and project to insular cortex. *Nature Neuroscience, 5,* 900-904.

Perl, E.R. (1984). Pain and nociception. In I. Darian-Smith (Ed.), *Handbook of physiology, sec. 1, The nervous system,* vol. 3, *Sensory processes* (pp. 915-975). Bethesda, MD: American Physiological Society.

Pickar, J.G., Hill, J.M., & Kaufman, M.P. (1994). Dynamic exercise stimulates group III muscle afferents. *Journal of Neurophysiology, 71*, 753-760.

Potts, J.T. (2001). Exercise and sensory integration. Role of the nucleus tractus solitarius. *Annals of the New York Academy of Sciences, 940*, 221-236.

Prechtl, J.C., & Powley, T.L. (1990). B-afferents: A fundamental division of the nervous system mediating homeostasis. *Behavioral and Brain Sciences, 13*, 289-332.

Richerson, G.B. (2004). Serotonergic neurons as carbon dioxide sensors that maintain pH homeostasis. *Nature Reviews: Neuroscience, 5,* 449-461.

Sanchez, M.M., Young, L.J., Plotsky, P.M., & Insel, T.R. (1999). Autoradiographic and in situ hybridization localization of corticotropin-releasing factor 1 and 2 receptors in nonhuman primate brain. *Journal of Comparative Neurology, 408*, 365-377.

Saper, C.B. (2002). The central autonomic nervous system: Conscious visceral perception and autonomic pattern generation. *Annual Review of Neuroscience, 25*, 433-469.

Sato, A., & Schmidt, R.F. (1973). Somatosympathetic reflexes: Afferent fibers, central pathways, discharge characteristics. *Physiological Reviews, 53,* 916-947.

Simone, D.A., Marchettini, P., Caputi, G., & Ochoa, J.L. (1994). Identification of muscle afferents subserving sensation of deep pain in humans. *Journal of Neurophysiology, 72,* 883-889.

Sinoway, L.I., Hill, J.M., Pickar, J.G., & Kaufman, M.P. (1993). Effects of contraction and lactic acid on the discharge of group III muscle afferents in cats. *Journal of Neurophysiology, 69*, 1053-1059.

Smith, S.A., Querry, R.G., Fadel, P.J., Gallagher, K.M., Stromstad, M., Ide, K., Raven, P.B., & Secher, N.H. (2003). Partial blockade of skeletal muscle somatosensory afferents attenuates baroreflex resetting during exercise in humans. *Journal of Physiology, 551,* 1013-1021.

Swanson, L.W. (2000). Cerebral hemisphere regulation of motivated behavior. *Brain Research, 886,* 113-164.

van den Pol, A.N. (1999). Hypothalamic hypocretin (orexin): Robust innervation of the spinal cord. *Journal of Neuroscience, 19*, 3171-3182.

Williamson, J.W., McColl, R., Mathews, D., Ginsburg, M., & Mitchell, J.H. (1999). Activation of the insular cortex is affected by the intensity of exercise. *Journal of Applied Physiology, 87*, 1213-1219.

Wilson, L.B., Andrew, D., & Craig, A.D. (2002). Activation of spinobulbar lamina I neurons by static muscle contraction. *Journal of Neurophysiology, 87,* 1641-1645.

Wilson, L.B., & Hand, G.A. (1997). The pressor reflex evoked by static contraction: Neurochemistry at the site of the first synapse. *Brain Research Reviews, 23,* 196-209.

Yasui, Y., Breder, C.D., Saper, C.B., & Cechetto, D.F. (1991). Autonomic responses and efferent pathways from the insular cortex in the rat. *Journal of Comparative Neurology, 303,* 355-374.

3

Brain Activation During Physical Activity

Jon W. Williamson, PhD

Our fascination with the human brain is long-standing, and significant advances have been made toward our understanding of brain function, more commonly termed the mind–body relationship, over the last century. These advancements were especially evident during the "Decade of the Brain" encompassing the 1990s. The majority of this work focused on what can be termed the cognitive neurosciences, involving topics related to thinking, learning, sensation, perception, language processing, visual recognition, and memory. However, there have also been significant advancements in our understanding of the relationship between physical activity or exercise and brain function.

Some of the earliest "brain and exercise" studies involved measuring changes in global cerebral blood flow during exercise (Roland, 1993). As the technology advanced, more emphasis was placed on assessing patterns of regional cerebral blood flow (rCBF), as an index of local brain activation, during various types of motor tasks (Olesen, 1971). Concerning the motor system, many of the earlier motor function studies focused on defining somatotopic organization, identification of areas recruited to perform specific types of movements, and the role of primary and supplementary motor regions in the planning and execution of movement. These studies have provided a wealth of information regarding the role of the brain in motor function and have been reviewed in great detail (Roland, 1993). With a greater understanding of how the sensorimotor system typically responds to complex and simple movement, the stage has been set for studies that directly address how the brain can be "reorganized" in response to injury toward facilitating the restoration of function through the use of physical therapy and rehabilitation.

Physical activity is also capable of eliciting changes in autonomic function, with the brain playing a role in cardiovascular modulation. Some of the earliest studies indicated that the higher brain (cerebral cortex) was largely involved in the overall cardiovascular responses to exercise (Johansson, 1895). Although a link between the higher brain and brainstem regions of cardiovascular integration was well accepted, there were few data to suggest which specific regions of the higher brain were driving the cardiovascular responses. Animal studies have identified the neural pathways and reciprocal connections between various regions of the higher brain and brainstem nuclei involved in cardiovascular regulation (Ruggierio et al., 1987; Cechetto & Saper, 1990; Waldrop et al., 1996; Verberne & Owens, 1998). However, while evidence of regional involvement is accumulating, the specific areas of the human brain involved in the modulation of cardiovascular responses during physical activity have not been definitively established.

As with many research topics involving humans, there is a large dependency upon technology, and this is especially true for human brain imaging. Advances in our understanding of brain processes have gone hand in hand with the evolution of imaging equipment. Neuronal activation in the brain is typically accompanied by changes in local metabolism, blood flow, and blood oxygenation. There are specific imaging techniques that utilize each of these types of changes to assess brain activity: positron emission tomography (PET)—metabolism; single photon emission computed tomography (SPECT)—regional cerebral blood flow; and functional magnetic resonance imaging (fMRI)—blood oxygenation. While the following descriptions of these techniques are very brief, more detailed information for each of these methodologies can be found in Orrison and colleagues (1995).

Developed in the early 1970s, PET involves the intravenous injection of short-lived radioactive compounds. These compounds travel into the brain and can track brain metabolism. Subjects must have their head positioned within the confines of the imaging device during the task or activity being assessed, and they must keep their head very still while performing the task or activity. Sensitive detectors positioned around the subject's head track positron emissions, and a computer is used to develop a spatial distribution of the radioactivity within the brain. Areas of increased or decreased metabolism will show up as areas of increased or decreased radioactivity, respectively.

Another technique similar to PET is SPECT, which also involves intravenous injection (or inhalation) of radiopharmaceuticals. These agents are distributed throughout the brain according to patterns of rCBF and can provide good indices of neuronal activation (Raichle, 1987). A major difference between PET and SPECT is that the SPECT radiopharmaceuticals, once in the brain, undergo a conformational change so that they are temporarily "retained" in brain tissue. In other words, a SPECT tracer can be injected during treadmill running to map the patterns of brain activity during running. Within about 2 min of injection, the blood flow tracer is trapped in the brain. The actual imaging part of the study using the detectors can be performed at a later time with the subject resting supine in the camera. While the ability to accurately assess activity for smaller brain regions (spatial resolution) is better with PET (6-8 mm^3) than for SPECT (10-12 mm^3), the SPECT offers the unique opportunity to assess brain activity during larger-muscle exercise.

A newer method for assessing brain activation is fMRI. The fMRI is noninvasive and can be used to assess regional changes in levels of blood oxygenation. As neuronal activity increases during a task, local metabolism and blood flow increase, resulting in changes in ratios of oxygenated to deoxygenated blood. It is the intrinsic paramagnetic properties of deoxyhemoglobin that allow for patterns of brain activity to be assessed using magnetic resonance imaging technology. The spatial resolution is very good for fMRI (1-3 mm^3), but the subject must be inside the magnet with the head remaining very still during imaging. While these techniques offer unique advantages (and disadvantages), all have been employed by investigators to provide important information toward our understanding of brain function during physical activity.

The focus of this chapter is to provide an overview of scientific literature involving physical activity and human brain mapping with particular attention to the topics of the cerebral cortical regions involved in (a) the modulation of cardiovascular responses during physical activity and (b) functional reorganization in the injured brain accompanying physical therapy interventions.

Central Cardiovascular Modulation

Central modulation of the cardiovascular system via descending signals from the cerebral cortex has been well recognized for over a century, yet the specific regions of the human brain involved in this exercise-related response have remained speculative. Since exercise can simultaneously activate motor and cardiovascular systems, brain mapping studies performed during both exercise and nonexercise conditions have been required to provide information toward establishing the cerebral cortical structures in the human brain specifically involved in modulation of autonomic function, as opposed to those activated in response to task-specific "motor programming." The concept of descending signals from higher brain centers capable of influencing cardiovascular responses during exercise (Zuntz & Geppert, 1886; Johansson, 1895), later termed central command, has been well studied and is widely accepted throughout the scientific community.

Most would concur that the magnitude of central command during exercise can be largely dictated by an individual's perception of effort (or effort sense) during actual or even attempted physical exertion, independent of the actual workload or force production (Mitchell, 1990). While increases in an individual's rating of perceived exertion or effort sense during exercise are coupled with elevated cardiovascular responses, the specific region or regions within the higher brain responsible for generating the neural signals resulting in autonomic adjustments have remained elusive. It is postulated that these signals can affect neural activity within the thalamus, hypothalamus, and mesencephalon prior to reaching brainstem regions of cardiovascular integration. Animal investigations have employed stimulation of both diencephalic and mesencephalic regions to represent the descending central command signals (Kaufman & Forster, 1996; Waldrop et al., 1996) and have provided valuable information as to the role of central command in cardiovascular regulation. Mapping the human brain during exercise makes it possible to gain further insight regarding the specific regions involved in central command or, more specifically, the neural networks altered by changes in one's perception of effort resulting in cardiovascular adjustments.

Functional Anatomy

Primary regions of the cerebral cortex with the capacity for modulation of autonomic function were carefully reviewed by Cechetto and Saper (1990) and Verberne and Owens (1998); and it was concluded that both the insular cortex and the infralimbic cortex, more specifically the medial prefrontal cortex, were well suited for this role. Efferent pathways from the insular cortex to well-recognized sites of cardiovascular control, including the lateral hypothalamus, rostral ventrolateral medulla, and nucleus of the solitary tract, have been documented (Yasui et al., 1991). Changes in heart rate and blood pressure have been reported in response to activation of the insular cortex in both the rat (Ruggierio et al., 1987) and human (Oppenheimer et al., 1992). Saper (1982) noted a convergence of autonomic and limbic connections within the rat insula. There also exist reciprocal connections between the insular cortex and the infralimbic cortex (medial prefontal region), suggesting a potential for interaction between these regions.

The medial prefrontal cortex has multiple limbic sensory inputs and appears to have a significant role in "stress-related modulation" of sympathetic outflow (Verberne & Owens, 1998). Rainville and colleagues (1997) have reported that the anterior cingulate is involved in the perceived unpleasantness of painful stimuli, which can elicit autonomic responses. Likewise, emotional (e.g., fear, anxiety) or mental stressors (e.g., arithmetic) can evoke autonomic adjustments, and Critchley and col-

leagues (2000) have shown activation of the insular region during arithmetic stress. Kuniecki and colleagues (2003) have suggested that activation of the insular cortex is most likely related to any autonomic arousal that might accompany emotional arousal. Taken together, the insular cortex and medial prefrontal cortex may function in concert or independently to interpret various forms of sensory input and elicit appropriate autonomic adjustments.

It would seem plausible to predict that these same brain regions altering cardiovascular responses during nonexercise conditions could also be activated during exercise conditions. It should be noted that the act of exercise per se can evoke both motor and cardiovascular responses, with both generally responding to the exercise in an intensity-dependent manner. Nowak and colleagues (1999) and others (Williamson et al., 2002) have concluded that it is unlikely that activation of the sensorimotor cortex during exercise represents a central command influence on the cardiovascular system. Therefore, central command during exercise may actually involve the simultaneous activation of two separate networks, one for central motor control and one for central cardiovascular control. Given the importance of the insular and medial prefrontal regions in overall cortical modulation of autonomic function, human studies have been performed to assess their possible role in central neural regulation of autonomic function during exercise.

Neuroimaging Studies

Studies investigating the functional anatomy of central command-induced changes in rCBF have identified a network of structures activated in the human brain. These regions include the insular cortex (Critchley et al., 2000; King et al., 1999; Nowak et al., 1999; Williamson et al., 1999, 2001, 2002; Williamson, McColl, & Mathews, 2003) and anterior cingulate cortex or the medial prefrontal region (Thornton et al., 2001; Critchley et al., 2000; King et al., 1999; Williamson et al., 2001, 2002; Williamson, McColl, & Mathews, 2003), as well as thalamic regions (King et al., 1999; Thornton et al., 2001; Williamson et al., 2001, 2002; Williamson, McColl, & Mathews, 2003). These regions represent a combination of limbic, paralimbic, autonomic, and sensory regions, which together may serve as a central command network. Further, these structures appear to be activated in response to an increased perception of effort during exercise when heart rate and blood pressure are elevated.

Focusing first on the insular cortex, it is possible that the observed rCBF changes within the insular cortex were related to the blood pressure increases (Zhang & Oppenheimer, 1997) or skeletal muscle afferent activation (Waldrop & Iwamoto, 1994), or both, during exercise. While muscle afferent signals can result in changes in activation within specific regions of the insular cortex, insular activation during attempted movement was reported in subjects with spinal cord injuries when afferent feedback was absent (Nowak, 2000) and also during imagined exercise, but only when the imagined effort elicited cardiovascular responses (Williamson et al., 2002). With regard to the latter study, an experiment was designed that permitted a contrast between patterns of brain activity during "attempted movement" both with and without cardiovascular activation. To accomplish this, brain activation was compared during actual and imagined handgrip exercise in subjects screened for either high or low hypnotizability. The goal of this investigation was to uncouple "central motor command" from "central cardiovascular command." The hypothesis was that the insular cortex and anterior cingulate cortex would be activated only when there were significant increases in cardiovascular responses. Subjects were screened for hypnotizability, and groups were studied under two hypnotic conditions involving 3 min of static handgrip exercise (SHG) at 30% of their maximal voluntary contraction (MVC) and an imagined handgrip exercise at 30% of MVC. Data for muscle force, forearm integrated electromyography (iEMG), ratings of perceived exertion (RPE), heart rate, and blood pressure were collected. Regional cerebral blood flow distribution in several cerebral cortical regions was assessed during actual and imagined exercise using SPECT.

During the actual SHG, both groups showed significant increases in heart rate (+13 ± 5 bpm) and mean blood pressure (+17 ± 3 mmHg) at 3 min. However, during the imagined SHG, only the highly hypnotizable subject group showed increases in heart rate (+10 ± 2 bpm) and mean blood pressure (+12 ± 2 mmHg). The subjects scoring low for hypnotizability could not elicit changes in heart rate (+1 ± 2 bpm) or mean blood pressure (+3 ± 1 mmHg) while they imagined performing SHG. Notably, there were no significant differences in force or iEMG activity between groups during the imagined SHG or increases from resting baseline EMG activity. The RPE was significantly increased for the highly hypnotizable group in both conditions, but was lower during imagined SHG. When patterns of brain activation between groups were compared, the lower-hypnotizable group showed significantly lower activity in the anterior cingulate (–6 ± 2%) and insular cortices (–9 ± 4%) during the imagined SHG, and they did not elicit cardiovascular responses.

Taken together, these findings suggest that cardiovascular responses elicited during imagined exercise by the highly hypnotizable subjects involve a "centrally mediated" activation of insular and anterior cingulate cortices, independent of muscle afferent feedback. While this does not negate the possibility that there may be regions of the insular cortex responding to muscle afferent input, as seen by Waldrop and Iwamoto (1994), it is likely that there are different regions within the insular cortex responsive to muscle afferent input and to central command during exercise. However, the potentially confounding effects of concomitant blood pressure elevations on insular cortex activation were not addressed.

As noted previously, the insular cortex responds to blood pressure changes (Zhang & Oppenheimer, 1997), and prior studies demonstrating insular activation have reported blood pressure elevations. In an attempt to localize regions of the insular cortex responding to central command independent of muscle metaboreflex input or blood pressure elevations, blood pressure increases were matched for volitional SHG (central command, muscle metaboreflex) and postexercise cuff occlusion (no central command, muscle metaboreflex) (Williamson, McColl, & Mathews, 2003). The goal of this investigation was to "uncouple" the effects of central command on rCBF from those of blood pressure elevations occurring during exercise. Central command is generally thought to have a greater effect on heart rate and cardiac output (Leonard et al., 1985; Williamson et al., 1996) than on blood pressure, with the latter being attributed to a pressor reflex response generated by the contracting skeletal muscle (Kaufman & Forster, 1996). It was hypothesized that there would be regions of the insular cortex that would be activated only during the handgrip. The handgrip force was continually adjusted such that mean blood pressure could be elevated by ~15 mmHg and then sustained at that level via reductions in force as needed. At the end of SHG, an arm cuff was rapidly inflated to trap the metabolites within the muscle and sustain metaboreflex activation to keep blood pressure elevated by ~15 mmHg.

As shown in figure 3.1, the blood pressure elevations were similar between SHG and postexercise cuff occlusion (PECO), suggesting that muscle metaboreflex activation was most likely driving the blood pressure increases during both conditions. Over the last minute of the handgrip with the blood pressure maintained, the RPE remained relatively constant at 15 ± 2 units, indicating that the level of central command was sustained during this period. As would be expected with central command activation during SHG, heart rate was elevated, but returned toward resting levels during PECO. Thus, with similar activation of muscle metaboreflexes and blood pressure elevation

between conditions, differences in patterns of rCBF would likely be related to the presence of central command during SHG (or absence during PECO). The primary finding of this investigation was that there were distinct regions of the insular cortex and anterior cingulate cortex activated during SHG by central command (as shown in figure 3.2), independent of muscle metaboreflex activation or blood pressure elevations. More specifically, the right inferior posterior and left inferior anterior insular regions were activated to a greater extent during exercise, but not during PECO with elevated blood pressure. Findings of the left inferior anterior activation are consistent

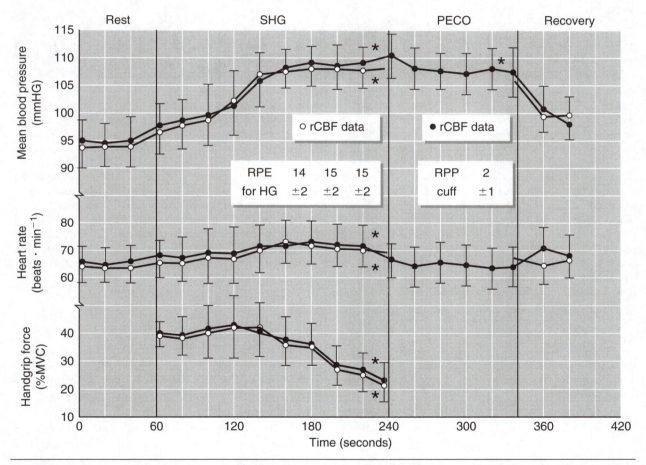

Figure 3.1 Cardiovascular and force responses during handgrip exercise (open circles) and during handgrip followed by postexercise circulatory occlusion (filled circles). Data are presented as 20 sec averages for mean blood pressure (MBP), heart rate (HR), and force (%MVC, maximal voluntary contraction) across testing periods of rest, static handgrip (SHG) exercise, postexercise cuff occlusion (PECO), and recovery. Time frames for regional cerebral blood flow (rCBF) assessment are shown for SHG and PECO. Averages for ratings of perceived exertion (RPE) using a 6-20 scale (Borg, 1973) for SHG and rating of pain and discomfort (RPP) using a 1-10 scale taken during PECO are also shown. The two trials were similar in all regards during the SHG. During the last minute of SHG, when rCBF was assessed, the RPE remained constant despite a fall in %MVC. The MBP was maintained during PECO, as HR returned to resting levels. The asterisk denotes significance ($p < 0.05$) from resting levels (from first minute for force) for both SHG and PECO trials.

Data from Williamson et al., *Journal of Applied Physiology,* 2003.

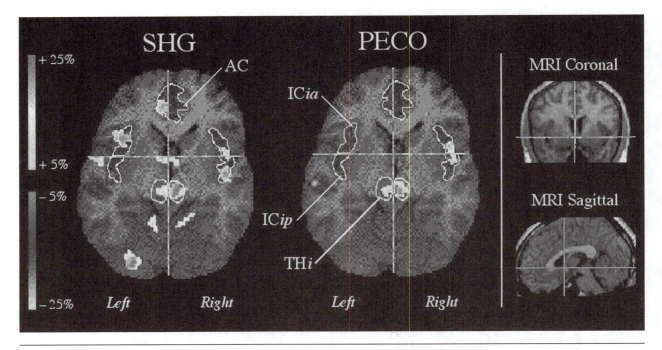

Figure 3.2 Differences in patterns of brain activation from rest for static handgrip (SHG) and postexercise cuff occlusion (PECO) matched for the same mean blood pressure elevation. Figure shows coregistered single photon emission computed tomography (SPECT) and magnetic resonance imaging (MRI) data representing a transaxial slice from one subject. The coronal and sagittal MRI figures (far right) show lines of orientation for the transaxial slice. The top and bottom of the transaxial figures correspond to an anterior and posterior orientation, respectively. Changes in regional cerebral blood flow (rCBF) distribution from SPECT data were mapped on the MRI using an arbitrary color scale with a positive range from 5% to 25% (from green through yellow to red in the original image, represented here as lighter areas) and negative range from –5% to –25% (from purple through dark blue to light blue in the original image, represented here as lighter areas). The white lines denote the specific regions of interest assessed (in this brain slice) and encompass the right and left insular cortices for inferior anterior (ICia) and inferior posterior (ICip) regions, right and left inferior thalamic regions (THi), and anterior cingulate cortex (AC). The image shows the significant increases in activation for both anterior cingulate and insular regions for this subject during the handgrip exercise with blood pressure matched to PECO. While these regions were not activated during PECO, there is significant activation in the thalamus and right inferior anterior insula, similar to that observed for the SHG.

Data from Williamson et al., *Journal of Applied Physiology,* 2003.

with previous work demonstrating a significant correlation with heart rate and RPE (Williamson et al., 1999).

From closer examination of data provided by King and colleagues (1999) during a brief bout of handgrip exercise, it appears that the right posterior insular region was activated during the handgrip, but not immediately postexercise. Critchley and colleagues (2000) also reported activation of the right posterior insular region during handgrip, as well as in response to mental stress. Insular activation during mental stress supports the concept of similar cortical regions modulating cardiovascular responses for both exercise and nonexercise conditions. It should be noted that activation of the right inferior posterior insular region was also reported to covary with blood pressure changes (Critchley et al., 2000; William-

son et al., 1999). These studies further support the contention that the insular cortex is involved in central command or central cardiovascular modulation during exercise.

With regard to a specific role of the anterior cingulate cortex as related to central command, it is largely involved in the discrimination of peripheral somatosensory input. Thus, it could serve to interpret an individual's level of central command (or sense of effort or exertion). This region, defined as the anterior cingulate cortex by both Critchley and colleagues (2000) and Williamson, McColl, and Mathews (2003), is included within the region termed the medial prefrontal cortex by King and colleagues (1999). These authors reported that activation of this medial prefrontal region during handgrip exercise was associated with cardiovascular activation. Reviews by Cechetto and Saper

(1990) and Verberne and Owens (1998) have defined a significant role for the medial prefontal cortex in cardiovascular regulation, and this area appears to have a role in central command during exercise (Williamson et al., 2001, 2002; Williamson, McColl, & Mathews, 2003). This suggests that the anterior cingulate cortex may work in cooperation with portions of the insular cortex as a "central command network," functioning to interpret an individual's sense of effort and then eliciting an appropriate autonomic adjustment to affect cardiovascular responses.

Regions of the thalamus appear to be involved in the pathway from higher brain regions to midbrain areas. As noted previously, animal investigations often elicit central command signals via stimulation of mesencephalon and posterior hypothalamic regions (Waldrop et al., 1996; Kaufman & Forster, 1996). Findings of thalamic activation coupled with that of higher brain centers provide some indirect evidence toward establishing a central command pathway to brainstem structures. From human studies, activation of the right and left inferior thalamic regions has been reported during both handgrip exercise and postexercise circulatory occlusion (Williamson, McColl, & Mathews, 2003).

The inferior (or ventral) region of the thalamus activated was analogous to the ventroposterior region previously demonstrated to have reciprocal connections with the insular cortex (Cechetto & Saper, 1990; Saper, 1982) and may be further related to baroreceptor activation (Cechetto & Saper, 1990). Blood pressure changes have been shown to elicit activation in the thalamus (Cechetto & Saper, 1990; Zhang & Oppenheimer, 2000). Zhang and Oppenheimer (1997) determined that a significant portion of baroreceptor-related neurons from the ventrobasal thalamus were reciprocally connected with the posterior insula in the rat. Further, it has been reported that regions of the human ventrocaudal nucleus of the thalamus are involved in the integration of afferent baroreceptor information (Oppenheimer et al., 1998). When directly stimulated, these thalamic regions can elicit increases in heart rate and blood pressure in humans (Thornton et al., 2002). Thus, regions of the human thalamus appear to have a key role in the overall regulation of blood pressure via baroreflex mechanisms and most likely play a role in central command-induced changes in baroreflex function.

The neural circuitry of central command appears to encompass regions of the insular cortex and anterior cingulate cortex that interact with thalamic and brainstem structures of cardiovascular integration, although there may be additional cerebral cortical regions involved. Further, it is probable that the same regions of the higher brain that are involved in cardiovascular modulation during exercise are involved in cardiovascular modulation during nonexercise conditions. It remains to be seen whether these regions implicated in central cardiovascular modulation or central command are involved in central neural adaptations associated with exercise training.

Brain Reorganization

Extensive research dealing with the role of the brain in motor function (Roland, 1993) has led to greater understanding of these processes and has established a solid foundation for further study of brain reorganization following damage to brain tissue. The goal of this section is to provide an overview of current knowledge and concepts using selected examples as opposed to defining the roles of specific regions, as well reviewed by others (Roland, 1993; Rouiller & Olivier, 2004). The recovery of the brain following insult or injury can be attributed, at least in part, to neural plasticity or a reorganization of the brain to compensate for nonfunctioning or abnormally functioning regions. Neural plasticity can entail redundancy (utilization of parallel distributed pathways), changes in synaptic strength, axonal sprouting with formation of new synapses, assumption of function by contralateral homologous cortex, substitution of uncrossed pathways, or a combination of these (Green, 2003).

While imaging technology cannot always differentiate specific mechanisms of recovery in humans, it is an important tool in assessing and understanding human brain reorganization and recovery. Animal studies have allowed and will continue to allow for more mechanistic study of specific recovery processes (Rouiller & Olivier, 2004), but human research is still critical to our full understanding of brain reorganization, as there are differences between human and animal brains. Interestingly, within the human brain, Penfield (1966) noted relatively larger regions of "uncommitted" cortex or areas for which there appeared to be no designated function. While these regions of uncommitted cortex may or may not serve a specific function under normal circumstances, they may serve as regions of tissue with a higher potential for "neural plasticity" and further facilitate brain reorganization.

Injury- or disability-related changes in human brain reorganization present a challenging area of investigation for several reasons. First, one must assume that there can be significant individual variation in the exact nature and extent of tissue damage, affecting different areas of the brain. These variations in specific sites of injured and noninjured tissue may in part dictate how and where reorganization takes place. Secondly, changes in the type and magnitude of afferent input received from the periphery following brain injury may influence patterns of brain activation, and may also produce changes independent of any reorganization. For example, increases or decreases in muscle strength within affected limbs may alter the way in which the brain responds to a given task. Lastly, there is certainly individual variation regarding the location and magnitude of brain activation in response to a specific stimulus (Senda et al., 1994). In other words, one cannot always be sure that a "deviation" from an expected pattern of activation is due to reorganization; it may simply be that the response is unique to that individual, even prior to injury. Through an understanding of the use-dependent changes in motor cortex organization following therapy, more optimal rehabilitation strategies can be developed. This type of research has the potential to drive the development of clinical rehabilitation and clinical practice (Shepherd, 2001). However, the point should not be lost that while assessment of brain reorganization is of scientific importance, the functional recovery made by the patients and their improvement following rehabilitation must not be neglected, independent of any brain reorganization or lack thereof.

Studies have documented brain reorganization following activity-related therapeutic interventions associated primarily with stroke (for review, see Rouiller & Olivier, 2004) and, more recently, spinal cord injury (Winchester et al., in press). Evaluation of use-dependent changes in motor cortex reorganization suggests that functional changes may also occur in response to disability per se, even prior to intervention (Reddy et al., 2002). From a broad perspective, the factors underlying the brain's manner of accomplishing optimal functional reorganization of different motor areas following injury vary greatly. It is likely that the different strategies of reorganization may be dependent upon the size and location of the injury (Friel & Nudo, 1998).

Injury following stroke typically produces problems with motor function and atypical patterns of brain activation for limbs affected by the insult.

In hemiplegic patients, functional recovery after a unilateral lesion depends on the contribution of other cortical areas, in both ipsilateral and contralateral (lesioned) hemispheres. Functional imaging data have provided evidence for a displacement or an enlargement of hand representation (or both) into most of the nonprimary motor areas (Chollet et al., 1991). In general agreement with this assessment, figure 3.3 shows a greater area of brain activation during movement with an affected limb following stroke.

These data are from a single hemiparetic patient, at 12 months postinsult following a relatively large middle cerebral artery stroke, performing single-leg bicycling in a recumbent position with both the affected and unaffected limbs. The patient had made significant recovery and was capable of walking independently with the use of a cane. While she was capable of performing the single-leg cycling activity with the affected limb, a much greater effort was involved. Using a Borg 6-20 rating scale (Borg, 1973), the RPE was 10 units (fairly light) for the unaffected leg as opposed to 16 units (hard) for the affected leg using the same 20 W workload. Movement in the affected leg was less coordinated, and the areas of related brain activation were much larger and more diffuse as compared to those patterns generated with use of the unaffected limb (figure 3.3).

This observation is in agreement with findings of Liepert and colleagues (2000), who noted that an enlargement of activation zones during performance of a task with the paretic limb may reflect the increased difficulty in performing the task. Ward and colleagues (2003) also reported that patients showing incomplete recovery of motor function following stroke were more likely to recruit a greater number of motor-related regions, as would typically be needed, during a motor task. Therefore, it could be postulated that as the paretic limb undergoes therapy and recovers function, patterns of brain activation may tend to match the "normal response" as observed for the nonparetic limb.

Regarding spinal cord injury, a substantial body of evidence indicates that body weight–supported ambulation training on treadmills (BWSTT) can be very effective in restoring overground locomotor performance in people with incomplete spinal cord injury (Barbeau, 2003; Columbo, Witz, & Dietz, 1998; Wernig & Muller, 1992; Winchester et al., 2005). The BWSTT involves assisting patients with trunk and limb kinematics while they are suspended (with a portion of their body weight

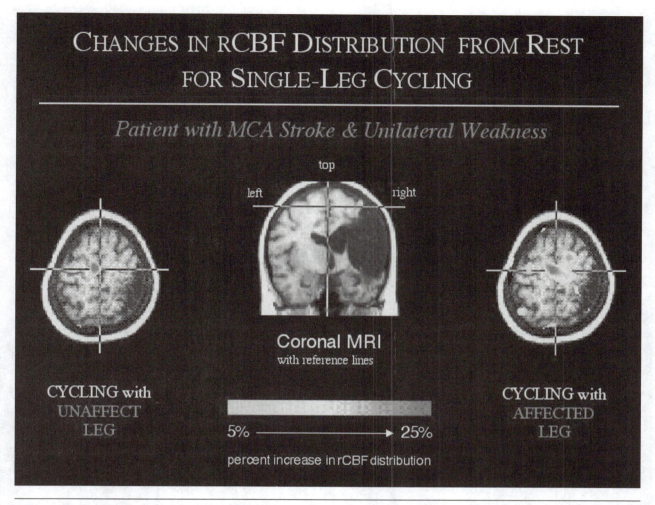

CHANGES IN rCBF DISTRIBUTION FROM REST FOR SINGLE-LEG CYCLING

Patient with MCA Stroke & Unilateral Weakness

top
left — right

Coronal MRI
with reference lines

CYCLING with UNAFFECT LEG

5% ———————→ 25%

percent increase in rCBF distribution

CYCLING with AFFECTED LEG

Figure 3.3 Differences in brain activation for single-leg cycling with affected and unaffected limbs poststroke (of the middle cerebral artery, MCA). Figure shows coregistered single photon emission tomography (SPECT) and magnetic resonance imaging (MRI) data representing a transaxial slice from one subject. The coronal MRI figure (center) shows lines of orientation corresponding to the transaxial slices and the extent of the stroke. The top and bottom of the transaxial figures correspond to an anterior and posterior orientation, respectively. Changes in regional cerebral blood flow (rCBF) distribution from SPECT data were mapped on the MRI using an arbitrary color scale with a positive range from 5% to 25% (from green through yellow to red in the original image, represented here as lighter areas, particularly visible near the orientation lines). The images show the significant increases in activation (from rest) of leg sensorimotor regions during single-leg cycling for both conditions. However, patterns of rCBF were more widespread during cycling with the affected limb.

Data represent unpublished observations from our laboratory courtesy of Dr. Patricia Smith.

supported) over a treadmill using a harness system. Therapists assist patients in maintaining an upright symmetrical posture while manually simulating normal lower limb kinematics for walking by helping to move the patients' lower limbs. These training effects may be due to reversal of "learned nonuse," a theoretical failure of neuronal circuitry that results from nonuse of motor systems (Young, 1996). However, the specific mechanisms related to the functional improvements are not well understood. Dobkin (2000) has suggested that this task-specific practice engages residual

cortical as well as spinal networks involved in locomotion. As noted previously, changes in patterns of brain activity related to a specific task have been reported following use-dependent therapy in stroke (Liepert et al., 2000; Ward et al., 2003).

Toward evaluating the possible role of brain reorganization following BWSTT, Winchester and colleagues (in press) have assessed changes in brain activation to specific tasks before and after BWSTT. Training effects were tested on both upper (finger tapping) and lower (toe curling) extremities in paraplegic patients, with the idea that BWSTT, as primarily a lower body therapeutic intervention, should affect the lower limbs to a greater extent than the upper limbs. A toe-curling task was selected as it is a fairly complex task and tends to produce a greater degree of cortical activation when contrasted with larger muscle contractions. Subjects were tested using fMRI before and after six months of BWSTT. For the finger tapping task or control task, there were no changes in patterns of brain activity when the pre- and postintervention data were compared. This was to be expected, since the subject's upper extremity was not directly treated during BWSTT. However, as can be seen in figure 3.4, there were significant differences between pre- and posttraining responses in the toe-curling task.

These changes—basically a greater extent of brain activation following BWSTT in response to the toe curling—in sensorimotor and cerebellar regions are a very consistent observation for the incomplete SCI subjects tested to date. These data show that the voluntary toe curling activated more regions of the brain and cerebellum following BWSTT. The patient also made significant gains in gait speed (24 to 62 cm/sec [9.4 to 24.4 in./sec]) and on the walking index for spinal cord injury (WISCI from 6 to 15 units). While the changes in brain activation are intriguing, we cannot definitively link them to improved functional outcome. However, data were also obtained from a subject with a complete SCI as a means of determining if changes in brain activation were associated

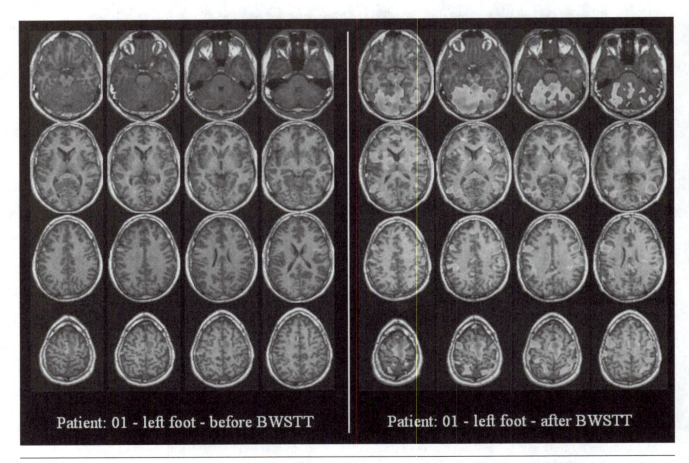

Patient: 01 - left foot - before BWSTT

Patient: 01 - left foot - after BWSTT

Figure 3.4 This figure shows sequential transaxial slices from one patient before and after BWSTT. Slices begin at the top of the head (bottom right corner) to level of the eyes (top left corner). The patient had an incomplete SCI and achieved independent ambulation with an artificial foot orthosis and cane following training. The red and yellow regions denote regions of brain activation corresponding to voluntary repetitive toe curling (here visible as lighter sections). The right panel (post-BWSTT) shows greater activation in sensorimotor (S1, S2) and parietal regions (bottom row of slices). Also, there is greater activation of cerebellar regions following BWSTT (top row of slices, right panel).

Data used with permission from Dr. Patricia Winchester.

with functional outcomes. Following training, the patient with the complete SCI showed no change in gait speed (pre-BWSTT = 0 cm/sec) or WISCI (pre-BWSTT = 0 units). Interestingly, there were no changes within the cerebellar regions for the complete SCI subject as observed for the incomplete SCI patients showing functional gains.

Taking together the lack of differences for finger tapping before and after BWSTT, coupled with differences for the incomplete and complete subject regarding cerebellar responses, it is likely that BWSTT may serve to reactivate neural networks involved in motor programming, possibly in both spinal and higher brain centers. The cerebellum, located in the posterior cranial fossa, influences the timing and force of contractions of voluntary muscles, which result in smooth, coordinated movements. One possible explanation for the changes seen in cortical network activation following BWSTT is that with BWSTT, the subject receives constant afferent input, including proprioception, kinesthesia, and cutaneous input, which could result in increased efferent activity in the motor cortex.

Interestingly, from the data presented, there appear to be different responses in the patterns of brain reorganization between stroke and SCI patients following physical rehabilitation. While the stroke patients tended to decrease patterns of activation with improved function, the SCI patients tended to show increased activation with improved functional outcomes. Any speculation should be tempered with the understanding that these changes may be related to the length of therapy in relation to the time from onset of injury, as well as other factors yet to be determined. For example, Johansen-Berg and colleagues (2002) have reported therapy-related improvements in hand function correlated with increases in fMRI activity following stroke. It is not unreasonable to suggest that initial responses involving expanded or different areas of activation may be followed by a period of more limited or "refined" activation as patterns are optimized. While the idea is speculative, these observations support the concept that different strategies of reorganization may be dependent on not only the size and location of the injury (Friel & Nudo, 1998), but also the specific nature of the injury. Researchers seek to determine the optimal modes and duration of physical rehabilitation needed to achieve the greatest functional outcomes, as well as to further establish specific mechanisms underlying changes in patterns of brain activity related to use-dependent therapy.

Weaknesses and Limitations in the Literature

Inherent to almost any area of research are various weaknesses and limitations, and human brain mapping is no exception. In human work, most research questions will be limited by their ability to delineate true mechanisms of function. This is primarily to ensure that human research ethics, as dictated by the Declaration of Helsinki, are maintained. On the other hand, while animal studies provide for a more invasive and mechanistic approach, the findings can sometimes be challenged on their ability to be extrapolated to accurately reflect the human condition. This may be especially true in brain research, where human subjects can provide more quantitative data based on constructs related to cognitive functions (e.g., pain, exertion, perception, sensation). Yet both animal and human investigations are critical to ensure our complete understanding of brain reorganization. As noted previously, brain mapping during physical activity represents a challenging area of study, with limitations in both methodology and interpretation.

Methodological considerations often entail a compromise between the amount of movement involved in the activity and the level of spatial resolution. For example, the SPECT methodology allows for assessment of patterns of brain activation during almost any activity but yields a lower spatial resolution (10-12 mm³) as compared with PET (6-8 mm³) or fMRI (1-3 mm³). Thus, SPECT may allow for assessment of brain activation during actual running, but information concerning smaller regions may be compromised. Both PET and fMRI approaches can improve spatial resolution, but subjects must be within the confines of the imaging unit with the head remaining very still.

The term *brain activation* has been used throughout this section to imply "neuronal activation." Neuronal activation in the brain is typically accompanied by changes in local metabolism, blood flow, and blood oxygenation. The specific details of the various methodologies used in functional brain mapping have been well documented (see Orrison et al., 1995). From a simple point of view, both PET and SPECT methods provide good indices of neuronal activation (Raichle, 1987), PET based largely on changes in local cerebral metabolism and SPECT based more on patterns of rCBF. The fMRI techniques can also be used to assess neuronal activation and are more sensitive to the local changes in blood oxygenation. An inherent limitation with all these approaches is that the type of neuronal activity cannot be determined—specifically whether the activity is of an excitatory or inhibitory nature. Nevertheless, despite these limitations, brain imaging technology remains an important research tool in furthering our understanding of human brain function during and in response to physical activity.

Directions for Future Investigation

The focus of brain imaging research is and will be ever evolving. This chapter has stressed selective aspects of brain activation during physical activity, primarily involving central modulation of cardiovascular responses during exercise and brain reorganization in response to physical therapy following brain injury. However, many questions remain with respect to both of these topics. Researchers seek to determine the optimal modes and duration of physical rehabilitation needed to achieve the greatest functional outcomes, and to further establish specific mechanisms underlying changes in patterns of brain activity related to use-dependent therapy. It remains to be seen whether these regions implicated in central cardiovascular modulation or central command are involved in central neural adaptations associated with exercise training. Future investigations must be performed in humans to more clearly define the specific foci within these cerebral cortical regions responsible for changes in autonomic function and how they interact to effectively modulate cardiovascular responses. It is also important to determine if the same regions of the higher brain involved in cardiovascular modulation during exercise are involved in cardiovascular modulation during nonexercise conditions, as this may have implications for other aspects of brain research. The interaction between physical activity and the human brain is not limited simply to cardiovascular modulation and neural plasticity. Physical activity has the capacity to affect many aspects of our overall "mental health and well-being," with broad implications for investigators studying cognition, emotional status, stress reactivity, sleep patterns, pain modulation, and immune responses. These topics represent important areas of future investigation. The study of the human brain during and in response to physical activity presents many challenges, but more importantly can and will yield enormous benefit.

References

Barbeau, H. (2003). Locomotor training in neurorehabilitation: Emerging rehabilitation concepts. *Neurorehabilitation and Neural Repair, 17,* 3-11.

Borg, G. (1973). Perceived exertion: A note on history and methods. *Medicine and Science in Sports and Exercise, 5,* 90-93.

Cechetto, D.F., & Saper, C.B. (1990). Role of the cerebral cortex in autonomic function. In A.D. Loewy & K.M. Spyer (Eds.), *Central regulation of autonomic function* (pp. 208-223). New York: Oxford University Press.

Chollet, F., DiPiero, V., Wise, R.J.S., Brooks, D.J., Dolan, R.J., & Frackowiak, R.S.J. (1991). The functional anatomy of motor recovery after stroke in humans: A study with positron emission tomography. *Annals of Neurology, 29,* 63-71.

Columbo, G., Witz, M., & Dietz, V. (1998). Effect of locomotor training related to clinical and electrophysiological examinations in spinal cord injured humans. *Annals of the New York Academy of Sciences, 860,* 536-538.

Critchley, H.D., Corfield, D.R., Chandler, M.P., Mathis, C.J., & Dolan, R.J. (2000). Cerebral correlates of autonomic cardiovascular arousal: A functional neuroimaging investigation in humans. *Journal of Physiology, 523.1,* 259-270.

Dobkin, B.H. (2000). Functional rewiring of the brain and spinal cord after injury: The three R's of neural repair and neurological rehabilitation. *Current Opinion in Neurology, 13,* 655-659.

Friel, K.M., & Nudo, R.J. (1998). Recovery of motor function after focal cortical injury in primates: Compensatory movement patterns used during rehabilitative training. *Somatosensory Motor Research, 15,* 173-189.

Green, J.B. (2003). Brain reorganization after stroke. *Topics in Stroke Rehabilitation, 10*(3), 1-20.

Johansen-Berg, H., Dawes, H., Guy, C., Smith, S.M., Wade, D.T., & Matthews, P.M. (2002). Correlation between motor improvements and altered fMRI activity after rehabilitative therapy. *Brain, 125* (pt. 12), 2731-2742.

Johansson, J.E. (1895). Uber die Einwirkung der Muskelthatigkeit auf die Athmung und die Herzthatigkeit. *Skandinavica Archives Physioliologica, 5,* 20-66.

Kaufman, M., & Forster, H.V. (1996). Reflexes controlling circulatory, ventilatory and airway responses to exercise. In L.B. Rowell & J.T. Shephard (Eds.), *Handbook of physiology*, sec. 12, *Exercise: Regulation and integration of multiple systems* (pp. 381-447). New York: Oxford University Press.

King, A.B., Menon, R.S., Hachinski, V., & Cechetto, D.F. (1999). Human forebrain activation by visceral stimuli. *Journal of Comparative Neurology, 413,* 572-582.

Kuniecki, M., Urbanik, A., Sobiecka, B., Kozub, J., & Binder, M. (2003). Central control of heart rate changes during visual affective processing revealed by fMRI. *Acta Neurobiologiae Experimentalis, 63*(1), 39-48.

Leonard, B., Mitchell, J.H., Mizuno, M., Rube, N., Saltin, B., & Secher, N.H. (1985). Partial neuromuscular blockade and cardiovascular responses to static exercise in man. *Journal of Physiology, 359,* 365-379.

Liepert, J., Bauder, H., Wolfgang, H.R., Miltner, W.H., Taub, E., & Weiller, C. (2000). Treatment-induced cortical reorganization after stroke in humans. *Stroke, 31,* 1210-1216.

Mitchell, J.H. (1990). Neural control of the circulation during exercise. *Medicine and Science in Sports and Exercise, 22,* 141-154.

Nowak, M. (2000). *The insula and central command influence on cardiovascular regulation during exercise—a PET and fMRI study.* Dissertation, University of Copenhagen, pp. 1-93.

Nowak, M., Olsen, K., Law, I., Holm, S., Paulson, O., & Secher, N.H. (1999). Command-related distribution of regional cerebral blood flow during attempted hand-grip. *Journal of Applied Physiology, 86*(3), 819-824.

Olesen, J. (1971). Contralateral focal increase of cerebral blood flow in man during arm work. *Brain, 94,* 635-646.

Oppenheimer, S.M., Gelb, A., Girvin, J.P., & Hachinski, V.C. (1992). Cardiovascular effects of human insular cortex stimulation. *Neurology, 42,* 1727-1732.

Oppenheimer, S.M., Kulshreshtha, N., Lenz, F.A., Zhang, Z., Rowland, L.H., & Dougherty, P.M. (1998). Distribution of cardiovascular related cells within the human thalamus. *Clinical Autonomic Research, 8*(3), 173-179.

Orrison, W.W., Lewine, J.D., Sanders, J.A., & Hartshone, M.F. (1995). *Functional brain imaging.* St. Louis: Mosby.

Penfield, W. (1966). Speech, perception and the uncommitted cortex. In J.C. Eccles (Ed.), *Brain and conscious experience* (pp. 217-237). Berlin: Springer-Verlag.

Raichle, M.E. (1987). Circulatory and metabolic correlates of brain function in normal humans. In *Handbook of physiology,* sec. 1, vol. 1, *The nervous system: Higher functions of the brain* (sec. 1, vol. 5, pt. 1, pp. 643-674). Bethesda, MD: American Physiological Society.

Rainville, P., Duncan, G.H., Price, D.D., Carrier, B., & Bushnell, M.C. (1997). Pain affect encoded in the anterior cingulate but not somatosensory cortex. *Science, 277,* 968-970.

Reddy, H., Narayanan, S., Woolrich, M., Mitsumori, T., Lapierre, Y., Arnold, D.L., & Matthews, P.M. (2002). Functional brain reorganization for hand movement in patients with multiple sclerosis: Defining distinct effects of injury and disability. *Brain, 125* (pt. 12), 2646-2657.

Roland, P.E. (1993). *Brain activation.* New York: Wiley-Liss.

Rouiller, E.M., & Oliver, E. (2004). Functional recovery after lesions of the primary motor cortex. *Progress in Brain Research, 143,* 467-475.

Ruggiero, D.A., Mraovitch, S., Granata, A.R., Anwar, M., & Reis, D.J. (1987). A role of insular cortex in cardiovascular function. *Journal of Comparative Neurology, 257,* 189-207.

Saper, C.B. (1982). Convergence of autonomic and limbic connections in the insular cortex of the rat. *Journal of Comparative Neurology, 210,* 163-173.

Senda, M., Kanno, I., Yonekura, Y., Fujita, H., Ishii, K., Lyshkow, H., Miura, S., Oda, K., Sadato, N., & Toyama, H. (1994). Comparison of anatomical standardization methods regarding the sensorimotor foci localization and between-subjects variation in H2(15)O PET activation, a three center collaboration study. *Annals of Nuclear Medicine, 8*(30), 210-217.

Shepherd, R.B. (2001). Exercise training to optimize functional motor performance in stroke: Driving neural reorganization. *Neural Plasticity, 8,* 111-129.

Thornton, J.M., Aziz, T., Schlugman, D., & Paterson, D.J. (2002). Electrical stimulation of the midbrain increases heart rate and arterial blood pressure in awake humans. *Journal of Physiology, 539(pt.2),* 615-621.

Thornton, J.M., Guz, A., Murphy, K., Griffith, A.R., Petersen, D.L., Kardos, A., Leff, A., Adams, L., Casadei, B., & Paterson, D.J. (2001). Identification of higher brain centers that may encode the cardiorespiratory response to exercise in humans. *Journal of Physiology, 533(pt.3),* 823-836.

Verberne, A.J.M., & Owens, N.C. (1998). Cortical modulation of the cardiovascular system. *Progress in Neurobiology, 54,* 149-168.

Waldrop, T.G., & Iwamoto, G.A. (1994). Neurons in the insular cortex are responsive to muscular contraction and have sympathetic and/or cardiac-related discharge. *Society for Neuroscience Abstracts, 20,* 1370.

Waldrop, T.G., Eldridge, F.L., Iwamoto, G.A., & Mitchell, J.H. (1996). Central neural control of respiratory and circulation during exercise (pp. 333-380). In *Handbook of physiology,* sec. 12, vol. 1, *Exercise: Regulation and integration of multiple systems* (sec. 2, ch. 9). Bethesda, MD: American Physiological Society.

Ward, N.S., Brown, M.M., Thompson, A.J., & Frackowiak, R.S. (2003). Neural correlates of outcome after stroke: A cross-sectional fMRI study. *Brain, 126* (pt. 6), 1430-1448.

Wernig, A.M., & Muller, S. (1992). Treadmill locomotion with body weight support in persons with severe spinal cord injury. *Paraplegia, 30,* 229-238.

Williamson, J.W., McColl, R., & Mathews, D. (2003). Evidence for central command activation of the human insular cortex during exercise. *Journal of Applied Physiology, 94,* 1726-1734.

Williamson, J.W., McColl, R., Mathews, D., Ginsburg, M., & Mitchell, J.H. (1999). Activation of the insular cortex is affected by the intensity of exercise. *Journal of Applied Physiology, 87*(3), 1213-1219.

Williamson, J.W., McColl, R., Mathews, D., Mitchell, J.H., Raven, P.B., & Morgan, W.P. (2002). Brain activation by central command during actual and imagined hand-grip under hypnosis. *Journal of Applied Physiology, 92,* 1317-1324.

Williamson, J.W., McColl, R., Mathews, D., Raven, P.B., Mitchell, J.H., & Morgan, W.P. (2001). Hypnotic manipulation of effort sense during dynamic exercise: Cardiovascular responses and brain activation. *Journal of Applied Physiology, 90,* 1392-1399.

Williamson, J.W., Olesen, H.L., Pott, F., Mitchell, J.H., & Secher, N.H. (1996). Central command increases cardiac output during static exercise in humans. *Acta Physiologica Scandinavica, 156,* 429-434.

Winchester, P.K., Martin, S., Foreman, N., Tansey, K., Querry, R., & Williamson, J.W. (2005). *Predicting overground locomotor function in spinal cord injury following body weight-supported treadmill training.* Manuscript submitted for publication.

Winchester, P.K., McColl, R., Querry, R., Foreman, N., Mosby, J., Tansey, K., & Williamson, J.W. (in press). Changes in supraspinal activation patterns following robotic locomotor therapy in motor incomplete spinal cord injury. *Neurorehabilitation and Neural Repair.*

Yasui, Y., Breder, C.D., Saper, C.B., & Cechetto, D.F. (1991). Autonomic responses and efferent pathways from the insular cortex in the rat. *Journal of Comparative Neurology, 303,* 355-374.

Young, W. (1996). Spinal cord regeneration [comment]. *Science, 273*(5274), 451.

Zhang, Z., & Oppenheimer, S.M. (1997). Characterization, distribution and lateralization of barorecep-tor-related neurons in the rat insular cortex. *Brain Research, 760,* 243-250.

Zhang, Z.H., & Oppenheimer, S.M. (2000). Baroreceptive and somatosensory convergent thalamic neurons project to the posterior insular cortex in the rat. *Brain Research, 861*(2), 241-256.

Zuntz, N., & Geppert, J. (1886). Uber die Natur der normalen Atemreize und den Ort ihrer Wirkung. *Pfugers Archives, 38,* 337-338.

II

Physical Activity and Cognition

The two chapters in the section examining the relationship between physical activity and cognition, chapter 4 by Art Kramer and Chuck Hillman and chapter 5 by Henriette van Praag, describe two modern scientific revolutions that the authors have spearheaded, two bona fide cases of "paradigm shifts" as defined by Kuhn (1996). The implications of these breakthroughs extend well beyond the boundaries of a single scientific discipline and are of interest to scientists in general and society at large. This is underscored by the fact that the original research reviewed in both of these chapters has been published in the world's leading science journals, including *Nature* and the *Proceedings of the National Academy of Sciences of the United States of America.*

Once again, as editors, we have chosen to highlight the topic from two different yet complementary perspectives, one from human research and one from basic animal research. In chapter 4, Kramer and Hillman shed light on what had been an area of research characterized by a history of conflicting results, namely the effects of aerobic exercise training and aerobic fitness on cognitive function in older human adults. The idea that Kramer proposed, and that Kramer and Hillman elaborate on in this chapter, is that the effects of exercise and fitness are specific to those tasks that show the largest age-related decline, namely tasks that require a substantial executive control component. The chapter examines both behavioral and neuroimaging evidence that supports this idea. To fully appreciate the research contributions reviewed in chapter 4, readers should have an understanding of the neurobiology of aging (Hof & Mobbs, 2001) and research on the effects of physical activity on the aging body (Spirduso, 2005). To fully appreciate the behavioral evidence,

readers should also have some familiarity with standard neurocognitive tests (Spreen & Strauss, 1998). To fully appreciate the psychophysiological evidence, it would be desirable to consult a text detailing the technical aspects of the methodology involved in studying event-related potentials (Handy, 2004; Misulis & Fakhoury, 2001; Rugg & Coles, 1997). Some understanding of the principles of positron emission tomography (Cherry & Phelps, 2002) and functional magnetic resonance imaging (Mandeville & Rosen, 2002) would help readers better comprehend the evidence derived from these brain imaging methods.

Henriette van Praag starts chapter 5 with the sentence, "Up until quite recently it was assumed that neurogenesis, or the production of new neurons, occurs only during development and never in the adult organism." This is a notion that most readers who have not followed the amazing developments in this literature in recent years probably still believe to be axiomatic. Yet van Praag demonstrates not only that neurogenesis is possible (in rodents, nonhuman primates, and even humans), particularly in the hippocampus, an area known to be involved in memory, but also that it is a process promoted by exercise. Interestingly, this research is not limited to findings of new neurons in an area of the brain in which they should, conceptually, play a functional role in enhancing cognition; it is nicely complemented by behavioral evidence showing that exercise improves learning in mice (i.e., locating a platform in the water maze task). To fully appreciate the research reviewed in chapter 5, having some understanding of the methods of immunocytochemistry (Polak & Van Noorden, 2004), as well as the process of neurogenesis (Bronner-Fraser & Hatten, 2003), would be desirable.

Suggested Background Readings

Bronner-Fraser, A., & Hatten, M.B. (2003). Neurogenesis and migration. In L.R. Squire, F.E. Bloom, S.K. McConnell, J.L. Roberts, N.C. Spitzer, & M.J. Zigmond (Eds.), *Fundamental neuroscience* (2nd ed., pp. 391-416). San Diego: Academic Press.

Cherry, S.R., & Phelps, M.E. (2002). Imaging brain function with positron emission tomography. In A.W. Toga & J.C. Mazziotta (Eds.), *Brain mapping: The methods* (2nd ed., pp. 485-511). San Diego: Academic Press.

Handy, T.C. (Ed.) (2004). *Event-related potentials: A methods handbook.* Cambridge, MA: MIT Press.

Hof, P.R., & Mobbs, C.V. (2001). *Functional neurobiology of aging.* San Diego: Academic Press.

Kuhn, T.S. (1996). *The structure of scientific revolutions* (3rd ed.). Chicago: University of Chicago Press.

Mandeville, J.B., & Rosen, B.R. (2002). Functional MRI. In A.W. Toga & J.C. Mazziotta (Eds.), *Brain mapping: The methods* (2nd ed., pp. 315-349). San Diego: Academic Press.

Misulis, K.E., & Fakhoury, T. (2001). *Spehlmann's evoked potential primer.* Boston: Butterworth-Heinemann.

Polak, J.M., & Van Noorden, S. (2004). *Introduction to immunocytochemistry* (3rd ed.). Oxford, UK: BIOS Scientific.

Rugg, M.D., & Coles, M.G.H. (1997). *Electrophysiology of mind: Event-related brain potentials and cognition.* New York: Oxford University Press.

Spirduso, W.W. (2005). *Physical dimensions of aging* (2nd ed.). Champaign, IL: Human Kinetics.

Spreen, O., & Strauss, E. (1998). *A compendium of neuropsychological tests: Administration, norms, and commentary* (2nd ed.). New York: Oxford University Press.

Aging, Physical Activity, and Neurocognitive Function

Arthur F. Kramer, PhD

Charles H. Hillman, PhD

Over the past several decades, numerous researchers have examined age-related differences and changes in perception, cognition, and motor function. Cross-sectional studies have, for the most part, shown relatively linear declines in the great majority of these processes from the 20s through the end of life (Park et al., 2002). Furthermore, the slope of the linear functions is quite similar across different cognitive processes. The potential problem with cross-sectional studies, however, is that age effects are confounded with cohort effects. That is, age-related differences in cognition could be due, in part, to differences in nutrition, medical care, education, and other factors among the different age groups in the studies (Hofer, Sliwinski, & Flaherty, 2002). One way around these potential interpretative difficulties is to examine age-related changes in a within-individual fashion in longitudinal studies. Indeed, there are currently a number of such studies under way. The general consensus from such studies is that while age-related decrements are observed across a wide variety of perceptual, cognitive, and motor abilities, many of these deficits are not observed until after 60 years of age (Schaie, 2004).

Despite the different trajectories observed in cognitive processes in cross-sectional and longitudinal studies of aging, an interesting common observation is that age-related decline is quite broad. However, there are some notable exceptions. For example, it has generally been observed that knowledge-based or crystallized abilities (i.e., the extent to which a person has absorbed the content of culture) such as verbal knowledge and comprehension continue to be maintained or improve over the life span. This is in contrast to process-based or fluid abilities (i.e., reasoning, speed, and other basic abilities not dependent on experience), which display earlier and more dramatic age-related declines. Another interesting observation in the literature on cognitive aging is that there is a large amount of variability in the rate of change of cognitive abilities among older adults (Wilson et al., 2002). An important question, one that we will address in the present chapter, is why such variability is observed.

However, before turning to the main topic of the chapter—the influence of physical activity differences and aerobic fitness training on brain and mind—we provide a brief overview of the literature that has addressed neuroanatomical and neurophysiological changes during the course of aging. Mirroring the cognitive literature, recent studies have shown differences in the time course and magnitude of age-related changes in brain structure. Correlations between age and cortical volume have been reported to be largest for prefrontal regions, somewhat smaller for temporal and parietal areas, and small and often nonsignificant for sensory and motor cortices (Head et al., 2002; Raz, 2000). In general, the disproportionate changes in brain structure across the adult life span parallel findings of age-specific changes in executive control (i.e., processes that involve scheduling, planning, working memory, coordination, and inhibitory control), which are supported in large part by prefrontal and temporal regions of the brain (Robbins et al., 1998; Schretlen et al., 2000).

Changes in human brain function, as indexed by positron emission tomography (PET) and functional magnetic resonance imaging (fMRI) studies, have also recently been examined; and these studies have resulted in a number of tentative general observations. For example, it has often been reported that older adults show lower levels of activation in a wide variety of tasks and brain regions than younger adults (Logan et al., 2002; Madden et al., 1996). Two different interpretations have been offered for such data. One is that aging is associated with an irreversible loss of neural resources. Another possibility is that resources are available but inadequately recruited. Although the reason or reasons for underrecruitment remain to be determined, some evidence points toward the second possibility. Logan and colleagues (2002) found that underrecruitment of prefrontal regions could be reduced when older adults were instructed to use semantic association strategies during word encoding.

Another frequent observation in PET and fMRI studies is that older adults show nonselective recruitment of brain regions. That is, relative to younger adults performing the same task, older adults often show the recruitment of different brain areas in addition to those activated in the younger adults. Indeed, one variety of nonselective recruitment, the bilateral activation of homologous brain regions, has been codified into a model of neurocognitive aging proposed by Cabeza (2002). The model, referred to as Hemispheric Asymmetry Reduction in Older Adults (HAROLD), suggests that under similar circumstances, cortical activity tends to be less lateralized in older than in younger adults. An important question with regard to this asymmetry is whether the additional activity observed for the older adults is compensatory or a marker of cortical decline (i.e., a failure to recruit specialized neural processors). At present, this is an open question, with some studies indicating that older adults who perform better on a task show bilateral recruitment of homologous areas while older adults who perform more poorly show unilateral activation (Cabeza et al., 2003; Reuter-Lorenz et al., 2000). Other studies have either failed to find a relationship between laterality and performance (Logan et al., 2002) or have shown unilateral prefrontal activation for better-performing older adults and bilateral activation for poorer-performing older adults (Colcombe et al., 2002). However, studies thus far have examined performance–brain activation pattern differences across subjects. Clearly, future studies are needed to examine these relationships within individuals

as a function of levels and types of cognitive challenges as well as a function of training and practice. Finally, as with the cognitive literature already described, it has become clear from the human neuroimaging literature that a good deal of individual variability exists in both brain structure and function during the course of aging (see, for example, O'Sullivan et al., 2001).

Despite the picture of aging painted by the literature just discussed, in recent years a number of studies have begun both to characterize the factors that lead to successful aging and to examine interventions that can improve cognition, brain structure, and function of older adults. An extensive review of this literature is clearly beyond the scope of the present chapter (see Kramer et al., 2004, for a discussion of this literature); however, cognitive and aerobic exercise training are two interventions that have been found to improve the cognitive and brain function of older humans.

Fitness and Behavioral Indices of Cognition

As discussed in the preceding section, although decrements in cognition occur during aging, certain lifestyle factors and interventions have been found to moderate age-related changes in selective aspects of cognition. One such moderating factor, and the central topic of this chapter, is physical activity or exercise. There is a relatively extensive history of studies examining the influence of aerobic exercise training on the cognitive function of older adults. Unfortunately, however, the results of these studies, with regard to whether or not beneficial effects of exercise training are observed on behavioral indices of cognition, have been mixed. The ambiguous nature of these results could be due to a number of factors, including relatively small sample sizes and therefore low statistical power in the great majority of intervention studies. Colcombe and Kramer (2003) performed a meta-analysis of randomized intervention trials in an effort to increase the power to detect potential effects of fitness training, most notably aerobic exercise training, and also to examine the influence of moderating factors on the relationship between fitness and cognition.

Physical activity intervention studies published from 1966 through 2001 were included in the analysis. Several interesting and potentially important results were obtained in the meta-analysis. First, a clear and significant effect of aerobic exercise training was found. Thus, when one aggregates across studies, exercise training does indeed have positive effects on the cognitive function of older humans. Second, exercise training had both general and selective effects on cognitive function. Although exercise effects were observed across a wide variety of tasks and cognitive processes, the effects were largest for those tasks that involved executive control processes (Kramer et al., 1999; i.e., planning, scheduling, working memory, interference control, task coordination). Executive control processes have been found to decline substantially as a function of aging (Kramer et al., 1994; West, 1996), as have the brain regions that support them (Raz, 2000). Therefore, the results of the meta-analysis suggest that even processes that are quite susceptible to age-related changes appear to be amenable to intervention.

The meta-analysis also revealed that a number of other moderator variables influenced the relationship between exercise training and cognition. For example, aerobic exercise training programs that were combined with strength and flexibility training regimens had a greater positive effect on cognition than exercise training programs that included only aerobic components. This effect may be the result of increases in the production of insulin-like growth factor-1 (IGF-1), which has been shown to accompany improvements in strength. Insulin-like growth factor-1 is a neuroprotective factor involved in neuronal growth and differentiation (Carro et al., 2001; Cotman & Berchtold, 2002). Exercise training programs also had a larger impact on cognition if the study samples included more than 50% females. This effect may be due, in part, to the positive influence of estrogen (in the present case estrogen replacement therapy) on both brain-derived neurotrophin factor (BDNF) and increased exercise participation (Cotman & Berchtold, 2002). Estrogen has been found to upregulate BDNF, a neurotrophic molecule that is also increased by exercise. Apparently, a normal estrogen level in exercising animals is necessary for maintaining voluntary activity levels (Berchtold et al., 2001). Both estrogen and BDNF are important for synaptogenesis and neurogenesis, especially in the hippocampal region (Klintsova & Greenough, 1999; Tanapat et al., 1999). Finally, exercise effects on cognition were found to be largest for exercise training interventions that exceeded 30 min per session.

A number of recent prospective studies with fairly large numbers of older participants have also shown that fitness training and physical activity are beneficial for maintaining cognitive vitality in old age. For example, Yaffe and colleagues (2001) reported a study of 5,925 high-functioning community-dwelling women, all greater than 65 years of age, who reported their activities including the number of blocks that they walked per week. The central question addressed in the study was whether higher levels of activity, particularly the number of blocks walked per week, would serve a protective function for cognition six to eight years in the future. Indeed, women with greater physical activity levels at baseline were less likely to experience cognitive decline as assessed with the mini-mental status exam (MMSE) during six to eight years of follow-up. This effect remained even after adjustment for age, educational level, health status, depression, stroke, diabetes, hypertension, smoking, and estrogen use. A similar study (Barnes et al., 2003) with a smaller male and female sample of older adults (349 participants 55 years of age and older at time 1) also showed that fitness level at baseline predicted higher levels of cognitive performance six years later. This study was noteworthy in that it used an objective measure of aerobic fitness, $\dot{V}O_2$peak, and also assessed a wider variety of cognitive processes. Indeed, higher levels of aerobic fitness at baseline predicted sparing of a number of different measures of attention and executive function.

Other studies have also shown that physical activity can have protective effects on the cognition function of middle-aged individuals. Richards, Hardy, and Wadsworth (2003) reported that physical activity level at 36 years of age was predictive of higher levels of verbal memory in a sample of 1,919 participants from 43 to 53 years of age. Interestingly, spare time activities such as game playing, attending religious services, or playing a musical instrument were not predictive of memory performance in these individuals from 43 to 53 years of age. Finally, Laurin and colleagues (2001) reported that compared to no exercise, physical activity level at baseline was associated with lower risks of cognitive impairment, Alzheimer's disease, and dementia of any type five years after assessment. All of the participants in this study (4,615 individuals) were high-functioning 65[+]-year-olds at the baseline assessment (see also Teri et al., 2003).

The results of these investigations suggest that modest levels of physical activity and aerobic fitness can have beneficial effects on a number of cognitive processes, especially executive control processes, of middle-aged and older individuals.

Fitness Effects on Brain Function and Structure

We turn now to an examination of the literature that has gone beyond performance-based measures of cognition in an effort to examine the influence of fitness levels and training on brain function and structure.

Event-Related Brain Potentials

As first discovered by Berger (1929/1969), neural activity in the cerebral cortex and subcortical areas produces electrical potentials at the scalp, and the electroencephalogram (EEG) can be recorded as a time series of the fluctuating voltages. The recorded neuroelectric activity (i.e., EEG) can be decomposed along two basic properties, frequency and amplitude. The amplitude of EEG, which is the topic of the current section, is measured in microvolts (μV) and is indicative of the relative size of the bioelectrical signal. The frequency of the recorded EEG signal is discussed in detail in chapter 8 of this volume.

Research on the temporal dynamics of the neuroelectric system has further focused on a class of EEG activity known as event-related brain potentials (ERPs), which have been found to be particularly susceptible to physical activity and aerobic exercise participation. ERPs reflect neuroelectric activity time-locked to a stimulus or response. In particular, the P3, a positive waveform that peaks approximately 300 to 800 msec after stimulus onset, is an endogenous component of an ERP that has captured considerable attention in the literature and has been related to attentional allocation and updating of memory. The amplitude of the P3 component reflects changes in the neural representation of the environment and is proportional to the amount of attentional resources needed to engage in a given task, with more attention increasing P3 amplitude (Polich & Heine, 1996). The latency of P3 is a measure of stimulus classification speed, with longer latencies reflecting increased processing time (Duncan-Johnson, 1981).

To the best of our knowledge, only a few studies have been conducted that have examined acute aerobic exercise effects on the P3 (see table 4.1). Specifically, two of the studies examined the effects of an acute bout of running on cognitive function using an auditory discrimination paradigm, known as the oddball task. This task requires participants to discriminate between two stimuli with differing probabilities and to respond selectively to the infrequent stimulus while ignoring the more frequent stimulus. Results indicated an increase in P3 amplitude (Magnie et al., 2000; Nakamura et al., 1999) and a decrease in P3 latency (Magnie et al., 2000) following acute aerobic exercise when compared to baseline. These results suggest that acute bouts of aerobic exercise may aid cognitive function related to both attentional allocation and memory updating, as well as increase stimulus-processing speed. Hillman, Snook, and Jerome (2003) measured the same relationship using a flanker task, which requires variable amounts of inhibitory control—one component of executive control. This task requires participants to respond as quickly as possible to a centrally presented target letter that appears among an array of distracting letters. In the Hillman, Snook, and Jerome (2003) study, neutral and incompatible conditions were presented to examine variable amounts of inhibitory control. In the neutral condition, the target letter was flanked by other letters with no response assignment. In the incompatible condition, the target letter was flanked by other letters requiring an alternate response. Hillman, Snook, and Jerome (2003) found an increase in P3 amplitude following exercise, suggesting that acute aerobic exercise may enhance attentional allocation. P3 latency was unchanged for the condition requiring less inhibitory control (i.e., neutral flanker condition) and decreased for the condition requiring greater inhibitory control (i.e., incompatible flanker condition) following exercise. The increase in P3 latency in the neutral condition may be the result of fatigue, while the decrease in P3 latency in the incompatible condition suggests enhanced inhibitory control. It is important to point out that in all three studies, posttesting occurred only after participants' heart rate had returned to preexercise baseline levels; hence, the observed differences in the P3 measures can be associated with the beneficial effects of exercise participation rather than a more general physiological arousal.

The majority of research examining the influence of chronic exercise participation on cognition has done so with older adults. The goal in these studies was to determine whether greater amounts of aerobic exercise participation can reduce age-related cognitive decline. Aging effects on the P3 component have been found to be robust. For example, Picton and colleagues (1984) employed auditory stimuli to elicit the P3 from participants

Table 4.1 Summary of Event-Related Brain Potential Studies on Acute and Chronic Physical Activity Influences on Cognition

Investigators	Subjects	Design	Procedure and task	Findings
Acute exercise				
Hillman et al. (2003)	20 males and females (M = 20.5 yr)	Within-subjects; pre-post design	E: 30 min treadmill run C: preexercise baseline Eriksen flanker task	*P3 amplitude:* increased at all sites *P3 latency:* condition effect at baseline, no condition effect following exercise
Magnie et al. (2000)	20 males (18-30 yr)	Pre-post design; cross-sectional	E: graded exercise stress test on cycle ergometer C: preexercise baseline P3—auditory oddball task N4—sentence task	*P3 amplitude:* increased amplitude at all sites for posttest regardless of fitness level *P3 latency:* decreased latency at all sites for posttest regardless of fitness level *N4 amplitude:* increased amplitude at posttest regardless of fitness level; effect observed only for incongruent sentences
Nakamura et al. (1999)	7 males (29-44 yr)	Within-subjects; pre-post design	E: 30 min self-paced jogging C: preexercise baseline Auditory oddball task	*P3 amplitude:* increased amplitude at central and parietal sites for posttest *P3 latency:* no exercise effect
Chronic exercise				
Bashore (1989)	90 older males (60-84 yr) 50 younger males (20-35 yr)	Age × fitness; cross-sectional	Speeded perceptual task	*Statistical analyses were not performed, descriptive results only* *P3 amplitude:* increased amplitude for high- compared to low-fit older males *P3 latency:* faster latency for high- compared to low-fit older males
Hillman et al. (2005)	24 male and female children (7-11 yr), 27 male and female adults (18-22 yr)	Age × physical activity; cross-sectional	Visual oddball task	*P3 amplitude:* increased amplitude for high-fit children compared to other groups *P3 latency:* faster latency for the high-fit compared to the low-fit group
Dustman et al. (1990)	30 older (50-62 yr) and 30 younger (20-31 yr) males	Age × fitness; cross-sectional	Visual oddball task	*P3 amplitude:* not reported *P3 latency:* faster latency for older high- compared to low-fit males *A/I slope:* larger for low- compared to high-fit males

(continued)

Table 4.1 (continued)

Investigators	Subjects	Design	Procedure and task	Findings
			Chronic exercise	
Hillman et al. (2002)	48 older (64.2 yr) and younger (22.8 yr) males and females	Age × fitness; cross-sectional	Speeded perceptual task	*P3 amplitude:* no fitness effect *P3 latency:* faster for older fit adults compared to older sedentary adults *CNV amplitude:* decreased amplitude for fit compared to sedentary adults *SPN amplitude:* no fitness effect
Hillman et al. (2004)	32 older (M = 66.8 yr) and younger (M = 20.4 yr) males and females	Age × physical activity; cross-sectional	Eriksen flanker task	*P3 amplitude:* increased amplitude at frontal sites for moderate- and high-active older adults compared to younger adults *P3 latency:* increased physical activity related to decreased latency in older adults
Hillman et al. (in press)	66 older (M = 64.8 yr) and younger (19.4 yr) males and females	Age × physical activity; cross-sectional	Task switching	*P3 amplitude:* increased amplitude at frontal sites for high-active compared to low-active older adults and high- and low-active younger adults *P3 latency:* faster latency for active compared to sedentary, regardless of age
McDowell et al. (2003)	36 older (M = 67.7 yr) and 37 younger (22.7 yr) males	Age × fitness; cross-sectional	Visual oddball task	*P3 amplitude:* increased amplitude for high-fit subjects, regardless of age *P3 latency:* no fitness effect *P3 AUC:* increased AUC for older low- compared to high-fit males
Polich & Lardon (1997)	11 high- (M = 30.0 yr) and 11 low-active (M = 34.7 yr) adults	Physical activity; cross-sectional	Visual and auditory oddball tasks	*P3 amplitude:* increased amplitude for high compared to low active *P3 latency:* no physical activity effects

Note: A/I slope: Amplitude/Intensity slope; CNV: Contingent Negative Variation; SPN: Stimulus Preceding Negativity; AUC: Area Under the Curve.

of different age groups (20-79 years, 12 from each decade). P3 amplitude declined with age at a rate of 0.18 μV per year after age 40, and the scalp distribution became more frontal due to age-related decreases in amplitude at the vertex (Cz) of the scalp. Further, P3 latency was observed to increase at a rate of 1.36 msec per year, indicating decreased stimulus classification speed with age.

To date, few reports on the P3 potential have appeared in the physical activity and cognition literature, with two other reports from our laboratory that are currently under review (see table 4.1). The relationship between physical activity and P3 latency appears robust, since decreased latency has been related to increased aerobic exercise participation in most reports (Bashore, 1989; Dustman et al., 1990; Hillman et al., 2002, 2004, in press). As already noted, findings have revealed that older individuals show increased latency compared to younger adults (Polich, 1996), indicating slower processing speed. However, habitual participation in aerobic exercise or physical activity has been shown to decrease P3 differences between older and younger individuals, indicating that aerobic exercise, in part, may help to maintain overall central nervous system (CNS) health (Dustman et al., 1993). Dustman and colleagues (1990) observed that P3 latency was faster in aerobically trained, compared to sedentary, older men in response to an auditory oddball task. In fact, the decrease in P3 latency was observed between older fit and both fit and sedentary younger adults, suggesting that aerobic exercise may help to reduce age-related slowing of cognitive processing—supporting aerobic fitness as a potential mediator of CNS degradation in older adults. Other studies have supported this finding (Bashore, 1989; Hillman et al., 2002, 2004, in press); but most notably, Hillman and colleagues (2004) measured P3 latency in older adults with a history of low, moderate, and high amounts of physical activity participation and a younger adult control group using a flanker task. Results indicated that P3 latency decreased with increased levels of exercise participation.

However, two other studies failed to find physical activity effects on P3 latency using oddball tasks. In the case of Polich and Lardon's study (1997), the observed lack of relationship between physical activity and P3 latency may be explained by their participant sample, which was composed of young adults (i.e., 34.7 and 30.0 years for low and high exercisers, respectively) who were rather heterogeneous in their physical activity participa-

tion (i.e., aerobic exercisers, racket sport athletes, etc.). As mentioned earlier, previous P3 research has not evidenced slowing of P3 latency until approximately 40 years of age; thus the observed similarity between high and low exercisers may have been due to a ceiling effect related to CNS health in younger adults. McDowell et al. (2003) also failed to observe significant differences in P3 latency as a function of physical activity level. However, an explanation of this lack of significance is not readily obvious given that several other studies have observed this relationship using similar tasks.

P3 amplitude has also been found to be affected by chronic physical activity participation. In a sample of young adults, those who participated in greater amounts of exercise had larger P3 amplitude along midline recording sites in response to both visual and auditory oddball tasks (Polich & Lardon, 1997). Other researchers have corroborated these findings (Hillman et al., in press; McDowell et al., 2003). Specifically, Hillman and colleagues (in press) observed increased P3 amplitude, but only at electrode sites overlying the frontal and parietal scalp regions, using a task switching paradigm that requires individuals to alternate between two different tasks. In this study, high physically active older adults had increased amplitude at frontal scalp sites, and high physically active younger adults had increased amplitude at parietal scalp sites, when compared to the other three groups. Hillman and colleagues (2005) corroborated these findings in a sample of high- and low-fit preadolescent children and fitness-matched young adult groups, as increased P3 amplitude was observed across midline sites for the high-fit children compared to the other three groups using a visual oddball task. Taken together, the results of these studies indicate that increased participation in aerobic exercise is related to changes in the neuroelectric system that underlie improvements in cognitive processing.

Several mechanisms for the relationship between aerobic exercise and differences or changes in neuroelectric activity have been suggested. One mechanism by which physical activity has been theorized to affect the P3 component is through underlying EEG activity (Polich & Lardon, 1997). In support of this notion, Kubitz and her colleagues (Kubitz & Mott, 1996; Kubitz & Pothakos, 1997) showed increased spectral EEG alpha activation (8-13 Hz activity) following acute bouts of submaximal aerobic exercise and suggested that exercise may serve to increase neuronal synchrony (also see Petruzzello, Ekkekakis, & Hall, chapter 8 in this text). Further, Polich (1997) has shown that interparticipant variations in spectral alpha power are related to individual variability in the P3 component, indicating that changes in resting EEG activity may directly influence ERPs. According to this view, aerobic exercise helps to increase the amount of alpha activity, which in turn increases P3 amplitude and decreases P3 latency. Some support for the relationship between the P3 component and resting EEG alpha has been reported (Bashore, 1989; Dustman et al., 1990; Lardon & Polich, 1996). Less clear, though, is the relationship between aerobic exercise and changes in alpha activity. Dustman and colleagues (1990, 1994) surmised that aerobic exercise promotes increased cerebral blood flow, which improves neurotransmitter function and cerebral vascularization among other neurobiological changes. Further discussion regarding potential mechanisms for aerobic exercise effects on cognitive function is presented later in this chapter.

Aging, Fitness, and Brain Structure

As discussed previously, a number of age-related changes have been observed in both human gray (brain tissue composed of neuronal cell bodies and supporting structures) and white matter (brain tissue composed primarily of myelinated nerve fibers), and these changes have in turn been related to changes in the efficiency of cognitive processes. Regionally specific age-related decreases in the volume of gray matter have been related to declines in a variety of cognitive processes. For example, Raz and colleagues (1998) reported that age-related differences in frontal gray matter volume were predictive of increases in the number of preservative errors on the Wisconsin Card Sorting Test, while Head and colleagues (2002) reported that decreases in prefrontal cortical volume were associated with reduced solution speed on the Tower of Hanoi puzzle and working memory performance (see also Meguro et al., 2001). Changes in gray matter volume could be the result of a number of factors, including neuron loss, neuron shrinkage, reduction in dendritic arborization, and changes in glia (Scheibel, 1996; Vinters, 2001). Age-related decreases in white matter volume and therefore connectivity have also been reported. These changes relate to decreases in the performance on a number of cognitive tasks (Davatzikos & Resnick, 2002; O'Sullivan et al., 2001; Sullivan et

al., 2002) and are likely the result of demyelination of axons.

Given previous reports (see van Praag, chapter 5 in this volume, for a detailed discussion of this literature) of cortical plasticity in older animals placed in enriched environments (Kempermann, Kuhn, & Gage, 1998; Kolb, Gibb, & Robinson, 2003; Rosenzweig & Bennett, 1996) and with aerobic exercise training interventions (Black et al., 1990; Cotman & Berchtold, 2002; van Praag, Kempermann, & Gage, 1999), one could ask whether similar changes would be observed in humans. Three recent studies suggest that this might indeed be the case. These studies employed a technique called Voxel-based morphology (VBM). In VBM analyses, high-resolution brain scans are segmented into gray and white matter maps, spatially warped into a common coordinate system, and examined for systematic changes in tissue density or volume as a function of some other variable. This technique allows examination of the entire brain in a point-by-point fashion, revealing spatially precise estimates of systematic variation in brain tissues. Voxel-based morphology provides a substantial advantage over other techniques, such as global estimates of gray and white matter volume, in that it allows researchers to localize the effects of a given variable to a specific region of the brain.

In a cross-sectional examination of 55 older adults, Colcombe and colleagues (2003) found that, consistent with previous findings, age-related losses in gray and white matter tended to be greatest in the frontal, prefrontal, and temporal regions (e.g., Raz, 2000; O'Sullivan et al., 2001). Moreover, consistent with predictions derived from the human and animal literatures, there was a significant reduction of declines in these areas as a function of aerobic fitness. That is, older adults who had better aerobic fitness also tended to lose much less tissue in the frontal, parietal, and temporal cortices as a function of age. Subsequent analyses, factoring out other potential moderating factors such as hypertension, hormone replacement therapy, caffeine, tobacco, and alcohol consumption, confirmed that none of these other variables moderated the effect of aerobic fitness.

Draganski and colleagues (2004) asked whether change in brain structure could be observed when a group of young adults were trained to juggle. Voxel-based morphology analysis was applied to high-resolution magnetic resonance imaging (MRI) scans obtained before and after a three-month training period, as well as three months after the cessation of training. Individuals who participated in the training were compared to individuals who were not trained to juggle. Bilateral increases in gray matter were found for the trained group in midtemporal regions (MT/V5) and in the left posterior intraparietal sulcus when the MRIs obtained before training were compared to those obtained immediately after the three-month training intervention. Both of the regions in which increased volume was observed have been related to the processing of motion. Interestingly, the volumes in these regions decreased at the last assessment, that is, when subjects were no longer juggling.

Finally, Colcombe and colleagues (2004) examined the influence of a six-month aerobic fitness training on the brain structure of older healthy but sedentary adults. High-resolution MRIs were obtained from 30 subjects in the aerobic exercise training group (i.e., walking) and from another 30 control subjects in a stretching and toning training group. Although preliminary, the results for changes in brain volume were quite similar to those obtained in the cross-sectional exercise training study conducted by Colcombe and colleagues (2003).

In summary, although there are still few studies on the influence of physical activity (i.e., both aerobic and motor skills) on human brain structure, the initial findings are quite promising. Of course, there is much left to discover, including the influence of the observed brain changes on selective components of perception, cognition, and motor processes; the amount and types of training required to induce changes in brain structure; the amount of training required to maintain increases in volume; and the nature of the morphological changes that underlie the measures obtained from the high-resolution MRIs.

Aging, Fitness, and Brain Function

In recent years, both PET and fMRI have been increasingly used to examine changes in the cortical dynamics that underlie cognition and aging. Given their relatively high spatial resolution, both of these techniques provide an ideal complement to the high temporal but poor spatial resolution of EEG and ERP measures. Both PET and fMRI are used to image functional activity in the brain, often as an individual is performing a specific task. Both of these techniques involve inferring changes in neuronal activity from changes in blood flow or metabolic activity in the brain (Reiman et al., 2000). In PET, cerebral blood flow and metabolic activity are measured on the basis of clearance of radionuclides from cortical tissues. These radionuclides, which are either inhaled or injected, decay by the emission of positrons that combine with electrons to produce gamma rays, which are detected by a series of sensors placed around the head. Each PET image, which is acquired over an interval of anywhere from 1 to 45 min depending on the nature of the radionuclide employed, represents all of the brain activity during the integration period. These PET images are then coregistered with structural scans, often obtained from MRIs, to indicate the location of the functional activity. Functional MRI is similar to PET in that it provides a map of functional activity of the brain. However, fMRI activity can be obtained more quickly (within a few seconds), does not depend on the inhalation or injection of radioactive isotopes, and can be collected in the same system as the structural information. The blood oxygen level dependent technique (BOLD) of fMRI uses the perturbation of local magnetic fields due to changes in the oxygen content of blood during increased blood flow to image functional brain activity (Belliveau et al., 1991; Ogawa & Lee, 1990).

Neuroimaging techniques like those described earlier were used in two studies examining the relationships among fitness or activity level, cognition, and brain function. Rogers, Meyer, and Mortel (1990) conducted a prospective study with 90 older adults to determine the relationship between physical activity, cerebral blood flow, and cognition. Measures of regional cerebral blood flow and physical activity were obtained from 60+-year-olds who were either still employed or retired. Over a four-year follow-up period, individuals who reduced their activity level were also found to have reductions in global measures of brain blood flow and on general measures of cognitive function. Although this study did not have the benefits of randomized assignment of subjects to experimental groups, it does suggest that further study of the relationship among physical activity, cognition, and brain function should be pursued.

To that end, Colcombe and colleagues (2004) examined the influence of a six-month program of exercise training designed to improve aerobic fitness, as compared to a program in which a control group of older adults were trained in stretching and toning, on brain function and cognition. Participants in the randomized intervention performed a flanker task, in which they were asked to identify the orientation of a central arrow presented among an array of distracting stimuli, while brain function was recorded using fMRI. On 50% of the trials, the orientation of the distracting stimuli was consistent with the central cue (e.g. "<<<<<"), while on the other 50% the distracting stimuli were oriented inconsistently with the central cue (e.g. ">><<>>"). On inconsistent trials, participants were required to suppress the information provided by the flanking stimuli in order to make a correct response. This paradigm was employed because it has previously been found to be sensitive to age-related decrements in attentional control as well as to show improvements in performance with increments in aerobic fitness (Kramer et al., 1999).

Results indicated that after six months of aerobic exercise training the older adults showed improved performance, particularly in terms of reducing their response times to the incompatible trials (in which subjects would need to selectively process the target and ignore the incompatible distractors), while the participants in the nonaerobic stretching and toning group did not. Furthermore, the aerobically trained participants showed increased activation in the superior parietal cortex and middle frontal gyrus, brain regions responsible for assisting in the focus of spatial attention and maintaining task goals in working memory, respectively. On the other hand, individuals in the nonaerobic group showed increased activation in the anterior cingulate cortex, a brain region that assists in resolving response conflicts. One interpretation of this pattern of results is that higher levels of aerobic fitness lead to more efficient prefrontal control of extrastriate and parietal regions of cortex that are responsible for the selective processing of stimulus attributes (Corbetta, 1998; Posner & DiGirolamo, 1998). Thus, these results suggest that exercise participation leading to improved aerobic fitness may provide a prophylactic effect to the functional integrity of the older adult brain.

Potential Mechanisms

An in-depth discussion of the mechanisms that underlie physical activity effects on brain and cognition is beyond the scope of this chapter (see van Praag in the present volume). However, there appear, at present, to be at least several different plausible biological mechanisms. First, a growing body of animal research has demonstrated a variety of molecular, vascular, and cellular changes in the brain in response to increased aerobic fitness (often engendered through wheel running). For example, aerobic exercise training in aging animals has been shown to increase levels of key neurochemicals that improve plasticity and neuronal survival, such as BDNF and IGF-1 (BDNF, Neeper et al., 1995; IGF-1, Carro et al., 2001), serotonin (Blomstrand et al., 1989), and dopamine (Spirduso & Farrar, 1981). Other studies have shown that aerobic exercise interventions increase the development of new capillaries, presumably to support increased neuronal firing, in rodents (Black et al., 1990; Isaacs et al., 1992) and primates (Rhyu et al., 2003). Indeed, this added vasculature has been demonstrated to be functional: Activity wheel–exercised rats have both a greater resting blood flow and a greater "reserve capacity" in response to increased oxygen demand compared with those not allowed to exercise (Swain et al., 2003). Finally, there have been a number of recent demonstrations of enhanced learning and memory (Anderson et al., 2000; van Praag, Kempermann, & Gage, 1999) and hippocampal neurogenesis (van Praag, Kempermann, & Gage, 1999; Rhodes et al., 2003; Trejo, Carro, & Torres-Aleman, 2001) with aerobic exercise training. These changes occur throughout the course of training and suggest a direct effect of fitness training on neurochemistry and brain structure.

Second, aerobic exercise training can exert its influence on cognition and brain through the reduction of vascular disease, including diabetes, hypertension, and heart disease. Each of these diseases can negatively influence cognition and hasten the development of Alzheimer's dementia (Fenster, Darley-Usmar, & Patel, 2002; Launer et al., 2000). Finally, inflammatory and immunological mechanisms are increasingly implicated in the pathogenesis of several age-related diseases including Alzheimer's (AD) and vascular dementias. Hallmarks of AD include chronic inflammation and significantly elevated levels of the acute-phase reactant C-reactive protein (CRP) and the proinflammatory cytokine interleukin-6 (IL-6) in amyloid plaques and microvessels. Furthermore, recent studies have indicated that elevated blood serum levels of CRP and IL-6 are also associated with cognitive deficits cross-sectionally and that they predict cognitive decline prospectively in nonpathological aged samples (Weaver et al., 2002; Yaffe et al., 2003). This suggests that elevated CRP and IL-6 may play a role in accelerating "normal" age-related neurocognitive decline or, conversely, that reducing CRP and IL-6 levels may slow deleterious changes in the aging brain. Although acute bouts of exercise transiently increase inflammatory markers, recent evidence suggests that chronic physical activity may reduce inflammatory markers in nonpathological humans (Ford, 2002; Reuben et al., 2003). Such findings hint that exercise may also exert positive effects on the CNS by reducing serum levels of proinflammatory molecules such as CRP and IL-6.

Thus, in summary, physical activity—and in particular exercise aimed at improving aerobic fitness—likely influences cognition and brain structure and function, both directly through its effects on brain structure and neurochemistry and indirectly by reducing inflammatory and other processes that are responsible, in part, for increased incidence of vascular disease.

Directions for Future Investigation

The studies reviewed in this chapter clearly suggest that physical activity and aerobic exercise training can serve to moderate undesirable age-related changes in cognition, brain function, and brain structure. Importantly, these data add substantially to the growing literature suggesting that cognitive and brain plasticity is maintained, albeit to a lesser extent than for younger individuals, well into old age. Such results have important implications both for our understanding of aging and from a public health standpoint.

There are, however, many unanswered questions with regard to the relationship between physical activity, aging, cognition, and the brain. For example, we do not yet know how much and what types of physical activity training produce the most rapid and robust effects on cognition and the brain. We are also ignorant about the extent to which the same or different biological mechanisms subserve exercise training and other interventions, such as cognitive training, social interventions, and nutritional programs, that have shown promise in reducing age-related declines in cognition and brain function. Indeed, to our knowledge there have been only two studies that contrasted the separate and joint effects of cognitive and fitness training on performance-based metrics of selective aspects of cognition, and these studies have come to opposite conclusions with regard to whether the effects of these two training modes are additive or interactive (Fabre et al., 1999, 2002).

There is also little knowledge about the moderating influences of specific genotypes on the magnitude of cognitive and brain effects of interventions such as aerobic exercise training. A recent study showed that physical activity level strongly interacted with the presence of an e4 allele on the APOE gene, a gene implicated in cognitive deficits and AD. Indeed, the researchers observed that high levels of activity reduced the negative effects of an e4 allele on the MMSE (Schuit et al., 2001). Given the rapidly developing knowledge about the relationship of allelic variation of genes with single nucleotide polymorphisms to neurotransmitter systems and neurotrophins and, in turn, the influence on specific aspects of cognition, the marriage of molecular genetics and intervention-based research is another fertile area for future inquiry (Greenwood & Parasuraman, 2003).

References

Anderson, B.J., Rapp, D.N., Baek, D.H., McCloskey, D.P., Coburn-Litvak, P.S., & Robinson, J.K. (2000). Exercise influences spatial learning in the radial arm maze. *Physiology and Behavior, 70,* 425-429.

Barnes, D.E., Yaffe, K., Satariano, W.A., & Tager, I.B. (2003). A longitudinal study of cardiorespiratory fitness and cognitive function in healthy older adults. *Journal of the American Geriatric Society, 51,* 459-465.

Bashore, T.R. (1989). Age, physical fitness, and mental processing speed. *Annual Review of Gerontology and Geriatrics, 9,* 120-144.

Belliveau, J.W., Kennedy, D.L., Jr., Mckinstry, C., Buchbinder, B.R., Eisskoff, R.M., Cohen, M.S., Vevea, J.M., Brady, T.J., & Rosen, B.R. (1991). Functional mapping of the human visual cortex by magnetic resonance imaging. *Science, 254,* 716-719.

Berchtold, N.C., Kesslak, J.P., Pike, C.J., Adlard, P.A., & Cotman, C.W. (2001). Estrogen and exercise interact to regulate brain-derived neurotropic factor mRNA and protein expression in the hippocampus. *European Journal of Neuroscience, 14,* 1992-2002.

Berger, H. (1929/1969). Uber das elektrenkephalogramm des menschen. Translated and reprinted in Pierre Gloor, Hans Berger on the electroencephalogram of man. *Electroencephalography and Clinical Neurophysiology, Suppl. 28.*

Black, J.E., Isaacs, K.R., Anderson, B.J., Alcantara, A.A., & Greenough, W.T. (1990). Learning causes synaptogenesis, whereas motor activity causes angiogenesis, in cerebellar cortex of adult rats. *Proceedings of the National Academy of Sciences, 87,* 5568-5572.

Blomstrand, E., Perrett, D., Parry-Billings, M., & Newsholme, E.A. (1989). Effect of sustained exercise on plasma amino acid concentrations and on 5-hydroxytryptamine metabolism in six different brain regions in the rat. *Acta Physiologica Scandinavica, 136,* 473-481.

Cabeza, R. (2002). Hemispheric asymmetry reduction in old adults: The HAROLD model. *Psychology and Aging, 17,* 85-100.

Cabeza, R., Anderson, N.D., Locantore, J.K., & McIntosh, A. (2003). Aging gracefully: Compensatory brain activity in high performing older adults. *Neuroimage, 17,* 1394-1402.

Carro, E., Trejo, L.J., Busiguina, S., & Torres-Aleman, I. (2001). Circulating insulin-like growth factor 1 mediates the protective effects of physical exercise against brain insults of different etiology and anatomy. *Journal of Neuroscience, 21,* 5678-5684.

Colcombe, S.J., Erickson, K.I., Raz, N., Webb, A.G., Cohen, N.J., McAuley, E., & Kramer, A.F. (2003). Aerobic fitness reduces brain tissue loss in aging humans. *Journal of Gerontology: Medical Sciences, 58,* 176-180.

Colcombe, S., & Kramer, A.F. (2003). Fitness effects on the cognitive function of older adults: A meta-analytic study. *Psychological Science, 14,* 125-130.

Colcombe, S., Kramer, A.F., Erickson, K., Belopolsky, A., Webb, A., Cohen, N., McAuley, E., & Wszalek, T. (2002). An fMRI examination of models of age-related decline in cognitive functioning. Paper presented at the 2002 Cognitive Aging Conference, Atlanta.

Colcombe, S.J., Kramer, A.F., Erickson, K.I., Scalf, P., McAuley, E., Cohen, N.J., Webb, A., Jerome, G.J., Marquez, D.X., & Elavsky, S. (2004). Cardiovascular fitness, cortical plasticity, and aging. *Proceedings of the National Academy of Sciences, 101*(9), 3316-3321.

Corbetta, M. (1998). Frontoparietal cortical networks for directing attention and the eye to visual locations: Identical, independent, or overlapping neural systems. *Proceedings of the National Academy of Sciences, 95,* 831-838.

Cotman, C.W., & Berchtold, N.C. (2002). Exercise: A behavioral intervention to enhance brain health and plasticity. *Trends in Neuroscience, 25,* 295-301.

Davatzikos, C., & Resnick, S.M. (2002). Degenerative age changes in white matter connectivity visualized in vivo using magnetic resonance imaging. *Cerebral Cortex, 12,* 767-771.

Draganski, B., Gaser, C., Busch, V., Schuierer, G., Bogdahn, U., & May, A. (2004). Changes in gray matter induced by training. *Nature, 427,* 311-312.

Duncan-Johnson, C.C. (1981). P3 latency: A new metric of information processing. *Psychophysiology, 18,* 207-215.

Dustman, R.E., Emmerson, R.Y., & Shearer, D.E. (1990). Electrophysiology and aging: Slowing, inhibition, and aerobic fitness. In M.L. Howe, M.J. Stones, & C.J. Brainerd (Eds.), *Cognitive and behavioral performance factors in atypical aging* (pp. 103-149). New York: Springer-Verlag.

Dustman, R.E., Emmerson, R.E., & Shearer, D.E. (1994). Physical activity, age, and cognitive-neurophysiological function. *Journal of Aging and Physical Activity, 2,* 143-181.

Dustman, R.E., Shearer, D.E., & Emmerson, R.E. (1993). EEG and event-related potentials in normal aging. *Progress in Neurobiology, 41,* 369-401.

Fabre, C., Charmi, K., Mucci, P., Masse-Biron, J., & Prefaut, C. (2002). Improvement of cognitive function and/or individualized aerobic training in healthy elderly subjects. *International Journal of Sports Medicine, 23,* 415-421.

Fabre, C., Masse-Biron, J., Charmi, K., Varray, A., Mucci, P., & Prefaut, C. (1999). Evaluation of quality of life in elderly healthy subjects after aerobic and/or mental training. *Archives of Gerontology and Geriatrics, 28,* 9-22.

Fenster, C.P., Darley-Usmar, V.M., & Patel, R.P. (2002). Obesity, aerobic exercise, and vascular disease: The role of oxidant stress. *Obesity Research, 10,* 964-968.

Ford, E.S. (2002). Does exercise reduce inflammation? Physical activity and c-reactive protein among U.S. adults. *Epidemiology, 13,* 561-568.

Greenwood, P.M., & Parasuraman, R. (2003). Normal genetic variation, cognition, and aging. *Behavioral and Cognitive Neuroscience Reviews, 2,* 278-306.

Head, D., Raz, N., Gunning-Dixon, F., Williamson, A., & Acker, J.D. (2002). Age-related differences in the course of cognitive skill acquisition: The role of regional cortical shrinkage and cognitive resources. *Psychology and Aging, 17,* 72-84.

Hillman, C.H., Belopolsky, A., Snook, E.M., Kramer, A.F., & McAuley, E. (2004). Physical activity and executive control: Implications for increased cognitive health during older adulthood. *Research Quarterly for Exercise and Sport, 75,* 176-185.

Hillman, C.H., Castelli, D., & Buck, S.M. (2005). Aerobic fitness and cognitive function in healthy preadolescent children. *Medicine and Science in Sports & Exercise, 37.*

Hillman, C.H., Kramer, A.F., Belopolsky, A.V., & Smith, D.P. (in press). A cross-sectional examination of age and physical activity on performance and event-related brain potentials in a task switching paradigm. *International Journal of Psychophysiology.*

Hillman, C.H., Snook, E.M., & Jerome, G.J. (2003). Acute cardiovascular exercise and executive control function: A P3 study. *International Journal of Psychophysiology, 48,* 307-314.

Hillman, C.H., Weiss, E.P., Hagberg, J.M., & Hatfield, B.D. (2002). The relationship of age and cardiovascular fitness to cognitive and motor processes. *Psychophysiology, 39,* 1-10.

Hofer, S.M., Sliwinski, M.J., & Flaherty, B.P. (2002). Understanding aging: Further commentary on the limitations of cross-sectional designs for aging research. *Gerontology, 48,* 22-29.

Isaacs, K.R., Anderson, B.J., Alcantara, A.A., Black, J.E., & Greenough, W.T. (1992). Exercise and the brain: Angiogenesis in the adult rat cerebellum after vigorous physical activity and motor skill learning. *Journal of Cerebral Blood Flow and Metabolism, 12,* 110-119.

Kempermann, G., Kuhn, H.G., & Gage, F.H. (1998). Experience-induced neurogenesis in the senescent dentate gyrus. *Journal of Neuroscience, 18,* 3206-3212.

Klintsova, A.Y., & Greenough, W.T. (1999). Synaptic plasticity in cortical systems. *Current Opinion in Neurobiology, 9,* 203-208.

Kolb, B., Gibb, R., & Robinson, T.E. (2003). Brain plasticity and behavior. *Current Directions in Psychological Science, 12,* 1-5.

Kramer, A.F., Bherer, L., Colcombe, S., Dong, W., & Greenough, W.T. (2004). Environmental influences on cognitive and brain plasticity during aging. *Journals of Gerontology: Series A, Biological Sciences and Medical Sciences, 59,* M940-M957.

Kramer, A.F., Hahn, S., Cohen, N., Banich, M., McAuley, E., Harrison, C., Chason, J., Vakil, E., Bardell, L., Boileau, R.A., & Colcombe, A. (1999). Aging, fitness, and neurocognitive function. *Nature, 400,* 418-419.

Kramer, A.F., Humphrey, D.G., Larish, J.F., Logan, G.D., & Strayer, D.L. (1994). Aging and inhibition: Beyond a unitary view of inhibitory processing in attention. *Psychology and Aging, 9,* 491-512.

Kubitz, K.A., & Mott, A.A. (1996). EEG power spectral densities during and after cycle ergometer exercise. *Research Quarterly for Exercise and Sport, 67,* 91-96.

Kubitz, K.A., & Pothakos, K. (1997). Does aerobic exercise decrease brain activation? *Journal of Sport and Exercise Psychology, 19,* 291-301.

Lardon, M.T., & Polich, J. (1996). EEG changes from long-term physical exercise. *Biological Psychology, 44,* 19-30.

Launer, L.J., Ross, G.W., Petrovitch, H., Masaki, K., Foley, D., White, L.R., & Havlik, R.J. (2000). Midlife blood pressure and dementia: The Honolulu-Asia aging study. *Neurobiology of Aging, 21,* 49-55.

Laurin, L., Verreault, R., Lindsay, J., MacPherson, K., & Rockwood, K. (2001). Physical activity and risk of cognitive impairment and dementia in elderly persons. *Archives of Neurology, 58,* 498-504.

Logan, J.M., Sanders, A.L., Snyder, A.Z., Morris, J.C., & Buckner, R.L. (2002). Under-recruitment and non-selective recruitment: Dissociable neural mechanisms associated with cognitive decline in older adults. *Neuron, 33,* 827-840.

Madden, D.J., Turkington, T.G., Coleman, R.E., Provenzale, J.M., Degrado, T.R., & Hoffman, J.M. (1996). Adult age differences in regional cerebral blood flow during visual word identification: Evidence from PET. *Neuroimage, 3,* 127-142.

Magnie, M., Bermon, S., Martin, F., Madany-Lounis, M., Suisse, G., Muhammad, W., & Dolisi, C. (2000). P300, N400, aerobic fitness, and maximal aerobic exercise. *Psychophysiology, 37,* 369-377.

McDowell, K., Kerick, S.E., Santa Maria, D.L., & Hatfield, B.D. (2003). Aging, physical activity, and cognitive processing: An examination of P300. *Neurobiology of Aging, 24,* 597-606.

Meguro, K., Shimada, M., Yamaguchi, S., Ishizaki, J., Ishii, H., Sato, M., Yamadori, A., & Sekita, Y. (2001). Cognitive function and frontal lobe atrophy in normal elderly adults: Implications for dementia not as age-related disorders and the reserve hypothesis. *Psychiatry and Clinical Neurosciences, 55,* 565-572.

Nakamura, Y., Nishimoto, K., Akamatu, M., Takahashi, M., & Maruyama, A. (1999). The effect of jogging on P300 event related potentials. *Electromyography and Clinical Neurophysiology, 39,* 71-74.

Neeper, S., Gomez-Pinilla, F., Choi, J., & Cottman, C. (1995). Exercise and brain neurotrophins. *Nature, 373,* 109.

Ogawa, S., & Lee, T.M. (1990). Magnetic resonance imaging of blood vessels at high fields: In vivo and in vitro measurements and image simulation. *Magnetic Resonance Medicine, 16,* 9-18.

O'Sullivan, M., Jones, D.K., Summers, P.E., Morris, R.G., Williams, S.C.R., & Markus, H.S. (2001). Evidence for cortical "disconnection" as a mechanism of age-related cognitive decline. *Neurology, 57,* 632-638.

Park, D.C., Lautenschlarger, G., Hedden, T., Davidson, N., Smith, A.D., & Smith, P.K. (2002). Models of visuospatial and verbal memory across the lifespan. *Psychology and Aging, 17,* 299-320.

Picton, T.W., Stuss, D.T., Champagne, S.C., & Nelson, R.F. (1984). The effects of age on human event-related potentials. *Psychophysiology, 21,* 312-325.

Polich, J. (1996). Meta-analysis of P3 normative aging studies. *Psychophysiology, 33,* 334-353.

Polich, J. (1997). EEG and ERP assessment of normal aging. *Electroencephalography and Clinical Neurophysiology, 104,* 244-256.

Polich, J., & Heine, M.R.D. (1996). P3 topography and modality effects from a single-stimulus paradigm. *Psychophysiology, 33,* 747-752.

Polich, J., & Lardon, M.T. (1997). P300 and long-term physical exercise. *Electroencephalography and Clinical Neurophysiology, 103,* 493-498.

Posner, M.I., & DiGirolamo, G.J. (1998). Executive control: Conflict, target detection, and cognitive control. In R. Parasuraman (Ed.), *The attentive brain* (pp. 401-424). Cambridge, MA: MIT Press.

Raz, N. (2000). Aging of the brain and its impact on cognitive performance: Integration of structural and functional findings. In F.I.M. Craik & T.A. Salthouse (Eds.), *The handbook of aging and cognition* (2nd ed., pp. 1-90). Mahwah, NJ: Erlbaum.

Raz, N., Gunning-Dixon, F.M., Head, D., Dupuis, J.H., & Acker, J.D. (1998). Neuroanatomical correlates of cognitive aging: Evidence from structural magnetic resonance imaging. *Neuropsychology, 12,* 95-114.

Reiman, E.M., Lane, D., Van Petten, C., & Bandetinni, P.A. (2000). Positron emission tomography and functional magnetic resonance imaging. In J.T. Cacioppo, L.G. Tassinary, & G.G Berntson (Eds.), *Handbook of psychophysiology* (2nd ed., pp. 85-118). New York: Cambridge University Press.

Reuben, D.B., Judd-Hamilton, L., Harris, T.B., Seeman, T.E., MacArthur Studies of Successful Aging. (2003). The associations between physical activity and inflammatory markers in high-functioning older persons: MacArthur Studies of Successful Aging. *Journal of the American Geriatrics Society, 51,* 1125-1130.

Reuter-Lorenz, P.A., Jonides, J., Smith, E.E., Hartley, A., Miller, A., Marshuetz, C., & Koeppe, R.A. (2000). Age differences in the frontal lateralization of verbal and spatial working memory revealed by PET. *Journal of Cognitive Neuroscience, 12,* 174-87.

Rhodes, J.S., van Praag, H., Jeffrey, S., Giard, I., Mitchell, G.S., Garland, T., & Gage, F.H. (2003). Exercise increases hippocampal neurogenesis to high levels but does not improve spatial learning in mice bred for increased voluntary wheel running. *Behavioral Neuroscience, 117,* 1006-1016.

Rhyu, I.J., Boklewski, J., Ferguson, B., Lee, K., Lange, H., Bytheway, J., Lamb, J., McCormick, K., Williams, N., Cameron, J., & Greenough, W.T. (2003). Exercise training associated with increased cortical vascularization in adult female cynomologus monkeys. *Society for Neuroscience Abstracts, 920.1.*

Richards, M., Hardy, R., & Wadsworth, M.E.J. (2003). Does active leisure protect cognition? Evidence from a national birth cohort. *Social Science and Medicine, 56,* 785-792.

Robbins, T.W., James, M., Owen, A.M., Shaakian, B.J., Lawrence, A.D., McInnes, L., & Rabbit, P.M.A. (1998). A study of performance from tests from the CANTAB battery sensitive to frontal lobe dysfunction in a large sample of normal volunteers: Implications for theories of executive functioning and cognitive aging. *Journal of the International Neuropsychological Society, 4,* 474-490.

Rogers, R.L., Meyer, J.S., & Mortel, K.F. (1990). After reaching retirement age physical activity sustains cerebral perfusion and cognition. *Journal of the American Geriatric Society, 38,* 123-128.

Rosenzweig, M.R., & Bennett, E.L. (1996). Psychobiology of plasticity: Effects of training and experience on brain and behavior. *Behavioral Brain Research, 78,* 57-65.

Schaie, K.W. (2004). Cognitive aging. In R.W. Pew & S.B. Can Hemel (Eds.), *Technology for adaptive aging* (pp. 43-63). Washington, DC: National Research Council.

Scheibel, A.B. (1996). Structural and functional changes in the aging brain. In J.E. Birren & K.W. Schaie (Eds.), *Handbook of the psychology of aging* (pp. 105-128). San Diego: Academic Press.

Schretlen, D., Pearlson, G.D., Anthony, J.C., Aylward, E.H., Augustine, A.M., Davis, A., & Barta, P. (2000). Elucidating the contributions of processing speed, executive ability, and frontal lobe volume to normal age-related differences in fluid intelligence. *Journal of the International Neuropsychological Society, 6,* 52-61.

Schuit, A.J., Feskens, E.J.M., Launer, L.J., & Kromhout, D. (2001). Physical activity and cognitive decline, the role of apolipoprotein e4 allele. *Medicine and Science in Sports and Exercise, 33,* 772-777.

Spirduso, W.W., & Farrar, R.P. (1981). Effects of aerobic training on reactive capacity: An animal model. *Journal of Gerontology, 36,* 654-662.

Sullivan, E.V., Pfefferbaum, A., Adalsteinsson, E., Swan, G.E., & Carmelli, D. (2002). Differential rates of regional brain change in callosal and ventricular size: A 4 year longitudinal MRI study of elderly men. *Cerebral Cortex, 12,* 438-445.

Swain, R.A., Harris, A.B., Wiener, E.C., Dutka, M.V., Morris, H.D., Theien, B.E., Konda, S., Engberg, K., Lauterbur, P.C., & Greenough, W.T. (2003). Prolonged exercise induces angiogenesis and increases cerebral blood volume in primary motor cortex of the rat. *Neuroscience, 117,* 1037-1046.

Tanapat, P., Hastings, N.B., Reeves, A.J., & Gould, E. (1999). Estrogen stimulates a transient increase in the number of new neurons in the dentate gyrus of the adult female rat. *Journal of Neuroscience, 19,* 5792-5801.

Teri, L., Gibbons, L., McCurry, S., Logsdon, R., Buchner, D., Barlow, W., Kukull, W., LaCroix, A., McCormick, W., & Larson, E. (2003). Exercise plus behavioral management in patients with Alzheimer disease: A randomized control trial. *Journal of the American Medical Association, 290,* 2015-2022.

Trejo, J.L., Carro, E., & Torres-Aleman, I. (2001). Circulating insulin-like growth factor mediates exercise-induced increases in the number of new neurons in the adult hippocampus. *Journal of Neuroscience, 21,* 1628-1634.

van Praag, H., Kempermann, G., & Gage, F.H. (1999). Running increases cell proliferation and neurogenesis in the adult mouse dentate gyrus. *Nature Neuroscience, 2,* 266-270.

Vinters, H.V. (2001). Aging and the human nervous system. In J. Birren (Ed.), *Handbook of the psychology of aging* (5th ed., pp. 135-159). San Diego: Academic Press.

Weaver, J.D., Huang, M.H., Albert, M., Harris, T., Rower, J.W., & Seeman, T.E. (2002). Interleukin-6 and risk of cognitive decline: MacArthur studies of successful aging. *Neurology, 59,* 371-378.

West, R.L. (1996). An application of prefrontal cortex function theory to cognitive aging. *Psychological Bulletin, 120,* 272-292.

Wilson, R.S., Beckett, L.A., Barnes, L.L., Schneider, J.A., Bach, J., Evans, D.A., & Bennett, D.A. (2002). Individual differences in rates of change in cognitive abilities of older persons. *Psychology and Aging, 17,* 179-193.

Yaffe, K., Barnes, D., Nevitt, M., Lui, L.Y., & Covinsky, K. (2001). A prospective study of physical activity and cognitive decline in elderly women. *Archives of Internal Medicine, 161,* 1703-1708.

Yaffe, K., Lindquist, K., Pennink, B.W., Simonsick, E.M., Pahor, M., Kritchevsky, S., Launer, L., Kuller, L., Rubin, S., & Harris, T. (2003). Inflammatory markers and cognition in well functioning African American and white elders. *Neurology, 61,* 76-80.

5

Exercise, Neurogenesis, and Learning in Rodents

Henriette van Praag, PhD

Up until quite recently, it was assumed that neurogenesis, or the production of new neurons, occurs only during development and never in the adult organism. As the famous neuroanatomist Santiago Ramón y Cajal (1928) stated, "Once development was ended, the fonts of growth and regeneration of the axons and dendrites dried up irrevocably. In adult centers, the nerve paths are something fixed and immutable: everything may die, nothing may be regenerated" (p. 750). This statement holds true for most of the regions of the adult brain. However, there are two adult brain areas in which neurogenesis is observed. The subventricular zone of the anterior lateral ventricles gives rise to cells that become neurons in the olfactory bulb; and the subgranular zone in the dentate gyrus of the hippocampus, a brain region that is important for learning and memory, generates new granule cell neurons.

The initial studies suggesting that the adult brain could generate new neurons were largely ignored. In the 1960s, Joseph Altman and coworkers published a series of papers reporting that some dividing cells in the adult brain survived and differentiated into cells with morphology similar to that of neurons (Altman & Das, 1965). The technique Altman used to label the cells was tritiated thymidine autoradiography. Tritiated thymidine is incorporated into the DNA of dividing cells. The highest density of labeling was in the subventricular zone and in the dentate gyrus of the hippocampus. It was known that the dentate gyrus of the hippocampus is essentially devoid of glia. Therefore, the labeling in this region was attributed to the uptake of thymidine by dentate granule cells. However, it could not be proven that the adult-generated cells were neurons rather than glia, since no phenotypic markers were available that could be used in conjunction with thymidine autoradiography. The absence of specific markers for neurons and glia, as well as continued skepticism surrounding the concept of adult neurogenesis, limited further development of the research.

In the mid-1970s and the early 1980s, these initial observations were reexamined using the electron microscope, adding substantial confidence that neurogenesis could occur in the adult brain. Through a combination of electron microscopy and tritiated thymidine labeling it was shown that labeled cells in the rat dentate gyrus have ultrastructural characteristics of neurons, such as dendrites (Kaplan & Hinds, 1977). However, these data also were not considered evidence of significant neurogenesis in adult mammals by most researchers. It was still not possible to prove definitively that the new cells were neurons. In addition, the concept that there may be neuronal stem cells that could proliferate, migrate, and then differentiate into new neurons had not yet been introduced. It was therefore thought that mature neurons would have to replicate, an idea that most researchers found incredible. Furthermore, the possible relevance of the findings for humans was underestimated because there was no evidence of neurogenesis in adult primates.

In the mid-1980s, this fledgling field was stimulated by astonishing findings in adult canaries. It was discovered that neurogenesis occurs in brain areas that mediate song learning (Goldman &

Nottebohm, 1983). Using a combination of tritiated thymidine with ultrastructural and electrophysiological techniques, the researchers provided evidence that the new cells were neurons (Paton & Nottebohm, 1984). In addition, they showed that there is a peak in the production of new neurons at the time of year birds acquire songs (Barnea & Nottebohm, 1994). It was also shown that neurogenesis in the hippocampal complex of adult chickadees is correlated with seed-storing behavior. In fact, the hippocampus is relatively larger in seed-storing than nonstoring birds and appears to play an important role in spatial learning. Chickadees store seeds in the fall and then retrieve them after days or weeks. In one of the studies, the birds were captured at different times of the year, injected with tritiated thymidine, released, and recaptured six weeks later. It was found that there was significant seasonality in the number of hippocampal cells labeled with tritiated thymidine. Birds that had received the label in October had more labeled cells than chickadees that had received the label at other times during the year (Barnea & Nottebohm, 1994). Taken together, these results raised the possibility that new neurons play a functional role in the mature brain and led to a revived interest in possible neurogenesis in adult mammals.

Despite the observations of neurogenesis in the adult avian brain, confusion over the mechanistic origin of cell genesis in the adult brain persisted. However, in the early 1990s it was revealed that cells with stem cell properties could be isolated and expanded in culture (Reynolds & Weiss, 1992). Using a variety of culture conditions with different factors, these isolated cells can be induced to proliferate and differentiate into glia or neurons. These observations in vitro provided a mechanism for neurogenesis in the adult brain in vivo. Mature committed neurons were not dividing; rather a population of immature stemlike cells exists in the brain, and it is likely that the proliferation and differentiation of this population results in neurogenesis.

Following the discovery of the mechanism by which new neurons could arise in the adult brain in vivo, great conceptual and technical progress was made. The thymidine analog 5-bromo-3'-deoxyuridine (BrdU), a traceable analog of uridine, which is incorporated into the genome of cells undergoing division, was used to label new cells in vivo. The advantage of BrdU over thymidine autoradiography is that the cells can be visualized using immunocytochemistry. This method allows for a more accurate estimate of the number of new cells using stereological techniques. In addition, BrdU immunocytochemistry can be used in combination with now available specific markers for neurons, such as NeuN (neuronal nuclear antigen A60, a neuron-specific, DNA binding nuclear protein) and calbindin, and for glia, such as s100β and glial fibrillary acidic protein (GFAP). Double labeling for BrdU and NeuN has been used extensively over the past decade to demonstrate whether a newborn cell has become a neuron (Kuhn et al., 1996; Gage, 2002). Using this method it has also been shown that there is a time course over which neurogenesis occurs. When BrdU-labeled cells were examined a few days after the last BrdU injection, the majority of the cells did not colabel for any of the mature neuronal or glial markers, suggesting that these are immature, proliferating cells. At four weeks after the last BrdU injection, about 60% of the BrdU-positive cells colabeled with the neuronal marker NeuN, suggesting that it takes about a month for a newly born cell to become a neuron (Kuhn et al., 1996). These findings were recently confirmed and extended using retroviral labeling selective for dividing cells. Using this method, it was demonstrated that although new neurons have acquired the functional and morphological characteristics of neurons at one month, they continue to increase in size and complexity for several months (van Praag et al., 2002).

Up until quite recently, studies that provided evidence for neurogenesis were considered irrelevant to the primate or human brain. It was assumed that neurogenesis had become restricted throughout evolution as the brain became more intricate. Thus, lizards and other reptiles can regenerate and replace neurons following damage, whereas in the complex human brain, the addition of new neurons could conceivably disturb the intricate wiring of neuronal connections. However, it was reported in 1999 that neurogenesis occurs in the hippocampus of nonhuman primates (Kornack & Rakic, 1999; Gould et al., 1999). At about the same time, the possible occurrence of neurogenesis in humans was being studied. Administration of BrdU followed by examination of cell proliferation in tumor biopsies is occasionally done to monitor tumor progression in patients with cancer. Because BrdU is a small soluble molecule, it is distributed throughout the body, including the brain, and thus can be a marker for cell division and neurogenesis in humans. It was reported that five cancer patients who had received BrdU between 15 days and 2$^+$ years earlier showed neurogenesis as revealed by colabel-ing of BrdU with markers of mature neurons in the dentate gyrus. These studies clearly demonstrated that neurogenesis, at least in the dentate gyrus, is a process that persists throughout life in mammalian species, including humans (Eriksson et al., 1998; Gage, 2002; Kornack & Rakic, 1999).

Although neurogenesis in the dentate gyrus of the hippocampus of adult mammals is now a generally accepted phenomenon, the functional significance of the new neurons is unknown. In fact, up until very recently it was not known whether the newborn neurons are functionally integrated into the hippocampal circuitry. All the evidence in mammals described so far is based on morphological studies, since the use of ^{3}H-thymidine and BrdU requires extensive processing of the tissue for visualization of the cells. Moreover, only the soma can be observed with these methods. In a recent study using a retrovirus expressing green fluorescent protein (GFP) that infects only dividing cells, newly born cells were visualized directly in live hippocampal slices. It was demonstrated that new granule neurons in the hippocampus exhibit neuronal morphology (GFP is expressed in the cytoplasm) and have passive membrane potentials, action potentials, and synaptic inputs that are similar to those of mature dentate neurons. Interestingly, this study also showed that new neurons become functionally mature over several weeks, a time course of integration that is longer than the parallel process in development (van Praag et al., 2002).

It is now well established that neurogenesis occurs in the adult mammalian nervous system. However, the function of the new cells remains unclear. Interestingly, a variety of environmental, behavioral, genetic, neuroendocrine, and neurochemical factors can influence the proliferation and survival of newborn cells. Treatments and manipulations that enhance the production of new cells have been associated with enhanced cognition and mental health, whereas reductions in new cell number correlate with impaired memory, stress, and depression. Several of these factors are outlined in table 5.1.

Environmental Enrichment and Neurogenesis

Initial work shows that the number of new cells in the adult hippocampus can be regulated using a paradigm of environmental enrichment (Kempermann et al., 1997b). In the late 1940s, Donald Hebb was the first to propose an "enriched environment" as an experimental concept. He reported anecdotally that rats that he took home as pets showed behavioral improvements over their littermates kept at the laboratory (Hebb, 1947). Rosenzweig and colleagues introduced enriched environments as a testable scientific concept in the early 1960s (Rosenzweig, 1966). In an experimental setting, an enriched environment is "enriched" in relation to standard laboratory housing conditions. In general the "enriched" animals are kept in larger cages, in larger groups, with the opportunity for more complex social interaction. The environment is complex and varied over the period of the experiments: tunnels, nesting material, toys, and food locations are frequently changed. In addition, animals are often given the opportunity for voluntary physical activity on running wheels. The standard definition of an enriched environment is "a combination of complex inanimate and social stimulation" (Rosenzweig et al., 1978).

In the initial studies, the effects of environmental stimuli on parameters such as "total brain weight," "total DNA or RNA content," or "total brain protein" were measured (Rosenzweig, Bennett, & Diamond, 1967). Subsequently, a great number of studies have demonstrated that environmental stimulation elicits a variety of plastic responses in the adult brain, ranging from biochemical parameters to dendritic arborization and gliogenesis, as well as improved learning (Cummins et al., 1973; Holloway, 1966; Diamond et al., 1976; Greenough & Volkmar, 1973). Very early, a debate began as to whether environmental enrichment had any influence on cell number in the adult brain. Joseph Altman, the first to describe adult neurogenesis in the hippocampus (Altman, 1962), investigated as early as 1964 whether environmental enrichment could affect the production of neurons—at that time with no result (Altman & Das, 1964).

Using BrdU labeling, Gerd Kempermann and colleagues showed that mice housed in an enriched environment do have increased neurogenesis. Specifically, mice were housed in either enriched or control conditions and then injected with BrdU over 12 days. A subset of mice that were sacrificed 24 hr after the last injection was used to study cell proliferation. The remaining mice were maintained for another four weeks to allow for maturation and differentiation of the BrdU-labeled newborn cells. Since the number of labeled cells declines with time after labeling (since not all dividing cells become mature neural cells), this is called the "survival"

Table 5.1 Factors Affecting in Vivo Cell Proliferation and Neurogenesis in Adult Hippocampus and Subventricular Zone (SVZ)/Olfactory Bulb*

Factor	Proliferation	Glial genesis	Neurogenesis	References
Genetic background	Yes	Yes	Yes	Kempermann & Gage (2002); Kempermann et al. (1997a)
FGF-2	No change Increase*	No change Increase*	No change Increase*	Kuhn et al. (1997) Wagner et al. (1999)
EGF	No change	Increase	Decrease	Craig et al. (1996); Kuhn et al. (1997)
IGF	Increase	No change	Increase	Aberg et al. (2000)
VEGF	Increase	n.d.	Increase	Jin et al. (2002)
BDNF	Increase*	n.d.	Increase*	Lee et al. (2002)
Serotonin	Increase	n.d.	Increase	Malberg et al. (2000); Santarelli et al. (2003)
Norepinephrine	Increase	No change	No change	Kulkarni et al. (2002)
Glutamate	Decrease Increase	n.d. n.d.	n.d. n.d.	Cameron et al. (1995) Bai et al. (2003)
(Antagonist: MK801)	Increase	n.d.	Increase	Cameron et al. (1998)
Stress	Decrease	n.d.	n.d.	Gould et al. (1997)
Glucocorticoids	Decrease	n.d.	n.d.	Cameron & Gould (1994)
Adrenalectomy	Increase	n.d.	Increase	Gould et al. (1992)
Estrogen	Increase	No change	No change	Tanapat et al. (1999)
Prolactin	Increase*	n.d.	Increase*	Shingo et al. (2003)
cAMP/CREB	Increase	n.d.	No change	Nakagawa et al. (2002)
Methamphetamine	Decrease	n.d.	n.d.	Teuchert-Noodt et al. (2000)
Opiates/heroin	Decrease	n.d.	n.d.	Eisch et al. (2000)
Enriched environment	No change	No change	Increase	Kempermann et al. (1997a)
Wheel running	Increase	No change	Increase	van Praag et al. (1999a, 1999b)
Learning	No change	n.d.	Increase No change	Gould et al. (1999) van Praag et al. (1999b)
Dietary restriction	Increase	n.d.	n.d.	Lee et al. (2002)
Aging	Decrease	n.d.	Decrease	Kuhn et al. (1996)
Vitamin E deficiency	Increase	n.d.	n.d.	Ciaroni et al. (1999)
Traumatic brain injury	Increase	Increase	Increase	Kernie et al. (2001)
Epilepsy	Increase	n.d.	Increase	Parent et al. (1997)
Stroke/ischemia	Increase	n.d.	Increase	Liu et al. (1998); Nakatomi et al. (2002)
X-irradiation	Decrease	Increase	Decrease	Monje et al. (2002)

*In SVZ/olfactory bulb only; n.d.= not determined.

time point. It was found that there was no change in cell division as a result of enrichment. However, an increased number of new neurons survived in the enriched as compared to control mice. These mice were also tested in a spatial memory task, the Morris water maze, whereby mice are trained to find a platform hidden under the surface of the pool in which the water is colored with paint. Mice can learn to find the platform based on cues on the walls of the testing room (Morris, 1984). The enriched mice learned faster than controls, raising the possibility that new neurons may contribute to enhanced cognition.

Exercise and Neurogenesis

Environmental enrichment consists of many different variables including increased opportunity for learning, socialization, and physical activity. In an attempt to determine which variables may contribute to the effect on cell genesis, mice were assigned to groups with a learning task, wheel running, enrichment, or standard housing. Mice were injected with BrdU for the first 10 days of the experiment. A subset of mice was killed after the last BrdU injection to study cell proliferation, whereas the remaining mice were allowed to survive an additional four weeks. Similar to environmental enrichment, voluntary exercise in a running wheel enhanced the survival of newborn neurons in the dentate gyrus, whereas none of the other conditions had any effect on cell genesis (van Praag et al., 1999b). In addition, wheel running increased cell division dramatically as compared to that in all the other groups. These findings (see figure 5.1.) suggest that physical activity is an important factor for neurogenesis, an observation that has been confirmed by other investigators (Trejo et al., 2001; Fabel et al., 2003; Kitamura, Mishina, & Sugiyama, 2003; Overstreet et al., 2004).

In a subsequent study we investigated whether the amount of running influences the number of new cells produced. Our initial studies were done in C57Bl/6 mice, which show little variation in distance run between animals. In contrast, a different strain of mice, 129SvEv, shows a wide range of wheel revolutions between individuals. In these mice we found a significant positive correlation between cell proliferation and distance run, and similar findings for cell survival (Allen et al., 2001). Thus, animals that ran the most had the greatest increase in neurogenesis.

The increase in the number of new neurons with wheel running strengthened the idea that neurogenesis may be important for brain function. A recent study addressed whether exercise influences neurogenesis in the olfactory bulb as well as the dentate gyrus of the hippocampus. Interestingly, there was no effect of exercise on neurogenesis in the olfactory bulb (Brown et al., 2003). Other researchers, however, showed that the production of new olfactory neurons can be enhanced by exposure to an odor-enriched environment (Rochefort et al., 2002). In summary, only hippocampal cell genesis is enhanced by running. Given that the hippocampus is important for learning and memory, elevated neurogenesis in that brain area may lead to improved cognitive function.

Other Anatomical Changes Associated With Exercise

Apart from effects on production of new neurons in the dentate gyrus of the hippocampus, exercise results in additional morphological changes. Motor skill learning has been shown to increase cortical thickness and synaptogenesis (Kleim et al., 1996), as well as the number of synapses per neuron in the cerebellum (Black et al., 1990; Isaacs et al., 1992). Activity matched to a skill-learning task has been reported to enhance capillary density or angiogenesis in the cerebellum, but not synaptogenesis (Black et al., 1990). In more recent studies, voluntary wheel running was found to increase angiogenesis in the motor cortex (Kleim, Cooper, & VandenBerg, 2002; Swain et al., 2003) and thickness of motor cortex (Anderson et al., 2002).

Exercise Improves Learning and Memory in Rodents

Both voluntary wheel running and treadmill training have been shown to enhance spatial learning (Fordyce & Farrar, 1991; Fordyce & Wehner, 1993; van Praag et al., 1999b). In the exercise studies, differences between sedentary and active animals were best observed when tasks were made more challenging with use of the water maze (Fordyce & Wehner, 1993; van Praag et al., 1999b). In our studies we showed that mice housed with a running wheel performed better in the Morris water maze

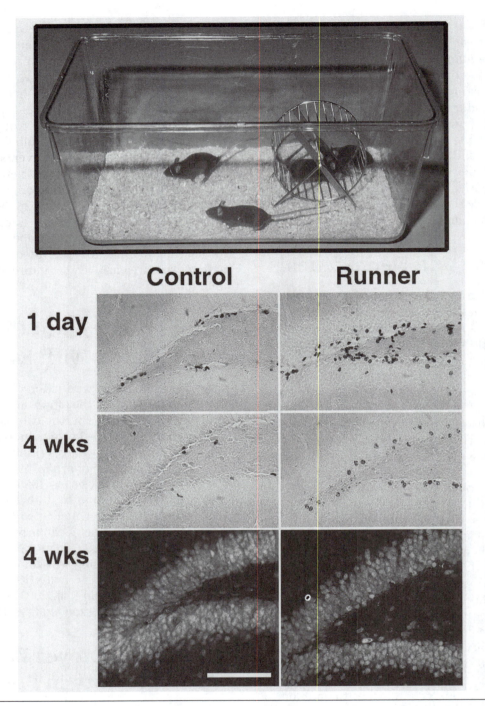

Control   **Runner**

1 day

4 wks

4 wks

Figure 5.1 Exercise increases cell proliferation and neurogenesis in the adult mouse hippocampus. Mice were housed either with or without a running wheel. At the onset of the experiment, animals received daily injections of 5-bromo-3'-deoxyuridine (BrdU, 50 mg/kg) over 10 days. Mice were killed either one day or four weeks after the last BrdU injection. Mice housed with a running wheel (b) had a significant increase in cell division as compared to controls (a). In addition, runners (d) showed more cell survival after four weeks than controls (c). Analysis of cell phenotype (red = BrdU; green = NeuN, neuronal marker; blue = S100β, glial marker) indicated that relatively more cells became neurons in runners (f) than controls (c); an overlap of BrdU + NeuN = orange, indicating that these cells were new neurons. *(Colors in original publication, visible here in shading only.)

than sedentary controls when mice were tested with only two trials per day over six days. On day 6, a probe trial was carried out 4 hr after completion of testing. In the probe trial, the platform is removed and the mice are allowed to search in the pool for the missing platform for 1 min. Mice that have learned the task well will spend most of their time in the quadrant of the pool where the platform was previously located. In our study the runners showed a preference for the platform quadrant whereas the sedentary controls did not, suggesting that retention of the task was improved by running (van Praag et al., 1999b; van Praag et al., 2005). A study by other researchers concerned the effect of exercise on learning in the radial arm maze. In this case, rats ran in wheels attached to their home cage for seven weeks before and throughout testing. The rats that exercised voluntarily took 30% fewer trials to reach criterion performance than sedentary controls (Anderson et al., 2000).

In a subsequent study, we investigated the effect of wheel running on learning and neurogenesis in mice bred for high levels of voluntary exercise over 26 generations (Rhodes et al., 2003). The hyperactive mice ran about 12 km/day (7.5 mi/day) whereas controls ran an average of 5 km/day (3.1 mi/day). Mice in this study were housed with or without running wheels. All mice were injected with BrdU daily for the first 10 days of the study and then allowed to survive for an additional four weeks. Spatial learning was tested in a subset of animals. There was no difference between sedentary control and hyperactive animals in the number of BrdU-positive cells. However, when mice were housed with a running wheel, there was a fivefold increase in cell genesis in the hyperactive mice versus a fourfold increase relative to sedentary conditions in controls. Interestingly, there was a strong positive correlation between cell genesis and running in the control mice, but no relationship between neurogenesis and distance run in the hyperactive mice. Furthermore, when spatial learning was tested in the Morris water maze, the control mice improved when housed with a running wheel, as shown in our previous work (van Praag et al., 1999a). The hyperactive mice, however, did not benefit from wheel running. In fact, their performance was slightly worse than that of sedentary hyperactive controls. Thus, excessive running is not necessarily beneficial for function. In fact, we propose that the selective breeding for hyperactivity is associated with neurological deficits that affect behavior (Rhodes et al., 2001).

Electrophysiological Changes Associated With Exercise

The relationship between physical and neuronal activity has been well documented. Discharge frequency of hippocampal pyramidal cells and interneurons has been shown to increase with increased wheel running velocity in rats (Czurko et al., 1999). In addition, locomotion is correlated with the hippocampal theta rhythm (Vanderwolf, 1969). The theta rhythm occurs naturally in the hippocampal electroencephalogram (EEG) and has long been considered important for memory function. Long-term potentiation (LTP), a physiological model of certain forms of learning and memory (Bliss & Collingridge, 1993), is best induced when stimulation follows the pattern of the theta rhythm (Larson, Wong, & Lynch, 1986). In a recent study, EPSP (excitatory postsynaptic potential) amplitudes, as well as LTP, were compared in hippocampal slices from running and control mice. The EPSPs were unchanged in both groups. However, LTP amplitude was enhanced in the dentate gyrus in slices from running mice as compared to controls. Recordings from another hippocampal subfield, area CA1, showed no change in LTP in response to running (van Praag et al., 1999a). Thus, electrophysiologically measurable changes occurred in the same region where neurogenesis was stimulated by running, suggesting that the newborn cells may have a functional role, possibly associated with learning and memory.

In a subsequent study, dentate gyrus LTP was examined in vivo in urethane-anesthetized rats. Specifically, rats given access to a running wheel exhibited significantly more short-term potentiation and LTP with theta-patterned conditioning stimulation in vivo than age-matched littermates. The increase in LTP may reflect an alteration in the induction threshold for synaptic plasticity that accompanies voluntary exercise. Comparisons were made between strong and weak theta-patterned stimulation. Strong stimulation induced LTP in both runners and controls, but to a greater degree in runners. Weak stimulation, which did not produce LTP in control subjects, produced a robust and long-lasting LTP in runners, suggesting that a shift in induction threshold had occurred. Long-term potentiation induction in both groups was dependent upon the activation of N-methyl-

D-aspartate (NMDA) receptors, and could be blocked by the competitive antagonist [+/-]-3-[2-carboxypiperazin-4-yl] propanephosphonic acid (Farmer et al., 2004).

Although the new cells are a small percentage of the granule cell layer, it is possible that they have greater plasticity than do mature cells. Indeed, in immature rats, dentate gyrus LTP lasts longer than in adults (Bronzino et al., 1994). In one study, electrophysiological properties of granule cells from the inner and outer layer of the dentate gyrus were compared. Inner layer cells were considered "young" cells and the outer layer cells "old" cells. It was found that putative young cells had a lower threshold for LTP and were unaffected by GABA (gamma aminobutyric acid) A inhibition, indicating enhanced plasticity in the young cells (Wang, Scott, & Wojtowicz, 2000). The problem with such a study is that the definition of "young" cells is ambiguous. In our studies we have found new neurons throughout the granule cell layer, although they do appear to arise initially from the subgranular layer. In a more recent study, recordings were made from young neurons identified by electrophysiological criteria established during early postnatal development of dentate gyrus neurons, immunoreactivity for immature neuronal markers, and developing dendritic morphology. Results showed that LTP can be induced more easily in young neurons than in mature neurons under identical conditions. Thus, newly generated neurons may have unique synaptic plasticity, which may be important for the formation of new memories (Schmidt-Hieber, Jonas, & Bischofberger, 2004).

Growth Factor Effects on Neurogenesis and Running

During development, growth factors provide important extracellular signals regulating proliferation and differentiation of stem and progenitor cells in the brain and spinal cord (Calof, 1995). Several investigations have addressed the role of these factors in the adult brain. Researchers have found that in the mature organism these factors may play a role in synaptic plasticity (Kang & Schuman, 1995), learning (Fischer et al., 1987), exercise, and neurogenesis. Growth factors that have been shown to affect adult neurogenesis include basic fibroblast growth factor (FGF-2), epidermal growth factor (EGF), brain-derived neurotrophic factor (BDNF), insulin-like growth factor I (IGF-I), and vascular endothelial growth factor (VEGF).

Two of the major growth factors that influence neural progenitor cell proliferation both in vivo and in vitro are FGF-2 and EGF. Intracerebroventricular (ICV) infusion of FGF-2 and EGF results in increased neurogenesis in the subventricular zone (SVZ), but not in the dentate gyrus (DG) of the hippocampus (Craig et al., 1996; Kuhn et al., 1997; Wagner et al., 1999). ICV administration of BDNF increased the number of new neurons in adult olfactory bulb (Zigova et al., 1998), whereas ICV VEGF enhanced cell proliferation in both SVZ and DG (Jin et al., 2002). In addition, peripheral infusion of IGF-1 increased adult neurogenesis (Aberg et al., 2000) and reversed the aging-related reduction in new neuron production (Lichtenwalner et al., 2001). Increased neurogenesis in adult songbirds is also associated with elevated levels of BDNF, VEGF, and VEGF receptor (R2) (Louissaint et al., 2002).

Exercise elevated gene expression of IGF-1 (Carro et al., 2000), FGF (Gomez-Pinilla, Dao, & So, 1997; Gomez-Pinilla, So, & Kesslak, 1998), nerve growth factor, and BDNF (Neeper et al., 1995; Widenfalk, Olson, & Thoren, 1999) in the hippocampus. The exercise-induced stimulation of hippocampal neurogenesis may be mediated in part by greater uptake of IGF-1 and VEGF into the brain from serum (Trejo et al., 2001; Fabel et al., 2003). Indeed, physical activity increases serum levels of IGF (Carro et al., 2000) and VEGF (Fabel et al., 2003). Moreover, blockade of peripheral VEGF and IGF-1 antiserum inhibited the increase in neurogenesis observed with running (Trejo et al., 2001; Fabel et al., 2003).

The Role of Neurotransmitters in Running and Neurogenesis

Physical activity can change the activity of several neurotransmitter systems in the brain. Exercise influences cholinergic parameters, affecting choline uptake in the hippocampus and cortex (Fordyce & Farrar, 1991). In addition, the activity of opioid systems is enhanced (Sforzo et al., 1986). Furthermore, monoamines such as norepinephrine and serotonin are activated by running or physical activity (Chaouloff, 1989). Indeed, the antidepressant effect of exercise has been shown to be just as potent as that of serotonergic medications (Babyak et al., 2000). Interestingly, both physical activity and antidepressants increase levels of BDNF (Russo-Neustadt et al., 2000). Moreover, it has been found that both acute and chronic voluntary exercise affect the expression of many hippocampal genes related to synaptic plasticity and neurotrophin function (Tong et al., 2001). In particular, genes related to the glutamatergic system are upregulated, whereas those related to the GABA system are downregulated (Molteni, Ying, & Gomez-Pinilla, 2002). In a recent study in rats, we found that mRNA levels for the NR2B subtype of the NMDA receptor, as well the glutamate receptor 5 gene expression, were increased by exercise in the DG but not in other nonneurogenic hippocampal subfields (Farmer et al., 2004). Interestingly, in mice lacking the NMDA receptor 1 subunit, the increase in neurogenesis with wheel running does not occur. In addition, BDNF protein levels did not change with exercise in these mice (Kitamura, Mishina, & Sugiyama, 2003).

All of the neurotransmitters mentioned have been reported to influence learning and synaptic plasticity in the adult brain. It has been suggested that the monoamines play a role in neurogenesis as well. Prolonged exposure to monoaminergic agonists can enhance the level of cell proliferation in rats. In particular, serotonergic antidepressants have been shown to stimulate granule cell production (Malberg et al., 2000), whereas administration of the serotonin 5-HT (1A) receptor antagonists decreases cell proliferation in the DG (Radley & Jacobs, 2002). Moreover, 5HT-1A receptor knockout mice showed increased anxiety and a reduced neurogenic response when treated with fluoxetine (Santarelli et al., 2003). Depletion of norepinephrine by neurotoxin DSP-4 results in a 63% reduction in DG cell proliferation with no influence on percentage of cells that differentiate into neurons (Brezun & Daszuta, 1999; Kulkarni, Jha, & Vaidya, 2002). Administration of the dopaminergic antagonist haloperidol, however, enhanced hippocampal neurogenesis in gerbils (Dawirs et al., 1998). Opiates, on the other hand, reduced hippocampal cell genesis (Eisch et al., 2000), suggesting that endorphins released by exercise are not necessarily neurogenic.

Directions for Future Investigation

Over the past decade, neurogenesis in the adult brain has become a well-accepted phenomenon. Neurogenesis is a process including cell proliferation, survival, migration, fate choices, differentiation, and integration. The addition of new neurons occurs in the olfactory bulb and DG of the hippocampus in all mammals studied, from mouse to human. The process of neurogenesis is highly regulated by experience, and we are only at the very beginning of understanding all the factors that affect neurogenesis; but certainly environment and exercise are key factors. In particular, exercise has been shown not only to increase neurogenesis but also to enhance learning, synaptic plasticity, and angiogenesis, as well as levels of neurotransmitters and neurotrophins. Several of these changes associated with exercise are specific to the hippocampus. Although it is clear that exercise is beneficial for brain health and function, it remains to be determined whether the effect of exercise on cell genesis is essential. Indeed, our insight into the significance of neurogenesis for brain function is still very limited. We do not know why neurogenesis has been selected for evolutionarily or why it occurs only in specific areas of the brain. Further investigation into the behavioral and cellular regulation of the genesis of new neurons is needed if we are to begin answering these questions.

References

Aberg, M.A., Aberg, N.D., Hedbacker, H., Oscarsson, J., & Eriksson, P.S. (2000). Peripheral infusion of IGF-I selectively induces neurogenesis in the adult rat hippocampus. *Journal of Neuroscience, 20,* 2896-2903.

Allen, D.M., van Praag, H., Ray, J., Weaver, Z., Winrow, C.J., Carter, T.A., Braquet, R., Harrington, E., Ried, T., Brown, K.D., Gage, F.H., & Barlow, C. (2001). Ataxia telangiectasia mutated is essential during adult neurogenesis. *Genes and Development, 15*(5), 554-566.

Altman, J. (1962). Are new neurons formed in the brains of adult mammals? *Science, 135,* 1127-1128.

Altman, J., & Das, G.D. (1964). Autoradiographic examination of the effects of enriched environment on the rate of glial multiplication in the adult rat brain. *Nature, 204,* 1161-1163.

Altman, J., & Das, G.D. (1965). Autoradiographic and histological evidence of postnatal neurogenesis in rats. *Journal of Comparative Neurology, 124,* 319-335.

Anderson, B.J., Rapp, D.N., Baek, D.H., McCloskey, D.P., Coburn-Litvak, P.S., & Robinson, J.K. (2000). Exercise influences spatial learning in the radial arm maze. *Physiology and Behavior, 70*(5), 425-429.

Anderson, M.F., Aberg, M.A., Nilsson, M., & Eriksson, P.S. (2002). Insulin-like growth factor-I and neurogenesis in the adult mammalian brain. *Brain Research: Developmental Brain Research, 134,* 115-122.

Babyak, M., Blumenthal, J.A., Herman, S., Khatri, P., Doraiswamy, M., Moore, K., Craighead, W.E., Baldewicz, T.T., & Krishnan, K.R. (2000). Exercise treatment for major depression: Maintenance of therapeutic benefit at 10 months. *Psychosomatic Medicine, 62*(5), 633-638.

Barnea, A., & Nottebohm, F. (1994). Seasonal recruitment of hippocampal neurons in adult free-ranging black-capped chickadees. *Proceedings of the National Academy of Sciences, 91,* 11217-11221.

Black, J.E., Isaacs, K.R., Anderson, B.J., Alcantara, A.A., & Greenough, W.T. (1990). Learning causes synaptogenesis, whereas motor activity causes angiogenesis, in cerebellar cortex of adult rats. *Proceedings of the National Academy of Sciences, 87,* 5568-5572.

Bliss, T.V., & Collingridge, G.L. (1993). A synaptic model of memory: Long-term potentiation in the hippocampus. *Nature, 361,* 31-39.

Brezun, J.M., & Daszuta, A. (1999). Depletion in serotonin decreases neurogenesis in the dentate gyrus and the subventricular zone of adult rats. *Neuroscience, 89,* 999-1002.

Bronzino, J.D., Abu-Hasaballah, K., Austin-LaFrance, R.J., & Morgane, P.J. (1994). Maturation of long-term potentiation in the hippocampal dentate gyrus of the freely moving rat. *Hippocampus, 4*(4), 439-446.

Brown, J., Cooper-Kuhn, C.M., Kempermann, G., van Praag, H., Winkler, J., Gage, F.H., & Kuhn, H.G. (2003). Enriched environment and physical activity stimulate hippocampal but not olfactory bulb neurogenesis. *European Journal of Neuroscience, 17*(10), 2042-2046.

Cajal, S.R. (1928). *Degeneration and regeneration of the nervous system* (Transl. by R. May). New York: Hafner.

Calof, A.L. (1995). Intrinsic and extrinsic factors regulating vertebrate neurogenesis. *Current Opinion in Neurobiology, 5*(1), 19-27.

Carro, E., Nunez, A., Busiguina, S., & Torres-Aleman, I. (2000). Circulating insulin-like growth factor I mediates effects of exercise on the brain. *Journal of Neuroscience, 20,* 2926-2933.

Chaouloff, F. (1989). Physical exercise and brain monoamines: A review. *Acta Physiologica Scandinavica, 137,* 1-13.

Craig, C.G., Tropepe, V., Morshead, C.M., Reynolds, B.A., Weiss, S., & van der Kooy, D. (1996). In vivo growth factor expansion of endogenous subependymal neural precursor cell populations in the adult mouse brain. *Journal of Neuroscience, 16,* 2649-2658.

Cummins, R.A., Walsh, R., Budtz-Olsen, O.E., Konstantinos, T., & Horsfall, C.R. (1973). Environmentally-induced changes in the brains of elderly rats. *Nature, 243,* 516-518.

Czurko, A., Hirase, H., Csicsvari, J., & Buzsaki, G. (1999). Sustained activation of hippocampal pyramidal cells by "space clamping" in a running wheel. *European Journal of Neuroscience, 11,* 344-352.

Dawirs, R.R., Hildebrandt, K., & Teuchert-Noodt, G. (1998). Adult treatment with haloperidol increases dentate granule cell proliferation in the gerbil hippocampus. *Journal of Neural Transmission, 105,* 317-322.

Diamond, M.C., Ingham, C.C., Johnson, R.E., Bennett, E.L., & Rosenzweig, M.R. (1976). Effects of environment on morphology of rat cerebral cortex and hippocampus. *Journal of Neurobiology, 7,* 75-85.

Eisch, A.J., Barrot, M., Schad, C.A., Self, D.W., & Nestler, E.J. (2000). Opiates inhibit neurogenesis in the adult rat hippocampus. *Proceedings of the National Academy of Sciences, 97,* 7579-7584.

Eriksson, P.S., Perfilieva, E., Bjork-Eriksson, T., Alborn, A.M., Nordborg, C., Peterson, D.A., & Gage, F.H. (1998). Neurogenesis in the adult human hippocampus. *Nature Medicine, 4,* 1313-1317.

Fabel, K., Fabel, K., Tam, B., Kaufer, D., Baiker, A., Simmons, N., Kuo, C.J., & Palmer, T.D. (2003). VEGF is necessary for exercise-induced adult hippocampal neurogenesis. *European Journal of Neuroscience, 18*(10), 2803-2812.

Farmer, J., Zhao, X., van Praag, H., Wodtke, K., Gage, F.H., & Christie, B.R. (2004). Effects of voluntary exercise on synaptic plasticity and gene expression in the dentate gyrus of adult male Sprague-Dawley rats in vivo. *Neuroscience, 124*(1), 71-79.

Fischer, W., Wictorin, K., Bjorklund, A., Williams, L.R., Varon, S., & Gage, F.H. (1987). Amelioration of cholinergic neuron atrophy and spatial memory impairment in aged rats by nerve growth factor. *Nature, 329,* 65-68.

Fordyce, D.E., & Farrar, R.P. (1991). Enhancement of spatial learning in F344 rats by physical activity and related learning-associated alterations in hippocampal and cortical cholinergic functioning. *Behavioral Brain Research, 46,* 123-133.

Fordyce, D.E., & Wehner, J.M. (1993). Physical activity enhances spatial learning performance with an associated alteration in hippocampal protein kinase C activity in C57BL/6 and DBA/2 mice. *Brain Research, 619,* 111-119.

Gage, F.H. (2002). Neurogenesis in the adult brain. *Journal of Neuroscience, 22,* 612-613.

Goldman, S.A., & Nottebohm, F. (1983). Neuronal production, migration, and differentiation in a vocal control nucleus of the adult female canary brain. *Proceedings of the National Academy of Sciences, 80,* 2390-2394.

Gomez-Pinilla, F., Dao, L., & So, V. (1997). Physical exercise induces FGF-2 and its mRNA in the hippocampus. *Brain Research, 764,* 1-8.

Gomez-Pinilla, F., So, V., & Kesslak, J.P. (1998). Spatial learning and physical activity contribute to the induction of fibroblast growth factor: Neural substrates for increased cognition associated with exercise. *Neuroscience, 85,* 53-61.

Gould, E., Reeves, A.J., Fallah, M., Tanapat, P., Gross, C.G., & Fuchs, E. (1999). Hippocampal neurogenesis in adult Old World primates. *Proceedings of the National Academy of Sciences, 96,* 5263-5267.

Greenough, W.T., & Volkmar, F.R. (1973). Pattern of dendritic branching in occipital cortex of rats reared in complex environments. *Experimental Neurology, 40,* 491-504.

Hebb, D.O. (1947). The effects of early experience on problem-solving at maturity. *American Psychologist, 2,* 306-307.

Holloway, R.L. (1966). Dendritic branching: Some preliminary results of training and complexity in rat visual cortex. *Brain Research, 2,* 393-396.

Isaacs, K.R., Anderson, B.J., Alcantara, A.A., Black, J.E., & Greenough, W.T. (1992). Exercise and the brain: Angiogenesis in the adult rat cerebellum after vigorous physical activity and motor skill learning. *Journal of Cerebral Blood Flow and Metabolism, 12,* 110-119.

Jin, K., Zhu, Y., Sun, Y., Mao, X.O., Xie, L., & Greenberg, D.A. (2002). Vascular endothelial growth factor (VEGF) stimulates neurogenesis in vitro and in vivo. *Proceedings of the National Academy of Sciences, 99,* 11946-11950.

Kang, H., & Schuman, E.M. (1995). Longlasting neurotrophin-induced enhancement of synaptic transmission in the adult hippocampus. *Science, 267,* 1658-1662.

Kaplan, M.S., & Hinds, J.W. (1977). Neurogenesis in the adult rat: Electron microscopic analysis of light radioautographs. *Science, 197,* 1092-1094.

Kempermann, G., Kuhn, H.G., & Gage, F.H. (1997a). Genetic influence on neurogenesis in the dentate gyrus of adult mice. *Proceedings of the National Academy of Sciences, 94,* 10409-10414.

Kempermann, G., Kuhn, H.G., & Gage, F.H. (1997b). More hippocampal neurons in adult mice living in an enriched environment. *Nature, 386,* 493-495.

Kitamura, T., Mishina, M., & Sugiyama, H. (2003). Enhancement of neurogenesis by running wheel exercises is suppressed in mice lacking NMDA receptor epsilon 1 subunit. *Neuroscience Research, 47*(1), 55-63.

Kleim, J.A., Cooper, N.R., & VandenBerg, P.M. (2002). Exercise induces angiogenesis but does not alter movement representations within rat motor cortex. *Brain Research, 934*(1), 1-6.

Kleim, J.A., Lussnig, E., Schwarz, E.R., Comery, T.A., & Greenough, W.T. (1996). Synaptogenesis and FOS expression in the motor cortex of the adult rat after motor skill learning. *Journal of Neuroscience, 16,* 4529-4535.

Kornack, D.R., & Rakic, P. (1999). Continuation of neurogenesis in the hippocampus of the adult macaque monkey. *Proceedings of the National Academy of Sciences, 96,* 5768-5773.

Kuhn, H.G., Dickinson-Anson, H., & Gage, F.H. (1996). Neurogenesis in the dentate gyrus of the adult rat: Age-related decrease of neuronal progenitor proliferation. *Journal of Neuroscience, 16,* 2027-2033.

Kuhn, H.G., Winkler, J., Kempermann, G., Thal, L.J., & Gage, F.H. (1997). Epidermal growth factor and fibroblast growth factor-2 have different effects on neural progenitors in the adult rat brain. *Journal of Neuroscience, 17,* 5820-5829.

Kulkarni, V.A., Jha, S., & Vaidya, V.A. (2002). Depletion of norepinephrine decreases the proliferation, but does not influence the survival and differentiation, of granule cell progenitors in the adult rat hippocampus. *European Journal of Neuroscience, 16,* 2008-2012.

Larson, J., Wong, D., & Lynch, G. (1986). Patterned stimulation at the theta frequency is optimal for the induction of hippocampal long-term potentiation. *Brain Research, 368*(2), 347-350.

Lichtenwalner, R.J., Forbes, M.E., Bennett, S.A., Lynch, C.D., Sonntag, W.E., & Riddle, D.R. (2001). Intracerebroventricular infusion of insulin-like growth factor-I ameliorates the age-related decline in hippocampal neurogenesis. *Neuroscience, 107,* 603-613.

Louissaint, A. Jr., Rao, S., Leventhal, C., & Goldman, S.A. (2002). Coordinated interaction of neurogenesis and angiogenesis in the adult songbird brain. *Neuron, 34,* 945-960.

Malberg, J.E., Eisch, A.J., Nestler, E.J., & Duman, R.S. (2000). Chronic antidepressant treatment increases neurogenesis in adult rat hippocampus. *Journal of Neuroscience, 20,* 9104-9110.

Molteni, R., Ying, Z., & Gomez-Pinilla, F. (2002). Differential effects of acute and chronic exercise on plasticity-related genes in the rat hippocampus revealed by microarray. *European Journal of Neuroscience, 16*(6), 1107-1116.

Morris, R. (1984). Development of a water-maze procedure for studying spatial learning in the rat. *Journal of Neuroscience Methods, 11*(1), 47-60.

Neeper, S.A., Gomez-Pinilla, F., Choi, J., & Cotman, C. (1995). Exercise and brain neurotrophins. *Nature, 373*(6510), 109.

Overstreet, L.S., Hentges, S.T., Bumaschny, V.F., de Souza, F.S., Smart, J.L., Santangelo, A.M., Low, M.J., Westbrook, G.L., & Rubinstein, M. (2004). A transgenic marker for newly born granule cells in dentate gyrus. *Journal of Neuroscience, 24*(13), 3251-3259.

Paton, J.A., & Nottebohm, F.N. (1984). Neurons generated in the adult brain are recruited into functional circuits. *Science, 225,* 1046-1048.

Radley, J.J., & Jacobs, B.L. (2002). 5-HT1A receptor antagonist administration decreases cell proliferation in the dentate gyrus. *Brain Research, 955,* 264-267.

Reynolds, B.A., & Weiss, S. (1992). Generation of neurons and astrocytes from isolated cells of the adult mammalian central nervous system. *Science, 255,* 1646.

Rhodes, J.S., Hosack, G.R., Girard, I., Kelley, A.E., Mitchell, G.S., & Garland, T. Jr. (2001). Differential sensitivity to acute administration of cocaine, GBR 12909, and fluoxetine in mice selectively bred for hyperactive wheel-running behavior. *Psychopharmacology (Berlin), 158*(2), 120-131.

Rhodes, J.S., van Praag, H., Jeffrey, S., Girard, I., Mitchell, G.S., Garland, T. Jr., & Gage, F.H. (2003). Exercise increases hippocampal neurogenesis to high levels but does not improve spatial learning in mice bred for increased voluntary wheel running. *Behavioral Neuroscience, 117*(5), 1006-1016.

Rochefort, C., Gheusi, G., Vincent, J.D., & Lledo, P.M. (2002). Enriched odor exposure increases the number of newborn neurons in the adult olfactory bulb and improves odor memory. *Journal of Neuroscience, 22*(7), 2679-2689.

Rosenzweig, M.R. (1966). Environmental complexity, cerebral change, and behavior. *American Psychologist, 21,* 321-332.

Rosenzweig, M.R., Bennett, E.L., & Diamond, M.C. (1967). Effects of differential environments on brain anatomy and brain chemistry. *Proceedings of the Annual Meeting of the American Psychopathological Association, 56,* 45-56.

Rosenzweig, M.R., Bennett, E.L., Hebert, M., & Morimoto, H. (1978). Social grouping cannot account for cerebral effects of enriched environments. *Brain Research, 153,* 563-576.

Russo-Neustadt, A.A., Beard, R.C., Huang, Y.M., & Cotman, C.W. (2000). Physical activity and antidepressant treatment potentiate the expression of specific brain-derived neurotrophic factor transcripts in the rat hippocampus. *Neuroscience, 101,* 305-312.

Santarelli, L., Saxe, M., Gross, C., Surget, A., Battaglia, F., Dulawa, S., Weisstaub, N., Lee, J., Duman, R., Arancio, O., Belzung, C., & Hen, R. (2003). Requirement of hippocampal neurogenesis for the behavioral effects of antidepressants. *Science, 301*(5634), 805-809.

Schmidt-Hieber, C., Jonas, P., & Bischofberger, J. (2004). Enhanced synaptic plasticity in newly generated granule cells of the adult hippocampus. *Nature, 429*(6988), 184-187.

Sforzo, G.A., Seeger, T.F., Pert, C.B., Pert, A., & Dotson, C.O. (1986). In vivo opioid receptor occupation in the rat brain following exercise. *Medicine and Science in Sports and Exercise, 18,* 380-384.

Swain, R.A., Harris, A.B., Wiener, E.C., Dutka, M.V., Morris, H.D., Theien, B.E., Konda, S., Engberg, K., Lauterbur, P.C., & Greenough, W.T. (2003). Prolonged exercise induces angiogenesis and increases cerebral blood volume in primary motor cortex of the rat. *Neuroscience, 117*(4), 1037-1046.

Tong, L., Shen, H., Perreau, V.M., Balazs, R., & Cotman, C.W. (2001). Effects of exercise on gene-expression profile in the rat hippocampus. *Neurobiology of Disease, 8*(6), 1046-1056.

Trejo, J.L., Carro, E., & Torres-Alemán, I. (2001). Circulating insulin-like growth factor I mediates exercise-induced increases in the number of new neurons in the adult hippocampus. *Journal of Neuroscience, 21,* 1628-1634.

Vanderwolf, C.H. (1969). Hippocampal electrical activity and voluntary movement in the rat. *Electroencephalography and Clinical Neurophysiology, 26*(4), 407-418.

van Praag, H., Christie, B.R., Sejnowski, T.J., & Gage, F.H. (1999a). Running enhances neurogenesis, learning, and long-term potentiation in mice. *Proceedings of the National Academy of Sciences, 96,* 13427-13431.

van Praag, H., Kempermann, G., & Gage, F.H. (1999b). Running increases cell proliferation and neurogenesis in the adult mouse dentate gyrus. *Nature Neuroscience, 2,* 266-270.

van Praag, H., Schinder, A.F., Christie, B.R., Toni, N., Palmer, T.D., & Gage, F.H. (2002). Functional neurogenesis in the adult hippocampus. *Nature, 415,* 1030-1034.

van Praag, H., Shubert, T., Zhao, C., and Gage, F.H. (2005). Exercise enhances learining and hippocampal neurogenesis in aged mice. *Journal of Neuroscience, 25*(38), 8680-8685.

Wagner, J.P., Black, I.B., & DiCicco-Bloom, E. (1999). Stimulation of neonatal and adult brain neurogenesis by subcutaneous injection of basic fibroblast growth factor. *Journal of Neuroscience, 19,* 6006-6016.

Wang, S., Scott, B.W., & Wojtowicz, J.M. (2000). Heterogenous properties of dentate granule neurons in adult rat. *Journal of Neurobiology, 42,* 248-257.

Widenfalk, J., Olson, L., & Thoren, P. (1999). Deprived of habitual running, rats downregulate BDNF and

TrkB messages in the brain. *Neuroscience Research, 34,* 125-132.

Zigova, T., Pencea, V., Wiegand, S.J., & Luskin, M.B. (1998). Intraventricular administration of BDNF increases the number of newly generated neurons in the adult olfactory bulb. *Molecular and Cellular Neuroscience, 11,* 234-245.

Physical Activity and Emotion

This section contains four chapters highlighting different aspects of the relationship between physical activity and the broadly defined psychological construct of emotion. The order of the chapters follows a progression from a broad conceptual understanding of the evolutionary basis of the exercise–emotion link (chapter 6) to the role of neurotransmitter molecules (chapter 9). Three of the chapters (chapters 6, 7, and 8) are based primarily on evidence from human research, and one chapter (chapter 9) is based primarily on evidence from basic animal research. This approach should provide readers with a multilevel view of the exercise–emotion connection, from the level of the intact human organism functioning within the environmental conditions that shaped human evolution to the level of the synapse.

Michel Cabanac, the author of chapter 6, was the first researcher to place the relationship between exercise and pleasure–displeasure within a conceptual framework grounded in evolutionary considerations. In a seminal paper published in *Science* in 1971 (cited in his chapter), Cabanac encapsulated this framework in the simple but powerful equation "pleasant = useful" and the novel concept of alliesthesia, the idea that a given stimulus can induce a pleasant or unpleasant sensation depending on the internal state and the adaptational needs of the organism. In this chapter, Cabanac reexamines the rationale behind these groundbreaking ideas and reviews his research pertaining specifically to their application to the context of exercise. As a companion to this chapter, besides Cabanac's own theoretical works on pleasure (see references in the chapter), readers may wish to consult texts on the evolution of the mind and brain (Preuss, 2000; Tooby & Cos-

mides, 2000) and the evolution of emotions (Cosmides & Tooby, 2000). A fresh reading of Darwin's (1872/1998) classic *The Expression of the Emotions in Man and Animals* is also recommended.

In chapter 7, Ekkekakis and Acevedo review the latest developments on the relationship between exercise intensity and affective responses, an area of research with a 35-year history and, until recently, mostly ambiguous results. They demonstrate how a series of changes in critical aspects of the methodology, including the ways of operationalizing and standardizing exercise intensity, have brought clarity and consistency. On the basis of the idea that the affective responses to exercise represent a multifaceted rather than a unitary phenomenon, they also sketch a new "dual-mode" psychobiological model that takes into account the role of both bottom-up (exercise-induced interoceptive stimuli) and top-down factors (relevant cognitive appraisals). Readers would benefit from a careful study of the chapters by Craig (chapter 2) and Williamson (chapter 3) in this volume, as well as from consulting texts on the neuroanatomy and neurophysiology of the amygdala (Aggleton, 2000) and its role in affective responses (LeDoux & Phelps, 2000). More comprehensive texts on affective neuroscience would give readers a broader perspective on the brain mechanisms involved in affect and emotion (Borod, 2000; Lane & Nadel, 2000; Panksepp, 1998; Rolls, 1999). These texts are also useful as companion references for the remaining chapters in this section.

In chapter 8, Petruzzello, Ekkekakis, and Hall examine patterns of interhemispheric asymmetries in the activation of the brain's frontal cortex as indices of affective style and affective responses to exercise. Although numerous studies over the years have examined the effects of exercise on brain electrocortical activity through electroencephalography (EEG), the integration and interpretation of this information have been nearly impossible due to the absence of an appropriate and adequately supported theoretical framework. Petruzzello, Ekkekakis, and Hall propose that such an integration is possible using the model proposed by Richard Davidson (2003, 2004) and review evidence that supports this claim. Readers would benefit from a good understanding of the various aspects of the EEG methodology (Davidson, Jackson, & Larson, 2000; Fisch, 1999; Rowan & Tolunsky, 2003).

In chapter 9, Romain Meeusen completes the section by providing the perspective from neuroscience, the most basic level of analysis. Meeusen examines exercise-induced acute and chronic changes in brain monoamines and their implications for anxiety and depression. Study-ing the effects of exercise on neurotransmitters in real time is an undertaking with tremendous potential for enhancing our understanding of the exercise–emotion link but also a highly challenging one from a technical standpoint. Meeusen has been a pioneer in use of the technique of microdialysis for this purpose. His results have opened a new window into the brain of the exercising animal. To fully appreciate the evidence reviewed in this chapter, readers should have a fairly good grasp of the function and psychopharmacology of the monoamine neurotransmitters (Cooper, Bloom, & Roth, 2003; Feldman, Meyer, & Quenzer, 1997). Although Meeusen has done an excellent job in describing the technical aspects of microdialysis in easy-to-understand terms, interested readers might want to consult additional sources for a more detailed presentation (Kehr, 1999).

Suggested Background Readings

Aggleton, J.P. (Ed.) (2000). *The amygdala: A functional analysis* (2nd ed.). New York: Oxford University Press.

Borod, J.C. (Ed.) (2000). *The neuropsychology of emotion.* New York: Oxford University Press.

Cooper, J.R., Bloom, F.E., & Roth, R.H. (2003). *The biochemical basis of neuropharmacology* (8th ed.). New York: Oxford University Press.

Cosmides, L., & Tooby, J. (2000). Evolutionary psychology and the emotions. In M. Lewis & J.M. Haviland-Jones (Eds.), *Handbook of emotions* (2nd ed., pp. 91-115). New York: Guilford Press.

Darwin, C. (1872/1998). *The expression of the emotions in man and animals* (3rd ed.). New York: Oxford University Press.

Davidson, R.J. (2003). Affective neuroscience and psychophysiology: Toward a synthesis. *Psychophysiology, 40,* 655-665.

Davidson, R.J. (2004). What does the prefrontal cortex "do" in affect: Perspectives on frontal EEG asymmetry research. *Biological Psychology, 67,* 219-233.

Davidson, R.J., Jackson, D.C., & Larson, C.L. (2000). Human electroencephalography. In J.T. Cacioppo, L.G. Tassinary, & G.G. Berntson (Eds.), *Handbook of psychophysiology* (2nd ed., pp. 27-52). Cambridge, UK: Cambridge University Press.

Feldman, R.S., Meyer, J.S., & Quenzer, L.F. (1997). *Principles of neuropsychopharmacology.* Sunderland, MA: Sinauer Associates.

Fisch, B.J. (1999). *Fisch and Spehlmann's EEG primer: Basic principles of digital and analog EEG* (3rd ed.). Amsterdam: Elsevier Science.

Kehr, J. (1999). Monitoring chemistry of brain microenvironment: Biosensors, microdialysis and related techniques. In W. Windhorst & H. Johansson (Eds.), *Modern techniques in neuroscience research* (pp. 1149-1198). New York: Springer-Verlag.

Lane, R.D., & Nadel, L. (Eds.) (2000). *Cognitive neuroscience of emotion.* New York: Oxford University Press.

LeDoux, J.E., & Phelps, E.A. (2000). Emotional networks in the brain. In M. Lewis & J.M. Haviland-Jones (Eds.), *Handbook of emotions* (2nd ed., pp. 157-172). New York: Guilford Press.

Panksepp, J. (1998). *Affective neuroscience: The foundations of human and animal emotions.* New York: Oxford University Press.

Preuss, T.M. (2000). What's human about the human brain. In M.S. Gazzaniga (Ed.), *The new cognitive neurosciences* (2nd ed., pp. 1219-1234). Cambridge, MA: MIT Press.

Rolls, E.T. (1999). *The brain and emotion.* New York: Oxford University Press.

Rowan, A.J., & Tolunsky, E. (2003). *Primer of EEG with a mini-atlas.* Philadelphia: Butterworth-Heinemann.

Tooby, J., & Cosmides, L. (2000). Toward mapping the evolved functional organization of mind and brain. In M.S. Gazzaniga (Ed.), *The new cognitive neurosciences* (2nd ed., pp. 1167-1178). Cambridge, MA: MIT Press.

6

Exertion and Pleasure From an Evolutionary Perspective

Michel Cabanac, PhD

In the sweat of your face you will eat bread.
—*Genesis 3:19*

Our knowledge of the world, including ourselves, is filtered twice—once by the narrow physical or chemical window of our senses, and again by the biological or cultural programming of our brains. Both filters are the result of evolution; that is, they have been passed down to us because they proved their worth in our ancestors. Such filtering might therefore affect the way we sense and perceive our own bodies.

But, first, what do words like "sense" and "perceive" mean? Sensation is the irruption into consciousness of any nervous message carried to the brain by an afferent pathway. From it, the brain creates a mental object that has four dimensions: quality, or the kind of stimulus; intensity, or how strong it is; hedonicity, or how useful or noxious it is; and duration, or how long it lasts. Quality, intensity, and duration are positive and multiplicative. Only hedonicity is additive, and it can be positive, negative, or nil. Such a definition of sensation is simple and has two advantages:

1. It lumps all of the different categories of sensations into one category, whereas classical categorization would list many different sorts of sensations with different attributes.

2. It points to a fundamental unity of sensory input to the central nervous system.

More complex than sensation, perception is the simultaneous entry of several afferent messages, including those retrieved from memory, into consciousness (Cabanac, 1995).

This book is about humans. Our species, however, evolved from earlier life forms, and this chapter addresses the origin of conscious sensation among our nonhuman ancestors. Clearly, the earliest animals were not conscious creatures, their behavior resulting only from tropisms and reflexes. So when, in phylogeny, did consciousness emerge? My research team has sought an answer in the evolutionary origin of emotional responses.

When we gently handled mammals, birds (*Gallus domesticus* [Cabanac & Aizawa, 2000]), and reptiles (lizards, tortoises [Cabanac & Bernieri, 2000]), their body temperature rose, producing an emotional fever. This response was produced in reptiles only through behavioral means and was lacking altogether in amphibians (Cabanac & Cabanac, 2004) and fish. Gentle handling also accelerated heart rate, another sign of emotion, in mammals, birds (Cabanac & Aizawa, 2000), tortoises (Cabanac & Bernieri, 2000), and lizards, but not in frogs (Cabanac & Cabanac, 2000). Because emotional fever and emotional tachycardia exist in mammals, birds, and reptiles, but not in amphibians, the mental experience of emotion may have emerged in the evolutionary lineage between amphibians and reptiles (for references before 1999, see Cabanac, 1999).

Just as ancient is "hedonicity", that is, the capacity to associate different sensations with pleasant or unpleasant responses. Mammals, birds, and reptiles learn to avoid the flavor of a novel food when digestive illness follows ingestion. Such learning is absent from amphibians (Paradis & Cabanac, 2004). Again, the transition from amphibians to reptiles seems to have been a critical evolutionary threshold.

These results are consistent with the hypothesis that specific mental capacities emerged with reptiles. According to Darwinian theory, sensory messages should have become conscious because consciousness had proved useful to the organisms first acquiring it. To be useful, these sensations had to describe the quality, the intensity, and above all the usefulness of environmental stimuli; therefore, it is likely that they were multidimensional from the outset, as defined earlier. The very persistence of consciousness over such a long time span demonstrates its formidable selective advantage. It provided the first sensorially conscious animals with a decision-making edge by optimizing their behavior and by freeing them from the need for an infinitely complex network of hardwired reflexes.

If consciousness has a single phylogenetic origin, it is likely that conscious events all share the same basic four-dimensional structure (Cabanac, 1996). We may now turn to a specific case: the self-optimizing nature of feelings aroused by muscular exertion (Ulmer, 1996). All that we have defined in the general case of sensation should also hold true here.

Sensations From Muscular Exertion

Borg has extensively studied the feelings aroused by muscular exertion and has proposed a scale from 6 to 20 called "rating of perceived exertion" (RPE) (Borg, 1962, 1982). The feelings measured by Borg's RPE scale are global perceptions arising from various parts of the body; they are not broken down into their various inputs. Where, then, do they originate? During exertion, nervous messages emerge into consciousness not only from the working muscles, tendons, and joints but also from other loci in the body.

Muscles and Tendons

In the working apparatus itself, the muscles and tendons, local conditions are modified by exertion. Conscious messages are sent via mechanical (Blomstrand & Essen-Gustavsson, 1987; Gandevia & McCloskey, 1977; Roland, 1975), chemical (Starkie et al., 1999), and temperature signals (Saltin, Gagge, & Stolwijk, 1968) in relation to the degree of exertion by the muscles. Sensation of muscular exertion thus originates peripherally (Sanes & Shadmehr, 1995; Wade, 2003).

Muscle temperature is an important signal of fatigue but, unexpectedly, not of heat. Cooling significantly shortens the time to reach fatigue and more than halves the work capacity. This is unexpected because cooler muscles require less effort, make less demand on reserves, and create lower concentrations of waste products and by-products. It is not yet understood why fatigue occurs at a particular point or why local cooling reduces work capacity (Wade et al., 2000).

Heart and Respiration

Many authors have shown that rates of perceived exertion and fatigue are independent of peripheral stimuli. Perceived exertion correlates most highly with blood pressure and not at all with electromyogram readings (Kilbom et al., 1983). Knibestöl and Valbo (1980) concluded that the signal for perceived exertion is central, not peripheral. For Pandolf (1978), muscular fatigue is fundamentally based on a central signal: cardiorespiratory stress. Indeed, dyspnea provides a conscious signal that reliably describes the underlying physiological state (Mahler & Horowitz, 1994).

Although heart rate is critical to perceived exertion, it is not the only factor. Heart rate is significantly raised by sleep deprivation even though perceived exertion remains unchanged (Martin & Haney, 1982). The findings of Jackson and colleagues (1981) do not support a central control model that links perceived exertion solely to cardiovascular stress.

Other Internal Influences

If neither peripheral inputs nor cardiorespiratory signals can explain perceived exertion, other factors may be involved. An important one seems to be lactacidemia: When subjects inhale air with less oxygen, lactacidemia rises with perceived exertion while endurance falls (Hogan & Welch, 1984). Conversely, intravenous glucose perfusion lowers heart rate and respiratory quotient while lowering perceived exertion (Tabata & Kawakami, 1991). Hyperthermia raises lactacidemia and in turn logarithmically increases perceived exertion (Bergh et al., 1986), a result also obtained by Kozlowski and colleagues (1985).

Core body temperature is thus a limiting factor that may increase discomfort and limit exertion. Temperature has a real but indirect influence. Hyperthermia does not seem to affect the activation pattern of the muscles. Rather, the linear correlation among core temperature, electroencephalographic recording (EEG), and perceived exertion indicates that changes in cerebral activity may be associated with hyperthermia-induced fatigue during prolonged exercise in hot environments (Nybo & Nielsen, 2001). A rise in ambient temperature increases oxygen consumption for a constant workload and raises the anaerobic fraction. Thus, heat stress causes some blood flow to be dedicated to thermolysis rather than to muscles (Dimri et al., 1980).

Finally, as may be expected, the sensation of exertion depends on the *type of work performed* by the muscle. At the start of exercise, sensation is a function of the muscle's resistance to the force and is largely independent of whether the work is static or dynamic (Cafarelli, 1982). When the work is extended over time, the sensation of exertion is of course a function of duration; the relationship between workload and work duration is hyperbolic when subjects maintain a steady sensation of exertion (Cafarelli, Cain, & Stevens, 1977). Different types of work arouse different sensations and also modify the internal environment differently: For an identical workload, light and prolonged aerobic pedaling or weightlifting modifies ventilatory flow, heart rate, and levels of lactate, cortisol, insulin, and blood glucose less than intense but intermittent work (VanHelder et al., 1985).

Conclusion

The conscious signal is neither purely muscular nor purely central. It is a combination of both (Löllgen, Graham, & Sjøgaard, 1980; Robertson, 1982). There are sensations from the working muscles and from the heart, yet perceived exertion is not a single sensation but rather an overall perception, as defined earlier. It is worth noting that the rating of perceived exertion, that is, a mental signal, measures exercise intensity at least as well as heart rate, that is, a physiological index (Eston, Davies, & Williams, 1987; Ueda & Kurokawa, 1991). In numerous experimental studies, the subjects' rating of perceived exertion predicted their relative metabolic demand, especially at higher workloads (Noble, 1982). This mental signal reliably adapts behavior to physiological capacity.

Thus, Borg's scale of overall perceived exertion effectively describes what is taking place overall in the mind of a person exerting effort. Is it possible to push this analysis further? By dissociating hedonicity from overall perception, we may find a tool with which to analyze perception. If the hedonic dimension of perception is what motivates and optimizes behavior, this will be especially obvious in the case of muscular exertion and the perceptions it arouses.

Hedonicity of Muscular Exertion

Humans, unlike animal subjects, can verbally describe their sensations. Human experimentation thus enables us to explore the mental experience of muscular exertion and, especially, to analyze the hedonic content of the perceptions it arouses. To this end, we recorded human sensations in the chest (variable x) and the lower limbs (variable y) and how human perceptions combine in subjects simply walking on a treadmill with five slopes (x) and five speeds (y) (Cabanac, 1985). The subjects separately estimated displeasure for chest and leg sensations. Figure 6.1 plots these ratings as isohedonic lines (left box: displeasure in the lower limbs; middle box: displeasure in the chest; right box: sum of the two ratings). These ratings were then compared with actual behavior in other sessions when the subjects had to climb 300 m (328 yd) on the treadmill at varying speeds and slopes. In these new sessions, when a set speed was imposed, the subject could adjust slope, and vice versa. The dots on figure 6.1 show the actual behavior of one subject. The dots fall along the lines, though not generating them, and were from different sessions. Behavior (dots) was strikingly adapted to the sum of perceived displeasure in the chest and in the lower limbs.

Thus, in the situations explored, chest versus lower limbs, behavior was repeatedly consistent: In the bidimensional sensory situations imposed by the experimenters, the subjects described maps of bidimensional pleasure in sessions investigating pleasure and tended to move to areas of minimal displeasure on these maps in sessions investigating behavior.

Figure 6.2 compares the behavioral choice (dots) at the end of a session with the theoretical time (lines) needed to climb 300 m (328 yd) as directed, the subject manipulating speed *or* slope. It can be seen that behavioral choice coincided with the 40 min isochronal curve; that is, the subject tended to walk with constant time for a constant work. He exercised at a constant power for the various combinations of slopes and speeds. This makes sense from the standpoint of physiology.

The results confirm that perception of muscular exertion (figure 6.1) integrates all afferent

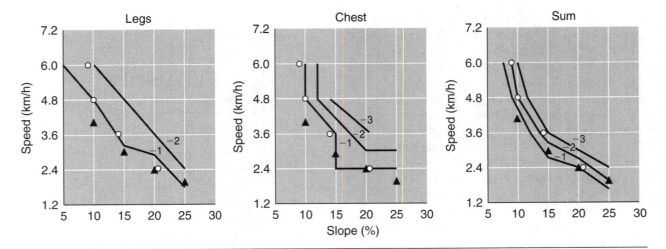

Figure 6.1 The lines indicate thresholds for discomfort (–1) and clear discomfort (–2) in the lower limbs (legs, left box) and chest (middle box) for various combinations of slopes and speeds. The dots indicate the subject's actual behavior. The line in the right box is the sum of the lines in the other two boxes. Of the three lines, the sum correlates the most highly with behavior.

From Cabanac (1985).

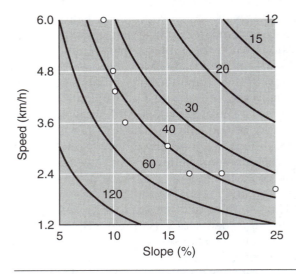

Figure 6.2 The lines and numbers indicate the time needed to climb 300 m (328 yd) at varying combinations of slopes and speeds. The dots show actual behavior when one of these two variables was fixed and the other could be adjusted by the subject.

From Cabanac (1985).

sensory inputs. In addition, behavior is not only motivated by the hedonic dimension of perception, but also optimized through minimization of displeasure (figure 6.2). These conclusions were repeatedly borne out by the findings of other research teams.

When subjects performed a mechanical task, that is, pointing at a target with their arm in various more or less functional positions, their precious sion and efficacy were maximal when their posture was most comfortable (figure 6.3). Performance deteriorated with increasing discomfort (Rossetti, Meckler, & Prablanc, 1994).

When subjects performed a short (10 min) incremental exercise on an electrically stabilized exercise bicycle, their oxygen uptake, leg effort, and dyspnea varied significantly with different pedaling frequencies. Oxygen uptake was minimal at 60 rpm and increased at both higher and lower pedaling frequencies. Both leg effort and dyspnea were minimal at 80 rpm; leg effort intensified at higher and lower pedaling frequencies, and dyspnea was most intense at 100 rpm. Thus, there was some conflict between minimization of energy expenditure and leg effort at expenditures less than 180 W. Leg effort was minimized at the cost of increased energy expenditure (Chen, Jones, & Killian, 1999), but the general trend was similar to that of our other experiment.

Pleasure aroused by muscular exertion decreased when the intensity of exertion reached maximum aerobic power and bordered on anaerobiosis (Acevedo et al., 2003). The same conclusions also been reached by Ekkekakis, Hall, and Petruzzello (2005): When exertion became anaerobic, formerly pleasurable muscular effort now aroused displeasure. Oxygen consumption tended spontaneously to be minimal when subjects could select their own pace (Zarrugh, Todd, & Ralston, 1974); indeed, this was what they did (Zarrugh & Radcliffe, 1978). The same type of optimization also took place in swimming; the stroke

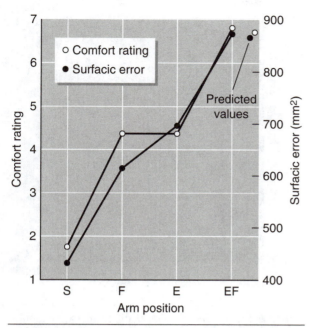

Figure 6.3 A subject was asked to point his finger at a target. Discomfort rate and performance error varied with arm position. In S, the subject adopted the most comfortable natural position; in F, the wrist was flexed as far as possible; in E, the arm was extended vertically as far as possible; and in EF, the subject adopted both F and E.

From Rossetti et al. (1994).

frequency spontaneously selected to achieve maximum speed was indeed the optimal one for oxygen consumption (Swaine & Reilly, 1983).

When the intensity of treadmill work rose, the perception of activation also rose from 2 to 5 (scale 1 to 6) and shifted from agreeable to disagreeable, +3 to –1.5 (scale –5 to +5). The working muscles produced a clearly negative alliesthesia of –2 to –3 points. The same stimulus, that is, muscular exertion, can thus arouse either pleasure or displeasure according to the circumstances. When exertion is interrupted, the general perception becomes immediately pleasurable. Thus, hedonicity is actually the means whereby the muscular system is optimized and whereby sentient organisms become aware of challenges to homeostasis (Hall, Ekkekakis, & Petruzzello, 2002). This is the very definition of alliesthesia (Cabanac, 1971).

Exercise intensity beyond the point of transition from aerobic to anaerobic metabolism is accompanied by an exponential decline in affective valence. This change in affect may be a useful guide in helping exercisers recognize their phase of metabolism and thus more effectively self-monitor and self-regulate the intensity of their efforts

(Ekkekakis, Hall, & Petruzzello, 2004). Ekkekakis distinguishes five types of hedonic responses to muscular exertion:

1. Brief episodes of pleasure, even at high intensity
2. Strong interindividual differences when exertion is prolonged
3. Universal clear-cut pleasure when exertion ends
4. Universal clear-cut displeasure when exertion borders on exhaustion
5. Universal clear-cut pleasure when intense exertion is interrupted (Ekkekakis, 2003)

When mediated by perceptions of exertion, the pursuit of pleasure optimizes behavior, as assessed by physiological criteria. Pleasure indexes usefulness. Thus, muscular exercise may be intrinsically motivated; that is, muscular exertion in itself might be rewarding. Some daily walking does improve mood (Thayer et al., 2004). Muscular exertion might also be rewarding because, though unpleasant, it procures another reward that offsets the unpleasantness of fatigue, for example, fighting the cold by heating oneself through physical exercise.

If hedonicity is indeed the signal for behavior optimization, as shown in figures 6.2 and 6.3, it is worth noting that constant muscular exertion was governed by thresholds of negative hedonicity. Thus behavior was optimized by minimizing bidimensional displeasure. Such a result does not change the conclusions: Hedonicity is still the optimizer. Yet one may wonder why our subjects would indulge in unpleasant behavior. The answer is that they were motivated to do so. They had the pleasure of being useful participants in research and receiving a modest financial compensation. Whatever their motivation, they were motivated to experience displeasure. The hedonicity of exertion had to compete inside them with other hedonicities. We will now turn to the problem of conflicting motivations.

Hedonicity in Motivational Conflicts

An organism must rank its priorities because behavior is a final common path: It is not possible to dine and sleep at the same time. To compare motivations and rank them in order of priority, one needs a common currency (McFarland & Sibly, 1975). I have proposed elsewhere that pleasure is this common currency (Cabanac, 1992). The perception of pleasure, as measured operationally and quantitatively by behavioral choices (in the case of animals) or by ratings of the intensity of pleasure or displeasure (in the case of humans), can serve as such a common currency for various motivations. Decisions would be made simply through maximization of the sum of different hedonic values. Is this true in the case of muscular exertion, when fatigue is pitted against other motivations?

Thermal Discomfort Versus Fatigue

The hypothesis was verified in treadmill versus ambient temperature experiments in which a clear cost was involved, either fatigue or cold discomfort. In these experiments the subjects were placed in a bidimensional (x, y) sensory space and had to make a trade-off. The results show that their behavior tended to place them in pleasurable areas of this space. The perception of a thermal environment was pitted against that of walking on a treadmill (Cabanac & LeBlanc, 1983). Thermal comfort (x) could be improved at the cost of fatigue (y). Dressed in swimsuits and tennis shoes, the subjects walked at 3 km/hr (1.9 mi/hr) on a treadmill in a climatic chamber. In an initial series of measurements, the treadmill's slope was varied from 0% to 24%, and this condition was combined with an ambient temperature ranging from 25° C to 5° C in a 25-node matrix. The subjects separately rated the pleasure or displeasure evoked by ambient temperature and by exercise. Actual ratings of pleasure/displeasure of x and y were obtained at ambient temperatures 5°, 10°, 15°, 20°, and 25° C in combination with 0%, 6%, 12%, 18%, and 24% slopes. The ratings of x and y were then totaled. Figure 6.4 gives the sum of the two ratings as isohedonic lines interpolated between the nodes. The figure is a map of pleasure/displeasure in a bidimensional sensory space (exertion vs. ambient temperature).

In a second series of measurements, one variable was imposed, either treadmill slope or ambient temperature, and the subject could manipulate the other one. The results are also given on figure 6.4 as dots. The subjects reciprocally adjusted exertion intensity and ambient temperature. When a steep slope was imposed, they selected a low ambient temperature, and

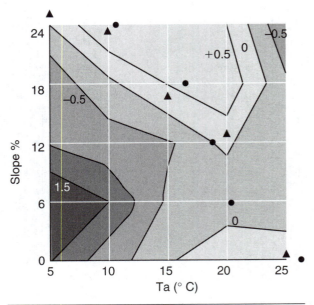

Figure 6.4 Results of several different experimental sessions on one subject walking at constant speed on a treadmill in a climatic chamber. In one series (map with isohedonic lines), ambient temperature (Ta) and treadmill slope were both imposed at various combinations, and the subject's ratings of pleasure/displeasure were recorded. On the map, both ratings were added algebraically, and isoclines indicate zones sharing the same hedonic perceptions. The darker the zone, the more unpleasant the perception. White = most pleasant. In a second series of five sessions (filled circles), treadmill slope was imposed and the subject could manipulate ambient temperature. In a third series of five sessions (filled triangle), ambient temperature was imposed and the subject could manipulate treadmill slope. The subject tried to remain in the white "pleasant" zone. This behavior was obviously thermoregulatory as the intensity of exertion—and thermogenesis—was inversely proportional to ambient temperature.

From Cabanac & LeBlanc (1983).

when walking on a level slope was imposed, they selected a lukewarm ambient temperature. When the subjects were allowed to adjust treadmill slope, with various ambient temperatures being imposed, they selected steep slopes at low ambient temperature and zero slopes at high ambient temperature. Quite strikingly, the dots showing the finally selected experimental conditions (in quasi-steady states at the end of 1 hr sessions) are in the white areas indicating bidimensional pleasure. Operant behavior was guided by a tendency to minimize displeasure (or maximize pleasure) in a bidimensional space.

Heat production in working muscles may be estimated to be three times the amount of mechanical energy produced by the muscle due to the relatively low rentability of the muscle engine. When the subjects walked on the treadmill, the heat production was inversely proportional to the ambient temperature. Behavioral heat production was proportional to the need to offset heat loss and was therefore optimal for temperature regulation. Taken separately from verbal reports of pleasure/displeasure, these results are consistent with animal observations (Krebs & Davies, 1981) or experiments (Collier & Rovee-Collier, 1981), which show a good fit between animal behavior and physiological need. This has been repeatedly demonstrated and needs no further demonstration. Here, however, I have gone beyond simple behavior measurement to compare variations in behavior with variations in sensory pleasure, as judged from ratings obtained in separate sessions. Behavior and pleasure follow the same patterns.

Thus, the tendency to maximize sensory pleasure serves the purpose of physiological regulation not only in the perception of exercise but also in motivational conflict. In both cases, pleasure coincides with a clearly adaptive physiological aim. This strongly suggests that pleasure is the key to optimal behavior and that maximizing pleasure leads to optimal physiological performance.

If sensory pleasure is the common currency that mediates competing motivations for behaviors with physiological outcomes, it may also mediate other, purely mental motivations. Pleasure may be felt even when no physiological need is being addressed. This was tested in a conflict between exertion and money.

Static Exertion Versus Money

In this experiment, human volunteers could earn money by simply exposing themselves to unpleasant, painful sensations from isometric contractions in their thighs (Cabanac, 1986). They sat with their backs against a wall and their legs at 90° angles, without any chair or stool for support. The longer they remained and endured the pain, the more money they earned. In several sessions, the rate of pay was varied. It was found that the discomfort or pain, as rated by the subjects, increased linearly as a function of time. The subjects also tolerated more intense pain for a longer time when the monetary reward was higher (figure 6.5). This finding is consistent with common sense. It can be assumed that the subjects decided to end a session just when the displeasure of the sensation became greater than

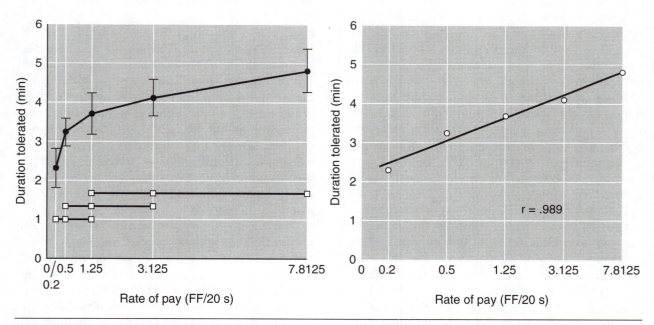

Figure 6.5 Ten volunteers were subjected to the natural pain of isometric muscular contraction. They could end the session whenever they wanted to. The longer they stayed, the more money they earned. For different sessions, the rates of pay varied. Mean duration and standard error (vertical lines) of pain tolerance are plotted as a function of rate of pay. In the left-hand graph, means not underscored by the same line (x—x) are significantly different. It can be seen that the two motivations, money and pain, could "speak" to one another quantitatively. FF/20 s means French francs per 20-second period.

From Cabanac (1986).

the pleasure of the anticipated monetary reward. The relation between reward and duration of tolerated displeasure was logarithmic. The hypothesis may thus cover behavioral motivations other than simple sensory hedonicity. The pursuit of pleasure may involve nonphysiological motivations.

The hedonic dimension of sensation seems to be the common currency that mediates the ranking of priorities. The sensations and perceptions aroused by muscular exertion are among many that may be mediated (Cabanac, 1986).

Animal Studies

This conclusion is supported by several animal experiments in which animals had to work for their reward. The amount of work an animal did for an increasingly infrequent reward was used to measure its rewarding effect. Three groups of rats were trained for this experimental design, the rewards being food pellets containing 1%, 10%, and 95% sucrose. When the food pellets were provided continuously, the 10% sucrose ones maintained the highest work response rates. When, however, the food pellets were provided less and less often, performance was consistently related to sucrose concentration (Cheeta, Brooks, & Willner, 1995).

When fed a tasty diet, rats tend to ingest more. When quinine, a bitter substance, is added to their food, they tend to ingest less and lose weight. In an experiment in which rats had to work for their food, their body weight was the same as when quinine was added to their food, an indirect indication that work was aversive (Peck, 1978). When rats had to run on a treadmill for sweet drinks, drinking was related to speed and, to a lesser degree, to distance. Thus, the rats must have been comparing information from their own bodies (rate of energy expenditure) with their use of a commodity (sweet reward) (Gannon, Smith, & Tierney, 1986). Other experiments pitted reproduction (insemination, lactation, nursing), which costs energy, against food intake, which was also costly, as the rats had to earn food by working on a treadmill (Perrigo, 1987).

These experiments provide convincing, albeit indirect, evidence that animals optimize their behavior through hedonic signals. Is it possible to gain more direct evidence that animals will seek sensory *pleasure* just for the sake of it and even will be ready to trade off some displeasure for it?

Light work must be pleasant to animals, as experiments show that rats will run indefinitely on a treadmill if it is made available (Jonsdottir et al., 1996) even when no special reward is obtainable through running. It may be, then, that work can be pleasurable in itself. As intensity or duration increases, however, work becomes aversive. When monkeys had to pull a chain for heat in a cold environment, they obviously linked the muscular exertion to the warm reward: The increasing force requirement was met with increasing tolerance for larger air temperature fluctuations and longer intervals between responses. Eventually they stopped and just sat and shivered (Adair & Wright, 1976).

In the obstruction method used by Warden (1931), rats could reach a bait at the cost of stepping on an unpleasant electrified meshed floor. In a similar but more natural situation, rats were trained to feed in a nest placed at one end of a 16 m (17.5 yd) zigzag alley (Cabanac & Johnson, 1983). The nest was provided with water and food in excess of the rats' needs. On the day of an experimental session, the nest was heated and tasty food (shortcake, peanut butter) was placed 16 m away, but the environment outside the warm nest was cooled to −15° C, a temperature potentially lethal to rats. The rats ran to the cold feeder for the palatable bait, not out of necessity (chow was provided at no cost in their warm nest) but for the pleasure of ingesting the tasty food. The number of trips was related to the tastiness of the food. When chow was placed in the cold feeder instead of shortcake, the rats went to it once and did not return. The rats were quantitatively comparing the pleasure of eating the food with the displeasure of enduring the cold. Other mammals thus seem to behave as humans do in situations in which conflicting motivations have to be resolved, with a central role for pleasure and hedonicity. If such a mechanism exists in mammals, which we can more easily accept as having consciousness, would it also exist in reptiles?

The role of sensory pleasure in decision making was verified in iguanas placed in a motivational conflict. The iguanas had to leave a warm refuge, provided with standard food, to reach a tasty but unnecessary bait (lettuce) in a cold environment. They nonetheless ventured out into the cold, trading off the coldness of the outside environment for the tastiness of the bait, but only in mild cold. When ambient temperature was 0° C, they remained under the infrared lamp. Like humans, the iguanas seemed to be maximizing their sensory pleasure; thus, they optimized their behavior (Balaskó & Cabanac, 1998).

Conclusions

Information on our physiological status is transmitted via signals to the human mind. These signals are critical to survival and must be analyzed, prioritized, and adjudicated to produce an appropriate behavioral response, such as during muscular exertion. This is the role of hedonicity in sensation and perception: to select a behavioral response that is appropriate to both the organism's needs and its physiological capacities. Pleasure/displeasure is the optimizer of behavior.

Hedonicity must have been an efficacious solution to the problems of life, as it has been retained by successive reptilian and mammalian lineages down to us. Because behavior is a final common path, all motivations, including the autohedonicity of exertion itself, compete for access to it. If a motivation to accomplish a given task is given so high a priority that other hedonic messages are ignored, the resulting overexertion may lead to injury or even death, as with Phedippides, the famous marathon runner (Cabanac & Bonniot-Cabanac, 1997). In most cases, however, the inconvenience of fatigue is simply less than the rewards of work. Work is disliked but done nevertheless for the rewards that flow from it. This was the very point of the verse in Genesis.

Conversely, acute and chronic physical activity influence brain function, resulting in changes to brain morphology, neuronal firing rates, cellular metabolism, neurotransmitter concentrations and release, number and sensitivity of receptors, and level of gene transcription and protein production (Hoomissen, 2004). In the absence of activity, boredom itself becomes a hedonic motivation (Mageau, Green-Demers, & Pelletier, 2000).

References

Acevedo, E.O., Kramer, R.R., Haltom, R.W., & Tryniecki, J.L. (2003). Perceptual responses proximal to the onset of blood lactate accumulation. *Journal of Sports Medicine and Physical Fitness, 43*, 267-273.

Adair, E.R., & Wright, B.A. (1976). Behavioral thermoregulation in the squirrel monkey when response effort is varied. *Journal of Comparative and Physiological Psychology, 90*, 179-184.

Balaskó, M., & Cabanac, M. (1998). Behavior of juvenile lizards (*Iguana iguana*) in a conflict between temperature regulation and palatable food. *Brain Behavior and Evolution, 52*, 257-262.

Bergh, U., Danielsson, U., Wennberg, L., & Sjödin, B. (1986). Blood lactate and perceived exertion during heat stress. *Acta Physiologica Scandinavica, 126*, 617-618.

Blomstrand, E., & Essen-Gustavsson, B. (1987). Influence of reduced muscle temperature on metabolism in type I and type II human muscle fibres during intensive exercise. *Acta Physiologica Scandinavica, 131*, 569-574.

Borg, G. (1962). Physical performance and perceived exertion. *Studia Psychologica et Paedologica, 11*, 1-64.

Borg, G. (1982). Psychophysical bases of perceived exertion. *Medicine and Science in Sports and Exercise, 14*, 377-381.

Cabanac, A., & Cabanac, M. (2000). Heart rate response to gentle handling of frog and lizard. *Behavioural Processes, 52*, 89-95.

Cabanac, A.J., & Cabanac, M. (2004). No emotional fever in toads. *Journal of Thermal Biology, 29*, 669-673.

Cabanac, M. (1971). Physiological role of pleasure. *Science, 173*, 1103-1107.

Cabanac, M. (1985). Optimisation du comportement par la minimisation du déplaisir dans un espace sensoriel à deux dimensions. *Comptes Rendus de l'Académie des Sciences, 301, Série III*, 607-610.

Cabanac, M. (1986). Money versus pain: Experimental study of a conflict in humans. *Journal of the Experimental Analysis of Behavior, 46*, 37-44.

Cabanac, M. (1992). Pleasure: The common currency. *Journal of Theoretical Biology, 155*, 173-200.

Cabanac, M. (1995). What is sensation? In R. Wong (Ed.), *Biological perspectives on motivated activities* (pp. 409-428). Norwood, NJ: Ablex.

Cabanac, M. (1996). On the origin of consciousness, a postulate and its corollary. *Neuroscience and Biobehavioral Reviews, 20*, 33-40.

Cabanac, M. (1999). Emotion and phylogeny. *Japanese Journal of Physiology, 49*, 1-10.

Cabanac, M., & Aizawa, S. (2000). Fever and tachycardia in a bird (*Gallus domesticus*) after simple handling. *Physiology and Behavior, 69*, 541-545.

Cabanac, M., & Bernieri, C. (2000). Behavioral rise in body temperature and tachycardia by handling of a turtle (*Clemys insculpta*). *Behavioural Processes, 49*, 61-68.

Cabanac, M., & Bonniot-Cabanac, M.-C. (1997). De quoi serait mort le courreur de Marathon? *Médecine sciences, 13*, 838-842.

Cabanac, M., & Johnson, K.G. (1983). Analysis of a conflict between palatability and cold exposure in rats. *Physiology and Behavior, 31*, 249-253.

Cabanac, M., & LeBlanc, J. (1983). Physiological conflict in humans: Fatigue vs cold discomfort. *American Journal of Physiology, 244*, R621-R628.

Cafarelli, E. (1982). Peripheral contributions to the perception of effort. *Medicine and Science in Sports and Exercise, 14*, 382-389.

Cafarelli, E., Cain, W.S., & Stevens, J.C. (1977). Effort dynamic exercise: Influence of load, duration, and task. *Ergonomics, 20,* 147-158.

Cheeta, S., Brooks, S., & Willner, P. (1995). Effects of reinforcer sweetness and the D2/D3 antagonist raclopride on progressive ratio operant performance. *Behavioural Pharmacology, 6,* 127-132.

Chen, B.Y., Jones, N.L., & Killian, K.J. (1999). Is there a conflict between minimizing effort and energy expenditure with increasing velocities of muscle. *Journal of Physiology, 518,* 933-940.

Collier, G., & Rovee-Collier, C.K. (1981). A comparative analysis of optimal foraging behavior: Laboratory simulations. In A.C. Kamil & T.D. Sargent (Eds.), *Foraging behavior* (pp. 39-76). New York: Garland STPM.

Dimri, G.P., Malhotra, S., SenGupta, J., SampathKumar, T., & Arora, B.S. (1980). Alteration in aerobic-anaerobic proportions of metabolism during work in heat. *European Journal of Applied Physiology, 45,* 43-50.

Ekkekakis, P. (2003). Pleasure and displeasure from the body: Perspectives from exercise. *Cognition and Emotion, 17,* 312-239.

Ekkekakis, P., Hall, E.E., & Petruzzello, S.J. (2005). Variation and homogeneity in affective responses to physical activity of varying intensities: An alternative perspective on dose-response based on evolutionary considerations. *Journal of Sports Sciences, 23,* 477-500.

Ekkekakis, P., Hall, E.E., & Petruzzello, S.J. (2004). Practical markers of the transition from aerobic to anaerobic metabolism during exercise: Rationale and a case for affect-based exercise prescription. *Preventive Medicine, 38,* 149-159.

Eston, R.G., Davies, B.L., & Williams, J.G. (1987). Use of perceived effort ratings to control exercise intensity in young healthy adults. *European Journal of Applied Physiology, 56,* 222-224.

Gandevia, S.C., & McCloskey, D.I. (1977). Sensation of heaviness. *Brain, 100,* 345-354.

Gannon, K.N., Smith, H.V., & Tierney, K.J. (1986). Effects of rate and distance of procurement wheel-running on saccharin-and-sucrose solution drinking by non-deprived rats. *Physiology and Behavior, 36,* 539-543.

Hall, E.E., Ekkekakis, P., & Petruzzello, S.J. (2002). The affective beneficence of vigorous exercise revisited. *British Journal of Health Psychology, 7,* 47-66.

Hogan, M.C., & Welch, H.G. (1984). Effect of varied lactate levels on bicycle ergometer performance. *Journal of Applied Physiology, 57,* RE507-RE513.

Hoomissen, J.V. (2004). Exercise and the brain: What do we know? Paper presented at the SSIB Annual Meeting, Cincinnati, July 20-24.

Jackson, A., Dishman, R.K., Lacroix, S., Patton, R., & Weinberg, R. (1981). The heart rate, perceived exertion, and pace of the 1.5 mile run. *Medicine and Science in Sports and Exercise, 13,* 224-228.

Jonsdottir, I.H., Asea, A., Hoffmann, P., Dahlgren, U.I., Andersson, B., Hellstrand, K., & Thoren, P. (1996). Voluntary chronic exercise augments in vivo natural immunity in rats. *Journal of Applied Physiology, 80,* 1799-1803.

Kilbom, Å., Gamberale, F., Persson, J., & Annwall, G. (1983). Physiological and psychological indices of fatigue during static contractions. *European Journal of Applied Physiology, 50,* 179-193.

Knibestöl, M., & Valbo, A.B. (1980). Intensity of sensation related to activity of slowly adapting mechanoreceptive units in the human hand. *Journal of Physiology, 300,* 251-267.

Kozlowski, S., Brzezinska, Z., Kruk, B., Kaciuba-Uscillo, H., Greenleaf, J.E., & Nazar, K. (1985). Exercise hyperthermia as a factor limiting physical performance: Temperature effect on muscle metabolism. *Journal of Applied Physiology, 59,* 766-773.

Krebs, J.R., & Davies, N.B. (1981). *An introduction to behavioural ecology.* Sunderland, MA: Sinauer Associates.

Löllgen, H., Graham, T., & Sjøgaard, G. (1980). Muscle metabolites, force, and perceived exertion bicycling at various pedal rates. *Medicine and Science in Sports and Exercise, 12,* 345-351.

Mageau, G.A., Green-Demers, I., & Pelletier, L.G. (2000). Mental control of boredom. *Canadian Journal of Behavioural Science (Revue Canadienne des Sciences du Comportement), 32,* 29-39.

Mahler, D.A., & Horowitz, M.B. (1994). Perception of breathlessness during exercise in patients with respiratory disease. *Medicine and Science in Sports and Exercise, 26,* 1078-1081.

Martin, B., & Haney, R. (1982). Self selected exercise intensity is unchanged by sleep loss. *European Journal of Applied Physiology, 49,* 79-86.

McFarland, D.J., & Sibly, R.M. (1975). The behavioural final common path. *Philosophical Transactions of the Royal Society, 270,* 265-293.

Noble, B.J. (1982). Clinical applications of perceived exertion. *Medicine and Science in Sports and Exercise, 14,* 406-411.

Nybo, L., & Nielsen, B. (2001). Perceived exertion is associated with an altered brain activity during exercise with progressive hyperthermia. *Journal of Applied Physiology, 91,* 2017-2023.

Pandolf, K.B. (1978). Influence of local and central factors in dominating rated perceived exertion during physical work. *Perceptual and Motor Skills, 46,* 683-698.

Paradis, S., & Cabanac, M. (2004). Taste aversion learning in reptiles but not in amphibians. *Behavioural Processes, 67,* 11-18.

Peck, J.W. (1978). Rats defend different body weights depending on palatability and accessibility of their food. *Journal of Comparative and Physiological Psychology, 92,* 555-570.

Perrigo, G. (1987). Breeding and feeding strategies in deer mice and house mice when females are challenged to work for their food. *Animal Behaviour, 35,* 1298-1316.

Robertson, R.J. (1982). Central signals of perceived exertion during dynamic exercise. *Medicine and Science in Sports and Exercise, 14,* 390-396.

Roland, P.E. (1975). Do muscular receptors in man evoke sensations of tension and kinesthesia? *Brain Research, 100,* 162-165.

Rossetti, Y., Meckler, C., & Prablanc, C. (1994). Is there an optimal arm posture? Deterioration of finger localization precision and comfort sensation in extreme arm-joint postures. *Experimental Brain Research, 99,* 131-136.

Saltin, B., Gagge, A.P., & Stolwijk, J.A.J. (1968). Muscle temperature during submaximal exercise in man. *Journal of Applied Physiology, 25,* 679-688.

Sanes, J.N., & Shadmehr, R. (1995). Sense of muscular effort and somesthesic afferent information in humans. *Canadian Journal of Physiology and Pharmacology, 73,* 223-233.

Starkie, R.L., Hargreaves, M., Lambert, D.L., Proietto, J., & Febbraio, M.A. (1999). Effect of temperature on muscle metabolism during submaximal exercise in humans. *Experimental Physiology, 84,* 775-784.

Swaine, I., & Reilly, T. (1983). The freely-chosen swimming stroke rate in a maximal swim and on a biokinetic swim bench. *Medicine and Science in Sports and Exercise, 15,* 370-375.

Tabata, I., & Kawakami, A. (1991). Effects of blood glucose concentration on ratings of perceived exertion during prolonged low-intensity physical exercise. *Japanese Journal of Physiology, 41,* 203-215.

Thayer, R.E., Godes, O., Lobato, N.E., Youpa, M., & Cecil, C. (2004). Walking more each day elevates mood, especially energy, a central mood element. Paper presented at the 16th Annual Convention of the American Psychological Society, Chicago May 27-30, 2004.

Ueda, T., & Kurokawa, T. (1991). Validity of heart rate and ratings of perceived exertion as indices of exercise intensity in a group of children while swimming. *European Journal of Applied Physiology, 63,* 200-204.

Ulmer, H.V. (1996). Concept of an extracellular regulation of muscular metabolic rate during heavy exercise in humans by psychophysiological feedback. *Experientia, 52,* 616-420.

VanHelder, W.P., Radomski, M.W., Goode, R.C., & Casey, K. (1985). Hormonal and metabolic responses to three types of exercise of equal duration and external work output. *European Journal of Applied Physiology, 54,* 337-342.

Wade, A.J., Broadhead, M.W., Cady, E.B., Llewelyn, M.E., Tong, H.N., & Newham, D.J. (2000). Influence of muscle temperature during fatiguing work with the first dorsal interosseous muscle in man: A P-31-NMR spectroscopy study. *European Journal of Applied Physiology, 81,* 203-209.

Wade, N.J. (2003). The search for the sixth sense: The cases for vestibular, muscle, and temperature senses. *Journal of the History of the Neurosciences, 12,* 175-202.

Warden, C.S. (1931). *Animal motivation, experimental studies on the albino rat.* New York: Columbia University Press.

Zarrugh, M.Y., & Radcliffe, C.W. (1978). Predicting metabolic cost of level walking. *European Journal of Applied Physiology, 38,* 215-223.

Zarrugh, M.Y., Todd, F.N., & Ralston, H.J. (1974). Optimization of energy expenditure during level walking. *European Journal of Applied Physiology, 33,* 293-296.

Affective Responses to Acute Exercise

Toward a Psychobiological Dose–Response Model

Panteleimon Ekkekakis, PhD, FACSM

Edmund O. Acevedo, PhD, FACSM

The study of the affective responses that accompany single bouts of exercise has been a prominent research direction within exercise psychology for approximately 35 years. Based on hundreds of studies conducted during this period, the main conclusion is that participation in a bout of exercise produces a so-called "feel-better" effect, which in most cases is defined operationally as a decrease in state anxiety, an increase in perceived vigor, or a general improvement in various mood states. As described in a recent literature review, "Both survey and experimental research . . . provide support for the well publicized statement that *exercise makes you feel good*" (Fox, 1999, p. 413, italics in the original). This is the same sentiment found in exercise psychology textbooks and touted in most media reports. It is now time to focus on other, finer points of the complex relationship between exercise and affect. In the last 10 or so years, the focal issue has been the shape of the dose–response relationship between the intensity of exercise and the nature of the affective response.

The Intensity–Affect Relationship

The relationship between the intensity of exercise and affective responses is important for two main reasons. One is its theoretical interest. Although the body and its activation are recognized as having an important role in most major theories of emotion, the nature and the extent of this role are and have been a hotly debated issue. Since exercise provides a way to precisely regulate the degree of bodily activation, it could potentially serve as a useful investigative platform in delineating the role of such activation in the generation of affective responses. The second reason is the practical significance of the dose–response relationship for the maintenance of exercise adherence and the prevention of dropout, two major public health concerns. Approximately 40% of the adults in the United States aged 18 years and older report no regular physical activity (United States Department of Health and Human Services

[USDHHS], 2000); two-thirds do not meet the current physical activity recommendations of 30 min of daily moderate activity (Jones et al., 1998); and only 15% participate in activities of sufficient intensity, duration, and frequency to improve or maintain cardiorespiratory fitness (USDHHS, 1996). Moreover, of those who make the decision to start an exercise program, approximately 50% drop out within the first few months (Dishman & Buckworth, 1996). The intensity of exercise might be one of the reasons contributing to this problem, as several studies have shown an inverse relation between intensity and adherence (Lee et al., 1996; Perri et al., 2002). Likewise, a meta-analysis of interventions for increasing exercise participation showed that interventions are more effective when the intensity of physical activity is lower (i.e., 50% of maximal capacity or less) rather than higher (Dishman & Buckworth, 1996). It seems reasonable to suggest that the negative relationship between the intensity of exercise and adherence is partly mediated by affect. Higher intensity might entail less pleasant or more unpleasant affect; and this may, in turn, lead to reduced adherence and increased risk of dropout, as people, in the long run, generally choose what makes them feel good and avoid what makes them feel bad.

In this chapter, we first present and critique a conceptual formulation, named the inverted U, that has served as a popular model of the dose–response relationship for many years. Second, we identify a number of critical conceptual and methodological problems in the previous dose–response literature that might have contributed to inconsistent findings. Third, we review some recently conducted dose–response studies that were based on a new research platform and have produced the first evidence of a reliable dose–response pattern. Fourth, we sketch a new theoretical framework for the dose–response relationship, named the dual-mode model. Fifth, based on neuroanatomical and neurophysiological data, we propose a possible neural basis for the dual-mode model. Sixth, we present some practical implications of the new theoretical formulation and suggest directions for future investigations.

The Inverted U
As a Dose–Response Model
and Its Limitations

The closest thing to a conceptual model of the dose–response relationship between the intensity

of exercise and affective responses is the time-honored inverted-U model. According to this idea, moderately vigorous exercise provides the optimal stimulus for positive affective change, whereas low-intensity exercise is insufficient to produce significant changes in affect and high-intensity exercise is either ineffective or experienced as aversive (Kirkcaldy & Shephard, 1990; Ojanen, 1994). However, it is becoming increasingly obvious that the inverted U has some serious limitations impeding further progress and thus cannot serve as the basis for future research.

First and foremost, the model does not appear to be consistent with emerging data. For example, it has been found that low-intensity and short-duration exercise can produce transient but significant positive changes (Ekkekakis et al., 2000; Saklofske, Blomme, & Kelly, 1992; Thayer, 1987); that high-intensity exercise, such as an incremental exercise protocol to volitional exhaustion, in addition to negative changes such as increases in fatigue, may also lead to some positive changes such as improvements in self-esteem (Pronk, Crouse, & Rohack, 1995); and that, during moderate-intensity exercise, some individuals may respond positively whereas others may respond negatively (Van Landuyt et al., 2000). Second, the inverted-U model is descriptive, not mechanistic. As such, it cannot provide any insights into the psychobiological processes underlying the observed responses. And, third, the model is nomothetic, making no provisions for patterns of interindividual variability in affective responses to the same intensity of exercise. It is clear that not all individuals respond in the same way to the same exercise stimulus (Gauvin & Brawley, 1993; Van Landuyt et al., 2000).

Previous Dose–Response
Findings and Weaknesses
in the Literature

In total, the relationship between the intensity of exercise and affective responses has been examined in approximately 55 studies. Of these, 31, conducted until 1998, were reviewed by Ekkekakis and Petruzzello (1999). These studies could be divided into two groups. One group contained 26 studies that examined affective changes from before the exercise to various time points after. Of these, the majority (14 of the 26 or 54%) did not show reliable evidence of a dose–response effect. The other group contained studies that examined affective responses during the exercise bouts. In these studies, there was a consistent dose–response pattern, with higher intensities being associated with less positive or more negative affective responses (e.g., Acevedo, Rinehardt, & Kraemer, 1994; Hardy & Rejeski, 1989; Parfitt & Eston, 1995; Parfitt, Eston, & Connolly, 1996; Parfitt, Markland, & Holmes, 1994). Similar findings, distinguishing between assessments from before to after exercise and assessments during exercise, have also emerged from the studies conducted since 1998.

The Ekkekakis and Petruzzello (1999) review also described some of the limitations in previous studies that might have obscured the identification of dose–response effects. The first limitation is apparent from the aforementioned findings of the review and pertains to the timing of affect assessments. In the majority of the studies, affect was assessed from before to after exercise, presumably based on the assumption that any changes that take place in the interim would be linear. However, it is clear that this is not the case. The studies that have examined responses during the exercise bout have shown that, depending on the intensity, the trajectory of change could be nonlinear. Specifically, when the intensity is high enough to induce a negative change, the decline follows a quadratic trend during exercise (even when the workload is continuously adjusted to keep the rate of oxygen consumption stable) and is followed by a rapid rebound once the exercise bout is terminated (e.g., Acevedo et al., 1996). Given this pattern, the failure to find consistent dose–response effects in studies that used before-to-after assessments is not surprising, since dose–response differences that might have appeared during exercise had likely dissipated by the time the postexercise assessment took place (in many cases, after a cool-down or a period of recovery).

The second problem pertains to the assessment of affective responses. In most dose–response studies, researchers used multi-item self-report measures of state anxiety or mood states (see Ekkekakis & Petruzzello, 2000, for a review). This, however, was not based on evidence that these are the only affective variables relevant to exercise across various intensities. Instead, it was based on the fact that standardized self-report measures of state anxiety and mood states, appropriate for use with nonclinical samples, were commonly available and becoming popular at the time that this line of research got under way (i.e., in the early 1970s). Thus, in essence, the outcome variables were dictated by the available measures rather than the other way around. In actuality, the affective responses that are likely to occur in different individuals under different conditions across the range of exercise intensities are impossible to predict at this stage. Therefore, in the context of dose–response studies, it would be advantageous to assess affective responses from a broad perspective, one that could capture all major variants of affective experience. Of course, because it would be impractical to ask participants whether they do or do not feel every affective state represented in the English vocabulary, this approach would have to involve a compromise; some degree of specificity must be sacrificed in exchange for breadth of scope. This can be accomplished by dimensional models of affect. According to the conceptual basis of dimensional models, affective states are systematically interrelated, such that their similarities and differences can be modeled parsimoniously along as few as two basic dimensions. The dimensional model with the longest history in affective psychology and the most extensive research base is the circumplex (Russell, 1980). In the circumplex model, the global affective space is defined by the orthogonal and bipolar dimensions of affective valence (ranging from displeasure to pleasure) and perceived activation (ranging from low to high). Given its breadth of scope, parsimony, balance, and domain-general nature, the circumplex model can be used as a template of affective space upon which the responses to various intensities of exercise can be mapped and compared (Ekkekakis & Petruzzello, 2002a).

The third problem is the standardization of exercise intensity. In the first wave of dose–response studies, participants exercised at the same level of heart rate or against the same level of resistance. The failure of this approach to take into account individual fitness levels soon became apparent, so the norm in most subsequent studies was to use percentages of measured or estimated maximal exercise capacity (maximal heart rate or oxygen uptake). Even this approach, however, is problematic for at least two reasons. First, the levels of intensity were essentially selected on an arbitrary basis (i.e., there was no conceptual reason for selecting, for example, 40%, 60%, and 80% as opposed to 30%, 50%, and 70%). Second, percentages of maximal capacity fail to take into account differences in the underlying metabolic processes, namely the contribution of aerobic and anaerobic metabolism. This is a problem identified in exercise physiology in the 1950s (Wells, Balke, & Van Fossan, 1957) and one that has resurfaced numerous times since then (e.g., Katch et al., 1978). At 75% of maximal oxygen uptake, for example, it is possible that one individual uses almost entirely aerobic sources whereas another requires substantial anaerobic supplementation. Given the rather profound ventilatory, cardiovascular, and endocrine changes that occur as the organism transitions to anaerobic supplementation, it cannot be argued that a percentage of maximal capacity, such as 70%, can provide an effective method of standardizing the intensity of exercise across individuals. The solution is to take the underlying metabolic processes into account by selecting intensities in relation to a transition marker, such as the lactate or the gas exchange ventilatory threshold (Wells, Balke, & Van Fossan, 1957).

The fourth problem stems from the phenomenon of interindividual variability in affective responses. Statistical analyses of change in dose–response studies were conducted at the level of group aggregates, and thus individual differences were treated as error. However, individual differences could have considerable psychological significance. For example, they could be accounted for by relevant traits or situational appraisals. Furthermore, it is important to keep in mind that, perhaps unlike most other affect-inducing stimuli, exercise can have a bidirectional impact on affect, producing pleasure or displeasure. Therefore, in the context of exercise, individual differences may manifest themselves not only in the form of quantitative differences in the extent to which an individual feels better or worse, but also in the form of qualitatively different responses to the same stimulus (such as changes toward pleasure or displeasure). In fact, in a study involving a 30 min bout of moderate-intensity (60% of estimated maximal aerobic capacity) stationary cycling, 44.4% of the participants reported gradual improvements in affective valence during the bout, whereas 41.3% reported gradual declines (Van Landuyt et al., 2000). As a result of these divergent patterns, the average rating across the entire sample appeared unchanged. Clearly, however, this conclusion would have misrepresented the actual responses. Therefore, the examination of patterns of change at the individual level, in addition to the traditional aggregate-level analyses, is necessary.

The "Next Generation" of Dose–Response Studies

A series of studies addressing most of the limitations of previous research has appeared in recent years and has provided the first reliable evidence of a dose–response relationship between the intensity of exercise and affective responses. The main finding, which has now been replicated by at least three independent laboratories, is that the point of transition from aerobic metabolism to anaerobic supplementation, operationally defined as either the gas exchange threshold or the lactate threshold, seems to be the turning point toward a decline in affective valence (reduced pleasure and, ultimately, increased displeasure) during exercise.

Bixby, Spalding, and Hatfield (2001) compared the effects of two exercise intensities, one corresponding to the gas exchange threshold and one corresponding to 75% of the gas exchange threshold, among 27 university students. Affect was assessed not only before and after exercise, but also during exercise. Specifically, the Positive and Negative Affect Schedule (PANAS; Watson, Clark, & Tellegen, 1988) was administered immediately before exercise, at the 20th minute of a 30 min bout on the cycle ergometer, and at the 20th minute of a 30 min recovery period. Furthermore, a visual analog scale of affective valence (pleasure–displeasure) was administered three times at baseline, three times during exercise (min 10, 20, 30), and three times during recovery (min 10, 20, 30). The results showed that the lower-intensity exercise led to an improvement, whereas the higher intensity led to a decline in affective valence during exercise. However, there were no significant differences between the two conditions after exercise, as there was a rapid "rebound" in affective valence in the higher-intensity condition as soon as the exercise bout ended.

Hall, Ekkekakis, and Petruzzello (2002) reported the results of a study examining ratings of affective valence, using the Feeling Scale (FS; Hardy & Rejeski, 1989), obtained at 1 min intervals during an incremental treadmill test to volitional exhaustion. The FS is an 11-point, single-item, bipolar measure of pleasure–displeasure, ranging from –5 to +5, and anchors at zero ("Neutral") and all odd integers, from "Very Good" (+5) to "Very Bad" (–5). The participants were 30 university students. To standardize the intensity of the activity despite variable test durations until the point of exhaustion, the first 2 min, the 4 min surrounding the gas exchange threshold (the minute before, the minute of, and the 2 min following it), and the last 2 min were retained for further analysis. The results showed that it was only once the participants exceeded the gas exchange threshold that significant and nearly homogeneous declines in affective valence occurred. Consistent with the results of Bixby, Spalding, and Hatfield (2001), there was a significant improvement in the affective state within just the first minute of a cool-down walk.

Ekkekakis, Hall, and Petruzzello (2004) replicated this finding using two different treadmill protocols, with 30 participants in each, to eliminate the possibility that the decline in affective valence that was initiated with the gas exchange threshold was protocol specific. They used a data reduction method similar to that used by Hall, Ekkekakis, and Petruzzello (2002). Consistent with the previous results, trend analyses demonstrated that during both protocols, the only 3-point segments for which the quadratic declining trends in self-ratings of affective valence were significant were those initiated with the minute at which the gas exchange threshold occurred.

Ekkekakis, Hall, and Petruzzello (2001) extended this line of research by examining affective responses to constant-speed treadmill exercise, as opposed to the incremental protocols used in the two previous studies. Thirty volunteers ran on a treadmill for 15 min at three intensities (on separate days, in random order): 20% of maximal aerobic capacity below, at, and 10% above their gas exchange threshold. The changes in self-ratings of affective valence during exercise were not statistically significant for the conditions below and at the level of the gas exchange threshold. Only the responses during the run above the gas exchange threshold showed a significant quadratic declining trend. Eighty percent of the participants (24 of the 30) in this condition reported declines in affective valence by an average of 3.17 units on the 11-point FS. It is important to point out that the differences in treadmill speed between the conditions at and 10% above the gas exchange threshold were very small (typically less than one-half mile per hour) and so were the differences in heart rate (10 bpm difference from condition to condition at the end of the runs). Yet the significant differences in the pattern of affective responses underscore the importance of exceeding the gas exchange threshold. Also consistent with previous studies (Bixby, Spalding, & Hatfield, 2001; Hall, Ekkekakis, & Petruzzello, 2002), there were no differences between the three conditions after a cool-down, since affective valence showed a very rapid rebound as soon as the runs stopped.

Acevedo and colleagues (2003) examined the FS responses to three running intensities, one 10% of maximal aerobic capacity below, one at, and one 10% of maximal aerobic capacity above the onset of blood lactate accumulation (by convention, a concentration of 4 mM lactate per liter of blood) among 11 distance runners. Each run lasted for 5 min. The FS declined significantly and became negative only when the intensity exceeded the onset of blood lactate accumulation.

Collectively, these studies provide considerable support to the idea that the transition to anaerobic supplementation represents an important event from an adaptational standpoint and, as such, is accompanied by a strong signal to conscious awareness in the form of a decline in affective valence. Ekkekakis, Hall, and Petruzzello (2004) and Acevedo and colleagues (2003) expressed the view that perhaps this affective change, since it is apparently perceptible and salient, could be used by exercisers as a guide in regulating their exercise intensity. Importantly, a considerable literature suggests that an intensity at or just below the aerobic–anaerobic transition is effective in improving fitness and maintaining health (see Ekkekakis, Hall, & Petruzzello, 2004, for a review).

On the basis of this idea, Lind, Joens-Matre, and Ekkekakis (2005) examined the intensity that a sample of 23 middle-aged, healthy, but sedentary women self-selected when they were asked to exercise on a treadmill for 20 min. On average, at the 15th and the 20th minute of the exercise session, their treadmill speed, oxygen uptake, rating of perceived exertion, and rating of affective valence were not different from the values corresponding to their gas exchange threshold as identified from a previous graded treadmill test. This suggests that, even intuitively, without being taught to do so, exercisers might use the aerobic–anaerobic transition as a guide in regulating their intensity. Stated differently, it is possible that exercisers tend to choose an intensity that is not high enough to induce unpleasant affective responses. In fact, ratings of affective valence remained positive and stable throughout the session at self-selected intensity. Lind, Joens-Matre, and Ekkekakis (2005), however, found that, beyond the average trend, individuals within the group selected intensities that were from as low as 60% to as high as 160% of the oxygen uptake corresponding to the gas exchange threshold. It could be argued, then, that this is where the challenge for future research lies; namely, in developing an understanding for the sources of this variability and appropriate intervention methods for teaching both the overestimators and the underestimators to select intensities that are effective, safe, and likely to elicit positive (or, at least, nonnegative) affective responses.

The Dual-Mode Theory

From the data reviewed so far, it seems clear that the aerobic–anaerobic transition acts as a turning point, beyond which affective valence begins to decline. It is interesting to ponder why this would be the case. The answer perhaps lies in the adaptational significance of this event.

Although exercise performed within the aerobic range can be continued for a long period of time, exercise that significantly exceeds the point of transition from aerobic metabolism to anaerobic supplementation precludes the maintenance of a physiological steady state, induces fatigue, and creates the need to stop the activity. Activity that requires a substantial anaerobic contribution increasingly depends on a relatively limited reservoir of metabolic resources (i.e., the adenosine triphosphate and creatine phosphate pool in the muscles and anaerobic glycolysis) compared to the resources available to aerobic metabolism (i.e., muscle and liver glycogen, free fatty acids from adipose tissue, and, to a lesser degree, body proteins). Furthermore, beyond the aerobic–anaerobic transition, a multitude of physiological adjustments takes place, drastically transforming the internal environment. Primarily, there is a rapid accumulation of lactate and hydrogen ions dissociated from lactic acid. This, in turn, has been linked to several processes that contribute to fatigue, including the accelerated breakdown of creatine phosphate (McCann, Mollé, & Caton, 1995), the gradual inhibition of glycolysis and glycogenolysis (Spriet et al., 1989), the inhibition of lipolysis (Boyd et al., 1974), and the interference with the calcium triggering of muscle contractions (Favero et al., 1995). In addition, lactic acidosis stimulates the release of catecholamines (Goldsmith et al., 1990), and thus the lactate threshold has been found to occur in close proximity to a catecholamine threshold (Urhausen et al., 1994; Weltman et al., 1994). In turn, catecholamines have widespread effects that further push the organism toward its functional limits, including a breakpoint in the relationship between the double product (the product of heart rate and systolic blood pressure) and work rate (Riley et al., 1997; Tanaka et al., 1997). Moreover, to compensate for metabolic acidosis, above the point of transition to anaerobic supplementation there is an increase in the frequency and depth of ventilation (Wasserman, 1978). Finally, the transition to anaerobic supplementation is accompanied by the recruitment of low-efficiency fast-twitch muscle fibers (Helal, Guezennec, & Goubel, 1987; Nagata et al., 1981; Shinohara & Moritani, 1992), thus increasing the oxygen cost of work and disrupting coordination patterns.

Overall, these conditions begin to pose a challenge to the maintenance of homeostasis. Damasio (1995) has written that "certain configurations of body state" (p. 21), such as during a heart attack, induce an innate, preorganized affective response. We would argue that the aforementioned physiological adjustments that occur beyond the aerobic–anaerobic transition constitute a quintessential example of such a "configuration of body state." Given the possible implications of this condition for adaptation and survival, it would make good sense if this "configuration of body state" induced a pronounced negative affective response. In fact, studies have shown that as exercise intensity increases, the negative correlations between affective valence and various indices of metabolic strain (heart rate, ventilation, respiratory rate, oxygen consumption, blood lactate) increase in magnitude (Acevedo, Rinehardt, & Kraemer, 1994; Hardy & Rejeski, 1989).

Importantly, Acevedo and colleagues (2003) reported that, although affective valence shows no significant relationships with physiological variables below or at the onset of blood lactate accumulation, valence was significantly related in a negative direction to both heart rate and ventilation when the intensity exceeded the onset of blood lactate accumulation. Ekkekakis (2003, see p. 232) has also reviewed evidence showing that during exercise performed at an intensity exceeding the gas exchange threshold, but not below, physiological variables (respiratory exchange ratio, percentage of peak heart rate) accounted for significant portions of the variance in affective valence. Collectively, these findings suggest that, once exercise intensity exceeds the level of transition from aerobic metabolism to anaerobic supplementation, affective valence is strongly related to physiological indices of metabolic strain.

Besides physiological variables, affective responses to exercise have also been shown to have significant relationships with cognitive variables. Of these, self-efficacy has been studied most extensively. Although the strength of the relationship between self-efficacy and affective responses appears to differ as a function of exercise intensity, the pattern is still not entirely clear. On the basis of the idea that the role of self-efficacy as a media-tor of affective responses is strengthened in the face of challenging stimuli, McAuley and Courneya (1992) first proposed that the association between physical self-efficacy and affect should become stronger when exercise intensity reaches a level where bodily cues become unequivocally aversive (tentatively specified as above 70% of maximal heart rate). At such an intensity level, a highly efficacious person is expected to exhibit more positive affect compared to a less self-efficacious one. More recently, McAuley and colleagues (2000) extended the earlier hypothesis of McAuley and Courneya (1992) by proposing that "at high intensi-ties, physiological cues . . . override cognitive pro-cessing" (p. 312). Therefore, cognitive influences on affective responses are theorized to become stronger when the intensity of exercise presents a substantial but not overwhelming challenge. Conversely, the influence of cognitive factors should be relatively weaker when the challenge posed by the exercise stimulus is either trivial or overwhelming. The studies conducted since then have produced conflicting results (Blanchard et al., 2002; McAuley et al., 2000; Tate, Petruzzello, & Lox, 1995; Treasure & Newbery, 1998).

Although the inconsistencies could be partly due to differences in the age and physical con-dition of the participants and the measures of affect, it is also possible that they are due to the arbitrarily selected levels of exercise intensity. Ekkekakis (2003) examined the results of a series of unpublished studies in which the intensity of exercise was determined in relation to the gas exchange threshold. These studies showed that self-efficacy was significantly related to affective responses when the intensity was proximal to the gas exchange threshold but not when it was sig-nificantly below or above it. In multiple regression analyses, in which both self-efficacy and physi-ological variables were entered as predictors of affective valence, self-efficacy accounted for the majority of the variance near the gas exchange threshold, whereas physiological variables were dominant when the intensity was higher and approached maximal capacity.

On the basis of these data, Ekkekakis (2003, 2005; Ekkekakis, Hall, & Petruzzello, 2005) formu-lated a new conceptual model of exercise-induced affective responses, named the dual-mode theory. A central thesis underpinning this conceptual model is that physical activity must be consid-ered from an adaptational perspective. Thus, the dual-mode theory is based on the following core

assumptions (see Ekkekakis, Hall, & Petruzzello, 2005, for a more detailed discussion and refer-ences). (a) Physical activity has been an essential component of the conditions that shaped human evolution; (b) affective responses are manifes-tations of evolved psychological mechanisms, selected for their ability to promote health and well-being or to solve recurrent adaptational problems, with pleasure signifying utility and displeasure signifying danger (Cabanac, 1971, 1979; also see chapter 6); (c) affective responses, including those that originate in the body, depend on a hierarchically organized system involving multiple layers of control, from oligosynaptic, subcortical, and evolutionarily primitive path-ways at the bottom and polysynaptic, evolution-arily recent, cortical pathways at the top; and (d) evolutionarily primitive functions show less interindividual variation, whereas functions that are evolutionarily recent show larger variability, as they are mostly shaped by individual develop-mental histories.

Based on these core assumptions, the dual-mode theory (Ekkekakis, 2003) posits that affec-tive responses to exercise are the products of the continuous interplay between two general factors, namely (a) relevant cognitive processes originat-ing primarily in the frontal cortex and involving such processes as appraisals of the meaning of exercise, goals, self-perceptions including self-efficacy, attributions, and considerations of the social context of exercise; and (b) interoceptive cues from a variety of receptors stimulated by exercise-induced physiological changes, which reach the affective centers of the brain via oli-gosynaptic subcortical pathways. The relative salience of these two factors is hypothesized to shift systematically as a function of exercise intensity. Specifically, cognitive factors should be dominant at intensities proximal to the aerobic–anaerobic transition, whereas interoceptive cues should gain salience when the intensity exceeds the aerobic–anaerobic transition and approaches an individual's maximal exercise capacity (see figure 7.1). The model, therefore, is consistent with extant findings showing that (a) the negative relationship between affective valence and physi-ological variables becomes increasingly stronger as the intensity of exercise increases and (b) the positive relationship between affective valence and self-efficacy appears to be strongest when the intensity approximates the aerobic–anaero-bic transition but is weakened when the intensity approaches maximal levels.

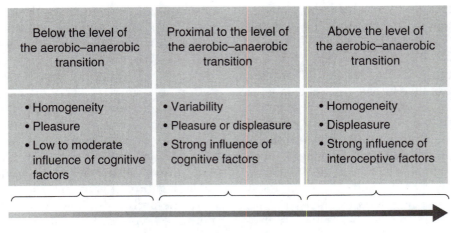

Below the level of the aerobic–anaerobic transition	Proximal to the level of the aerobic–anaerobic transition	Above the level of the aerobic–anaerobic transition
• Homogeneity • Pleasure • Low to moderate influence of cognitive factors	• Variability • Pleasure or displeasure • Strong influence of cognitive factors	• Homogeneity • Displeasure • Strong influence of interoceptive factors

Spectrum of exercise intensity

Figure 7.1   The dose–response model based on the dual-mode theory. Exercise intensity is considered in relation to the individually determined level of transition from aerobic metabolism to anaerobic supplementation. The model takes into account systematic patterns of change in the degree of interindividual variability and proposes a mechanistic basis for the type of affective responses that emerge at different intensities.

A Putative Neural Pathway

It is still not possible to take full advantage of the modern brain imaging technologies to examine the patterns of brain activity in response to vigorous exercise, due to problems associated with movement artifact (see chapter 3). This limitation makes examination of the dual-mode hypothesis at the neural level extremely difficult. Nevertheless, neuroscience has made considerable advances in delineating the neural network responsible for processing interoceptive cues, including those associated with exercise, and generating affective responses (see chapter 2). The extant information is sufficient to allow us to examine whether the predictions of the dual-mode theory are plausible at the level of the nervous system. This can be achieved through a review of evidence on whether neuroanatomical connections and neurophysiological mechanisms that would be needed for the model to function as hypothesized are in place.

To support the plausibility of the model, the neuroscientific evidence would have to indicate that

a.   the system that collects and relays interoceptive information to the brain is highly sensitive to variations in the intensity of internal signals;

b.   the processing of interoceptive signals in the brain is based on a hierarchically organized system that includes both corti-

cally mediated and noncortically mediated pathways; and

c.   there are appropriate gating mechanisms capable of redirecting interoceptive signals to the subcortical pathways when the intensity exceeds a certain critical threshold.

Before we present the relevant findings that support each of these statements, we must issue a caveat. Particularly in recent years, it has become increasingly clear that the amygdaloid complex (a part of the limbic system, situated in the anterior part of the temporal lobe; Sah et al., 2003) serves as a critical center for integrating affective information and assigning affective significance to sensory events (Aggleton & Young, 2000; LeDoux, 1986, 1989, 1996; Zald, 2003). Although, consistent with these accounts, the discussion here focuses on the amygdala, it is important to note that several other brain areas, such as the insula and cingulate cortex (Critchley et al., 2004), are activated by exercise and also appear to play important roles in the genesis of affective responses.

In humans, direct evidence of amygdala involvement during vigorous exercise is still lacking because of the aforementioned technical difficulties in obtaining brain imaging data free of movement artifacts. However, indirect evidence is available, in the form of studies showing that the amygdala is activated in response to noxious somatic stimuli (Bingel et al., 2002; Bornhövd et al., 2002; Derbyshire et al., 1997; Schneider et al.,

2001), blood pressure elevations (Harper et al., 2000) and drops (Henderson et al., 2004), and induced dyspnea and "air hunger" sensations (Brannan et al., 2001; Evans et al., 2002; Liotti et al., 2001). However, most of the relevant evidence comes from animal studies. A study in rats showed that glucose utilization was increased in response to exercise by 56% in the central nucleus, 33% in the lateral nucleus, and 18% in the medial nucleus of the amygdala (Vissing, Andersen, & Diemer, 1996). This was not a surprising finding. Anatomical studies had already established that the amygdala receives afferent connections from various brain regions known to be involved in cardiovascular, respiratory, and endocrine regulation during exercise, including the hypothalamus and the ventrolateral medulla (Aggleton, Burton, & Passingham, 1980; Cechetto, Ciriello, & Calaresu, 1983; Ciriello, Schultz, & Roder, 1994; Ottersen, 1980; Roder & Ciriello, 1993, 1995; Turner & Herkenham, 1991; Volz et al., 1990; Zardetto-Smith & Gray, 1995). Moreover, physiological studies had shown that neurons in the amygdala respond to spontaneous increases in blood pressure (Ben-Ari et al., 1973), stimulation of baro- and chemoreceptors (Cechetto & Calaresu, 1984, 1985; Knuepfer et al., 1995; Schütze et al., 1987), and stimulation of the carotid sinus and aortic depressor nerves (Cechetto & Calaresu, 1983). Furthermore, discharges in amygdala neurons exhibit timing relationships with the cardiac and respiratory cycles (Frysinger & Harper, 1989; Frysinger, Zhang, & Harper, 1988). The amygdala had also been shown to receive extensive somatosensory input (Romanski et al., 1993; Uwano et al., 1995) and to be involved in the processing of noxious somatosensory stimuli (Bernard & Besson, 1990; Bernard, Bester, & Besson, 1996; Bernard, Huang, & Besson, 1990, 1992; Bernard, Peschanski, & Besson, 1989; Romanski et al., 1993).

From the perspective of the dual-mode theory, the key question is how the exercise-induced interoceptive cues reach the amygdala. Are there both subcortical and cortical routes, and is the intensity of stimulation important in determining which pathway is involved? As noted in the previous section, exercise generates a great variety of interoceptive signals, such as increases in heart rate and blood pressure, tissue ischemia, acidosis (drops in pH), increased concentration of protons (H^+) dissociated from lactic acid, breathlessness associated with hypoxia or hypercapnia, and muscle pain. In patient populations, exercise can generate additional signals, such as stimulation of articular nociceptors in arthritic joints, angina pectoris resulting from myocardial ischemia, or ischemic pain in leg muscles due to intermittent claudication.

All of these bits of information about the condition of the body are collected by primary afferent neurons that exist in virtually all tissues (also see chapter 2). Some of these, situated at strategic locations, also perform specialized functions, such as monitoring arterial pressure, the tension of respiratory gases, and changes in pH. Exercise appears to engage mainly two types of primary afferent neurons, both of small diameter and therefore having relatively slow conducting velocities, the thinly myelinated Aδ (or Group III) and the unmyelinated C (or Group IV). The majority of Aδ neurons are activated by deformations in contracting muscles and are, therefore, considered mechanoreceptors, whereas the majority of C neurons are activated by metabolic changes and are therefore considered chemo- or metaboreceptors (Kaufman & Forster, 1996; Mense, 1996).

Consistent with the notion that the interoceptive system is highly sensitive to variations in the intensity of stimulation, primary afferent neurons have different threshold properties and consequently respond to different levels of stimulation (Cervero, 1994; Cervero & Janig, 1992). One type is characterized by a low threshold and is therefore activated by innocuous intensities of stimulation. These receptors, which in the case of exercise-associated stimuli have been characterized as ergoreceptors, carry information necessary for basic regulatory adjustments and might be involved in relaying nonnoxious sensations. A second type of primary afferent neuron is characterized by a high threshold and is used to encode intensity by responding only to stimuli in the noxious range. These neurons are therefore characterized as nociceptors. Finally, a third type, called the "silent nociceptor," exhibits no response under normal circumstances but shows a large response in cases of prolonged stimulation involving the high-threshold neurons. Such cases may include acute tissue hypoxia or inflammation. The different thresholds of the three receptor types ensure that the intensity of stimulation, and therefore the extent of any deviations of physiological parameters from the normal range, will be properly and reliably encoded as this information enters the central nervous system.

Aδ and C afferents enter the spinal cord mainly through the dorsal horn and synapse with spinal neurons in several laminae but primarily with lamina I (Craig, 1996; also see chapter 2). In turn, lamina I neurons have several major targets in the brain. These include the nucleus of the solitary tract, the parabrachial nucleus of the pons, the periaqueductal gray, the ventrolateral medulla, and the sensory thalamus (Iwamoto et al., 1996).

After this point, from the perspective of cognitive theories of emotion, the only relevant pathway is the one that projects from the thalamus to the somatosensory and frontal cortices. Anatomical studies have shown that the amygdala receives extensive input from several cortical areas (McDonald, 1998). This pathway is consistent with a view of emotions as driven by cognitive appraisals (LeDoux, 1994, 1989). The somatosensory cortices enable the recognition and localization of the source of the stimulation, and the frontal cortex can analyze its significance and possible implica-

tions for survival, well-being, and the goals of the individual. However, LeDoux (1986, 1996) showed that the thalamocorticoamygdala pathway is not necessary for fear conditioning to acoustic stimuli and therefore that this may not be the only pathway involved in emotional responses. He demonstrated that a direct thalamoamygdala projection that bypasses the cortex could suffice. He named this direct projection the "low road," as opposed to the "high road" via the cortex (LeDoux, 1996; see figure 7.2a). Speculating on the functional significance of this "low road," LeDoux (1996) noted that it represents an "evolutionary relic" (p. 163) that, since it has continued to exist for millions of years despite the evolution of the more advanced "high road," must still serve some useful function. According to LeDoux (1996), the capacity of the "low road" to activate the amygdala several mil-

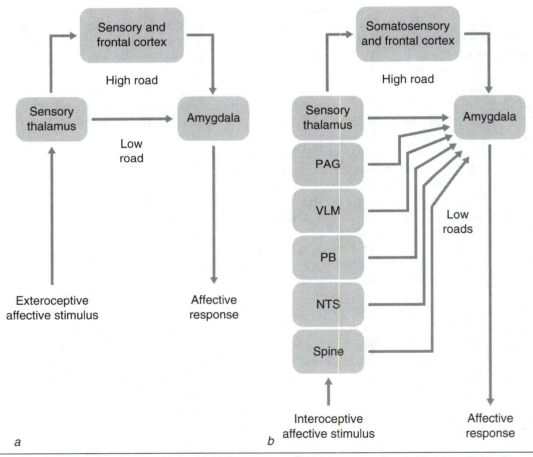

Figure 7.2 *(a)* The model of affective response generation proposed by LeDoux (1986, 1996) for exteroceptive stimuli. *(b)* A proposed modification specifically for exercise-associated interoceptive stimuli. In addition to the sensory thalamus, subcortical pathways to the amygdala originate in the spine, nucleus of the solitary tract (NTS), parabrachial nucleus (PB), ventrolateral medulla (VLM), and periaqueductal gray (PAG). The presence of multiple "low roads" in the case of interoceptive stimuli can be explained from an evolutionary standpoint, since in general, intense stimuli from the internal environment of the body probably have more immediate and potentially severe implications for survival and adaptation than exteroceptive stimuli.

liseconds more rapidly than the "high road" can make the difference between "the quick and the dead" (p. 163).

LeDoux's interpretation of the functional significance of the "low road" as an alternative non-cognitive pathway for the elicitation of affective responses, which questions the long-held belief in social-cognitive psychology that cognitive appraisal is a prerequisite for such responses, has met with criticism. Emotion theorists have argued that LeDoux's model essentially begs the invocation of a homunculus at the subcortical level. Clore and Ortony (2000), for example, noted that, for the amygdala to be activated via the "low road" when a snake is seen on the ground, as LeDoux had suggested, some recognition and evaluation of the adaptational significance of the snake must take place. However, by most definitions, these functions constitute cognitive processing.

Here, we use LeDoux's basic idea of a system that involves both a cortically mediated and a noncortically mediated route for the activation of the amygdala and, therefore, both a cognitively mediated and a noncognitively mediated mode of eliciting affective responses. However, our model differs from LeDoux's in an important way that avoids the homunculus problem. Although LeDoux's model pertained to exteroceptive stimuli, such as auditory and visual cues, which must undergo some—even rudimentary—recognition and interpretation before they can acquire adaptational significance, most of the adaptational significance of interoceptive stimuli, such as those induced by exercise, is already encoded in their intensity. This fundamental property (intensity) can be "interpreted" by as basic and simple a mechanism as a neural gate that allows only impulses exceeding a certain threshold to flow through. From an evolutionary perspective, the intensity of interoceptive stimulation has critical survival value (Schneirla, 1959), and consequently "responses to stimulus intensity are highly conserved throughout the neuraxis" (Coghill et al., 1999, p. 1940). According to Damasio (1999),

The range of possible states of the internal milieu and of the viscera is tightly limited. This limitation is built into the organism specifications since the range of states that is compatible with life is small. The permissible range is indeed so small and the need to respect its limits so absolute for survival that organisms spring forth equipped with an automatic regulation system to ensure that

life threatening deviations do not occur or can be rapidly corrected. (p. 141)

Another difference between the structures of the systems that process exteroceptive and interoceptive stimuli is also very important. Unlike what happens with the singular thalamoamygdala pathway that functions as the "low road" in LeDoux's model, interoceptive stimuli are forwarded to the amygdala by a multitude of subcortical routes, or several "low roads" (see figure 7.2b). Specifically, interoceptive information can reach the amygdala via the thalamus (Ottersen & Ben-Ari, 1979; Turner & Herkenham, 1991), the nucleus of the solitary tract (Ottersen, 1981; Ricardo & Koh, 1978; Zardetto-Smith & Gray, 1990), the parabrachial nucleus (Bernard, Alden, & Besson, 1993; Bernard, Peschanski, & Besson, 1989; Ma & Peschanski, 1988; Ottersen, 1981), the periaqueductal gray (Rizvi et al., 1991), and a direct spinal projection (Burstein & Potrebic, 1993; Cliffer, Burstein, & Giesler, 1991; Giesler, Katter, & Dado, 1994; Menétrey & de Pommery, 1991). Furthermore, as noted earlier, the amygdala also receives projections from other subcortical areas involved in cardiovascular, respiratory, and endocrine regulation, including the ventrolateral medulla and the hypothalamus.

A remaining important issue pertains to the presence of appropriate intensity-sensitive gating mechanisms that would permit the activation of the amygdala through the aforementioned subcortical pathways once the intensity of exercise exceeds the level of the aerobic–anaerobic transition and the barrage of interoceptive stimuli from throughout the body intensifies (see the summary of the peripheral physiological changes that accompany the aerobic–anaerobic transition in the previous section). Based on what is presently known, such gating can occur at least at the following four points. First, the sensory thalamus is the primary gate that can control information flow to both the cortex and the amygdala (McCormick & Bal, 1994). Second, the nucleus of the solitary tract, a major recipient of interoceptive information from the spinal cord and a major source of projections to the amygdala, has been proposed to serve a gating function for various modalities of interoceptive afferents (Mifflin, Spyer, & Withington-Wray, 1988b; Toney & Mifflin, 2000; Zhang & Mifflin, 2000). Its inhibitory effect is, at least in part, under the control of GABA-ergic (gamma-aminobutyric acid) projections from the central nucleus of the amygdala (Saha, Batten, & Henderson, 2000) and the hypothalamus (Jordan, Mifflin, & Spyer, 1988; Mifflin, Spyer, & Withington-Wray, 1988a). Third, the parabrachial nucleus, a recipient of interoceptive information from the spinal cord and nucleus of the solitary tract and also a major source of projections to the amygdala, has been postulated to serve as a modulator of this information, under the influence of input from the periaqueductal gray (Krout, Jansen, & Loewy, 1998). Fourth, the lateral nucleus of the amygdala, the entry point of most sensory input to the amygdala, can also function as a gating mechanism, regulating information flow through the rest of the amygdaloid complex (Lang and Paré, 1998; Paré et al., 2003; Royer, Martina, & Paré, 1999).

Theoretically, these gates make it possible for interoceptive impulses to be directed toward the cortex or directly toward the amygdala, depending on their intensity. Preliminary data are consistent with this scenario. Imaging studies in humans have shown that, in general, "as the stimulus rating increases in intensity, an increasing number of brain regions become active" (Derbyshire et al., 1997, p. 438). This suggests that certain intensity-sensitive gating mechanisms must exist that permit the flow of information to additional areas as the intensity rises. Specifically regarding the amygdala, an imaging study in humans involving thermal stimuli ranging from innocuous to painful showed that the amygdala is activated once a painful threshold is exceeded and that, thereafter, additional increases in stimulus intensity are reflected by linear increases in amygdala activation (Bornhövd et al., 2002). In rats, somatosensory stimulation using an air puff resulted in a mean latency of 61 msec for the response of the lateral nucleus of the amygdala (Uwano et al., 1995), whereas the mean value using an electric foot shock was only 17 msec (Romanski et al., 1993). This difference suggests that the two stimuli reached the lateral nucleus through different pathways, with the more innocuous one likely having followed the longer and, therefore, slower thalamocorticoamygdala route and the more intense one likely having reached the target via one or more of the shorter and faster subcortical routes.

In summary, there appears to be enough evidence to consider the dual-mode theory plausible at the neural level. The data we reviewed indicate that

a. the intensity of interoceptive information is a feature of paramount adaptational importance that is well preserved from the level of the primary afferents to the higher levels of the brain,

b. interoceptive information reaches the amygdala (and other areas involved in affective responses) via both cortical and subcortical routes, and

c. appropriate gating mechanisms exist at critical locations that could permit the flow of interoceptive cues either to the cortical or to the subcortical routes depending on their intensity.

Therefore, as the dual-mode theory postulates, once the level of the aerobic–anaerobic transition is exceeded and a multitude of peripheral physiological cues initiate a positively accelerated response, it seems reasonable to suggest that the flow of this information to the amygdala will be primarily via the previously described subcortical pathways. Following the rationale of LeDoux's (1986, 1989, 1994, 1996) model, this would suggest that, when the intensity of exercise exceeds the level of the aerobic–anaerobic transition, the role of cortically mediated cognitive influences on affective responses would be attenuated and these responses would more directly reflect the perturbed physiological condition of the body.

Conclusions

The following conclusions can be drawn from the data summarized in this chapter. First, contrary to the widely popularized view that exercise, in general, makes people feel better, substantial evidence indicates that the relationship between exercise and affective responses is complex, with affective responses, under certain conditions, being negative rather than positive. In fact, the positive affective responses are limited to (a) during and after low-intensity and self-paced exercise and (b) recovery from vigorous exercise. In contrast, exercise intensity that exceeds the level of the aerobic–anaerobic transition (or the level of intensity associated with the onset of other symptoms, such as muscular, skeletal, or cardiorespiratory) is associated with declines in affective valence.

Second, a midrange intensity (i.e., not "too low," not "too high") is not necessarily the optimal stimulus for positive affective change. It is only the recovery from such activity that brings about unified positive responses. During exercise performed at a midrange intensity, there appears to be great interindividual variability, with some individuals experiencing positive and others experiencing negative changes in affective valence.

Third, the patterns of interindividual variability in affective responses appear to be systematic and dependent on the intensity of exercise. Specifically, homogeneity emerges during exercise of low intensity (below the aerobic–anaerobic transition), when most responses are positive, and during exercise of high intensity (above the aerobic–anaerobic transition), when most responses are negative. On the other hand, variability emerges during activity performed near the level of the aerobic–anaerobic transition.

Fourth, the influence of cognitive factors (e.g., self-efficacy) on affective responses to exercise appears to be modulated by the intensity of exercise and is gradually reduced once the intensity exceeds the level of the aerobic–anaerobic transition (or symptom onset). Conversely, the influence of peripheral physiological cues, such as those associated with respiration and blood lactate concentration (or symptom-related nociception), is gradually increased and becomes dominant as the intensity exceeds the level of the aerobic–anaerobic transition (or symptom onset).

This last point has significant implications for interventions aimed at helping exercisers cope with the unpleasant sensations particularly during the critical early stages of exercise involvement. Based on the dual-mode theory, the effectiveness of some of the popular cognitive techniques for coping with such sensations might be limited to intensities below or near the aerobic–anaerobic transition (or symptom onset). Such techniques include attentional dissociation (i.e., "turn your attention away from your body"), cognitive restructuring (i.e., "think of these unpleasant symptoms as something positive, as signs of improvement"), and bolstering one's sense of physical self-efficacy (i.e., "believe that you can do it"). Insistence on the part of an exercise leader on these techniques, when the intensity exceeds a critical level that renders them ineffective, might lead to persistent negative affective responses to exercise, frustration, reduction of intrinsic motivation for exercise, and eventually dropout.

Directions for Future Investigation

From the standpoint of basic research, perhaps the most important condition for substantial progress is the abandonment of the exclusive focus on the positive affective responses to exercise. It should be clear that the affective responses to exercise can be complex and multifaceted and, therefore, driven by a variety of underlying mechanisms.

Future basic studies should seek to replicate and thus establish the reliability of the recent dose–response findings reviewed here. That the aerobic–anaerobic transition is the turning point toward a decline in affective valence has now been found in three different laboratories (Acevedo et al., 2003; Bixby, Spalding, & Hatfield, 2001; Hall, Ekkekakis, & Petruzzello, 2002) and replicated in one (Ekkekakis, Hall, & Petruzzello, 2001, 2004). That there are systematic intensity-dependent changes in the patterns of interindividual variation in affective valence responses has been examined in only one laboratory (Ekkekakis, Hall, & Petruzzello, 2005). Although several laboratories have found that the magnitude of the negative relationship between affective valence and physiological variables increases as the intensity of exercise increases (e.g., Acevedo, Rinehardt, & Kraemer, 1994; Ekkekakis, 2003; Hardy & Rejeski, 1989), the relationship of affective valence with cognitive variables across different levels of exercise intensity remains unclear (Blanchard et al., 2002; McAuley & Courneya, 1992; McAuley et al., 2000; Tate, Petruzzello, & Lox, 1995; Treasure & Newbery, 1998). As noted earlier, this is possibly due to the fact that different laboratories have defined exercise intensity in different ways, using arbitrarily selected percentages of maximal capacity. Preliminary evidence indicates that clarity might be established once the intensity is defined in relation to the level of the aerobic–anaerobic transition (Ekkekakis, 2003). What other cognitive variables, besides self-efficacy, are related to affective responses during exercise is also a question that warrants attention. In general, as basic research on the dose–response relationship moves forward, it is necessary to consider the methodological issues that were outlined here (also see Ekkekakis & Petruzzello, 1999, 2000).

Additional steps are also clearly needed in deciphering the neural underpinnings of the affective responses to various intensities of exercise. The putative model we presented here appears reasonable based on the extant evidence but remains speculative. Given the current technical difficulty with testing the model in a human brain imaging study, priority should be given to animal research. As noted, only one known study (Vissing, Andersen, & Diemer, 1996) has directly examined the acute response of the amygdala to exercise. This appears to be the unfortunate consequence of the fact that most neuroanatomical and neurophysiological studies of exercise responses focus on cardiovascular and respiratory regulation and thus rarely venture into areas beyond the brainstem. It is also important to reiterate that, although here we focused on the amygdala, the role of other areas, including the insula, the cingulate, the prefrontal cortex, and the nucleus accumbens, should be investigated as well.

From the standpoint of practical applications, the data and conceptual model presented here raise some interesting possibilities for future applied research. First, there is the possibility of using the significant decline in affective valence that accompanies the transition to anaerobic metabolism as a practical aid in self-monitoring and self-regulating exercise intensity (Acevedo et al., 2003; Ekkekakis, Hall, & Petruzzello, 2004). Research has shown that novice exercisers, on average, intuitively select an intensity corresponding to the level of the aerobic–anaerobic transition (Lind, Joens-Matre, & Ekkekakis, 2005). It is interesting to ponder whether increasing the awareness of affective changes could be used as a guide for helping those individuals who inadvertently select intensities either significantly below or significantly above this level to improve their self-regulatory skills.

Applied studies should also examine the range of effectiveness of cognitive techniques aimed at helping novice exercisers cope with the unpleasant affective responses to exercise (e.g., attentional dissociation, cognitive restructuring, self-efficacy), particularly during the critical early stages of exercise participation. We have suggested here that the effectiveness of these techniques might be limited to intensities below or near the level of the aerobic–anaerobic transition. Intensities that exceed this level are probably not only ineffective at conferring any additional fitness or health benefits to exercisers, but will also raise the risk of muscular and skeletal injuries, cardiac complications, and so on. Therefore, the proper solution would not be to learn to tolerate these intensities but rather to develop the appropriate skills to detect and avoid them. Techniques based on the principles of biofeedback, aimed at increasing interoceptive acuity specifically for the physiological, perceptual, and affective symptoms characteristic of the aerobic–anaerobic transition, might be helpful in this regard (Ekkekakis & Petruzzello, 2002b).

Finally, the long-term goal should be to examine the intensity–affect–adherence hypothesized causal chain in its entirety. There are presently no studies that have manipulated exercise intensity, examined the impact of these manipulations on adherence and dropout, and tested the mediational role of affective responses. This is clearly a significant void. To repeat our statement in the introduction, in the long run, people generally choose to do what makes them feel good and avoid what makes them feel bad. Therefore, it is possible that improving our understanding of the relationship between exercise intensity and affective responses might be one of the keys to solving the critical public health problem of physical inactivity.

References

Acevedo, E.O., Gill, D.L., Goldfarb, A.H., & Boyer, B.T. (1996). Affect and perceived exertion during a two-hour run. *International Journal of Sport Psychology, 27*, 286-292.

Acevedo, E.O., Kraemer, R.R., Haltom, R.W., & Tryniecki, J.L. (2003). Perceptual responses proximal to the onset of blood lactate accumulation. *Journal of Sports Medicine and Physical Fitness, 43*, 267-273.

Acevedo, E.O., Rinehardt, K.F., & Kraemer, R.R. (1994). Perceived exertion and affect at varying intensities of running. *Research Quarterly for Exercise and Sport, 65*, 372-376.

Aggleton, J.P., Burton, M.J., & Passingham, R.E. (1980). Cortical and subcortical afferents to the amygdala of the rhesus monkey (macaca mulatta). *Brain Research, 190*, 347-368.

Aggleton, J.P., & Young, A.W. (2000). The enigma of the amygdala: On its contribution to human emotion. In R.D. Lane & L. Nadel (Eds.), *Cognitive neuroscience of emotion* (pp. 106-128). New York: Oxford University Press.

Ben-Ari, Y., Le Gal la Salle, G., & Champagnat, J. (1973). Amygdala unit activity changes related to a spontaneous blood pressure increase. *Brain Research, 52*, 394-398.

Bernard, J.F., Alden, M., & Besson, J.M. (1993). The organization of the efferent projections from the pontine parabrachial area to the amygdaloid complex: A phaseolus vulgaris leucoagglutinin (PHA-L) study in the rat. *Journal of Comparative Neurology, 329*, 201-229.

Bernard, J.F., & Besson, J.M. (1990). The spino(trigemino)pontoamygdaloid pathway: Electrophysiological evidence for an involvement in pain processes. *Journal of Neurophysiology, 63*, 473-490.

Bernard, J.F., Bester, H., & Besson, J.M. (1996). Involvement in the spino-parabrachio-amygdaloid and -hypothalamic pathways in the autonomic and affective emotional aspects of pain. *Progress in Brain Research, 107,* 243-255.

Bernard, J.F., Huang, G.F., & Besson, J.M. (1990). Effects of noxious somesthetic stimulation on the activity of neurons of the nucleus centralis of the amygdala. *Brain Research, 523,* 347-350.

Bernard, J.F., Huang, G.F., & Besson, J.M. (1992). Nucleus centralis of the amygdala and the globus pallidus ventralis: Electrophysiological evidence for an involvement in pain processes. *Journal of Neurophysiology, 68,* 551-569.

Bernard, J.F., Peschanski, M., & Besson, J.M. (1989). A possible spino(trigemino)-ponto-amygdaloid pathway for pain. *Neuroscience Letters, 100,* 83-88.

Bingel, U., Quante, M., Knab, R., Bromm, B., Weiller, C., & Büchel, C. (2002). Subcortical structures involved in pain processing: Evidence from single-trial fMRI. *Pain, 99,* 313-321.

Bixby, W.R., Spalding, T.W., & Hatfield, B.D. (2001). Temporal dynamics and dimensional specificity of the affective response to exercise of varying intensity: Differing pathways to a common outcome. *Journal of Sport and Exercise Psychology, 23,* 171-190.

Blanchard, C.M., Rodgers, W.M., Courneya, K.S., & Spence, J.C. (2002). Moderators of the exercise/feeling-state relationship: The influence of self-efficacy, baseline, and in-task feeling states at moderate- and high-intensity exercise. *Journal of Applied Social Psychology, 32,* 1379-1395.

Bornhövd, K., Quante, M., Glauche, V., Bromm, B., Weiller, C., & Büchel, C. (2002). Painful stimuli evoke different stimulus-response functions in the amygdala, prefrontal, insula and somatosensory cortex: A single-trial fMRI study. *Brain, 125,* 1326-1336.

Boyd, A.E., Giamber, S.R., Mager, M., & Lebovitz, H.E. (1974). Lactate inhibition of lypolysis in exercising man. *Metabolism, 23,* 531-542.

Brannan, S., Liotti, M., Egan, G., Shade, R., Madden, L., Robillard, R., Abplanalp, B., Stofer, K., Denton, D., & Fox, P.T. (2001). Neuroimaging of cerebral activations and deactivations associated with hypercapnia and hunger for air. *Proceedings of the National Academy of Sciences, 98,* 2029-2034.

Burstein, R., & Potrebic, S. (1993). Retrograde labeling of neurons in the spinal cord that project directly to the amygdala or the orbital cortex in the rat. *Journal of Comparative Neurology, 335,* 469-485.

Cabanac, M. (1971). Physiological role of pleasure. *Science, 173,* 1103-1107.

Cabanac, M. (1979). Sensory pleasure. *Quarterly Review of Biology, 54,* 1-29.

Cechetto, D.F., & Calaresu, F.R. (1983). Response of single units in the amygdala to stimulation of buffer nerves in cat. *American Journal of Physiology, 244,* R646-R651.

Cechetto, D.F., & Calaresu, F.R. (1984). Units of the amygdala responding to activation of carotid baro- and chemoreceptors. *American Journal of Physiology, 246,* R832-R836.

Cechetto, D.F., & Calaresu, F.R. (1985). Central pathways relaying cardiovascular afferent information to amygdala. *American Journal of Physiology, 248,* R38-R45.

Cechetto, D.F., Ciriello, J., & Calaresu, F.R. (1983). Afferent connections to cardiovascular sites in the amygdala: A horseradish peroxidase study in the cat. *Journal of the Autonomic Nervous System, 8,* 97-110.

Cervero, F. (1994). Sensory innervation of the viscera: Peripheral basis of visceral pain. *Physiological Reviews, 74,* 95-138.

Cervero, F., & Janig, W. (1992). Visceral nociceptors: A new world order? *Trends in Neurosciences, 15,* 374-378.

Ciriello, J., Schultz, C.G., & Roder, S. (1994). Collateral axonal projections from ventrolateral medullary non-catecholaminergic neurons to central nucleus of the amygdala. *Brain Research, 663,* 346-351.

Cliffer, K.D., Burstein, R., & Giesler, G.J. (1991). Distributions of spinothalamic, spinohypothalamic, and spinotelencephalic fibers revealed by anterograde transport of PHA-L in rats. *Journal of Neuroscience, 11,* 852-868.

Clore, G.L., & Ortony, A. (2000). Cognition in emotion: Always, sometimes, or never? In R.D. Lane & L. Nadel (Eds.), *Cognitive neuroscience of emotion* (pp. 24-61). New York: Oxford University Press.

Coghill, R.C., Sang, C.N., Maisog, J.M., & Iadarola, M.J. (1999). Pain intensity processing within the human brain: A bilateral, distributed mechanism. *Journal of Neurophysiology, 82,* 1934-1943.

Craig, A.D. (1996). An ascending general homeostatic afferent pathway originating in lamina I. *Progress in Brain Research, 107,* 225-242.

Critchley, H.D., Wiens, S., Rothstein, P., Öhman, A., & Dolan, R.J. (2004). Neural systems supporting interoceptive awareness. *Nature Neuroscience, 7,* 189-195.

Damasio, A.R. (1995). Toward a neurobiology of emotion and feeling: Operational concepts and hypotheses. *Neuroscientist, 1,* 19-25.

Damasio, A.R. (1999). *The feeling of what happens: Body and emotion in the making of consciousness.* New York: Harcourt Brace.

Derbyshire, S.W.G., Jones, A.K.P., Gyulai, F., Clark, S., Townsend, D., & Firestone, L.L. (1997). Pain processing during three levels of noxious stimulation produces differential patterns of central activity. *Pain, 73,* 431-445.

Dishman, R.K., & Buckworth, J. (1996). Increasing physical activity: A quantitative synthesis. *Medicine and Science in Sports and Exercise, 28,* 706-719.

Ekkekakis, P. (2003). Pleasure and displeasure from the body: Perspectives from exercise. *Cognition and Emotion, 17,* 213-239.

Ekkekakis, P. (2005). The study of affective responses to acute exercise: The dual-mode model. In R. Stelter & K.K. Roessler (Eds.), *New approaches to exercise and sport psychology (pp. 119-146).* Oxford, United Kingdom: Meyer & Meyer Sport.

Ekkekakis, P., Hall, E.E., & Petruzzello, S.J. (2001). Intensity of acute exercise and affect: A critical reexamination of the dose-response relationship [abstract]. *Medicine and Science in Sports and Exercise, 33,* S50.

Ekkekakis, P., Hall, E.E., & Petruzzello, S.J. (2004). Practical markers of the transition from aerobic to anaerobic metabolism during exercise: Rationale and a case for affect-based exercise prescription. *Preventive Medicine, 38,* 149-159.

Ekkekakis, P., Hall, E.E., & Petruzzello, S.J. (2005). Variation and homogeneity in affective responses to physical activity of varying intensities: An alternative perspective on dose-response based on evolutionary considerations. *Journal of Sports Sciences, 23,* 477-500.

Ekkekakis, P., Hall, E.E., Van Landuyt, L.M., & Petruzzello, S.J. (2000). Walking in (affective) circles: Can short walks enhance affect? *Journal of Behavioral Medicine, 23,* 245-275.

Ekkekakis, P., & Petruzzello, S.J. (1999). Acute aerobic exercise and affect: Current status, problems, and prospects regarding dose-response. *Sports Medicine, 28,* 337-374.

Ekkekakis, P., & Petruzzello, S.J. (2000). Analysis of the affect measurement conundrum in exercise psychology: I. Fundamental issues. *Psychology of Sport and Exercise, 2,* 71-88.

Ekkekakis, P., & Petruzzello, S.J. (2002a). Analysis of the affect measurement conundrum in exercise psychology: IV. A conceptual case for the affect circumplex. *Psychology of Sport and Exercise, 3,* 35-63.

Ekkekakis, P., & Petruzzello, S.J. (2002b). Biofeedback in exercise psychology. In B. Blumenstein, M. Bar-Eli, & G. Tenenbaum (Eds.), *Brain and body in sport and exercise: Biofeedback application in performance enhancement* (pp. 77-100). Chichester, England: Wiley.

Evans, K.C., Banzett, R.B., Adams, L., McKay, L., Frackowiak, R.S.J., & Corfield, D.R. (2002). BOLD fMRI identifies limbic, paralimbic, and cerebellar activation during air hunger. *Journal of Neurophysiology, 88,* 1500-1511.

Favero, T.G., Zable, A.C., Bowman, M.B., Thompson, A., & Abramson, J.J. (1995). Metabolic end products inhibit sarcoplasmic reticulum Ca^{2+} release and [^{3}H]ryanodine binding. *Journal of Applied Physiology, 78,* 1665-1672.

Fox, K.R. (1999). The influence of physical activity on mental well-being. *Public Health and Nutrition, 2,* 411-418.

Frysinger, R.C., & Harper, R.M. (1989). Cardiac and respiratory correlations with unit discharge in human amygdala and hippocampus. *Electroencephalography and Clinical Neurophysiology, 72,* 463-470.

Frysinger, R.C., Zhang, J., & Harper, R.M. (1988). Cardiovascular and respiratory relationships with neuronal discharge in the central nucleus of the amygdala during sleep-waking states. *Sleep, 11,* 317-332.

Gauvin, L., & Brawley, L.R. (1993). Alternative psychological models and methodologies for the study of exercise and affect. In P. Seraganian (Ed.), *Exercise psychology: The influence of physical exercise on psychological processes* (pp. 146-171). New York: Wiley.

Giesler, G.J., Katter, J.T., & Dado, R.J. (1994). Direct spinal pathways to the limbic system for nociceptive information. *Trends in Neurosciences, 17,* 244-250.

Goldsmith, S.R., Iber, C., McArthur, C.D., & Davies, S.F. (1990). Influence of acid-base status on plasma catecholamines during exercise in normal humans. *American Journal of Physiology, 258,* R1411-R1416.

Hall, E.E., Ekkekakis, P., & Petruzzello, S.J. (2002). The affective beneficence of vigorous exercise revisited. *British Journal of Health Psychology, 7,* 47-66.

Hardy, C.J., & Rejeski, W.J. (1989). Not what, but how one feels: The measurement of affect during exercise. *Journal of Sport and Exercise Psychology, 11,* 304-317.

Harper, R.M., Bandler, R., Spriggs, D., & Alger, J.R. (2000). Lateralized and widespread brain activation during transient blood pressure elevation revealed by magnetic resonance imaging. *Journal of Comparative Neurology, 417,* 195-204.

Helal, J.N., Guezennec, C.Y., & Goubel, F. (1987). The aerobic-anaerobic transition: Re-examination of the threshold concept including an electromyographic approach. *European Journal of Applied Physiology, 56,* 643-649.

Henderson, L.A., Richard, C.A., Macey, P.M., Runquist, M.L., Yu, P.L., Galons, J.-P., & Harper, R.M. (2004). Functional magnetic resonance signal changes in neural structures to baroreceptor reflex activation. *Journal of Applied Physiology, 96,* 693-703.

Iwamoto, G.A., Wappel, S.M., Fox, G.M., Buetow, K.A., & Waldrop, T.G. (1996). Identification of diencephalic and brainstem cardiorespiratory areas activated during exercise. *Brain Research, 726,* 109-122.

Jones, D.A., Ainsworth, B.E., Croft, J.B., Macera, C.A., Lloyd, E.E., & Yusuf, H.R. (1998). Moderate leisure-time physical activity: Who is meeting the public health recommendations? A national cross-sectional study. *Archives of Family Medicine, 7,* 285-289.

Jordan, D., Mifflin, S.W., & Spyer, K.M. (1988). Hypothalamic inhibition of neurones in the nucleus tractus solitarius of the cat is GABA mediated. *Journal of Physiology, 399,* 389-404.

Katch, V., Weltman, A., Sady, S., & Freedson, P. (1978). Validity of the relative percent concept for equating training intensity. *European Journal of Applied Physiology, 39,* 219-227.

Kaufman, M.P., & Forster, H.V. (1996). Reflexes controlling circulatory, ventilatory and airway responses to exercise. In L.B. Rowell & J.T. Shephard (Eds.), *Handbook of physiology, Exercise: Regulation and integration of multiple systems* (pp. 381-447). New York: Oxford University Press.

Kirkcaldy, B.C., & Shephard, R.J. (1990). Therapeutic implications of exercise. *International Journal of Sport Psychology, 21,* 165-184.

Knuepfer, M.M., Eismann, A., Schütze, I., Stumpf, H., & Stock, G. (1995). Response of single neurons in amygdala to interoceptive and exteroceptive stimuli in conscious cats. *American Journal of Physiology, 268,* R666-R675.

Krout, K.E., Jansen, A.S.P., & Loewy, A.D. (1998). Periaqueductal gray matter projection to the parabrachial nucleus in rat. *Journal of Comparative Neurology, 401,* 437-454.

Lang, E.J., & Paré, D. (1998). Synaptic responsiveness of interneurons of the cat lateral amygdaloid nucleus. *Neuroscience, 83,* 877-889.

LeDoux, J.E. (1986). Sensory systems and emotion: A model of affective processing. *Integrative Psychiatry, 4,* 237-248.

LeDoux, J.E. (1989). Cognitive-emotional interactions in the brain. *Cognition and Emotion, 3,* 267-289.

LeDoux, J.E. (1994). The degree of emotional control depends on the kind of response system involved. In P. Ekman & R.J. Davidson (Eds.), *The nature of emotion: Fundamental questions* (pp. 270-272). New York: Oxford University Press.

LeDoux, J.E. (1996). *The emotional brain: The mysterious underpinnings of emotional life.* New York: Simon & Schuster.

Lee, J.Y., Jensen, B.E., Oberman, A., Fletcher, G.F., Fletcher, B.J., & Raczynski, J.M. (1996). Adherence in the Training Levels Comparison Trial. *Medicine and Science in Sports and Exercise, 28,* 47-52.

Lind, E., Joens-Matre, R.R., & Ekkekakis, P. (2005). What intensity of physical activity do previously sedentary middle-aged women select? Evidence of a coherent pattern from physiological, perceptual, and affective markers. *Preventive Medicine, 40,* 407-419.

Liotti, M., Brannan, S., Egan, G., Shade, R., Madden, L., Abplanalp, B., Robillard, R., Lancaster, J., Zamarripa, F.E., Fox, P.T., & Denton, D. (2001). Brain responses associated with consciousness of breathlessness (air hunger). *Proceedings of the National Academy of Sciences, 98,* 2035-2040.

Ma, W., & Peschanski, M. (1988). Spinal and trigeminal projections to the parabrachial nucleus in the rat: Electron-microscopic evidence of a spino-ponto-amygdalian somatosensory pathway. *Somatosensory Research, 5,* 247-257.

McAuley, E., Blissmer, B., Katula, J., & Duncan, T.E. (2000). Exercise environment, self-efficacy, and affective responses to acute exercise in older adults. *Psychology and Health, 15,* 341-355.

McAuley, E., & Courneya, K.S. (1992). Self-efficacy relationships with affective and exertion responses to exercise. *Journal of Applied Social Psychology, 22,* 312-326.

McCann, D.J., Mollé, P.A., & Caton, J.R. (1995). Phosphocreatine kinetics in humans during exercise and recovery. *Medicine and Science in Sports and Exercise, 27,* 278-387.

McCormick, D.A., & Bal, T. (1994). Sensory gating mechanisms of the thalamus. *Current Opinion in Neurobiology, 4,* 550-556.

McDonald, A.J. (1998). Cortical pathways to the mammalian amygdala. *Progress in Neurobiology, 55,* 257-332.

Menétrey, D., & de Pommery, J. (1991). Origins of spinal ascending pathways that reach ventral areas involved in visceroception and visceronociception in the rat. *European Journal of Neuroscience, 3,* 249-259.

Mense, S. (1996). Group III and IV receptors in skeletal muscle: Are they specific or polymodal? *Progress in Brain Research, 113,* 83-100.

Mifflin, S.W., Spyer, K.M., & Withington-Wray, D.J. (1988a). Baroreceptor inputs to the nucleus tractus solitarius in the cat: Modulation by the hypothalamus. *Journal of Physiology, 399,* 369-387.

Mifflin, S.W., Spyer, K.M., & Withington-Wray, D.J. (1988b). Baroreceptor inputs to the nucleus tractus solitarius in the cat: Postsynaptic actions and the influence of respiration. *Journal of Physiology, 399,* 349-367.

Nagata, A., Muro, M., Moritani, T., & Yoshida, T. (1981). Anaerobic threshold determination by blood lactate and myoelectric signals. *Japanese Journal of Physiology, 31,* 585-597.

Ojanen, M. (1994). Can the true effects of exercise on psychological variables be separated from placebo effects? *International Journal of Sport Psychology, 25,* 63-80.

Ottersen, O.P. (1980). Afferent connections to the amygdaloid complex of the rat and cat: II. Afferents from the hypothalamus and the basal telencephalon. *Journal of Comparative Neurology, 194,* 267-289.

Ottersen, O.P. (1981). Afferent connections to the amygdaloid complex of the rat with some observations in the cat: III. Afferents from the lower brain stem. *Journal of Comparative Neurology, 202,* 335-356.

Ottersen, O.P., & Ben-Ari, Y. (1979). Afferent connections to the amygdaloid complex of the rat and cat: I. Projections from the thalamus. *Journal of Comparative Neurology, 187,* 401-424.

Paré, D., Royer, S., Smith, Y., & Lang, E.J. (2003). Contextual inhibitory gating of impulse traffic in the intra-amygdaloid network. *Annals of the New York Academy of Sciences, 985,* 78-91.

Parfitt, G., & Eston, R. (1995). Changes in ratings of perceived exertion and psychological affect in the early stages of exercise. *Perceptual and Motor Skills, 80,* 259-266.

Parfitt, G., Eston, R., & Connolly, D. (1996). Psychological affect at different ratings of perceived exertion in high-and low-active women: A study using a production protocol. *Perceptual and Motor Skills, 82,* 1035-1042.

Parfitt, G., Markland, D., & Holmes, C. (1994). Responses to physical exertion in active and inactive males and females. *Journal of Sport and Exercise Psychology, 16,* 178-186.

Perri, M.G., Anton, S.D., Durning, P.E., Ketterson, T.U., Sydeman, S.J., Berlant, N.E., Kanasky, W.F., Newton, R.L., Limacher, M.C., & Martin, A.D. (2002). Adherence to exercise prescriptions: Effects of prescribing moderate versus higher levels of intensity and frequency. *Health Psychology, 21,* 452-458.

Pronk, N.P., Crouse, S.F., & Rohack, J.J. (1995). Maximal exercise and acute mood response in women. *Physiology and Behavior, 57,* 1-4.

Ricardo, J.A., & Koh, E.T. (1978). Anatomical evidence of direct projections from the nucleus of the solitary tract to the hypothalamus, amygdala, and other forebrain structures in the rat. *Brain Research, 153,* 1-26.

Riley, M., Maehara, K., Pórszász, J., Engelen, M.P.K.J., Barstow, T.J., Tanaka, H., & Wasserman, K. (1997). Association between the anaerobic threshold and the break-point in the double product/work rate relationship. *European Journal of Applied Physiology, 75,* 14-21.

Rizvi, T.A., Ennis, M., Behbehani, M.M., & Shipley, M.T. (1991). Connections between the central nucleus of the amygdala and the midbrain periaqueductal gray: Topography and reciprocity. *Journal of Comparative Neurology, 303,* 121-131.

Roder, S., & Ciriello, J. (1993). Innervation of the amygdaloid complex by catecholaminergic cell groups of the ventrolateral medulla. *Journal of Comparative Neurology, 332,* 105-122.

Roder, S., & Ciriello, J. (1995). Convergence of ventrolateral medulla and aortic baroreceptor inputs onto amygdala neurons. *Brain Research, 705,* 71-78.

Romanski, L.M., Clugnet, M.C., Bordi, F., & LeDoux, J.E. (1993). Somatosensory and auditory convergence in the lateral nucleus of the amygdala. *Behavioral Neuroscience, 107,* 444-450.

Royer, S., Martina, M., & Paré, D. (1999). An inhibitory interface gates impulse traffic between the input and output stations of the amygdala. *Journal of Neuroscience, 19,* 10575-10583.

Russell, J.A. (1980). A circumplex model of affect. *Journal of Personality and Social Psychology, 39,* 1161-1178.

Sah, P., Faber, E.S.L., Lopez De Armentia, M., & Power, J. (2003). The amygdaloid complex: Anatomy and physiology. *Physiological Reviews, 83,* 803-834.

Saha, S., Batten, T.F.C., & Henderson, Z. (2000). A GABAergic projection from the central nucleus of the amygdala to the nucleus of the solitary tract: A combined anterograde tracing and electron microscopic immunohistochemical study. *Neuroscience, 99,* 613-626.

Saklofske, D.H., Blomme, G.C., & Kelly, I.W. (1992). The effects of exercise and relaxation on energetic and tense arousal. *Personality and Individual Differences, 13,* 623-625.

Schneider, F., Habel, U., Holthusen, H., Kessler, C., Posse, S., Müller-Gärtner, H.-W., & Arndt, J.O. (2001). Subjective ratings of pain correlate with subcortical-limbic blood flow: An fMRI study. *Neuropsychobiology, 43,* 175-185.

Schneirla, T.C. (1959). An evolutionary and developmental theory of biphasic processes underlying approach and withdrawal. In M.R. Jones (Ed.), *Nebraska symposium on motivation* (vol. 7, pp. 1-42). Lincoln, NE: University of Nebraska Press.

Schütze, I., Knuepfer, M.M., Eismann, A., Stumpf, H., & Stock, G. (1987). Sensory input to single neurons in the amygdala of the cat. *Experimental Neurology, 97,* 499-515.

Shinohara, M., & Moritani, T. (1992). Increase in neuromuscular activity and oxygen uptake during heavy exercise. *Annals of Physiological Anthropology, 11,* 257-262.

Spriet, L.L., Lindinger, M.I., McKelvie, R.S., Heigenhauser, G.J.F., & Jones, N.L. (1989). Muscle glycogenolysis and H+ concentration during maximal intermittent cycling. *Journal of Applied Physiology, 66,* 8-13.

Tanaka, H., Kiyonaga, A., Terao, Y., Ide, K., Yamauchi, M., Tanaka, M., & Shindo, M. (1997). Double product response is accelerated above the blood lactate threshold. *Medicine and Science in Sports and Exercise, 29,* 503-508.

Tate, A.K., Petruzzello, S.J., & Lox, C.L. (1995). Examination of the relationship between self-efficacy and affect at varying levels of aerobic exercise intensity. *Journal of Applied Social Psychology, 25,* 1922-1936.

Thayer, R.E. (1987). Energy, tiredness, and tension effects of a sugar snack versus moderate exercise. *Journal of Personality and Social Psychology, 52,* 119-125.

Toney, G.M., & Mifflin, S.W. (2000). Sensory modalities conveyed in the hindlimb somatic afferent input to the nucleus tractus solitarius. *Journal of Applied Physiology, 88,* 2062-2073.

Treasure, D.C., & Newbery, D.M. (1998). Relationship between self-efficacy, exercise intensity, and feeling states in a sedentary population during and following an acute bout of exercise. *Journal of Sport and Exercise Psychology, 20,* 1-11.

Turner, B.H., & Herkenham, M. (1991). Thalamoamygdaloid projections in the rat: A test of the amygdala's role in sensory processing. *Journal of Comparative Neurology, 313,* 295-325.

United States Department of Health and Human Services. (1996). *Physical activity and health: A report of the Surgeon General.* Atlanta: U.S. Department of Health and Human Services, Centers for Disease Control and Prevention, National Center for Chronic Disease Prevention and Health Promotion.

United States Department of Health and Human Services. (2000). *Healthy people 2010.* Washington, DC: Author.

Urhausen, A., Weiler, B., Coen, B., & Kindermann, W. (1994). Plasma catecholamines during endurance exercise of different intensities as related to the individual anaerobic threshold. *European Journal of Applied Physiology, 69,* 16-20.

Uwano, T., Nishijo, H., Ono, T., & Tamura, R. (1995). Neuronal responsiveness to various sensory stimuli, and associative learning in the rat amygdala. *Neuroscience, 68,* 339-361.

Van Landuyt, L.M., Ekkekakis, P., Hall, E.E., & Petruzzello, S.J. (2000). Throwing the mountains into the lakes: On the perils of nomothetic conceptions of the exercise-affect relationship. *Journal of Sport and Exercise Psychology, 22,* 208-234.

Vissing, J., Andersen, M., & Diemer, N.H. (1996). Exercise-induced changes in the local cerebral glucose utilization in the rat. *Journal of Cerebral Blood Flow and Metabolism, 16,* 729-736.

Volz, H.P., Rehbein, G., Triepel, J., Knuepfer, M.M., Stumpf, H., & Stock, G. (1990). Afferent connections of the nucleus centralis amygdalae: A horseradish peroxidase study and literature survey. *Anatomy and Embryology, 181,* 177-194.

Wasserman, K. (1978). Breathing during exercise. *New England Journal of Medicine, 298,* 780-785.

Watson, D., Clark, L.A., & Tellegen, A. (1988). Development and validation of brief measures of positive and negative affect: The PANAS scales. *Journal of Personality and Social Psychology, 54,* 1063-1070.

Wells, J.G., Balke, B., & Van Fossan, D.D. (1957). Lactic acid accumulation during work: A suggested standardization of work classification. *Journal of Applied Physiology, 10,* 51-55.

Weltman, A., Wood, C.M., Womack, C.J., Davis, S.E., Blumer, J.L., Alvarez, J., Sauer, K., & Gaesser, G.A. (1994). Catecholamine and blood lactate responses to incremental rowing and running exercise. *Journal of Applied Physiology, 76,* 1144-1149.

Zald, D.H. (2003). The human amygdala and the emotional evaluation of sensory stimuli. *Brain Research Reviews, 41,* 88-123.

Zardetto-Smith, A.M., & Gray, T.S. (1990). Organization of peptidergic and catecholaminergic efferents from the nucleus of the solitary tract to the rat amygdala. *Brain Research Bulletin, 25,* 875-887.

Zardetto-Smith, A.M., & Gray, T.S. (1995). Catecholamine and NPY efferents from the ventrolateral medulla to the amygdala in the rat. *Brain Research Bulletin, 38,* 253-260.

Zhang, J., & Mifflin, S.W. (2000). Subthreshold aortic nerve inputs to neurons in nucleus of the solitary tract. *American Journal of Physiology, 278,* R1595-R1604.

Physical Activity, Affect, and Electroencephalogram Studies

Steven J. Petruzzello, PhD

Panteleimon Ekkekakis, PhD, FACSM

Eric E. Hall, PhD

Emotions are essential for successful adaptation, . . . they interact seamlessly with other cognitive processes, and . . . they support motivated behavior. (Davidson, 2003, p. 655)

Exercise has been linked with affective change for quite some time. It is generally accepted that exercise results in either reduced negative (e.g., tension, anxiety, depression) or increased positive (e.g., energy, vigor) affect or both. (Note that "affect" is the term used throughout this chapter, as it is the most basic component of all valenced [positive or negative, pleasant or unpleasant] responses, including, but not limited to, emotions and moods [for a more detailed discussion, see Ekkekakis & Petruzzello, 2000]). Indeed, the beneficial psychological effects of exercise are widely touted (Biddle, Fox, & Boutcher, 2000; Biddle & Mutrie, 2001), and research in this area is becoming increasingly prevalent. It is completely plausible to discuss the exercise–affect relationship as an exclusively psychological phenomenon. In fact, it could be argued that the majority of work in exercise psychology over the past 40 years has involved the study of psychological processes (e.g., affect) as though they were distinct from physiologic sources. Physiological inputs and systems are often overlooked, if considered at all, and psychological constructs (e.g., affect) are often viewed as disengaged from the body (Ekkekakis, 2003). Thinking along these lines limits the investigation of problems to a single level, disregarding the impact such phenomena might have

on adjacent levels of inquiry (e.g., physiological, social; see Petruzzello, 1999, 2001).

A more comprehensive perspective, however, would hold that the physical changes that inevitably occur as a result of exercise are intimately linked to such affective changes (see Petruzzello, 1999). This is not a new idea, as reflected in the comments of William James more than 100 years ago:

"Everyone knows the effect of physical exercise on the mood: how much more cheerful and courageous one feels when the body has been toned up, than when it is 'run down' . . . our moods are determined by the feelings which come up from our body. Those feelings are sometimes of worry, breathlessness, anxiety; sometimes of peace and repose. It is certain that physical exercise will tend to train the body toward the latter feelings. The latter feelings are certainly an essential ingredient in all perfect human character." (emphasis added, 1899, pp. 220-221)

The question that remains unanswered, however, is which of the myriad physiological changes that do occur can be useful in explaining why exercise typically results in improved affect, particularly during recovery from exercise. One place that should certainly be examined for its potential role in the affective domain is the brain itself. As LeDoux has stated, "Understanding emotions in the human brain is clearly an important quest, as most mental disorders are emotional disorders" (1996, pp. 18-19) and "once emotions occur they become powerful motivators of future behavior" (1996, p. 19).

A tremendous increase in research into the workings of the human brain began in the 1990s, fueled in part by the congressional declaration of the 1990s as the "Decade of the Brain." As already noted, within the exercise sciences there has also been a tremendous increase in interest regarding the affective consequences of physical exercise. It would seem reasonable to propose a case for the importance of the brain in this relationship. There is certainly a need for a clearer understanding of the linkage between brain function, exercise, and affect. Although a number of relatively brief reviews of the exercise–brain function literature have appeared periodically over the past 20 years (Dishman, 1992; Etnier & Landers, 1995; Hatfield & Landers, 1983, 1987), there is a need for a more comprehensive accounting of what has been done, what is known, and what remains to be done.

It is completely plausible to discuss exercise effects on the brain as an exclusively physiological phenomenon, examining changes in particular frequency bands or electrode sites (e.g., Crabbe & Dishman, 2004). Rather than such a dualistic, reductionistic approach, a potentially more informative approach involves embracing mind–body unity, an approach captured in the psychophysiological perspective. Psychophysiology, as a field of study, involves the examination of psychological phenomena (cognitive, affective [emotional], behavioral), viewing such phenomena as related to and revealed through physiological principles and events (Cacioppo & Tassinary, 1990). Perhaps the primary advantage of the psychophysiological approach is that it goes beyond single levels of analysis. As Cacioppo and Berntson (1992) have argued, a reliance on only singular levels of understanding (e.g., self-report [psychological] or neurochemical [physiological]) is narrow-minded. The prevailing perspective in exercise and sport psychology is one that seems to hold that there is no reality beyond our subjective experience (e.g., Dzewaltowski, 1994). Such a singular perspective runs counter to the multilevel integrative approach espoused by Cacioppo and Berntson. Psychological and physiological perspectives are complementary (i.e., each is fundamental to psychophysiological inquiries). Essentially, the point is that consideration of both physiological and psychological perspectives reduces the chances of errors related to operationalization,

measurement, and inference. Ultimately, this has the potential to enrich theory and research on human processes and behavior.

Davidson has been instrumental in advancing what he has termed "affective neuroscience" (Davidson & Sutton, 1995), a field of inquiry that certainly captures the essence of multilevel integration. A rich literature has developed over many years examining the role of the brain in affective regulation (Allen & Kline, 2004). A primary measure in this work has been the electroencephalogram (EEG), a measure of the electrical activity of the brain. This has been a particularly useful measure in work with humans, specifically in the investigation of affective responses (see Davidson, 1995), and has been utilized in numerous exercise studies as well.

In an era where functional neuroimaging methodologies, such as positron emission tomography (PET) and functional magnetic resonance imaging (fMRI), have seen an exponential increase in the study of emotion and psychopathology, one might question whether there remains a role for frontal EEG asymmetry in the study of emotion, motivation, and psychopathology. Aside from the obvious advantages of EEG as a measure that is less invasive, less expensive, and more widely available than many neuroimaging modalities, frontal EEG asymmetry has established—by virtue of the nearly 100 studies using this measure—a sizable literature that embeds the measure in a network of psychological and behavioral constructs, thus bestowing frontal EEG asymmetry with sizable construct validity as a measure of an underlying approach-related or withdrawal-related motivational style (e.g. Davidson et al., 2000; Harmon-Jones, 2004), or as an index of potential risk for emotion-related psychopathology (Coan and Allen, 2004). As such, frontal EEG asymmetry has greater construct validity as a measure of this motivational style than does any neuroimaging measure to date. (Allen & Kline, 2004, p. 1)

The EEG itself results from the recording of differences in electrical potentials between various points on the scalp. This is thought to reflect the activity of large groups of cortical neurons being synchronously depolarized. Said another way, the EEG reflects the spontaneous electrical activity of the brain, most likely from dendritic processes in the upper cortical layers. Electrode location on the scalp has traditionally utilized the standardized International 10-20 system (Jasper, 1958). This system uses four anatomical reference points (inion, nasion, left and right preauricular points) and then locates the 19 electrodes systematically around the scalp. In the literature, as a general rule, capital letters are used to refer to the electrode location in terms of the cortical lobe over which it sits (Frontal, Temporal, Central, Parietal, Occipital), and then either a zed (e.g., Fz, Cz) or a number (e.g., F3, T4) is used to further clarify position. Odd numbers indicate left-sided placement, even numbers indicate right-sided placement, and the zed indicates a midline placement. A full 10-20 montage yields 19 EEG leads, but many modern laboratories have increased the recording montages to 32, 64, 128, and even 256 leads to more accurately depict the electrical activity across the scalp and, in some cases, to assist in determining the source within the brain, from which such signals originate (referred to as source localization).

The recording of the electrical activity from the brain is actually a comparison of signals from two electrodes. The signal that is *not* common to both electrodes is recorded (i.e., common signal is canceled out). What is actually measured, then, is the electrical or potential *difference* between two electrodes. It is worth noting a number of important terms with respect to the recording of such activity. An active electrode is an electrode placed over scalp areas where EEG generators are assumed to be (e.g., frontal cortex). An inactive electrode, on the other hand, is placed over a site that would not reflect a source of EEG, thus allowing for a neutral reference site (i.e., mastoid process, tip of nose, earlobes). In a bipolar recording, each recording channel is connected to two active electrodes. It is sometimes difficult to determine what each electrode contributes to the overall signal in such a montage. Monopolar recording, on the other hand, uses one active and one inactive electrode, thus allowing a more reasonable localization of electrical activity. For example, an electrode over the earlobe and an electrode over the left frontal region (F3) would yield a difference potential likely reflecting the activity present at the F3 site. Another important consideration in recording the EEG is the decision regarding which reference montage to use. A linked-ears reference, wherein the earlobes are electrically connected, is the most widely used. More recently, some have advocated the use of a mathematically derived average reference (Miller, Lutzenberger, & Ebert, 1991).

The collection of spontaneous EEG typically produces a large amount of data. The number of channels being examined further multiplies this amount. Historically, EEG was analyzed visually and quantified by the amount of time a particular frequency was present in the written record. With the advent of computer technology, sophisticated signal-processing techniques have been applied to the EEG signal. The EEG signal occurs in the microvolt range; thus it is very small and requires amplification before it is written to a data medium and stored. The analog EEG signal coming from the subject is amplified by a polygraph, and this signal is then converted to digital form via an analog-to-digital converter. This converter samples the analog signal at a chosen rate, typically determined via the Nyquist Theorem, which states that the signal should be sampled at least twice as fast as the highest frequency of interest in the signal (usually up to ~30 Hz). The EEG signal is usually sampled three to five times the highest frequency. One of the most common signal-processing techniques used in analyzing EEG data is the Fourier analysis, also referred to as spectral analysis or power spectral analysis. It is a time-series technique that decomposes a signal into various frequency components (see Hugdahl, 1995, for a more detailed description). The EEG data are also sometimes referred to as percentages of the power spectra, that is, how much of the total EEG signal is composed of frequencies in the alpha range (% alpha), beta range (% beta), etc. (see table 8.1 for a definition of these frequency bands).

The EEG has traditionally been divided into several groups based on frequency bandwidths, including delta, theta, alpha, and beta rhythms. These rhythms have been shown to have high test–retest reliabilities, suggesting that normal EEG may be treated as a stable intraindividual trait. Alpha is discussed in more detail here because most of the research to be considered later has examined this frequency range and it has important theoretical implications for understanding emotion or affect. The alpha rhythm is a regular waveform of characteristic frequency (7-13 Hz). The thalamus was regarded early on as the anatomical locus for the generation of alpha rhythms. That pyramidal cells in the cortex are kept in synchrony by pacemaker neurons in the thalamus is another possibility, among others. This connection is often referred to as the "thalamocortical" pathway. The involvement of nonthalamic cortical regions, wherein input to a particular brain region comes from other cortical regions via association fibers, is referred to as the "corticocortical" pathway (Hugdahl, 1995).

The traditional interpretation of the alpha rhythm is that it reflects behavioral awareness to a certain extent. Alpha activity is typically attenuated during arousal; thus the absence or reduction of alpha would be interpreted as indicative of greater cortical activation. It is often assumed that the presence of alpha activity is equivalent to relaxation or positive feelings or both, but this is certainly not always a valid assumption. Evidence has clearly shown that alpha activity can be unrelated to mood state. For example, Plotkin, Maczer, and Lowey (1976) demonstrated the lack of a relationship between mood and the amount of alpha produced. Lindholm and Lowry (1976) also showed no reliable relationship between the amount of alpha activity produced and subjective reports of mood state. In a study from the exercise domain, Boutcher and Landers (1988) actually showed the opposite relationship between alpha activity and state anxiety, with greater alpha being associated with greater anxiety. In essence, it cannot be assumed that EEG alpha reflects a particular subjective state. This highlights the need for multilevel analysis. It has not been reliably demonstrated that there is a one-to-one correspondence between the psychological and physiological domain in this regard. This is a point that will come up again and again in the exercise–EEG literature discussed in this chapter.

EEG Changes As a Result of Acute Exercise

The EEG has actually been used to examine changes in brain activity as a result of exercise for quite some time. One of the earliest studies in the exercise literature dates to 1958. Beaussart and colleagues examined EEG in boxers before and 6 to 10 min after boxing matches. There is very little detail of the actual methodology, but Beaussart, Niquet, and Beaussart-Boulenge (1958) noted EEG changes in 10 of the 18 cases they studied. Six of the boxers showed a clear alpha asymmetry, with increased amplitude in the right parietal region. Three boxers showed increased slow waves, and one showed a symmetrical depression of background EEG activity. With this study as a backdrop, the next section reviews what has now been over 40 years of EEG–exercise research.

Descriptive Research

In the more than 45 years since the first published work by Beaussart, Niquet, and Beaussart-Boulenge (1958), relatively few studies have reported on EEG activity as a consequence of an acute bout of exercise in humans. Many of these are often cited in discussions of affective change accompanying exercise (Dishman, 1992; Hatfield & Landers, 1983, 1987), in spite of the fact that very few actually assessed affective responses. A few exemplar studies are discussed next.

Pineda and Adkisson conducted one of the classic EEG–exercise studies in 1961. Graded treadmill exercise to exhaustion was used as the exercise stimulus, with durations ranging from 35 to 70 min because of individual variability in fitness levels. The EEG was assessed before and after exercise, recording from the left and right frontal, central, and occipital locations using a bipolar montage. Although Pineda and Adkisson did not statistically analyze their data, they did provide the raw data for each subject in the text of their paper. Secondary analysis of these data revealed the following: (a) a significant Hemisphere main effect, with a greater amount of "percent of alpha" and maximum amplitude of the EEG signal obtained in the left relative to the right hemisphere, and (b) a significant Time main effect, with a greater increase in percent alpha and greater maximum amplitude following exercise relative to preexercise for the frontal-central leads. Only the Time main effect (post- greater than preexercise) was significant for the central-occipital leads. Although objective, self-reported affect was not assessed, Pineda and Adkisson noted that the subjects were in a "median state of consciousness" (1961, p. 340) and that "in the subjective analysis of the person tested he was in a state of fatigue" (p. 338). Interestingly, four of the subjects showed greater activation (i.e., less alpha) in the left relative to the right frontal-central leads following the exercise bout; eight showed greater activation in the right relative to the left; and four subjects showed no change.

A few studies were conducted after the Pineda and Adkisson work (Hughes & Hendrix, 1968; Scheich & Simonova, 1971; Kamp & Troost, 1978; Farmer et al., 1978; Wagemaker & Goldstein, 1980), but the most often cited study was done by Wiese, Singh, and Yeudall (1983). Using variable-intensity cycle ergometer exercise lasting a total of 40 min (25 min at 40% $\dot{V}O_2$max, then 15 min at 60% $\dot{V}O_2$max), a significant increase in alpha (8-12 Hz) occurred from pre- to postexercise. There was also a significant change during exercise in the right/left hemisphere power ratios toward equality. The authors concluded:

> *Increased alpha power after exercise could contribute to an altered state of consciousness and could help explain the psychological benefits, including reductions in anxiety and depression, that have been reported with regular exercise. The R/L changes suggest a decrease in hemispherization in the cortex during exercise which could further facilitate an atmosphere for psychological change. (p. 117)*

Unfortunately, this work was never published as a journal article, existing only as a published abstract. Thus it is impossible to ascertain what the change in the power ratios entailed (e.g., increase in left coupled with decrease in right, decrease in left coupled with increase in right). In addition, given that no self-report measures were used, it is erroneous to assume that such EEG changes actually reflect what the subjects might have been experiencing (cf. Cacioppo & Tassinary, 1990). In spite of these limitations, this study is often used as evidence that a more positive psychological state results from acute exercise (cf. Hatfield, 1991).

Youngstedt et al. (1993) examined the effects of cycling exercise (in both thermoneutral and warm water) on EEG and state anxiety. Eleven males (26 ± 5.8 years) cycled for 20 min at 70% $\dot{V}O_2$peak. EEG was assessed at left and right occipital leads (O1, O2) along with state anxiety before and at 15 and 25 min postexercise. No hemisphere differences were observed. Percent of EEG in the alpha frequency band (8-12 Hz) showed significant increases pre- to 15 min postexercise, but returned to prevalues by 25 min postexercise. Percent of EEG in the beta frequency band (13-40 Hz) showed significant increases pre- to 15 min postexercise with further increases 15 to 25 min postexercise. It is important to note that no anxiety reduction was seen in the study and no significant relationships between EEG and anxiety were reported.

Mechau and colleagues (1998) reported a provocative study that examined exercise intensity issues and related changes in EEG. Subjects (17 males, 2 females) ran five or six discontinuous stages, with each successive stage increasing in velocity by 0.3 m/sec (0.3 yd/sec). The protocol was devised so that the first three stages would be run at an intensity below the individual's lactate threshold, while the remaining stages would result in increased lactate accumulation. Resting EEG was obtained before any exercise was undertaken; and within 1 min following each stage, 2 min of EEG was recorded. Interstage intervals ranged from 4.5 to 5.5 min. As heart rates (HR) increased from ~75 bpm at rest to ~135 bpm after Stage 1, increases were seen in alpha$_1$ spectral power (7.0-9.5 Hz) across all scalp sites, with large increases ($p < 0.001$) across all frontal sites (F3, F7, Fz, F4, F8). Following Stage 3 (HR ~155 bpm), a small ($p < 0.02$) increase in alpha$_1$ spectral power was seen, but only at the F7 site, compared to Stage 1. Following Stage 5 (HR ~175 bpm), which was associated with a blood lactate concentration of ~5.5 mMol/L, small decreases in alpha$_1$ spectral power were seen in F7 and F8 along with a medium ($p < 0.005$) decrease at F3, compared to Stage 3. It should be noted that such decreases would be interpreted as a relative increase in activation of that brain region. Finally, comparing EEG following Stage 5 with that seen after 15 min of recovery (HR ~95 bpm), there were again small decreases in alpha$_1$ spectral power at F7 and F8 coupled with small to medium decreases in alpha$_2$ spectral power (9.75-12.5 Hz) across all frontal sites.

Of particular interest is the fact that increases in alpha activity occurred during early, less intense stages of exercise, followed by decreases in alpha activity after intensities exceeded a certain threshold (i.e., lactate threshold). This is consistent with studies showing increases in cerebral blood flow at lower intensities with subsequent declines after intensities exceed the anaerobic threshold (Moraine et al., 1993). Although Mechau and colleagues (1998) do discuss the implications of these findings for affective changes that might occur with exercise, there are no data from this work to support such assertions. These findings were apparently replicated in a study by Sasaki (1998), wherein alpha spectral densities were lower at exercise intensities at and above the anaerobic threshold compared to exercise below this threshold.

Generally, the studies that have examined EEG–exercise relationships before and after aerobic exercise have shown an increase in EEG activity (operationalized in a variety of ways) following aerobic exercise, particularly in the slower frequencies (i.e., delta, theta, alpha). This conclusion is supported by the meta-analytic findings of Crabbe and Dishman (2004; see table 8.1). In addition to its predominantly atheoretical nature, however, this literature has been plagued by numerous methodological shortcomings that

Table 8.1   Average Effect Sizes for EEG–Exercise Studies Reported by Crabbe and Dishman (2004)

Frequency band	# of studies	# of ESs	Mean ES	95% CI	Fail-safe n
Alpha	18[b]	58	.54	.43-.65	96
Alpha$_1$ (~8-10 Hz)[a]	2	12	.75	.54-.97	33
Alpha$_2$ (~11-13 Hz)[a]	2	12	.57	.36-.78	22
Beta	10	28	.38	.23-.53	25
Beta$_1$ (~13-20 Hz)[a]	3	13	.70	.50-.89	33
Beta$_2$ (~21-30 Hz)[a]	3	13	.38	.18-.56	12
Delta (~1-3 Hz)	6	17	.50	.32-.68	26
Theta (~4-7 Hz)	8	20	.53	.36-.70	33

Fail-safe n refers to the number of additional null effects needed to attenuate the observed ES to a cumulative effect of 0.20. [a]These ESs derived from studies in which alpha, beta, or both were measured concurrently with other frequencies in the same study, as distinct from studies that measured only alpha or beta frequencies. [b]It is worth noting that this analysis includes a study by Fernhall and Daniels (1984) that has since been retracted as it contained questionable data. ES: Effect size; CI: Confidence interval.

make its interpretation difficult. Nevertheless, given relationships with other physiological parameters during exercise (e.g., cerebral blood flow), such increases seem consistent.

Weaknesses and Limitations in the Literature

Trying to find order in the chaos that is the EEG–exercise literature is difficult for a number of reasons. There has been little consistency regarding the EEG sites examined in EEG–exercise research; EEG has been variously assessed at different scalp sites across the relevant studies. Further, few studies have measured EEG activity at the same locations. Adding to the confusion, both monopolar and bipolar recording montages (when these are reported) have been used. When such basic information is not reported, it becomes difficult to determine any regional effects that exercise may (or may not) have.

An issue related to electrode site involves the rationale for the EEG site with respect to affect. In this regard, there is little theoretical support for the majority of the EEG sites that have been examined in the exercise–affect literature. For example, there is no reasonable rationale, theoretical or empirical, for expecting to see changes in occipital (i.e., posterior) brain areas concomitant with affective changes (recall the Youngstedt et al., 1993 study). Given the 25-year history of the Davidson model (Allen & Kline, 2004), examination of anterior brain locations (i.e., frontal, anterior temporal) makes theoretical sense for establish-

ing associations with affective processes (this is discussed in more detail later). Of the published studies, only those by Boutcher and Landers (anterior temporal; 1988), Pineda and Adkisson (frontal; 1961), Petruzzello and Landers (frontal; 1994), Kubitz and Mott (frontal, anterior temporal; 1996), Kubitz and Pothakos (frontal, anterior temporal; 1997), Petruzzello and Tate (frontal; 1997), Hall and Petruzzello (frontal; 1999), Hall et al. (frontal; 2000), Bixby, Spalding, and Hatfield (frontal; 2001), and Petruzzello, Hall, and Ekkekakis (frontal; 2001) have measured EEG at these anterior sites. It is also worth noting that in a number of studies (Bixby, Spalding, & Hatfield, 2001; Petruzzello & Tate, 1997; Petruzzello, Hall, & Ekkekakis, 2001), posterior EEG sites have also been examined, but activity at these brain regions was not related to any affective changes seen. This highlights the potential specificity of the brain activation–affect relationships.

It is also difficult to compare studies because a wide variety of exercise stimuli have been used, again with little consistency across studies. Cycle ergometry has been the most often used mode of exercise, with the remainder of the studies using running or a combination of walking and running. Exercise intensity has ranged from self-selected pace (Hangartner et al., 1994) to maximal aerobic capacity (Farmer et al., 1978). Intensity has also varied from percentages of heart rate maximum to percentages of maximal aerobic capacity. It is of interest that studies that have specifically examined intensities below and above the anaerobic threshold (e.g., Mechau et al., 1998) have revealed some potentially intriguing findings with respect to EEG–affect. Duration of the exercise stimulus has ranged from as short as 5 min to as long as 70 min. Given such inconsistencies with the various exercise components, it is difficult to make any definitive generalizations about the findings in this area.

Finally, and perhaps most importantly, most of the EEG–exercise studies have failed to provide corroborating self-report evidence that EEG alpha activity is associated with reduced anxiety or any other changes in affect. It remains to be demonstrated that EEG alpha activity is an index of exercise-related affective states. The implicit assumption in much of this work has been that the relationship between EEG alpha and anxiety (as the most common affective state examined) is invariant (cf. Cacioppo & Tassinary, 1990). As outlined by Cacioppo and Tassinary (1990), such a relationship exists when a physiological element (in this case, EEG alpha) is present *if and only if* a specific psychological element (anxiety, or lack thereof) is present. Although the traditional activation approach assumes that EEG alpha is reflective of a relaxed state, it needs to be shown that EEG alpha is actually a measure of exercise-related affect. In its simplest form, this would entail comparing EEG alpha to a valid criterion measure of affect. Until this has been done, making the assumption that exercise-related EEG alpha directly reflects improved affect (e.g., reduced anxiety) is strictly hypothetical. This is especially relevant since Boutcher (1986) reported a positive relationship between anxiety and EEG alpha activity (i.e., anxiety increased as alpha increased), and Hangartner and colleagues (1994) and Youngstedt and colleagues (1993) found no change in anxiety from pre- to postexercise even though changes were seen in brain activity. (A potential reason for the lack of concordance between EEG alpha and anxiety in these latter two studies could have been the inappropriate measurement site for EEG [i.e., occipital] with respect to affect.)

Failure to obtain an invariant relationship does not necessitate an abandonment of physiological measures. As Cacioppo and Tassinary (1990) have noted, a great deal of information can be obtained about psychological significance from physiological measures even if invariance does not exist. It is crucial to emphasize that, despite assumptions that changes in EEG activity reflect changes in some psychological construct, the psychological construct in question is rarely assessed in the same studies. Our level of knowledge is not at the stage where it is possible to ascribe psychological significance (affective or otherwise) based solely on measures of EEG activity.

A Model for EEG–Exercise–Affect Research

Although the case can certainly be made for examining the effects of exercise on the EEG (as a measure of brain activity), that alone is a fairly descriptive, single-level approach to understanding the role of the brain in the exercise–affect relationship. A more desirable approach would involve examination at multiple levels of analysis that integrates brain activity as well as, at the very least, some measure of self-reported affective response. There is a growing body of literature that consistently finds differential activation of the two hemispheres, specifically in anterior regions, with respect to affective states. Tucker and colleagues (1981) found that the frontal lobes differentiated between positive and negative affective arousal. Compared to what happened in the left hemisphere, they found relatively greater right frontal activation during negative emotion (i.e., induced depression). In examining EEG in response to positive and negative emotion-eliciting statements, Ahern and Schwartz (1985) found relatively greater activation (i.e., less alpha activity) in the left frontal area for positive versus negative statements. Davidson, Schaffer, and Saron (1985) examined the effects of lateralized presentations of happy, sad, and neutral faces on EEG asymmetries and self-reported affect. Subjects reported more positive affect when happy faces were presented to the left hemisphere (i.e., via the right visual field) than when the same faces were presented to the right hemisphere. Davidson, Schaffer, and Saron also found that frontal EEG asymmetry was significantly related to self-reported affect ($r = 0.74$), indicating that as anterior left hemisphere activation increased relative to the right (i.e., right frontal alpha activity increased), so did ratings of positive affect. Finally, Davidson and colleagues (1990) examined EEG asymmetry in response to film clips designed to elicit happiness and amusement (i.e., positive emotion) or disgust (i.e., negative emotion). Disgust was associated with relatively greater activation of the right frontal area, while happiness was associated with greater relative activation of the left frontal area.

Not only does evidence show that brain activation changes in response to emotion-eliciting events (i.e., state dependent), but resting EEG asymmetry has also been shown to be a state-independent index of an individual's predisposition to respond affectively. Henriques and Davidson (1990) were able to differentiate previously, but not currently, depressed subjects from never-depressed controls on the basis of resting anterior EEG asymmetry, with previously depressed subjects having greater activation in right relative to left anterior regions. Tomarken, Davidson, and Henriques (1990) showed that resting EEG asymmetry in frontal regions significantly predicted self-reported affective responses to film clips. Greater right frontal activation, relative to left, was associated with greater negative affective responses to negative film clips, with the effects being independent of mood ratings at the time of resting EEG assessment. Finally, Tomarken et al. (1992) demonstrated that resting EEG asymmetry was linked to dispositional measures of affect. Subjects with relatively greater left frontal activation reported more dispositional positive affect and less negative affect compared to subjects with relatively greater right frontal activation.

Appropriate Theoretical Frameworks

From the existing research, it is apparent that resting asymmetrical anterior brain activation (i.e., EEG asymmetry) can serve as a biological marker of affect and affective style (for reviews, see Davidson, 1992, 1993a, 1993b, 1994, 1995, 1998, 2003; Davidson & Irwin, 1999; Davidson et al., 1999). From this perspective, individual differences in hemispheric activation can serve both as a neurobehavioral substrate of affect (i.e., predisposing an individual to have generally positive or negative affect; Henriques & Davidson, 1990; Tomarken et al., 1992) and as a "neural threshold" for reactivity to affective stimuli (Tomarken, Davidson, & Henriques, 1990; Wheeler, Davidson, & Tomarken, 1993). Specifically, Davidson (1992) proposed a framework wherein anterior brain asymmetries reflect a basic neuroanatomical asymmetry implicated in the control of approach- and withdrawal-related behaviors. To approach or withdraw from a situation is a fundamental adaptive response, with approach behavior being associated with positive affect and withdrawal behavior being related to negative affect (Davidson, 1993a; Konorski, 1967). Greater left frontal activation relative to right is thus proposed to be associated with the approach system and positive affect, and greater right frontal

activation relative to left is associated with the withdrawal system and negative affect. Davidson (1993b) has suggested that the anterior regions of the brain may act as an emotion convergence zone that integrates emotional input and output.

In this framework, baseline measures of asymmetric anterior activation are associated with a propensity to experience positive or negative emotions, given the requisite environmental elicitors (Davidson, 1993a). Frontal EEG asymmetry is theorized to reflect a diathesis that, in conjunction with an emotion-eliciting stimulus of sufficient intensity, will result in a change in positive or negative affect appropriate to the emotion-eliciting stimulus. For example, individuals who show greater right relative to left frontal activation may currently be nondepressed, but may be more vulnerable to depression and may display more intense negative affect in response to negative affective elicitors (e.g., death of a loved one, watching a sad movie). Tomarken, Davidson, and Henriques (1990) demonstrated that resting frontal EEG asymmetry significantly predicted negative affective responses to film clips and global affective valence (positive affect minus negative affect). Additionally, there was a strong relationship between frontal asymmetry and fear responses to films. With these findings, the authors proposed that resting anterior asymmetry might be a state-independent index of an individual's predisposition to respond affectively. Similar results were obtained by Wheeler, Davidson, and Tomarken (1993), who showed that greater left frontal activation was associated with reports of more intense positive affect in response to positive film clips and that greater right frontal activation was associated with more intense reports of negative affect in response to the negative film clips.

There have been some attempts at modification and improvement of Davidson's basic model. For example, Heller (1993) proposed that because the right parietal region has been shown to reflect cardiovascular and autonomic arousal, affect might be further distinguished by an arousal component via parietal region activity. Thus, with the Heller extension, affective valence should be reflected by relative activation in the anterior regions, with affective arousal being reflected by activation of the parietal regions.

Theory-Based Exercise Research

Recall the work of Pineda and Adkisson (1961). It is always difficult to know what authors might mean, but it is interesting to speculate that the "median state of consciousness" that some subjects in their study were purported to be in may have occurred in those who showed greater relative left-sided activation on the frontal-central leads. Conversely, relatively greater right-sided activation may have been associated with those reporting "fatigue." In an effort to overcome the methodological inadequacies in the extant exercise–EEG literature, Petruzzello and Landers (1994) examined brain activation within the Davidson framework as a potential explanation for exercise-related changes in affect. Bilateral anterior (i.e., frontal) EEG alpha activity and state anxiety were assessed in 19 physically fit ($\dot{V}O_2$max = 54 ml · kg^{-1} · min^{-1}), right-handed males immediately before and at 5, 10, 20, and 30 min following a 30 min treadmill run at 75% of each subject's maximal aerobic capacity (i.e., $\dot{V}O_2$max).

Comparison of preexercise resting EEG to postexercise EEG revealed a shift in brain activation such that the left frontal area became more activated (i.e., less alpha) relative to the right. Significant reductions in anxiety also occurred at these times. The relationship between frontal asymmetry (right EEG alpha minus left EEG alpha; a higher value indicates relatively greater left-sided activation) and anxiety at each of the time periods was strongly negative ($r = -.70$), indicating that as the anterior left hemisphere became relatively more activated following exercise, anxiety decreased. Within-subject correlations examining the change in anxiety and changes in brain activation revealed predicted relationships for the right frontal area ($r = -.32$; as anxiety decreased from pre- to postexercise, alpha activity increased). Resting EEG asymmetry was also strongly related to trait anxiety ($r = -.61$), consistent with previous findings that resting brain activation can serve as a biological marker of dispositional affect (Tomarken et al., 1992). Finally, resting frontal asymmetry predicted postexercise anxiety responses, even when preexercise anxiety levels were controlled for ($\beta = -.57$). Thus, resting brain activation was a significant predictor of affective responsivity to an acute bout of exercise. This initial evidence suggested that the relationship between exercise and affect might be mediated in part by alterations in brain activation such that exercise results in greater activation of the anterior left hemisphere compared to the right. Such differential cardiovascular effects have already been noted (Davidson et al., 1981; Walker & Sandman, 1979, 1982; Zamrini et al., 1990). A limitation of this study, however, was

the inability to ascribe these changes directly to the exercise stimulus and not to some other factors, since no control condition was employed.

A second study (Petruzzello & Tate, 1997) was undertaken to replicate and extend the Petruzzello and Landers (1994) work. As the previous study could not rule out alternative explanations for the findings, and in an effort to examine the exercise stimulus more carefully, three conditions were used. Subjects ($N = 20$; 15 males, 5 females) were randomly assigned to either a control condition or one of two exercise conditions on separate days. The two exercise conditions differed in terms of intensity so that this variable could be examined. Thus, subjects either sat quietly on a bicycle ergometer for 30 min or cycled for 30 min at either 55% or 70% of their $\dot{V}O_2$max. As an important methodological feature of the study, subjects never knew which of the three conditions they would participate in on any given day until after baseline measures of EEG and affect were obtained. A number of important results emerged from this study. First, resting frontal EEG asymmetry was able to significantly predict unique variance in postexercise anxiety reduction at both 5 ($\beta = -0.57$) and 10 min ($\beta = -0.52$) postexercise, but *only* for the 70% condition. This not only replicates the earlier work, but also indicates that there is perhaps a dose–response effect for this phenomenon. This study also examined positive affective changes, thus extending the previous work into other affective domains. It was found that resting frontal EEG asymmetry significantly predicted unique variance in postexercise positive affect immediately upon cessation of exercise ($\beta = 0.48$). This again occurred only in the 70% intensity condition.

A more recent effort in this line of research has been to examine the extent to which aerobic fitness might mediate the brain activation–affective responsivity relationship. Petruzzello, Hall, and Ekkekakis (2001) examined EEG (right/left frontal and parietal sites) and affect in both "high-fit" (10 females: $\dot{V}O_2$max = 52 ml · kg^{-1} · min^{-1}; 12 males: $\dot{V}O_2$max = 58 ml · kg^{-1} · min^{-1}) and "low/moderate-fit" (20 females: $\dot{V}O_2$max = 42 ml · kg^{-1} · min^{-1}; 25 males: $\dot{V}O_2$max = 46 ml · kg^{-1} · min^{-1}) individuals before and after a 30 min treadmill run at an intensity of 75% $\dot{V}O_2$max. As with the prior studies, resting EEG asymmetry predicted postexercise affect, specifically an increase in activated pleasantness at 10 (24% unique variance), 20 (23%), and 30 min (17%). Importantly, this effect was mediated by fitness level, with the relationship being seen only in the high-fit group. These findings were interpreted as indicating that aerobic fitness influenced the relationship between resting anterior asymmetry and exercise-related affective responsivity. This study also revealed ongoing relations between EEG and affect during the postexercise recovery period. Specifically, at the next time point when it was assessed (e.g., post-10 asymmetry was related to post-20 energy), significant relationships were seen, and these relationships grew in strength over time. These relationships were significant even after preexercise energy was partialled out (this was done because preexercise energy was moderately correlated with each postexercise energy measure, r_s = .62-.68, p_s ≤ .001). In addition, frontal asymmetry was significantly related to concurrent energy at 10, 20, and 30 min postexercise, again with preexercise energy controlled for (partial r_s = .62, .60, and .61, p_s ≤ .005). These relationships were found only for energy and only in the high-fit group.

Researchers in other laboratories have seen similar findings using the same basic protocol. Bixby, Spalding, and Hatfield (2001) examined EEG and affect before, during, and following 30 min of cycle ergometer exercise at either a "low" intensity, corresponding to a workload at 75% of the observed ventilatory breakpoint (mean HR = 119 bpm, rating of perceived exertion [RPE] = 10), or a "high" intensity, corresponding to a workload at the ventilatory breakpoint (mean HR = 159 bpm, RPE = 14). EEG was recorded from multiple anterior sites (F3, F4, F7, F8) as well as parietal sites (P3, P4) using a Cz reference. Affect was assessed using both a single-item visual analog scale ("How is your mood right now?") and the Positive and Negative Affect Schedule (PANAS). There was a general increase in left-sided activation (as indicated by greater R/L ratio scores) along with increased positive affect scores on the PANAS during exercise compared to both baseline and recovery periods. Bixby, Spalding, and Hatfield noted that the observed asymmetry changes were significant only at the lateral-frontal sites (F8-F7) and not at the medial-frontal sites (F4-F3); however, the pattern was the same for both. It is also of note that there were no intensity differences, although inspection of the means presented in the paper reveals a somewhat greater increase in alpha activity in the low-intensity condition compared to the high-intensity condition. This is consistent with the findings of Mechau and colleagues (1998) discussed earlier given that the high-intensity condition occurred at the ventilatory breakpoint.

Other studies have failed to demonstrate the ability of resting frontal asymmetry to predict affective responses to exercise. Hall and colleagues (2000) were unable to find resting frontal asymmetry to be predictive of affective responses to a 10 min walk at a self-selected pace on a treadmill. These results were replicated on two separate days. It is worth noting, however, that resting frontal asymmetry did predict self-selected walking speed, with those having greater relative left-sided activation choosing a faster treadmill speed than those with greater relative right-sided activation. (This was interpreted in light of the fact that selecting a faster walking speed is indicative of greater approach motivation, a finding completely in line with the predictions of the theoretical model.) Additionally, VanLanduyt (1999) was unable to predict affective responses to a 30 min cycling session at 60% of predicted $\dot{V}O_2$max with resting frontal asymmetry. Petruzzello, Hall, and Ekkekakis (1999) found that resting EEG did predict affective responses following maximal exercise (via graded exercise test), but the EEG predicted changes in both tiredness and calmness. A number of recent studies has also examined the EEG–affect relationship in the exercise domain (Crabbe, O'Connor, & Dishman, 2002; Crabbe, Smith, & Dishman, 1999; He, Landers, & Lochbaum, 1999; Kubitz & Pothakos, 1998); but because these have not appeared in the peer-reviewed published literature yet (and the important details are inaccessible to us), it is difficult to evaluate them appropriately. It is encouraging, however, that more work of this type is being done.

Overall, what these studies show is that there appears to be a dose–response relationship in the ability of resting frontal asymmetry to predict affective responses to exercise. When low intensities of exercise are used (walking at a self-selected pace [Hall et al., 2000]; cycling at 55% $\dot{V}O_2$max [Petruzzello & Tate, 1997]; or cycling at 60% predicted $\dot{V}O_2$max [VanLanduyt, 1999]), the intensity of the stimulus does not appear to allow frontal asymmetry to predict affective responses. However, at higher intensities (cycling at 70% $\dot{V}O_2$max [Petruzzello & Tate, 1997]; running at 70% $\dot{V}O_2$max [Petruzzello & Landers, 1994]; running at 75% $\dot{V}O_2$max [Petruzzello, Hall, & Ekkekakis, 2001]; graded maximal exercise test [Petruzzello, Hall, & Ekkekakis, 1999]), frontal asymmetry is able to predict affective responses; and this appears to be influenced by fitness (Petruzzello, Hall, & Ekkekakis, 2001, 1999). The fact that there might be a dose–response relationship does not come as a surprise. Davidson (1998) wrote,

> there are probably intrinsic differences in certain components of emotional responding. There are likely individual differences in the threshold for eliciting components of a particular emotion, given a stimulus of a certain intensity. Thus, some individuals are likely to produce facial signs of disgust on presentation of a particular intensity of noxious stimulus, whereas other individuals may require a more intense stimulus for the elicitation of the same response at a comparable intensity. This suggestion implies the dose–response function may reliably differ across individuals. Unfortunately, systematic studies of this kind have not been performed, in part because of the difficulty in creating stimuli that are graded in intensity and designed to elicit the same emotion. (p. 309)

It is also worthwhile noting the instances of "state-dependent" relationships between ongoing EEG and affect. Recall that Petruzzello Hall, and Ekkekakis (2001) noted significant relationships between frontal asymmetry and self-reported energy (i.e., activated pleasant affect) during the postexercise recovery period. Thus, there is not only evidence that the relative activation balance at rest predicts affective responses to exercise; there is also evidence that such relationships hold when examined concurrently.

The lack of concordance in the findings at the various intensities of exercise is a bit puzzling. It is possible that frontal asymmetry predicts cognitively driven affective changes, but not affective changes that may be driven more by somatic-physiological responses. If such logic is correct, then in response to more physically demanding intensities (e.g., maximal exercise, like that seen at the end of a graded exercise test), at which affective changes are likely to be driven primarily by somatic-physiological factors (with cognitive factors likely playing a much reduced role), it makes sense that a relationship between EEG and affective change wouldn't necessarily be seen. If, as suggested earlier, EEG asymmetry can predict cognitively mediated affective responses, why doesn't EEG asymmetry predict affective responses to walking? Because there are affective changes that occur with low-intensity activity like walking, cognitive factors should be causing them. However, from correlational analyses that we have done, neither self-efficacy nor physiological variables seem to correlate with affect at low intensities. So, if not cognitive factors, then what?

While speculative, a number of observations are worth noting. Rowland (1998) has discussed the notion of an "activity-stat," a built-in biological mechanism that "makes" us move to maintain an energy balance. It could be that walking (or other low-intensity activities) makes us feel good because the activity-stat gives the activation associated with such activity some positive affective quality. If true, this would point toward a noncognitive mechanism. We (Ekkekakis, Hall, & Petruzzello, 2005) have also proposed the possibility that low-intensity activities (e.g., walking) and subsequent affective responses are generated primarily through subcortical mechanisms and thus a relative absence of cognitive mediation. Finally, it is also possible that affective responses to low-intensity activities may not be related to measures of peripheral physiological activity either because those measures examined to date (e.g., heart rate, oxygen uptake) have been irrelevant or have been influenced by a restriction of range, or because the most relevant physiological measures are central (but perhaps subcortical) and not peripheral. Obviously, the veracity of such possibilities awaits further research.

Directions for Future Investigation

A number of issues remain to be resolved. One of these involves determining the cause of the asymmetries. A number of viable alternatives are plausible, as discussed in the next section. It is also important, perhaps as much or more so, to integrate the findings from theoretically driven studies with what is known about brain function from both human and animal studies. Such integration can focus investigators as to what types of variables might be important to manipulate to isolate relevant as well as irrelevant aspects of the EEG–exercise paradigm. For example, while it is possible that the effects replicated in numerous studies for anterior brain regions in the alpha frequency range may indeed be localized to those regions, further study of other brain regions (e.g., posterior), as well as other frequency bands, will help to either eliminate other regions or frequencies from the realm of the possible or to show that they should indeed continue to be studied.

Potential Mechanisms Underlying Asymmetry

The findings from the recent exercise studies (Bixby, Spalding, & Hatfield, 2001; Petruzzello & Landers, 1994; Petruzzello & Tate, 1997; Petruzzello, Hall, & Ekkekakis, 2001), and the growing body of literature from Davidson and colleagues, are interesting in their own right. A fundamentally unanswered issue, however, concerns the mechanism underlying the differential hemispheric activation seen in both areas of research. In other words, as Davidson (1993b) has noted, "What is the reason for the asymmetry?" One potential explanation argues that the asymmetry is simply due to anatomical differences (Davidson, 1993). The electrical asymmetries noted at the scalp could be caused by asymmetrical differences in skull thickness. Davidson (1993) reports on work done in his lab that has essentially ruled this out. By comparing magnetic resonance image scans of subjects with extreme asymmetry scores, Davidson and colleagues have shown that structural differences cannot account for the electrical asymmetries. Other possibilities outlined by Davidson (1993) include genetic contributions and environmental influences, both of which might explain at least some of the variance in scalp-recorded asymmetries. Several possibilities have been examined in the exercise domain as well, including regional cerebral blood flow, activation of the amygdala, and changes in calcium levels in the brain. Each of these is briefly discussed next.

A number of other plausible mechanisms could be put forth to explain the differential hemispheric activation that has been shown in the more recent exercise–EEG studies. Cerebrovascular factors, notably cerebral blood flow (CBF), have been examined in response to both static and dynamic forms of exercise. Cerebral blood flow has been shown to increase with dynamic forms of exercise (Hollman et al., 1994; Jorgensen et al., 1992; Thomas et al., 1989), although this may be driven by factors beyond simple oxygen demands (Nybo & Secher, 2004). There is some evidence, however, showing that exercise above certain intensities (e.g., anaerobic threshold) results in declines of CBF back toward baseline values (Moraine et al., 1993). Sizable increases have been shown in anterior brain regions, particularly at higher intensi-

ties, in some studies (Herholz et al., 1987) but not in others (Jorgensen, Perko, & Secher, 1992). As EEG alpha has been shown to be related to CBF at rest (Okyere, Ktonas, & Meyer, 1986), it is possible that increased CBF as a result of dynamic (i.e., aerobic) exercise may drive EEG alpha activity during and following exercise. There is presently no evidence of differential CBF for the left versus right hemispheres specific to the frontal cortices (but see the work of Williamson et al. [1999, 2001], chapter 3 for differential CBF to insular cortices), so this possibility remains untested.

It is also possible that the differential activation may be driven by cardiovascular influence. The classic early work of Bonvallet, Dell, and Hiebel (1954) demonstrated that distension of the carotid sinus (in cats), which causes increased pressure, resulted in a shift in electrocortical activity from low-voltage fast-frequency to high-voltage slow-frequency activity. This would classically be interpreted as a change from beta activity to alpha activity. In essence, the increased pressure in the carotid sinus resulted in electrocortical inhibition. Rau and colleagues (1993) showed that baroreceptor manipulation altered electrical activity at the scalp, with the changes being greatest at the frontal electrode site. Koriath, Lindholm, and Landers (1987) essentially showed the same phenomenon during cycling exercise in humans. They examined the influence of changes in heart rate (induced via varying exercise loads on a bicycle ergometer) on EEG activity recorded from the center of the scalp (Cz). As heart rate increased from no exercise, to low exercise (94.6 bpm), to high exercise (122.6 bpm), EEG activity increased in slower-frequency bands. As with Bonvallet, Dell, and Hiebel (1954), it is possible that the increased heart rate, and resultant increase in blood pressure, served to inhibit electrocortical activity.

Zamrini and colleagues (1990) further highlighted the link between the cardiovascular and central nervous systems as well as demonstrated a differential effect for the two hemispheres. They showed a differential heart rate response to unilateral injections of sodium amytal. This procedure results in deactivation, or sedation, of one hemisphere but not the other. Following left hemisphere deactivation, heart rate increased from 83.6 to 85.8 bpm, whereas following right hemisphere deactivation the heart rate decreased from 83.8 to 81.4 bpm. The work of Walker and Sandman (1979) also showed different effects of the cardiovascular system on the cerebral hemispheres. They examined the influence of heart rate on evoked potentials recorded from the left and right hemispheres. Their findings indicated that changes in heart rate were more clearly shown in the right than in the left hemisphere. These findings suggest the possibility that the short-term effects of exercise influence the right hemisphere more than the left hemisphere, resulting in less activation of the right relative to the left. It is also possible that long-term exercise may make the right hemisphere more sensitive to cardiovascular influence and result in resting activation differences at the scalp. Although all of these studies are relevant and interesting, none specifically examined differences between left and right baroreceptor function and asymmetrical hemispheric effects.

When considered in total, the studies just outlined (and those discussed in the next section) provide the interesting possibility that there may indeed be differential activation of left and right hemispheric regions of the brain that could ultimately be reflected in the electrical activity recorded at the scalp. This possibility awaits not only future research on regional cerebral blood flow (rCBF), but also work that links rCBF to EEG changes.

The Amygdala Connection

It is also possible that the asymmetrical electrocortical effects are due to differences occurring in deeper, subcortical brain structures. A primary structure that has received a great deal of research focus is the amygdala. As Davidson (2003) notes, the amygdala has a role in directing attention to affective stimuli that have particular salience. The amygdala also issues "a call for further processing of stimuli that have major significance for the individual" (Davidson, 2003, pp. 656-657). In the exercise domain, recent animal work (in rats) has shown that local cerebral glucose utilization (LCGU) changes as a result of exercise. Vissing, Andersen, and Diemer (1996) demonstrated that LCGU increased approximately 35% during running at 85% $\dot{V}O_2$max in the central, lateral, and medial amygdala. This is important for a number of reasons. First, Schulz and colleagues (1996) have shown that discharge patterns of neurons in the central nucleus of the amygdala are related to both blood pressure fluctuations and cortical activity. Second, the amygdala is thought to be a key structure in extracting affective significance from external stimuli. Irwin and colleagues (1996) have shown bilateral amygdala activation using functional magnetic resonance imaging (fMRI),

with the changing valence of the affective stimuli being related to the asymmetrical activation, particularly in the prefrontal cortex. Together these findings show that the amygdala is an important brain structure for emotional integration, that activity in the amygdala is related to cortical activity, and that exercise can have a significant impact on amygdala activation. This could be an important avenue for future research to carefully explicate the relationships among these factors. It is also possible that these interactions might differ in more fit individuals, but again, more research is needed to better understand this connection.

The Calcium-Dopamine Hypothesis

Another potential explanation revolves around increases in calcium levels in the brain (Sutoo & Akiyama, 1996). Sutoo and Akiyama demonstrated that exercise leads to elevations in serum calcium levels followed in time by elevated levels of calcium in the mouse brain, particularly in the neostriatum and nucleus accumbens. Sutoo and Akiyama hypothesize that the increased calcium levels lead to increased synthesis of brain dopamine, which subsequently influences behavior, including psychological changes. They do caution that other catecholamine synthesis is driven by the calcium-calmodulin-dependent system. While this is intriguing, it is unknown to what extent elevated calcium levels in the brain relate to changes reflected in the EEG.

Interdisciplinary and Multi-Level Research

It is important to point out that such kinds of research increasingly will need to rely on work from other fields, perhaps most notably neuroscience. An excellent example of this type of work can be seen in Davidson's progression of research since its beginnings back in the late 1970s. His laboratory has been instrumental in pushing the envelope of research to include sophisticated neuroimaging techniques to delve further into important brain–affect questions. Davidson (2003) has recently outlined much of this recent work that not only utilized EEG methodologies but also incorporated both positron emission tomography (PET) and fMRI technologies. This allows (potentially) for convergence between what is seen at the scalp and what is occurring at deeper brain levels (e.g., subcortical structures like the amygdala). Admittedly, such technologies are difficult to effectively use in acute exercise–affect paradigms at present, but that does not mean that the situation will continue indefinitely. Exercise scientists are encouraged to collaborate with neuroscientists to continue developing methodologies and paradigms that will allow further understanding to develop.

Theoretical Framework

Perhaps the most important thing that needs to continue to happen in future research is to continue to build on existing knowledge and to do so from relevant theoretical perspectives. The most glaring aspect of previous research into EEG–exercise relationships has been its almost exclusive reliance on being *atheoretical*. The outcome of this research has been lots of data with relatively minimal psychologically substantive informational yield. Interesting facts have been uncovered, but they are not as substantial as those gleaned from the relatively few studies that have utilized a theoretical foundation. Incorporating Davidson's approach–withdrawal model has helped in furthering the understanding of EEG–affect in the exercise domain, and what has been learned can be used to help inform the model within the exercise context. Recent work by Harmon-Jones (2003) has also shown that EEG asymmetries in the frontal cortex may reflect motivational direction rather than affective valence (positive, negative). His findings present some potentially interesting methodological and theoretical possibilities for future research. Using existing theory, investigators have a road map that informs them about which sites to measure EEG from, what type of recording montage to use, what kind of psychological construct to examine, and how to interpret the results.

In general, future work should utilize concurrent EEG and fMRI where possible as well as incorporating animal models where possible. In the exercise domain, further examination of the psychological meaning of state-independent relationships needs to take place from a trait approach–withdrawal perspective. For example, traits like extraversion or the behavioral activation system could prove useful in furthering our understanding. Further investigation is also needed of the pattern of correlations between EEG and affective variables above a certain threshold (e.g., anaerobic threshold), as well as under such thresholds. It is also important for future investigations to examine fitness and training effects, as these might prove important in the exercise domain.

Conclusions

At the present time, a number of issues confront research in this area. It is no longer acceptable to "simply" measure EEG at some scalp locations before, during (when possible), and after exercise. At the very least, this needs to be coupled with the assessment of relevant affective variables. More importantly, future research needs to be couched within a theoretical framework. Such an approach not only will provide a road map leading to the relevant psychological and physiological variables, but also will advance the understanding of what the EEG changes might mean, under what conditions relationships between EEG variables and affective responses hold or do not hold, and where the research might go next.

References

Ahern, G.L., & Schwartz, G.E. (1985). Differential lateralization for positive and negative emotion in the human Brain: EEG spectral analysis. *Neuropsychologia, 23,* 745-756.

Allen, J.J.B., & Kline, J.P. (2004). Frontal EEG asymmetry, emotion, and psychopathology: The first, and the next 25 years. *Biological Psychology, 67,* 1-5.

Beaussart, M., Niquet, G., & Beaussart-Boulenge, L. (1958). EEG changes recorded in boxers immediately after the fight [abstract]. *Encephalography and Clinical Neurophysiology, 10,* 763.

Biddle, S.J.H., Fox, K.R., & Boutcher, S.H. (Eds.) (2000). *Physical activity and psychological well-being.* New York: Routledge.

Biddle, S.J.H., & Mutrie, N. (2001). *Psychology of physical activity: Determinants, well-being and interventions.* New York: Routledge.

Bixby, W.R., Spalding, T.W., & Hatfield, B.D. (2001). Temporal dynamics and dimensional specificity of the affective response to exercise varying of intensity: Differing pathways to a common outcome. *Journal of Sport and Exercise Psychology, 23,* 171-190.

Bonvallet, M., Dell, P., & Hiebel, G. (1954). Tonus sympathique et activite electrique corticale. *Electroencephalography and Clinical Neurophysiology, 6,* 119-144.

Boutcher, S.H. (1986). *The effects of running and nicotine on mood states.* Unpublished doctoral dissertation, Arizona State University, Tempe, Arizona.

Boutcher, S.H., & Landers, D.M. (1988). The effects of vigorous exercise on anxiety, heart rate, and alpha activity of runners and nonrunners. *Psychophysiology, 25*(6), 696-702.

Cacioppo, J.T., & Berntson, G.G. (1992). Social psychological contributions to the decade of the brain: Doctrine of multilevel analysis. *American Psychologist, 47,* 1019-1028.

Cacioppo, J.T., & Tassinary, L.G. (1990). Psychophysiology and psychophysiological inference. In J.T. Cacioppo & L.G. Tassinary (Eds.), *Principles of psychophysiology: Physical, social, and inferential elements* (pp. 3-33). New York: Cambridge.

Crabbe, J.B., & Dishman, R.K. (2004). Brain electrocortical activity during and after exercise: A quantitative synthesis. *Psychophysiology, 41,* 563-574.

Crabbe, J.B., O'Connor, P.J., & Dishman, R.K. (2002). Effects of cycling exercise on mood and brain electrocortical activity after sleep deprivation [abstract]. *Medicine and Science in Sports and Exercise, 34,* S93.

Crabbe, J.B., Smith, J.C., & Dishman, R.K. (1999). EEG and emotional response after cycling exercise [abstract]. *Medicine and Science in Sports and Exercise, 31,* S173.

Davidson, R.J. (1992). Anterior cerebral asymmetry and the nature of emotion. *Brain and Cognition, 20,* 125-151.

Davidson, R.J. (1993a). The neuropsychology of emotion and affective style. In M. Lewis & J.M. Haviland (Eds.), *Handbook of emotions* (pp. 143-154). New York: Guilford Press.

Davidson, R.J. (1993b). Parsing affective space: Perspectives from neuropsychology and psychophysiology. *Neuropsychology, 7,* 464-475.

Davidson, R.J. (1994). Asymmetric brain function, affective style, and psychopathology: The role of early experience and plasticity. *Development and Psychopathology, 6,* 741-758.

Davidson, R.J. (1995). Cerebral asymmetry, emotion, and affective style. In R.J. Davidson & K. Hugdahl (Eds.), *Brain asymmetry* (pp. 361-387). Cambridge, MA: MIT Press.

Davidson, R.J. (1998). Affective style and affective disorders: Perspectives from affective neuroscience. *Cognition and Emotion, 12,* 307-330.

Davidson, R.J. (2003). Affective neuroscience and psychophysiology: Toward a synthesis. *Psychophysiology, 40,* 655-665.

Davidson, R.J., Abercrombie, H., Nitschke, J.B., & Putnam, K. (1999). Regional brain function, emotion and disorders of emotion. *Current Opinions in Neurobiology, 9,* 228-234.

Davidson, R.J., Ekman, P., Saron, C.D., Senulis, J.A., & Friesen, W.V. (1990). Approach-withdrawal and cerebral asymmetry: Emotional expression and brain physiology. Part I. *Journal of Personality and Social Psychology, 58,* 330-341.

Davidson, R.J., Horowitz, M.E., Schwartz, G.E., & Goodman, D.M. (1981). Lateral differences in the latency between finger tapping and the heart beat. *Psychophysiology, 18,* 36-41.

Davidson, R.J., & Irwin, W. (1999). The functional neuroanatomy of emotion and affective style. *Trends in Cognitive Sciences, 3,* 11-21.

Davidson, R.J., Schaffer, C.E., & Saron, C. (1985). Effects of lateralized presentations of faces on self-reports of emotion and EEG asymmetry in depressed and non-depressed subjects. *Psychophysiology, 22,* 353-364.

Davidson, R.J., & Sutton, S.K. (1995). Affective neuroscience: The emergence of a discipline. *Current Opinion in Neurobiology, 5,* 217-224.

Dishman, R.K. (1992). Psychological effects of exercise for disease resistance and health promotion. In R.R. Watson & M. Eisinger (Eds.), *Exercise and disease* (pp. 179-207). Boca Raton, FL: CRC Press.

Dzewaltowski, D.A. (1994). Physical activity determinants: A social cognitive perspective. *Medicine and Science in Sports and Exercise, 26,* 1395-1399.

Ekkekakis, P. (2003). Pleasure and displeasure from the body: Perspectives from exercise. *Cognition and Emotion, 17,* 213-239.

Ekkekakis, P., Hall, E.E., & Petruzzello, S.J. (2005). Variation and homogeneity in affective responses to physical activity of varying intensities: An alternative perspective on dose-response based on evolutionary considerations. *Journal of Sports Sciences, 23* (5), 477-500.

Ekkekakis, P., & Petruzzello, S.J. (2000). Analysis of the affect measurement conundrum in exercise psychology: I. Fundamental issues. *Psychology of Sport and Exercise, 2,* 71-88.

Etnier, J.L., & Landers, D.M. (1995). Brain function and exercise: Current perspectives. *Sports Medicine, 19*(2), 81-85.

Farmer, P.K., Olewine, D.A., Comer, D.W., Edwards, M.E., Coleman, T.M., Thomas, G., & Hames, C.G. (1978). Frontalis muscle tension and occipital alpha production in young males with coronary prone (Type A) and coronary resistant (Type B) behavior patterns: Effects of exercise [abstract]. *Medicine and Science in Sports, 10*(1), 51.

Fernhall, B., & Daniels, F.S. (1984). Electroencephalographic changes after a prolonged running period: Evidence for a relaxation response [abstract]. *Medicine and Science in Sports and Exercise, 16,* 181.

Hall, E.E., Ekkekakis, P., Van Landuyt, L.M., & Petruzzello, S.J. (2000). Resting frontal asymmetry predicts self-selected walking speed but not affective responses to a short walk. *Research Quarterly for Exercise and Sport, 71,* 74-79.

Hall, E.E., & Petruzzello, S.J. (1999). Frontal asymmetry, dispositional affect, and physical activity in older adults. *Journal of Aging and Physical Activity, 7,* 76-90.

Hangartner, J.A., Dishman, R.K., DuVal, H.P., & Firth, M.R. (1994). Effects of walking on anxiety, blood pressure and brain electrocortical activity in older adults [abstract]. *Medicine and Science in Sports and Exercise, 26,* S139.

Harmon-Jones, E. (2003). Clarifying the emotive functions of asymmetrical frontal cortical activity. *Psychophysiology, 40,* 838-848.

Hatfield, B.D. (1991). Exercise and mental health: The mechanisms of exercise-induced psychological states. In L. Diamant (Ed.), *Psychology of sports, exercise, and fitness: Social and personal issues* (pp. 17-49). New York: Hemisphere.

Hatfield, B.D., & Landers, D.M. (1983). Psychophysiology: A new direction for sport psychology. *Journal of Sport Psychology, 5,* 243-259.

Hatfield, B.D., & Landers, D.M. (1987). Psychophysiology in exercise and sport: An overview. *Exercise and Sport Sciences Reviews, 15,* 351-387.

He, C., Landers, D.M., & Lochbaum, M. (1999). Resting frontal EEG asymmetric index and mood changes under different exercise intensities and durations [abstract]. *Medicine and Science in Sports and Exercise, 31,* S173.

Heller, W. (1993). Neuropsychological mechanisms of individual differences in emotion, personality, and arousal. *Neuropsychology, 7,* 476-489.

Henriques, J.B., & Davidson, R.J. (1990). Regional brain electrical asymmetries discriminate between previously depressed and healthy control subjects. *Journal of Abnormal Psychology, 99,* 22-31.

Herholz, K., Buskies, W., Rist, M., Pawlik, G., Hollmann, W., & Heiss, W.D. (1987). Regional cerebral blood flow in man at rest and during exercise. *Journal of Neurology, 234,* 9-13.

Hollman, W., Fischer, H.G., DeMeirleir, K., Herzog, H., Herholz, K., & Feinendegen, L.-E. (1994). The brain: Regional cerebral blood flow, metabolism, and psyche during ergometer exercise. In C. Bouchard, R.J. Shephard, & T. Stephens (Eds.), *Physical activity, fitness, and health* (pp. 490-503). Champaign, IL: Human Kinetics.

Hugdahl, K. (1995). *Psychophysiology: The mind-body perspective.* Cambridge, MA: Harvard University.

Hughes, J.R., & Hendrix, D.E. (1968). Telemetered EEG from a football player in action. *Encephalography and Clinical Neurophysiology, 24,* 183-186.

Irwin, W., Davidson, R.J., Lowe, M.J., Mock, B.J., Sorenson, J.A., & Turski, P.A. (1996). Human amygdala activation detected with echo-planar functional magnetic resonance imaging. *NeuroReport, 7,* 1765-1769.

James, W. (1899). Physical training in the educational curriculum. *American Physical Education Review, 4,* 220-221.

Jasper, H.H. (1958). The ten-twenty electrode system of the International Federation. *Electroencephalography and Clinical Neurophysiology, 10,* 371-375.

Jorgensen, L., Perko, M., Hanel, B., Schroder, T.V., & Secher, N.H. (1992). Middle cerebral artery flow velocity and blood flow during exercise and muscle ischemia in humans. *Journal of Applied Physiology, 72,* 1123-1132.

Jorgensen, L., Perko, M., & Secher, N.H. (1992). Regional cerebral artery mean flow velocity and blood flow during dynamic exercise in humans. *Journal of Applied Physiology, 73,* 1825-1830.

Kamp, A., & Troost, J. (1978). EEG signs of cerebrovascular disorder, using physical exercise as a provocative method. *Encephalography and Clinical Neurophysiology, 45,* 295-298.

Konorski, J. (1967). *Integrative activity of the brain: An interdisciplinary approach.* Chicago: University of Chicago Press.

Koriath, J.J., Lindholm, E., & Landers, D.M. (1987). Cardiac-related cortical activity during variations in mean heart rate. *International Journal of Psychophysiology, 5,* 289-299.

Kubitz, K.A., & Mott, A.A. (1996). EEG power spectral densities during and after cycle ergometer exercise. *Research Quarterly for Exercise and Sport, 67*(1), 91-96.

Kubitz, K.A., & Pothakos, K. (1997). Does aerobic exercise decrease brain activation? *Journal of Sport and Exercise Psychology, 19,* 291-301.

Kubitz, K.A., & Pothakos, K. (1998). Exercise and brain activation in individuals with and without Type II diabetes [abstract]. *Medicine and Science in Sports and Exercise, 30,* S128.

LeDoux, J. (1996). *The emotional brain: The mysterious underpinnings of emotional life.* New York: Simon & Schuster.

Lindholm, E., & Lowry, S. (1976). Alpha production in humans under conditions of false feedback. *Bulletin of the Psychonomic Society, 11*(2), 106-108.

Mechau, D., Mucke, S., Weiss, M., & Liesen, H. (1998). Effect of increasing running velocity on electroencephalogram in a field test. *European Journal of Applied Physiology, 78,* 340-345.

Miller, G.A., Lutzenberger, W., & Elbert, T. (1991). The linked-reference issue in EEG and ERP recording. *Journal of Psychophysiology, 5,* 273-276.

Moraine, J.J., Lamotte, M., Berre, J., Niset, G., Leduc, A., & Naeije, R. (1993). Relationship of middle cerebral artery blood flow velocity to intensity during dynamic exercise in normal subjects. *European Journal of Applied Physiology and Occupational Physiology, 67,* 35-38.

Nybo, L., & Secher, N.H. (2004). Cerebral perturbations provoked by prolonged exercise. *Progress in Neurobiology, 72,* 223-261.

Okyere, J.G., Ktonas, P.Y., & Meyer, J.S. (1986). Quantification of the alpha EEG modulation and its relation to cerebral blood flow. *IEEE Transactions in Biomedical Engineering, 33,* 690-696.

Petruzzello, S.J. (1999). Recent advances in mind/body understandings. In J. Rippe (Ed.), *Lifestyle medicine* (pp. 947-956). Malden, MA: Blackwell Science.

Petruzzello, S.J. (2001). Reflecting, recognizing and re-integrating. *Journal of Sport and Exercise Psychology, 23,* 265-267.

Petruzzello, S.J., Hall, E.E., & Ekkekakis, P. (1999). Regional brain activation as a biological marker of affective responsivity to maximal exercise [abstract]. *Medicine and Science in Sports and Exercise, 31,* S174.

Petruzzello, S.J., Hall, E.E., & Ekkekakis, P. (2001). Regional brain activation as a biological marker of responsivity to acute exercise: Influence of fitness. *Psychophysiology, 38,* 99-106.

Petruzzello, S.J., & Landers, D.M. (1994). State anxiety and exercise: Does hemispheric activation reflect such changes? *Medicine and Science in Sports and Exercise, 26*(8), 1028-1035.

Petruzzello, S.J., & Tate, A.K. (1997). Brain activation, affect, and aerobic exercise: An examination of both state-independent and state-dependent relationships. *Psychophysiology, 34,* 527-533.

Pineda, A., & Adkisson, M.A. (1961). Electroencephalographic studies in physical fatigue. *Texas Reports on Biology and Medicine, 19*(2), 332-341.

Plotkin, W.B., Mazer, C., & Lowey, D. (1976). Alpha enhancement and the likelihood of an alpha experience. *Psychophysiology, 13,* 466-471.

Rau, H., Pauli, P., Brody, S., Elbert, T., & Birbaumer, N. (1993). Baroreceptor stimulation alters cortical activity. *Psychophysiology, 30,* 322-325.

Rowland, T.W. (1998). The biological basis of physical activity. *Medicine and Science in Sports and Exercise, 30,* 392-399.

Sasaki, H. (1998). Effects of the exercise intensities standardized by anaerobic threshold on EEG and heart rate variability (in Japanese). *Hokkaido Igaku Zasshi, 73*(4), 327-341.

Scheich, H., & Simonova, O. (1971). Parameters of alpha activity during the performance of motor tasks. *Encephalography and Clinical Neurophysiology, 31,* 357-363.

Schulz, G., Knuepfer, M., Lambertz, M., Langhorst, P., & Stock, G. (1996). Relationship between rhythmic discharge patterns of neurons in the central nucleus of the amygdala, blood pressure fluctuations and cortical activity. *Journal of the Autonomic Nervous System, 57,* 158-162.

Sutoo, D., & Akiyama, K. (1996). The mechanism by which exercise modifies brain function. *Physiology and Behavior, 60,* 177-181.

Thomas, S.N., Schroeder, T., Secher, N.H., & Mitchell, J.H. (1989). Cerebral blood flow during submaximal and maximal dynamic exercise in humans. *Journal of Applied Physiology, 67,* 744-748.

Tomarken, A.J., Davidson, R.J., & Henriques, J.B. (1990). Resting frontal asymmetry predicts affective responses to films. *Journal of Personality and Social Psychology, 59,* 791-801.

Tomarken, A.J., Davidson, R.J., Wheeler, R.E., & Doss, R.C. (1992). Individual differences in anterior brain asymmetry and fundamental dimensions of emotion. *Journal of Personality and Social Psychology, 62*(4), 676-687.

Tucker, D.M., Stenslie, C.E., Roth, R.S., & Shearer, S.L. (1981). Right frontal lobe activation and right hemisphere performance. Decrement during a depressed mood. *Archives of General Psychiatry, 38,* 169-174.

VanLanduyt, L.M. (1999). *Unique approaches to exercise: Frontal asymmetry predicts consistent perceived arousal but variable affective valence.* Unpublished master's thesis, University of Illinois at Urbana-Champaign, Urbana, Illinois.

Vissing, J., Andersen, M., & Diemer, N.H. (1996). Exercise-induced changes in local cerebral glucose utilization in the rat. *Journal of Cerebral Blood Flow and Metabolism, 16,* P729-P736.

Wagemaker, H., & Goldstein, L. (1980). The runner's high. *Journal of Sports Medicine and Physical Fitness, 20,* 227-229.

Walker, B.B., & Sandman, C.A. (1979). Human visual evoked responses are related to heart rate. *Journal of Comparative and Physiological Psychology, 93,* 717-729.

Walker, B.B., & Sandman, C.A. (1982). Visual evoked potentials change as heart rate and carotid pressure change. *Psychophysiology, 19,* 520-527.

Wheeler, R.E., Davidson, R.J., & Tomarken, A.J. (1993). Frontal brain asymmetry and emotion reactivity: A biological substrate of affective style. *Psychophysiology, 30,* 82-89.

Wiese, J., Singh, M., & Yeudall, L. (1983). Occipital and parietal alpha power before, during and after exercise [abstract]. *Medicine and Science in Sports and Exercise, 15*(2), 117.

Williamson, J.W., McColl, R., Mathews, D., Ginsburg, M., & Mitchell, J.H. (1999). Activation of the insular cortex is affected by the intensity of exercise. *Journal of Applied Physiology, 87,* 1213-1219.

Williamson, J.W., McColl, R., Mathews, D., Mitchell, J.H., Raven, P.B., & Morgan, W.P. (2001). Hypnotic manipulation of effort sense during dynamic exercise: Cardiovascular responses and brain activation. *Journal of Applied Physiology, 90,* 1392-1399.

Youngstedt, S.D., Dishman, R.K., Cureton, K.J., & Peacock, L.J. (1993). Does body temperature mediate anxiolytic effects of acute exercise? *Journal of Applied Physiology, 74*(2), 825-831.

Zamrini, E.Y., Meador, K.J., Loring, D.W., Nichols, F.T., Lee, G.P., Figueroa, R.E., & Thompson, W.O. (1990). Unilateral cerebral inactivation produces differential left/right heart rate responses. *Neurology, 40,* 1408-1411.

9

Physical Activity and Neurotransmitter Release

Romain Meeusen, PhD

Exercise is a very powerful physiologic perturbation experienced by the human body. It requires major metabolic and cardiovascular adjustments to increase the supply of oxygen and fuels to the working muscles while maintaining internal homeostasis. At the same time, the central nervous system needs to be provided with sufficient glucose and oxygen to control these functions. Maintaining brain health and plasticity throughout life is an important public health goal, and it is increasingly clear that behavioral stimulation and exercise can help us to achieve it (Dunn & Dishman, 1991; van Praag, Kempermann, & Gage, 1999; Gross, 2000). Over the past decade, a number of studies on humans have shown the benefits of exercise on brain health and function, particularly in aging populations. Exercise participation has consistently emerged as a key indicator of improved cognitive function (Kubesch et al., 2003; Cotman & Berchtold, 2002).

But what is really happening in the brain during exercise? In contrast with research that has expanded our knowledge about the peripheral adaptations to exercise, studies relating exercise to brain neurotransmitter levels are scarce. Therefore, it is of interest to examine the effect of acute and chronic exercise on neurotransmitter release, since several motor functions, movement initiation, and control of locomotion, as well as emotions and cognitive functions, have been shown to be related to brain neurotransmitter systems (Meeusen & De Meirleir, 1995).

There are numerous levels at which central neurotransmitters can affect motor behavior, from sensory perception and sensory-motor integration to motor effector mechanisms. However, the crucial point concerns whether or not the latter changes trigger or reflect changes in monoamine release, since until now most studies have been done on homogenized tissue, which gives us no indication of the dynamic release of neurotransmitters in the extracellular space of living organisms (Meeusen & De Meirleir, 1995). This chapter focuses on the effects of exercise on neurotransmission, especially the influence of exercise on the monoaminergic systems.

Biosynthesis of Brain Monoamines

The biogenic amines include the catecholamines dopamine (DA), norepinephrine (NOR), and epinephrine (see figure 9.1), as well as the indolamine 5-hydroxytryptamine or serotonin (5-HT) (see figure 9.2). Tyrosine (TYR) is the common amino acid precursor of all catecholamines, while the precursor of serotonin is the essential amino acid tryptophan (TRP).

Monoaminergic neurons modulate a wide range of functions in the central nervous system (Dunn & Dishman, 1991; Meeusen & De Meirleir, 1995). Norepinephrine neurons are involved in cardiovascular function, sleep, depression, and analgesic responses; dopaminergic neurons are linked with motor function (Freed & Yamamoto, 1985; Meeusen & De Meirleir, 1995), and serotonergic activity is associated with pain, fatigue, appetite, and sleep (Dunn & Dishman, 1991; Jacobs & Fornal, 1993; Meeusen & De Meirleir, 1995).

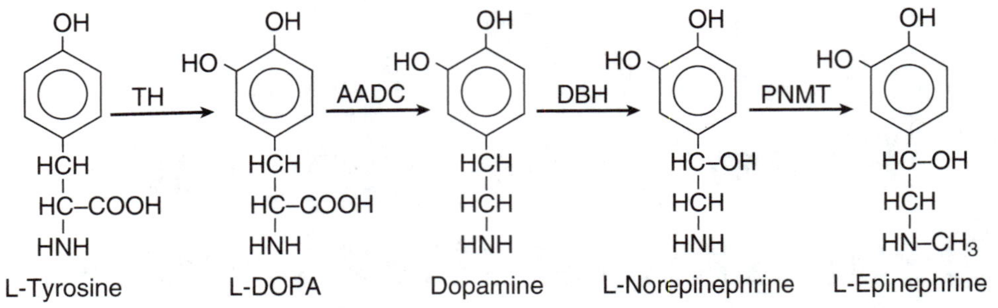

Figure 9.1 Catecholamine biosynthesis.

Reprinted, by permission, from R. Meeusen, S. Sarre, K. De Meirleir, G. Ebinger, Y. Michotte, 2003, "The effects of running speed and running duration on extracellular dopamine levels in rat striatum, measured with microdialysis," *Medicina Sportive* 7 (1): 29-36.

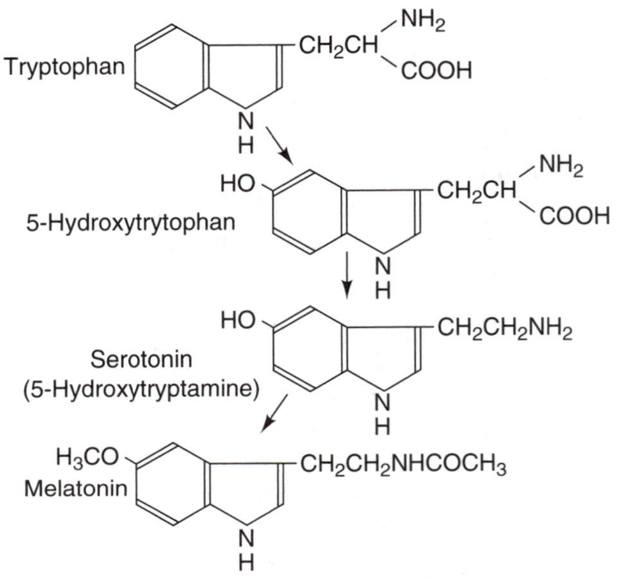

Figure 9.2 Indolamine biosynthesis.

The Effects of Physical Activity on Anxiety and Depression

Aerobic exercise seems to be effective in improving general mood and symptoms of depression and anxiety in healthy individuals and psychiatric patients (Brosse et al., 2002; Meyer & Broocks, 2000; Martinsen & Morgan, 1997). A variety of biological and psychosocial pathways have been hypothesized to mediate these effects. Brain neurotransmitter activity has been implicated in the regulation of cardiovascular (Ishide et al., 2000a, 2000b, 2003; Nauli et al., 2001) and endocrine (Chaouloff, 1993; Hand et al., 2002; Meeusen, 1999; Porter et al., 2004) responses during exercise; and it seems that of these neurotransmitters, the central monoamines are the strong candidates

as neurochemical supports for the mood-elevating and anxiolytic effects of exercise (Chaouloff, 1989). There is certainly an interaction between central 5-HT, NOR, DA, and physical exercise, and it has been suggested that altered brain monoamine activity explains the reductions in major depression and anxiety reported by humans after exercise (Brosse et al., 2002; Martinsen & Morgan, 1997; Raglin, 1997; Dunn & Dishman, 1991; Dishman, 1997a, 1997b; Chaouloff, 1989, 1997; Fulk et al., 2004; Meyer & Broocks, 2000). The recent progress in 5-HT receptor pharmacology has helped to define a portion of the mechanisms through which antidepressant and anxiolytic therapies exert their positive effects.

If depression is the result of low monoamine levels, then raising these levels should alleviate symptoms of depression in a matter of hours. However, clinical responses from antidepressant drugs generally are not observed for 10 to 20 days (Dishman, 1997b); this indicates that the antidepressant effects of these drugs (and probably also of exercise) involve chronic adaptations in neural regulation (Siever & Davis, 1985; Chaouloff, 1993). The role of monoamines in the functioning of specific brain regions and the hypothesis that monoamines play a key role in the positive effects of exercise on mood, suggest that central monoaminergic activity is affected by physical activity. It has been shown in animal studies that central dopaminergic, noradrenergic, and serotonergic activity, release, and metabolism are influenced by exercise (Meeusen & De Meirleir, 1995; Meeusen & Piacentini, 2001) and that training will produce specific adaptations in basal neurotransmitter output in rat striatum (Meeusen et al., 1997b). Thus, there is ample evidence that depression and anxiety are associated with altered central monoamine functioning and that exercise influences brain neurotransmitter levels.

Exercise and Brain Neurotransmitter Concentrations

The first reports on the influence of exercise on brain neurotransmitters appeared 40 years ago (Barchas & Freedman, 1963; Gordon et al., 1966; Moore & Larivière, 1964; Moore, 1986). These studies mostly used exercise as a stress model, or compared exercise with other stressors such as exposure to cold (Gordon et al., 1966), foot shock (Speciale et al., 1986), or tail pinch, immobilization, or restraint (Brown et al., 1992; Bliss & Aillion, 1971).

It is difficult to draw conclusions from these studies because there has been no uniformity in the methods used. Neurotransmitter concentrations in whole brain or brain regions are just an indication of the amount of neurotransmitter, and give us no information concerning neuronal activity. Receptor binding studies are not specific to one receptor type.

Furthermore, there has been no uniformity in study designs, exercise protocols, brain regions of interest, or measuring methods. Furthermore, the strains of animals used were different, with each strain having unique implications. But despite the great discrepancies in experimental protocols, the results indicate that there is evidence in favor of changes in synthesis and metabolism of monoamines during exercise.

Microdialysis

Because of shortcomings with postmortem methods and in part because of the desire to be able to directly relate neurochemistry to behavior, there has been considerable interest in the development of in vivo neurochemical methods. Total tissue levels may easily mask small but important neurochemical changes related to activity; it is therefore important to sample directly from the extracellular compartment of nervous tissue in living animals. Since the chemical interplay between cells occurs in the extracellular fluid, there has been a need to access this compartment in the intact brain of living and freely moving animals. Estimation of the transmitter content in this compartment is believed to be directly related to the concentration at the site where these compounds are functionally released: in the synaptic cleft. As measurements in the synapse are not yet possible, in vivo measurements in the extracellular fluid appear to provide the most directly relevant information currently available (Meeusen, Piacentini & De Meirleir, 2001 Westerink & Justice, 1991).

The idea of using the principles of dialysis to sample extracellular fluid has been continuously refined, and today it is applied in a large variety of experiments for bioanalytical sampling of substances from the brain and other tissues (Meeusen & Piacentini, 2001). The microdialysis technique employs the dialysis (from Greek, "to separate") principle in which a membrane, permeable to water and small solutes, separates two fluid compartments. The principle is based on the kinetic dialysis principle: The membrane is continuously flushed on one side with a solution that lacks the substances of interest, whereas the other side is in contact with the extracellular space. Provided that no osmolarity (pressure) or electrical potential differences exist across the membrane, solute transport between the two compartments is governed only by diffusion, that is, concentration gradients. A concentration gradient is created that causes diffusion of substances from the extracellular space into the dialysis probe (and vice versa).

A microdialysis probe is therefore a convenient way of introducing a dialysis tube into the tissue. A dialysis membrane is connected with in- and outlet tubings, allowing fluid to enter and leave the microdialysis probe. The continuous flow through the probe carries substances to the sampling site for further analysis. Because the dialysis probe is continuously flushed, the concentrations of substances in the dialysate (outflow solution) are only reflections of the true extracellular fluid (Meeusen, Piacentini, & De Meirleir, 2001).

Microdialysis makes it possible to sample continuously for hours or days in a single animal, which in addition to other advantages, decreases the number of animals needed in an experiment. Because the microdialysis probe may remain implanted in a single animal over a full experimental period, sampling via microdialysis can be used to reduce intersubject variation. This method can be used for recovering or introducing into the tissue endogenous or exogenous substances (or both). Microdialysis collects a representative sample of all substances in the extracellular fluid (provided that they pass through the membrane) and carries them out of the body for further analysis (Westerink & Justice 1991). The samples are relatively clean and ready for analysis, because large molecules (enzymes) do not pass through the membrane owing to its molecular cutoff weight (Meeusen, Piacentini, & De Meirleir, 2001).

Microdialysis and Behavior

A primary advantage of in vivo microdialysis is that it can be used to examine neurochemistry in behaving animals. Several kinds of behavior have been studied using microdialysis.

Many behaviorally induced changes in neurochemical output are subtle, that is, on the order of 20% to 50% of baseline levels. In contrast, pharmacologically induced changes typically range from 100% to 500% or more. In order to reliably interpret the results of behavioral studies it becomes important to establish very stable baseline levels upon which the effects of experimental manipulations can be assessed (Mark et al., 1991; Passetti et al., 2000). Baseline levels of serotonin and DA are known to be affected by several types of "disturbances" such as food deprivation (Pothos, Mark, & Hoebel, 1989) and of course circadian rhythms (Feenstra, Botterblom, & Mastenbroek, 2000; Stanley et al., 1989). Microdialysis studies can also help us to gain more insight into the daily variations in spontaneous transmitter release and help us to interpret various results.

Behavioral Studies

The list of different "types of behavior" that have been investigated is almost endless. Microdialysis provides a useful method for the study of extracellular neurotransmitters of conscious rats during active behavior (Kalen et al., 1989; Cenci & Kalen, 2000). Several experiments have indicated a role for neurotransmitter pathways in the mediation of a wide spectrum of behaviors, such as feeding and drinking (e.g., Voigt et al., 2000; Rada et al., 2000), orientation to sensory stimuli (e.g., Paredes et al., 1999), locomotion (e.g., Di Chiara, Morelli, & Consolo, 1994; Rada et al., 2000; Takahashi et al., 2000), and exploratory behavior and stress (for review: Westerink, 1995; Meeusen, Piacentini, & De Meirleir, 2001).

Several studies have been performed to examine neurotransmitter release in different brain regions during feeding behavior (e.g., Hernandez et al., 1991; Rada et al., 2000). Hernandez and colleagues (1991), for instance, examined hypothalamic serotonin in treatments for feeding disorders and depression. Hypothalamic serotonin increased significantly relative to that in controls in response to TRP loading, in the context of dietary control of 5-HT. Serotonin also increased significantly following the smelling of food and eating of a meal, in the context of food anticipation, satiety, and circadian rhythm (Hernandez et al., 1991). Chronic food deprivation and subsequent weight loss have been found to increase drug-seeking behavior and voluntary drug intake in animals. Chronic food deprivation may alter basal DA release in the nucleus accumbens (Pothos, Creese, & Hoebel, 1995).

Stress

The activation of central catecholaminergic systems by stressful stimuli has been the focus of many studies. Several studies have shown that brain increases in monoamines following stress are dependent on the form of stress used (Pei, Zetterström, & Fillenz, 1990). It is well established that exposure to stress increases the monoaminergic (e.g., Abercrombie et al., 1989; Finlay, Zigmond, & Abercrombie, 1995; Jedema & Moghaddam, 1994) and glutamatergic (e.g., Keefe, Zigmond, & Abercrombie, 1992; Moghaddam, 1993; Moghaddam et al., 1994) activity in several brain areas. Many acute stressors increase the extracellular concentration of NOR and DA in a number of brain regions, indicating that stress can elicit widespread activation of catecholaminergic neurons.

Cortical NOR and DA projections may represent a component of a globally activated catecholaminergic system that is responsible for stress-induced anxiety (Finlay, Zigmond, & Abercrombie, 1995; Inglis & Moghaddam, 1999). Norepinephrine release in the hippocampus has been reported to increase during immobilization stress or intermittent tail shocks, as well as during application of mildly stressful stimuli such as gentle handling of the animals or tail pinch (Cenci et al., 1992). Cenci and colleagues (1992) made a systematic comparison of changes in DA overflow in several brain regions during exposure to a wide variety of stimuli other than stress. They compared mild stressors such as handling or tail pinch with nonstressful, rewarded behavior, such as eating not preceded by food deprivation. Their results support the idea that mesocortical and mesostriatal DA systems are differentially regulated during ongoing behavior and that they respond quite differently to stressful and rewarding stimuli, and also that NOR release can be selectively activated in different cortical and striatal terminal subfields (Cenci et al., 1992). Animals are also confronted with repeated or prolonged exposure to stressors, and it is clear that exposure to chronic stress can alter an animal's response to subsequent stressors (Cadoni, Solinas, & Di Chiara, 2000; Gresch et al., 1994; Ronan et al., 2000).

Following the acute administration of amphetamine (AMPH), there is a marked dose-dependent increase in motor activity that is accompanied by a dose-dependent increase in the extracellular concentration of DA in both the nucleus accumbens and caudate nucleus (Zetterström et al., 1983; Robinson & Camp, 1990; Whishaw et al., 1992). The repeated, intermittent administration of cocaine produces a progressive enhancement in the behavioral response to subsequent exposure to cocaine, a phenomenon known as behavioral sensitization. As with psychostimulants, previous exposure to environmental stress, whether given repeatedly or as a single exposure, results in both behavioral sensitization and enhanced DA neurotransmission (Sorg & Kalivas, 1991). The striking similarities in the changes that are produced by stress and psychostimulant-induced sensitization have led to studies demonstrating behavioral and neurochemical cross-sensitization between these stimuli (Sorg & Kalivas, 1991). Until now, most of the studies on motor behavior were conducted to measure the effect of AMPH or other stimulants on the animals' locomotor activity. In these cases, intracerebral transmitter release was provoked by drugs, and the subsequent increase (or decrease) in locomotor behavior was measured. There is a possible interaction between DA and glutamate (GLU) in the nucleus accumbens in the initiation of locomotion (Di Chiara, Morelli, & Consolo, 1994; Boldry & Uretski, 1988; Boldry et al., 1991; Kalivas & Stewart, 1991; Wu, Brudzynski, & Mogenson, 1993). The relation between other transmitters and locomotion has also been examined (Di Chiara, Morelli, & Consolo, 1994; De Parada et al., 2000; Kretschmer, Goiny, & Herrera-Marschitz, 2000). Direct injection of excitatory transmitter agonists into several brain regions increases locomotion (Wu, Brudzynski, & Mogenson, 1993).

Activity State

There are substantial fluctuations in neurotransmitter release in freely moving animals that correlate with the activity state of the animals (Kalen et al., 1989; Jacobs & Reuter, 1995). Because animals are motorically more active during darkness than during the day, it is possible that the observed changes in neurotransmitter overflow are associated with the level of arousal or vigilance, or with gross body movements (Jacobs & Reuter, 1995). Systemic administration of a variety of 5-HT drugs, including precursors, agonists, and releasers, produces a motor syndrome in rats (Jacobs & Fornal, 1993). Its most conspicuous signs are hyperactiv-

ity, head shakes or "wet dog shakes," tremor, rigidity, hindlimb abduction, Straub tail, lateral head weaving, and reciprocal forepaw treading. This so-called 5-HT syndrome has served as an important research tool because it represents one of the few pure behavioral signs of central 5-HT activity (Jacobs & Fornal, 1993). Because brain 5-HT is thought to be important in a wide variety of behavioral (aggression, feeding, sleep) and physiologic (thermoregulation, cardiovascular control, glucoregulation) processes, several studies have examined 5-HT neuronal activity under a diversity of conditions.

Jacobs and his coworkers (1991, 1993, 1995) performed several studies to examine the electrophysiological activity of 5-HT neurons in a number of behavioral and environmental or physiological challenges. As predicted, extracellular 5-HT increased and decreased in parallel with behavioral state (Jacobs & Reuter, 1995). The results of these studies indicate that during periods of low motor activity, the activity of the 5-HT neurons may be suppressed (Jacobs, 1991). Since in some forms of depression there is a deficit in 5-HT neurotransmission, it could be beneficial for these patients to train their tonic motor activity. One of the possibilities is to engage in some form of repetitive locomotion such as walking, riding a bicycle, or jogging. These arguments are in agreement with the sometimes anecdotal information but also with other research data on the effects of exercise on depression. Jacobs (1991) states that since obsessive-compulsive disorders are a form of psychopathology in which 5-HT appears to play an important role, and reuptake inhibitors are often effective in the treatment of these disorders (and also of depression), it is likely that repetitive motor acts that increase 5-HT neuronal activity, such as exercise or locomotion, will activate brain 5-HT in a nonpharmacological manner.

Intracerebral Microdialysis During Exercise

The ability to accurately sample continuously the interstitial brain environment in vivo is a technical challenge not only for the neuroscientist (Bourne, 2003), but also for those studying neurochemical mechanisms behind brain functioning during exercise (Meeusen, Piacentini, & De Meirleir, 2001). Since its introduction into the study of the nervous system, microdialysis has become a popular tool for the measurement of brain chemistry. Researchers looking at possible neurochemical explanations for psychobiological phenomena have used microdialysis especially because of one of its features: The sample collected from the brain area of interest contains the various neurotransmitters and their metabolites, as well as metabolic precursors and waste products in transit between cellular components of the nervous system (Bourne, 2003).

Since the 1980s, microdialysis has been used extensively in studies correlating the time course of behaviors and events in brain chemistry; and beginning in the mid-1990s the possible effects of exercise on extracellular neurotransmitter levels have also been investigated. Most of the studies used treadmill walking (speed <10 m/min [<11 yd/min]) (e.g., Castaneda, Whishaw, & Robinson, 1990; Kurosawa et al., 1993; Sabol, Richard, & Freed, 1990; McCullough & Salamone, 1992; Bland, Gonzale, & Schallert, 1999; Westerink, 1995; Gerin, Becquet, & Privat, 1994; Gerin, Legrand, & Privat, 1995; Gerin & Privat, 1996, 1998) or running (speed >10 m/min) (e.g., Hattori, Li, Matsui, & Nishino, 1993; Hattori, Naoi, & Nishino, 1994; Meeusen et al., 1994, 1995, 1996, 1997b, 2003; Wilson & Marsden, 1996, Pagliari & Peyrin, 1995a, 1995b; Bequet et al., 2000) to measure the exercise effects on extracellu-

lar neurotransmitter concentrations. It was shown that in most brain regions the neurotransmitter levels increased, but that there seems to be a "threshold speed" above which neurotransmitter release begins (Meeusen, Piacentini, & De Meirleir, 2001).

It is clear that the running duration will also influence neuronal output; this has been demonstrated by several authors (Meeusen et al., 1994, 1995, 1996, 1997b, 2003; Pagliari & Peyrin, 1995a, 1995b). Pagliari and Peyrin (1995a, 1995b) used a chronic probe implantation in the frontal cortex. Norepinephrine turnover and release increased during exercise and even further increased when exercise time was prolonged to 2 hr of running.

In order to clarify the influence of different exercise protocols on extracellular DA levels in rat striatum, Meeusen and colleagues (2003) used groups of animals that ran at different speeds and for different running durations. The authors concluded that extracellular DA levels are more likely to be linked to the exercise duration than to exercise speed, and that the perturbation of extracellular DA levels lasts for a longer time period when exercise duration is longer (see figure 9.3).

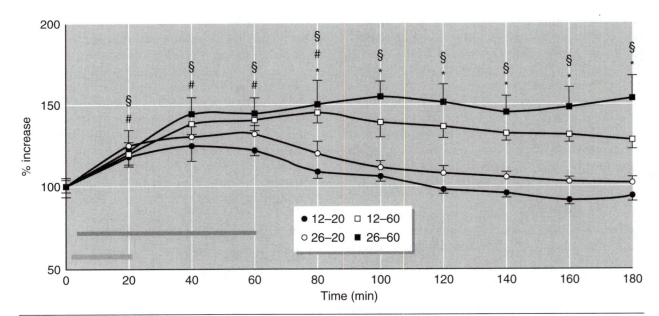

Figure 9.3 Extracellular dopamine levels in rat striatum during 20 or 60 min of exercise at two different speeds (12 or 26 m/min [13 or 28 yd/min]) and during the recovery from exercise. Extracellular DA levels increased significantly in all groups during and following exercise (i.e., until minute 80 for the short-duration groups and until the end of the experiment for the long-duration groups).

Bars indicate running duration: Open bar = 20 min of exercise; solid bar = 60 min of exercise. # Significant increase from baseline for the short-duration exercise ($p < .05$). § Significant increase from baseline for the long-duration exercise ($p < .05$). * Significant difference between the two 60 min duration and 20 min duration groups ($p < .05$).

Reproduced with the permission from Meeusen et al., 2003.

The effects of training on extracellular neurotransmitter levels were examined by Meeusen and colleagues (1997b). Male Wistars were randomly assigned to a training or control group. The exercise training consisted of running on a treadmill for six weeks, five days per week; running time and speed gradually increased from 30 min at 19 m/min (21 yd/min) during the first week to 80 min at 26 m/min (28 yd/min) during the final training week. Basal concentrations of DA, NOR, and GLU were significantly lower for the trained compared to control animals (see table 9.1). Sixty minutes of exercise significantly increased extracellular DA, NOR, and GLU levels in both control and trained animals, but there was no significant difference in the exercise-induced increase (expressed as percent increase above baseline) between trained and control animals. The results indicate that exercise training appears to result in diminished basal activity of striatal neurotransmitters while maintaining the necessary sensitivity for responses to acute exercise.

That prior physical conditioning greatly influences central NA response was shown by Pagliari and Peyrin (1995a, 1995b), since in their study 1 hr-trained rats experienced 2 hr running as extremely stressful whereas the 2 hr-trained animals exhibited a progressive sustained NA efflux.

Central Fatigue

Fatigue during prolonged exercise has traditionally been attributed to the occurrence of a "metabolic endpoint," at which muscle glycogen concentrations are depleted, plasma glucose concentrations are reduced, and plasma free fatty acid levels are elevated (Bailey, Davis, & Ahlborn, 1993a, 1993b; Meeusen & De Meirleir, 1995). But there is also a "central fatigue hypothesis," which is based on the assumption that the concentration of brain 5-HT increases during exercise (Newsholme, Acworth, & Blomstrand, 1987). Serotonin is a neurotransmitter that has been shown to induce sleep, depress motor neuron excitability, influence autonomic and endocrine function, and suppress appetite (Acworth, Nicolass, & Morgan, 1986; Blomstrand, Celsing, & Newsholme, 1988; Newsholme, Acworth, & Blomstrand, 1987). Since brain 5-HT synthesis depends on the plasma concentration of its precursor TRP, treatments that elevate plasma TRP will promote accelerated 5-HT synthesis, metabolism, or both (Chaouloff, 1993; Meeusen & De Meirleir, 1995). It is known from animal studies that cerebral serotonin content increases during prolonged exercise (Bequet et al., 2001; Chaouloff et al., 1985, 1986a, 1986b; Chaouloff, Laude, & Elghozi, 1987, 1989; Meeusen et al., 1996), and therefore it is hypothesized that central nervous system fatigue is associated with an increase in brain concentration of 5-HT.

In well-controlled laboratory experiments on animals and humans, the administration of branched chain amino acids (BCAA), utilized to reduce TRP entrance into the brain, failed to show positive effects on performance during prolonged exercise, while it is well known that carbohydrate supplementation enhances performance (Davis, Alderson, & Welsh, 2000), possibly by maintaining blood glucose homeostasis and therefore maintaining the "central drive" to working muscles during prolonged exercise (Nybo, 2003).

Central fatigue may thus be postponed by carbohydrate ingestion, mainly because glucose ingestion attenuates the exercise-induced rise in

Table 9.1 Basal Extracellular Neurotransmitter Levels in Striatum of Trained and Untrained Rats

	Control (n = 8)	Trained (n = 8)
DA (fmol · 20 min^{-1})	178.4 ± 32.6	57.1 ± 13.1*
NA (fmol · 20 min^{-1})	27.7 ± 6.1	8.3 ± 2.6*
GLU (mM · 20 min^{-1})	0.86 ± 0.179	0.28 ± 0.034*
GABA (mM · 20 min^{-1})	0.018 ± 0.004	0.019 ± 0.006

Dopamine (DA), Noradrenaline (NA) or norepinephrine, Glucose (GLU), Gamma-aminobutyric acid (GABA). Data are presented as means ± SEM. * $p < .01$ for comparison of trained vs. control animals.

Reprinted, by permission, from R. Meeusen, I. Smolders, S. Sarre, K. De Meirleir, H. Keizer, M. Serneels, G. Ebinger, and Y. Michotte, 1997, "Endurance training effects on striatal neurotransmitter release, an 'in vivo' microdialysis study," *Acta Physiol. Scand* 159: 335-341.

free TRP. Several studies also used microdialysis to clarify what really happens with 5-HT (and other neurotransmitters) during prolonged exercise. We examined whether exercise-elicited increases in brain TRP availability (and in turn 5-HT synthesis) alter 5-HT release in the hippocampus of food-deprived rats (Meeusen et al., 1996). We found that exercise stimulates 5-HT release in the hippocampus of fasted rats, and that a pretreatment with TRP (at a dose increasing extracellular 5-HT levels) amplifies exercise-induced 5-HT release. It should be noted that in this study none of the animals showed any sign of fatigue during the exercise session, although extracellular 5-HT levels increased markedly, especially in the TRP and exercise trial. Furthermore, since it was shown that during exercise 5-HT, DA, NOR, and GLU release increased in striatum (Meeusen et al., 1994, 1995), as did 5-HT release in hippocampus (Meeusen et al., 1996), without affecting the running capacity of the animals, the direct relationship between increased 5-HT release and fatigue could not be established.

In order to determine whether or not brain glucose could influence the brain 5-HT system, several other studies were performed. Wang and colleagues (2002) showed that after exhausting swimming, the concentration of glucose in hypothalamus decreased. Bequet and colleagues (2001, 2002) also used the microdialysis technique to monitor the effects of a direct injection of glucose in rat brain hippocampus on serotonergic metabolism during high-intensive treadmill running. Their studies demonstrate clearly that exercise induces changes in brain glucose and 5-HT levels. They also showed that brain glucose can act on serotonergic metabolism and thus can prevent exercise-induced increase of 5-HT levels. Taking into account the implications of brain 5-HT in central fatigue, they suggest that if glucose supplementation before and during exercise undoubtedly increased performance because of its peripheral positive action, it would have a negative impact on the quality of recovery after the end of the exercise. The fact that not only is 5-HT influenced during exhaustive exercise, but also the extracellular concentration of several amino acids increases (Zhang et al., 2001) and administration of L-valine can prevent the exercise-induced 5-HT increase (Gomez-Merino et al., 2001), supports the likelihood that serotonin is not the only neurotransmitter to explain the central fatigue hypothesis.

Because there were indications that brain neurotransmission is certainly influenced by exercise (Meeusen & De Meirleir, 1995; Meeusen, Piacentini, & De Meirleir, 2001), we performed several human studies in which brain NOR, dopaminergic, and serotonergic activity was manipulated (Meeusen et al., 1997a, 2001; Piacentini et al., 2002a, 2002b, 2004). In these studies we tried to affect exercise time by supplementing the subjects with a dopamine precursor (L-dopa) or a specific 5-HT$_{2a/2c}$ antagonist (Meeusen et al., 1997a), or by manipulating the central neurotransmitter systems through supplementation with fluoxetine (5-HT reuptake inhibitor; Meeusen et al., 2001), venlafaxine (combined 5-HT/NOR reuptake inhibitor; Piacentini et al., 2002a), reboxetine (NOR reuptake inhibitor; Piacentini et al., 2002b), and bupropion (DA reuptake inhibitor; Piacentini et al., 2004). Results showed that performance during the specific time trial was not influenced by the reuptake inhibitors; however, most of the hormones (peripheral output) showed a specific pattern that could be linked to central nervous system action.

Our recent microdialysis studies (Piacentini et al., 2003a, 2003b) confirmed the specific influence of these reuptake inhibitors on extracellular neurotransmitter levels in the hippocampus of rats, while peripheral hormones were also affected by the drugs. Due to the dual reuptake properties of the drugs and the mutual interaction of the different neurotransmitter systems, the observed effects on peripheral hormones are possibly mediated by a combined action of the neurotransmitter systems (Piacentini et al., 2003a, 2003b).

The results from these studies emphasize the importance of DA, NOR, and 5-HT (and probably other neurotransmitter) interactions during exercise. However, any possible role of these neurotransmitters in motor function should be perceived as a continuum. This continuum not only is important at the brain level, but also has its own importance in the interaction between central neurotransmission and the peripheral processes during exercise, including the neuroendocrine system, especially the activity of the hypothalamic pituitary adrenal (HPA) axis. Neurotransmitter systems not only influence each other but also are intimately linked to the HPA (Chaouloff, 1989; Meeusen & De Meirleir, 1995) because peripheral feedback modulates physiological and behavioral responses to stressors (Hand et al., 2002; Chaouloff, 1993; Porter et al., 2004).

Neurotransmission and Overtraining

To adjust the disturbance in resting homeostasis produced by an exercise stimulus, a number of regulatory systems are called upon to return the body to a new level of homeostasis. Principal among these is the central nervous system, which is capable of making very rapid adjustments to large segments of the body, and the endocrine system, which can have a more global and far-reaching effect but requires more time to respond (Mazzeo, 1991; Meeusen, 1999). The symptoms associated with overtraining, such as changes in emotional behavior, sleep disturbances, and hormonal dysfunctions, are indicative of changes in the regulation and coordinative function of the hypothalamus (Keizer, 1998). The HPA, together with the autonomic nervous system, is the most important stress system in the body. There is evidence that central serotonergic systems act upon the sympathetic nervous system and the HPA and that, reciprocally, glucocorticoids and catecholamines (derived from sympathetic nerves and the adrenomedulla) affect central serotonergic systems (Chaouloff, 1993). Norepinephrine is also linked to the regulation of the HPA, which is dysregulated not only in overtraining (Keizer, 1998) but also in conditions such as major depression and certain anxiety disorders (Chaouloff, 1997; Dishman, 1997a). In these conditions, glucocorticoids and brain monoaminergic systems apparently fail to restrain the HPA response to stress. Activation of the brain noradrenergic and serotonergic systems during stress is believed to increase the secretion of adrenocorticotropin hormone (ACTH) by stimulating the secretion of corticotrophin releasing hormone (CRH) (Plotsky, Cunninham, & Widmaier, 1989; Tuomisto & Mannisto, 1985). Furthermore, stress-induced CRH release within the central nucleus of the amygdala varies with the type of stressor (Hand et al., 2002). In pathological situations such as in major depression (Dishman, 1997b), and probably also in overtraining (Meeusen, 1999; Meeusen et al., 2004), the glucocorticoids and the brain monoaminergic systems apparently fail to restrain the HPA response to stress.

In overtraining it is assumed that a "maladaptation" to chronic exercise (and other) stress occurs. There is evidence that apart from other brain areas, the hippocampus downregulates the HPA in both rats and primates. Previously, we have analyzed the impact of streptozotocin (STZ)-elicited diabetes (a chronic stress for the body) on hippocampal extracellular 5-HT levels both under basal conditions and during restraint stress. Restraint stress is a procedure known to stimulate 5-HT synthesis/metabolism and release. In this microdialysis experiment, the chronic stress decreased hippocampal 5-HT metabolism, but did not alter baseline 5-HT release (compared to controls). Restraint stress increased extracellular 5-HT levels in controls, but did not increase 5-HT in the diabetic animals (Thorré et al., 1997). This might indicate that in the chronically stressed animals the central response to an acute stressor (restraint) is impaired. The examples cited previously illustrate that in several brain nuclei, chronic stress creates an adaptation mechanism (autoreceptor mediated, neurotransmitter interactions, or other mechanisms). When an animal is confronted with a novel stressful stimulus, a sensitization occurs. However, in chronic, very intense stress situations (as in STZ diabetes, where other peripheral hormonal mechanisms also play an important role), this sensitization of hippocampal 5-HT release does not occur. One might speculate that in overtraining (the step beyond coping with stress), a comparable mechanism occurs. Whether or not these results from a "nonexercise" chronic stress situation can be translated to another chronic stress scenario such as overtraining remains to be elucidated.

Several neurotransmitters might play an important role in the onset of the central dysfunctions that occur in the maladaptation to chronic exercise stress or overtraining. We are aware of the fact that this multifactorial disturbance in the onset of overtraining could give rise to more questions than answers, yet it is quite clear that several neurotransmitters and neuromodulators are involved in the disturbed adaptation to chronic exercise stress that we call overtraining.

Weaknesses and Limitations in the Microdialysis Literature

Neurotransmitters are released from neurons during a brief period following depolarization. In order to reach the microdialysis membrane, neurotransmitters released from the nerve terminals have to travel a relatively long distance in the extracellular space (Kehr, 1993; Di Chiara, 1990, 1991). The extracellular space is not simply a uniform volume of distribution of released neurotransmitters. Many events, such as efflux, the encounter with catabolic enzymes, and uptake and binding sites occur between the "release" of the transmitter substance and the recovery via the probe. These processes will affect the free concentration of the neurotransmitter and therefore the amount harvested through the probe. Neurotransmitters are present only in small amounts in the extracellular fluid, primarily due to the efficiency of clearing processes. When these clearing mechanisms change during ongoing behavior (e.g., fluctuations in blood flow), they might cause changes in the extracellular content of neurotransmitters (Westerink, 1995).

Conclusions

There is substantial evidence that individuals who engage in physical activity experience positive health effects, including both physiological and psychological benefits. Physical exercise may also have positive effects in mood disturbances, anxiety, and other psychiatric situations. The role of neurotransmitters in these exercise-induced mechanisms has been the subject of several studies. Until now, most studies have been performed on homogenized tissue, which gives us no indication of the dynamic release of neurotransmitters in the extracellular space of living organisms. Recently microdialysis was introduced to measure in vivo release of neurotransmitters in exercise science. This method can be used to collect virtually any substance from the brains of freely moving animals with a limited amount of tissue trauma. It allows the measurement of local neurotransmitter release in combination with ongoing behavioral changes such as exercise. Although the first results are very promising, researchers should be aware of possible discrepancies between studies. There is no uniformity in study designs, exercise protocols, brain regions of interest, and measuring methods. Many studies used other stressors in addition to running that could influence results.

The effects of exercise on neurotransmission should be explored in a multidimensional way because there is a constant interaction between several neurotransmitters and their respective receptors during locomotion. Many neurotransmitters or neuromodulators influence an individual's ability to exercise via actions in both the peripheral and central nervous system.

Directions for Future Investigation

We need to develop standard experimental strategies in order to examine the effects of exercise on brain functions. Neurotransmitter interrelationships are important since these interactions reflect the multidimensional image of the different processes that happen in the brain during exercise, training, and possibly overtraining.

The arguments we proposed in this chapter may illustrate the regrettable limitation of research in this field: Most investigations have attempted to concentrate on one or just a few aspects of the cascade of events that occur during exercise and training. Many questions remain to be answered regarding the hypothesized mechanisms of action and the physiological and psychological effects of endurance exercise.

What remains to be seen is how individual elements of the several neurotransmitters and neuromodulators contribute to this scheme: how modulation of pre- and postsynaptic receptors, coupled with rapid or delayed changes in transmitter synthesis and release, account for the behavioral and performance impact of a stress called exercise.

Finally, we need not look at the present research data as totally contradictory or inconsistent—the current state of the research probably just means that we are only at the beginning of the "age of the brain."

References

Abercrombie, E., Keefe, K., DiFrischia, D., & Zigmond, M. (1989). Differential effect of stress on in vivo dopamine release in striatum, nucleus accumbens, and medial frontal cortex. *Journal of Neurochemistry, 52,* 1655-1658.

Acworth, I., Nicolass, J., & Morgan, B. (1986). Effect of sustained exercise on concentrations of plasma aromatic and branched chain amino acids and brain amines. *Biochemical and Biophysical Research Communications, 137*(1), 149-153.

Bailey, S., Davis, J., & Ahlborn, E. (1993a). Neuroendocrine and substrate responses to altered brain 5-HT activity during prolonged exercise to fatigue. *Journal of Applied Physiology, 74*(6), 3006-3012.

Bailey, S., Davis, J., & Ahlborn, E. (1993b). Serotonergic agonists and antagonists affect endurance performance in the rat. *International Journal of Sports Medicine, 14*(6), 330-333.

Barchas, J., & Freedman, D. (1963). Brain amines: Response to physiological stress. *Biochemical Pharmacolology, 12,* 1232-1235.

Bequet, F., Gomez-Merino, D., Berthelot, M., & Guezennec, C.Y. (2001). Exercise-induced changes in brain glucose and serotonin revealed by microdialysis in rat hippocampus: Effect of glucose supplementation. *Acta Physiologica Scandinavica, 173,* 223-230.

Bequet, F., Gomez-Merino, D., Berthelot, M., & Guezennec, C.Y. (2002). Evidence that brain glucose availability influences exercise-enhanced extracellular 5-HT level in hippocampus: A microdialysis study in exercising rats. *Acta Physiologica Scandinavica, 176,* 76-79.

Bequet, F., Peres, M., Gomez-Merino, D., Berthelot, M., Satabin, P., Pierard, C., & Guezennec, Y. (2000). Simultaneous NMR microdialysis study of brain glucose metabolism in relation to fasting or exercise in the rat. *Journal of Applied Physiology, 88*(6), 1949-1954.

Bland, S., Gonzale, R., & Schallert, T. (1999). Movement related glutamate levels in rat hippocampus, striatum, and sensorimotor cortex. *Neuroscience Letters, 277*(2), 119-122.

Bliss, E., & Aillion, J. (1971). Relationship of stress and activity on brain dopamine and homovanillic acid. *Life Sciences, 10,* 1161-1169.

Blomstrand, E., Celsing, F., & Newsholme, E. (1988). Changes in plasma concentrations of aromatic and branched chain amino acids during sustained exercise in man and their possible role in fatigue. *Acta Physiologica Scandinavica, 133,* 115-121.

Boldry, R., & Uretsky, N. (1988). The importance of dopaminergic neurotransmission in the hypermobility response produced by the administration of *N*-methyl-D-aspartate into the nucleus accumbens. *Neuropharmacology, 27,* 569-577.

Boldry, R., Willins, D., Wallace, L., & Uretsky, N. (1991). The role of endogenous dopamine in the hypermobility response to intra-accumbens AMPA. *Brain Research, 559,* 100-108.

Bourne, J. (2003). Intracerebral microdialysis: 30 years as a tool for the neuroscientist. *Clinical and Experimental Pharmacology and Physiology, 30,* 16-24.

Brosse, A., Sheets, E., Lett, H., & Blumenthal, J. (2002). Exercise and the treatment of clinical depression in adults. Recent findings and future directions. *Sports Medicine, 32*(12), 741-760.

Brown, B., Piper, E., Riggs, C., Gormann, D., Garzo, E., & Dykes, D. (1992). Acute and chronic effects of aerobic and anaerobic training upon brain neurotransmitters and cytochrome oxidase activity in muscle. *International Journal of Sports Medicine, 13,* 92-93.

Cadoni, C., Solinas, M., & Di Chiara, G. (2000). Psychostimulant sensitization: Differential changes in accumbal shell and core dopamine. *European Journal of Pharmacology, 388*(1), 69-76.

Castaneda, E., Whishaw, I., & Robinson, T. (1990). Changes in striatal dopamine neurotransmission assessed with microdialysis following recovery from a bilateral 6-OHDA lesion: Variation as a function of lesion size. *Journal of Neuroscience, 10*(6), 1847-1854.

Cenci, A., Kalen, P., Mandel, R., & Bjorklund, A. (1992). Regional differences in the regulation of dopamine and noradrenaline release in medial frontal cortex, nucleus accumbens and caudate-putamen: A microdialysis study in the rat. *Brain Research, 581,* 217-228.

Cenci, M.A., & Kalen, P. (2000). Serotonin release from mesencephalic raphe neurons grafted to the 5,7-dihydroxytryptamine-lesioned rat hippocampus: Effects of behavioral activation and stress. *Experimental Neurolology, 164*(2), 351-361.

Chaouloff, F. (1989). Physical exercise and brain monoamines: A review. *Acta Physiologica Scandinavica, 137,* 1-13.

Chaouloff, F. (1993). Physiolopharmacological interactions between stress hormones and central serotonergic systems. *Brain Research Reviews, 18,* 1-32.

Chaouloff, F. (1997). The serotonin hypothesis. In W.P. Morgan (Ed.), *Physical activity and mental health* (pp. 179-198). Washington, DC: Taylor and Francis.

Chaouloff, F., Elghozi, J.L., Guezennec, Y., & Laude, D. (1985). Effects of conditioned running on plasma, liver and brain tryptophan and on brain 5-hydroxytryptamine metabolism in the rat. *British Journal of Pharmacology, 86,* 33-41.

Chaouloff, F., Kennett, G., Serrurier, B., Merino, D., & Curzon, G. (1986a). Amino acid analysis demonstrates that increased plasma free tryptophan causes the increase of brain tryptophan during exercise in the rat. *Journal of Neurochemistry, 46,* 1647-1650.

Chaouloff, F., Laude, D., & Elghozi, J.L. (1987). Brain serotonin response to exercise in the rat: The influence of training duration. *Biogenic Amines, 4,* 99-106.

Chaouloff, F., Laude, D., & Elghozi, J. (1989). Physical exercise: Evidence for differential consequences of tryptophan on 5-HT synthesis and metabolism in central serotonergic cell bodies and terminals. *Journal of Neural Transmission, 78,* 121-130.

Chaouloff, F., Laude, D., Guezennec, Y., & Elghozi, J.L. (1986b). Motor activity increases tryptophan, 5-hydroxyindoleacetic acid, and homovanillic acid in ventricular cerebrospinal fluid of the conscious rat. *Journal of Neurochemistry, 46,* 1313-1316.

Chaouloff, F., Laude, D., Meringo, D., Serrurier, B., & Guezennec, Y. (1987). Amphetamine and α-methyl-p-tyrosine affect the exercise induced imbalance between the availability of tryptophan and synthesis of serotonin in the brain of the rat. *Neuropharmacology, 26*(8), 1099-1106.

Cotman, C., & Berchtold, N. (2002). Exercise: A behavioural intervention to enhance brain health and plasticity. *Trends in Neurosciences, 25*(6), 295-301.

Davis, J.M., Alderson, N., & Welsh, R. (2000). Serotonin and central nervous system fatigue: Nutritional considerations. *American Journal of Clinical Nutrition, 72* (suppl.), 573S-578S.

De Parada, M.P., Parada, M.A., Rada, P., Hernandez, L., & Hoebel, B.G. (2000). Dopamine-acetylcholine interaction in the rat lateral hypothalamus in the control of locomotion. *Pharmacology, Biochemistry and Behavior, 66*(2), 227-234.

Di Chiara, G. (1990). In vivo brain dialysis for neurotransmitters. *Trends in Pharmacological Sciences, 11,* 116-121.

Di Chiara, G. (1991). Brain dialysis of monoamines. In T.E. Robinson & J.B. Justice (Eds.), *Microdialysis in the neurosciences* (pp. 175-185). Amsterdam: Elsevier Science.

Di Chiara, G., Morelli, M., & Consolo, S. (1994). Modulatory functions of neurotransmitters in the striatum: ACh/dopamine/NMDA interactions. *Trends in Neurosciences, 17*(6), 228-233.

Dishman, R. (1997a). Brain monoamines, exercise, and behavioral stress: Animal models. *Medicine and Science in Sports and Exercise, 29*(1), 63-74.

Dishman, R. (1997b). The norepinephrine hypothesis. In W.P. Morgan (Ed.), *Physical activity and mental health* (pp. 199-212). Washington, DC: Taylor and Francis.

Dunn, A., & Dishman, R. (1991). Exercise and the neurobiology of depression. *Exercise and Sport Sciences Reviews, 19,* 41-98.

Feenstra, M.G., Botterblom, M.H., & Mastenbroek, S. (2000). Dopamine and noradrenaline efflux in the prefrontal cortex in the light and dark period: Effects of novelty and handling and comparison to the nucleus accumbens. *Neuroscience, 100*(4), 741-748.

Finlay, J., Zigmond, M., & Abercrombie, E. (1995). Increased dopamine and norepinephrine release in medial prefrontal cortex induced by acute and chronic stress effects of diazepam. *Neuroscience, 64*(3), 619-628.

Freed, C., & Yamamoto, B. (1985). Regional brain dopamine metabolism: A marker for the speed, direction and posture of moving animals. *Science, 229,* 62-65.

Fulk, L., Stock, H., Lynn, A., Marshall, J., Wilson, M., & Hand, G. (2004). Chronic physical exercise reduces anxiety-like behaviors in rats. *International Journal of Sports Medicine, 25,* 78-82.

Gerin, C., Becquet, D., & Privat, A. (1995). Direct evidence for the link between monoaminergic descending pathways and motor activity: I. A study with microdialysis probes implanted in the ventral funiculus of the spinal cord. *Brain Research, 704,* 191-201.

Gerin, C., Legrand, A., & Privat, A. (1994). Study of 5-HT release with chronically implanted microdialysis probe in the ventral horn of the spinal cord of unrestrained rats during exercise on a treadmill. *Journal of Neuroscience Methods, 52,* 129-141.

Gerin, C., & Privat, A. (1996). Evaluation of the function of microdialysis probes permanently implanted into the rat CNS and coupled to an on-line HPLC system of analysis. *Journal of Neuroscience Methods, 66*(2), 81-92.

Gerin, C., & Privat, A. (1998). Direct evidence for the link between monoaminergic descending pathways and motor activity: II. A study with microdialysis probes implanted in the ventral horn of the spinal cord. *Brain Research, 794*(1), 169-173.

Gomez-Merino, D., Bequet, F., Berthot, M., Riverain, S., Chennaoui, M., & Guezennec, C. (2001). Evidence that the branched chain amino acid valine prevents exercise-induced release of 5-HT in rat hippocampus. *International Journal of Sports Medicine, 22*(5), 317-322.

Gordon, R., Spector, A., Sjoerdsma, A., & Undenfriend, S. (1966). Increased synthesis of norepinephrine and epinephrine in the intact rat during exercise and exposure to cold. *Journal of Pharmacology and Experimental Therapies, 153,* 440-447.

Gresch, P., Sved, A., Zigmond, M., & Finlay, J. (1994). Stress-induced sensitization of dopamine and norepinephrine in medial prefrontal cortex of the rat. *Journal of Neurochemistry, 63,* 575-583.

Gross, C. (2000). Neurogenesis in the adult brain: Death of a dogma. *Nature Reviews: Neuroscience, 1*(1), 67-73.

Hand, G., Hewitt, C., Fulk, L., Stock, H., Carson, J., Davis, M., & Wilson, M. (2002). Differential release of corticotrophin-releasing hormone (CRH) in the amygdale during different types of stressors. *Brain Research, 949,* 122-130.

Hattori, S., Li, Q., Matsui, N., & Nishino, H. (1993). Treadmill running test for evaluating locomotor activity after 6-OHDA lesions and dopaminergic cell grafts in the rat. *Brain Research Bulletin, 31,* 433-435.

Hattori, S., Naoi, M., & Nishino, H. (1994). Striatal dopamine turnover during treadmill running in the rat: Relation to the speed of running. *Brain Research Bulletin, 35*(1), 41-49.

Hernandez, L., Parada, M., Baptista, T., Schwartz, D., West, H., Mark, G., & Hoebel, B. (1991). Hypothalamic serotonin in treatments for feeding disorders and depression as studied by brain microdialysis. *Journal of Clinical Psychiatry, 52* (suppl.), 32-40.

Inglis, F.M., & Moghaddam, B. (1999). Dopaminergic innervation of the amygdala is highly responsive to stress. *Journal of Neurochemistry, 72*(3), 1088-1094.

Ishide, T., Hara, Y., Maher, T., & Ally, A. (2000a). Glutamate neurotransmission and nitric oxide interaction within the ventrolateral medulla during cardiovascular responses to muscle contraction. *Brain Research, 874*(2), 107-115.

Ishide, T., Mancini, M., Maher, T.J., Chayaikul, P., & Ally, A. (2000b). Rostral ventrolateral medulla opioid receptor activation modulates glutamate release and attenuates the exercise pressor reflex. *Brain Research, 865*(2), 177-185.

Ishide, T., Nauli, S., Mahler, T., & Ally, A. (2003). Cardiovascular responses and neurotransmitter changes following blockade of nNOS within the ventrolateral medulla during static muscle contraction. *Brain Research, 977*(1), 80-89.

Jacobs, B. (1991). Serotonin and behaviour: Emphasis on motor control. *Journal of Clinical Psychiatry, 52*(12, suppl.), 17-23.

Jacobs, B., & Fornal, C. (1993). 5-HT and motor control: A hypothesis. *Trends in Neurosciences, 16*(9), 346-350.

Jacobs, B., & Reuter, L. (1995). Changes in extracellular brain serotonin during the light/dark transition: Release is correlated with behavioural activity rather than the circadian cycle. *Society for Neuroscience Abstracts, 21*(3), 1691.

Jedema, H., & Moghaddam, B. (1994). Glutamatergic control of dopamine release during stress in the rat prefrontal cortex. *Journal of Neurochemistry, 63*, 785-788.

Kalen, P., Rosengren, E., Lindvall, O., & Björklund, A. (1989). Hippocampal noradrenaline and serotonin release over 24 hours as measured by the dialysis technique in freely moving rats—correlation to behaviour activity state, effect of handling and tail-pinch. *European Journal of Neuroscience, 1*, 181-188.

Kalivas, P., & Stewart, J. (1991). Dopamine transmission in the initiation and expression of drug- and stress-induced sensitization of motor activity. *Brain Research Reviews, 16*, 223-244.

Keefe, K., Zigmond, M., & Abercrombie, E. (1992). Extracellular dopamine in striatum: Influence of nerve impulse activity in medial forebrain bundle and local glutamatergic input. *Neuroscience, 47*(2), 325-332.

Kehr, J. (1993). A survey on quantitative microdialysis: Theoretical models and practical implications. *Journal of Neuroscience Methods, 48*, 251-261.

Keizer, H. (1998). Neuroendocrine aspects of overtraining. In R.B. Kreider, A.C. Fry, & M.L. O'Toole (Eds.), *Overtraining in sport* (pp. 145-167). Champaign, IL: Human Kinetics.

Kretschmer, B.D., Goiny, M., & Herrera-Marschitz, M. (2000). Effect of intracerebral administration of NMDA and AMPA on dopamine and glutamate release in the ventral pallidum and on motor behavior. *Journal of Neurochemistry, 74*(5), 2049-2057.

Kubesch, S., Bretschneider, V., Freudenmann, R., Weidenhammer, N., Lehmann, M., Spitzer, M., & Gron, G. (2003). Aerobic endurance exercise improves executive functions in depressed patients. *Journal of Clinical Psychiatry, 64*(9), 1005-1012.

Kurosawa, M., Okada, K., Sato, A., & Uchida, S. (1993). Extracellular release of acetylcholine, noradrenaline and serotonin increases in the cerebral cortex during walking in conscious rats. *Neuroscience Letters, 161*, 73-76.

Mark, G., Schwartz, D., Hernandez, L., West, H., & Hoebel, B. (1991). Application of microdialysis to the study of motivation and conditioning: Measurement of dopamine and serotonin in freely behaving rats. In T.E. Robinson & J.B. Justice (Eds.), *Microdialysis in the neurosciences* (pp. 369-388). Amsterdam: Elsevier Science.

Martinsen, E., & Morgan, W. (1997). Antidepressant effects of physical activity. In W.P. Morgan (Ed.), *Physical activity and mental health* (pp. 93-106). Washington, DC: Taylor and Francis.

Mazzeo, R. (1991). Catecholamine responses to acute and chronic exercise. *Medicine and Science in Sports and Exercise, 23*(7), 839-845.

McCullough, L., & Salamone, J. (1992). Involvement of nucleus accumbens dopamine in the motor activity induced by periodic food presentation. A microdialysis and behavioural study. *Brain Research, 592*, 29-36.

Meeusen, R. (1999). Overtraining and the central nervous system—the missing link? In M. Lehman, C. Foster, U. Gastmann, H. Keizer, J.M. Steinacker (Eds.), *Overload, performance incompetence, and regeneration in sport* (ch. 15, pp. 187-202). New York: Kluwer Academic/Plenum.

Meeusen, R., Chaouloff, F., Thorré, K., Sarre, S., De Meirleir, K., Ebinger, G., & Michotte, Y. (1996). Effects of tryptophan and/or acute running on extracellular 5-HT and 5-HIAA levels in the hippocampus of food-deprived rats. *Brain Research, 740*, 245-252.

Meeusen, R., & De Meirleir, K. (1995). Exercise and brain neurotransmission. *Sports Medicine, 20*(3), 160-188.

Meeusen, R., & Piacentini, M.F. (2001). Exercise and neurotransmission: A window to the future? *European Journal of Sport Science, 1*(1), 1-6 *(Electronic Journal ECSS)*.

Meeusen, R., Piacentini, M.F., Busschaert, B., Buyse, L., De Schutter, G., & Stray-Gundersen, J. (2004). Hormonal responses in athletes: The use of a two bout exercise protocol to detect subtle differences in (over)training status. *European Journal of Applied Physiology, 91*, 140-146.

Meeusen, R., Piacentini, M.F., & De Meirleir, K. (2001a). Brain microdialysis in exercise research. *Sports Medicine, 31*(14), 965-983.

Meeusen, R., Piacentini, M.F., Van Den Eynde, S., Magnus, L., & De Meirleir, K. (2001b). Exercise performance is not influenced by a 5-HT reuptake inhibitor. *International Journal of Sports Medicine, 22,* 239-336.

Meeusen, R., Roeykens, J., Magnus, L., Keizer, H., & De Meirleir, K. (1997a). Endurance performance in humans: The effect of a dopamine precursor or a specific serotonin antagonist. *International Journal of Sports Medicine, 18,* 571-577.

Meeusen, R., Sarre, S., De Meirleir, K., Ebinger, G., & Michotte, Y. (2003). The effects of running speed and running duration on extracellular dopamine levels in rat striatum, measured with microdialysis. *Medicina Sportiva, 7*(1), 29-36.

Meeusen, R., Sarre, S., Michotte, Y., Ebinger, G., & De Meirleir, K. (1994). The effects of exercise on neurotransmission in rat striatum, a microdialysis study. In A. Louilot, T. Durkin, U. Spampinato, & M. Cador (Eds.), *Monitoring molecules in neuroscience* (pp. 181-182). Proceedings of the 6th International Conference on in vivo Methods, September 17-20, Seignosse 'Les Tuquets,' Gradigan France PubliType.

Meeusen, R., Smolders, I., Sarre, S., De Meirleir, K., Ebinger, G., & Michotte, Y. (1995). The effects of exercise on extracellular glutamate (GLU) and GABA in rat striatum, a microdialysis study. *Medicine and Science in Sports and Exercise, 27*(5), S215.

Meeusen, R., Smolders, I., Sarre, S., De Meirleir, K., Keizer, H., Serneels, M., Ebinger, G., & Michotte, Y. (1997b). Endurance training effects on striatal neurotransmitter release, an "in vivo" microdialysis study. *Acta Physiologica Scandinavica, 159,* 335-341.

Meyer, T., & Broocks, A. (2000). Therapeutic impact of exercise on psychiatric diseases. Guidelines for exercise testing and prescription. *Sports Medicine, 30*(4), 269-279.

Moghaddam, B. (1993). Stress preferentially increases extraneuronal levels of excitatory amino acids in the prefrontal cortex: Comparison to hippocampus and basal ganglia. *Journal of Neurochemistry, 60,* 1650-1657.

Moghaddam, B., Bolinao, M., Stein-Behrens, B., & Sapolsky, R. (1994). Glucocorticoids mediate the stress-induced extracellular accumulation of glutamate. *Brain Research, 655,* 251-254.

Moore, K. (1986). Development of tolerance to the behavioural depressant effect of α-methyltyrosine. *Journal of Pharmacy and Pharmacology, 20,* 805-806.

Moore, K., & Larivière, E. (1964). Effects of stress and d-amphetamine on rat brain catecholamines. *Biochemical Pharmacology, 13,* 1098-1100.

Nauli, S., Mahler, T., Pearce, W., & Ally, A. (2001). Effects of opioid receptor activation on cardiovascular responses and extracellular monoamines within the rostral ventrolateral medulla during static contraction of skeletal muscle. *Neuroscience Research, 41,* 373-383.

Newsholme, E., Acworth, I., & Blomstrand, E. (1987). Amino acids, brain neurotransmitters and a functional link between muscle and brain that is important in sustained exercise. In G. Benzi (Ed.), *Advances in myochemistry* (pp. 127-138). London: John Libby Eurotext.

Nybo, L. (2003). CNS fatigue and prolonged exercise—effect of glucose supplementation. *Medicine and Science in Sports and Exercise, 35,* 589-594.

Pagliari, R., & Peyrin, L. (1995a). Norepinephrine release in the rat frontal cortex under treadmill exercise: A study with microdialysis. *Journal of Applied Physiology, 78*(6), 2121-2130.

Pagliari, R., & Peyrin, L. (1995b). Physical conditioning in rats influences the central and peripheral catecholamine responses to sustained exercise. *European Journal of Applied Physiology, 71,* 41-52.

Paredes, D., Rada, P., Bonilla, E., Gonzalez, L.E., Parada, M., & Hernandez, L. (1999). Melatonin acts on the nucleus accumbens to increase acetylcholine release and modify the motor activity pattern of rats. *Brain Research, 850*(1-2), 14-20.

Passetti, F., Dalley, J.W., O'Connell, M.T., Everitt, B.J., & Robbins, T.W. (2000). Increased acetylcholine release in the rat medial prefrontal cortex during performance of a visual attentional task. *European Journal of Neuroscience, 12*(8), 3051-3058.

Pei, Q., Zetterström, T., & Fillenz, M. (1990). Tail pinch-induced changes in the turnover and release of dopamine and 5-hydroxytryptamine in different brain regions of the rat. *Neuroscience, 35,* 133-138.

Piacentini, M.F., Clinckers, R., Meeusen, R., Sarre, S., Ebinger, G., & Michotte, Y. (2003a). Effect of Bupropion on hippocampal dopamine, serotonin and noradrenaline and on peripheral hormonal concentrations in the rat. *Journal of Applied Physiology, 95,* 652-656.

Piacentini, M.F., Clinckers, R., Meeusen, R., Sarre, S., Ebinger, G., & Michotte, Y. (2003b). Effects of Venlafaxine on extracellular 5-HT, dopamine and noradrenaline in the hippocampus and on peripheral hormonal concentrations in the rat in vivo. *Life Sciences, 73,* 2433-2442.

Piacentini, M.F., Meeusen, R., Buyse, L., De Schutter, G., & De Meirleir, K. (2002a). No effect of a selective serotonergic/noradrenergic reuptake inhibitor on endurance performance. *European Journal of Sport Science, 2,* 1-6 *(Electronic Journal ECSS).*

Piacentini, M.F., Meeusen, R., Buyse, L., De Schutter, G., & De Meirleir, K. (2004). Hormonal responses during prolonged exercise are influenced by a selective DA/NA reuptake inhibitor. *British Journal of Sports Medicine, 38,* 129-133.

Piacentini, M.F., Meeusen, R., Buyse, L., De Schutter, G., Kempenaers, F., Van Nijvel, J., & De Meirleir, K. (2002b). No effect of a noradrenergic reuptake inhibitor on performance in trained cyclists. *Medicine and Science in Sports and Exercise, 34*(7), 1189-1193.

Plotsky, P., Cunninham, E., & Widmaier, E. (1989). Catecholaminergic modulation of corticotropin-releasing factor and adrenocorticotropin secretion. *Endocrine Reviews, 10,* 437-458.

Porter, R., Gallagher, P., Watson, S., & Young, A. (2004). Corticosteroid-serotonin interactions in depression: A review of the human evidence. *Psychopharmacology, 173,* 1-17.

Pothos, E., Creese, I., & Hoebel, B. (1995). Restricted eating with weight loss selectively decreases extracellular dopamine in the nucleus accumbens and alters dopamine response to amphetamine, morphine and food intake. *Journal of Neuroscience, 15*(10), 6640-6650.

Pothos, E., Mark, G., & Hoebel, B. (1989). Dopamine release is reduced in the nucleus accumbens of underweight rats. *Society for Neuroscience Abstracts., 15,* 559.

Rada, P.V., Mark, G.P., Yeomans, J.J., & Hoebel, B.G. (2000). Acetylcholine release in ventral tegmental area by hypothalamic self-stimulation, eating, and drinking. *Pharmacology, Biochemistry and Behavior, 65*(3), 375-379.

Raglin, J. (1997). Anxiolytic effects of physical activity. In W.P. Morgan (Ed.), *Physical activity and mental health* (pp. 107-126). Washington, DC: Taylor and Francis.

Robinson, T., & Camp, D. (1990). Does amphetamine preferentially increase the extracellular concentration of dopamine in the mesolimbic system of freely moving rats? *Neuropsychopharmacology, 3,* 163-173.

Ronan, P.J., Steciuk, M., Kramer, G.L., Kram, M., & Petty, F. (2000). Increased septal 5-HIAA efflux in rats that do not develop learned helplessness after inescapable stress. *Journal of Neuroscience Research, 61*(1), 101-106.

Sabol, K., Richard, J., & Freed, C. (1990). In vivo dialysis measurements of dopamine and DOPAC in rats trained to turn on a circular treadmill. *Pharmacology, Biochemistry and Behavior, 36,* 21-28.

Siever, L., & Davis, K. (1985). Overview toward a dysregulation hypothesis of depression. *American Journal of Psychiatry, 142,* 1017-1031.

Sorg, B., & Kalivas, P. (1991). Effects of cocaine and footshock stress on extracellular dopamine levels in the ventral striatum. *Brain Research, 559*(1), 29-36.

Speciale, S., Miller, J., McMillen, B., & German, D. (1986). Activation of specific central dopamine pathways: Locomotion and footshock. *Brain Research Bulletin, 16,* 33-38.

Stanley, B., Schwartz, D., Hernandez, L., Hoebel, B., & Leibowitz, S. (1989). Patterns of extracellular 5-hydroxyindoleacetic acid (5-HIAA) in the paraventricular nucleus (PVN): Relation to circadian rhythm and deprivation-induced eating behaviour. *Pharmacology, Biochemistry and Behavior, 33,* 257-260.

Takahashi, H., Takada, Y., Nagai, N., Urano, T., & Takada, A. (2000). Serotonergic neurons projecting to hippocampus activate locomotion. *Brain Research, 869*(1-2), 194-202.

Thorré, K., Chaouloff, F., Sarre, S., Meeusen, R., Ebinger, G., & Michotte, Y. (1997). Differential effects of restraint stress on hippocampal 5-HT metabolism and extracellular levels of 5-HT in streptozotocin-diabetic rats. *Brain Research, 772,* 209-216.

Tuomisto, J., & Mannisto, P. (1985). Neurotransmitter regulation of anterior pituitary hormones. *Pharmacology Reviews, 37,* 249-332.

van Praag, H., Kempermann, G., & Gage, F. (1999). Running increases cell proliferation and neurogenesis in the adult mouse dendate gyrus. *Nature Neuroscience, 2,* 266-270.

Voigt, J.P., Kienzle, F., Sohr, R., Rex, A., & Fink, H. (2000). Feeding and 8-OH-DPAT-related release of serotonin in the rat lateral hypothalamus. *Pharmacology, Biochemistry and Behavior, 65*(1), 183-189.

Wang, L., Dong, Y., Shangguan, D., Zhao, R., Han, H., & Liu, G. (2002). Analysis of glucose and lactate in dialysate from hypothalamus of rats after exhausting swimming using microdialysis. *Biomedical Chromatography, 16*(7), 427-431.

Westerink, B. (1995). Brain microdialysis and its application for the study of animal behaviour. *Behavioural Brain Research, 70,* 103-124.

Westerink, B., & Justice, J. (1991). Microdialysis compared with other in vivo release models. In T.E. Robinson & J.B. Justice (Eds.), *Microdialysis in the neurosciences* (pp. 23-46). Amsterdam: Elsevier Science.

Whishaw, I., Fiorino, D., Mittleman, G., & Castaneda, E. (1992). Do forebrain structures compete for behavioural expression? Evidence from amphetamine-induced behaviour, microdialysis, and caudate-accumbens lesions in medial frontal cortex damaged rats. *Brain Research, 576,* 1-11.

Wilson, W., & Marsden, C. (1996). In vivo measurement of extracellular serotonin in the ventral hippocampus during treadmill running, *Behavioural Pharmacology, 7,* 101-104.

Wu, M., Brudzynski, S., & Mogenson, G. (1993). Functional interaction of dopamine and glutamate in the nucleus accumbens in the regulation of locomotion. *Canadian Journal of Physiology and Pharmacology, 71,* 407-413.

Zetterström, T., Sharp, T., Collin, A., & Ungerstedt, U. (1983). In vivo measurement of extracellular dopamine and its metabolites by intracerebral dialysis: Changes after d-amphetamine. *Journal of Neurochemistry, 41,* 1769-1773.

Zhang, D., Zhang, J., Ma, W., Chen, D., Han, H., Shu, H., & Liu, G. (2001). Analysis of trace amino acid neurotransmitters in hypothalamus of rats after exhausting exercise using microdialysis. *Journal of Chromatography: B, Biomedical Sciences and Applications, 758*(2), 277-282.

Physical Activity and Psychosomatic Health

The chapters in this section examine the relationship between exercise and various aspects of psychosomatic health, including cardiovascular health, immune system function, and pain. The central hypothesis that ties these chapters together is that exercise can lead to an adaptive pattern of response to various types of stressors, thus ultimately improving health and promoting well-being. Although exercise is often touted as a powerful stress management intervention in the popular press and stress relief is often cited in anecdotal reports as a reason for exercise participation, the general picture emerging from the research literature is one of considerable complexity and few definitive answers. The chapters in this section put the current knowledge base in perspective, summarizing what is known, pointing out what remains unclear, identifying factors that have been overlooked, and outlining directions for future research.

It could be argued that chapters 10 and 11, in particular, were developed to serve as starting blocks for a new phase of research into the exercise–stress connection, a phase characterized by hypotheses that are now, after more than two decades of research, considerably more mature and refined. In chapter 10, Mark Sothmann first sets the stage for the rest of this section by defining the concept of stress, presenting a historical overview of the stress field, and describing the cardiovascular and neuroendocrine responses associated with stress. He then offers a state-of-the-science review on the cross-stressor adaptation hypothesis, the idea that exercise-induced cardiovascular and neuroendocrine adaptations will also manifest themselves in responses to non-exercise (i.e., psychosocial) stressors. This critical review, focusing primarily on neuroendocrine reac-

tivity (i.e., the sympathetic adrenomedullary and hypothalamic-pituitary-adrenocortical systems), reveals several of the limitations of past research. These include the adherence to the notion of the nonspecificity of the stress response, the inattention to the modifiers of the stress response (such as habituation and sensitization), the lack of systematic investigations, and the problematic methods of experimental stress induction and response assessment. It is recommended that readers who are now beginning to explore this area of research consult contemporary overviews of the stress response (Chrousos, 1998; Tsigos & Chrousos, 2002) and the neuroendocrine responses to stress (Lovallo & Thomas, 2000; McEwen, 2001).

In chapter 11, Steve Boutcher and Mark Hamer focus on the effects of exercise on cardiovascular stress reactivity. They provide significant background information on the implications of stress reactivity for cardiovascular health and the methods of assessing cardiovascular reactivity. But the centerpiece of their analysis is a multifactorial model that takes into account the multitude of factors that account for variability in stress reactivity. As demonstrated in their review of the literature on the effects of exercise on cardiovascular stress reactivity, controlling for these sources of variability when examining exercise effects is critical, since the reactivity-dampening effects of exercise are likely to be larger when reactivity is exaggerated due to individual and situational differences. As useful companions to this chapter, readers might wish to consult texts on the function of the autonomic nervous system during stress (Jänig, 2003), the pathophysiology of cardiovascular disease (Lilly, 1997; Lusis, 2000), the role of stress in cardiovascular disease (Goldstein, 1995; Krantz & McCeney, 2002; Rozanski, Blumenthal,

& Kaplan, 1999; Stansfeld & Marmot, 2002), and the technical aspects of assessing cardiovascular responses (Brownley, Hurwitz, & Schneiderman, 2000; Stern, Ray, & Quigley, 2001).

In chapter 12, Suzi Hong and Paul Mills explore a relatively new and fascinating field, exercise psychoneuroimmunology (PNI). The development of this field is based on the premise that, since (a) immune function is affected by stress and is, to a large extent, under the influence of neuroendocrine modulation and (b) exercise could produce a more adaptive pattern of neuroendocrine responses to stress (see chapter 10), it follows that exercise could also lead to a more effective and resilient immune response to stress. This is yet another example of an area in which research has produced sobering evidence of the complexity of the issues involved. For example, two frequently echoed assumptions have been that cortisol has an immunosuppressive effect, whereas opioids have an immunoenhancing effect. There is now evidence that neither assumption is entirely accurate. Thus, exercise PNI is a field in transition, just beginning to contemplate the tremendous scope and difficulty of the task that lies ahead. It is also clear, however, that the early findings are promising and that the potential future payoff for health and well-being is enormous. To fully appreciate the effects of exercise, readers should have some understanding of the components (Westermann & Exton, 1999) and functions (Jacobs & Schmidt, 1999) of the immune system, endocrine–immune interactions (Mastorakos, Bamberger, & Chrousos, 1999; Schedlowski & Benschop, 1999), and the effects of stress on immunity (Biondi, 2001; Sanders, Iciek, & Kasprowicz, 2000; Uchino, Kiecolt-Glaser, & Glaser, 2000).

In chapter 13, Greg Hand, Ken Phillips, and Marlene Wilson examine exercise effects on the brain mechanisms involved in the initiation and coordination of the stress response. Their review covers such critical structures as the paraventricular nucleus of the hypothalamus (the initial link in the hypothalamic-pituitary-adrenocortical chain), the locus ceruleus (the origin of the brain's network of noradrenergic neurons), and the amygdala (point of integration of affective information in the brain, influencing both cardiovascular and neuroendocrine adjustments to stressful and emotional situations through connections with hypothalamic and medullary nuclei). Although the research on the effects of exercise on the central regulatory mechanisms of the stress response is a relatively recent endeavor, the emerging findings offer additional insights on the role of exercise in stress adaptation. As with other chapters that deal with brain mechanisms, a well-illustrated neuroanatomy text (e.g., Paxinos & Mai, 2003) will serve as a useful companion to this chapter. Readers might also benefit from additional overviews of the brain networks involved in responding to stress (Winters et al., 2000).

In chapter 14, Dane Cook examines the neuroanatomy and neurobiology of pain and presents a state-of-the-science review of the relationships betweeen physical activity and musculoskeletal pain. Pain is a significant public health problem, as it is one of the main factors affecting quality of life among various patient populations. Moreover, pain is a potential barrier to physical activity participation, particularly among persons who are elderly, those who are obese, and patients with muscular or skeletal problems (e.g., arthritis). Cook's review focuses on several aspects of pain exercise including the phenomenon of exercise-induced analgesia, a reliably established effect whose basis, however, remains unclear. Texts offering detailed coverage on the neuroanatomy, neurophysiology, and neuropharmacology of pain (Millan, 1999; Wall & Melzack, 1999) and the methods of pain assessment (Turk & Melzack, 2001) could serve as useful companions.

Suggested Background Readings

Biondi, M. (2001). Effects of stress on immune function: An overview. In R. Ader, D.L. Felten, & N. Cohen (Eds.), *Psychoneuroimmunology* (3rd ed., vol. 2, pp. 189-226). San Diego: Academic Press.

Brownley, K.A., Hurwitz, B.E., & Schneiderman, N. (2000). Cardiovascular psychophysiology. In J.T. Cacioppo, L.G. Tassinary, & G.G. Berntson (Eds.), *Handbook of psychophysiology* (2nd ed., pp. 224-264). Cambridge, UK: Cambridge University Press.

Chrousos, G.P. (1998). Stressors, stress, and neuroendocrine integration of the adaptive response: The 1997 Hans Selye memorial lecture. *Annals of the New York Academy of Sciences, 851,* 311-335.

Goldstein, D.S. (1995). *Stress, catecholamines, and cardiovascular disease.* New York: Oxford University Press.

Jacobs, R., & Schmidt, R.E. (1999). Foundations in immunology. In M. Schedlowski & U. Tews (Eds.), *Psychoneuroimmunology: An interdisciplinary introduction* (pp. 39-62). New York: Kluwer Academic.

Jänig, W. (2003). The autonomic nervous system and its coordination by the brain. In R.J. Davidson, K.R. Scherer, & H.H. Goldsmith (Eds.), *Handbook of affective sciences* (pp. 135-186). New York: Oxford University Press.

Krantz, D.S., & McCeney, M.K. (2002). Effects of psychological and social factors on organic disease: A critical assessment of research on coronary heart disease. *Annual Review of Psychology, 53,* 341-369.

Lilly, L.S. (Ed.) (1997). *Pathophysiology of heart disease* (2nd ed.). Philadelphia: Lippincott, Williams & Wilkins.

Lovallo, W.R., & Thomas, T.L. (2000). Stress hormones in psychophysiological research: Emotional, behavioral, and cognitive implications. In J.T. Cacioppo, L.G. Tassinary, & G.G. Berntson (Eds.), *Handbook of psychophysiology* (2nd ed., pp. 342-367). Cambridge, UK: Cambridge University Press.

Lusis, A.J. (2000). Atherosclerosis. *Nature, 407,* 233-241.

Mastorakos, G., Bamberger, C., & Chrousos, G.P. (1999). Neuroendocrine regulation of the immune process. In N.P. Plotnikoff, R.E. Faith, A.J. Murgo, & R.A. Good (Eds.), *Cytokines: Stress and immunity* (pp. 17-37). Boca Raton, FL: CRC Press.

McEwen, B.S. (Ed.) (2001). *Coping with the environment: Neural and endocrine mechanisms* (*Handbook of physiology,* sec. 7, vol. 4). New York: Oxford University Press.

Millan, M.J. (1999). The induction of pain: An integrative review. *Progress in Neurobiology, 57,* 1-164.

Paxinos, G., & Mai, J.K. (2003). *The human nervous system* (2nd ed.). San Diego: Elsevier Science.

Rozanski, A., Blumenthal, J.A., & Kaplan, J. (1999). Impact of psychological factors on the pathogenesis of cardiovascular disease and implications for therapy. *Circulation, 99,* 2192-2217.

Sanders, V.M., Iciek, L., & Kasprowicz, D.J. (2000). Psychosocial factors and humoral immunity. In J.T. Cacioppo, L.G. Tassinary, & G.G. Berntson (Eds.), *Handbook of psychophysiology* (2nd ed., pp. 425-455). Cambridge, UK: Cambridge University Press.

Schedlowski, M., & Benschop, R.J. (1999). Neuroendocrine system and immune functions. In M. Schedlowski & U. Tews (Eds.), *Psychoneuroimmunology: An interdisciplinary introduction* (pp. 185-207). New York: Kluwer Academic.

Stansfeld, S.A., & Marmot, M.G. (Eds.) (2002). *Stress and the heart: Psychosocial pathways to coronary heart disease.* London: BMJ.

Stern, R.M., Ray, W.J., & Quigley, K.S. (2001). *Psychophysiological recording* (2nd ed.). New York: Oxford University Press.

Tsigos, C., & Chrousos, G.P. (2002). Hypothalamic-pituitary-adrenal axis, neuroendocrine factors and stress. *Journal of Psychosomatic Research, 53,* 865-871.

Turk, D.C., & Melzack, R. (Eds.) (2001). *Handbook of pain assessment* (2nd ed.). New York: Guilford Press.

Uchino, B.N., Kiecolt-Glaser, J.K., & Glaser, R. (2000). Psychological modulation of cellular immunity. In J.T. Cacioppo, L.G. Tassinary, & G.G. Berntson (Eds.), *Handbook of psychophysiology* (2nd ed., pp. 397-424). Cambridge, UK: Cambridge University Press.

Wall, P.D., & Melzack, R. (Eds.) (1999). *Textbook of pain* (4th ed.). New York: Churchill Livingstone.

Westermann, J., & Exton, M.S. (1999). Functional anatomy of the immune system. In M. Schedlowski & U. Tews (Eds.), *Psychoneuroimmunology: An interdisciplinary introduction* (pp. 1-37). New York: Kluwer Academic.

Winters, R.W., McCabe, P.M., Green, E.J., & Schneiderman, N. (2000). Stress responses, coping, and cardiovascular neurobiology: Central nervous system circuitry underlying learned and unlearned affective responses to stressful stimuli. In P.M. McCabe, N. Schneiderman, T. Field, & A.R. Wellens (Eds.), *Stress, coping, and cardiovascular disease* (pp. 1-49). Mahwah, NJ: Erlbaum.

10

The Cross-Stressor Adaptation Hypothesis and Exercise Training

Mark S. Sothmann, PhD

Epidemiological research conducted over the last 30 years has clearly linked the incidence of numerous chronic diseases to lifestyle experiences of which "stress" is considered to be one precipitating factor (Heuser & Lammers, 2003; Rossi, 2003). The stress concept for health and disease is so pervasive that the World Health Organization Global Burden of Disease Survey estimates that stress-related disorders will be the second leading cause of disabilities by the year 2020 (Murray & Lopez, 1996). Moreover, economic studies estimate that disability caused by stress is just as great as disability caused by workplace accidents (Kalia, 2002). These trends clearly indicate that the stress concept, as well as its relationship to chronic illness and economic well-being, is very much alive and growing.

An important line of research concentrates on hypothesized intervention strategies that may alleviate stress and thus have beneficial outcomes for associated chronic illnesses. Such interventions have included, but are not limited to, counseling on perceived control and anger expression, social adjustment including developing support systems or altering the environment, pharmacological treatments, and nutrition (Gerber et al., 2003; Kamarck, Peterman, & Raynor, 1998; Pincus, 2001). Along this line, there is increasingly clear evidence that frequent physical activity is one lifestyle choice that may help forestall the emergence of chronic illnesses (American College of Sports Medicine, 2000). This association, when considered with the research linking stress and chronic disease, has led some scientists to question whether physical activity works in part by modifying the stress mechanism. This chapter presents a historical perspective of that hypothesis and some emerging directions for future research.

Evolution of the Cross-Stressor Adaptation Hypothesis

To fully appreciate the theoretical underpinnings for current research on physical activity and stress, one should be familiar with the historical evolution of the stress concept (Chrousos & Gold, 1992). The stress hypothesis traces its roots to the historical perspective that physiological disharmony is a natural, intrinsic process necessary for survival. However, it wasn't until the 19th century that the building blocks of modern-day stress theory started to emerge when Claude Bernard proposed that the *milieu interieur* has an internal physiological equilibrium that is necessary for the maintenance of health. In the early 1900s, Walter Cannon extended that concept to describe the term *homeostasis* as a coordinated set of biological mechanisms that interact to maintain an internal physiological steady state. In his work with the catecholamine epinephrine released from the adrenal medulla, Cannon also scientifically described the *fight or flight* reaction as the first defense against threatening stimuli. What emerged from that groundbreaking work was the appreciation of an overall *nonspecific response* of the body to many types of external challenge.

The individual ultimately credited with coining the term *stress* was the noted endocrinologist Hans Selye. Through his work with the adrenal cortex, Selye introduced many new terms to the scientific literature (e.g., corticoids, glucocorticoids, mineralocorticoids), but stress is perhaps the most ubiquitously used by researchers, health professionals, and the general public. It was Selye's 1936 publication in *Nature* that extended the nonspecificity of response previously observed by Cannon to include glucocorticoids and mineralocorticoids from the adrenal cortex (Selye, 1936). Selye's subsequent work showed that the same syndrome of neuroendocrine (hormonal) responses occurred across many different types of stimuli. Due to the amplifying effect of circulating hormones on physiological function, the result was a common (nonspecific) manifestation of arousal. According to Selye's belief, that particular syndrome had specific biological properties, so in the 1940s he borrowed the term *stress* from the physical sciences to better label its uniqueness. In his last writings Selye still referred to stress as the nonspecific response of the body to any demand placed on it (Selye, 1983).

Selye expanded his stress research to health status through his research on the *general adaptation syndrome,* in which he showed that with repeated exposure to a chronic noxious stimulus a "triad of stress" emerges, resulting in adrenal enlargement, gastrointestinal ulcers, and thymolymphatic atrophy (Szabo, 1998). With sufficiently prolonged exposure, cellular death occurs. Such findings led Selye to hypothesize that there are "diseases of adaptation" that have common neuroendocrine characteristics underlying many different disease conditions. This manifests as a "sickness syndrome" emerging from chronic stress as opposed to a specific etiology such as infection.

Two additional dimensions proposed by Selye are important to the stress concept. He maintained that hypostress and hyperstress are two extremes of optimal stress. Medical scientists have subsequently postulated that hyperstress may be part of the clinical syndrome of diseases of the circulatory system, melancholic depression, panic anxiety, anorexia nervosa, and obsessive-compulsive disorders, whereas hypostress may contribute to the sickness syndrome associated with obesity,

atypical depression, posttraumatic stress disorder, and chronic fatigue syndrome (Chrousos & Gold, 1992). The second dimension has to do with the qualitative nature of the stimuli. Selye maintained that there were positive stimuli resulting in good stress (eustress) and negative stimuli resulting in bad stress (distress) (Selye, 1983).

Over the years numerous challenges to Selye's original definition of stress have emerged. Many physiologists note that a tight match exists between a particular challenge and the resulting physiological responses, thus indicating a high degree of *specificity of response*. It is important here to note that stress theory recognizes specificity of response; it only argues that in addition there is a nonspecific response syndrome. Another trend has been to expand the definition of stress to incorporate psychological factors such as appraisal or perceived threat (Lazarus, 1991). There is no question that psychological stimuli can elicit a stress response, but the two are not mutually dependent. One can experience psychological distress without manifesting the neuroendocrine profile characteristic of stress, and vice versa. To date, no alternative unifying definition of stress has emerged to replace the original hypothesis put forth by Selye.

Basic Elements of the Stress Response

When one considers the physiological properties the human body has to achieve a "nonspecific response," it becomes immediately clear that multiple systems are fundamentally involved. These include the autonomic nervous system; sympathoadrenal system; hypothalamic-pituitary-adrenocortical axis; renin-angiotensin system; and systems involving vasopressin, endogenous opioids, and immune function. It is not within the scope of this chapter to detail the specific structure and functioning of each system and its role in whole-system physiological arousal. The reader is referred to other reviews for that understanding (Chrousos & Gold, 1992). Rather, the concentration here is on the prevailing evidence for the presence of an adaptation to exercise training that would suggest it as an intervention to influence the stress response. For purposes of this review, two systems are fundamentally important for an understanding of the basic theoretical concepts: (1) the hypothalamic-pituitary-adrenocortical axis (HPA) and

(2) the locus ceruleus-sympathetic-adrenomedullary (LCSA) system. The glucocorticoids released from the adrenal cortex and the catecholamines released from the adrenal medulla offer model systems for analysis.

Figure 10.1 reflects decades of science extending the groundbreaking research of Cannon and Selye pertaining to nonspecificity of response. With respect to the HPA system, in the presence of a challenging internal or external stimulus there is release of corticotropin releasing hormone (CRH) into the hypothalamic hypophyseal portal vessels that lead to the anterior pituitary gland. Corticotropin releasing hormone causes the precursor molecule proopiomelanocortin (POMC) to be secreted from which adrenocorticotropin

hormone (ACTH), B-endorphin, and other neuropeptides are released. Elevated secretion of circulating ACTH stimulates the release of glucocorticoids from the adrenal cortex.

Also depicted in figure 10.1 is the LCSA system. Nerve fibers project widely from a region of the lower brain called the locus ceruleus. Stimuli induced by physical or psychological challenge are a potent factor in the release of norepinephrine (NE) from the sympathetic nervous system (SNS) and NE and epinephrine (E) from the adrenal medulla. While the SNS has a high level of specificity of response for such physiological adjustments as heart rate increase or blood flow, the NE circulating in blood from SNS overflow or adrenal medulla secretion, coupled

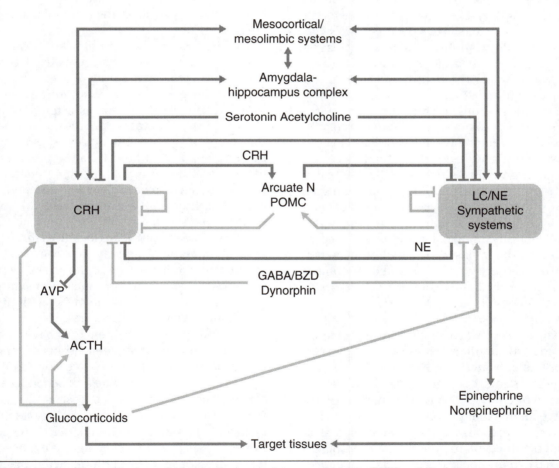

Figure 10.1 Integration of the hypothalamic-pituitary-adrenocortical axis (HPA) and the locus ceruleus-sympathetic-adrenomedullary (LCSA) stress response systems. See discussion in text.

Corticotropin Releasing Hormone (CRH), Arcuate nucleous (N), proopiomelanocortin (POMC), Locus Ceruleus/Norepinephrine Sympathetic systems (LC/NE Symp Syst), Norepinephrine (NE), Argenine Vasopressin (AVP), Gamma-aminobutyric acid/benzodiazepine (GABA/BZD), Adrenocorticotropin hormone (ACTH).

Reprinted, by permission, from M.S. Sothmann, J. Buckworth, R.P. Claytor, R.H. Cox, J.E. White-Whelkley, R.K. Dishman, 1996, "Exercise training and the cross-stressor adaptation hypothesis," *Exercise and Sport Sciences Reviews* 24: 267-288.

with the E released from the adrenal medulla, represents a principal mechanism for eliciting a stress response.

Collectively the HPA and LCSA systems result in a whole-system physiological arousal by such actions as increased gluconeogenesis, enhanced free fatty acid mobilization, increased heart rate and stroke volume, and heightened resistance to blood flow in nonpriority tissue. Moreover, there are certain critical properties of the HPA and LCSA systems for determining the magnitude and nature of the nonspecific (stress) response to any given challenge. A first property is that their regulation during the stress response occurs at multiple levels through feedforward and feedback mechanisms. One result is to maximize whole-system physiological arousal in the presence of novel, threatening, or challenging stimuli. From an evolutionary perspective, this would be considered beneficial in that it maximizes the organism's fight or flight capability. Another result is to preserve critical resources when the physiological system better understands the nature and intensity of internal or external stimuli (i.e., to become more efficient in the response). Thus, for example, one would not expect to observe the same circulating levels of E in threatening versus familiar yet comparably muscularly challenging situations.

A second property is that at both the central and peripheral levels, there is the potential for "single-system" and "dual-system" arousal depending upon the nature and intensity of the external stimuli. The physiological responses would be expected to differ based upon whether single- or dual-system activation is elicited (Sothmann et al., 1996). This is important for considering a "stimulus threshold" at which the stress response occurs.

A final property is that while there are profound physiological manifestations with the stress response as indicated by heart rate, blood pressure, and nutrients, there are correspondingly significant emotional and behavioral characteristics. Animals experimentally exposed to challenges that elicit a stress response manifest increased alertness, locomotor activity, rearing, and grooming; decreased exploration in the open field; enhanced fear-induced freezing and fighting; and vigilance, among other behaviors (Koop, 1992). Depending upon the nature of the stressor, humans may have correspondingly increased vigilance and changes in psychomotor properties, cognitive performance, and self-reported measures of emotional state (Sothmann et al., 1988).

Cross-Stressor Adaptation Hypothesis

The possibility that exercise training may beneficially impact one's stress level falls under the umbrella of an overarching stress-related concept termed the cross-stressor adaptation hypothesis. The fundamental question with that hypothesis is whether the physiological adaptation to one type of stimulus inducing a stress response (i.e., exercise) will "cross over" to other stimuli (e.g., environmental, behavioral stressors) eliciting a similar nonspecific response. To ask the question another way, regardless of the stressor, when the generalized response pattern has been chronically stimulated and subsequently adapted, would one expect that generalized adaptation to be manifested whenever the generalized systems are provoked?

McCarty, Konarska, and Stewart (1992) have offered learning theory as a construct through which the cross-stressor hypothesis might be scientifically explored. *Associative learning* would recognize that there is a temporal component to the adaptation process. In support of this, emotion and cognitive processes have long been recognized to be critical modulators of a neuroendocrine and autonomic activation pattern. If one changes such elements as perceived control or threat of the stressor, there are adaptations in both the nature and the magnitude of the response. In contrast, *nonassociative learning* suggests an underlying adaptation of the physiological structure and function of the stress response (e.g., tissue structure, neurotransmitter synthesis) to repeated stimuli that cannot be attributed to prevailing psychological factors.

Two additional critical concepts have emerged from the neuroendocrine/neurotransmitter fields that further define the cross-stressor adaptation hypothesis. Animals routinely exposed to a variety of stressors (foot shock, restraint, exercise, temperature) typically *habituate* (i.e., adapt) by manifesting a blunted neuroendocrine response. However, when that same animal is exposed to a novel stressor of sufficient intensity, it manifests an augmented response that exceeds the initial, nonhabituated levels. This is referred to as *sensitization*. Kvetnansky (1980) has proposed that habituation occurs because there is a tonic central nervous system inhibition that allows an animal to minimize the physiological response necessary to successfully meet a familiar (homeotypic) challenge. However, a second element of the habituation is the alteration of cellular tissue structure and function resulting in increased biosynthesis and storage of neurotransmitters and hormones. Under novel (heterotypic) or threatening challenges, the central nervous system inhibition is overridden and the animal's newly established, increased capacity is released, thus resulting in a greater response than in nonhabituated animals.

How do these theoretical perspectives apply to exercise? From the preceding discussion there are at least three separate but equally important routes by which one might investigate whether exercise training modifies the stress response. One could hypothesize that chronic exercise increases the maximal capacity of the stress response under threatening conditions while simultaneously enhancing the efficiency of response during submaximal, familiar challenges. A second question is whether exercise training changes the stimulus threshold at which the stress response occurs, not just for exercise but for nonexercise stressors as well. Finally, given that the precipitators and indicators of stress with some challenges likely incorporate psychological, behavioral, and physiological factors interwoven into a *psychobiological syndrome,* one might ask how exercise training impacts such a syndrome. As the reader will hopefully come to appreciate, and as is the case in many areas of science, these questions are of sufficient complexity that they do not lend themselves to easy answers.

A survey of the extant literature (Sothmann et al., 1996) will indicate that an acute bout of exercise eliciting a physiological response beneficial for enhancing aerobic fitness is generally carried out at an intensity and duration to also elicit a stress response. As it pertains to the habituation concept proposed, for both the HPA and LCSA systems scientific investigations have consistently shown that there tend to be lower circulating hormone levels at the same absolute exercise workload following as little as a few weeks of exercise training. Cellular changes are also apparent with the habituation process in that there is increased biosynthesis and storage of NE and E, as well as increased responsiveness of ACTH, NE, and E release, with maximal and supramaximal exercise. These findings suggest that exercise training does alter the stimulus threshold (i.e., submaximal exercise workload) at which a stress response occurs.

Evidence for a sensitization of response with exposure to nonexercise, novel, or threatening challenges is less clear. There is substantial evidence that highly exercise-trained humans have augmented circulating E levels with first exposure to certain physical (hypoglycemia, hypercapnia), behavioral, or cognitive challenges (Claytor & Cox, 1992, Kjaer, 1992; Sothmann et al., 1988). However, comparison of discrete fitness groups on their plasma NE response to such first-exposure challenges as orthostasis and cold pressor has not revealed marked differences (Claytor et al., 1988; Kohrt et al., 1993). Moreover, markedly discrete fitness groups have not differed on their ACTH or cortisol responses to a familiar cognitively challenging task (Blaney et al., 1990).

Research with animals allows one the opportunity to apply an intensity of physiological challenge not normally tolerated by humans to observe the capacity of the stress response system. In a series of studies with a novel (heterotypic) stressor, exercise-trained rats did not manifest the anticipated augmented E or NE release, either in the circulating blood or in the brain (McCoy et al., 1995, 1994; Soares et al., 1999). With respect to ACTH, investigators have reported no exercise-induced alteration with exposure to a novel stimulus (Dishman et al., 1997, 1995; Overton et al., 1991), whereas others have reported an attenuation (Dishman et al., 1998) or an augmentation (White-Welkey et al., 1995, 1996). No additional insight has been gleaned from studies on circulating cortisol. As is discussed in subsequent sections of this chapter, these apparently conflicting results with ACTH have accented the need to further refine the paradigm for considering how exercise training may relate to the cross-stressor adaptation hypothesis.

In summary, from the questions posed previously it is reasonable to make a few overarching statements pertaining to our extant knowledge of exercise training and cross-stressor adaptation. First, there is consistent evidence that the principal neuroendocrine systems eliciting the stress response to exercise habituate in terms of both an attenuated responsiveness to the same submaximal exercise challenge and a cellular biosynthesis and storage of key endocrines and neurotransmitters. Second, while there is consistent evidence that E manifests an augmented release to nonexercise challenges in the highly trained, this pattern is not so readily apparent with other neuroendocrines or neurotransmitters. Finally, an exercise training bout of several months in animals, while sufficient to induce a habituated response, has not been consistently shown to lead to a sensitization of the stress response upon exposure to nonexercise stressors.

Psychobiological Testing of the Cross-Stressor Hypothesis in Humans

A question previously asked in the chapter was whether exercise training and stress responsivity might manifest as a psychobiological syndrome in humans. This experimental approach would be relevant to an integration of associative and nonassociative learning theory and addresses the carryover value of animal studies to the human. Along this line, the hypothesized nonspecific adaptation to exercise training has been extensively discussed in this chapter. What should be additionally recognized is that *specificity of adaptation* also has a role in the generalized response and that both the nonspecific and specific adaptations can be modified by psychological factors.

As depicted in figure 10.2, specialty fields within exercise physiology have mapped the multitude of exercise-induced adaptations within singular physiological systems. Such specific adaptations likely have importance for the generalized stress response on two accounts. First, adaptations to a specific stimulus may be operative in the pres-

ence of other challenges. For example, alterations in tissue structure (such as in the heart) from exercise training typically induce a change in that tissue's overall function, and this change in function would be expected to be generalized because of the altered structural properties. Secondly, depending on the nature and intensity of an external challenge, such single-system physiological adaptations in structure and function may integrate across multiple systems to enhance or suppress the generalized stress response.

Figure 10.2 also recognizes that psychological processes can modify the intensity or duration of the response. For example, it has long been recognized that when a challenge is perceived as a psychological threat with little neuromuscular involvement, one is likely to observe elevations in ACTH and E, with NE having a minor role. In contrast, behavioral challenges inducing vigilance and physical performance elicit a principally NE response (Frankenhaeuser, Lundberg, & Forsman, 1980). An important area of exercise psychobiology is the theoretical perspective that exercise training influences such cognitive processes as self-perception, attentional focus, mastery, and anger. There remain compelling issues in this area that preclude definitive statements (Dishman, 1994).

Developing experimental studies that capture those integrative dynamics for stress responsivity

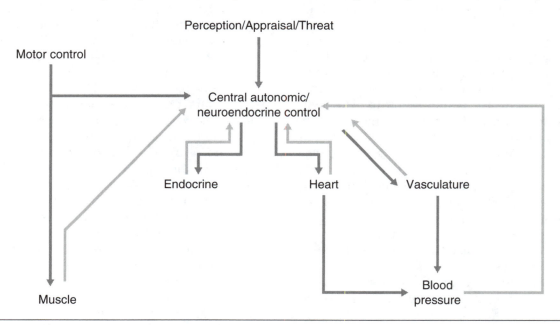

Figure 10.2   Postulated integrative mechanisms for exercise training and cross-stressor adaptation.

Reprinted, by permission, from M.S. Sothmann, J. Buckworth, R.P. Claytor, R.H. Cox, J.E. White-Whelkley, R.K. Dishman, 1996, "Exercise training and the cross-stressor adaptation hypothesis," *Exercise and Sport Sciences Reviews* 24: 267-288.

in ways that can be precisely measured has been a significant challenge. To illustrate the complexity of the experimental design and data interpretation, it is educational to consider the findings from a series of studies in which humans were exposed to a cognitive and behavioral challenge that elicited a significant neuroendocrine stress response with corresponding physiological, psychological, and behavioral manifestations integrated as a psycho-biological syndrome.

The experimental challenge (Sothmann et al., 1988) inducing the stress response was a double-conflict task (modified Stroop test) in which the words RED, GREEN, or BLUE were flashed on a screen in 2 sec intervals for 12 min; the font of the words were presented in colors that were in conflict with their meaning. Subjects responded to the conflict by moving a lightweight wooden arm to tap the appropriately colored lever to make a correct response. Subjects were monitored for their number of correct responses and reaction time, among other psychomotor properties. Immediately following the double-conflict task the individuals were administered a set of anagrams to assess their cognitive performance. Posttask cognitive performance scores were compared to pretask values to assess the level of cognitive fatigue, if any, induced by the double-conflict task. During the double-conflict and anagram tasks, venous blood samples were collected at periodic intervals for neuroendocrine (ACTH, cortisol, NE, E) monitoring. Moreover, at those same time intervals physiological measures (heart rate and blood pressures) were recorded, as were pre- and posttask self-reports of emotion (state anxiety, depression).

With the double-conflict protocol, the subject group experienced significant changes in all dimensions measured (i.e., their circulating hormones, physiological responses, performance, and self-report measures) indicating psychological distress and physiological arousal, thus suggestive of a stress response. A series of analyses was then performed to examine discrete fitness groups' responses to the stress protocol. The findings of these studies revealed that markedly lower-fit middle-aged males had higher NE secretion than their middle- or higher-fit counterparts (Sothmann, Horn, & Hart, 1991; Sothmann et al., 1987), and they also tended to manifest significantly more cognitive fatigue following the stress protocol (Sothmann et al., 1987). The groups did not differ on other circulating hormones, psychomotor

performance, selected physiological responses, or self-reported psychological states. The moderate- and higher-fit individuals did have lower resting heart rates and blood pressures at rest relative to their low-fit counterparts, and these absolute differences carried over to the double-conflict task; but there were no response differences between groups when the baseline values were statistically controlled.

While the cross-sectional comparisons revealed that discrete fitness groups differed on key psychological and physiological indicators of a stress response, it is important to note that the differences were isolated to just the markedly lower-fit group of middle-aged males, that the differences involved just a couple of the measured dimensions, and that even within the affected dimensions the differences were limited to a few specific variables. Such cross-sectional findings underlie the complexity of studying the relationship between physical activity and cross-stressor adaptation. A review of the extant literature with humans demonstrates the *inconsistency* of findings. This is probably due in large measure to the complexity of the stress response and the sophistication of the experimental design needed to capture any apparent fitness effect.

The relationship of high circulating NE and high cognitive fatigue manifested by the lower-fit middle-aged men in the set of studies just described did allow for the testing of the influence of an exercise training program on an experimentally derived psychobiological syndrome characteristic of low physical fitness levels (Sothmann, Hart, & Horn, 1992). Lower-fit, sedentary, middle-aged males were assigned to exercise training and sedentary groups. Their preintervention performance on the double-conflict task was established and then the exercise group underwent 16 weeks of training that improved their aerobic fitness by approximately 20%. No change in aerobic fitness occurred with the sedentary group over the same 16 weeks. Postintervention exposure to the double-conflict task revealed no differences between exercise-trained and sedentary counterparts on the cognitive fatigue and circulating NE responses. Moreover, all other physiological response, behavioral, and psychological self-report variables were similar to those in the control group except resting heart rate, which declined significantly in the exercise-trained group.

The findings from the exercise training studies further illustrate the difficulty of documenting an association between physical activity and stress reactivity. Cross-sectional comparisons of markedly discrete fitness groups under a short-term psychological challenge may reflect a syndrome of neuroendocrine, psychological, or behavioral patterns differentiating the fitness groups. However, the few studies conducted to date with humans suggest that while exercise training for three to four months may increase key physiological measures of fitness, it generally has not induced changes in stress reactivity as indicated by neuroendocrine measures where a short-term psychosocial challenge is the precipitating factor. Therefore, based on the neuroendocrine data one cannot substantively argue for an impact of exercise training in augmenting or reducing stress reactivity in psychosocial settings. It is theoretically reasonable to postulate that such a beneficial effect should be present, but the experimental approaches to date have offered limited confirming data in the human.

Weaknesses and Limitations in the Literature

The first studies on exercise training and the cross-stressor adaptation hypothesis emerged in the early 1980s, and while they presented important preliminary findings they also accented the limitations in several key areas that continue to the present. Such limitations were mentioned earlier and have been reviewed in detail (Dishman, 1997; Sothmann et al., 1996); but for purposes of this review, four overriding considerations are highlighted.

Lack of a Theoretical Underpinning for Experimental Designs

As this chapter has emphasized, the type of challenge is a predetermining factor in the nature and magnitude of the stress response. The equivocal findings from two decades of studies suggest that categorizing the nature of the stressor as homeotypic or heterotypic is valuable but not sufficient in studying the impact of exercise training on selected neuroendocrine response patterns. Unfortunately, there has been limited effort to perform series of investigations to test even the most basic of theoretical paradigms. This limitation significantly confounds the literature.

Nature of the Populations Investigated

The majority of studies have been performed with relatively young, healthy males. This has limited the research on two accounts. First, it is unlikely that one will see a beneficial impact of exercise training in those who already have a highly responsive, well-integrated stress response system. Older sedentary individuals or those experiencing chronic disease likely have the most potential gain from exercise training, but they have not been sufficiently studied. Secondly, it is becoming increasingly clear that stress responses influenced by exercise and physical fitness may not be similar for men and women (Dishman et al., 2003; White-Welkley et al., 1996). More research is needed in both areas to ascertain those differences and their meaning.

Limitations of the Neuroendocrine Measurements

Measuring plasma concentrations of a circulating hormone offers a very global view of the balance between release, metabolism, and clearance. There are significant differences between the concentration of a hormone in the arterial and venous (where sampling generally occurs) blood with any given stimulus. Moreover, neuroendocrines and neurotransmitters have individual properties in the time for their release and metabolism. Thus, the potential impact of exercise training on a stress response hormone may be masked by the location and the timing of blood sampling. This may explain part of the disparate findings with humans.

Lack of a Demonstrable Exercise Training Effect in Humans

As stated previously, there has been limited research in which sedentary individuals were exercise trained for a long enough time to markedly increase their physical fitness and then compared to an appropriately matched control group on their pre- and poststress responses. Most of the work done in this area has been limited to an analysis comparing discrete fitness groups. Until studies consistently demonstrate that the act of physical activity or exercise training in humans in fact alters the neuroendocrine response to nonexercise stressors, the findings with animal models and the comparisons of markedly different groups have little meaning for the effectiveness of intervention. In the author's opinion this is currently the field's biggest challenge.

Directions for Future Investigation

Certain specific limitations of the extant literature base with humans were cited in the preceding section and thus would form the basis on which recommendations for future research might be pursued. Clearly in all areas of research with the human, more concentration needs to be focused on *refining the measurement process* within the present conceptual paradigm. Existing studies lack uniformity in their measurement of fitness or physical activity, the nature of the protocols invoking a stress response, the behavioral factors involved (e.g., anger vs. effort), the measurement of the stress response, or a combination of these (Dishman et al., 2003; Sothmann et al., 1996). Given this, to better refine hypothesis formulation in human studies, more effort should be devoted to developing reliable, data-driven models of associations across multiple dimensions of stress reactivity (e.g., neuroendocrine, physiological, behavioral, self-report) with an established stress protocol. Such a priori models, if shown to be reliable in their response patterns, would then be more conducive to examination of the impact of exercise intervention.

While in this chapter the historic cross-stressor adaptation hypothesis has been principally defined as a blunted or magnified neuroendocrine/neurotransmitter response, more recent research is broadening the hypothesis in interesting ways. For example, there is evidence from animal models that exercise training may be *protective to the depletion of critical neurotransmitters regulating a neuroendocrine stress response*. Two studies (Dishman et al., 2000b; Soares et al., 1999) have examined the extent to which exercise training of rats will confer an adaptation of neurotransmitters in brain regions responsible for the regulation of the peripheral release of stress hormones such as ACTH. Those studies are experimentally designed to address the proposition that a healthy neuroendocrine stress response (i.e., one that is appropriate to the nature of the stimuli and efficient in response) is determined in part by the synthesis and depletion rates of neurotransmitters intimately involved in the regulation of that particular system. Thus, tracking the neurotransmitter adaptation with exercise training in those brain regions, and its response to novel stressors, offers insight on behavior of critical regulators of the neuroendocrine stress response. Preliminary examination of NE adaptation to exercise in brain regions involved with the regulation of the HPA axis suggests just such a protective effect.

Another emerging concept within the crossover adaptation hypothesis is that exercise training may *confer a protective effect through the habituation of the neuroendocrine response to heterotypic as well as homeotypic stressors*. The cross-stressor adaptation hypothesis has argued that animals will habituate to a familiar (homeotypic) challenge, but that there is a sensitization resulting in the unleashing of an augmented neuroendocrine/neurotransmitter response to a novel (heterotypic) stressor. Research conducted to date with exercise training is mixed in its validation of that preliminary view, in that studies on ACTH and NE secretion following exercise training of rats have noted both blunted and augmented responses to novel stressors (Dishman et al., 1998; McCoy et al., 1995; Soares et al., 1999). This raises the interesting possibility that a blunted (habituated) response may be physiologically preferred by the animal in most situations except where certain other stressor qualities are present, such as whether the novel stress is controllable or uncontrollable (Dishman et al., 1997). This possibility further reinforces the importance of a clear theoretical perspective on the nature of the challenge for interpreting the neuroendocrine response patterns with exercise training.

A third developing thought is that exercise training may *normalize the response of neuroendocrine/neurotransmitters during the stress response*. It is well documented that there is a high degree of brain region specificity in neurotransmitter release. A study by Kastello and Sothmann (1999) utilized a nine-day simulated weightlessness model with rats as a chronic stressor protocol to examine NE release in brain regions involved in the regulation of the HPA and LCSA systems. A characteristic of that particular protocol was that it elicited significantly elevated NE release in the locus ceruleus but, conversely, significantly blunted NE release in the hypothalamus compared to values in caged controls. Exercise-trained rats experiencing the protocol manifested a moderated response pattern when compared to their sedentary suspended counterparts. That is, whether there was an elevated or blunted response, exercise training tended to bring the response pattern closer to normal control values. The investigators suggested this as evidence of exercise training as a *global homeostatic regulator* in that it normalized the response pattern, with normalization operationally defined by the investigators as adaptational change toward control values. This concept has important implications for a theoretical approach to the postulated simultaneous benefit of exercise training for both the hyper- and hypostress clinical syndromes discussed previously in this chapter. These findings also suggest that the crossover adaptation hypothesis with exercise training should be interpreted as more of a bidirectional adaptation model than previously appreciated.

A final direction for future research includes extracting more insight into how such exercise-induced stress adaptations may affect mechanisms intricately involved in health and chronic disease. As an example, recent research (Dishman et al., 2000a, 2000c) has examined in the animal model whether exercise training confers an immunoprotective effect as a result of a generalized cross-stressor adaptation.

Conclusions

Sufficient evidence has accumulated from animal research to suggest that exercise training influences stress responsivity, but the nature and magnitude of stress response, and its relation to exercise training, are variable depending upon the challenge. This suggests more complexity to the cross-stressor adaptation hypothesis than originally thought. Human studies comparing discrete fitness groups indicate that physical fitness is a moderating variable in a psychobiological stress syndrome. However, to date, the few studies with exercise training intervention have not produced a reliable change. Until such research is forthcoming, one should be cautious about pronouncing the postulated beneficial aspects of exercise for stress reactivity in humans.

References

American College of Sports Medicine. (2000). *Guidelines for exercise testing and prescription* (6th ed.). Baltimore: Williams & Wilkins.

Blaney, J., Sothmann, M., Raff, H., Hart, B., & Horn, T. (1990). Impact of exercise training on plasma adrenocorticotropin hormone response to a well learned vigilance task. *Psychoneuroendocrinology, 15,* 453-462.

Chrousos, C., & Gold, P. (1992). The concept of stress and stress system disorders: Overview of physical and behavioral homeostasis. *Journal of the American Medical Association, 267,* 1244-1252.

Claytor, R., & Cox, R. (1992). Exercise training induced enhancement in sympathoadrenal response to a behavioral challenge [abstract]. *Medicine and Science in Sports and Exercise, 24,* S25.

Claytor, R., Cox, R., Howley, E., Lawler, A., & Lawler, J. (1988). Aerobic power and cardiovascular response to stress. *Journal of Applied Physiology, 65*(3), 1416-1423.

Dishman, R. (1994). Biological psychology, exercise, and stress. *Quest, 46,* 28-59.

Dishman, R. (1997). Brain monoamines, exercise, and behavioral stress: animal models. *Medicine and Science in Sports and Exercise, 29*(1), 63-74.

Dishman, R., Bunnell, B., Youngstedt, S., Yoo, H., Mougey, E., & Meyerhoff, J. (1998). Activity wheel running blunts increased plasma adrenocorticotropin (ACTH) after footshock and cage-switch stress. *Physiology and Behavior, 63*(5), 911-917.

Dishman, R., Hong, S., Soares, J., Edwards, G., Bunnell, B., Jaso-Friedman, L., & Evans, D. (2000a). Activity wheel running blunts suppression of splenic natural killer cell cytotoxicity after sympathectomy and footshock. *Physiology and Behavior, 71,* 297-304.

Dishman, R., Nakamura, Y., Jackson, E., & Ray, C. (2003). Blood pressure and muscle sympathetic nerve activity during cold pressure: Fitness and gender. *Psychophysiology, 40*(3), 370-380.

Dishman, R., Renner, K., Youngstedt, S., Reigle, T., Bunnell, B., Burke, K., Yoo, H., Mougey, E., & Meyerhoff, J. (1997). Activity wheel running reduces escape latency and alters brain monoamine levels after footshock. *Brain Research Bulletin, 42*(5), 399-406.

Dishman, R., Renner, K., White-Welkley, J., Burke, K., & Bunnell, B. (2000b). Treadmill exercise training augments brain norepinephrine response to familiar and novel stress. *Brain Research Bulletin, 52*(5), 337-342.

Dishman, R., Warren, J., Hong, S., Bunnell, B., Mougey, H., Meyerhoff, J., Jaso-Friedmann, L., & Evans, D. (2000c). Treadmill exercise training blunts suppression of splenic natural killer cell cytolysis after footshock. *Journal of Applied Physiology, 88*(6), 2176-2182.

Dishman, R., Warren, J., Youngstedt, S., Yoo, H., Bunnell, B., Mougey, E., Meyerhoff, J., Jaso-Friedmann, L., & Evans, D. (1995). Activity wheel running attenuates suppression of natural killer cell activity after footshock. *Journal of Applied Physiology, 78,* 1547-1554.

Frankenhaeuser, M., Lundberg, V., & Forsman, L. (1980). Dissociation between sympathetic-adrenal and pituitary-adrenal responses to an achievement situation characterized by high controllability: Comparison between type A and type B females. *Biological Psychology, 10,* 79-91.

Gerber, B., Muller, H., Reimer, T., Krause, A., & Friese, K. (2003). Nutrition and lifestyle factors on the risk of developing breast cancer. *Breast Cancer Research and Treatment, 79*(2), 265-276.

Heuser, I., & Lammers, C. (2003). Stress and the brain. *Neurobiology of Aging, 24,* S69-S76.

Kalia, M. (2002). Assessing the economic impact of stress—the modern day hidden epidemic. *Metabolism: Clinical and Experimental, 51*(6), 49-53.

Kamarck, T., Peterman, A., & Raynor, D. (1998). The effects of the social environment on stress-related cardiovascular activation: Current findings, prospects, and implications. *Annals of Behavioral Medicine, 20*(4), 247-256.

Kastello, G., & Sothmann, M. (1999). Brain norepinephrine changes with simulated weightlessness and relation to exercise training. *Physiology and Behavior, 66*(5), 885-891.

Kjaer, M. (1992). Regulation of hormonal and metabolic responses during exercise in humans. *Exercise and Sport Sciences Reviews, 20,* 161-184.

Kohrt, W., Spina, R., Ehsani, A., Cryer, P., & Holloszy, J. (1993). Effect of age, adiposity, and fitness level on plasma catecholamine responses to standing and exercise. *Journal of Applied Physiology, 75,* 1828-1835.

Koop, G. (1992). The behavioral neuroendocrinology of corticotrophin-releasing factor, growth hormone releasing factor, somatostatin, and gonadotropin releasing hormone. In C.B. Nemeroff (Ed.), *Neuroendocrinology* (pp. 353-364). Boca Raton, FL: CRC Press.

Kvetnansky, R. (1980). Recent progress in catecholamines under stress. In E. Usidin, R. Kvetnansky, & I. Kopin (Eds.), *Catecholamines and stress: Recent advances* (pp. 1-7). New York: Elsevier.

Lazarus, R. (1991). *Emotion and adaptation.* Oxford: Oxford University Press.

McCarty, R., Konarska, M., & Stewart, R. (1992). Adaptation to stress: A learned response? In R. Kvetnansky, R. McCarty, & J. Axelrod (Eds.), *Stress: Neuroendocrine and molecular approaches* (pp. 531-535). Philadelphia: Gordon Breach.

McCoy, D., Steele, J., Cox, R., & Wiley, R. (1995). Swim training alters sympathoadrenal and endocrine responses to hemorrhage in borderline hypertensive rats. *American Journal of Physiology, 269,* R124-R130.

McCoy, D., Steele, J., Cox, R., Wiley, R., & McGuire, G. (1994). Swim training alters renal and cardiovascular responses to stress in borderline hypertensive rats. *Journal of Applied Physiology, 75,* 1946-1954.

Murray, C.J.L., & Lopez, A.D. (Ed.) (1996). The global burden of disease and injury series, volume 1: A comprehensive assessment of mortality and disability from diseases, injuries, and risk factors in 1990 and projected to 2020. Cambridge, MA: Published by the Harvard School of Public Health on behalf of the World Health Organization and the World Bank, Harvard University Press.

Overton, M., Kregal, K., Gromon, G., Seals, D., Tipton, C., & Fisher, L. (1991). Effects of exercise training on responses to central injection of CRF and noise stress. *Physiology and Behavior, 49,* 93-98.

Pincus, T. (2001). Psychosocial influences and mortality: Ruberman et al. (1984). *Advances in Mind-Body Medicine, 17,* 24-28.

Rossi, E. (2003). The bioinformatics of psychosocial genomics in alternative and complementary medicine. *Forschende Komplementarmedizin und Klassische Naturheilkunde, 10*(3), 143-150.

Selye, H. (1936). A syndrome produced by diverse nocuous agents. *Nature, 138,* 32.

Selye, H. (1983). The stress concept: Past, present and future. In C.L. Cooper (Ed.), *Stress research* (pp. 1-20). New York: Wiley.

Soares, J., Holmes, P., Renner, K., Edwards, G., Bunnell, B., & Dishman, R. (1999). Brain norepinephrine responses to footshock after chronic activity-wheel running. *Behavioral Neuroscience, 113*(3), 558-566.

Sothmann, M., Buckworth, J., Claytor, R., Cox, R., White-Welkley, J., & Dishman, R. (1996). Exercise training and the cross stressor adaptation hypothesis. *Exercise ad Sport Sciences Reviews, 24,* 267-287.

Sothmann, M., Gustafson, A., Garthwaite, T., Hron, T., & Hart, B. (1988). Cardiovascular fitness and selected adrenal hormone responses to cognitive stress. *Endocrine Research, 14,* 59-69.

Sothmann, M., Hart, B., & Horn, T. (1992). Sympathetic nervous system and behavioral responses to stress following exercise training. *Physiology and Behavior, 51,* 1097-1103.

Sothmann, M., Hart, B., Horn, T., & Gustafson, A. (1988). Plasma catecholamine and performance associations during psychological stress: Evidence for peripheral noradrenergic involvement with an attention demanding task. *Human Performance, 1,* 31-43.

Sothmann, M., Horn, T., & Hart, B. (1991). Plasma catecholamine response to acute psychological stress in humans: Relation to aerobic fitness and exercise training. *Medicine and Science in Sports and Exercise, 23,* 860-867.

Sothmann, M., Horn, T., Hart, B., & Gustafson, A. (1987). Comparison of discrete cardiovascular fitness groups on plasma catecholamine and selected behavioral responses to psychological stress. *Psychophysiology, 24,* 47-54.

Szabo, S. (1998). Hans Selye and the development of the stress concept: Special reference to gastroduodenal ulcerogenesis. *Annals of the New York Academy of Sciences, 831,* 19-27.

White-Welkley, J., Bunnell, B., Mougey, E., Meyerhoff, J., & Dishman, R. (1995). Treadmill exercise training and estradiol differentially modulate hypothalamic-pituitary-adrenal cortical responses to acute running and immobilization. *Physiology and Behavior, 57*(3), 533-540.

White-Welkley, J., Warren, G., Bunnell, B., Mougey, E., Meyerhoff, J., & Dishman, R. (1996). Treadmill exercise training and estradiol increase plasma ACTH and prolactin after novel footshock. *Journal of Applied Physiology, 80*(3), 931-939.

Psychobiological Reactivity, Physical Activity, and Cardiovascular Health

Stephen H. Boutcher, PhD

Mark Hamer, PhD

Cardiovascular reactivity can be defined as a statistically reliable increase or decrease in cardiovascular response from baseline (Blascovich & Katkin, 1993). Cardiovascular reactivity responses primarily involve the sympathetic-adrenomedullary and hypothalamic-pituitary axes that are called into play to bring about defensive measures against stimuli that threaten to disrupt the body's ability to maintain homeostasis. Reactivity has typically been assessed by measuring heart rate (HR) and blood pressure (BP). A variety of psychosocial and physical stimuli can elicit cardiovascular reactivity; however, not all stimuli that induce cardiovascular reactivity are perceived to be stressful or threatening. Also factors such as genetic characteristics, age, gender, body composition, blood lipids, personality characteristics, and appraisals appear to contribute to the size and pattern of cardiovascular reactivity.

Other factors can amplify or help exaggerate the cardiovascular reactivity response. For example, salt sensitivity, caffeine, nicotine, and sleep deprivation have been shown to elevate cardiovascular reactivity in certain individuals. Also patterns of reactivity vary depending on the nature of the task and stimulus. For example, some tasks elicit significant cardiovascular responses, whereas other tasks barely perturb the cardiovasculature. Some tasks elicit central responses such as increases in HR and cardiac output, whereas others bring about increases in BP and vascular resistance. It is likely that certain reactivity patterns are more harmful to cardiovascular health than others. Exaggerated cardiovascular reactivity is associated with cardiovascular disease and hypertension; however, the pathophysiological mechanisms that mediate the relationship between excessive cardiovascular reactivity and disease are undetermined. Chronic and acute aerobic exercise have been shown to reduce or dampen certain aspects of cardiovascular reactivity, although mechanisms are unclear. Whether exercise-reduced cardiovascular reactivity leads to reduced cardiovascular disease or prevents the development of hypertension is unknown.

The purpose of this chapter is to provide an overview of the effects of physical activity on cardiovascular reactivity. Specific goals are to outline a model of cardiovascular reactivity, to describe assessment of cardiovascular reactivity, to summarize the effect of reactivity on cardiovascular disease and hypertension, to summarize the effects of chronic and acute exercise on reactivity, and to examine issues confronting future research into the reactivity–health–exercise relationship.

A Multifactorial Model of Cardiovascular Reactivity

Figure 11.1 illustrates a model describing reactivity factors and responses that could lead to the development of cardiovascular disease and hypertension. An example of excessive reactivity may serve to illustrate the complexity and multifactorial nature of the reactivity response. A viscerally obese middle-aged businessman with a history of hypertension in his family spends much of his working day interfacing with a computer. His interaction with the computer is attentionally demanding and also requires a constant motor response (manipulating the mouse). To help increase and sustain his attention he constantly drinks coffee and eats high-glycemic, sugary foods (e.g., doughnuts). As can be seen from figure 11.1 the attentionally demanding computer task, family history of hypertension, excessive visceral fat, and intake of caffeine and sugar all have the ability to bring

about an excessive reactivity response through the sympathetic-adrenomedullary and hypothalamic-pituitary axes. Enhanced sympathetic-adrenomedullary axis activity can result in elevated catecholamine levels in the blood, whereas enhanced hypothalamic-pituitary axis activity can elevate blood cortisol levels. Constant turning on and off of these axes produces responses that could result in damage to the cardiovasculature (see figure 11.1). This model indicates a number of intervention possibilities. For example, reducing time on the computer, losing visceral fat, cutting out hyperreactive foods, and lowering blood lipids are all possible ways of reducing reactivity. As will

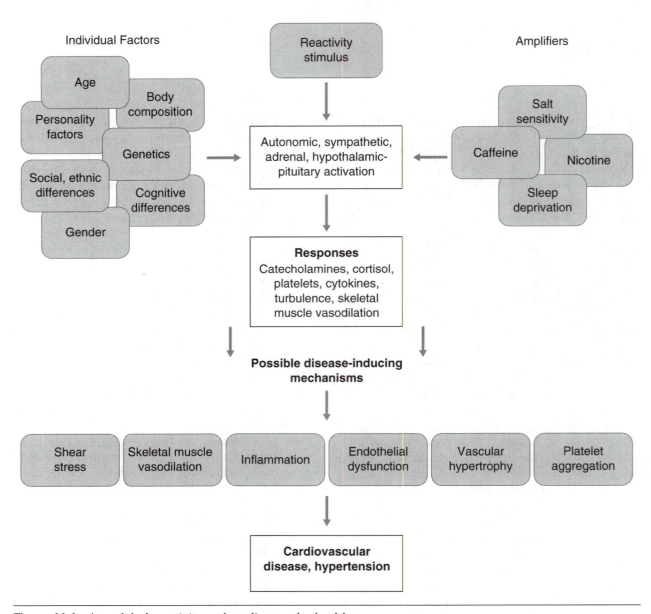

Figure 11.1 A model of reactivity and cardiovascular health.

be discussed more fully later, both chronic and acute aerobic exercise could also contribute by directly or indirectly reducing reactivity. Exercise has the potential to directly reduce certain aspects of reactivity to mental challenge (e.g., decreasing catecholamine response) and also has the ability to help indirectly by reducing the effect of individual and amplifying factors (e.g., lowering visceral fat). The various components of the model are briefly highlighted and discussed next.

Reactivity-Inducing Stimuli

Reactivity research has typically examined the psychophysiological response to laboratory stressors (e.g., mental arithmetic, the Stroop task) that produce elevated levels of perceived stress. So an important aspect of reactivity appears to be stressful stimuli. Not all stimuli that induce cardiovascular reactivity, however, are perceived to be stressful or threatening. For example, playing interesting computer games can result in elevated blood catecholamine levels (Patkai, 1971). Thus, seemingly benign tasks such as working on a computer or driving a car may also have the ability to induce excessive reactivity responses. Categorization of the nature and type of reactivity-inducing stimuli and tasks has included active versus passive coping (Obrist, 1981), defense reaction or striving versus aversive vigilance (Schneiderman & McCabe, 1989), and sensory rejection versus sensory intake (Lacey, 1967). Laboratory stressors have included both mental and physical challenge such as the Stroop task, mental arithmetic, interviews, reaction time, cold pressor, tracing task, and isometric exercise (Steptoe & Vogele, 1991). These tasks typically elicit cardiovascular reactivity. For example, a much-used laboratory reactivity task is the Stroop color-word task that typically results in a HR increase of 10 to 15 bpm and an increase in mean arterial BP of 10+ mmHg. The Stroop typically produces increased α- and β-adrenergic activation with a concomitant decrease in vascular resistance in skeletal muscle. In contrast, tasks such as the cold pressor produce vascular constriction through enhanced α-adrenergic activity.

Individual Differences Affecting Reactivity

Individual factors such as cognitive set, genetic characteristics, age, gender, body composition, personality characteristics, ethnic differences, and social factors also have been shown to contribute to the size and pattern of the cardiovascular reactivity response.

Cognitive Set

Cognitive set refers to the expectations and appraisal of an individual with regard to a particular task or situation. Most would agree that awareness of a stressor is an important aspect of the reactivity response. Theories on the mechanisms by which awareness comes about, however, vary greatly. Some feel that appraisals and interpretation are essential, whereas others suggest that there are occasions when cognitive variables are less important. The evidence seems to suggest that although appraisal processes are often carried out automatically without direct awareness, often some sort of appraisal typically occurs (Lazarus & Folkman, 1984).

Genetic Characteristics

Genetic characteristics reflect the inheriting of "reactivity" genes that contribute to exaggerated cardiovascular response. Variability within α- and β-adrenoreceptor genes has been shown to predict the BP response to stressors (Li et al., 2001). These data demonstrate that variation within the adrenoreceptor gene plays an important role in determining individual reactivity response.

Age

Older adults have significant neural and receptor age-related changes that have been shown to influence peripheral resistance and cardiac contractility (Baker et al., 1985). With regard to reactivity, studies have shown that the aging cardiovasculature is less reactive but is under greater hemodynamic stress during both rest and mental challenge (Boutcher & Stocker, 1996). We have also found that aerobically trained compared to untrained older males displayed greater HR, systolic BP, and total peripheral resistance reactivity to mental challenge (Boutcher, Nurhayati, & McLaren, 2001). Thus, it appears that participation in aerobic exercise by older individuals is associated with greater α- and β-adrenoreceptor sensitivity.

Gender

It has been shown that untrained premenopausal women, compared to men, possess a reduced cardiovascular response to psychological stressors. For example, women's epinephrine and systolic BP response to mental challenge was significantly lower than that of men (Matthews & Stoney, 1988).

Thus, compared to age-matched men, premenopausal women possessed reduced reactivity to mental challenge.

Body Composition

The major body composition factor that affects cardiovascular reactivity appears to be the amount and distribution of body fat. For example, Alvarez and colleagues (2002) have shown that individuals possessing visceral adiposity have greater muscle sympathetic nerve activity than nonobese individuals. Also, Agapitov and colleagues (2002) found that obese compared to lean adults possessed a significantly reduced forearm vasodilation response to mental arithmetic. Kuniyoshi and colleagues (2003) showed that muscle sympathetic nervous activity and forearm vascular resistance were augmented during Stroop challenge in healthy obese compared with healthy lean individuals. Thus, elevated abdominal visceral fat is a tissue linking obesity with sympathetic neural activation.

Blood Lipids

Animal studies suggest that cholesterol may alter vascular smooth muscle reactivity. Hypercholesterolemia has been shown to reduce renal blood flow in baboons (Bomzon, Kew, & Rosendorff, 1978) and to enhance vascular responsiveness to noradrenaline in isolated rabbit femoral and basilar arteries (Bloom, McCalden, & Rosendorff, 1975). Elevated levels of low-density lipoprotein cholesterol may be responsible for increased vascular reactivity in hypercholesterolemia (Galle, Mulsch, & Bassenge, 1989). The effect of serum lipid levels on cardiovascular reactivity to laboratory stressors, however, is equivocal (van Doornen, Sneider, & Boomsma, 1998).

Personality Characteristics

Certain personality characteristics are associated with exaggerated reactivity response, with the most important being social inhibition (Cole et al., 2003). For example, socially inhibited individuals who also display irritability and hostility show heightened autonomic reactivity. Exaggerated HR and BP, elevated blood catecholamines, and elevated skin conductance to mental challenge have been documented (Cole et al., 2003; Miller et al., 1999). The occurrence of social inhibition and irritability or hostility has been shown to be a significant risk factor for cardiovascular disease (Denollet et al., 1996).

Ethnic and Social Factors

A number of investigations have examined black–white differences in cardiovascular reactivity as a potential mediator of hypertension. Most studies have shown that both American black adults and children show significantly greater BP reactivity than whites (Anderson, 1989). Anderson, McNeilly, and Myers (1993) contend that black Americans, on average, are exposed to a wider array of chronic stressors than whites. These chronic stressors interact with biological, behavioral, and psychological risk factors to increase sympathetic nervous system activity, which in turn leads to the release of norepinephrine and adrenocorticotropin hormone, augmented sodium retention, and enhanced vasoconstriction (Anderson, McNeilly, & Myers, 1993).

Reactivity Amplifiers

Other factors can amplify or help exaggerate the cardiovascular reactivity response. For example, salt sensitivity, ingestion of caffeine, smoking, and sleep deprivation have been shown to influence cardiovascular reactivity.

Salt Sensitivity

Increased reactivity has been shown to be a consequence of salt loading. For example, salt-sensitive subjects demonstrate elevated HR to mental challenge (Buchholz et al., 1999). Buchholz and colleagues (2003) found that the mechanisms underlying the increased HR reactivity in salt-sensitive individuals were reduced vagal and increased sympathetic tone. Also Falkner and colleagues (1986) observed greater BP at rest and in response to stress during salt loading in salt-sensitive adolescents. As salt-sensitive people are genetically susceptible to hypertension development, it is likely that exaggerated cardiovascular reactivity contributes to hypertension in these individuals (Buchholz et al., 2003).

Caffeine

Caffeine has been shown to possess significant stimulatory effects on the cardiovascular and neuroendocrine systems. Laboratory studies have shown that a caffeine dose equivalent to two to three cups of coffee can raise resting BP by 7 to 10 mmHg (Pincombe et al., 1988). Studies have also shown that caffeine can raise plasma levels of the major stress hormones such as norepinephrine, epinephrine, and cortisol (Lane et al., 1989). Laboratory studies have indicated that caffeine can intensify both cardiovascular and humoral response to experimental stressors, amplify increases in cardiac output and skeletal muscle blood flow, and increase plasma levels of epinephrine and cortisol (Pincombe et al., 1988).

Nicotine

Cigarette smoking induces rapid changes in cardiovascular function and produces changes similar to those of a stressor. Heart rate, BP, and cardiac output increase during smoking and remain elevated for as long as 2 hr (Spohr & Hoffman, 1979). Also, catecholamines have been found to significantly increase during smoking (Cryer & Haymond, 1976). Smoking and stress interact in cardiovascular reactivity, so that the cardiovascular response is larger for someone who smokes under stress than for someone who smokes during normal conditions (MacDougall & Dembroski, 1983).

Sleep Deprivation

Sleep insomnia is highly prevalent in the general population, with between 10% and 50% of individuals reporting difficulty in sleeping (Johnson, 1999). There are now emerging data to suggest that sleep deprivation may have consequences for health, leading to pronounced changes in neuroendocrine, hormonal, and inflammatory status (Spiegel, Leproult, & Van Cauter, 1999).

Patterns of Reactivity Response

Patterns of reactivity are influenced by the nature of the task, amplifiers, and individual differences (figure 11.1). Also reactivity patterns vary across individuals performing the same task or challenge. Thus, some subjects display an exaggerated cardiovascular response (hot reactors), whereas others display far less reactivity to the same task. Saab and Schneiderman (1993) suggest that laboratory tasks elicit two major patterns of cardiovascular reactivity: Pattern 1 reactivity is characterized by skeletal muscle vasodilation, BP elevation caused by cardiac output increases, tachycardia, increased β-adrenergic activity, and decreased vagal tone. In contrast, pattern 2 reactivity evokes muscle vasoconstriction, BP elevation caused by total peripheral resistance increase, bradycardia, increased α-adrenergic activity, and increased vagal tone. Saab and Schneiderman (1993) suggest that laboratory stressors that typically generate pattern 1 reactivity are active

coping, mental work, and defense behavior. Those that typically produce pattern 2 are aversive vigilance, inhibitory coping, and passive avoidance (Saab & Schneiderman, 1993). Other researchers have labeled pattern 1 and pattern 2 reactivity as myocardial and vascular reactivity and β-adrenergic and α-adrenergic activity.

Certain patterns of reactivity appear to be better predictors than others of the development of cardiovascular disease and hypertension. Thus, individuals who display exaggerated or heightened reactivity are likely to increasingly become the focus of reactivity research. A number of physiological factors that vary across individuals may underlie the hot reactor's exaggerated reactivity response. These include excessive sympathetic outflow, greater receptor density and sensitivity, and abnormal baroreceptor sensitivity. The identification of those reactivity patterns that affect cardiovascular health is likely to be a major focus for reactivity researchers in the future.

Cardiovascular Reactivity Assessment

Further understanding of the reactivity–disease–exercise relationship will be dependent on the ability to assess complex cardiovascular reactivity patterns. It is likely that greater use of multiple measures will be needed to disentangle reactivity patterns and their contribution to cardiovascular disease. Ideally, it would be desirable to assess cardiovascular reactivity by measuring cardiac output, peripheral resistance, beat-by-beat BP, cardiac contractility, HR, blood flow in different vascular beds, heart and coronary artery status, endothelium status, hormonal response, and blood platelet and lipid response. It is typically not possible to assess all these measures simultaneously, so researchers must make a compromise. Following are brief descriptions of measures that have been used to assess cardiovascular reactivity. Table 11.1 lists studies that have utilized these techniques and overviews that discuss these techniques in greater depth.

Cardiac and Vascular Measures

Cardiac reactivity measures have typically included HR, vagal assessment, cardiac output, stroke volume, and cardiac contractility. The noninvasive technique of impedance cardiography

Table 11.1 Cardiovascular Measures With References That Discuss in Greater Depth

Method	Measures	References
Impedance cardiography	Cardiac output, stroke volume, cardiac contractility, total peripheral resistance	Sherwood et al. (1990); Miles & Gotshall (1989)
Finapres	Beat-to-beat blood pressure	Parati et al. (1989)
Venous occlusion plethysmography	Skeletal muscle blood flow, vascular resistance, flow	Formel & Doyle (1957); Whitney (1953)
Vascular ultrasound	Mediated vasodilation (endothelial function)	Faulx et al. (2003); Radegran (1999)
Microneurography and spectral analysis of heart rate and blood pressure	Muscle sympathetic nerve activity, sympathovagal balance	Grassi & Esler (1999)
Neck pressure, lower body negative pressure	Baroreceptor function	Raven et al. (2000)

has been used extensively in reactivity research (Sherwood et al., 1990). This technique allows the rapid assessment of cardiac output, cardiac contractility, and peripheral resistance. If HR is recorded using a data acquisition system, then vagal influence on the heart can be assessed by spectral analysis of the interbeat interval (Grassi & Esler, 1999). Assessment of vagal influence on the heart is also termed heart period variability analysis and reflects the amount of parasympathetic influence on the sinoatrial node. Other measures obtained through data acquisition systems include pulse amplitude, skin electrodermal activity, and respiration. Vascular reactivity measures include skeletal muscle blood flow, flow-mediated vasodilation (FMD), BP, and baroreceptor reflex assessment. Skeletal muscle blood flow has been assessed using venous occlusion plethysmography, whereas FMD has been assessed using high-resolution ultrasound. Blood pressure has typically been measured beat by beat (e.g., the Finapres), whereas baroreceptor reflex has typically been assessed using lower body negative pressure, neck pressure, and the Valsalva maneuver (see table 11.1).

Biochemical Indices of Reactivity

Hormonal reactivity measures include epinephrine, norepinephrine, and cortisol. Liquid chromatography, radioimuunoassay, and radioenzymatic procedures are commonly used in measuring hormones and other reactivity-related biochemi-cal substances (Goldstein & McDonald, 1986). However, kits exist for both catecholamine and cortisol analysis (Wassell et al., 1999). Other blood variable reactivity measures include platelets and blood lipids (Patterson et al., 1995).

Reactivity Effects on Health

The relationship between heightened reactivity and disease is likely to manifest itself through exposure to repeated episodes of acute reactivity. Heightened cardiovascular reactivity has been linked to unfavorable health outcomes that include the development of cardiovascular disease and hypertension.

Cardiovascular Disease

The evidence for reactivity-induced influences on cardiovascular disease is supported directly and indirectly by animal and human evidence.

Animal Research

A series of studies conducted by Kaplan and colleagues provides the strongest evidence linking reactivity and cardiovascular disease. Kaplan and coworkers carried out a series of reactivity studies using a monkey model (cynomolgus macaques). These monkeys, when fed a high-fat diet, quickly develop atherosclerosis. The stressor was the disruption of status hierarchy that is well developed in macaques. Kaplan and colleagues (1983) first showed that dominant monkeys fed a high-fat diet and constantly exposed to stress over a 22-month period had more extensive atherosclerosis than monkeys experiencing less stress. This study demonstrated that psychological stress in monkeys was associated with the development of atherosclerosis. These findings were further replicated in female monkeys (Manuck et al., 1989), and collectively suggest that cardiac responsivity to behavioral challenge is atherogenic.

Human Research

In human research the evidence is not as strong; however, it is supportive of the results of the animal studies. For example, Jiang and colleagues (1996) exposed infarct patients to mental stress and then monitored mortality and incidence of cardiovascular incidents over a five-year period. Patients who recorded mental challenge–induced ischemia compared with nonischemic patients possessed significantly more cardiac problems. Jain and colleagues (1995), using a similar paradigm, produced similar results. Also Stone, Krantz, and McMahon (1999) examined the relationship between ischemia during daily life and mental stress-induced ischemia. Results indicated that patients with daily life ischemia exhibited exaggerated cardiovascular reactivity to mental challenge. Mental challenge response was more predictive of daily ischemia than other laboratory markers. Williams and colleagues (2000) have also provided support for the effects of reactivity on heart health risk by showing that subjects who were at increased risk of coronary artery disease exhibited high trait anger.

Hypertension

Heightened cardiovascular reactivity has also been linked to the development of hypertension (Matthews, Wood, & Allen, 1993). As with the cardiovascular disease research, evidence supporting the role of reactivity-induced development of hypertension is provided by both animal and human work.

Animal Research

A series of studies has shown that chronic exposure to stressors such as shock and social crowding in normotensive rats is accompanied by increased resting BP (Henry, Ely, & Stephens, 1972). Vander and colleagues (1978) have suggested that the hypertension resulting from exposure to stressors was caused by the effect of sympathetically produced circulatory neurohormones.

Other researchers have used the spontaneously hypertensive rat (SHR) to study reactivity-induced hypertension. The SHR begins to show elevated BP at about six weeks of age and develops established hypertension by about six months. In response to aversive stimuli, the young SHR displays greater sympathetic nervous system activity and exaggerated cardiovascular reactivity as compared to non-SHR controls (Hallback & Folkow, 1975). Hallback and Folkow (1975) have shown that hypertension is a consequence of the SHR's hyperreactivity to stressful environmental stimulation. Other studies have shown that shocking and immobilizing SHRs produce centrally mediated increases in catecholamines (McCarty, Chiveh, & Kopin, 1978). Also, a series of studies by Henry and colleagues (Henry et al., 1975) showed that the development of hypertension in SHRs can be averted through a reduction in cardiovascular reactivity. Collectively, these results indicate that hypertension in the SHR can be caused by exposure to stressors, whereas removal of aversive stimulation can prevent hypertension development.

Human Research

Researchers studying humans have shown that BP reactivity predicts future increases in resting BP. For example, Carroll and colleagues (2003) exposed 990 subjects to laboratory stressors and found that BP reactivity significantly predicted a five-year increase in resting systolic and diastolic BP. Also, data from the CARDIA study showed that among 3,308 black and white American adults, the psychosocial factors "time urgency/impatience" and "hostility" were associated with an increase in the long-term risk of hypertension (Yan et al., 2003). Family history of hypertension has also been shown to be a significant hypertension risk factor (Alleman & Weidmann, 1995). Subjects with a parental history of hypertension have been shown to demonstrate exaggerated BP, HR (Muldoon et al., 1993), forearm blood flow responses (Miller & Ditto, 1991), sympathetic nervous activity, and endothelin-1 release (Noll et al., 1996) in response to mental challenge. Interestingly, certain aspects of hyperreactivity do not seem to be evident in hypertensive individuals. For example, Cardillo and colleagues (1998) found that hypertensive subjects possessed a significantly blunted forearm blood flow response to mental stress in comparison with healthy controls. The reduced vasodilatory reactivity was due to impaired nitric oxide–dependent vasodilation. Collectively, these findings demonstrate that reactivity can cause cardiovascular disease and hypertension in susceptible animals. In humans, reactivity and psychosocial factors are associated with the development of cardiovascular disease and hypertension.

Chronic Aerobic Exercise and Reactivity

Researchers examining the effects of chronic exercise (e.g., regular walking, jogging) on reactivity have utilized both cross-sectional and longitudinal approaches.

Cross-Sectional Studies

Cross-sectional studies typically have compared the reactivity responses of aerobically trained or physically active individuals with those of the untrained or sedentary. Some studies have shown different HR and BP reactivity responses (e.g., baseline HR minus HR response to the stressor) between trained and untrained adults (Light et al., 1987; Turner et al., 1987), whereas others have found no differences (Brooke & Long, 1987; Hollander & Seraganian, 1984; Hull, Young, & Ziegler, 1984; Sinyor et al., 1986; Sothmann et al., 1987). Meta-analysis by Crews and Landers (1987) showed that chronic aerobic exercise was associated with a small reactivity reduction. In summary, studies indicate that reactivity, as defined by cardiovascular responses (e.g., HR, BP) from baseline, are associated with an insignificant or negligible reactivity-reducing effect.

An issue, however, is whether HR responsivity or absolute HR level during mental challenge is most relevant for cardiovascular health. For example, all studies comparing HR of aerobically trained subjects who display resting bradycardia (HR below 60 bpm) with that of untrained subjects have demonstrated a lower absolute HR level during mental challenge for the trained subjects (e.g., Boutcher, Nugent, & Weltman, 1995). This difference in absolute HR response may have important implications for cardiovascular health. Lower HRs during rest and during mental challenge in the trained are thought to be due to enhanced cardiac parasympathetic influence. Thus, the parasympathetic and sympathetic response to mental challenge may be different in trained and untrained subjects. For example, Boutcher and colleagues (1998) reported that trained compared to untrained males exhibited a greater decrease in parasympathetic control of

the heart during Stroop challenge (see figure 11.2), even though the HR reactivity responses of the two groups were similar. Parasympathetic control of the heart was measured by assessment of heart period variability using spectral analysis of the interbeat interval (Boutcher et al., 1998). These results suggest that trained individuals show a greater reliance on the parasympathetic system and a lower activation of the sympathetic nervous system during mental challenge. This greater parasympathetic withdrawal to mental challenge of trained subjects has been replicated in older males (Boutcher, Nurhayati, & McLaren, 2001), prepubescent boys (Franks & Boutcher, 2003), and postmenopausal women (Boutcher, Craig, & Nurhayati, 1999). Reduced sympathetic activation to mental challenge may prevent the deleterious long-term effects of excessive catecholamine production. Studies comparing parasympathetic and sympathetic response of trained and untrained subjects to mental challenge need to be carried out to verify this relationship.

All the aforementioned cross-sectional studies examined exercise–reactivity relationships in low-risk, healthy individuals. It is feasible, however, that aerobic exercise training may produce a far greater reduction in reactivity in those subjects who display greater reactivity. Support for this

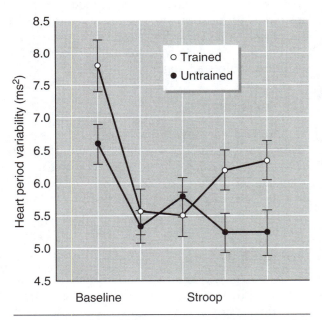

Figure 11.2 The vagal response (heart period variability) of trained and untrained males to Stroop mental challenge.

Reprinted, by permission, from S. Boutcher, F.W. Nugent, P.F. McLaren and A. Weltman, 1998, "Heart period variability of trained and untrained men at rest and during mental challenge," *Psychobiology* 35: 16-22.

notion comes from the hypertension literature. The development of hypertension has a genetic influence, and it has been estimated that up to 50% of hypertension risk is inherited (Alleman & Weidmann, 1995). Offspring of hypertensives (having a parent or grandparent with high BP) also consistently display exaggerated reactivity to mental challenge. For example, Holmes and Cappo (1987) have shown that inactive offspring hypertensives record significantly greater reactivity to mental challenge than fit and active offspring hypertensives. We have also compared vascular reactivity responses of aerobically trained and untrained offspring hypertensives to Stroop challenge (Hamer, Boutcher, & Boutcher, 2002). As can be seen in figure 11.3, vascular reactivity (skeletal muscle blood flow) to the Stroop, measured by occlusion plethysmography, was significantly lower in the trained offspring hypertensives. Thus, aerobic exercise training may produce a far greater reduction in reactivity in those subjects who display greater initial reactivity.

Longitudinal Studies

Longitudinal studies typically have compared the reactivity responses of healthy individuals before and after an exercise program with those of nonexercising controls. Longitudinal results

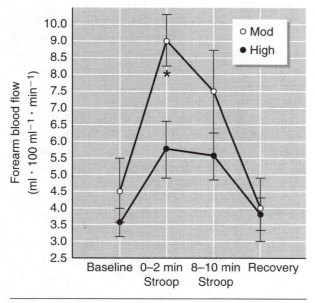

Figure 11.3 Forearm blood flow response to Stroop mental challenge in highly (High) and moderately active (Mod) offspring hypertensives. *Significantly different change between groups from baseline.

Adapted from Hamer et al., 2002.

have provided no clear evidence to suggest that exercise training reduces relative HR and BP reactivity. However, as with the cross-sectional results previously mentioned, aerobically trained subjects who display a reduction in their resting HR with chronic training also record a lower absolute HR level during mental challenge compared to that of untrained subjects (e.g., Stein & Boutcher, 1992).

Similar to the situation with the offspring hypertensive cross-sectional results, there is preliminary longitudinal evidence in offspring hypertensives that supports the ability of aerobic exercise training to produce a far greater reduction in reactivity in those subjects who initially are more reactive. For example, in one of the few studies that has examined the effect of chronic exercise on reactivity in hypertensive subjects, systolic and diastolic BP, total peripheral resistance, and HR were all significantly reduced during mental challenge after six months of aerobic exercise training (Georgiades et al., 2000).

Mechanisms

Perhaps the major finding of the chronic exercise research is that chronic exercise lowers the absolute HR response of healthy individuals to laboratory mental challenge. Evidence exists to show that trained compared to untrained males exhibit a greater decrease in parasympathetic control of the HR during mental challenge. This response may indicate a greater reliance on the parasympathetic system and a lower activation of the sympathetic nervous system, resulting in reduced catecholamine response to mental challenge. The reduced sympathetic activation to mental challenge may help prevent the deleterious effects of excessive catecholamine production.

The research results discussed in the preceding section also show that the ability of chronic exercise to reduce reactivity is likely to be far greater in those individuals who display exaggerated reactivity. Exaggerated reactivity is displayed by individuals with no apparent risk factors and by those who inherit risk factors (e.g., offspring of hypertensives). The mechanisms underlying the hyperreactivity of these individuals are unclear but may include abnormal receptor sensitivity or density and abnormal baroreceptor sensitivity. For example, we have shown that the exaggerated forearm skeletal muscle blood flow response of offspring hypertensives to Stroop challenge is reduced by over 80% when the cardiopulmonary receptors are inhibited (Hamer, Boutcher, & Boutcher, 2003). These results suggest that the abnormal vascular reactivity of these offspring hypertensives was likely brought about by overly sensitive cardiopulmonary baroreceptors. Thus, offspring hypertensives, despite displaying normal resting BP and body composition, may possess abnormal cardiopulmonary baroreceptor sensitivity. Interestingly, it has been shown that chronic exercise that results in plasma volume expansion can decrease cardiopulmonary baroreceptor sensitivity (Mack et al., 1991). Whether chronic exercise-decreased cardiopulmonary sensitivity also results in a reduced blood flow response to mental challenge in offspring hypertensives or hot reactors is undetermined.

In summary, there is evidence to suggest that chronic physical activity may decrease certain aspects of reactivity to mental challenge. The decrease in absolute HR has been consistently found in those cross-sectional studies that have examined individuals displaying resting bradycardia and in longitudinal studies that have resulted in decreases in resting HR. In contrast, the results of studies of the effects of chronic exercise on other reactivity measures such as relative HR and BP are equivocal. Inactive offspring hypertensives typically show significantly greater BP and vascular reactivity to mental challenge than active offspring hypertensives. Also HR, BP, and peripheral resistance reactivity were significantly reduced after training in offspring hypertensive subjects. Thus, the ability of chronic exercise to reduce reactivity is likely to be far greater in individuals who display exaggerated reactivity.

Acute Aerobic Exercise and Reactivity

The rationale behind studying the effects of acute exercise on reactivity is that repeated acute exercise effects may accumulate to generate sustained reactivity dampening. For example, significant reductions in BP, lasting hours, follow a vigorous bout of aerobic exercise (Pescatello et al., 1991). With regard to cardiovascular reactivity, the research evidence is again equivocal; however, there is more evidence to support an acute exercise reactivity-lowering effect than for chronic exercise. This is possibly due to the absence of the confounding variable genetic fitness, which has been problematic in chronic exercise research. The majority of studies in this area have shown a reactivity-lowering effect to mental challenge after an acute bout of aerobic exercise (Boone

et al., 1993; Probst, Bulbulian, & Knapp, 1997; Rejeski et al., 1992; Steptoe, Kearsley, & Walters, 1993; West, Brownley, & Light, 1998), whereas a minority have shown no effect (Cleroux et al., 1992; Floras et al., 1989; Peronnet et al., 1989). The reactivity-lowering effects of acute exercise have mainly been observed as a reduction in BP reactivity (Brownley et al., 2003; Probst, Bulbulian, & Knapp, 1997; Rejeski et al., 1992; Steptoe, Kearsley, & Walters, 1993; West, Brownley, & Light, 1998), although West, Brownley, and Light (1998) also noted a postexercise reduction in total peripheral resistance.

The lack of significant findings in some studies may be a function of the intensity and duration of exercise employed and the length of time between the aerobic exercise bout and the postexercise reactivity stressor. It is apparent that studies yielding significant results have employed higher-intensity aerobic exercise (>60% $\dot{V}O_2$max) for at least 20 min with reactivity testing completed within the first hour of exercise recovery. For example, Steptoe, Kearsley, and Walters (1993) employed two different exercise intensities (50% and 70% $\dot{V}O_2$max) on a stationary bike and found a significant stress reactivity-lowering effect only for the higher-intensity exercise. In summary, there is evidence to suggest that vigorous acute aerobic activity may decrease certain aspects of reactivity to mental challenge. A decrease in BP reactivity has been consistently found in those studies that used a high-intensity bout of exercise.

Possible mechanisms underlying the acute exercise damping reactivity effect include reduced catecholamines, β-adrenergic receptor responsiveness, α-adrenergic-mediated vasoconstriction, and opioidergic inhibition response to stressors. For example, reductions in catecholamine reactivity to stress tasks following an acute bout of exercise have been demonstrated. Peronnet and colleagues (1989) found a 56% reduction in plasma epinephrine reactivity to the Stroop task following a 2 hr bout of moderate-intensity exercise. Also, Brownley and colleagues (2003) recorded significant reductions in epinephrine and norepinephrine reactivity to a speech stress task after a 25 min bout of moderate-intensity exercise. Furthermore, Brownley and colleagues (2003) showed that reduced norepinephrine reactivity was the best single predictor of postexercise reduced BP reactivity.

Brownley and colleagues (2003) also assessed β-adrenergic receptor responsiveness before and after exercise. The authors used a β-adrenergic agonist (isoproterenol) to determine the dose required to elicit a HR increase of 25 bpm and a peripheral vascular resistance decrease of 50%. The results showed significant increases in postexercise $\beta 1$- and $\beta 2$-receptor responsiveness evidenced by reductions in both HR and peripheral resistance throughout the 2 hr postexercise period. Results indicate that the BP reactivity was primarily blunted by enhancement of $\beta 2$-mediated vasodilation.

An important aspect of reactivity that does not appear to have been examined is the effect of acute exercise on vascular reactivity. We have shown that offspring of hypertensives typically display exaggerated vascular reactivity to mental challenge (Hamer, Boutcher, & Boutcher, 2002). The effect of acute exercise on the exaggerated vascular reactivity response of special populations such as offspring hypertensives, however, is undetermined. Similarly, the effect of acute exercise on the transient endothelial dysfunction that is observed following acute mental challenge also appears to be unexamined. Given that sympathetic activation appears to be involved with a reduction in endothelium-dependent vasodilation (Hijmering et al., 2002), it is plausible that exercise could reduce or eliminate stress-induced endothelial dysfunction. For example, exercise may blunt α-adrenergic-mediated vasoconstriction in vascular beds such as muscle. A reduction in α-adrenergic-mediated vasoconstriction during stress is likely to contribute to the increased muscle blood flow that typically occurs in mental challenge. α-adrenergic-mediated vasoconstriction is significantly influenced by cardiopulmonary baroreceptors. Thus, it is plausible that exercise-induced changes in cardiopulmonary baroreceptor sensitivity could result in decreased stress-induced muscle blood flow. Although Halliwill, Dinenno, and Dietz (2003) have recently shown that vascular responsiveness to $\alpha 1$- and $\alpha 2$-agonists was maintained during a 60 min postexercise hypotension period, the authors did not examine reactivity response to stressors.

β-Endorphin, which is produced during exercise and has stress-modulatory characteristics, has also been suggested to play a role in the postexercise reduction in BP reactivity. McCubbin, Surwit, and Williams (1985, 1988) have shown that the opiate antagonist naloxone increases BP responses to psychological stress. Also, McCubbin and colleagues (1992) showed that the lower BP reactivity observed in aerobically trained males was abolished after opiate antagonist treatment, suggesting a role for opioidergic inhibition of cardiovascular reactivity.

Directions for Future Investigation

Issues facing future research on the reactivity–exercise relationship include the use of multiple reactivity measures, the identification of exercise–reactivity mechanisms, a focus on individuals who display exaggerated reactivity, and identification of health outcomes related to exercise–reactivity.

As the reactivity response is complex, it follows that multiple measures of reactivity are needed to identify patterns of reactivity. What is needed is rapid multiple cardiac, vascular, and blood assessment. Given the important role of vascular abnormality in both cardiovascular disease and hypertension, increased use of vascular assessment and the development of new vascular assessment techniques would be desirable.

As previously discussed, the mechanisms underlying the reactivity-reducing effect of chronic and acute exercise are undetermined. It is feasible that different mechanisms are influenced by different kinds of exercise performed at different intensities. This may be especially true of individuals prone to cardiovascular disease and hypertension. The identification of mechanisms that are fundamental to the development of disease and are positively influenced by exercise would be especially helpful.

It is clear that exercise has a far greater effect on the reactivity of individuals who display hyperreactivity compared to others. This is an exciting area for future research because people who display hyperreactivity are typically more prone than others to cardiovascular disease and hypertension. Thus, research examining the effect of chronic and acute exercise on the hyperreactivity of clinical subgroups is required.

Traditionally, exercise psychophysiologists have focused on individual differences affecting the reactivity response and the nature of the reactivity response itself. There has been a paucity of research examining the relationship between reactivity and clinical health outcomes. Consequently, the effects of exercise-induced reductions in cardiac, vascular, hormonal, baroreceptor, lipid, and platelet reactivity on cardiovascular disease and hypertension need to be determined.

Conclusions

Cardiovascular reactivity is a multifactorial phenomenon influenced by the nature of the reactivity stimulus, individual differences, and reactivity amplifiers. Exaggerated cardiovascular reactivity is associated with both cardiovascular disease and hypertension, and therefore interventions for lowering reactivity will play an important role in the future. Both chronic and acute aerobic exercise have been shown to ameliorate certain aspects of cardiovascular reactivity. The exercise-induced reactivity dampening is greater for individuals who exhibit greater reactivity initially, although the mechanisms are undetermined. The major issues for future research in this area include better methods of reactivity assessment, discovery of the exercise damping reactivity mechanisms, and the identification of exercise–reactivity clinical outcomes.

References

Agapitov, A.V., Correia, M.L., Sinkey, C.A., Dopp, J.M., & Haynes, W.G. (2002). Impaired skeletal muscle and skin microcirculatory function in human obesity. *Journal of Hypertension, 20*(7), 1401-1495.

Alleman, Y., & Weidmann, P. (1995). Cardiovascular, metabolic and hormonal dysregulations in normotensive offspring of essential hypertensive parents. *Journal of Hypertension, 13,* 163-173.

Alvarez, G.E., Beske, S.D., Ballard, T.P., & Davy, K.P. (2002). Sympathetic neural activation in visceral obesity. *Circulation, 106,* 2533-2542.

Anderson, N.B. (1989). Racial differences in stress-induced cardiovascular reactivity and hypertension: Current status and substantive issues. *Psychological Bulletin, 105,* 89-105.

Anderson, N.B., McNeilly, M., & Myers, H. (1993). A biopsychological model of race differences in vascular reactivity. In J. Blascovich & E.S. Katkin (Eds.), *Cardiovascular reactivity to psychological stress and disease* (pp. 83-108). Washington, DC: American Psychological Association.

Baker, S.P., Marchand, S.M., O'Neil, E., Nelson, C.A., & Posner, P. (1985). Age-related changes in cardiac muscarinic receptors. *Journal of Gerontology, 40,* 141-146.

Blascovich, J., & Katkin, E.S. (1993). *Cardiovascular reactivity to psychological stress and disease.* Washington, DC: American Psychological Association.

Bloom, D., McCalden, T.A., & Rosendorff, C. (1975). The effects of hypercholesterolemic plasma on vascular sensitivity to norepinephrine. *British Journal of Pharmacology, 54,* 421-427.

Bomzon, L., Kew, M.C., & Rosendorff, C. (1978). Renovascular hypersensitivity to norepinephrine in dietary induced hypercholesterolemia in baboons. *Clinical Experimental Pharmacology, 5,* 181-185.

Boone, J.B., Probst, M.M., Rogers, M.W., & Berger, R. (1993). Postexercise hypotension reduces cardiovascular responses to stress. *Journal of Hypertension, 11,* 449-453.

Boutcher, S.H., Craig, G., & Nurhayati, Y. (1999). Cardiovascular response of trained and untrained postmenopausal females to mental challenge. *Medicine and Science in Sports and Exercise, 31*(5), S290.

Boutcher, S.H., Nugent, F.W., McLaren, P.F., & Weltman, A.L. (1998). Heart period variability of trained and untrained men at rest and during mental challenge. *Psychophysiology, 35,* 16-22.

Boutcher, S.H., Nugent, F.W., & Weltman, A.L. (1995). Cardiac response to psychological stressors of individuals possessing low resting heart rate. *Behavioral Medicine, 21,* 42-46.

Boutcher, S.H., Nurhayati, Y., & McLaren, P. (2001). Cardiovascular response to mental challenge in trained and untrained older males. *Medicine and Science in Sports and Exercise, 33,* 659-664.

Boutcher, S.H., & Stocker, D. (1996). Cardiovascular response of young and older males to mental challenge. *Journals of Gerontology, Psychology, 51,* 261-267.

Brooke, S.T., & Long, B.C. (1987). Efficiency of coping with a real life stressor: A multimodal comparison of aerobic fitness. *Psychophysiology, 24,* 173-180.

Brownley, K.A., Hinderlitter, A.L., West, S.G., Girdler, S.S., Sherwood, A., & Light, K.A. (2003). Sympathoadrenergic mechanisms in reduced hemodynamic stress responses after exercise. *Medicine and Science in Sports and Exercise, 35,* 978-986.

Buchholz, K., Schanger, H., Wagner, M., Sharma, A.M., & Deter, H.C. (2003). Reduced vagal activity in salt-sensitive subjects during mental challenge. *American Journal of Hypertension, 16,* 531-536.

Buchholz, K., Schorr, U., Turan, S., Sharma, A.M., & Deter, H.C. (1999). Emotional irritability and anxiety in salt-sensitive persons at risk for essential hypertension. *Psychotherapie, Psychosomatik, Medizinische Psychologie, 49,* 284-289.

Cardillo, C., Kilcoyne, C.M., Cannon, R.O., & Panza, J.A. (1998). Impairment of the nitric oxide-mediated vasodilator response to mental stress in hypertensive but not in hypercholesterolemic patients. *Journal of the American College of Cardiology, 32*(5), 1207-1213.

Carroll, D., Ring, C., Hunt, K., Ford, G., & Macintyre, S. (2003). Blood pressure reactions to stress and the prediction of future blood pressure: Effects of sex, age, and socioeconomic position. *Psychosomatic Medicine, 65,* 58-64.

Cleroux, J., Kouame, N., Nadeau, A., Coulombe, D., & Lacourciere, Y. (1992). Baroreflex regulation of forearm vascular resistance after exercise in hypertensive and normotensive humans. *American Journal of Physiology, 263,* H1523-H1531.

Cole, S.W., Kemeny, M.E., Fahey, J.L., Zack, J.A., & Naliboff, B.D. (2003). Psychological risk factors for HIV pathogenesis: Mediation by the autonomic nervous system. *Biological Psychiatry, 54,* 1444-1456.

Crews, D.J., & Landers, D.M. (1987). A meta-analytic review of aerobic fitness and reactivity to psychosocial stressors. *Medicine and Science in Sports and Exercise, 19,* S114-S120.

Cryer, P.E., & Haymond, J.W. (1976). Norepinephrine and epinephrine release and adrenergic mediation of smoking-associated hemodynamic and metabolic events. *New England Journal of Medicine, 295,* 573-577.

Denollet, J., Sys, S.U., Stroobant, N., Rombouts, H., Gillebert, T.C., & Brutsaert, D.L. (1996). Personality as an independent predictor of long-term mortality in patients with coronary heart disease. *Lancet, 347,* 417-421.

Falkner, B., Katz, S., Canessa, M., & Kushnerm, H. (1986). The response to long-term sodium loading in young Blacks. *Hypertension, 8,* I165-I168.

Faulx, M.D., Wright, A.T., & Hoit, B.D. (2003). Detection of endothelial dysfunction with brachial artery ultrasound scanning. *American Heart Journal, 145*(6), 943-951.

Floras, J.S., Sinkey, C.A., Aylward, P.E., Seals, D.R., Thoren, P.N., & Mark, A.L. (1989). Post exercise hypotension and sympathoinhibition in borderline hypertensive men. *Hypertension, 14,* 28-35.

Formel, P.F., & Doyle, J.T. (1957). Rationale of venous occlusion plethysmograph. *Circulation Research, 5,* 354-356.

Franks, P., & Boutcher, S.H. (2003). Cardiovascular response to mental challenge in trained and untrained pre-teenage boys. *Medicine and Science in Sports and Exercise, 35,* 1429-1435.

Galle, J., Mulsch, A., & Basssenge, E. (1989). Oxidatively modified low density lipoproteins enhance agonist-induced vasoconstriction. *European Heart Journal, 10,* 37.

Georgiades, A., Sherwood, A., Gullette, E.D., Babyak, M.A., Hinderliter, A., Waugh, R., Tweedy, D., Craighead, L., Bloomer, R., & Blumenthal, J.A. (2000). Effects of exercise and weight loss on mental stress-induced cardiovascular responses in individuals with high blood pressure. *Hypertension, 36,* 171-176.

Goldstein, D.S., & McDonald, R.H. (1986). Biochemical indices of cardiovascular reactivity. In K.A. Matthews, S.M. Weiss, T. Detre, T.M. Dembroski, B. Falkner, S.B. Manuck, & R.B. Williams (Eds.), *Handbook of stress, reactivity, and cardiovascular disease* (pp. 187-206). New York: Wiley.

Grassi, G., & Esler, M. (1999). How to assess sympathetic activity in humans. *Journal of Hypertension, 17*(6), 719-734.

Hallback, M., & Folkow, B. (1975). Cardiovascular response to acute mental stress in spontaneously hypertensive rats. *Acta Physiolologica Scandinavica, 90,* 684-698.

Halliwill, J.R., Dinenno, F.A., & Dietz, N.M. (2003). Alpha-adrenergic vascular responsiveness during postexercise hypotension in humans. *Journal of Physiology, 550* (pt. 1), 279-286.

Hamer, M., Boutcher, Y., & Boutcher, S.H. (2002). Cardiovascular and renal responses to mental challenge in highly and moderately active males with a family history of hypertension. *Journal of Human Hypertension, 16,* 319-326.

Hamer, M., Boutcher, Y., & Boutcher, S.H. (2003). The role of cardiopulmonary baroreceptors during the forearm vasodilation response to mental stress in humans. *Psychophysiology, 40,* 249-253.

Henry, J.P., Ely, D.L., & Stephens, P.M. (1972). Changes in catecholamine-controlling enzymes in response to psychosocial activation of the defence and alarm reactions: Physiology, emotion and psychosomatic illness. *Ciba Foundation Symposium, 8,* 225-251.

Henry, J.P., Stephens, P.M., Axelrod, J., & Santisteban, G.A. (1975). A model of psychosocial hypertension showing reversibility and progression of cardiovascular complications. *Circulation Research, 36,* 156-164.

Hijmering, M.L., Stroes, E.S., Olijhoek, J., Hutten, B.A., Blankestijn, P.J., & Rabelink, T.J. (2002). Sympathetic activation markedly reduces endothelium-dependent, flow-mediated vasodilation. *Journal of the American College of Cardiology, 39*(4), 683-688.

Hollander, A., & Seraganian, P. (1984). Aerobic fitness and psychophysiological reactivity. *Canadian Journal of Behavioral Science, 16,* 257-261.

Holmes, D.S., & Cappo, B.M. (1987). Prophylactic effect of aerobic fitness on cardiovascular arousal among individuals with a family history of hypertension. *Journal of Psychosomatic Research, 31*(5), 601-605.

Hull, E.M., Young, S.H., & Ziegler, M.G. (1984). Aerobic fitness affects cardiovascular and catecholamine responses to stressors. *Psychophysiology, 21,* 353-360.

Jain, D., Burg, M., Soufer, R., & Zaret, B.L. (1995). Prognostic implications of mental stress induced silent left ventricular dysfunction in patients with stable angina pectoris. *American Journal of Cardiology, 76,* 31-35.

Jiang, W., Babyak, M., Krantz, D., Waugh, R.A., Coleman, E., Hanson, M.M., Frid, D.J., McNulty, S., Morris, J.J., O'Conner, C.M., & Blumenthal, J.A. (1996). Mental stress-induced myocardial ischemia and cardiac events. *Journal of the American Medical Association, 275,* 1651-1656.

Johnson, E. (1999). *Sleep in America.* Washington, DC: National Sleep Foundation.

Kaplan, J.R., Manuck, S.B., Clarkson, T.B., Lusso, F.M., Taub, D.M., & Miller, E.W. (1983). Social stress and atherosclerosis in normocholesterolemic monkeys. *Science, 22,* 733-735.

Kuniyoshi, F.H., Trombetta, I.C., Batalha, L.T., Rondon, M.U., Laterza, M.C., Gowdak, M.M., Barretto, A.C., Halpern, A., Villares, S.M., Lima, E.G., & Negrao, C.E. (2003). Abnormal neurovascular control during sympathoexcitation in obesity. *Obesity Research, 11*(11), 1411-1419.

Lacey, J.I. (1967). Somatic response patterning and stress. Some revisions of activation theory. In M.H. Appley & R. Trumbull (Eds.), *Issues in research* (pp. 14-44). New York: Appleton-Century-Crofts.

Lane, J.D., Adcock, R.A., Williams, R.B., & Kuhn, C.M. (1989). Caffeine affects on cardiovascular and neuroendocrine responses to acute psychosocial stress and their relationship to level of habitual caffeine consumption. *Psychosomatic Medicine, 51,* 373-380.

Lazarus, R.S., & Folkman, S. (1984). *Stress, appraisal, and coping.* New York: Springer.

Li, G.H., Faulhaber, H.D., Rosenthal, M., Schuster, H., Jordan, J., Timmermann, B., Hoehe, M.R., Luft, F.C., & Busjahn, A. (2001). Beta-2 adrenergic receptor gene variations and blood pressure under stress in normal twins. *Psychophysiology, 38*(3), 485-489.

Light, K.C., Obrist, P.A., James, S.A., & Strogatz, D.S. (1987). Cardiovascular responses to stress: II. Relationships to aerobic exercise patterns. *Psychophysiology, 24,* 79-86.

MacDougall, J.M., & Dembroski, T.M. (1983). Cardiovascular effects of stress and cigarette smoking. *Journal of Human Stress, 9,* 13-21.

Mack, G.W., Thompson, C.A., Doerr, D.F., Nadel, E.R., & Convertino, V.A. (1991). Diminished baroreflex control of forearm vascular resistance following training. *Medicine and Science in Sports and Exercise, 23,* 1367-1374.

Manuck, S.B., Kaplan, J.R., Adams, M.R., & Clarkson, T.B. (1989). Behaviorally elicited heart rate reactivity and atherosclerosis in Cynomolgus monkeys. *Psychosomatic Medicine, 45,* 95-108.

Matthews, K.A., & Stoney, C.M. (1988). Influences of sex and age on cardiovascular responses during stress. *Psychosomatic Medicine, 50,* 46-56.

Matthews, K.A., Wood, K.L., & Allen, M.T. (1993). Cardiovascular reactivity to stress predicts future blood pressure status. *Hypertension, 22,* 479-485.

McCarty, R., Chiveh, C.C., & Kopin, I.J. (1978). Behavioral and cardiovascular responses of spontaneously hypertensive and normotensive rats to inescapable footshock. *Behavioral Biology, 22,* 405-411.

McCubbin, J.A., Cheung, R., Montgomery, T.B., Bulbulian, R., & Wilson, J.F. (1992). Aerobic fitness and opioidergic inhibition of cardiovascular stress reactivity. *Psychophysiology, 29*(6), 687-697.

McCubbin, J.A., Surwit, R.S., & Williams, R.B. Jr. (1985). Endogenous opiate peptides, stress reactivity, and risk for hypertension. *Hypertension, 7*(5), 808-811.

McCubbin, J.A., Surwit, R.S., & Williams, R.B. Jr. (1988). Opioid dysfunction and risk for hypertension: Naloxone and blood pressure responses during different types of stress. *Psychosomatic Medicine, 50*(1), 8-14.

Miles, D.S., & Gotshall, R.W. (1989). Impedance cardiography: Noninvasive assessment of human central hemodynamics at rest and during exercise. *Exercise and Sport Sciences Reviews, 17,* 231-263.

Miller, G.E., Cohen, S., Rabins, B.S., Skoner, D.P., & Doyle, W.J. (1999). Personality and tonic cardiovascular, neuroendocrine, and immune parameters. *Brain Behavior, Immunity, 13,* 109-123.

Miller, S.B., & Ditto, B. (1991). Exaggerated sympathetic nervous system response to extended psychological stress in offspring of hypertensives. *Psychophysiology, 28,* 103-113.

Muldoon, M.F., Terrell, D.F., Bunker, C.H., & Manuck, S.B. (1993). Family history studies in hypertension research. Review of the literature. *American Journal of Hypertension, 6,* 76-88.

Noll, G., Wenzel, R.R., Schneider, M., Oesch, V., Binggeli, C., Shaw, S., Weidmann, P., & Luscher, T.F. (1996). Increased activation of sympathetic nervous system and endothelin by mental stress in normotensive offspring of hypertensive parents. *Circulation, 93*(5), 866-869.

Obrist, P. (1981). *Cardiovascular psychophysiology: A perspective.* New York: Plenum Press.

Parati, G., Casadei, R., Groppeli, A., Rienzo, M.D., & Mancia, G. (1989). Comparison of finger and intra-arterial blood pressure monitoring at rest and during laboratory testing. *Hypertension, 13,* 647-655.

Patkai, P. (1971). Catecholamine excretion in pleasant and unpleasant situations. *Acta Psychologica, 35,* 352-363.

Patterson, S.M., Krantz, D.S., Gottdiener, J.S., Hecht, G., Vargot, S., & Goldstein, D.S. (1995). Prothrombotic effects of environmental stress: Changes in platelet function, hematocrit, and total plasma protein. *Psychosomatic Medicine, 57*(6), 592-599.

Peronnet, F.D., Massicotte, D., Paquet, J., Brisson, G., & De Champlain, J. (1989). Blood pressure and plasma catecholamine responses to various challenges during exercise recovery in man. *European Journal of Applied Physiology, 58,* 551-555.

Pescatello, L.S., Fargo, A.E., Leach, C.N., & Scherzer, H.H. (1991). Short-term effect of dynamic exercise on arterial blood pressure. *Circulation, 83,* 1557-1561.

Pincombe, G.A., Lovallo, W.R., Passey, R.B., & Wilson, M.F. (1988). Effect of behavior state on caffeine's ability to alter blood pressure. *American Journal of Cardiology, 61,* 798-802.

Probst, M., Bulbulian, R., & Knapp, C. (1997). Hemodynamic responses to the Stroop and cold pressor tests after submaximal cycling exercise in normotensive males. *Physiology and Behavior, 62,* 1283-1290.

Radegran, G. (1999). Limb and skeletal muscle blood flow measurements at rest and during exercise in human subjects. *Proceedings of the Nutrition Society, 58*(4), 887-898.

Raven, P.B., Potts, J.T., Shi, X., & Pawelczyk, J. (2000). Baroceptor-mediated reflex regulation of blood pressure during exercise. In B. Saltin, R. Boushel, N. Secher, & J. Mitchell (Eds.), *Exercise and circulation in health and disease* (pp. 3-24). Champaign, IL: Human Kinetics.

Rejeski, J.W., Thompson, A., Brubaker, P.H., & Miller, H.S. (1992). Acute exercise: Buffering psychosocial stress responses in women. *Health Psychology, 11,* 355-362.

Saab, P.G., & Schneiderman, N. (1993). Biobehavioral stressors, laboratory investigation, and the risk of hypertension. In J. Blascovich & E.S. Katkin (Eds.), *Cardiovascular reactivity to psychological stress and disease* (pp. 49-82). Washington, DC: American Psychological Association.

Schneiderman, N., & McCabe, P.M. (1999). Psychophysiologic strategies in laboratory research. In N. Schneiderman, S.M. Weiss, & P.G. Kaufmann (Eds.), *Handbook of research methods in cardiovascular behavioral medicine* (pp. 349-364). New York: Plenum Press.

Sherwood, A., Allen, M.T., Fahrenberg, J., Kelsey, R.M., Lovallo, W.R., & van Doornen, L. (1990). Methodological guidelines for impedance cardiography. *Psychophysiology, 27*(1), 1-23.

Sinyor, D., Peronnet, F., Brisson, G., & Seraganian, P. (1986). Failure to alter sympathoadrenal response to psychosocial stress following aerobic training. *Physiological Behavior, 42,* 293-296.

Sothmann, M.S., Horn, T.S., Hart, B.A., & Gustafson, A.B. (1987). Comparison of discrete cardiovascular fitness groups on plasma catecholamine and behavioural responses to psychological stress. *Psychophysiology, 24,* 47-54.

Spiegel, K., Leproult, R., & Van Cauter, E. (1999). Impact of sleep debt on metabolic and endocrine function. *Lancet, 354,* 1435-1439.

Spohr, U., & Hoffman, W. (1979). Evaluation of smoking-induced effects on sympathetic, hemodynamic and metabolic variables with respect to plasma nicotine and COHb levels. *Atherosclerosis, 33,* 271-283.

Stein, P.K., & Boutcher, S.H. (1992). The effect of participation in an exercise training program on cardiovascular reactivity in sedentary middle-aged men. *International Journal of Psychophysiology, 13,* 215-223.

Steptoe, A., Kearsley, N., & Walters, N. (1993). Cardiovascular activity during mental stress following vigorous exercise in sportsmen and inactive men. *Psychophysiology, 30,* 245-252.

Steptoe, A., & Vogele, C. (1991). Methodology of mental stress testing in cardiovascular research. *Circulation, 83,* II-14–II-24.

Stone, P.H., Krantz, R.P., & McMahon, R.P. (1999). Relationship among mental-induced ischemia and ischemia during daily life and during exercise: The psychophysiologic investigations of myocardial ischemia (PIMI) study. *Journal of the American College of Cardiology, 33,* 1476-1484.

Turner, J.R., Costello, M., Carroll, D., & Sims, J. (1987). The effects of aerobic fitness on additional heart rate during active psychological challenge: A cross-sectional study [abstract]. *Psychophysiology, 24,* 571.

Vander, A.J., Henry, J.P., Stephens, P.M., Kay, L.L., & Mouw, D.R. (1978). Plasma renin activity in psychosocial hypertension of CBA mice. *Circulation Research, 42,* 496-502.

van Doornen, L.J.P., Sneider, H., & Boomsma, D.I. (1998). Serum lipids and cardiovascular reactivity to stress. *Biological Psychology, 47*(3), 279-297.

Wassell, J., Reed, P., Kane, J., Weinkove, C. (1999). Freedom from drug interference in new immunoassays for urinary catecholamines and metanephrines. *Clinical Chemistry, 45*(12), 2216-2223.

West, S.G., Brownley, K.A., & Light, K.C. (1998). Postexercise vasodilatation reduces diastolic blood pressure responses to stress. *Annals of Behavioral Medicine, 20,* 77-83.

Whitney, R.J. (1953). The measurement of volume changes in human limbs. *Journal of Physiology, 121,* 1-27.

Williams, J.E., Paton, C.C., Siegler, I.C., Eigenbrodt, M.L., & Tyroler, H.A. (2000). Anger proneness predicts coronary heart disease risk: Prospective analysis from the atherosclerosis in communities (ARIC) study. *Circulation, 101,* 2034-2039.

Yan, L.L., Liu, K., Matthews, K.A., Daviglus, M.L., Ferguson, T.F., & Kiefe, C.I. (2003). Psychosocial factors and risk of hypertension: The Coronary Artery Risk Development in Young Adults (CARDIA) study. *Journal of the American Medical Association, 290*(16), 2138-2148.

12

Physical Activity and Psychoneuroimmunology

Suzi Hong, PhD

Paul J. Mills, PhD

Most people know that the phrase "sick to my stomach" does not refer to mere indigestion. Many can instantly associate it with emotional reactions from their anecdotal experiences, including anxiety, fear, disgust, and so on. Many people also believe that "distress" is a cause of or largely contributes to mild to severe illnesses, ranging from flu to cancer. In our everyday lives we encounter or experience events that are seemingly intuitive, although mechanistically unclear, examples of a connection between mind and body. It is a common belief for most of us that our emotional state can influence our physical condition, yet we have little knowledge of how and why this occurs.

Immunology is a science of the organism's defense system against a variety of disease-causing agents, including viruses, bacteria, fungi, parasites, and cancer. Research in immunology has grown exponentially since Edward Jenner successfully demonstrated vaccination against smallpox in 1798. Conventionally, the immune system was considered to be self-regulating, independent of other regulatory mechanisms. Hence, the interaction of the immune system with other systems of the organism received little attention among researchers in the past. During the past two decades, however, a deeper appreciation of the manifold communication between the nervous and immune systems began to draw attention among researchers and spawned the field of psychoneuroimmunology (PNI). Broadly speaking, PNI is the study of the reciprocal interactions among the

behavioral, neural, endocrine, and immune systems (Ader, Cohen, & Felten, 1995). This chapter briefly describes this rapidly emerging area and, on the basis of a review of the literature, discusses exercise as a promising model for PNI research.

The number of studies examining the effects of exercise on the immune system has grown significantly in the past decade. This phenomenally growing body of literature clearly shows that exercise affects diverse aspects of the immune system (Hong & Mills, 2003). However, studies that address the effects of exercise in the context of PNI are still limited and merit further inquiry. Thus, this chapter focuses on a review of the exercise studies with an emphasis on cellular immunity and on a discussion of health implications of those studies. Before starting this review, for the purpose of establishing a basis for understanding the current exercise and PNI literature, we present a brief overview of the immune system.

The Immune System

The mammalian immune system consists of different subsets of cell populations and molecules that are responsible for immune responses. It is a complex and intricately orchestrated system that modern technology and science are still far from fully understanding. The immunological host defense mechanism involves recognition of a foreign entity that has entered the body or mutated cells (i.e., cancer) and elimination of the entity through various reactions. These reactions can be categorized into innate and adaptive immunity. This distinction depends on the characteristics of antigen (immunological target molecule) recognition, defensive capabilities, and immunologic history or memory. Innate immunity, which is a barrier of low specificity to various infectious agents and cancer with low antigen specificity, consists of phagocytic cells such as macrophages and neutrophils, as well as natural killer (NK) cells, a subset of lymphocytes. Innate immunity also includes blood proteins that are components of the complement system, as well as other inflammation-causing mediators, including interleukins. Adapted immunity is highly specific in its recognition of antigens, has memory of previous exposure, and differentially responds to different types of pathogens. Lymphocytes such as T and B cells (including their products, antibodies) compose adaptive immunity.

Cells

Leukocytes (white blood cells) include a number of types of immune cells: lymphocytes, monocytes, granulocytes, and dendritic cells. Lymphocytes are major mediators of adaptive immunity in mammals. They originate in the bone marrow and are differentiated into distinct subpopulations depending on the site of maturation. In mammals, B lymphocytes mature in bone marrow and produce antibodies after interaction with antigens, and this composes humoral immunity. T lymphocytes mature in the thymus and are classified into CD4$^+$ and CD8$^+$ cells depending on their surface molecule cluster of differentiation (CD). They are also named according to their functional differences as helper T (T$_H$, CD4$^+$) and cytotoxic T (T$_C$, CD8$^+$) cells. The main function of T$_C$ cells is lysis of tumor and virus-infected cells, and T$_H$ cells secrete cytokines upon activation. Cytokines promote growth and differentiation of T cells and other lymphocytes and activate inflammatory cells such as mononuclear phagocytes, neutrophils, and eosinophils. There are a number of classes of cytokines (e.g., colony-stimulating factors, chemokines, interleukins) that are produced and released by different types of immune cells, including mononuclear phagocytes and T lymphocytes upon their activation. The term *interleukin* (IL) (e.g., IL-6, IL-8) implies being responsible for the communication between leukocytes. Later, this chapter reviews and discusses in further detail studies of ILs and exercise in the context of PNI research.

Natural killer cells represent another class of lymphocytes found in blood and lymphoid organs, especially the spleen. Natural killer cells play an important role in early defense against pathogens through lysis or apoptosis (morphological processes of genetically programmed cell death characterized by cell shrinkage, DNA fragmentation, etc.) of virus-infected cells and tumor cells. Monocytes are derived from the bone marrow and mature to become macrophages that are major phagocytic cells and cytokine producers. Dendritic cells are the most efficient antigen-presenting cells and are present in relatively low numbers in the body. Granulocytes, which originate in the bone marrow, include neutrophils, eosinophils, basophils, and mast cells. Granulocytes represent about 90% of the immune cells in peripheral blood, and neutrophils are the predominant subpopulation of granulocytes.

Organs

Immune cells migrate to and are concentrated in the primary and secondary lymphoid organs that are distributed throughout the body. The primary lymphoid organs are the bone marrow, where hematopoiesis (generation of blood cells) occurs, and the thymus. The secondary lymphoid organs, where lymphocytes encounter antigens, include lymph nodes, the spleen, tissues of the mucosal immune system (e.g., Peyer's patches in the small intestine and the tonsils), and the cutaneous immune system (e.g., epidermic or dermic lymphocytes). Foreign antigens are collected and transported to the lymph nodes through lymphatic vessels. The spleen stores immune cells and provides an environment for immune responses to blood-borne antigens.

Exercise As a Model for Psychoneuroimmunology Research

Psychoneuroimmunology is the study of the reciprocal interactions among the behavioral, neural, endocrine, and immune systems (Ader, Cohen, & Felten, 1995). Thus, the term "psycho-neuro-endocrino-immunology" (Solomon, 1987) may be more descriptive of the area of research. Research in the area of PNI has flourished since the early 1980s, but the communication between the brain and immune system was initially examined as early as the 1960s. Solomon reported stress-induced immunomodulation such that higher serum antibody titers were found in a group of rats that were handled neonatally by humans compared to those of the control (nonhandled) rats (Solomon, 1969). Furthermore, documentation of stress-induced lymphocytosis (increased number of lymphocytes in circulation) in humans dates back to the 1920s (Mora, Amtmann, & Hoffmann, 1926).

Findings of psychosocial influences on immunity in humans provide early evidence of a link between psychology and immunity; immunosuppression (e.g., decreased NK cell function, decreased lymphocyte proliferation), for example, was observed during or following acute stressful events (e.g., final examinations among medical school students) or prolonged stress (i.e., depression caused by prolonged stressful events) (Kiecolt-Glaser & Glaser, 1987). These indicators of compromised immunity are also associated with increased disease susceptibility (Kemeny & Gruenewald, 1999).

In an effort to further investigate the underlying mechanisms of the link between immune responses and psychosocial factors, experimental laboratory studies have been conducted to document the neuroendocrine–immune relationship. In order to examine the role of catecholamines in immune cell responses to psychosocial stress, a series of studies utilized injection or infusion of epinephrine and norepinephrine (NE) and showed concomitant increases in numbers of certain lymphocytes such as NK and T_C cells (see Benschop, Rodriguez-Feuerhahn, & Schedlowski, 1996, for review). In addition, brain lesions have been used in animals to study the neural links between the central nervous system and immune system. Lesions in brain areas that govern emotions such as the hypothalamus, limbic system, and cortex resulted in decreased immune function (Ader, Cohen, & Felten, 1995). In summary, the evidence of the communication "from" the brain "to" the immune system is rather clear. However, the effects of the immune system on the psychoneuroendocrine system or behavior have been studied to a much lesser extent in spite of the fact that PNI research emphasizes investigations of the bidirectional communications between systems.

The Neuroendocrine System and Exercise

What is the nature of the neuroendocrine response to exercise? It is well known that plasma catechol-amine levels significantly increase during acute exercise (Dishman, 1997; Dishman et al., 2000; Mazzeo, 1991). Plasma levels of adrenocorticotropin hormone (ACTH), cortisol, and prolactin also increase in an intensity- and duration-dependent manner during acute exercise (Dishman et al., 1998). These data indicate the activation of the hypothalamic-pituitary-adrenal (HPA) system during acute exercise.

These acute responses of the sympathetic nervous and HPA systems to exercise appear to change after repeated exercise bouts. Exercise training results in changes in end-organ responsiveness through adaptations in the sympathoadrenal system. For example, decreased heart rate after exercise training is well known as "training-induced bradycardia" (Sigvardsson, Svanfeldt, & Kilbom, 1977). On the other hand, low physical fitness or detraining can lead to augmented plasma NE responses to stress depending on the type of stressor (Sothmann, Hart, & Horn, 1991). Exercise training also leads to decreased circulating NE levels at rest and to blunted NE responses to acute exercise in humans (Kjaer, Secher, & Galbo, 1987) or to a laboratory stressor in animals (Fleshner et al., 2002). Downregulation of β-adrenergic receptors occurs as a result of chronic exercise training in humans (Ohman et al., 1987). Lower resting heart rate among physically active subjects as compared to inactive subjects further suggests that regular exercisers may have less sensitive β-adrenergic receptors (Hong et al., 2004).

The HPA system also appears to partially adapt after chronic exercise training in humans (Dishman et al., 1998). However, whether chronic exercise alters HPA responses to other stressors remains unclear (Sothmann et al., 1996). It is evident that exercise affects the neuroendocrine system such that acute exercise activates the system, and that regular exercise or training may lead to partial adaptations (downregulation) of the system.

This chapter has only briefly reviewed the effects of exercise on the neuroendocrine system as a segue to the discussion of PNI and exercise. Thus, other chapters in the book should be referred to for a detailed review of the exercise–neuroendocrine literature.

Effects of Physical Activity on Neuroendocrine–Immune Associations

Given the evidence of effects of exercise on the neuroendocrine system and the large body of literature in exercise immunology (Hong & Mills, 2003), it is clear that there is an association between exercise and the neuroendocrine–immune linkage. Exercise training leads to downregulation of β-adrenergic receptor density on lymphocytes at rest (Kjaer, Secher, & Galbo, 1987). Regular physical activity or exercise training leads to blunted lymphocyte adhesion molecule expression responses to stress, in part via an adaptation of the adrenergic system (Hong et al., 2004).

Figure 12.1 is a schematic model to depict exercise as a paradigm for PNI research and an overview of the associations among exercise, psychology, the neuroendocrine system, and the immune system. However, evidence of the asso-

ciations is mainly based on studies examining the separate effects of exercise on psychology, the neuroendocrine system, or the immune system, as marked by unfilled arrows. As noted throughout this chapter, the effects of exercise on these systems are highly dependent on the nature of the exercise—acute versus chronic, mild versus vigorous, short versus prolonged duration, and aerobic versus resistance.

Enumerative Responses of the Immune System to Exercise

The research on the enumerative responses of the immune system to exercise has focused on the circulation and migration of immune cells, immune cells in blood, and cellular adhesion molecules (CAMs).

Circulation and Migration of Immune Cells

Recirculation and migration of immune cells to the different sites of antigen localization within the body are critical in host defense providing surveillance for foreign microorganisms. Foreign antigens are also transported to lymphoid tissues where they can be recognized by lymphocytes. Migration of lymphocytes to the various sites of antigen localization within the body is critical in immune responses. Naive lymphocytes (those that have not encountered antigens) in the blood circulation randomly and loosely adhere to the vessel walls (marginal pool) for a fraction of a second and are detached by the force of flowing blood. Once they migrate and attach to the endothelial surface of lymph nodes and mucosal lymphoid tissues, lymphocytes are activated upon encountering specific antigens; but naive lymphocytes that do not encounter antigens return to the circulation. Homing (recruitment to the infected areas of the body) of leukocytes begins with sensing the presence of infectious microbes in specific areas. Initial trafficking, rolling, and firm adhesion of leukocytes to the site of infection are mediated by adhesion molecules, which are homing receptors on the lymphocytes (e.g., L-selectin, LFA-1, VLA-4, CD44) and their ligands (molecules that bind to a macromolecule, such as receptors) on endothelial cells (e.g., GlyCAM-1, ICAM-1, VCAM-1). Inflammatory stimuli (e.g., tumor necrosis factor-α [TNF-α], IL-1,

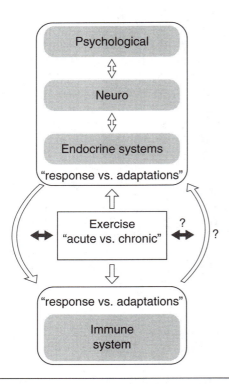

Figure 12.1 Conceptual diagram of exercise as a model for PNI research. The effects of exercise on the psychoneuroendocrine (PNE) and immune systems are relatively well documented separately as depicted with unfilled arrows (see the sections in this chapter titled, "The Neuroendocrine System and Exercise" and "Enumerative/Functional Responses of the Immune System to Exercise"). The effects of PNE system on immunity are well documented whereas immune system effects on PNE system (marked with "?") are not. Most importantly, black (filled) arrows depict exercise as a model to study the immune-PNE association. It is also noted that responses versus adaptations of the PNE and immune systems should be clearly distinguished in reponse to acute exercise or as a result of chronic exercise.

chemokines) and antigen recognition by immune cells lead to the expression of those molecules. Leukocytes then attach to endothelial cells lining the infected areas ("firm adhesion"), penetrate into the tissue ("transmigration"), and destroy the pathogen. Most studies examine exercise-induced immune cell trafficking to peripheral blood (i.e., leukocytosis) and expression of the CAMs on these cells as discussed next.

Immune Cells in Blood

Leukocytosis is normally observed during and after a bout of exercise. This immune cell response to exercise varies among subpopulations of leukocytes and is dependent upon the intensity and duration of the exercise challenge. Increases in numbers of most lymphocyte subsets, monocytes, and granulocytes are observed; however, small or no changes are typically seen in numbers of B lymphocytes after exercise of a moderate to high intensity (i.e., 50-85% $\dot{V}O_2$max) (Nehlsen-Cannarella, 1998; Nielsen et al., 1996; Rhind et al., 1999). Mild exercise (i.e., 40% $\dot{V}O_2$max), on the other hand, results in smaller changes in cell numbers in blood (Strasner et al., 1997). The effect of exercise (whether mild, moderate, or high in intensity) is most dramatic for NK cell numbers, such that the number of NK cells can increase two- to fourfold above resting levels (Shek et al., 1995). Eccentric exercise using relatively small muscle groups also affects circulating immune cells (Palmo et al., 1995; Malm, Lenkei, & Sjodin, 1999). The exercise dose–response in leukocytosis is also correlated with the recovery time after exercise, ranging from 15 min to 2 hr (Goebel & Mills, 2000; Hong et al., 2004) for the leukocyte numbers to return to the baseline values depending on the intensity of the exercise. The recovery time is also dependent on the type of leukocytes. In contrast to the relatively rapid transient increases in numbers among lymphocytes, monocytes and granulocytes exhibit a more gradual and slower recovery after exercise (Shek et al., 1995).

The origins of the leukocytes that acutely traffic to the circulation during exercise are not entirely clear. However, increases in numbers of immune cells do not appear to be simply caused by decreases in plasma volume postexercise. Possible candidates include the marginal pool, the spleen, lungs, and bone marrow. Leukocytes may "demarginate" to the peripheral blood compartment during exercise in part as increased hemodynamic forces detach cells that are loosely adherent to the vessel wall at rest. In addition, cells that are mobilized to the circulation during exercise appear to be from the secondary lymphoid organs such as the spleen and lymph nodes, rather than from the primary lymphoid organs (the thymus and the bone marrow), given the findings that a greater percentage of activated memory T cells demarginate as compared to naive cells (Nielsen et al., 1996, 1997). What causes these lymphocytes to be redistributed to the blood compartment from the spleen and lymph nodes? Noradrenergic projections and NE-containing nerve terminals found in the spleen are the evidence of sympathetic innervation of the spleen (Felten et al., 1987). In addition, high-affinity β_2-adrenergic receptors are found on lymphocytes and monocytes (Carlson, Fox, & Abell, 1997). β-adrenergic receptor activation leads to increased circulating numbers of lymphocytes (Murray et al., 1992) and NK cells (Benschop et al., 1997). Attachment of NK cells to human endothelial cells is decreased in a dose-dependent manner after addition of β_2-adrenergic agonists in vitro (Benschop et al., 1993). Infusing β-adrenergic agonists such as epinephrine or isoproterenol leads to a demargination and trafficking of leukocyte subsets similar to that seen following an exercise challenge (Mills et al., 2002). Thus, it appears that sympathetic innervation of the spleen, as well as increases in the levels of circulating catecholamines, contributes to the dramatic lymphocytosis seen during exercise.

It is interesting to note that exhaustive and prolonged exercise (e.g., a marathon) results in decreased immune cell numbers (leukocytopenia) in the circulation. For example, T and NK cell numbers are decreased in peripheral blood after a triathlon in trained athletes and return to the baseline numbers within 18 hr after completion of the race (Staats et al., 2000). It is unclear what aspects of prolonged exercise contribute to an immune cell number response opposite to that normally observed after shorter exercise. The sustained activation of the HPA axis resulting in high cortisol levels or muscular tissue injury may be a contributing factor. Whether the leukocytopenia seen after a marathon reflects the homing of the cells to the fatigued or damaged muscle tissue is not known.

Cellular Adhesion Molecules

The recruitment of immune cells to sites of infection and cell–cell interactions are critical in host defense, and CAMs mediate the adhesion processes. Selectins (e.g., L-selectin: CD62L) are critical in rolling and initial tethering of immune cells on endothelial surfaces. Integrins (LFA-1: CD11a/CD18, Mac-1: CD11b/CD18) cause cells to firmly attach and to migrate through the endothelium by binding to endothelial adhesion molecules (ICAM-1, VCAM-1).

Studies show that the expression of CD62L and CD11a is highly responsive to exercise. Maximal exercise leads to significantly reduced CD62L expression on leukocytes, while CD11b density increases on peripheral blood mononuclear cells (PBMC) and lymphocytes (Van Eeden et al., 1999). No change in CD11b and decreased CD11a levels are shown after a 3 hr run; however, increased CD11b expression may be seen after a maximal aerobic test (Jordan, Beneke, & Hutler, 1997). A preferential increase of CD62L^{low} and CD11a^{hi} T cells has been reported following intensive exercise (Kurokawa et al., 1995). An increase in the density of CD11a and a decrease in the density of CD62L on lymphocytes have been reported after moderate aerobic exercise (Gabriel et al., 1994; Goebel & Mills, 2000). Thus, the effects on these selectins and integrins are variable depending on the intensity and duration of exercise.

The activated forms of integrins, necessary for effective high-avidity binding, bind to ICAM family molecules (i.e., ICAM-1, ICAM-2, and MAdCAM-1) and extracellular matrix proteins (e.g., fibronectin, fibrinogen) on the endothelium, resulting in firm attachment of leukocytes to the endothelial wall. Cellular activation through receptor cross-linkage or endotoxin stimulation results in activation of these integrins. In spite of the evidence that exercise leads to an increased expression of LFA-1 in circulating leukocytes (Goebel & Mills, 2000; Kurokawa et al., 1995), its implications in adhesion processes need further examination. Since the binding of leukocytes to endothelial cells requires activated integrins, it would be more meaningful to determine whether or not exercise increases the avidity of the molecule than to assess expression levels. A greater increase in the number of T_C lymphocytes with high expression of CD11a (CD8$^+$CD11a^{high}) compared with low expression of CD11a (CD8$^+$CD11a^{low}) has been reported following intensive exercise (Kurokawa et al., 1995). However, given the limited literature, it is premature to presume that exercise leads to trafficking of cells with high expression of activated integrins into the circulation. Regarding mechanisms, although it has been shown that exercise leads to a selective recruitment of immune cells into the circulation

depending on the profiles of adhesion molecule expression (Mills et al., 1998), and that this effect can be blocked with the nonspecific β_2-adrenergic antagonist propranolol (Mills et al., 1999), it is still unclear whether the elevation in catecholamine levels or sympathetic outflow to lymphoid organs (or both) causes an actual up- or downregulation of leukocyte adhesion molecules.

Functional Responses of the Immune System to Exercise

In order to investigate changes in functionality of the immune system in response to exercise, researchers have employed several different types of laboratory assays to examine the functions of immune cell populations. Natural killer cell cytotoxicity (NKCC), lymphocyte proliferation in vitro, and in vivo lung clearance of tumor cells in animals have been the main parameters examined in the literature.

Natural Killer Cell Cytotoxicity

The chromium (Cr^{51})-release assay has been used widely as a standard assay to assess the ability of NK cells to destroy tumor cells in vitro. In this assay, NK (effector) cells are cocultured with radioactive-labeled tumor (target; YAC-1, K-562, etc.) cells, and free radioactivity level is assessed as an indication of the number of lysed tumor cells. Some animal studies have utilized in vivo lung clearance of injected tumor cells as an indicator of NKCC (e.g., Jonsdottir et al., 1997). Recently, a new method using flow cytometry (detection of fluorescent-labeled cells in a stream) to assess NKCC has emerged (e.g., Hoppner et al., 2002). Transient increases in NKCC during or immediately after moderate- to high-intensity exercise are followed by NKCC that is below baseline level about 2 hr after the completion of exercise (Rhind et al., 1999; Espersen et al., 1996). Questions remain as to whether there is a possible effect of demargination of NK cells during exercise on their cytotoxic function, given that postexercise NKCC did not differ from the baseline value when the function was assessed and reported on a per NK cell basis (Miles et al., 2002; Palmo et al., 1995).

Involvement of the neuroendocrine system in NKCC responses to exercise is shown by a number of studies. Norepinephrine released from the sympathetic nerve endings leads to suppression of NKCC (Hellstrand, Hermodsson, & Strannegard,

1985), and β-adrenergic receptors are identified on lymphocytes, including NK cells (Maisel et al., 1990). Adrenergic agonist infusion leads to suppression of NKCC, yet sympathetic denervation blocks stress-induced suppression of NKCC (Katafuchi, Take, & Hori, 1993). In addition, chemical sympathectomy (destruction or blocking of sympathetic nerves or outflow) leads to reduction of NE in the spleen (Hong et al., 1998) and elevated NKCC (Livnat et al., 1987), and also restored NKCC that was attenuated following corticotropin releasing hormone (Irwin et al., 1988). Hypothalamic-pituitary-adrenocortical axis mediation of NKCC is evidenced by the finding that injection of cortisol leads to a transient increase (Onsrud & Thorsby, 1981) and subsequent significant attenuation of NKCC (Bodner, Ho, & Kreek, 1998). Thus, findings clearly suggest that transient increases in NKCC during and following exercise are mediated in part by both the adrenergic system and the HPA axis (Hong, 2000).

Leukocyte Proliferation

By incubation of whole blood or isolated lymphocytes with mitogens, including phytohemagglutinin (PHA), pokeweed mitogen (PWM), and concanavalin A (ConA), proliferative functions of immune cells can be assessed in vitro. Decreased lymphocyte proliferation responses to PHA are shown after aerobic exercise regardless of physical training status of the subjects (Green, Rowbottom, & Mackinnon, 2002; Tvede et al., 1989), or no effects of exercise are found on lymphocyte proliferation in response to ConA or PWM (Nehlsen-Cannarella et al., 1991). Mixed findings on lymphocyte proliferation responses are also seen after resistance exercise (Dohi et al., 2001). It is not clear whether these inconclusive findings are due to the nature of the different mitogens used, inconsistent experimental methods across the studies, or sample size that is insufficient to produce significant differences.

Cytokine Responses to Exercise

In recent years, a growing number of researchers have been actively investigating the effects of exercise on cytokine levels. Acute exercise induces an inflammation-like response marked by increased cytokine secretion in a dose-dependent manner. Exercise affects the levels of cytokines, including a variety of colony-stimulating factors, chemokines, and ILs produced by different cells such as IL-6, IL-1β, and TNF. Activation of immune cells following exercise leads to a cascade of cellular events and results in an orchestrated secretion of ILs beginning with IL-1 and TNF-α (Hong & Mills, 2003). The kinetics of cytokine secretion during and following exercise differ for various cytokines, and the elevated levels of IL-1β, IL-6, and TNF-α (Brenner et al., 1999; Nemet et al., 2002) are followed by increased levels of their antagonists (i.e., soluble receptors and anti-inflammatory cytokines) including IL-1ra, TNF-2R, IL-4, and IL-10 (Goebel et al., 2000). Lipopolysaccharide (LPS)-stimulated IL-6 and TNF-α levels also increase significantly after exhaustive exercise (Goebel et al., 2000; Scheett et al., 1999). Additionally, a recent review suggests that highly intense exercise may have immunosuppressive effects mediated by increased cytokine levels in the blood (Suzuki et al., 2002).

Recent developments in laboratory techniques, including commercially available high-sensitivity enzyme-linked immunoabsorbent assay (ELISA) kits, provide reliable assessments of cytokines in plasma, serum, cell culture supernatant, and urine samples. Cytokine levels can be also measured in cell culture supernatant after stimulation of PBMCs using endotoxins (e.g., LPS). Intracellular cytokines are measured using flow cytometry; concomitantly different cell types producing these cytokines can be identified. The polymerase chain reaction (PCR) is used to measure cytokine gene expression in tissues (e.g., muscle).

Hormones (e.g., glucocorticoids, catecholamines) that are released during and after exercise may affect exercise-induced elevation of plasma cytokine levels. Activation of the immune system via either endotoxin challenge or proinflammatory cytokine injection leads to a cascade of cytokine release. This indicates additive, synergistic, or antagonistic effects of cytokines on immune cells. A sequential release of pro- and anti-inflammatory cytokines upon activation is also seen during and after exercise, implying that agonistic and antagonistic interactions of the cytokine system are displayed in response to exercise.

Cytokines usually exhibit autocrine (self-affecting) or paracrine (influencing adjacent cells) functions affecting a variety of leukocytes (i.e., pleiotropic). However, some cytokines have been shown to act in an endocrine fashion, traveling to target organs including the brain. For example, IL-6, IL-1, and interferon-gamma IFN-γ, or cytokine-producing cells, cross or traffic to the blood–brain barrier and influence mood and behavior. This mutual relationship between cytokines and the brain and behavior requires further investigation, and exercise may be a good paradigm to expand this research.

Regular Physical Activity and Psychoneuroimmunology

The literature on the effects of chronic exercise (training) or physical fitness on peripheral blood leukocyte numbers and adhesion molecule expression is inconclusive. No differences in circulating T_H, T_C, or NK cells were shown between trained and untrained individuals in two studies (Eliakim et al., 1997; Nieman et al., 2000). Aerobic exercise training led to increased circulating T_H, naïve T_H, T_C, and B lymphocyte numbers at rest (LaPerriere et al., 1994) or to no changes in T_H, T_C, and B cells in other subjects (Imrich et al., 2004; Pedersen et al., 2000). Findings from studies addressing how physical fitness affects leukocyte trafficking in response to stress, including acute exercise, are even more controversial. No effects of regular physical activity on lymphocyte subpopulations were shown in response to submaximal exercise (Moyna et al., 1996) or in response to a speech stressor (Moyna et al., 1999). However, physically active or fit individuals show attenuated lymphocytosis in selected lymphocyte subsets in response to a speech stressor (Hong et al., 2004) or moderate exercise (Hong et al., 2005). In addition, resistance exercise leads to an increase in leukocyte numbers in untrained individuals but to no change in trained individuals (Potteiger et al., 2001). Although adaptations in the adrenergic or endocrine systems are suggested to mediate possible adaptations of the immune system as a result of regular physical activity, it is still unclear what drives adaptations in immune cell trafficking.

The literature on NK cell function after exercise training is also less conclusive compared to the literature on NKCC in response to acute exercise. Exercise training ranging from three to six months does not affect NKCC in humans (Nieman et al., 1998; Woods et al., 1999). A number of animal studies do show relatively consistent benefits of exercise training on NKCC after either forced or voluntary exercise (Simpson & Hoffman-Goetz, 1990). However, some studies indicate no change in NKCC after 6 to 15 weeks of treadmill training in rats (Dishman et al., 1995, 2000). What appears to be rather clear

is that suppression of NKCC induced by electric foot shock stress is blunted in treadmill-trained rats (Dishman et al., 1995), suggesting that exercise training may have a protective effect against stress-induced immunosuppression.

The insignificant effects of exercise training on resting NK cell activity observed in the human literature raise questions regarding the nature of the exercise program (i.e., intensity, duration, etc.) as it may affect different adaptations in NK cell activity.

Directions for Future Investigation

Despite the significant progress in our understanding of the effects of acute exercise on psychological, neurohormonal, and immunological activity, it is remains inconclusive how repeated exercise (regular physical activity) leads to adaptations in the psychoneuroimmunological system. Furthermore, little is known about the possible effect of PNI interactions on exercise behavior or performance (see figure 12.1). In addition, the literature on the effects of immunological reactions or adaptations on the psychoneuroendocrine system is limited, as is our understanding of how increased levels of inflammatory cytokines upon injury or infection lead to "sickness behavior" (including fever, anorexia, decreased locomotion and social interaction, and fatigue) (Larson & Dunn, 2001). There is growing evidence that elevated levels of cytokines may be associated with psychosocial behavior or even mood disorders. All of these areas, in particular exercise-induced cytokine activation and its influence on psychosocial behavior and mood, present promising opportunities to researchers and merit further investigation.

As presented earlier in the chapter, moderate acute exercise transiently activates the immune system, although this is followed by decreased immunity. Prolonged and exhaustive exercise (e.g., marathon) has been shown to result in immunosuppression or leukocytopenia, which may lead to susceptibility to infections. It remains to be clarified whether these effects of exercise on the immune system are time dependent (i.e., is there a time window of greater susceptibility to infections after an exercise bout?), intensity dependent (i.e., does heavy exercise lead to decreased immunity?), or fitness dependent (i.e., do trained individuals exhibit different immune responses to acute exercise as compared to untrained individuals?). Finally, does regular physical activity have beneficial effects on immunity? Animal studies more clearly show enhanced immune functions after exercise training. Moreover, adaptations that occur in the brain, SNS, and HPA axis after exercise training are important phenomena in that regular physical activity may have protective effects against the immunosuppression commonly observed in response to acute or chronic psychosocial stress.

Possible protective effects against either immunosuppression or overactivation of the immune system brought about by regular physical activity may have clinical implications for patient groups with various diseases, including cardiovascular diseases. For example, the literature on exercise and leukocyte trafficking in human hypertension is surprisingly limited despite its significant clinical implications regarding vascular diseases, including atherosclerosis. Hypertension is a condition characterized by exaggerated activation of the SNS. Chronically elevated expression of CAMs in response to SNS activation in individuals with hypertension may result in unnecessary extravasation and transmigration of immune cells, vascular injury, and plague formation leading to atherosclerosis. A number of studies show increased expression and activation of CAMs in response to stress among patients with hypertension (Goebel & Mills, 2000; Mills et al., 2002, 2000). However, a limited number of studies have examined the potential benefits of exercise training on improving vascular physiology via changes in leukocyte trafficking and adhesion molecule expression. Thus, the significant clinical implications of exercise and PNI research in cardiovascular diseases should be further recognized.

Conclusions

Psychoneuroimmunology is the study of the reciprocal relationships among the psychological, neural, endocrine, and immune systems. Mechanistic studies provide evidence of the biological linkage between the brain (and the SNS) and the immune system such that SNS activation leads to redistribution of leukocytes and compromised functionality of lymphocytes. Activation of the HPA system has been shown to have similar effects. A large literature shows activation of the SNS and HPA systems in response to acute exercise. Those responses are also largely dependent upon the intensity, duration, and type of the exercise stimulus. A significant number of studies also

provide evidence for exercise-induced changes in the immune system: leukocytosis, transient increases in NKCC, elevated cytokine levels, and so on. Given the nature of acute exercise not only as a sympathoadrenergic and endocrine activator, but also as an immune system activator, it is a highly appropriate model for PNI research. In addition, the ability to accurately and objectively quantify exercise intensity enables systematic investigation of the true effects of exercise on the neuroendocrine and immune systems.

Exercise is unique in that repeated exposure leads to adaptations in various organs. Studies show that the brain noradrenergic system and SNS adapt to chronic exercise. Adaptation of the HPA axis is less evident. Currently, the literature on immunological adaptations is limited and inconclusive, although a few studies suggest blunted responsiveness of the immune system to stressors among fit individuals or exercise-trained rats. In spite of the rapidly increasing interest in research on exercise-induced cytokine activation, the effects of cytokines on the neuroendocrine system in response to exercise are also significantly understudied. Given the functions of cytokines influencing the brain, cytokines are a useful way to investigate the effects of immune activation with exercise on the neuroendocrine system and behavior. All in all, exercise presents researchers with nearly endless ways to examine the communications between the neuroendocrine and immune systems.

References

Ader, R., Cohen, N., & Felten, D. (1995). Psychoneuroimmunological interactions between nervous system and the immune system. *Lancet, 345,* 99-103.

Benschop, R.J., Oostveen, F.G., Heijnen, C.J., & Ballieux, R.E. (1993). β_2-adrenergic stimulation causes detachment of natural killer cells from cultured endothelium. *European Journal of Immunology, 23,* 3242-3247.

Benschop, R.J., Rodriguez-Feuerhahn, M., & Schedlowski, M. (1996). Catecholamine-induced leukocytosis: early observations, current research, and future directions. *Brain, Behavior, and Immunity, 10,* 77-91.

Benschop, R.J., Schedlowski, M., Wienecke, H., Jacobs, R., & Schmidt, R.E. (1997). Adrenergic control of natural killer cell circulation and adhesion. *Brain, Behavior, and Immunity, 11,* 321-332.

Bodner, G., Ho, A., & Kreek, M.J. (1998). Effect of endogenous levels on natural killer cell activity in healthy humans. *Brain, Behavior, and Immunity, 12,* 285-296.

Brenner, I.K.M., Natalie, V.M., Vasiliou, P., Moldoveanu, A.I., Shek, P.N., & Shephard, R.J. (1999). Impact of three different types of exercise on components of the inflammatory response. *European Journal of Applied Physiology, 80,* 452-460.

Carlson, S.L., Fox, S., & Abell, K.M. (1997). Catecholamine modulation of lymphocyte homing to lymphoid tissues. *Brain, Behavior, and Immunity, 11,* 307-320.

Dishman, R.K. (1997). Brain monoamines, exercise, and behavioral stress: Animal models. *Medicine and Science in Sports and Exercise, 29,* 63-74.

Dishman, R.K., Bunnell, B.N., Youngstedt, S.D., Yoo, H., Mougey, E.H., & Meyerhoff, J.L. (1998). Activity wheel running blunts increased plasma adrenocorticotrophin (ACTH) after footshock and cage-switch stress. *Physiology and Behavior, 63*(5), 911-917.

Dishman, R.K., Hong, S., Soares, J., Edwards, G.L., Bunnell, B.N., Jaso-Friedmann, L., & Evans, D.L. (2000). Activity-wheel running blunts suppression of splenic natural killer cell cytotoxicity after sympathectomy and footshock. *Physiology and Behavior, 71*(3-4), 297-304.

Dishman, R.K., Warren, J.M., Youngstedt, S.D., Yoo, H., Bunnell, B.N., Mougey, E.H., Meyerhoff, J.L., Jaso-Friedmann, L., & Evans, D.L. (1995). Activity-wheel running attenuates suppression of natural killer cell activity after footshock. *Journal of Applied Physiology, 78*(4), 1547-1554.

Dohi, K., Mastro, A.M., Miles, M.P., Bush, J.A., Grove, D.S., Leach, S.K., Volek, J.S., Nindl, B.C., Marx, J.O., Gotshalk, L.A., Putukian, M., Sebastianelli, W.J., & Kraemer, W.J. (2001). Lymphocyte proliferation in response to acute heavy resistance exercise in women: Influence of muscle strength and total work. *European Journal of Applied Physiology, 85*(3-4), 367-373.

Eliakim, A., Wolach, B., Kodesh, E., Gavrieli, R., Radnay, J., Ben-Tovim, T., Yarom, Y., & Falk, B. (1997). Cellular and humoral immune response to exercise among gymnasts and untrained girls. *International Journal of Sports Medicine, 18,* 208-212.

Espersen, G.T., Elbaek, A., Schmidt-Olsen, S., Ejlersen, E., Varming, K., & Grunnet, N. (1996). Short-term changes in the immune system of elite swimmers under competition conditions. Different immunomodulation induced by various types of sport. *Scandinavian Journal of Medicine and Science in Sports, 6*(3), 156-163.

Felten, D.L., Felten, S.Y., Bellinger, D.L., Carlson, S.L., Ackerman, K.D., Madden, K.S., Olschowki, J.A., & Livnat, S. (1987). Noradrenergic sympathetic neural interactions with the immune system: Structure and function. *Immunological Review, 100,* 225-260.

Fleshner, M., Campisi, J., Deak, T., Greenwood, B.N., Kintzel, J.A., Leem, T.H., Smith, T.P., & Sorensen, B. (2002). Acute stressor exposure facilitates innate immunity more in physically active than in sedentary rats. *American Journal of Physiology, 282,* R1680-R1686.

Gabriel, H., Brechtel, L., Urhausen, A., & Kindermann, W. (1994). Recruitment and recirculation of leukocytes after an ultramarathon run: Preferential homing of cells expressing high levels of the adhesion molecule LFA-1. *International Journal of Sports Medicine, 15,* S148-S153.

Goebel, M.U., & Mills, P.J. (2000). Acute psychological stress and exercise and changes in peripheral leukocyte adhesion molecule expression and density. *Psychosomatic Medicine, 62,* 664-670.

Goebel, M.U., Mills, P.J., Irwin, M.R., & Ziegler, M.G. (2000). Interleukin-6 and tumor necrosis factor-α production after acute psychological stress, exercise, and infused isoproterenol: Differential effects and pathways. *Psychosomatic Medicine, 62,* 591-598.

Green, K.J., Rowbottom, D.G., & Mackinnon, L.T. (2002). Exercise and T-lymphocyte function: A comparison of proliferation in PBMC and NK cell-depleted PBMC culture. *Journal of Applied Physiology, 92,* 2390-2395.

Hellstrand, K., Hermodsson, S., & Strannegard, O. (1985). Evidence for a β-adrenoreceptor-mediated regulation of human natural killer cells. *Journal of Immunology, 134,* 4095-4099.

Hong, S. (2000). Exercise and psychoneuroimmunology. *International Journal of Sports Psychology, 31,* 204-227.

Hong, S., Farag, N.H., Nelesen, R.A., Ziegler, M.G., & Mills, P.J. (2004). Effects of regular exercise on lymphocyte subsets and CD62L after psychological and physical stress. *Journal of Psychosomatic Research, 56*(3), 363-370.

Hong, S., & Mills, P.J. (2003). Physical stress/exercise and immune response. In M. Schafer & C. Stein (Eds.), *Mind over matter: Regulation of peripheral inflammation by the CNS* (PIR series; pp. 37-56). Basel, Switzerland: Birkhauser Verlag.

Hong, S., Johnson, T.A., Farag, N., Guy, H., Matthews, S., & Mills, P.J. (2005). Attenuation of T lymphocyte demargination and adhesion molecule expression in response to moderate exercise in physically fit individuals. *Journal of Applied Physiology, 98*(3), 1057-1063.

Hong, S., Soares, J., Bunnell, B.N., Edwards, G.L., Evans, D.L., & Dishman, R.K. (1998). Activity wheel running blunts suppression of natural killer cell cytotoxicity after footshock and sympathectomy [abstract]. *Medicine and Science in Sports and Exercise, 30*(5), suppl., S1700.

Hoppner, M., Luhm, J., Schlenke, P., Koritke, P., & Frohn, C. (2002). A flow-cytometry based cytotoxicity assay using stained effector cells in combination with native target cells. *Journal of Immunological Methods, 267,* 157-163.

Imrich, R., Tibenska, E., Koska, J., Ksinantova, L., Kvetnansky, R., Bergendiova-Sedlackova, K., Blazicek, P., & Vigas, M. (2004). Repeated stress-induced stimulation of catecholamine response is not followed by altered immune cell redistribution. *Annals of the New York Academy of Sciences, 1018,* 266-272.

Irwin, M., Hauger, R.L., Brown, M., & Britton, L. (1988). CRF activates autonomic nervous system and reduces natural killer cytotoxicity. *American Journal of Physiology, 5*(2), R744-R747.

Jonsdottir, I.H., Johansson, C., Asea, A., Johansson, P., Hellstrand, K., Thoren, P., & Hoffmann, P. (1997). Duration and mechanisms of the increased natural cytotoxicity seen after chronic voluntary exercise in rats. *Acta Physiologica Scandinavica, 160*(4), 333-339.

Jordan, J., Beneke, R., & Hutler, M. (1997). Moderate exercise leads to decreased expression of β1 and β2 integrins on leukocytes. *European Journal of Applied Physiology, 76,* 192-194.

Katafuchi, T., Take, S., & Hori, T. (1993). Roles of sympathetic nervous system in the suppression of cytotoxicity of splenic natural killer cells in the rat. *Journal of Physiology (London), 465,* 343-357.

Kemeny, M.E., & Gruenewald, T.L. (1999). Psychoneuroimmunology update. *Seminar in Gastrointestinal Disease, 10*(1), 20-29.

Kiecolt-Glaser, J.K., & Glaser, R. (1987). Psychosocial moderators of immune function. *Annals of Behavioral Medicine, 9*(2), 16-20.

Kjaer, M., Secher, N.H., & Galbo, H. (1987). Physical stress and catecholamine release. *Clinics in Endocrinology and Metabolism, 1,* 279-298.

Kurokawa, Y., Shinkai, S., Torii, J., Hino, S., & Shek, P.N. (1995). Exercise-induced changes in the expression of surface adhesion molecules on circulating granulocytes and lymphocytes subpopulations. *European Journal of Applied Physiology, 71,* 2245-2252.

LaPerriere, A., Antoni, M.H., Ironson, G., Perry, A., McCabe, P., Klimas, N., Helder, L., Schneiderman, N., & Fletcher, M.A. (1994). Effects of aerobic exercise training on lymphocyte subpopulations. *International Journal of Sports Medicine, 15*(Suppl. 3), S127-S130.

Larson, S.J., & Dunn, A.J. (2001). Behavioral effects of cytokines. *Brain, Behavior, and Immunity, 15,* 371-387.

Livnat, S., Madden, K.S., Felten, D.L., & Felten, S.Y. (1987). Regulation of the immune system by sympathetic neural mechanisms. *Progress in Neuropsychopharmacology and Biological Psychiatry, 11*(2-3), 145-152.

Maisel, A.S., Harris, T., Rearden, C.A., & Michel, M.C. (1990). β-adrenergic receptors in lymphocyte subsets after exercise: Alterations in normal individuals and patients with congestive heart failure. *Circulation, 82*(6), 2003-2010.

Malm, C., Lenkei, R., & Sjodin, B. (1999). Effects of eccentric exercise on the immune system in men. *Journal of Applied Physiology, 86*(2), 2003-2010.

Mazzeo, R.S. (1991). Catecholamine responses to acute and chronic exercise. *Medicine and Science in Sports and Exercise, 23,* 839-845.

Miles, M.P., Mackinnon, L.T., Grove, D.S., Williams, N.I., Bush, J.A., Marx, J.O., Kraemer, W.J., & Mastro, A.M. (2002). The relationship of natural killer cell counts, perforin mRNA and CD2 expression to post-exercise natural killer cell activity in humans. *Acta Physiologica Scandinavica, 174,* 317-325.

Mills, P.J., Farag, N.H., Perez, C., & Dimsdale, J.E. (2002). Peripheral blood mononuclear cell CD62L and CD11a expression and soluble interstitial cell adhesion molecule-1 levels following infused isoproterenol in hypertension. *Journal of Hypertension, 20*(2), 311-316.

Mills, P.J., Maisel, A.S., Ziegler, M.G., Dimsdale, J.E., Carter, S.M., Kennedy, B., & Woods, V.L. Jr. (2000). Peripheral blood mononuclear cell-endothelial adhesion in human hypertension following exercise. *Journal of Hypertension, 18,* 1801-1806.

Mills, P.J., Rehman, J., Ziegler, M.G., Carter, S.M., Dimsdale, J.E., & Maisel, A.S. (1999). Nonselective beta blockade attenuates the recruitment of CD62L(-)T lymphocytes following exercise. *European Journal of Applied Physiology and Occupational Physiology, 79,* 531-534.

Mills, P.J., Ziegler, M.G., Rehman, J., & Maisel, A.S. (1998). Catecholamines, catecholamine receptors, cell adhesion molecules, and acute stressor-related changes in cellular immunity. *Advances in Pharmacology, 42,* 587-590.

Mora, J.M., Amtmann, L.E., & Hoffmann, S.J. (1926). Effect of mental and emotional states on the leukocyte count. *Journal of the American Medical Association, 86,* 945-946.

Moyna, N.M., Acker, G.R., Weber, K.M., Fulton, J.R., Goss, F.L., Robertson, R.J., & Rabin, B.S. (1996). The effects of incremental submaximal exercise on circulating leukocytes in physically active and sedentary males and females. *European Journal of Applied Physiology, 74*(3), 211-218.

Moyna, N.M., Bodnar, J.D., Goldberg, H.R., Shurin, M.S., Robertson, R.J., & Rabin, B.S. (1999). Relation between aerobic fitness level and stress induced alterations in neuroendocrine and immune function. *International Journal of Sports Medicine, 20*(2), 136-141.

Murray, D.R., Irwin, M., Rearden, C.A., Ziegler, M., Motulsky, H., & Maisel, A.S. (1992). Sympathetic and immune interactions during dynamic exercise. Mediation via a beta 2-adrenergic-dependent mechanism. *Circulation, 86,* 203-213.

Nehlsen-Cannarella, S.L. (1998). Cellular responses to moderate and heavy exercise. *Canadian Journal of Physiology and Pharmacology, 76,* 485-489.

Nehlsen-Cannarella, S.L., Nieman, D.C., Jessen, J., Chang, L., Gusewitch, G., Blix, G.G., & Ashley, E. (1991). The effects of acute moderate exercise on lymphocyte function and serum immunoglobulin levels. *International Journal of Sports Medicine, 12*(4), 391-398.

Nemet, D., Hong, S., Mills, P.J., Ziegler, M.G., Hill, M., & Cooper, D.M. (2002). Systemic vs. local cytokine and leukocyte responses to unilateral wrist flexion exercise. *Journal of Applied Physiology, 93,* 546-554.

Nielsen, H.B., Secher, N.H., Kappel, M., Hanel, B., & Pedersen, B.K. (1996). Lymphocyte, NK and LAK cell responses to maximal exercise. *International Journal of Sports Medicine, 17,* 60-65.

Nielsen, H.B., Secher, N.H., Kristensen, J.H., Christensen, N.J., Espersen, K., & Pedersen, B.K. (1997). Splenectomy impairs lymphocytosis during maximal exercise. *American Journal of Physiology, 272,* R1847-R1852.

Nieman, D.C., Nehlsen-Cannarella, S.L., Fagoaga, O.R., Henson, D.A., Shannon, M., Hjertman, J.M., Schmitt, R.L., Bolton, M.R., Austin, M.D., Schilling, B.K., & Thorpe, R. (2000). Immune function in female elite rowers and non-athletes. *British Journal of Sports Medicine, 34,* 181-187.

Nieman, D.C., Nehlsen-Cannarella, S.L., Henson, D.A., Koch, A.J., Butterworth, D.E., Fagoaga, O.R., & Utter, A. (1998). Immune response to exercise training and/or energy restriction in obese women. *Medicine and Science in Sports and Exercise, 30*(5), 679-686.

Ohman, E.M., Butler, J., Kelly, J., Horgan, J., & O'Malley, K. (1987). Beta-adrenoceptor adaptation to endurance training. *Journal of Cardiovascular Pharmacology, 10,* 728-731.

Onsrud, M., & Thorsby, E. (1981). Influence of in vivo hydrocortisone on some human blood lymphocyte subpopulations. *Scandinavian Journal of Immunology, 13,* 573-579.

Palmo, J., Asp, S., Daugaard, J.R., Richter, E.A., Klokker, M., & Pedersen, B.K. (1995). Effect of eccentric exercise on natural killer cell activity. *Journal of Applied Physiology, 78*(4), 1442-1446.

Pedersen, B.K., Helge, J.W., Richter, E.A., Rohde, T., & Kiens, B. (2000). Training and natural immunity: Effects of diets rich in fat or carbohydrate. *European Journal of Applied Physiology, 82,* 98-102.

Potteiger, J.A., Chan, M.A., Haff, G.G., Mathew, S., Schroeder, C.A., Haub, M.D., Chirathaworn, C., Tibbetts, S.A., Mcdonald, J., Omoike, O., & Benedict, S.H. (2001). Training status influences T-cell responses in women following acute resistance exercise. *Journal of Strength and Conditioning Research, 15*(2), 185-191.

Rhind, S.G., Gannon, G.A., Suzui, M., Shepard, R.J., & Shek, P.N. (1999). Indomethacin inhibits circulating PGE2 and reverses postexercise suppression of natural killer cell activity. *American Journal of Physiology, 276*(5 Pt. 2), R1496-R1505.

Rhind, S.G., Shek, P.N., Shinkai, S., & Shephard, R.J. (1996). Effects of moderate endurance exercise and training on in vitro lymphocyte proliferation, interleukin-2 (IL-2) production, and IL-2 receptor expression. *European Journal of Applied Physiology and Occupational Physiology, 74*(4), 348-360.

Scheett, T.P., Mills, P.J., Ziegler, M.G., Stoppani, J., & Cooper, D. (1999). Effect of exercise on cytokines and growth mediators in prepubertal children. *Pediatric Research, 46,* 429-434.

Shek, P.N., Sabiston, B.H., Buguet, A., & Radomski, M.W. (1995). Strenuous exercise and immunological changes: A multiple-time-point analysis of leukocyte subsets, CD4/CD8 ratio, immunoglobulin production and NK cell response. *International Journal of Sports Medicine, 16,* 466-474.

Sigvardsson, K., Svanfeldt, E., & Kilbom, A. (1977). Role of the adrenergic nervous system in development of training-induced bradycardia. *Acta Physiologica Scandinavica, 101,* 481-488.

Simpson, J.R., & Hoffman-Goetz, L. (1990). Exercise stress and murine natural killer cell function. *Proceedings of Society for Experimental Biology and Medicine, 195,* 129-135.

Solomon, G.F. (1969). Early experience and immunity. *Nature, 220*(23), 821-822.

Solomon, G.F. (1987). Psychoneuroimmunology: Interactions between central nervous system and immune system. *Journal of Neuroscience Research, 18,* 1-9.

Sothmann, M.S., Buckworth, J., Claytor, R.P., Cox, R.H., White-Welkley, J.E., & Dishman, R.K. (1996). Exercise training and the cross-stressor adaptation hypothesis. *Exercise and Sport Sciences Reviews, 24,* 247-267.

Sothmann, M.S., Hart, B.A., & Horn, T.S. (1991). Plasma catecholamine response to acute psychological stress in humans: Relation to aerobic fitness and exercise training. *Medicine and Science in Sports and Exercise, 23,* 860-867.

Staats, R., Balkow, S., Sorichter, S., Northoff, H., Matthys, H., Luttmann, W., Berg, A., & Virchow, J.C. (2000). Change in perforin-positive peripheral blood lymphocyte (PBL) subpopulations following exercise. *Clinical and Experimental Immunology, 120*(3), 434-439.

Strasner, A., Davis, J.M., Kohut, M.L., Pate, R.R., Ghaffar, A., & Mayer, E. (1997). Effects of exercise intensity on natural killer cell activity in women. *International Journal of Sports Medicine, 18*(1), 56-61.

Suzuki, K., Nakaji, S., Yamada, M., Totsuka, M., Sato, K., & Sugawara, K. (2002). Systemic inflammatory response to exhaustive exercise. Cytokine kinetics. *Exercise and Immunology Review, 8,* 6-48.

Tvede, N., Pedersen, B.K., Hansen, F.R., Bendix, T., Christensen, L.D., Galbo, H., & Halkjaer-Kristensen, J. (1989). Effect of physical exercise on blood mononuclear cell subpopulations and in vitro proliferative responses. *Scandinavian Journal of Immunology, 29,* 383-389.

Van Eeden, S.F., Granton, J., Hards, J.M., Moore, B., & Hogg, J.C. (1999). Expression of the cell adhesion molecules on leukocytes that demarginate during acute maximal exercise. *Journal of Applied Physiology, 86*(3), 970-976.

Woods, J.A., Ceddia, M.A., Wolters, B.W., Evans, J.K., Lu, Q., & McAuley, E. (1999). Effects of 6 months of moderate aerobic exercise training on immune function in the elderly. *Mechanisms of Ageing and Development, 109*(1), 1-19.

Central Regulation of Stress Reactivity and Physical Activity

Gregory A. Hand, PhD

Kenneth D. Phillips, PhD, RN

Marlene A. Wilson, PhD

The purpose of this chapter is to synthesize the current knowledge concerning central nervous system adjustments to physical exercise into the broader topic of the neurobiology of stress. The review is limited predominantly to acute adjustments during exercise and other stressors. A significant amount of information regarding central chronic adaptations to exercise is covered in other chapters of this text. Only in situations in which there are different changes during acute and chronic exercise, which occurs often, will we note the specific chronic adaptations. We use the term *exercise* interchangeably with *physical activity*. The use of the term *exercise* is appropriate for this review since the majority of data were gathered from animal studies. A growing exclusivity of the term *exercise,* defined as only structured physical activity regimens for the purpose of obtaining health benefits, would exclude a large portion of animal research, including all voluntary wheel running by rodents and spontaneous activity in a number of models. We apologize in advance to investigators in the field for reference omissions due to the relatively brief bibliography requirement.

The Physiological Stress Response

Historically, stress has been defined by physiologic changes including activation of the hypo-thalamic-pituitary-adrenal (HPA) axis; changes in the autonomic nervous system highlighted by sympathetic activation; and adaptations in central neural pathways involving the hypothalamus, limbic system (amygdala, hippocampus), frontal cortex, and brainstem (locus ceruleus, dorsal raphe) structures.

The neurobiological regulation of interpreting and responding to stressful events is a well-studied, yet poorly understood, physiological phenomenon. This confusion is due in part to differing definitions for stress and in part to individual variability in responding to environmental stimulation. Simply put, what is perceived as a threat and evokes a physiological stress response in one person may not be stressful (perceptually or physically) to another. However, there is no question about the profound impact of a traumatic life event on neural and psychological development, or about the significant health risk associated with the sustained physiological adjustments to chronic stressful stimulation.

A number of factors are involved in an individual's appraisal of a potentially threatening situation. They are typically divided into inherent characteristics (genetic predisposition and physiological limitations) and environmental factors (situational context and previous experiences). The effects of these two types of characteristics on individual responses to stressful stimulation are illustrated well by the physiological adjustments during the challenge of public speaking.

Previous work indicates that most individuals habituate to the stress of speaking to an audience after a number of sessions. In other words, application of the same environmental stimulus over time evokes a progressively smaller release of catecholamines and the stress hormone cortisol from the adrenal glands. However, some individuals do not habituate over time and continue to secrete high levels of these hormones even after several sessions of public speaking. Positive social interactions (having someone to share the misery) reduce cortisol release during stressful sessions, while isolation accentuates the stress hormone response. Considering all of the variables associated with the response and adaptation to the stress of public speaking, one can see the difficulty in studying the neurobiological mechanisms for the stress response in a constantly changing environment. These same challenges to research design are inherent in the study of exercise as a physiological stressor.

The Practical Significance of Studying Physical Activity and Stress

The popular concept of "stress," as it applies today, originated from early work by Walter Cannon around the turn of the 20th century. While Cannon's research focused on the biological responses to physiological stressors such as hypoxia or hypoglycemia, he also used the term *stress* in the context of emotions. Cannon was the first to hypothesize that life challenges produce emotion-driven physiological adjustments. However, Hans Selye is correctly given credit as the driving force for our current understanding of the linkage between stress and health. Selye's work has, over the past 70 years, stimulated major scientific breakthroughs that show the detrimental effects of chronic physiological stress responses on virtually every system in the body. From cardiovascular disease to immunosuppression to depression and anxiety disorders, "chronic stress" has been shown to either cause or exacerbate the major public health challenges in Western society. It is not surprising, then, that a significant amount of research is focused on therapeutic modalities to manage the stress associated with daily life. And, all the better if the modality can elicit other health benefits such as normalizing blood lipids, increasing cardiorespiratory functional capac-

ity, and maintaining a healthy body weight. It is accepted generally that regular exercise participation can help reduce perceived stress levels and contribute to these other health benefits.

Measures of Stress Reactivity

Traditionally, human studies of the central regulation of stress reactivity have utilized stressors that generate "perceived stress" and have quantified indirect measures of central function such as the plasma levels of cortisol and catecholamines. The measurement of these stress-related hormones has a number of serious limitations (as will be discussed later), and has contributed to the confusion that surrounds stress physiology and effects of exercise on stress-related conditions.

Animal studies allow for much more invasive procedures than those utilized in human studies. Animal research has produced the majority of information related to central regulation of behavioral and physiological changes associated with stress, and virtually all of our understanding of the acute and chronic biochemical and morphological changes within the brain resulting from stressful stimulation. It should be emphasized that the use of animals as human analogs in the study of behavior is, by its very nature, based on anthropomorphic assumptions that may prove to be unfounded. However, a number of animal models have proven to provide a reasonable level of predictive validity to the human condition. Predictive validity indicates that an intervention, such as administration of a drug or some adverse stimulus, that induces a specific change in animal behavior can predictably evoke a particular response in humans. For example, a drug that increases the amount of time that a rat voluntarily spends on the open arms of a plus maze is also likely to reduce feelings of anxiety in an individual. Of course, the animal behaviorist cannot know if the intervention reduces anxiety in the rat, or even if rats have anxiety. However, a new drug that is found to increase the open arm activity will quickly be marked as a potential anxiolytic compound and be moved on to more advanced experiments.

Stimuli used as stressors in animal models include handling, physiological challenges (such as ambient cold), electric shock, restraint, noise, chronic mild stressors that are rotated over time such as wet cage and alternating cage mates, and restraint or immobilization. In addition, a number of models have been developed to examine behavior during situational stress, such as exposure to a novel environment or object. A number of these models have been used to study the effects of exercise on stress-related behaviors (Fulk et al., 2004; Burghardt et al., 2004).

Handling or transfer to a novel environment (or both) has been used as a stressor and managed as a confounding variable in studies utilizing other stressors. In either case, it is a variable that must be dealt with during any animal study. During handling, the animal exhibits a rapid and robust increased secretion of plasma stress hormones. Continued sessions of handling over weeks result in decreased corticosterone secretion, but no adaptation to the catecholamine response (Dobrakovova et al., 1993). Novel stimulation administered via changing the handler after two weeks of handling results in similar or enhanced corticosterone and catecholamine release. So, simply picking up the rats during a study cannot be underestimated as a confounding variable that has the potential, over time, for a profound effect on the experimental results.

Electric shock is a powerful stimulus that has been used as a novel and chronic stressor. It has also been used to examine the possibility of cross-stressor adaptation resulting from exercise. Rats shocked repeatedly over several days show an increased baseline corticosterone level in the morning, with increased adrenal weight and decreased thymus weight. Interestingly, rats exposed repeatedly to electric shock over a period of months show only moderate neuroendocrine adaptations to shock stress, but their responses to novel stressors are enhanced (Brodish & Odio, 1989; Odio & Brodish, 1989).

The effects of restraint stress on neuroendocrine systems are similar to those observed for electric shock. Rats restrained for 1 hr show a rapid and robust increase in amygdala and paraventricular nucleus of the hypothalamus (PVN) corticotropin releasing hormone (CRH) (Hand et al., 2002) with a concomitant increase in CRH mRNA (Kalin, Takahashi, & Chen, 1994). While rats adapt to restraint over time, there is no effect in these animals on the stress response to a novel stressor.

A common type of test used to examine animal behavior and neurobiology, especially as related to anxiety or depression, is the conflict paradigm. In this type of test, the animal is put in a novel situation such that its instincts for hiding and exploring come into conflict. The tests gener-ally provide for open areas and confined areas that the animal is free to traverse. Animals that receive stressful stimulation spend significantly more time in the enclosed areas, while animals that receive anxiolytic or antidepressant treatment (including exercise) usually spend more time in the open areas as compared to control animals (Fulk et al., 2004).

Neural and Endocrine Systems That Respond to Stressful Stimulation

Hypothalamic-pituitary-adrenal axis, autonomic nervous system, dorsal raphe nucleus, amygdala, and hippocampus are neural systems known to respond to stressful stimulation. In turn, these areas activate the response of corticotropin releasing hormone systems, central catecholamines, serotonin, and other endocrine systems. These systems and their responses to exercise are discussed below.

The Hypothalamic-Pituitary-Adrenal Axis

A variety of stressors activate the HPA axis, where ultimately the secretion of adrenocortical glucocorticoids (cortisol in primates, corticosterone in rodents) into the systemic circulation is regulated by adrenocorticotropin (ACTH) release from the pituitary. The increased levels of circulating glucocorticoids serve to help reestablish homeostasis through energy mobilization and increased cardiovascular tone, combined with inhibition of anabolic processes such as reproduction and inflammation. These effects are mediated through interactions with intracellular mineralocorticoid (Type I) and glucocorticoid (Type II) receptors in target organs that serve as transcription factors that modulate protein synthesis. These receptors are also localized throughout the limbic system, the brain areas associated with emotion; and data suggest that the higher-affinity Type I receptors help regulate the inherent neuronal sensitivity of the immediate stress response. The lower-affinity Type II receptors are activated by the heightened glucocorticoid levels associated with HPA activation, and appear to help restrain the stress response and facilitate recovery of the system.

The pituitary secretion of products derived from the precursor proopiomelanocortin (POMC) during stress, primarily ACTH and β-endorphin, is controlled by hypothalamic release of several secretagogs into the hypophyseal portal system at the median eminence. The peptidergic hormone CRH, synthesized in neurons localized in the PVN, plays the preeminent role in controlling ACTH release during stress. Many other secretagogs, including arginine vasopressin (AVP), oxytocin, epinephrine, serotonin, and angiotensin II, contribute to the regulation of ACTH release during a stressor, although many of these factors appear to modulate the primary CRH effects on ACTH secretion. Further, the CRH-induced HPA axis response to stress is independent of consciousness, as hemorrhage under anesthesia results in increased plasma glucocorticoids. Catecholaminergic inputs from the brainstem noradrenergic and adrenergic cell bodies in the locus ceruleus (LC) and nucleus of the solitary tract (NTS) provide dense innervation of the PVN and supraoptic nucleus (SON), helping to control the release of CRH, AVP, oxytocin, and other secretagogs, thus connecting sympathetic and noradrenergic activation during stress with activation of the HPA axis. Serotonergic inputs from the dorsal raphe nuclei, and afferent projections from limbic sites including hippocampus, amygdala, and bed nucleus of the stria terminalis (BNST), help integrate cognitive and behavioral adaptations with HPA activation during stress. There is also evidence that systemic catecholamines (epinephrine and norepinephrine) released by adrenal medullary sympathetic activation regulate HPA function and ACTH release as well (see Herman et al., 2003; Carrasco & De Kar, 2003).

Corticotropin Releasing Hormone Systems

A large body of research indicates that CRH and CRH-like peptides within the brain modulate the physiological and behavioral responses to stressors. Exogenous administration of CRH results in stress-like behavioral and physiological responses, which include increased activity of the sympathetic nervous system and HPA axis, plus anxiogenic responses in behavioral paradigms. The behavioral and physiological changes associated with CRH administration, as well as those observed during the administration of stressors, are attenuated by the central injection of CRH antagonists. Chronic stress induces distinct changes in CRH and CRH gene expression in limbic structures, the PVN, the LC, and the dorsal motor vagal nucleus

among other sites. Modulation of glucocorticoid levels primarily alters CRH expression in the PVN (see Carrasco & De Kar, 2003; Owens & Nemeroff, 1991; Herman et al., 2003).

Two G-protein-linked receptors mediate the actions of CRH and CRH-like peptides such as urocortin and stresscopins. Corticotropin releasing hormone binds with high affinity to the CRF_1 receptor site, which is highly expressed in the frontal cortex, cerebellum, amygdala, hippocampus, LC, and anterior pituitary. The CRF_2 receptor site, which has a high affinity for urocortin, is expressed in the PVN, lateral septal nucleus, ventromedial hypothalamic nucleus, medial amygdaloid nucleus, and hippocampus, along with many peripheral sites, the choroid plexus, and arterioles. Studies suggest that primates and rodents may differ in the potential roles of these receptor types and their splice variants in some brain sites. Studies using binding analysis, pharmacologic manipulations, and genetic alterations in expression have implicated distinct roles for CRH, urocortin, CRF_1, and CRF_2 receptors in various stress-related effects (Holsboer, 1999).

Effects of Exercise on HPA Axis Activity and CRH Systems

As with the intensity-dependent ACTH and glucocorticoid responses to other physiological stressors, the response to exercise is dependent on exercise duration and a relative workload intensity of >60% to 80% of maximal oxygen capacity (Howlett, 1987). Further, the relative amount of CRH and AVP release is dependent on the type of stimulus. For example, the acute effect of stressors that have been administered repeatedly over a period of time is usually a greater release of AVP from the hypothalamus than of CRH (Aguilera, 1994). This differential regulation of hypothalamic hormonal release may be true of high-intensity exercise in humans and other mammals. Studies indicate that short, intense exercise in trained individuals elicits an increase in plasma AVP and ACTH without a change in plasma CRH (Luger et al., 1987; Wittert et al., 1991). Similar work, based on the exercising horse model, that examined the levels of hormones in venous blood samples draining from the pituitary gland indicated an increased AVP and ACTH release with no change in CRH levels (Alexander et al., 1991). Lesser-intensity exercise for prolonged periods (1 hr or longer) also produces an HPA axis response (plasma CRH, ACTH, cortisol) to a lesser degree than higher-intensity workloads and appear to be dependent on plasma glucose levels (Harte, Eifert, & Smith, 1995; Tabata et al., 1991).

Recent work from our laboratory indicates that hypothalamic tissue samples from rats run to exhaustion during a 1 hr exercise bout, or restrained for a similar period of time, showed higher levels of tissue CRH, when compared to levels in cage controls or treadmill controls, of greater than two and threefold, respectively (Hand et al., 2002). While one can argue that the greater tissue CRH following restraint suggests a discrimination between stressor types, it is notable that plasma corticosterone levels were twice as high following exhaustive running when compared to concentrations induced by restraint. This dissociation between the magnitude of changes in tissue CRH and plasma corticosterone may result from a variety of factors, including a difference in the time courses of the two hormones. Alternatively, the dissociation could result from differential control of ACTH release from the pituitary gland by other hormones such as AVP, as would be suggested from our understanding of HPA regulation during acute stressors. Only recently have these control mechanisms begun to be studied during physical exercise stress.

Changes in CRF and AVP mRNA levels within the PVN usually occur several minutes or more following the onset of the stressor. In the case of exercise, treadmill running induces an enhanced production of CRH and CRH$_1$ mRNA in the PVN, as well as CRH binding protein in the medial pre-optic area (Timofeeva, Huang, & Richard, 2003). The enhanced expression of CRH$_1$ during treadmill running appears to be isolated to the PVN—a characteristic of a number of stressors including immune system challenge and immobilization (Timofeeva, Huang, & Richard, 2003).

The Autonomic Nervous System and Central Catecholamines

Stress alters autonomic activity, and the physiological results of this activation include increases in circulating epinephrine (E) and norepinephrine (NE), increases in heart rate and blood pressure, sweating, piloerection, and pupil dilation. A similar constellation of effects representing sympathetic activation is produced by stimulation of the lateral hypothalamus, although the amygdala, LC, and medullary NE projections help modulate sympathetic activation through the lateral hypothalamus. Parasympathetic changes through the

parabrachial nucleus (PBN) and dorsal motor nucleus of the vagus are influenced by projections from PVN, LC, and the amygdala.

Studies demonstrated that central angiotensin II and CRH administration enhanced cardiovascular function, with angiotensin II increasing mean arterial pressure via AVP release and subsequent increases in peripheral vascular resistance, whereas CRH induced increases in cardiac output (Owens & Nemeroff, 1991). Immunoneutralization of circulating CRH effects along with central CRH administration indicated that enhanced catecholamine release was independent of HPA activation and could be induced by activating various brain sites. The hypoglycemia induced by intracerebroventricular (i.c.v.) administration of CRH, and presumably stress, appears to result from altered circulating catecholamine levels, while increased sympathetic or decreased parasympathetic tone (or both) modulates effects on heart rate.

The pontine LC provides extensive efferent NE innervation throughout the central nervous system, innervating cortex, thalamus, limbic system, hypothalamus, brainstem nuclei, and the spinal cord (see Berridge & Waterhouse, 2003). The LC-NE system is critical for arousal and the maintenance of the waking state, and discharge activity of LC neurons is increased by a variety of both aversive and appetitive stimuli, as well as CRH administration. The electrophysiological properties of LC neurons, and their responsiveness to multimodal sensory stimuli, support their role facilitating the processing of salient information; and the level of LC activation is dependent upon the salience or arousing nature of the stimulus. Numerous stressors elevate NE release in various sites, and stimuli that activate LC discharge (including CRH administration) also increase forebrain NE release and neuronal activity. Even in anesthetized animals, internal challenges such as hemodynamic stress, colonic distension, and bladder distension induce LC activation, plus changes in encephalogram activity and NE release. Single exposure to stressors can induce a transient decrease in NE levels, presumably reflecting the activation-induced depletion of NE.

Intriguingly, LC activation by various forms of stress appears to involve distinct afferent systems and neurochemical mediators. For example, the responses to hemodynamic stress involve CRH afferents from central nucleus of the amygdala. Many of these afferent inputs, however, influence LC activity indirectly through projections to the pericerulear zone. Afferent connections including

CRH projections from PVN, Barrington's nucleus, nucleus paragigantocellularis (PGi), amygdala, and perivascular nucleus prepositus hypoglossi (PrH) help coordinate LC activity with autonomic and HPA responses to stress. Conversely, LC innervation helps regulate HPA function. It should be noted that although LC projections traverse multiple brain regions, the primary NE source for the hypothalamus, preoptic areas, and spinal cord arises from specific NE-containing cells in the medulla (A1, A2, A5, and C1 cells). Serotonic inputs also regulate LC activity, although these do not appear to arise from the raphe nuclei (Berridge & Waterhouse, 2003).

It is possible that LC-NE activation forms the "cognitive" aspect of autonomic activation during stress, and that LC connections with regions such as the PGi help coordinate peripheral autonomic responses and brain NE activity during stress. The activation of the LC-NE system during stress not only plays an important role in arousal, but also has been implicated in modulating anxiety state and altered immune function. Although CRH administration in the LC and PBN increases anxiety-like behaviors, data indicating that activation of the LC-NE system can actually decrease various measures of anxiety have led to the suggestion that this system may have a counterbalancing or restorative function associated with stress as well.

Effects of Exercise on Central Catecholamines

A large body of literature has been generated on the topic of exercise and its effects on central catecholamine levels in the brain. A variety of techniques have been used, ranging from biochemical analysis of samples from whole-brain extracts or tissue punched from specific brain regions, to the current gold standard of extracting extracellular fluid samples through microdialysis technology. Because of the various techniques that have been utilized, the literature contains a number of studies that provide conflicting data. In addition to the issues related to sampling techniques, the study of stress-induced brain catecholamine regulation must consider a wide variety of factors that contribute to local and systemic adjustments to NE levels. During exercise, catecholamine levels in the brain adjust in response to stimulation by arterial chemo- and baroreceptor activation, ergoreceptor activation in muscle and connective tissue, and direct stimulation of hypothalamic regions by changes in blood temperature and glucose levels.

Interestingly, the feedforward system commonly referred to as "central command" that is activated by the "intent" to evoke muscle activity elicits an increase in sympathetic nervous system outflow previous to peripheral feedback mechanisms (Mitchell, 1990).

As stated earlier, the primary NE input to the hypothalamus does not originate in the LC, but rather in regions of the dorsal and ventrolateral medulla that are sensitive to activation of motor pathways and arborations from the afferent sensory tracts. The distinctive nature of these divergent pathways is illustrated by data indicating that NE levels in the dialysate from the cortex of rats running on the treadmill correlate poorly with plasma NE levels (presumably arising as spillover from peripheral sympathetic fibers) (Pagliari & Peyrin, 1995). Further, blockade of adrenoreceptors in the hypothalamus appears to have no effect on the release of corticosterone in exercising rats (Scheurink, Steffens, & Gaykema, 1990). Additional factors in exercise studies that moderate central NE regulation are exercise intensity, motivational techniques such as electric shock, and the psychological component of the exercise paradigm. In addition to all of these factors that complicate the interpretation of experimental results, it appears that acute and chronic activity generally induce opposite effects on central NE systems.

Several studies have examined the NE concentration in whole-brain extracts following an acute bout of exercise. The results of these studies were either no significant change or a decrease in NE levels (Sheldon, Sorscher, & Smith, 1975; Moore, 1968). However, studies that examined the effect of acute exercise on NE concentrations in specific brain regions provide data that allude to a much more complex control of NE activity. Following an acute bout of exercise, NE levels were decreased in all regions of the hypothalamus, the hippocampus, and all major segments of the brainstem (Gordon et al., 1966; Stone, 1973; Rea & Hellhammer, 1984; Sudo, 1983). As noted earlier with other stressors, NE reuptake and storage mechanisms are not disrupted by exercise (Stone, 1973), so it is likely that the NE depletion in these brain regions results from accelerated neurotransmitter turnover. In contrast, acute exercise increases NE levels in the frontal cortex, the striatum, and the hypothalamic preoptic area (Lukaszyk, Buczko, & Wisniewski, 1983; Blomstrand et al., 1989; Broocks, Liu, & Pirke, 1990). One study (Pagliari & Peyrin, 1995) that utilized microdialysis technology to examine extracellular NE concentrations in the frontal cortex of rats during treadmill running showed a significant increase in NE. The nature of the stimulus that evokes these changes in NE levels during acute exercise remains to be determined. Studies using immobilization as a stimulus have shown increased NE release in regions of the amygdala, PVN of the hypothalamus, and frontal cortex. As these changes during immobilization are similar to those observed during treadmill running, wheel running, and swimming, the possibility exists that stressors with either a large psychological or physiological component activate the same neurochemical pathways in similar regions of the central nervous system.

The Dorsal Raphe Nucleus and Serotonin

Cell bodies in the midbrain raphe nuclei send serotonergic projections to multiple forebrain sites critical for stress responses, including the hypothalamus (PVN and median eminence), hippocampus, and amygdala. Numerous studies demonstrate the interactions between brain serotonergic systems, the sympathetic nervous system, and the HPA axis. Serotonin can modify PVN activity directly through ascending afferents from the midbrain serotonergic cell bodies, or indirectly through serotonergic modulation of hippocampal or amygdalar activity. The specific effects of serotonergic modulation on sympathetic effects and HPA function rely critically on the spectrum of serotonergic receptor sites that have distinct anatomical distributions (Owens & Nemeroff, 1991; Chaouloff, 1997; Carrasco & De Kar, 2003). For example, distinct effects of 5-HT1a and 5-HT2 receptors on sympathetic activity and HPA responses have been seen (Carrasco & De Kar, 2003; Herman et al., 2003). Such studies generally demonstrate that serotonin activates the HPA system, through predominantly 5-HT1a- and 5-HT2-type receptors. Serotonergic influences in hippocampus and amygdala serve to regulate not only HPA and autonomic consequences of stress, but also stress-related behavioral changes. The serotonergic effects on HPA activation are complicated by the potential for direct serotonergic modulation of pituitary and adrenomedullary hormone release.

Effects of Physical Activity on the Serotonergic System

Acute stress, chronic stress, and altered glucocorticoid levels modulate the serotonergic system; and changes in serotonin synthesis, metabolism, release, and receptor levels have been observed. Locomotion is associated with activation of the serotonergic system as exercise increases both release and reuptake of 5-HT in a time-dependent manner. These adaptive changes are seen both in the raphe nuclei and in target areas such as the hippocampus and hypothalamus. Further, physical activity has been shown to have a profound effect on serotonin autoreceptor expression in the dorsal raphe (Greenwood et al., 2003).

Much of the early work on the effect of exercise on central serotonergic systems was performed by Chaouloff and colleagues (Chaouloff, 1997). Treadmill running has been shown to increase the discharge rate of serotonergic caudal raphe neurons (Jacobs & Fornal, 1993; Veasey et al., 1995). And treadmill activity, performed in studies at varying intensities, increased 5-HT levels in the frontal cortex and hippocampus (Kurosawa et al., 1993; Meeusen et al., 1996). Stress initially serves to activate serotonin systems, although subsequent glucocorticoid downregulation of serotonin processes helps to "counterregulate" stress responses and reestablish homeostasis. Direct effects of CRH are also seen in the dorsal raphe nucleus (Carrasco & De Kar, 2003), suggesting reciprocal integration between serotonergic and HPA systems. This reciprocal activation is only one of a number of other confounding factors in examination of the exercise-induced effects on serotonergic systems. For example, studies indicate that levels of the serotonergic metabolite 5HIAA are not consistently correlated with changes in 5-HT levels (Gerin, Becquet, & Privat, 1995). Running has been shown to increase the serotonergic metabolite 5HIAA in frontal cortex but not raphe dorsalis (Clement et al., 1993). Meeusen and colleagues (1996) showed a similar pattern of change in 5-HT and 5HIAA levels in the hippocampus of exercising rodents, but the overall effect of 5HIAA was not statistically significant relative to baseline. The investigators concluded that with the multifactorial control of metabolite concentrations, it is virtually impossible to determine the functional significance of extraneuronal 5HIAA measurements.

The Amygdala

The amygdalar complex is a key component of the physiological and behavioral responses to stressful stimuli, and serves to provide external stimuli with emotional valence and integrate adaptive responses to stressors. Anatomical studies indicate that the amygdala consists of two macrostructures, the corticobasolateral and centromedial amygdala, that represent distinct but interconnected neuroanatomical, neurochemical, electrophysiological, and behavioral systems. The corticobasolateral amygdala serves as the sensory interface of the amygdala and is capable of associating information from various sensory modalities with their positive and negative emotional valences. The basolateral region (BLA) is thought to integrate information in several sensory domains and receives synaptic inputs from the thalamus and cortex for auditory and shock stimuli, peri-rhinal cortex for visual inputs, and hippocampus for contextual information. The central and medial extended amygdala is the effector system, and serves to alter the action of diencephalic or brainstem nuclei and their functionally specific effector systems. The central amygdala receives inputs from lateral, basal, and basolateral nuclei, and specific projections from the centromedial amygdala direct distinct aspects of stress-related responses. For example, projections to the lateral hypothalamus control blood pressure responses; projections to the BNST regulate HPA activation; and projections to the periaqueductal gray (PAG) mediate behavioral responses such as freezing.

The amygdala also influences responses of the HPA system, through direct projections from the central nucleus of the amygdala to the PVN and via amygdalar efferents to BNST, other hypothalamic nuclei, and brainstem (PBN, NTS) nuclei with extensive PVN inputs (Herman et al., 2003; Gray & Bingaman, 1996). Amygdalar activation stimulates HPA responses, although major amygdalar nuclei appear to modify HPA responses to distinct types of stressors (Herman et al., 2003; Hand et al., 2002). Amygdalar and BNST CRH systems may play an important role in regulating HPA responses and behavioral adaptations to stressors (Hand et al., 2002).

The amygdala plays a key role in emotional behaviors, fear conditioning, reward, nociception, and social behaviors; and studies suggest that this brain site is an essential component in emotional memory processes, particularly forming and storing "fear memories." The amygdala plays an essential role in simple associative learning processes that support acquisition of information concerning threatening stimuli in the environment, and amygdalar long-term potentiation (LTP) may provide an enduring form of synaptic plasticity that mediates at least some aspects of emotional memory processes. Glutamatergic processes appear to play a key role in both amygdalar LTP and the acquisition and expression of fear conditioning in the amygdala through inotropic and metabotropic receptor pathways.

Chronic stress in rodents modulates both neuronal morphology and markers of synaptic plasticity in the amygdala. Changes in anxiety-related behaviors and fear conditioning in animals, and in human imaging studies, indicate that these morphological changes in amygdala may have behavioral consequences (McEwen, 2003). As an emotion control region, the amygdala would be an attractive target for research on exercise-induced behavioral changes such as decreased or increased activity during depressive episodes. As we shall see in the next section, locomotor activity is also altered by experimental manipulation of the amygdala.

Effects of Exercise on the Amygdala

Injection of CRH i.c.v. in rats causes a dose-dependent increase in locomotor activity in familiar environments and increased anxiety-like behaviors, such as decreased locomotor activity, in the novel open field test. These responses appear to be independent of HPA axis activity, implying a suprahypothalamic mechanism (Herman et al., 2003). Our analysis of CRH activity in the amygdala during treadmill running included microdialysis sampling of CRH in extracellular fluid from the central nucleus and measurement of tissue CRH-immunoreactivity (IR) in soluble protein from amygdala tissue samples. During a 60 min exposure to moderate-intensity (approximately 60% $\dot{V}O_2$max) exercise, there was an initial transient increase in extracellular CRH levels within the central nucleus of the amygdala (CeA) that returned to preexercise levels during the middle 20 min collection period. It is notable that the initial rise at the onset of running was likely due to handling stress, as the change in CRH was not different than that following placement of the rats on an inactive treadmill. In contrast, the amygdalar CRH levels during the third and exhaustive 20 min collection period were higher than baseline samples or samples from rats exposed to the inactive treadmill. We could not distinguish the physical versus affective factors for the increased CRH in the last 20 min collection period during running;

however, CRH levels in the same animals exposed to restraint stress were significantly greater than levels measured during treadmill running. These data support previous work suggesting that amygdalar CRH systems are activated by stressors of a predominantly "psychological" nature.

The Hippocampus

The hippocampus plays a central role in regulating both the cognitive and endocrine adjustments to stress. A variety of studies support the overarching view that the hippocampus serves to exert an inhibitory role over HPA activity and plays a critical role in terminating HPA activity following a stressor (Herman et al., 2003). These functions are supported by the high density of both Type I and Type II glucocorticoid receptors in hippocampus. Type II glucocorticoid receptors are found in many other limbic brain sites, while the higher-affinity type I receptors are most abundant in hippocampus, although there appears to be some species variation in the distribution of Type I receptors. Activation of these hippocampal receptors by high glucocorticoid levels following stress serves to exert negative feedback regulation on the PVN, depress CRH synthesis and secretion, and ultimately restore prestress glucocorticoid function. Glucocorticoid release also serves to help counterregulate heightened hippocampal activity induced by acute stress via effects on various neurotransmitter systems, including downregulation of serotonin, NE, excitatory amino acids (EAA), and inhibitory $GABA_A$ (Gamma-aminobutyric acid-A) receptor signaling. The hippocampus also participates in maintaining the diurnal rhythm of the HPA axis, and glucocorticoids maintain survival of dentate gyrus neurons in the hippocampus via Type I receptor activity (Herman et al., 2003). Hippocampal influences over PVN activity involve projections from the subiculum to hypothalamic regions that project to PVN and the BNST (Herman et al., 2003).

Various forms of repeated stress or exposure to high glucocorticoid levels impairs spatial hippocampus-dependent cognitive tests in rodents, reduces hippocampal LTP, and induces dendritic remodeling in the CA3 region of hippocampus (McEwen, 2001). Stress-induced changes in the hippocampus involve glucocorticoid modulation of a variety of neurotransmitter systems, including the serotonergic, GABAergic, and glutamatergic systems. Collectively, these findings from clinical and preclinical studies suggest a dynamic interplay between glucocorticoids and several neurotransmitter systems that produce morphological changes associated with cognitive impairments.

With the finding from van Praag and colleagues that wheel running can significantly increase the rate of neurogenesis in the hypothalamic dentate gyrus of mice, and with similar results discovered later in rats (van Praag, Kempermann, & Gage, 1999; Farmer et al., 2004), a number of laboratories have explored the possible exercise-related biochemical signals and neurological pathways that elicit the proliferation of cells in the subgranular zone of the hippocampus. Investigations into the effect of exercise on hippocampal function have led to a general agreement that (1) the hippocampus, along with the frontal cortex, appears to be selectively suited to respond to theta rhythm signaling evoked by motor activity; and (2) the hippocampus displays an exercise-induced increase in brain-derived neurotrophic factor (BDNF) that is mediated through a number of biochemical mechanisms. Brain-derived neurotrophic factor has been shown to act as a modulator of neurotransmitter activity and to facilitate use-dependent neuronal growth in the hippocampus.

Brain-derived neurotrophic factor within the hippocampus, typically downregulated during stress, shows increased levels during exercise that are dependent on cAMP response element binding protein (CREB) activation. The activation of the CREB pathway within the hippocampal cells appears to be dependent on production of theta activity, such as that produced during a bout of exercise. A number of neurotransmitters and hormones have been associated with the hippocampal plasticity during exercise. In all cases, appropriate changes in these chemicals within the hippocampus during exercise lend biological feasibility to the possibility that each plays a mediating role in exercise-induced neurogenesis. For example, the results from one study suggest that brain uptake of insulin-like growth factor-1 (IGF-1) from the blood is necessary for exercise-induced hippocampal neurogenesis (Trejo, Carro, & Torres-Aleman, 2001). The same research group has shown that running rats have enhanced IGF-1 uptake into the brain as compared to sedentary rats, and that the neurogenic effects of IGF-1 may be mediated by increased neuronal sensitivity to stimulation, enhanced BDNF production, or both.

Traditional neurotransmitter systems, altered by exercise, appear to be involved in regulating the hippocampal cell proliferation resulting from physical activity. A number of studies examining hippocampal function have shown correlations between stress-induced changes in BDNF levels and glutamatergic N-methyl-D-aspartate (NMDA) receptor activity (Farmer et al., 2004). While BDNF-induced changes in hippocampal neuronal function do not require changes in NMDA receptor activity, it appears that amino acid receptors play a role in receptor-mediated changes in hippocampal function. This possibility is illustrated by the role of exercise in reducing the stress-induced efflux of hippocampal glutamate that has been shown to be detrimental to hippocampal structure and function. In contrast, NE levels appear to be critical for neurogenesis in the hippocampus, but not for cell survival or differentiation. Blockade of beta-adrenergic receptors in the hippocampus significantly reduced the exercise-evoked increase in BDNF mRNA. Increases in serotonin levels within the hippocampus have a profound positive effect on cell proliferation. Further, the effect of serotonin on neurogenesis is dependent on hippocampal region-specific 5-HT receptor types. 5-HT_{1A} receptor stimulation in the subgranular layer (SGL) and subventricular zone (SVL) of the dentate gyrus enhanced cell proliferation, while 5-HT_{2A} and 5-HT_{2C} receptor stimulation produced increased proliferation selectively in the SGL and SVL. Interestingly, Russo-Neustadt and colleagues (Ivy et al., 2003) showed that blockade of 5-HT_{1A} receptors did not inhibit the rise in dentate gyrus BDNF levels following exercise, but did enhance exercise-induced BDNF levels in the CA4 region. It was speculated that these latter findings suggest a minimal role for dentate gyrus 5-HT receptors in neurogenesis following physical activity. Clearly, much work remains to determine the role of the multiple, integrated neurochemical pathways that mediate the exercise-induced cell proliferation of the hippocampus.

Weaknesses and Limitations in the Literature

As the study of exercise from a neurobiological perspective is a relatively young field, it has not yet had the benefit of a broad base of literature or an extensive set of basic principles that underlie experimentation. Interestingly, although there is a long history of research on stress-related physiological adjustments, the psychobiology of

exercise has traditionally been represented by a schematic showing arrows pointing to and from a box with the phrase "central nervous system" written inside. As eloquently stated by Dishman in 1994 and still applicable today, "There has been little use of biological psychology traditions and methods in exercise science. This observation is consistent with a dualistic view of mind and body adopted by exercise scientists. . . ."(p. 52). There are a number of shortcomings that have led to gaps in the literature.

First, there is no clear understanding of the nature of exercise as a neurobiological stressor. This is partly due to an overemphasis on the major similarity of different types of exercise. That is, unlike most other types of stressors, all exercise requires muscular activity for locomotion with a resultant increase in energy expenditure. While there need not be agreement on what specific modality of locomotion will be defined as exercise (in fact, such an agreement would likely hinder our understanding of exercise as a stressor), it is important that the modality be characterized as specifically as possible. This characterization is critical, as physiological "load" on the nervous system, such as hypoglycemia or elevated temperature, can have effects analogous to that of neurogenic activity on sympathetic nervous system or HPA activity.

Second, since the stress of exercise is, by nature, significantly composed of peripheral afferent input to the nervous system, it has been easy for exercise science to dismiss the neurogenic component of exercise. While a significant amount of research has focused on the effects of exercise on regions of the brain that regulate physiological adjustments, only recently have exercise neurobiologists begun to examine brain regions implicated in emotional and cognitive functions. Using the model provided by decades of research on the integration of central command and peripheral feedback for the regulation of cardiorespiratory function during exercise, an emphasis should be placed on studies that examine the separate aspects of, and the integration of, neurogenic and myogenic mechanisms for central nervous system adjustments during exercise.

A third limitation, and one not confined to research on exercise, is our lack of data concerning the relationship between central neural pathways and neuroendocrine function. One example of this gap in the literature is the relatively unexplored relationship between exercise-induced adjustments in central catecholamine regulation and the effects of those changes on the wide variety of changes in endocrine function, mediated through HPA activation, during physical stress. Further, exercise neuroscience is only beginning to explore the activity-related changes in other systems, such as central and peripheral opiate systems, that appear to modulate many of the more well-described adjustments by the nervous system.

Directions for Future Investigation

An issue that often arises during comparison of various exercise studies using different modes of exercise is the question of comparable workloads. A need exists for a study that compares the functional capacity among commonly used strains of rats and mice. Since the majority of central neural responses to exercise are dependent on relative workload, a survey of each strain's energy expenditure at various workloads using different modes of exercise would enhance the ability to compare previous studies using different exercise regimens. Many discussions with animal experimentalists indicate that different strains of rodents have different abilities and temperaments as related to exercise capacity. Further, our experience has been that certain exercise regimens have the capacity to alter temperament. For example, male Sprague Dawley rats become very averse to human handling when given access for several weeks to a running wheel (Burghardt et al., 2004).

Future exercise neurobiology studies should include comparisons with the central adjustments to other stressors (both predominantly physical stressors and psychological stressors). Due to the inability to compare relative intensities of different stressors, this is possibly the most difficult aspect of psychobiological research on stress. However, uncovering the differences in central adjustments and adaptations that distinguish the stress of exercise from other well-described stressors may provide a better understanding of how, in contrast to other stressors, exercise can provide a therapeutic modality for many mental and physical ailments. Ultimately, the main goal of most exercise neurobiologists is to understand the neural mechanisms through which this therapeutic effect is manifested.

References

Aguilera, G. (1994). Regulation of pituitary ACTH secretion during chronic stress. *Frontiers in Neuroendocrinology, 15,* 321-350.

Alexander, S.L., Irvine, C.H.G., Ellis, M.J., & Donald, R.A. (1991). The effect of acute exercise on the secretion of corticotropin-releasing factor, arginine vasopressin, and adrenocorticotropin as measured in pituitary venous-blood from the horse. *Endocrinology, 128,* 65-72.

Berridge, C.W., & Waterhouse, B.D. (2003). The locus coeruleus-noradrenergic system: Modulation of behavioral state and state-dependent cognitive processes. *Brain Research Reviews, 42,* 33-84.

Blomstrand, E., Perrett, D., Parry-Billings, M., & Newsholme, E.A. (1989). Effect of sustained exercise on plasma amino acid concentrations and on 5-hydroxytryptamine metabolism in six different brain regions in the rat. *Acta Physiologica Scandinavica, 136,* 473-481.

Brodish, A., & Odio, M. (1989). Age-dependent effects of chronic stress on ACTH and corticosterone responses to an acute novel stress. *Neuroendocrinology, 49,* 496-501.

Broocks, A., Liu, J., & Pirke, K.M. (1990). Semistarvation-induced hyperactivity compensates for decreased norepinephrine and dopamine turnover in the mediobasal hypothalamus of the rat. *Journal of Neural Transmission: General Section, 79,* 113-124.

Burghardt, P.R., Fulk, L.J., Hand, G.A., & Wilson, M.A. (2004). The effect of chronic treadmill and wheel running on behavior in rats. *Brain Research, 1019,* 84-96.

Carrasco, G.A., & De Kar, L.D.V. (2003). Neuroendocrine pharmacology of stress. *European Journal of Pharmacology, 463,* 235-272.

Chaouloff, F. (1997). Effects of acute physical exercise on central serotonergic systems. *Medicine and Science in Sports and Exercise, 29,* 58-62.

Clement, H.W., Schafer, F., Ruwe, C., Gemsa, D., & Wesemann, W. (1993). Stress-induced changes of extracellular 5-hydroxyindoleacetic acid concentrations followed in the nucleus raphe dorsalis and the frontal cortex of the rat. *Brain Research, 614,* 117-124.

Dishman, R.K. (1994). Biological psychology, exercise, and stress. *Quest, 46,* 28-59.

Dobrakovova, M., Kvetnansky, R., Oprsalova, Z., & Jezova, D. (1993). Specificity of the effect of repeated handling on sympathetic-adrenomedullary and pituitary-adrenocortical activity in rats. *Psychoneuroendocrinology, 18,* 163-174.

Farmer, J., Zhao, X., van Praag, H., Wodtke, K., Gage, F.H., & Christie, B.R. (2004). Effects of voluntary exercise on synaptic plasticity and gene expression in the dentate gyrus of adult male Sprague-Dawley rats in vivo. *Neuroscience, 124,* 71-79.

Fulk, L.J., Stock, H.S., Lynn, A., Marshall, J., Wilson, M.A., & Hand, G.A. (2004). Chronic physical exercise reduces anxiety-like behavior in rats. *International Journal of Sports Medicine, 25,* 78-82.

Gerin, C., Becquet, D., & Privat, A. (1995). Direct evidence for the link between monoaminergic descending pathways and motor activity: I. A study with microdialysis probes implanted in the ventral funiculus of the spinal cord. *Brain Research, 704,* 191-201.

Gordon, R., Spector, S., Sjoerdsma, A., & Udenfriend, S. (1966). Increased synthesis of norepinephrine and epinephrine in the intact rat during exercise and exposure to cold. *Journal of Pharmacology and Experimental Therapies, 153,* 440-447.

Gray, T.S., & Bingaman, E.W. (1996). The amygdala: Corticotropin-releasing factor, steroids, and stress. *Critical Reviews in Neurobiology, 10,* 155-168.

Greenwood, B.N., Foley, T.E., Day, H.E.W., Campisi, J., Hammack, S.H., Campeau, S., Maier, S.F., & Fleshner, M. (2003). Freewheel running prevents learned helplessness/behavioral depression: Role of dorsal raphe serotonergic neurons. *Journal of Neuroscience, 23,* 2889-2898.

Hand, G.A., Hewitt, C.B., Fulk, L.J., Stock, H.S., Carson, J.A., Davis, J.M., & Wilson, M.A. (2002). Differential release of corticotropin-releasing hormone (CRH) in the amygdala during different types of stressors. *Brain Research, 949,* 122-130.

Harte, J.L., Eifert, G.H., & Smith, R. (1995). The effects of running and meditation on beta-endorphin, corticotropin-releasing hormone and cortisol in plasma, and on mood. *Biological Psychology, 40,* 251-265.

Herman, J.P., Figueiredo, H., Mueller, N.K., Ulrich-Lai, Y., Ostrander, M.M., Choi, D.C., & Cullinan, W.E. (2003). Central mechanisms of stress integration: Hierarchical circuitry controlling hypothalamo-pituitary-adrenocortical responsiveness. *Frontiers in Neuroendocrinology, 24,* 151-180.

Holsboer, F. (1999). The rationale for corticotropin-releasing hormone receptor (CRH-R) antagonists to treat depression and anxiety. *Journal of Psychiatric Research, 33,* 181-214.

Howlett, T.A. (1987). Hormonal responses to exercise and training—a short review. *Clinical Endocrinology, 26,* 723-742.

Ivy, A.S., Rodriguez, F.G., Garcia, C., Chen, M.J., & Russo-Neustadt, A.A. (2003). Noradrenergic and serotonergic blockade inhibits BDNF mRNA activation following exercise and antidepressant. *Pharmacology, Biochemistry and Behavior, 75,* 81-88.

Jacobs, B.L., & Fornal, C.A. (1993). 5-HT and motor control: A hypothesis. *Trends in Neuroscience, 16,* 346-352.

Kalin, N.H., Takahashi, L.K., & Chen, F.L. (1994). Restraint stress increases corticotropin-releasing hormone messenger-RNA content in the amygdala and paraventricular nucleus. *Brain Research, 656,* 182-186.

Kurosawa, M., Okada, K., Sato, A., & Uchida, S. (1993). Extracellular release of acetylcholine, noradrenaline and serotonin increases in the cerebral cortex during walking in conscious rats. *Neuroscience Letters, 161,* 73-76.

Luger, A., Deuster, P.A., Kyle, S.B., Gallucci, W.T., Montgomery, L.C., Gold, P.W., Gold, P.W., Loriaux, D.L., & Chrousos, G.P. (1987). Acute hypothalamic pituitary-adrenal responses to the stress of treadmill exercise—physiological adaptations to physical-training. *New England Journal of Medicine, 316,* 1309-1315.

Lukaszyk, A., Buczko, W., & Wisniewski, K. (1983). The effect of strenuous exercise on the reactivity of the central dopaminergic system in the rat. *Polish Journal of Pharmacology and Pharmacy, 35,* 29-36.

McEwen, B.S. (2001). Plasticity of the hippocampus: Adaptation to chronic stress and allostatic load. *Annals of the New York Academy of Sciences, 933,* 265-277.

McEwen, B.S. (2003). Mood disorders and allostatic load. *Biological Psychiatry, 54,* 200-207.

Meeusen, R., Thorre, K., Chaouloff, F., Sarre, S., De Meirleir, K., Ebinger, G., & Michotte, Y. (1996). Effects of tryptophan and/or acute running on extracellular 5-HT and 5-HIAA levels in the hippocampus of food-deprived rats. *Brain Research, 740,* 245-252.

Mitchell, J.H. (1990). Neural control of the circulation during exercise. *Medicine and Science in Sports and Exercise, 22,* 141-154.

Moore, K.E. (1968). Development of tolerance to the behavioral depressant effects of alpha-methyltyrosine. *Journal of Pharmacy and Pharmacology, 20,* 805-807.

Odio, M., & Brodish, A. (1989). Age-related adaptation of pituitary-adrenocortical responses to stress. *Neuroendocrinology, 49,* 382-388.

Owens, M.J., & Nemeroff, C.B. (1991). Physiology and pharmacology of corticotropin-releasing factor. *Pharmacological Reviews, 43,* 425-473.

Pagliari, R., & Peyrin, L. (1995). Norepinephrine release in the rat frontal-cortex under treadmill exercise—a study with microdialysis. *Journal of Applied Physiology, 78,* 2121-2130.

Rea, M.A., & Hellhammer, D.H. (1984). Activity wheel stress: Changes in brain norepinephrine turnover and the occurrence of gastric lesions. *Psychotherapy and Psychosomatics, 42,* 218-223.

Scheurink, A.J., Steffens, A.B., & Gaykema, R.P. (1990). Hypothalamic adrenoceptors mediate sympathoadrenal activity in exercising rats. *American Journal of Physiology, 259,* R470-R477.

Sheldon, M.I., Sorscher, S., & Smith, C.B. (1975). A comparison of the effects of morphine and forced running upon the incorporation of 14-C-tyrosine into 14-C-catecholamines in mouse brain, heart and spleen. *Journal of Pharmacology and Experimental Therapies, 193,* 564-575.

Stone, E.A. (1973). Accumulation and metabolism of norepinephrine in rat hypothalamus after exhaustive stress. *Journal of Neurochemistry, 21,* 589-601.

Sudo, A. (1983). Time course of the changes of catecholamine levels in rat brain during swimming stress. *Brain Research, 276,* 372-374.

Tabata, I., Ogita, F., Miyachi, M., & Shibayama, H. (1991). Effect of low blood-glucose on plasma CRF, ACTH, and cortisol during prolonged physical exercise. *Journal of Applied Physiology, 71,* 1807-1812.

Timofeeva, E., Huang, Q.L., & Richard, D. (2003). Effects of treadmill running on brain activation and the corticotropin-releasing hormone system. *Neuroendocrinology, 77,* 388-405.

Trejo, J.L., Carro, E., & Torres-Aleman, I. (2001). Circulating insulin-like growth factor I mediates exercise-induced increases in the number of new neurons in the adult hippocampus. *Journal of Neuroscience, 21,* 1628-1634.

van Praag, H., Kempermann, G., & Gage, F.H. (1999). Running increases cell proliferation and neurogenesis in the adult mouse dentate gyrus. *Nature Neuroscience, 2,* 266-270.

Veasey, S.C., Fornal, C.A., Metzler, C.W., & Jacobs, B.L. (1995). Response of serotonergic caudal raphe neurons in relation to specific motor activities in freely moving cats. *Journal of Neuroscience, 15,* 5346-5359.

Wittert, G.A., Stewart, D.E., Graves, M.P., Ellis, M.J., Evans, M.J., Wells, J.E., Donald, R.A., & Espiner, E.A. (1991). Plasma corticotropin releasing-factor and vasopressin responses to exercise in normal man. *Clinical Endocrinology, 35,* 311-317.

Physical Activity and Pain

Dane B. Cook, PhD

Pain is "an unpleasant sensory and emotional experience associated with actual or potential tissue damage, or described in terms of such damage" (IASP, 1979, p. 249). This is the most widely accepted and used definition of pain. It highlights the principal concept of the perception of pain—that it is a subjective experience. Nociception is a physiological process involving the reception of signals in the central nervous system (CNS) that are evoked by specialized sensory receptors (nociceptors) and transmitted along small peripheral afferent nerve fibers. These signals provide information about the physical and chemical environment within skeletal muscle.

The perception of musculoskeletal pain is a widely recognized phenomenon that occurs in both healthy and chronically diseased populations (O'Connor & Cook, 1999; Woolf & Pfleger, 2003). It is an integral consequence of repetitive muscular contractions and often of pathological states. However, the mechanisms of muscle pain, whether naturally occurring or chronically maintained, are poorly understood. The reason, in part, is that until recently the characteristics of the muscle nociceptive systems were relatively unexplored. Research aimed at understanding the phenomenon of musculoskeletal pain has the potential to contribute to a host of physical activity-related topics, including the mechanisms responsible for the experience of naturally occurring muscle pain, the phenomenon of exercise-induced analgesia, the adoption and maintenance of exercise behavior, exercise as a treatment for chronic musculoskeletal pain conditions, and limitations in athletic performance. The contents of this chapter are in large measure an abbreviated and updated version of previous reviews on this topic. For more detailed discussion of select

topics, the reader is referred to several reviews (Cook & Koltyn, 2000; Graven-Nielsen & Mense, 2001; Millan, 1999; O'Connor & Cook, 1999).

Epidemiology of Musculoskeletal Pain

Acute muscle pain is likely to be experienced by most individuals across their life span. Estimates of acute low back and neck pain are as high as 50% over a one-year span, and the lifetime prevalence is as much as 70% (Bovim, Schrader, & Sand, 1994; Frymoyer et al., 1980). For most people, this will be a relatively short-lived episode and they will recover. However, for a substantial number of people, acute muscle pain can become a chronic and debilitating musculoskeletal pain condition (Holbrook et al., 1984). Chronic pain generally associated with the musculoskeletal system affects up to 20% of the adult population (Woolf & Pfleger, 2003). According to the World Health Organization, musculoskeletal conditions are the most frequent cause of disability around the world (WHO, 2003; Woolf & Akesson, 2001). The economic burden of back pain alone is estimated at $33 billion annually (Waddell, 1998), with common pain conditions (e.g., back pain and muscle unspecified) accounting for an estimated $61.2 billion in lost productive time in the United States workforce (Stewart et al., 2003). Physical inactivity is an independent risk factor for a host of musculoskeletal and chronic pain conditions ("Surgeon General's Report," 1996). Unfortunately, much like the situation with their healthy counterparts, adherence to physical activity in chronic musculoskeletal pain patients is not optimal. Clearly, a better understanding of the mechanisms that underlie muscle pain would be useful for the treatment of chronic musculoskeletal pain conditions and help to ensure a high-quality and physically active lifestyle.

Neurobiology of Muscle Pain

Pain is a complex neurobiological process, and our knowledge of the interaction between the nociceptive signal and the perceptual experience has progressed dramatically in the past 40 years or so. Starting with Melzack and Wall's (1965) mechanistic theory of nociceptive modulation through gate control, and converging with modern-day knowledge of nociceptive synaptic plasticity, the Decarte concept of pain specificity (psychogenic pain versus "real" pain) has ultimately been discounted. Theories of pain perception now recognize the intricate interaction between the physiology and molecular biology of nociception and the psychology of perception.

Peripheral Nociception

The two primary sensory fibers that are capable of transmitting a nociceptive signal are the Type III and Type IV afferent fibers, also referred to as A-delta and C-fibers, respectively. Type III afferent fibers are wide-diameter, thinly myelinated fibers that respond preferentially to mechanical pressure resulting in tissue deformation. The signal transmission is relatively fast (5-30 m/sec [5.5-33 yd/sec]); and stimulation results in a sharp, pricking, and stabbing type of pain (Mitchell & Schmidt, 1996), although within skeletal muscle, stimulation of Type III fibers can result in a dull-aching or cramping type of pain (Marchettini et al., 1996). Type IV afferents are thin, unmyelinated fibers that respond preferentially to a noxious chemical environment. The signal is transmitted more slowly (0.5-2 m/sec [0.5-2.2 yd/sec]), and stimulation results in diffuse, dull, burning, and aching type of pain. Both nociceptive fiber types are present in tendon, muscle, and cutaneous tissues (Mense, 1993). Within skeletal muscle the nociceptive units are located along the walls of arterioles and the surrounding connective tissue, and their cell bodies are located in dorsal and trigeminal ganglia (Mense, 1993; Millan, 1999).

Propagation of a nociceptive signal occurs through stimulation (depolarization) of a nocicep-

tor. Muscle nociceptors are either free or unencapsulated nerve endings within the interstitial fluid of the muscle (Mense, 1993). The thresholds for depolarization are high compared to those of the larger, faster Type I and Type II fibers. However, the exact stimuli that are necessary and sufficient for the excitation of nociceptors in normal human muscle are unknown, and not all Type III and IV fibers transmit nociceptive information (Besson, 1999).

Nociceptors can be stimulated by a number of physical and chemical stimuli including exercise, mechanical pressure, heat, cold, and a plethora of endogenous molecules (Graven-Nielsen & Mense, 2001; Millan, 1999). Following prolonged or intense stimulation, muscle nociceptors can become sensitized; and there is evidence that repetitive nociceptive signaling from muscle is capable of producing acute, and sometimes prolonged, sensitivity at peripheral and spinal terminals (Tuveson, Lindblom, & Fruhstorfer, 2003; Vierck et al., 2001). The nociceptive unit is positioned and constituted to respond to stimuli via several different receptor-mediated mechanisms. Stimulation, in turn, results in increased membrane protein for the formation of tetrodotoxin-resistant Na^+ channels, heat-sensing vanilloid receptors (VR-1), acid-sensing ion channels (ASIC), and increased activity of second messenger systems such as protein kinase C (PKC) and cyclic adenosine monophosphate (cAMP) (Costigan & Woolf, 2000; Graven-Nielsen & Mense, 2001; Millan, 1999). Receptors for bradykinin (BK), serotonin (5-HT), norepinephrine (NE), adenosine, neuropeptide Y, prostaglandin E2 (PGE2), hydrogen ions (H^+), nerve growth factors, nitric oxide (NO), gamma aminobutyric acid (GABA), beta-endorphin, substance P (SP), and calcitonin gene-related peptide (CGRP) all reside or can be expressed on the nociceptive unit. Biochemicals that stimulate these receptors are released from several sources including the primary afferent fiber, platelets, neutrophils, lymphocytes, and macrophages (Besson, 1999; Millan, 1999). Importantly, skeletal muscle activity has been shown to result in the release of many of these same biochemicals (Kaufman & Forester, 1996). The role of these endogenous substances in naturally occurring muscle pain responses to exercise remains largely unknown. However, human models of experimental musculoskeletal pain through injection of algesic substances into skeletal muscle have shown that most of the aforementioned biochemicals are capable of causing the sensation of muscle pain in human volunteers (Graven-Nielsen & Mense, 2001).

Spinal Cord Nociception

From peripheral skeletal muscle, nociceptive afferent fibers first synapse at the dorsal horn, a finely structured system of laminae (I through X), within the spinal cord. The majority of nociceptive afferents terminate in the superficial dorsal horn, lamina I and II (substantia gelatinosa), and more deeply in lamina V (Besson, 1999; Mense, 1993; Millan, 1999). Within the spinal cord, nociceptive transmission is accomplished primarily with two types of neurons, the wide dynamic range neurons (WDR) and nociceptive-specific (NS) neurons (Millan, 1999). Nociceptive-specific neurons are predominantly located in lamina I and II, and WDR are predominately located in lamina V. As the name implies, the NS neurons respond preferentially to noxious stimuli, while the WDR neurons respond in a graded fashion to a multitude of stimuli, some of which are capable of sending nociceptive information. A third class of neurons, the silent nociceptive (SN), appears to become active only during inflammatory or chronic pain situations (Besson, 1999). These neurons may be good candidates for the enhanced pain sensitivity observed in delayed-onset muscle soreness.

Within the spinal cord, glutamate is a primary neurotransmitter for communication of acute nociceptive information (Millan, 1999). Glutamate binds to N-methyl D-aspartate (NMDA) and alpha-amino-3-hydroxy-5-methyl-4-isoxazole propionic acid (AMPA) receptor subtypes on WDR and NS neurons. The NMDA receptors are normally blocked by magnesium ions that effectively occupy ion channels, and require more intense and sustained stimulation for depolarization than do AMPA receptors (Costigan & Woolf, 2000; Millan, 1999). Glutamate, however, is certainly not the only biochemical involved in spinal nociception. In fact, nociceptive neurons within the dorsal horn of the spinal cord are equipped to respond to numerous signaling molecules including SP (NK1 and NK2 receptors), brain-derived neurotrophic factor (tyrosine kinase A receptors), adenosine triphosphate (P2X receptors), prostaglandins (PGE2 receptors), endogenous opioids (mu, delta, and kappa opioid receptors), GABA (GABA A and B receptors), and the monoamines (5-HT and alpha receptors) (Besson, 1999; Costigan & Woolf, 2000; Millan, 1999).

Spinal Cord Transmission

From the spinal cord, the nociceptive signal is transmitted via projection neurons to supraspinal sites along several afferent pathways, including the spinothalamic, spinoreticular, spinomesencephalic, spinoparabrachial, spinohypothalamic, and dorsal column pathway tracts. These pathways are composed of fibers originating in several spinal laminae, but have in common lamina I, II, or V (Millan, 1999). These tracts have first synapses in several pain-relevant areas involved in emotion, movement, cardiovascular regulation, and sensory perception. These include, but are not limited to, the medial and lateral components of the thalamus, the reticular formation of the brainstem, the midbrain periaqueductal gray, the parabrachial nuclei, the cuneiform nuclei, the amygdala, the hypothalamus, and the nucleus parogigantocellularis (Millan, 1999). In turn, these brainstem, medullary, and pontine systems relay nociceptive information to cortical and subcortical systems involved in integration and modulation of sensory, emotional, and cognitive aspects of pain perception. In fact, studies employing positron emission tomography (PET) and functional magnetic resonance imaging (fMRI) techniques have identified many of the brain areas involved in processing nociceptive signals in healthy people. The areas most consistently implicated in pain processing are the sensory cortex, prefrontal cortex, inferior parietal cortex, anterior cingulate cortex (ACC), insula, lentiform nucleus, and thalamus (Peyron, Laurent, & Garcia-Larrea, 2000). The distributed network of pain-related areas has confirmed the multidimensional nature of the human pain experience. Further, these studies have provided specific information regarding the cognitive, sensory, and emotional processes that are intrinsic components of pain perception, and suggest that persons engaging in physical activity or sport can have considerable control over the perception of muscle pain without the use of analgesics. This information is also helpful in understanding how pain can be such an intrusive sensation capable of interfering with skeletal muscle function.

Functional brain imaging of acute muscle pain suggests that acute skin and muscle pain are processed in similar areas of the brain (Niddam et al., 2002). Functional brain imaging has also been used to study the function of the nociceptive system in chronic musculoskeletal pain conditions. Fibromyalgia patients, who have medically unexplained and severe muscle pain symptoms, have been shown to exhibit exaggerated neural processing of sensory information in multiple pain-relevant regions of the brain compared to healthy controls (Cook et al., 2004b; Gracely et al., 2002).

The most consistent area identified as active during pain in functional imaging studies is the insular cortex (Peyron, Laurent, & Garcia-Larrea, 2000). This structure is particularly interesting from an exercise and muscle pain perspective because of the recognized interaction between pain and cardiovascular regulation (Lovick, 1993; Randich & Maixner, 1984), and the fact that regional cerebral blood flow (rCBF) is increased in the insular cortex during dynamic exercise in humans (Williamson, McColl, & Mathews, 2003). Connections between the insular cortex and the thalamus, ACC, periaqueductal gray (PAG), and supplementary motor cortex suggest a functional link among pain processing, autonomic regulation, and motor planning (Dubner & Ren, 1999).

Pain Modulation

Modulation of the nociceptive signal can occur in the periphery and at spinal and supraspinal sites. While modulation is most often discussed in terms of inhibition, it has excitatory components as well. It has been proposed that chronic musculoskeletal pain or pain originating from deep tissues may result from an imbalance of excitatory and inhibitory control, such that normally innocuous signals are interpreted by the central nervous system as noxious (Dubner & Ren, 1999). The hierarchy and redundancy of the system make it likely that all muscle nociceptive signals undergo some modulation during the course of transmission.

In peripheral tissue, endogenous opioids and competition from nonnociceptive signals act to decrease afferent nociceptive input to the dorsal horn (Melzack & Wall, 1965; Mense, 1993). This results from inhibition of calcium influx and potassium conductance leading to cell hyperpolarization and decreased release of SP from the dorsal root ganglia (Meintjes et al., 1995). This suggests that peripheral opioids are capable of modulating pain during exercise. Indeed, peripheral blood concentrations of beta-endorphins have been shown to increase during exercise (Goldfarb & Jamurtas, 1997). These increases are likely to be dependent on intensity and duration, suggesting that metabolic strain plays a role in beta-endorphin release (Cook & Koltyn, 2000). However, the relationship between muscle pain perception and beta-endorphin concentrations is presently unknown.

Within the dorsal horn, nociceptive signals are under both ascending and descending influence. Nociceptive neurons converge with nonnociceptive sensory neurons, a key to understanding the concept of Melzack and Wall's (1965) gate control theory of pain modulation. Numerous local interneurons, many of which contain enkephalins and amino acids and their associated receptors, have both excitatory and inhibitory effects on nociceptive projection neurons (Millan, 1999).

Perhaps the most intriguing of the pain modulatory networks are those of the supraspinal descending modulatory and facilitatory systems. These systems have classically involved the PAG, rostral ventromedial medulla (RVM), and dorsolateral pontine tegmentum (DPT) whereby descending signals traveling the dorsolateral funiculus of the brainstem act to inhibit spinal nociceptive projection neurons (Fields & Basbaum, 1994). Numerous neural pathways form a coordinated network that facilitates the antinociceptive action of the descending signal. Stimulation of the PAG, RVM, or dorsolateral pontine tegmentum (DLPT) results in analgesia via descending serotonergic and noradrenergic pathways (Fields & Basbaum, 1994; Yaksh & Malmberg, 1994), and endogenous opioids are heavily involved in this pain modulatory process (Millan, 1999; Yaksh & Malmberg, 1994). While the net effect of nociceptive modulation is inhibitory, there also exist descending excitatory influences via the nucleus reticularis gigantocellularis (NGC) (Dubner & Ren, 1999).

It is now recognized that several other cortical structures can have profound influences on the descending inhibitory signal and nociceptive processing. Direct forebrain inputs from the insular cortex, the ACC, and the prefrontal lobes to the PAG suggest that sensation, emotion, cognition, and autonomic regulation are capable of initiating descending modulation of the afferent nociceptive signals (Dubner & Ren, 1999; Millan, 1999). In humans, brain imaging of the cognitive modulation of pain has demonstrated that distraction from pain results in decreased fMRI responses in areas known to process pain (e.g., caudal anterior cingulate, midinsular, and sensory cortices) and increases in areas known to modulate or inhibit pain processing (e.g., rostral anterior cingulate, orbitofrontal cortex, the PAG; Bantick et al., 2002). Importantly, top-down initiation of descending modulatory networks suggests that nociceptive inputs are not necessary for central regulation of pain.

Measurement of Muscle Pain

Muscle pain is typically measured using one of four types of scales: pain threshold, pain tolerance, ratings of muscle pain, and multidimensional pain measures.

Pain Threshold

Pain threshold is defined as the minimum stimulus intensity that is *usually* (50% of the time in detection experiments) perceived as painful. Pain thresholds are easily obtained and quantified and can be measured in time (e.g., seconds to first pain report) or stimulus (e.g., temperature perceived as "just painful") parameters. Drawbacks are the high intraindividual and interindividual variability, the lack of intensity and affective dimensions, the failure to predict the type of muscle pain experienced by chronic pain patients, and the influence of nonsensory factors (e.g., personality, expectations, instructional sets) (Price & Harkins, 1992; Snodgrass, Levy-Berger, & Haydon, 1985). Limitations notwithstanding, pain thresholds are the single most utilized measure of pain perception. Psychophysical scaling methods such as the "method of limits," the "method of constant stimuli," and "staircase methods" all have been used to assess pain thresholds (Gracely et al., 1988; Price & Harkins, 1992).

Pain Tolerance

Pain tolerance can be defined as either the length of time an individual is willing to endure a noxious stimulus or the maximal stimulus intensity that one will endure. For most types of noxious stimuli (e.g., noxious pressure or electrical stimulation), true tolerance measures cannot be achieved because of the potential for extensive tissue damage or permanent injury. Therefore, arbitrary cutoffs such as maximal exposure times or intensities serve to truncate the range of possible true tolerance times, introducing a "ceiling effect." As with measures of pain threshold, pain tolerance measures are unlikely to generalize to the actual type of pain (muscle or cutaneous) experienced by the individual.

Ratings of Muscle Pain

Muscle pain ratings are the verbal reports of stimuli that are above pain threshold. Muscle pain ratings can be measured with a variety of scales including category, ratio, or visual analog (VAS). These scales usually range from "no pain" to "extremely intense pain" or "worst pain imaginable" (Cook et al., 1997; O'Connor & Cook, 1999). Pain ratings can be measured for both the sensory (intensity) and affective (unpleasantness) dimensions of pain, and therefore provide a more complete measure than either pain thresholds or tolerances. Muscle pain ratings may also be more likely to represent or generalize to the pain experienced during everyday physical activities such as walking stairs or carrying groceries, or to the phenomenon of chronic pain.

The validity and reliability of muscle pain ratings have been documented. Leg muscle pain intensity ratings during cycle ergometry have been shown to be highly reliable (intraclass correlations of .88 to .98) and reproducible across trials, strongly related to an objective measure of exercise intensity (power output in watts), and significantly correlated ($r = .79$ to .94) with muscle pain measured using a 10 cm (4 in.) VAS (Cook et al., 1997). Similar to perceived exertion, muscle pain during exercise can be reliably produced and maintained (O'Connor & Cook, 2001), suggesting that it is a potentially useful tool for the study of mechanisms that underlie muscle pain in general, as well as a potential guide for exercise prescription.

Multidimensional Pain Measures

Several approaches can be used to assess pain in even broader dimensions while controlling for some of the potential biases that are often inherent to pain research. For example, the Descriptor Differential Scale was developed to minimize potential response bias and can be used to make separate assessments of the sensory and emotional components of pain. These scales are based on the psychophysical approach of cross-modality matching and also provide a measure of internal consistency, in standard deviation units, used to identify subjects who may be responding in a biased manner (Gracely & Kwilosz, 1988). Another simple approach used to assess pain more thoroughly is to examine both the intensity and emotional components of pain with the use of two VAS. The ease and validity of measuring pain using these scales make this a practical approach to pain assessment (Jensen, Karoly, & Braver, 1986). The McGill Pain Questionnaire (MPQ) (Melzack, 1975; Wilkie et al., 1990) is another useful tool that has been used extensively to assess the sensory, affective, and overall evaluation of the pain experience. The MPQ has been applied to study both acute experimental pain and symptoms of chronic musculoskeletal pain (Cook et al., 1997; Wilkie et al., 1990). Finally, a number of questionnaires are available to measure differing aspects of pain perception such as expectancy, attention, fear, catastrophizing, beliefs, and the impact the pain has on an individual's life (Burckhardt, Clark, & Bennett, 1991; Mason, Anderson, & Meenan, 1988; Sullivan et al., 1998; Williams & Keefe, 1991). Thus, the tools are available for the researcher to assess pain in a multidimensional context.

Experimental Pain Stimuli

Experimental stimulations to cause muscle pain include pressure, electricity, chemical stimuli, ischemia, and naturally occurring muscle actions.

Pressure

Pressure algometry is a widely used method to assess muscle pain in both clinical and research settings. Mechanical pressure is commonly used to assess both pain thresholds and tolerances (Brennum et al., 1989; Cook et al., 1997). The rate of increase can be controlled; however, pressure algometry applied to the skin inevitably stimulates cutaneous as well as deep tissue receptors. This can result in gating of the nociceptive signal through stimulation of cutaneous nonnociceptive afferents or, with intense pressure, an exacerbation of the nociceptive input through cutaneous nociceptive afferents.

Electricity

Electrical stimulation is also commonly used to produce muscle pain. Electrical stimuli are highly reproducible and easy to control. However, the electrical stimulus excites afferent pathways in an unnatural, synchronized fashion, with the signal bypassing the afferent receptors. Moreover, in many cases, the electrical current stimulates both nociceptive and nonnociceptive afferent nerve fibers. Thus, it is unclear how well pain ratings during electrical stimulation generalize to natural pain experiences.

Chemical Stimuli

A number of noxious chemicals (e.g., saline, BK, and capsaicin) have been shown to produce transient muscle pain and prolonged sensitivity to nociceptive stimuli (Graven-Nielsen & Mense, 2001; Mork et al., 2003). These noxious chemicals are usually injected into the muscle at controlled concentrations (e.g., 10% vs. 20%). Both the pain produced by the chemical and the sensitivity to other experimental pain stimuli are measured to document the chemical's algesic properties and its influence on peripheral and central nociceptive processes. Unfortunately, this method is invasive, requiring multiple injections. This introduces several potential confounds such as anxiety, heightened attention, and the influence of painful needle sticks on subsequent pain ratings. It is also unclear to what extent the concentrations used are encountered during muscular activity or to what degree these substances produce or interact with endogenous biochemicals.

Ischemia

Compression ischemia is a muscle pain stimulus that has been employed in laboratory studies since the 1930s (Lewis, Pickering, & Rothschild, 1931). It has also been used extensively in studies addressing the influence of biochemical accumulation (i.e., chemoreceptor or Type IV afferent fiber stimulation) on muscle sympathetic nerve activity (MSNA) and cardiovascular regulation (Ray & Hume, 1998). Compression ischemia produces pain that increases over time and is dependent upon the energy expended by the muscle and the contraction frequency (O'Connor & Cook, 1999).

Naturally Occurring Muscle Actions

Experimental pain stimuli have many advantages for researching muscle pain. They can be precisely controlled, are often easy to administer, and have contributed to our understanding of noxious signal transmission from human muscle. However, the pain induced by experimental stimuli is often novel and not likely to generalize to muscle pain that an individual normally experiences. Hence, a potentially useful, and increasingly popular, pain stimulus is that produced by the natural processes that underlie muscular contractions (O'Connor & Cook, 1999). Naturally occurring muscle pain induced by exercise is described as exhausting, intense, sharp, burning, cramping, and pulling (Cook et al., 1997). These same descriptors have been used to characterize clinical pain conditions such as menstrual pain, arthritic pain, cancer pain, chronic back pain, and fibromyalgia (Cook et al., 2004b; Melzack & Katz, 1994). Thus, an advantage of studying naturally occurring muscle pain is that it may be more likely to generalize to the pain experienced by chronic pain patients. Another advantage is that it can be produced transiently, safely, and reproducibly (Cook et al., 1997; Cook, O'Connor, & Ray, 2000). Moreover, the interindividual pain ratings can be examined relative to each individual's maximum performance (i.e., percentage of peak power output), thus making between-group comparisons potentially more meaningful.

Naturally Occurring Muscle Pain

Authors of classic studies conducted in the 1930s examined muscle pain during limb ischemia and observed perceptions of aching pain similar to the obstructive leg pain described by claudication patients (Lewis, Pickering, & Rothschild, 1931). The pain experienced was found to be a function of the force and frequency of contraction, but was highly variable (Lewis, Pickering, & Rothschild, 1931; Perlow, Markle, & Katz, 1934). It was concluded that muscle pain arising from an exercising or ischemic limb was due to the presence of a substance named factor P. The stimulus for factor P was thought to be due to the hypoxic state of the tissue, resulting from metabolic demand and inadequate blood flow (Lewis, Pickering, & Rothschild, 1931; Perlow, Markle, & Katz, 1934). Candidates for factor P included potassium, acid metabolites, and histamine (Dorpat & Holmes, 1955). The role of these biochemicals in naturally occurring muscle pain is still unknown.

Naturally occurring muscle pain has been used to study numerous exercise-related topics including the influence of pain on exercise performance (Cook et al., 1997; O'Brien & O'Connor, 2000); the relationship between pain and effort during exercise (Cook et al., 1997, 1998; Hollander et al., 2003); the influence of demographic, social, and genetic factors on perceptions during exercise (Cook et al., 2004a, 1997); and the effect of pharmacological manipulations on pain and exertion during exercise (Cook et al., 1997; Cook, O'Connor, & Ray, 2000; Motl et al., 2003; O'Connor et al., 2004). Descriptively, muscle pain thresholds during exercise appear to occur at ~50% of peak exercise

intensity, but as shown in earlier studies, are highly variable (Cook et al., 1997, 1998; Cook, O'Connor, & Ray, 2000). Above the pain threshold, muscle pain ratings increase as a positively accelerating function of the exercise stimulus (see figure 14.1) (Cook et al., 2004a, 1997, 1998; Cook, O'Connor, & Ray, 2000; Hamilton et al., 1996), suggesting that tonic inhibitory influences serve to filter nociceptive information until higher exercise intensities are reached. The muscle pain experienced during exercise is characterized as diffuse and described as sharp, intense, exhausting, and burning in quality; is similar for large and small muscle mass; and does not appear to be a factor in the participant's decision to stop maximal exercise (Cook et al., 1997, 1998; Cook, O'Connor, & Ray, 2000). Pain during recovery from exercise is characterized by a fast initial component, presumably representing the loss of input from the muscle contraction (i.e.,

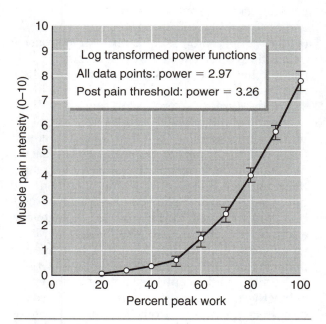

Figure 14.1 A composite of muscle pain intensity ratings for leg and forearm muscles during maximal exercise. The averaged response represents 177 data points (covering various exercise intensities) collected by the author, some of which have been published in the literature. Pain intensity during maximal exercise is characterized as a positively accelerating function of relative exercise intensity. Noticeable features are that pain rarely occurs prior to 50% of peak exercise intensity and then increases exponentially following pain threshold (~50% of peak capacity). Also shown are the power functions for the entire curve (20% to 100%) and for pain ratings following pain threshold. Power functions are based on linear regression of the Log10 transformed values for pain and power output (watts).

mechanoreceptor input), and a slower secondary component thought to represent the slow diffusion, metabolism, or washout of noxious chemicals (i.e., BK) (Cook et al., 1997; Cook, O'Connor, & Ray, 2000). Muscle pain ratings during sustained contractions are greater in ischemic compared to nonischemic conditions, and the total time that a contraction can be held is less (Caldwell & Smith, 1966; Dorpat & Holmes, 1955). Leg muscle pain ratings during exercise have been shown to be distinct from the perception of exertion (Cook et al., 1997, 1998; Cook, O'Connor, & Ray, 2000; Hamilton et al., 1996), and appear to be unrelated to experimentally induced pressure pain applied to the finger (Cook et al., 1997).

Several research groups have attempted to determine mechanisms that may underlie the experience of musculoskeletal pain during exercise. Pharmacological manipulations have been used in an attempt to block potential biochemical stimulation of muscle during exercise. Cook and colleagues (1997) found no effect of 20 mg/kg (~1,500 mg per subject) of aspirin on leg muscle pain ratings during maximal cycle ergometry, suggesting that prostaglandins do not play a critical role in the perception of pain during high-intensity, short-duration exercise. Subsequently, Cook, O'Connor, and Ray (2000) determined the effects of an opioid agonist (codeine) and antagonist (naltrexone) on muscle pain and MSNA during maximal handgrip exercise to exhaustion. Results demonstrated that neither 60 mg of codeine, 50 mg of naltrexone, or placebo altered the perception of muscle pain during exercise or recovery, and that neither drug had an influence on MSNA (see figure 14.2). Results from this investigation indicate that neither a mild agonist nor antagonist of the mu opioid receptor is sufficient to alter the subjective experience of muscle pain during exercise. Recent evidence from Motl and colleagues (Motl et al., 2003) suggests that adenosine receptor antagonism can have significant effects on the perception of muscle pain during exercise. They reported that ingestion of a high dose of caffeine (10 mg/kg body weight) resulted in significantly lower leg muscle pain ratings during 30 min of cycle ergometry compared to placebo. A follow-up study demonstrated a significant linear relationship between placebo, 5 mg/kg caffeine, and 10 mg/kg caffeine on leg muscle pain ratings, suggesting a dose–response effect (O'Connor et al., 2004). These results suggest that adenosine, a biochemical known to induce pain when injected into muscle (Graven-Nielsen & Mense, 2001) and known to be released during exercise (Costa et

al., 2001), plays an important role in the perception of naturally occurring muscle pain induced by exercise.

Aside from the direct manipulation of nociception, demographic, social, and genetic influences have demonstrated significant effects on muscle pain perception during exercise. For example, in a study by Cook and colleagues (1998), females reported higher leg muscle pain intensity ratings than males during cycle ergometry when the data were expressed as a function of absolute exercise intensity (i.e., 98 to 158 W). However, when the data were expressed relative to the participants' peak power output (i.e., 60% to 100%), females rated the leg muscle pain as significantly less intense than males. Recently, Cook and colleagues (2004a) reported that normotensive African American women with a positive family history of hypertension rated significantly lower leg muscle pain during exercise compared to African American women without a positive family history. These results were consistent with previous research demonstrating a significant negative relationship between risk for the development of hypertension and pain sensitivity (France, 1999), and support the hypothesis that decreased pain perception in at-risk individuals is the result of an underlying

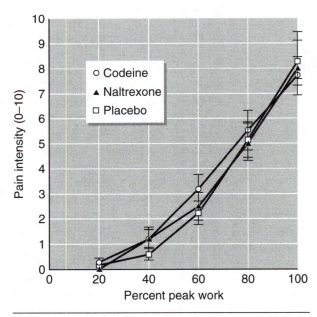

Figure 14.2 Pain intensity ratings at 20%, 40%, 60%, 80%, and 100% of peak work (J) during fatiguing handgrip for codeine, naltrexone, and placebo conditions. There were no effects of either drug on pain intensity or muscle sympathetic nerve activity (not shown) during exercise or recovery (not shown).

Adapted from Cook, O'Connor, & Ray, 2000.

pathophysiological process that leads to development of hypertension.

Analgesia During and Following Physical Activity

Reduced sensitivity to experimental pain stimuli presented during a bout of exercise suggests that exercise has an analgesic effect. Results from several investigations indicate that dental pain thresholds, induced by electrical stimulation of the tooth pulp, increase during exercise, with greater thresholds observed at higher compared to lower exercise intensities (Droste et al., 1991; Kemppainen et al., 1990; Pertovaara et al., 1984).

The analgesic response during exercise does not appear to be a transient phenomenon, but instead appears to translate into decreased pain sensitivity following exercise. The phenomenon of exercise-induced analgesia (EIA) has been demonstrated for a number of different experimental stimuli (for more detailed reviews see Cook & Koltyn, 2000), including ischemic, electrical, heat, and pressure pain, and is characterized by both increased pain thresholds and decreased pain ratings. Most of the investigations examining EIA have focused on exercise such as running and cycling, with the most consistent results occurring when the exercise stimulus is greater than 70% of maximal aerobic capacity or 200 W and duration is greater than 20 min. A limited number of studies have also reported analgesia following resistance exercise (Bartholomew et al., 1996; Koltyn & Arbogast, 1998). Thus, it appears that both aerobic exercise and anaerobic exercise are capable of inducing an analgesic effect. The exception to these findings comes from the research employing a noxious cold stimulus (e.g., the cold pressor), with exercise generally failing to result in an analgesic response (Janal et al., 1984; Padawer & Levine, 1992).

The mechanisms responsible for the analgesic effect are poorly understood. Hypotheses involving the endogenous opioid system have received limited support (Janal et al., 1984; Pertovaara et al., 1984). For example, a lack of EIA has been reported following the administration of naloxone, suggesting that circulating opioids during exercise have lasting effects postexercise (Janal et al., 1984; Pertovaara et al., 1984). However, others have failed to observe such an effect (Droste et al., 1991; Olausson et al., 1986). Similarly, data regarding the effects of peripheral stress hormones such as growth hormone, serotonin, adrenocorticotropic hormone, cortisol, and prolactin have been equivocal (Kemppainen et al., 1990; Pertovaara et al., 1984).

An interesting observation is that patients with chronic musculoskeletal pain (i.e., fibromyalgia) do not exhibit EIA, but instead exhibit a hyperalgesic response following exercise (Mengshoel, Vollestad, & Forre, 1995; Vierck et al., 2001). These studies have shown that exercise results in increased painful symptoms as well as increased sensitivity to experimental pain stimuli, and also provide further support that chronic muscle pain may be maintained by dysregulated central nervous system processing of sensory information.

Muscle Pain As a Barrier to Physical Activity

Does pain or the expectancy of pain affect someone's decision to exercise? In otherwise healthy individuals, the answer is essentially unknown. The recent emphasis toward educating people on the health benefits of low-intensity exercise (Pate et al., 1995) suggests that efforts are being made to make exercise more enjoyable and therefore less aversive (less painful?). While we know that physical inactivity is a major public health problem, we also know that multiple factors contribute to a physically active lifestyle. In older individuals, physical symptoms including shortness of breath, lack of energy, and painful joints have been reported as independent deterrents to engaging in physical activities (Crombie et al., 2004), while higher levels of physical activity are associated with improved quality of life and physical independence (Koltyn, 2001). For individuals with chronic musculoskeletal pain, the picture is less ambiguous. Symptoms of musculoskeletal pain are associated with reduced physical activity in individuals suffering from rheumatoid arthritis and osteoarthritis (Kaplan et al., 2003), low back pain (Taimela et al., 2000), and fibromyalgia (Granges, Zilko, & Littlejohn, 1994). In addition to painful symptoms, other deterrents to exercise in chronic pain conditions appear to be the same as in otherwise healthy individuals; specifically, self-efficacy has been shown to predict self-reported physical activity in fibromyalgia (Buckelew et al., 1995). Higher baseline levels of exercise are associated with decreased pain reporting and increased function in patients with chronic muscle pain (Stewart et al., 1994). Thus, exercise training may be an effective treatment for many muscle pain conditions.

Physical Activity As a Treatment for Chronic Musculoskeletal Pain

Exercise training and maintenance of a physically active lifestyle are important for chronic muscle pain patients for a host of reasons. The primary aim of most programs is to maintain physical function and avoid disability (Cooper et al., 1999). In peripheral arterial disease (PAD), exercise training results in vast improvements in terms of both pain onset during walking and maximal walking distance (Stewart et al., 2002). A recent meta-analysis of randomized, controlled trials of exercise in PAD concluded that exercise training resulted in 150% improvement in walking time (Leng, Fowler, & Ernst, 2000). In patients with unexplained muscle pain and fatigue, aerobic exercise training (60%-65% of predicted maximal heart rate) resulted in a lower number of symptoms; a lower number of general practitioner consultations; less prescribed medication; and improved ratings of pain, fatigue, anxiety, depression, and social interaction (Peters et al., 2002). In persons with rheumatoid arthritis, two weeks (3 hr/week) of low-impact aerobic exercise resulted in decreases in pain and fatigue with no detrimental effects on disease status in terms of joint count and sedimentation rate (Neuberger et al., 1997). In fibromyalgia, exercise training is considered one of the only efficacious treatments for management of patients' musculoskeletal pain symptoms (Busch et al., 2002; Sim & Adams, 2002). Thus, exercise appears to be beneficial for most chronic musculoskeletal pain conditions. However, the effect of exercise on pain is not always clear. Indeed, exercise may result in improved or maintained function without changes in muscle pain symptoms (Sim & Adams, 2002). In any case, physical activity appears critical to maintaining physical function, avoiding comorbid disease, and promoting independence.

Muscle Pain As a Limiting Factor in Sport Performance

It is a widely held belief that pain is a limiting factor during athletic competition. Athletes performing at extreme levels of human endurance must cope with intense muscle pain. This fact has translated into the consensus that pain tolerance can limit athletic performance, with speculations that "pain is the most critical differentiator between successful and unsuccessful athletes in endurance sports" (Anshel & Russell, 1994, p. 535). Anecdotal evidence abounds. Reigning Tour de France champion and Olympic athlete Lance Armstrong, in his recent book (*Every Second Counts,* with Sally Jenkins), makes this point very clear in the following excerpts:

> *There are parts unknown with regard to human performance, and those are the parts when it's just about pain and forfeit. . . . The experience of suffering is like the experience of exploring, of finding something unexpected and revelatory. When you find the outermost thresholds of pain, or fear, or uncertainty, what you experience afterward is an expansive feeling, a widening of your capabilities. Pain is good because it teaches your body and your soul to improve. It's almost as though your unconscious says, 'I'm going to remember this, remember how it hurt, and I'll increase my capacities so that the next time, it doesn't hurt as much.' The body literally builds on your experiences, and a physique and temperament that have gone through the Tour de France one year will be better the next year, because it has the memory to build upon. (pp. 222-223)*

There are several potentially interesting hypotheses relating to Armstrong's insights. Implied is that the body remembers pain, and there is evidence that this is the case (Ren & Dubner, 2002). Also implied is that the body (musculoskeletal system) adapts to pain and that pain during competition can be modified through training. Can athletes "harden" themselves against pain during competition? Can pain be an architect of human physiology in sport? There is currently no scientific evidence to support these contentions.

Apart from the anecdotal evidence in sport, indirect evidence concerning pain and performance comes from laboratory studies of muscle pain, exercise performance, and pain-related agents. Correlational evidence from early studies showed a moderate negative relationship (about −0.60) between muscle pain ratings and endurance performance during handgrip exercise (Caldwell & Smith, 1966; Dorpat & Holmes, 1955). However, Cook and colleagues (1997) found that during maximal cycle ergometry, all of the participants (19/19) reported stopping due to local leg fatigue and not leg muscle pain. In a follow-up study, Cook, O'Connor, and Ray (2000) reported that pain during maximal handgrip was a factor in the decision to stop exercising in 10 of 36 exercise tests, whereas fatigue was indicated in 34 of 36 tests.

Few studies have been conducted in which muscle pain was experimentally manipulated and performance determined. The ability to perform a complex golf putting task was hindered by the concurrent application of experimental pain stimuli, while a less complex weightlifting task was unaffected, suggesting that task complexity mediated the relationship between pain and performance (Brewer, Van Raalte, & Linder, 1990). One interesting study showed that cognitive dissociation, combined with the suggestion that the procedure would be analgesic, resulted in both attenuated pain ratings and a significant increase in leg raise endurance compared to a dissociation-only and a control condition (Spink, 1988). These results suggest that the cognitive modulation of pain can be a powerful tool during endurance exercise.

Several studies have examined the effects on exercise performance of drugs known to reduce musculoskeletal pain. Unfortunately, the majority of studies have failed to provide a concomitant measure of pain, thereby precluding any conclusions regarding pain and performance. A recent meta-analytic review indicated that the ingestion of sodium bicarbonate, resulting in a decrease in muscle hydrogen ion concentration, resulted in an overall improvement in anaerobic performance (Matson & Tran, 1993). However, no data on the effects of bicarbonate on muscle pain have been reported. Three randomized placebo-controlled experiments consistently showed that a moderate-to-large dose of aspirin (650 to 1,564 mg) taken 30 to 60 min prior to exercise had no influence on brief (<15 min) bouts of running or cycle ergometry (Cook et al., 1997; Lisse et al., 1991; Roi et al., 1994). Only one of these studies obtained muscle pain ratings, and that study showed no effect during exercise or recovery (Cook et al., 1997). Further, Cook, O'Connor, and Ray (2000) reported no effect of an opioid agonist (codeine, 60 mg) or antagonist (naltrexone, 60 mg) on exercise performance during maximal handgrip.

Directions for Future Investigation

There are a host of physical activity topics for which musculoskeletal pain is relevant. Unfortunately, most have not been systematically studied. The primary limitation for determining the influence of muscle pain on different aspects of physical activity is the scant knowledge concerning its basic mechanism. Significant advances in our knowledge of the molecular biology of nociception make plausible the notion of elucidating specific mechanisms involved in nociceptive transmission from active skeletal muscle. Physiological and psychological influences on the perception of experimental pain stimuli may or may not generalize to the perception of naturally occurring muscle pain, but for the most part they have yet to be tested. Assumptions that lactate results in muscle pain have been challenged, while biochemicals such as adenosine appear to be at least partially involved in the chemical stimulation of muscle nociceptors during exercise. Several other naturally occurring algesic substances are likely to contribute and remain to be studied. It is also plausible that a better understanding of the underlying mechanisms involved in the muscle nociceptive signal will aid in the treatment of chronic musculoskeletal pain. Consequently, exercise models may prove useful in determining how muscle pain can be treated.

Another important limitation has been the principal focus on pain intensity with less attention paid to other aspects of pain perception, such as affective and cognitive dimensions. These are critical features of the pain experience that are known to exert significant effects on how pain is processed and experienced. Pain thresholds are still the most widely used measure of pain, despite their documented limitations. There is a clear need for a multidimensional approach to the study of muscle pain during physical activity. How do the sensory, affective, and cognitive dimensions of pain contribute to muscle pain perception and its influence on physical activity? Moreover, how do these dimensions affect the efficacy of drugs designed to block nociceptive processes? It is recommended that muscle pain be studied from a perspective that recognizes the various qualitative (intensity, duration, and location), emotional (unpleasant and worrisome), and cognitive (appraisal, attention, and coping) aspects of the pain experience.

Fear and expectancy of pain appear to influence decisions concerning physical activity in chronic pain patients, but the influence in otherwise healthy people is essentially unknown. Therefore, research determining whether the perception of muscle pain influences an individual's decision to adopt or maintain a physically active lifestyle is warranted. Surprisingly, studies aimed at determining the effects of analgesic and algesic substances on exercise performance have generally failed to measure the perception of pain. This would seem to be a critical issue given the vast amount of anecdotal evidence indicating pain as a limiting factor in sport performance. The use of selective agonists and antagonists of opioid receptors requires further evaluation to determine what role the endogenous opioid system plays in the experience of muscle pain and EIA. Clearly, there are many challenges ahead for the exercise scientist interested in physical activity and pain. The field is open for exploration.

References

Anshel, M.H., & Russell, K.G. (1994). Effect of aerobic and strength training on pain tolerance, pain appraisal and mood of unfit males as a function of pain location. *Journal of Sports Science, 12,* 535-547.

Armstrong, L. & Jenkins, S. (2003). *Every second counts.* New York: Random House Inc.

Bantick, S.J., Wise, R.G., Ploghaus, A., Clare, S., Smith, S.M., & Tracey, I. (2002). Imaging how attention modulates pain in humans using functional MRI. *Brain, 125,* 310-319.

Bartholomew, J.B., Lewis, B.P., Linder, D.E., & Cook, D.B. (1996). Post-exercise analgesia: Replication and extension. *Journal of Sports Science, 14,* 329-334.

Besson, J.M. (1999). The neurobiology of pain. *Lancet, 353,* 1610-1615.

Bovim, G., Schrader, H., & Sand, T. (1994). Neck pain in the general population. *Spine, 19,* 1307-1309.

Brennum, J., Kjeldsen, M., Jensen, K., & Jensen, T.S. (1989). Measurements of human pressure-pain thresholds on fingers and toes. *Pain, 38,* 211-217.

Brewer, B.W., Van Raalte, J.L., & Linder, D.E. (1990). Effect of pain on motor performance. *Journal of Sport and Exercise Psychology, 12,* 353-365.

Buckelew, S.P., Murray, S.E., Hewett, J.E., Johnson, J., & Huyser, B. (1995). Self-efficacy, pain, and physical activity among fibromyalgia subjects. *Arthritis Care Research, 8,* 43-50.

Burckhardt, C.S., Clark, S.R., & Bennett, R.M. (1991). The fibromyalgia impact questionnaire: Development and validation. *Journal of Rheumatology, 18,* 728-733.

Busch, A., Schachter, C.L., Peloso, P.M., & Bombardier, C. (2002). Exercise for treating fibromyalgia syndrome. *Cochrane Database of Systematic Reviews,* CD003786.

Caldwell, L.S., & Smith, R.P. (1966). Pain and endurance of isometric muscle contractions. *Journal of Engineering Psychology, 5,* 25-32.

Cook, D.B., Jackson, E.M., O'Connor, P.J., & Dishman, R.K. (2004a). Muscle pain during exercise in normotensive African American women: Effect of parental hypertension history. *Journal of Pain, 5,* 111-118.

Cook, D.B., & Koltyn, K.F. (2000). Pain and exercise. *International Journal of Sports Medicine, 31,* 256-277.

Cook, D.B., Lange, G., Ciccone, D.S., Liu, W.C., Steffener, J., & Natelson, B.H. (2004b). Functional imaging of pain in patients with primary fibromyalgia. *Journal of Rheumatology, 31,* 364-378.

Cook, D.B., O'Connor, P.J., Eubanks, S.A., Smith, J.C., & Lee, M. (1997). Naturally occurring muscle pain during exercise: Assessment and experimental evidence. *Medicine and Science in Sports and Exercise, 29,* 999-1012.

Cook, D.B., O'Connor, P.J., Oliver, S.E., & Lee, Y. (1998). Sex differences in naturally occurring leg muscle pain and exertion during maximal cycle ergometry. *International Journal of Neuroscience, 95,* 183-202.

Cook, D.B., O'Connor, P.J., & Ray, C.A. (2000). Muscle pain perception and sympathetic nerve activity to exercise during opioid modulation. *American Journal of Physiology. Regulatory, Integrative and Comparative Physiology, 279,* R1565-R1573.

Cooper, R.A., Quatrano, L.A., Axelson, P.W., Harlan, W., Stineman, M., Franklin, B., Krause, J.S., Bach, J., Chambers, H., Chao, E.Y., Alexander, M., & Painter, P. (1999). Research on physical activity and health among people with disabilities: A consensus statement. *Journal of Rehabilitation Research and Development, 36,* 142-154.

Costa, F., Diedrich, A., Johnson, B., Sulur, P., Farley, G., & Biaggioni, I. (2001). Adenosine, a metabolic trigger of the exercise pressor reflex in humans. *Hypertension, 37,* 917-922.

Costigan, M., & Woolf, C.J. (2000). Pain: Molecular mechanisms. *Journal of Pain, 1,* 35-44.

Crombie, I.K., Irvine, L., Williams, B., McGinnis, A.R., Slane, P.W., Alder, E.M., & McMurdo, M.E. (2004). Why older people do not participate in leisure time physical activity: A survey of activity levels, beliefs and deterrents. *Age and Ageing, 33,* 287-292.

Dorpat, T.L., & Holmes, T. (1955). Mechanisms of skeletal muscle pain and fatigue. *AMA Archives of Neurology and Psychiatry, 74,* 628-640.

Droste, C., Greenlee, M.W., Schreck, M., & Roskamm, H. (1991). Experimental pain thresholds and plasma beta-endorphin levels during exercise. *Medicine and Science in Sports and Exercise, 23,* 334-342.

Dubner, R., & Ren, K. (1999). Endogenous mechanisms of sensory modulation. *Pain* (suppl. 6), S45-S53.

Fields, H.L., & Basbaum, A.I. (1994). Central nervous system mechanisms of pain modulation. In P.D. Wall & R. Melzack (Eds.), *Textbook of pain* (3rd ed., pp. 243-357). New York: Churchill Livingstone.

France, C.R. (1999). Decreased pain perception and risk for hypertension: Considering a common physiological mechanism. *Psychophysiology, 36,* 683-692.

Frymoyer, J.W., Pope, M.H., Costanza, M.C., Rosen, J.C., Goggin, J.E., & Wilder, D.G. (1980). Epidemiologic studies of low-back pain. *Spine, 5,* 419-423.

Goldfarb, A.H., & Jamurtas, A.Z. (1997). Beta-endorphin response to exercise: An update. *Sports Medicine, 24,* 8-16.

Gracely, R.H., & Kwilosz, D.M. (1988). The Descriptor Differential Scale: Applying psychophysical principles to clinical pain assessment. *Pain, 35,* 279-288.

Gracely, R.H., Lota, L., Walter, D.J., & Dubner, R. (1988). A multiple random staircase method of psychophysical pain assessment. *Pain, 32,* 55-63.

Gracely, R.H., Petzke, F., Wolf, J.M., & Clauw, D.J. (2002). Functional magnetic resonance imaging evidence of augmented pain processing in fibromyalgia. *Arthritis and Rheumatism, 46,* 1333-1343.

Granges, G., Zilko, P., & Littlejohn, G.O. (1994). Fibromyalgia syndrome: Assessment of the severity of the condition 2 years after diagnosis. *Journal of Rheumatology, 21,* 523-529.

Graven-Nielsen, T., & Mense, S. (2001). The peripheral apparatus of muscle pain: Evidence from animal and human studies. *Clinical Journal of Pain, 17,* 2-10.

Hamilton, A.L., Killian, K.J., Summers, E., & Jones, N.L. (1996). Quantification of intensity of sensations during muscular work by normal subjects. *Journal of Applied Physiology, 81,* 1156-1161.

Holbrook, T.L., Grazier, K., Kelsey, J.L., & Stauffer, R.N. (1984). *The frequency of occurrence, impact and cost of selected musculoskeletal conditions in the United States.* Park Ridge, IL: American Academy of Orthopedic Surgeons.

Hollander, D.B., Durand, R.J., Trynicki, J.L., Larock, D., Castracane, V.D., Hebert, E.P., & Kraemer, R.R. (2003). RPE, pain, and physiological adjustment to concentric and eccentric contractions. *Medicine and Science in Sports and Exercise, 35,* 1017-1025.

International Association for the Study of Pain. (1979). Pain terms: A list with definitions and notes on usage. *Pain, 6,* 249.

Janal, M.N., Colt, E.W., Clark, W.C., & Glusman, M. (1984). Pain sensitivity, mood and plasma endocrine levels in man following long-distance running: Effects of naloxone. *Pain, 19,* 13-25.

Jensen, M.P., Karoly, P., & Braver, S. (1986). The measurement of clinical pain intensity: A comparison of six methods. *Pain, 27,* 117-126.

Kaplan, M.S., Huguet, N., Newsom, J.T., & McFarland, B.H. (2003). Characteristics of physically inactive older adults with arthritis: Results of a population-based study. *Preventive Medicine, 37,* 61-67.

Kaufman, M.P., & Forester, H.V. (1996). Reflexes controlling circulatory, ventilatory and airway responses to exercise. In L.G. Rowell & J.T. Shepard (Eds.), *Handbook of physiology. Exercise: Regulation and integration of multiple systems* (pp. 381-447). New York: Oxford University Press.

Kemppainen, P., Paalasmaa, P., Pertovaara, A., Alila, A., & Johansson, G. (1990). Dexamethasone attenuates exercise-induced dental analgesia in man. *Brain Research, 519,* 329-332.

Koltyn, K.F. (2001). The association between physical activity and quality of life in older women. *Womens Health Issues, 11,* 471-480.

Koltyn, K.F., & Arbogast, R.W. (1998). Perception of pain after resistance exercise. *British Journal of Sports Medicine, 32,* 20-24.

Leng, G.C., Fowler, B., & Ernst, E. (2000). Exercise for intermittent claudication. *Cochrane Database of Systematic Reviews,* CD000990.

Lewis, T., Pickering, G.W., & Rothschild, P. (1931). Observations upon muscular pain in intermittent claudication. *Heart, 15,* 359-389.

Lisse, J.R., MacDonald, K., Thurmond-Anderle, M.E., & Fuchs, J.E. Jr. (1991). A double-blind, placebo-controlled study of acetylsalicylic acid (ASA) in trained runners. *Journal of Sports Medicine and Physical Fitness, 31,* 561-564.

Lovick, T.A. (1993). Integrated activity of cardiovascular and pain regulatory systems: Role in adaptive behavioural responses. *Progress in Neurobiology, 40,* 631-644.

Marchettini, P., Simone, D.A., Caputi, G., & Ochoa, J.L. (1996). Pain from excitation of identified muscle nociceptors in humans. *Brain Research, 740,* 109-116.

Mason, J.H., Anderson, J.J., & Meenan, R.F. (1988). A model of health status for rheumatoid arthritis. A factor analysis of the Arthritis Impact Measurement Scales. *Arthritis and Rheumatism, 31,* 714-720.

Matson, L.G., & Tran, Z.V. (1993). Effects of sodium bicarbonate ingestion on anaerobic performance: A meta-analytic review. *International Journal of Sport Nutrition, 3,* 2-28.

Meintjes, A.F., Nobrega, A.C., Fuchs, I.E., Ally, A., & Wilson, L.B. (1995). Attenuation of the exercise pressor reflex. Effect of opioid agonist on substance P release in L-7 dorsal horn of cats. *Circulation Research, 77,* 326-334.

Melzack, R. (1975). The McGill Pain Questionnaire: Major properties and scoring methods. *Pain, 1,* 277-299.

Melzack, R., & Katz, J. (1994). Pain measurement in persons in pain. In P.D. Wall & R. Melzack (Eds.), *Textbook of pain* (3rd ed., pp. 337-351). New York: Churchill Livingstone.

Melzack, R., & Wall, P.D. (1965). Pain mechanisms: A new theory. *Science, 150,* 971-979.

Mengshoel, A.M., Vollestad, N.K., & Forre, O. (1995). Pain and fatigue induced by exercise in fibromyalgia patients and sedentary healthy subjects. *Clinical and Experimental Rheumatology, 13,* 477-482.

Mense, S. (1993). Peripheral mechanisms of muscle nociception in local muscle pain. *Journal of Musculoskeletal Pain, 1,* 133-170.

Millan, M.J. (1999). The induction of pain: An integrative review. *Progress in Neurobiology, 57,* 1-164.

Mitchell, J.H., & Schmidt, R.F. (1996). Cardiovascular reflex control by afferent fibers from skeletal muscle receptors. In L.G. Rowell & J.T. Shepard (Eds.), *Handbook of physiology. Exercise: Regulation and integration of multiple systems* (pp. 623-658). New York: Oxford University Press.

Mork, H., Ashina, M., Bendtsen, L., Olesen, J., & Jensen, R. (2003). Experimental muscle pain and tenderness following infusion of endogenous substances in humans. *European Journal of Pain, 7,* 145-153.

Motl, R.W., O'Connor, P.J., & Dishman, R.K. (2003). Effect of caffeine on perceptions of leg muscle pain during moderate intensity cycling exercise. *Journal of Pain, 4,* 316-321.

Neuberger, G.B., Press, A.N., Lindsley, H.B., Hinton, R., Cagle, P.E., Carlson, K., Scott, S., Dahl, J., & Kramer, B. (1997). Effects of exercise on fatigue, aerobic fitness, and disease activity measures in persons with rheumatoid arthritis. *Research in Nursing and Health, 20,* 195-204.

Niddam, D.M., Yeh, T.C., Wu, Y.T., Lee, P.L., Ho, L.T., Arendt-Nielsen, L., Chen, A.C., & Hsieh, J.C. (2002). Event-related functional MRI study on central representation of acute muscle pain induced by electrical stimulation. *Neuroimage, 17,* 1437-1450.

O'Brien, P.M., & O'Connor, P.J. (2000). Effect of bright light on cycling performance. *Medicine and Science in Sports and Exercise, 32,* 439-447.

O'Connor, P.J., & Cook, D.B. (1999). Exercise and pain: The neurobiology, measurement, and laboratory study of pain in relation to exercise in humans. *Exercise and Sport Sciences Reviews, 27,* 119-166.

O'Connor, P.J., & Cook, D.B. (2001). Moderate-intensity muscle pain can be produced and sustained during cycle ergometry. *Medicine and Science in Sports and Exercise, 33,* 1046-1051.

O'Connor, P.J., Motl, R.W., Broglio, S.P., & Ely, M.R. (2004). Dose-dependent effect of caffeine on reducing leg muscle pain during cycling exercise is unrelated to systolic blood pressure. *Pain, 109,* 291-298.

Olausson, B., Eriksson, E., Ellmarker, L., Rydenhag, B., Shyu, B.C., & Andersson, S.A. (1986). Effects of naloxone on dental pain threshold following muscle exercise and low frequency transcutaneous nerve stimulation: A comparative study in man. *Acta Physiologica Scandinavica, 126,* 299-305.

Padawer, W.J., & Levine, F.M. (1992). Exercise-induced analgesia: Fact or artifact? *Pain, 48,* 131-135.

Pate, R.R., Pratt, M., Blair, S.N., Haskell, W.L., Macera, C.A., Bouchard, C., Buchner, D., Ettinger, W., Heath, G.W., King, A.C., Kriska, A., Leon, A.S., Marcus, B.H., Morris, J., Paffenbarger, R.S. Jr., Patrick, K., Pollock, M.L., Rippe, J.M., Sallis, J., Wilmore, J.H. (1995). Physical activity and public health. A recommendation from the Centers for Disease Control and Prevention and the American College of Sports Medicine. *Journal of the American Medical Association, 273,* 402-407.

Perlow, S., Markle, P., & Katz, L.N. (1934). Factors involved in the production of skeletal muscle pain. *Archives of Internal Medicine, 53,* 814-824.

Pertovaara, A., Huopaniemi, T., Virtanen, A., & Johansson, G. (1984). The influence of exercise on dental pain thresholds and the release of stress hormones. *Physiology and Behavior, 33,* 923-926.

Peters, S., Stanley, I., Rose, M., Kaney, S., & Salmon, P. (2002). A randomized controlled trial of group aerobic exercise in primary care patients with persistent, unexplained physical symptoms. *Family Practice, 19,* 665-674.

Peyron, R., Laurent, B., & Garcia-Larrea, L. (2000). Functional imaging of brain responses to pain. A review and meta-analysis. *Neurophysiologie Clinique, 30,* 263-288.

Price, D.D., & Harkins, S.W. (1992). Psychophysical approaches to pain measurement and assessment. In D.C. Turk & R. Melzack (Eds.), *Handbook of pain assessment* (pp. 111-134). New York: Guilford Press.

Randich, A., & Maixner, W. (1984). Interactions between cardiovascular and pain regulatory systems. *Neuroscience and Biobehavioral Reviews, 8,* 343-367.

Ray, C.A., & Hume, K.M. (1998). Sympathetic neural adaptations to exercise training in humans: Insights from microneurography. *Medicine and Science in Sports and Exercise, 30,* 387-391.

Ren, K., & Dubner, R. (2002). Descending modulation in persistent pain: An update. *Pain, 100,* 1-6.

Roi, G.S., Garagiola, U., Verza, P., Spadari, G., Radice, D., Zecca, L., & Cerretelli, P. (1994). Aspirin does not affect exercise performance. *International Journal of Sports Medicine, 15,* 224-227.

Sim, J., & Adams, N. (2002). Systematic review of randomized controlled trials of nonpharmacological interventions for fibromyalgia. *Clinical Journal of Pain, 18,* 324-336.

Snodgrass, J.G., Levy-Berger, G., & Haydon, M. (1985). Psychophysical methods. In *Human experimental psychology* (pp. 58-87). New York: Oxford University Press.

Spink, K.S. (1988). Facilitating endurance performance: The effects of cognitive strategies and analgesic suggestions. *Sport Psychologist, 2,* 97-104.

Stewart, A.L., Hays, R.D., Wells, K.B., Rogers, W.H., Spritzer, K.L., & Greenfield, S. (1994). Long-term functioning and well-being outcomes associated with physical activity and exercise in patients with chronic conditions in the Medical Outcomes Study. *Journal of Clinical Epidemiology, 47,* 719-730.

Stewart, K.J., Hiatt, W.R., Regensteiner, J.G., & Hirsch, A.T. (2002). Exercise training for claudication. *New England Journal of Medicine, 347,* 1941-1951.

Stewart, W.F., Ricci, J.A., Chee, E., Morganstein, D., & Lipton, R. (2003). Lost productive time and cost due to common pain conditions in the US workforce. *Journal of the American Medical Association, 290,* 2443-2454.

Sullivan, M.J., Stanish, W., Waite, H., Sullivan, M., & Tripp, D.A. (1998). Catastrophizing, pain, and disability in patients with soft-tissue injuries. *Pain, 77,* 253-260.

Surgeon General's report on physical activity and health. From the Centers for Disease Control and Prevention (1996). *Journal of the American Medical Association, 276,* 522.

Taimela, S., Diederich, C., Hubsch, M., & Heinricy, M. (2000). The role of physical exercise and inactivity in pain recurrence and absenteeism from work after active outpatient rehabilitation for recurrent or chronic low back pain: A follow-up study. *Spine, 25,* 1809-1816.

Tuveson, B., Lindblom, U., & Fruhstorfer, H. (2003). Experimental muscle pain provokes long-lasting alterations of thermal sensitivity in the referred pain area. *European Journal of Pain, 7,* 73-79.

Vierck, C.J. Jr., Staud, R., Price, D.D., Cannon, R.L., Mauderli, A.P., & Martin, A.D. (2001). The effect of maximal exercise on temporal summation of second pain (windup) in patients with fibromyalgia syndrome. *Journal of Pain, 2,* 334-344.

Waddell, G. (1998). *The back pain revolution.* Edinburgh: Churchill Livingstone.

Wilkie, D.J., Savedra, M.C., Holzemer, W.L., Tesler, M.D., & Paul, S.M. (1990). Use of the McGill Pain Questionnaire to measure pain: A meta-analysis. *Nursing Research, 39,* 36-41.

Williams, D.A., & Keefe, F.J. (1991). Pain beliefs and the use of cognitive-behavioral coping strategies. *Pain, 46,* 185-190.

Williamson, J.W., McColl, R., & Mathews, D. (2003). Evidence for central command activation of the human insular cortex during exercise. *Journal of Applied Physiology, 94,* 1726-1734.

Woolf, A.D., & Akesson, K. (2001). Understanding the burden of musculoskeletal conditions: The burden is huge and not reflected in national health priorities. *British Medical Journal, 322,* 1079-1080.

Woolf, A.D., & Pfleger, B. (2003). Burden of major musculoskeletal conditions. *Bulletin of the World Health Organization, 81,* 646-656.

World Health Organization. (2003). The burden of musculoskeletal conditions at the start of the new millennium. *World Health Organization Technical Report Series, 919, i-x, 1-218, back cover.*

Yaksh, T.L., & Malmberg, A.B. (1994). Central pharmacology of nociceptive transmission. In P.D. Wall & R. Melzack (Eds.), *Textbook of pain* (3rd ed., pp. 165-200). New York: Churchill Livingstone.

Psychobiology of Human Performance

This section includes three chapters focusing on applications of psychobiological research methods and intervention techniques to the problems of understanding and enhancing skilled athletic performance. In chapter 15, Brad Hatfield, Amy Haufler, and Tom Spalding review the results from a systematic line of inquiry spanning more than 20 years. Their chapter examines patterns of cortical activity (assessed through electroencephalography or EEG) associated with skilled performance in athletes of different sports. The presentation of the evidence is organized around the central theme of economy of effort. Due to space limitations the authors have provided a basic overview of EEG methodology. Readers seeking additional technical details could consult more specialized sources (Davidson, Jackson, & Larson, 2000; Fisch, 1999; Rowan & Tolunsky, 2003).

In chapter 16, Dave Collins and Alan McPherson examine the role of biofeedback in sport performance. He places emphasis on a number of critical methodological issues that could have a significant impact on the outcomes of biofeedback-based interventions. Readers interested in pursuing further study on this topic can find a wealth of practical information in texts focusing on biofeedback in general (Schwartz & Adrasik, 2003) or specifically in sport (Blumenstein, Bar-Eli, & Tenenbaum, 2002).

In chapter 17, Paul Holmes examines the application of imagery in the context of sport. Most of the hypotheses that have been proposed to explain why imagery (or "mental practice") would be effective in improving performance in physical tasks have psychobiological underpinnings. Holmes reviews neuroscientific data from a variety of sources to provide insight into the mechanisms involved in creating mental images and linking them to movement. Interested readers should consult the sources cited by Holmes on the neural bases of imagery in general (Farah, 2000) and motor imagery in particular (Decety, 1996).

Suggested Background Readings

Blumenstein, B., Bar-Eli, M., & Tenenbaum, G. (Eds.) (2002). *Brain and body in sport and exercise: Biofeedback applications in performance enhancement.* Chichester, UK: Wiley.

Davidson, R.J., Jackson, D.C., & Larson, C.L. (2000). Human electroencephalography. In J.T. Cacioppo, L.G. Tassinary, & G.G. Berntson (Eds.), *Handbook of psychophysiology* (2nd ed., pp. 27-52). Cambridge, UK: Cambridge University Press.

Decety, J. (1996). The neurological basis of motor imagery. *Behavioral Brain Research, 77,* 45-52.

Farah, M.J. (2000). The neural bases of mental imagery. In M.S. Gazzaniga (Ed.), *The new cognitive neurosciences* (2nd ed., pp. 965-974). Cambridge, MA: MIT Press.

Fisch, B.J. (1999). *Fisch and Spehlmann's EEG primer: Basic principles of digital and analog EEG* (3rd ed.). Amsterdam: Elsevier Science.

Rowan, A.J., & Tolunsky, E. (2003). *Primer of EEG with a mini-atlas.* Philadelphia: Butterworth-Heinemann.

Schwartz, M.S., & Adrasik, F. (Eds.) (2003). *Biofeedback: A practitioner's guide* (3rd ed.). New York: Guilford Press.

A Cognitive Neuroscience Perspective on Sport Performance

Bradley D. Hatfield, PhD

Amy J. Haufler, PhD

Thomas W. Spalding, PhD

A number of investigators have supported the notion that high-level athletic performance is characterized by economy of metabolic, physiological, and kinematic processes (i.e., motion) (Daniels, 1985; deVries, 1968; deVries & Housh, 1994; Hatfield & Hillman, 2001). This means that skilled athletes accomplish their work and perform their tasks with minimal effort. More specifically, Sparrow (2000) stated that the dynamics of coordinated muscle activity are organized on the basis of minimization of energy expenditure in a process of adaptation to constraints imposed by both task and environment. In this manner, the athlete sprinting in a 100 m track and field event may be engaged in an intense muscular effort because of the nature of the task. However, optimal performance would be characterized by the absence of nonessential muscle recruitment and of any unnecessary tension in both the prime movers (e.g., gluteal and upper "hamstring" action) and synergistic muscles that move the runner's center of mass in a rectilinear manner toward the finish line (deVries & Housh, 1994). To illustrate, Carl Lewis, the great American sprinter, anecdotally described his optimal sprinting performance as a state of "relaxed explosiveness." Such a state is based on essential recruitment of motor units for the intended movement, with little wasted effort, resulting in efficient metabolic activity and reduced effort sense. The

focal question that guides the present review is "Does such a state also characterize the mind or brain of the skilled performer?"

Phenomenological reports of high-performance athletes are supportive of such a position. Williams and Krane (1998) described a number of psychological qualities associated with the ideal performance state such as effortlessness, little "thinking" during performance, and an involuntary quality to the experience. Such subjective attributes are also consistent with the classic notion of automaticity of skilled motor behavior advanced by Fitts and Posner (1967). On the other hand, negative affect and the associated cognitive activity reduce efficiency of movement, thereby degrading the quality of motor performance (Beuter & Duda, 1985; Weinberg & Hunt, 1976). In this regard, Beuter and Duda observed alterations in the kinematic qualities of lower limb movement in young children during walking when they were subjected to psychological stress. The authors stated that the task of stepping, which was controlled automatically in a low-stress condition, became less smooth and efficient as volitional control took over under high stress. In addition, Weinberg and Hunt (1976), in a classic study, observed heightened motor unit activation and cocontraction (loss of reciprocal inhibition in the antagonists) of the involved muscles in an overhead throwing motion in college students subjected to stress relative to a control condition. The heightened musculoskeletal activity was also associated with reduced accuracy of throwing a ball at a target. According to these findings, the influence of cognitive-affective states on the quality of motor performance appears causal in nature, but the central (i.e., brain) mechanisms of effect are unclear from such studies.

Alternatively, the cognitive neuroscience perspective does offer insight as to how psychological states affect the quality of motor performance. Cognitive neuroscience, an area of behavioral science in which mental processes are explained in terms of neurobiology, typically uses neuroimaging or "brain imaging" tools to address research issues. As illustrated schematically in figure 15.1, the cortical association areas that underlie cognitive and affective processes are intricately interconnected to the "motor loop" mediated by the basal ganglia. The motor loop is composed of the striatum, globus pallidus, and the ventrolateral

nucleus of the thalamus, which then projects to the motor cortex and enables depolarization of the appropriate cell bodies for ultimate activation of skeletal muscle motor units (Bear, Conners, & Paradiso, 2002; Kandel & Schwartz, 1985). Practice results in "pruning" of nonessential brain processes (Bell & Fox, 1996). In this way the skilled performer eliminates task-irrelevant cerebral cortical and subcortical connections, thereby reducing complexity in the organization of his or her motor control processes. Such simplicity, or reduction in the degrees of freedom of neural network actions, likely leads to less interference with the "motor loop" and greater consistency of performance, and such a theoretical perspective can be empirically tested with the tools of cognitive neuroscience.

The present chapter illustrates that this fundamental dimension of superior psychomotor performance (i.e., economy) is also characteristic of cerebral cortical activity. The model illustrated in figure 15.1 leads to testable hypotheses with the

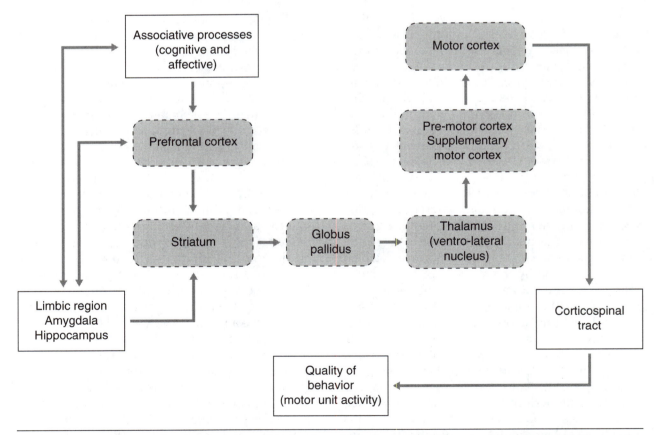

Cognitive neuroscience model of psychomotor performance

Figure 15.1 Various component structures involved in the interplay between cognitive (association), emotive (limbic lobe), and motor processes that result in motor behavior (motor unit activation). The motor loop is shown by the structures connected with the broken lines.

employment of neuroimaging techniques. It stands to reason that the brain would adapt to the stress of training and skill acquisition similarly to the peripheral musculature, since the central nervous system (CNS), indeed, controls the quality of muscle action. In this regard the human brain is highly plastic and seems to undergo significant change in response to the demands imposed on it (Elbert et al., 1995). With such a concept in mind, we overview the literature on cerebral cortical dynamics during psychomotor performance. The study of sport participants is useful in this regard in that they are highly motivated to attend to the tasks that are imposed (e.g., target shooting). In addition, the study of skilled performers who have undergone extensive practice over appreciable periods of time enables the observation of well-defined and stable patterns of electrocortical activity because of their long-term experience with the tasks (Hatfield et al., 2004). Typically, these tasks have included self-paced events such as rifle and pistol marksmanship (Hatfield, Landers, & Ray, 1984; Haufler et al., 2000; Hillman et al., 2000; Janelle et al., 2000a, 2000b; Kerick, Douglass, & Hatfield, 2004; Loze et al., 2001), archery (Salazar et al., 1990; Landers et al., 1994), golf putting (Crews & Landers, 1993), and preparatory periods for karate skills (Collins, Powell, & Davies, 1990). These events offer the opportunity for psychophysiological recording in light of the motionless hold or preparatory phase that reduces the likelihood of movement artifact while requiring intense attentive states.

Regional Cortical Activity in Elite Performers

Electroencephalography (EEG) has been the primary neuroimaging technique employed in this area of research, as it allows the study participant to engage in sport-related motor tasks while recordings of brain activity are obtained. Other techniques such as functional magnetic resonance imaging and positron emission tomography (PET) confine subjects spatially and restrict them from engaging in such tasks. In addition, these technologies may be cost prohibitive in many research settings. EEG represents a time series of electrical activity recorded from the brain via placement of electrodes at selected sites on the head. A standard electrode placement system specifies electrode locations based on anatomical landmarks on the head. This system, for example, specifies that key electrodes be placed 10%, 20%, and 50% of the

distance between such landmarks as the bridge of the nose, or nasion, and the small bump in the occipital region of the skull, or inion. As such, this standard recording strategy is referred to as the International 10-20 system, in light of the percent distances between landmark reference sites on the head, and it allows for comparison of results across various laboratories and clinical settings (Jasper, 1958).

The EEG sensor, typically composed of metal such as tin or chloride-coated silver, detects the transient or fluctuating summation of excitatory and inhibitory postsynaptic potentials (currents) from tens of thousands of neurons, and possibly glial cells, located below the scalp surface within the cortex of the brain, that collectively generate an electrical charge or potential. The vertically or radially oriented current detected by the EEG sensors emanates from the gyral surfaces or folds in the cortex below the scalp, and the signal is manifest on the order of millionths of volts or microvolts (μV). However, one major limitation of EEG is the problem of volume conduction or the spreading of electrical charge throughout the liquid medium of the brain so that the signal is detected by additional sensors beyond those overlying the tissue of interest. In this manner, the spatial resolution of EEG, or its ability to specifically localize the neural (i.e., brain) source of the time series, is poor; but there are methods to increase spatial precision by using large numbers of sensors, or what are called dense electrode arrays (as many as 250 sensors), along with sophisticated algorithms to solve the inverse problem.

The transient continuous potentials or analog signal, changing in magnitude over time, is sampled and converted to digital values in computer memory by an analog-to-digital (AD) converter and must be amplified 20 to 50 thousand times to be visible on a chart recorder or a computer screen. The current is conducted by wire leads to an amplifier and then subjected to a process termed differential amplification, whereby the resultant EEG record is actually a record of the difference in voltage between the recording sites placed on the scalp over the cerebral cortex and a reference site that is typically placed on a "nonbrain" region such as the earlobe or the tip of the nose. This "differential" recording strategy is designed to achieve common-mode rejection or the elimination of any nonbrain signals. The reasoning behind this recording strategy is that any electrical activity common to a recording site over the cerebral cortex and a neutral site must not be indicative of brain activity—the subtraction process removes any common activity. Thus each EEG recording derived from the scalp surface is actually the result of the amplified difference between the active sites and the common reference site and, as such, enables the investigator to be confident that the EEG record of oscillating electrical potentials is in fact reflective of cortical activity and not "noise."

The EEG record is a two-dimensional time series of voltage fluctuations characterized by amplitude and frequency that can be examined for the purpose of cognitive inference when combined with consideration of the neuroanatomical location of the recording site(s). The frequency range or spectrum extends from 1 to approximately 50 cycles per second (Hz), with higher frequencies indicative of greater activation. In order to accurately represent the time series, the sampling rate must be at least twice that of the highest frequency in the signal, so minimal sampling rates are 100 Hz; this requirement is termed the Nyquist frequency, and undersampling will result in a distortion of the time series or "aliasing." The amplitude of EEG, centered around a mean value for a given time sample of EEG or baseline, is approximately ± 50 μV. In essence, the raw signal is composed of a mixture of the frequencies in the spectrum and can be decomposed into its primary "ingredients" or sinusoidal frequency components in order to determine the degree of activation. The decomposition of the complex record or EEG wave for a given time period or epoch, termed spectral analysis, is accomplished mathematically by Fast Fourier Transformation or FFT. Lower frequencies, such as the high-amplitude delta (i.e., 1-3 Hz), theta (i.e., 4-7 Hz), and alpha bands (i.e., 8-13 Hz), are indicative of a relaxed state, while the low-amplitude higher frequencies (i.e., beta [13-30 Hz] and gamma bands [36-44 Hz]) are indicative of localized activation. Figure 15.2 illustrates the placement of EEG sensors and the recording of EEG during rifle marksmanship, an ideal task for psychophysiological recordings.

The alpha band frequencies reflect relaxation, as such high amplitudes are likely the result of similar or synchronous neuronal activity in the brain region of interest (ROI). Similar neuronal states, and the accompanying postsynaptic potentials, would enable summated or synchronous high-amplitude, slow-oscillatory activity; and such activity is more likely to occur during rest or inactivity within a given cortical ROI. Heightened metabolic activity in such a region would

likely result in differentiated neuron states, as the various neurons engage in specific functions, and desynchronous (i.e., lower amplitude) faster-oscillating, high-frequency potentials. In this manner the activation of brain ROIs can be determined for the purpose of inferring cognitive activity on the part of the subject (cognitive inference). Although it is somewhat oversimplified, the reader can subscribe to the rule of thumb that alpha power is positively related to regional relaxation (and inversely related to activation) while beta and gamma power are positively related to activation.

A related line of research by Konttinen and colleagues (Konttinen & Lyytinen, 1992, 1993a, 1993b; Konttinen, Lyytinen, & Konttinen, 1995; Konttinen, Lyytinen, & Viitasalo, 1998; Konttinen, Lyytinen, & Era, 1999; Konttinen, Landers, & Lyytinen, 2000), using slow potential (SP) recordings from the motor planning, motor cortex, and visual areas (i.e., SP recordings are time-averaged potentials that precede a self-initiated event such as the trigger pull in marksmanship), as well as event-related potentials recorded during reactive table tennis and baseball tasks (Hung et al., 2004; Radlo et al., 2001), offers further support for the notion of economy; but the present discussion is limited to spectral analysis of the EEG.

Early EEG and Motor Performance Research

One of the initial studies to employ EEG during motor behavior to assess cerebral cortical activity was conducted by Hatfield and colleagues (1982), who assessed EEG activity at left and right temporal and occipital sites during the aiming period prior to trigger pull in 15 elite world-class competitive marksmen. The impetus for this early investigation was the work of Beausey (cited in Pullum, 1977), who observed robust increases in EEG alpha power during superior marksmanship performance. This preliminary report by Beausey, along with the classic notions of hemispheric asymmetry in cognitive function (Galin & Ornstein, 1972; Springer & Deutsch, 1998), guided Hatfield and colleagues to address one of the prevalent themes in sport psychology at that time from a cognitive neuroscience perspective: the notion of attenuated self-talk during superior performance (Gallwey, 1974; Meichenbaum, 1977). At that time the employment of CNS-related psychophysiological measures in sport psychology studies was largely undeveloped (Hatfield & Landers, 1983).

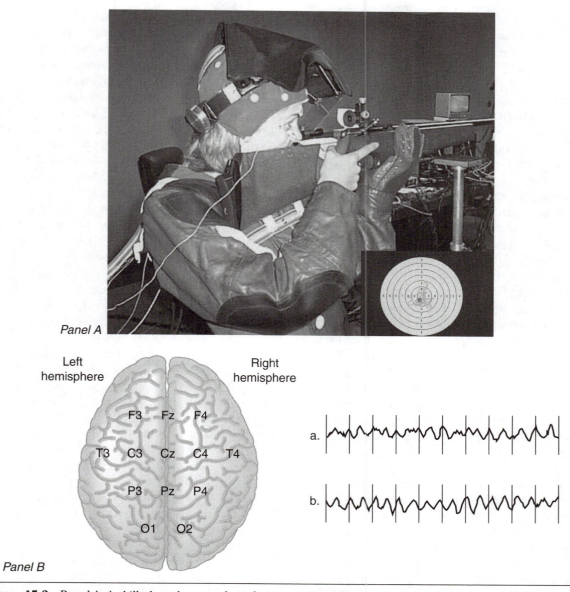

Panel A

Panel B

Figure 15.2   Panel A. A skilled marksman who is being monitored for electroencephalography (EEG) and eye movements during actual target shooting performance is pictured with an authentic illustration of the rifle barrel movement prior to the shot execution and shot accuracy. Performance accuracy is monitored by a computer system interfaced with a light-emitting device that is attached to the end of the rifle and, when pointed to a reflective target, tracks the path of the barrel and aiming point at the time of trigger pull. The performance accuracy and EEG systems are interfaced so that assessment of brain state may be conducted with respect to actual psychomotor performance. Panel B. The International 10-20 system (Jasper, 1958) with frontal (F), central (C), temporal (T), parietal (P), and occipital (O) electrode placements illustrated. Even numbers associated with electrodes designate the right hemisphere, and odd numbers designate the left hemisphere. Z placements are midline placements. EEG sensors placed on the scalp enable the recording of brain waves. Examples of raw EEG obtained at the parietal area while a subject is sitting quietly with eyes open (*a*) and closed (*b*) are provided. Note the differential amplitudes associated with eyes open and eyes closed.

Subscribing to the traditional view that increased EEG alpha power is indicative of decreased activation—the concept of "cortical idling" later advanced by Pfurtscheller (1992)—the investigators theorized that left temporal alpha power should be relatively higher than that observed in the right temporal region in highly skilled performers, indicative of less phonological processing. Such a finding would offer psychophysiological evidence for attenuated covert self-instructional activity or verbal-analytic processing in highly skilled athletes and is consistent with attainment of the stage of automaticity as described by Fitts and Posner (1967). No specific predictions were expressed for the occipital EEG recordings, but the O1 and O2 sites were monitored because of the visual demands inherently associated with the marksmanship task. In this completely within-subjects design, the relative EEG alpha power (i.e., the percentage of power in the 8 to 12 Hz band within a spectrum defined from 1 to 30 Hz) recorded at the four sites during the aiming period was contrasted to that observed during a resting state. Twelve of the 15 participants clearly showed a marked elevation in left temporal (T3) alpha power averaged across three successive 2.5 sec epochs (or time periods) during the aiming period, relative to a comparable period of rest, accompanied by desynchrony or less EEG alpha power in the right temporal region (T4). This difference in corresponding or homologous sites resulted in remarkable temporal EEG asymmetry during aiming, indicative of reduced left temporal activation. No such asymmetry was observed in these marksmen in the resting condition, during which the overall alpha power was also reduced.

As already suggested, the findings are consistent with the concept of a practice-induced reduction of self-instructional phonological processes in light of the reduced activity in the left temporal region. In addition, the results imply a reduction in feature detection of external and interoceptive stimuli with establishment of a memory-based internal model to guide performance (Kinsbourne, 1982). The findings can also be interpreted from the viewpoint of an intention to act, as outlined by Shaw (1996), as opposed to a simple reduction of attention or cognitive load, as the athlete is likely to have a well-established mental routine or approach to achieve his or her goal that internally guides the behavior with less emphasis on external feature detection. In either case, the significance of such neural adaptations lies in the possibility of a reduction in cognitive association processes and detailed analysis of environmental stimuli that could potentially influence motor control processes in a negative manner. That is, with heightened cognitive load, the involved motor processes may become more variable from increased corticocortical communication between association (e.g., phonological) and motor regions (see Networking Between Cortical Association and Motor Regions, page 234). The highly skilled marksmen studied by Hatfield and colleagues (1982) seemingly eliminated such "neuromotor noise." At the same time the desynchronous activity observed in the right temporal region (T4) during shooting, as compared to the resting state, is consistent with the notion of a reliance on visual-spatial processing during the aiming period, an event entirely consistent with the specific demands of target shooting.

The early work of Hatfield and colleagues (1982) spawned a number of subsequent investigations and instituted a guiding methodological approach for many of the EEG studies of athletes that followed. The paradigm is defined by EEG recording at homologous (i.e., both left and right hemisphere) sites to determine cerebral hemispheric activation during the final 3 to 8 sec of the preparatory period for a self-paced motor task, immediately prior to the self-initiated action, when motion artifact is minimal. Typically, several performance trials (e.g., 40 trials of target shooting) are examined, and the resultant spectral power estimates from each trial are then averaged to achieve a stable estimate of EEG activity during the aiming period.

Using this paradigm, Hatfield, Landers, and Ray (1984) conducted a two-part study. In Study 1, they replicated the results of Hatfield and colleagues (1982) while also computing temporal asymmetry scores during the aiming period that clearly revealed a dramatic shift from relative left temporal activation early in the aiming period to greater right temporal activation at the time of trigger pull. The temporal asymmetry scores were derived as "T4 alpha power/T3 alpha power" such that positive scores indicated relative left temporal activation and negative scores indicated relative right temporal activation.

Although the results of Study 1 were suggestive of the cognitive processes involved during skilled visuomotor behavior, Hatfield, Landers, and Ray (1984) conducted Study 2 in order to achieve cognitive inference with increased confidence. Essentially, the authors replicated and extended the procedures used in Study 1 with a different group (15 intercollegiate marksmen) by employing the shooting task and additionally challenging the subjects with verbal-analytic (i.e., paragraph comprehension and arithmetic problem solving) and visual-spatial tasks (i.e., geometric puzzle solving). These additional challenges were presented to the participants in order to deduce whether the mental processes involved during highly skilled marksmanship were more similar to those in the verbal-analytic or the visuospatial domain. The participants executed 20 trials of the comparative cognitive tasks, which were presented via projected images on a screen, while they assumed the same posture as employed during the shooting position in an attempt to equalize the motor demands of the tasks and any cardio-vascular effects on CNS processes (Lacey, 1967). EEG recorded during the cognitive challenges was also divided into three successive 2.5 sec epochs to allow contrast with the temporal dynamic of the EEG derived during target shooting. Again, temporal asymmetry metrics in the form specified in Study 1 were generated for analysis in a 3 × 3 (task × epochs) design.

The results of the analysis revealed stable asymmetry scores across the epochs during both cognitive challenges, with the scores during the "left hemisphere" challenges higher (i.e., more positive) than those during the "right hemisphere" challenges; however, those derived during the target aiming period revealed a dramatic shift over time (see figure 15.3). The asymmetry scores during the initial 2.5 sec epoch of aiming on the target were similar to those observed during the verbal-analytic challenge and significantly higher than those observed during the visual-spatial

tasks, while they were significantly reduced in magnitude during the final two epochs just prior to trigger pull as compared to those exhibited in the initial 2.5 sec epoch of aiming. By the third and final epoch of the aiming period, the asymmetry scores during the shooting task were significantly reduced relative to those during verbal-analytic processing and similar to those during visual-spatial processing (although lower in magnitude). Again, as in Study 1, such a shift in temporal asymmetry, in conjunction with inspection of EEG alpha power at the individual homologous sites, revealed a progressive decrease in activation of the left temporal region accompanied by relative stability of activation in the right temporal region that subserves visuospatial function.

Cognitive Inference

The comparison of the "unknown" preparatory state during shooting to states during the defined or "known" tasks in the verbal-analytic and visual-spatial dimensions represents a cognitive inference strategy described by Cacioppo and Tassinary (1990). In essence, the EEG signature during the task of interest, in this case the aiming period, is compared to other EEG signatures recorded during known referents to determine similarity (Hatfield et al., 2004). If the EEG signature during the task of interest is similar to that during a referent, then support is provided for similarity of the involved cognitive states. Of course, such metrics as asymmetry scores must be carefully considered along with the spectral power at the individual sites, as such ratio scores can change in magnitude in one direction for a variety of reasons. For example, a rise in T4/T3 magnitude over successive epochs could be due to relative stability in T3 with a progressive rise in T4 over epochs; it could also be due to relative stability in T4 alpha power and a progressive decline in T3 alpha power. Careful examination of both power and asymmetry, in conjunction with comparison to such measures during "known" mental states, allows a powerful tool for cognitive inference. In this manner, the study by Hatfield, Landers, and Ray (1984) offered a paradigmatic and conceptual base for subsequent investigations of cortical activity and psychomotor learning and performance. The interpretation of the results offered by the authors also appears consistent with phenomenological reports by athletes, such as the one offered by the Hall of Fame football player Walter Payton of the Chicago Bears, who was quoted by Attner (1984; pp. 2-3) as follows:

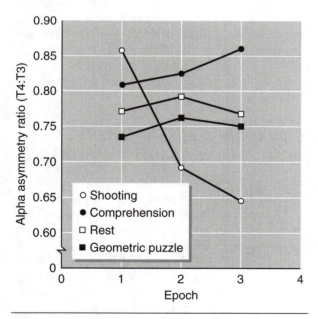

Figure 15.3 Mean electroencephalographic (EEG) alpha (8-12 Hz) asymmetry scores (T4:T3) across three consecutive 2.5 sec epochs immediately preceding the trigger pull in a rifle shooting task and in three comparison conditions. Alpha asymmetry scores in the shooting condition were significantly lower in epochs 2 and 3 as compared to epoch 1. Asymmetry scores did not change across epochs in the nonshooting tasks.

Reprinted, by permission, from B.D. Hatfield, A.J. Haufler, T. Hung and T.W. Spalding, 2004, "Electroencephalographic studies of skilled psychomotor performance," *Journal of Clinical Neurophysiology* 21(3): 148.

I'm Dr. Jekyll and Mr. Hyde when it comes to football. When I'm on the field sometimes I don't know what I am doing out there. People ask me about this move or that move, but I don't know why I did something, I just did it. I am able to focus out the negative things around me and just zero in on what I am doing out there. Off the field I become myself again.

In essence, it appears that the phenomenological and the psychophysiological levels of analyses converge on a common theme of automaticity of skilled performance (Fitts & Posner (1967). In this manner, the quote by Payton suggests a lack of left temporoparietal activation during performance as he reported "no thinking." At the same time, other areas of Payton's cerebral cortex involved with kinesthetic awareness and spatial processing must have been specifically and highly engaged in order for him to achieve such high-quality sport performance. On the model described earlier (figure 15.1), one could speculate that excessive rumination and self-talk (see "Associative processes" box in figure 15.1) would cause performance degradation by interfering with task-specific (e.g., rushing in football) attentional and motor processes (see the motor loop indicated by broken lines).

In support of this position, Rebert, Low, and Larsen (1984) published a report, during the same year that the Hatfield, Landers, and Ray (1984) paper appeared in the literature, on EEG alpha power in left temporal and parietal regions recorded during the performance of a video game that also demanded intense visual-spatial processing. Remarkably, the participants exhibited increasing right temporal activation during the course of the rallies (note: in this report, asymmetry metrics were employed by which increasing magnitude implied relative right activation), which began to decline or reversed direction just prior to the commission of an error that terminated the rally. Of note, the temporal and parietal asymmetry profiles observed during the course of the rallies were absent during the intervening rest intervals when the subjects were not actively engaged with the task. Again, it may be inferred that the move toward increased left temporal activation (increased verbal-analytic processing) observed in the participants just prior to initiation of error resulted in an attentive state that was inconsistent with the task demands of the video game. Although the interpretation is speculative, such an incongruent state may have interfered with the essential visuomotor processes and could be described as "overthinking" the task demands, resulting in "choking."

The interpretation of the studies discussed so far is also related to the work of Schneider and Shiffrin (1977) and Schneider and Chein (2003), who discussed the notion of controlled and automatic processing. Accordingly, the novice performer would be expected to show heightened frontal executive processing and effortful feature detection of environmental cues to perform the task (Kinsbourne, 1982), while the establishment of memory processes to guide the performance as a function of practice would result in reduced activation in such regions. During a task like rifle marksmanship, this developmental process would manifest as less left temporal-parietal activation or higher regional EEG alpha power; relative maintenance of activation in the right temporal-parietal region, indicated by a lack of progressive synchrony in T4 alpha, would occur because of the critical reliance on visuospatial processing. In contrast, the novice marksman would be expected to show heightened activation of the left temporal region perhaps due to verbal-analytic and feature detection as well as hippocampal processes involved in establishing a memory trace to guide the task. In fact, one would predict overall heightened cortical activation across a wide topographical distribution, relative to that observed in experts, in light of the novelty of the task demands on the performer.

Hemispheric EEG in Experts During Psychomotor Performance

A number of investigators have similarly observed higher EEG alpha power in the left (compared to right) temporal region of the cortex during the preparatory period for archery and rifle or pistol marksmanship (Bird, 1987; Hatfield, Landers, & Ray, 1987; Haufler et al., 2000; Hillman et al., 2000; Janelle et al., 2000a; Kerick et al., 2001; Kerick, Douglass, & Hatfield, 2004; Landers et al., 1991, 1994; Loze, Collins, & Holmes, 2001; Salazar et al., 1990). Although some investigators have failed to observe EEG alpha synchrony during such performances in this specific region (Collins, Powell, & Davies, 1990; Crews & Landers, 1993), they have observed alpha synchrony in other cortical areas. It may be that the specific demands of the tasks imposed on the subjects in these investigations (i.e., karate and golf putting, respectively) resulted in the allocation of different neural resources, and that the quiescence of left temporal activation noted during target shooting may have been highly specific to the neural processes involved with target shooting tasks.

Crews and Landers (1993), for example, assessed EEG activity at left and right temporal and central sites (C3, C4, T3, and T4) in 34 highly skilled golfers over a 3 sec period prior to the golf putt. The participants executed 40 trials and generally showed progressive desynchrony of alpha power in the right temporal and central regions (i.e., increasing activation), accompanied by progressive alpha synchrony (i.e., progressive relaxation) in the left central region across the epochs ending with initiation of the putting action. There was no evidence of left temporal alpha synchrony over the successive epochs. According to the cortical idling perspective of EEG alpha power advanced by Pfurtscheller (1992), the golfers observed by Crews and Landers were characterized by progressive activation in the right regions (C4 and T4) and attenuated cortical activation in the left central region (C3) as they prepared for initiation of the putt. Although cortical activity (i.e., desynchrony of EEG alpha) increased at site C4, the authors also noted that the best-performing participants displayed more alpha power at this site during the last second of preparation just prior to initiation of the putt. That is, the superior performers constrained the activation recorded at C4 or maintained regional relaxation. This effect was also associated with less error in ball placement from the cup. It may be that an optimal level of right hemispheric cortical activation (not too high in this case), in accompaniment with the progressive synchrony in the left motor cortex (C3), achieved the optimal zone of arousal.

Also, in contrast to the specific finding of relative left temporal EEG alpha power in target shooting studies, Collins, Powell, and Davies (1990) observed increasing alpha power bilaterally in both left and right temporal regions in eight high-level karate athletes preparing for an easy and a hard board-breaking task. The EEG was recorded during four successive epochs, with the last coinciding with the initiation of the decisive hand movement. Their results imply a progressive quieting of the motor cortex or a possible refinement of neuromotor processes as the participants achieved a state of readiness. It should be noted that the magnitude of this effect was enhanced in preparation for the more difficult challenge as the subjects were faced with an even greater need to achieve optimal readiness.

Although the specific findings of Crews and Landers (1993) and those of Collins and colleagues (1990) are different in detail than those of the earlier marksmanship studies, they are similar in kind or in principle. That is, adaptation to the imposed demands of training in such highly skilled athletes results in task-specific decrements in cerebral cortical activation such that superior psychomotor performance is achieved by allocation of task-specific cortical resources in an efficient and economical manner. Additionally, employment of a comparison group of lesser ability than the elite golfers examined by Crews and Landers might have revealed even less alpha power at T3 (i.e., heightened activation in this region) in the lower-ability group over the same preparatory period.

Validation of Cognitive Inference of Temporal EEG

All the studies described previously are merely suggestive of the complex cortical dynamics associated with skilled performance in light of the low number of recording sites, lack of spatial resolution, and failure to assess relevant networking patterns between appropriate cortical regions. Historically, investigators have used few electrode sites in this area of research, primarily due to the relative newness of EEG to the sport sciences and a corresponding lack of measurement sophistication. Accordingly, there is concern regarding whether the change in cortical activation observed at site T3 is, in fact, a valid indicator of regional associative (i.e., non-motor) activity or whether it is simply due to measurement error from the relatively poor spatial resolution of EEG as compared to other neuroimaging techniques. To address this concern, two investigations have been conducted to determine whether the EEG alpha synchrony typically observed at site T3 is, in fact, reflective of cognitive or cortical association processes or is simply due to motor activity in preparation to shoot (Kerick et al., 2001; Salazar et al., 1990). Exclusion of significant motor influence is necessary for a neurocognitive interpretation of the observed findings, as opposed to "spillover" of neural activity associated with simple motor activity due to volume conduction properties of the EEG (i.e., electrical activity in the brain spreads through the aqueous medium of the brain such that EEG recorded at one site is influenced by brain activity in different regions).

To address this concern, Salazar and colleagues (1990) monitored EEG at sites T3 and T4 in 28 elite right-handed archers during the 3 sec period before the release of the arrow at full draw. The participants executed 16 trials in each of four conditions. The condition of interest involved a full draw of the bow and arrow release after the preparatory aiming period with a regulation-weight bow (14-22 kg [31-49 lb]). Another condition was designed to mimic the physical demands of the task but excluded the aiming process. In other words, the participants held the arrow at full draw while simply "looking at the target." Two other comparative conditions involved a task similar to that just described with a lightweight bow (2 kg [4.4 lb]) and a final condition that simply consisted of no draw while looking at the target. Thus the first two conditions described imposed the same physical or motor demands, but the attentional demands differed. The authors observed relative EEG alpha synchrony in the left temporal region during the aiming and shooting condition with full draw compared to that observed during all other comparative conditions. Salazar and colleagues concluded that the T3 alpha synchrony effect observed in other target aiming studies was, in fact, due to relaxation of cognitive processes and not simply a reflection of motoric processes.

A similar conclusion was reached by Kerick and colleagues (2001), who recorded EEG activity in eight elite rifle marksmen in the left and right central and temporal regions, commonly referenced to Cz to focus on differences at the homologous sites, during three comparative conditions. During shooting, the participants performed 40 shooting trials on a standard indoor rifle range with air rifles aimed at a target distance of 50 ft (15 m). Participants assumed the same postural and gun-holding positions in two additional tasks; one involved trigger pull with no aiming on the target, while the other was absent any trigger pull. In order to minimize the volume conduction limitations of EEG recording, the investigators employed a Laplacian reference montage so as to transform the recorded time series at the central sites in order to correct them for any influence of the surrounding cortical regions (Hjorth, 1975). Unfortunately, such a recording and transformation strategy is not possible for the temporal sites because of anatomical restrictions. Specifically, this reference montage involves the placement of four neighboring sensors in a ring around the sensor of interest. The EEG record from each of the neighboring sites is subtracted from that of the centrally located site so as to increase the spatial specificity of the record and reduce the problems inherent with volume conduction. The ability to place sensors in a circular manner around T3 and T4 is anatomically obstructed by the ears. EEG activity was then examined over 8 sec epochs prior to trigger pull (or an 8 sec

period without triggering in the case of the last comparison condition described).

The authors noted the oft-described progressive EEG alpha synchrony in the left temporal region as the trigger pull approached, while relative stability and less average power over the aiming period were noted in the right. The observed synchrony effect at T3 was not noted during either of the two comparative conditions and, more importantly, was distinct in pattern from that observed from the transformed time series recorded from the left motor cortex (C3). As such, it would seem that the synchrony of EEG alpha in the left temporal region was not simply a reflection of ipsilateral motor cortex processes. Both of these investigations strengthen the notion that the observed EEG activity in the left temporal region is cognitive in nature and may well be due to the suppression of irrelevant cognitive processes.

In summary, the evidence obtained from EEG recordings during expert psychomotor performance implies attenuation of cortical association processes as the state of readiness is achieved during target aiming tasks. The regional relaxation is a result of practice and is characterized by pruning of irrelevant pathways and greater dependence on subcortical structures such as cerebellum (Grafton, Hari, & Salenius, 2000). The results of the various investigations imply a state of cortical simplification during self-paced motor performance—an adaptation critical to the conceptual model described earlier in the chapter, which illustrates that reductions in nonessential neurocognitive processes will reduce potential interference with the motor loop.

Expert–Novice Contrasts of EEG Power During Psychomotor Performance

The studies cited in the previous section were confined to the examination of cortical activity in a single-group or case study of highly skilled participants. Expert–novice contrasts have been largely absent in the literature but are critical to assessment of the practice-induced cortical efficiency concept. In a recent study, Haufler and colleagues (2000) compared regional cortical activation in expert marksmen and novice rifle shooters as indicated by a broad range of spectral power estimates. In this study, specifically designed to examine efficiency of cerebral cortical activity as a function of skill acquisition, Haufler and colleagues predicted that experts would demonstrate less global cortical activation than novices during the aiming period. The relatively dense topographical EEG assessment, compared to that employed in earlier studies, allowed the investigators to more fully determine the extent of any group differences via assessment of more cortical regions. In contrast to the predictions for the novices, the experts were expected to show reduced cortical activation during the target aiming period in light of the relaxation of greater areas of the cortex due to their experience with the task and emergence of an efficient neurocognitive strategy.

More specifically, EEG was recorded at homologous frontal (F3, F4), central (C3, C4), temporal (T3, T4), parietal (P3, P4), and occipital (O1, O2) sites, referenced to averaged ears, in 15 expert marksmen (i.e., national and international competitive experience) and 21 novice volunteers (i.e., little to no experience with firearms and no experience with position shooting) who were all right hand and ipsilateral eye dominant. A shooting simulation system using a laser tracking component was employed to track the kinematics or trajectory of the barrel throughout the aiming period. The diameter of the small-bore target was adjusted to achieve a visual angle similar to that elicited by a target at a distance of 50 ft (15 m), which is regulation distance. Experts demonstrated higher shooting scores as

compared to their novice counterparts (M = 339.8, SD = 44.7 and M = 90.7, SD = 38.9, respectively, out of a possible 400 points). Furthermore, Haufler and colleagues (2000) subjected the participants to psychometrically matched verbal and spatial tasks (Davidson et al., 1990) while recording EEG. The EEG derived during the aiming period was also compared to that recorded during the verbal and spatial tasks, which were also performed in the shooting stance, and in relation to which the groups were similar in terms of experience.

Overall, the findings of Haufler and colleagues (2000) revealed that the experts exhibited less cortical activation compared to the novices during the aiming period, which clearly supports the notion of increasing economy of cerebral cortical processes with task-specific practice. In short, robust differences were observed in cortical activation patterns between expert marksmen and novice rifle shooters as indicated by a broad range of spectral power estimates (i.e., reduced alpha power in novices along with heightened beta and gamma activity during target aiming), while few such differences in EEG spectral power were observed while the participants performed the comparative cognitive tasks with which the two groups were equally familiar. Figure 15.4 clearly shows the heightened cortical activation in the

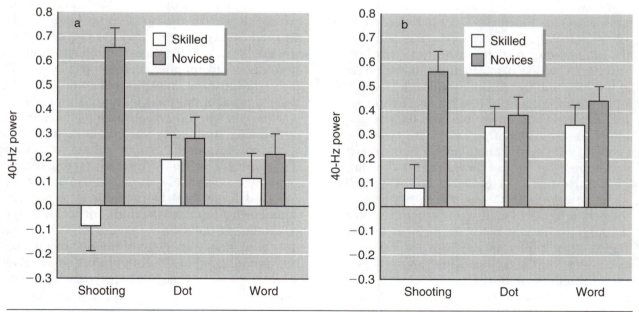

Figure 15.4 (a) Log-transformed electroencephalogram (EEG) gamma (40 Hz) power averaged across left and right frontal sites for expert marksmen and novice target shooters during the aiming period of target shooting and the comparative spatial (i.e., dot) and verbal (i.e., word) tasks. (b) Log-transformed EEG gamma power averaged across left and right temporal sites for expert marksmen and novice target shooters during the aiming period of target shooting and the comparative spatial (i.e., dot) and verbal (i.e., word) tasks.

Reprinted, by permission, from B.D. Hatfield, A.J. Haufler, T. Hung and T.W. Spalding, 2004, "Electroencephalographic studies of skilled psychomotor performance," *Journal of Clinical Neurophysiology* 21(3): 149.

novices during shooting (i.e., greater gamma power in the frontal and temporal regions), while no such difference was apparent during the comparative tasks. Although the design of the study was cross-sectional, the results illustrate task specificity of the observed EEG differences in the two groups and, on the basis of the kinematic data derived from the laser tracking system, showed that the "quiet" mind state in the experts was accompanied by less movement of the gun during aiming while the "noisy" mind of the novices was accompanied by an inefficient and variable trajectory of the gun.

Effects of Training on Cortical Activation

The majority of investigations of cortical processes during psychomotor performance have not involved extended practice or training periods (Bird, 1987; Crews & Landers, 1993; Hatfield, Landers, & Ray, 1984, 1987; Haufler et al., 2000, 2002; Hillman et al., 2000; Loze et al., 2001; Salazar et al., 1990), and as such the study designs leave open the possibility that the observed cortical activity patterns may be inherent to the performers as opposed to an adaptation resulting from practice and learning. In an attempt to determine the effects of training on cortical activation, Landers and colleagues (1994) conducted a study with 11 novice archers in which EEG was recorded from sites T3 and T4, referenced to left mastoid, during the aiming period just prior to arrow release before and after 12 weeks of instruction involving 27 sessions with an Olympic-caliber coach. All of the participants were right-handed and executed 16 archery trials and three resting trials before and after the instructional period. At the time of the pretest, no differences between the temporal sites were noted in spectral power during the aiming period. However, a significant increase in EEG alpha power at site T3 was noted after the training period, while no such practice-related increase in alpha power was noted in the right temporal region (T4). Target shooting performance also improved over the course of instruction. Of note, no such difference in the homologous temporal sites was noted during the resting trials either before or after training.

Kerick, Douglass, and Hatfield (2004) replicated and extended this finding with 11 midshipmen at the United States Naval Academy who underwent extensive pistol training as part of their effort to become proficient members of a competitive shooting team. The participants had had little or no experience with firearms prior to 12 to 14 weeks of supervised instruction with a qualified coach. EEG was recorded from 11 sites (F3, Fz, F4, C3, Cz, C4, T3, T4, P3, Pz, P4). It was hypothesized that mean alpha power and its rate of change would increase in the left temporal region during aiming from early to late season as participants improved their accuracy and reduced cognitive effort. The authors observed the EEG over a 5 sec aiming period during target shooting (40 trials) and two comparative tasks that involved either seated rest or postural simulation with no trigger pull. They achieved increased temporal resolution of the cortical activity by subscribing to a signal-processing technique employed by Pfurtscheller (1992). Although most of the previous studies in this area examined successive epochs during the preparatory period in the range of 1 to 2 sec of temporal resolution, the present technique allowed for 125 msec precision such that 40 successive estimates of alpha power were examined over the 5 sec aiming period. Such a procedure allowed greater detail in the assessment of any change in cerebral cortical activity during the aiming period; this is important, as brain processes change in a dynamic and rapidly fluctuating manner.

EEG alpha power increased at T3 from the beginning to the end of the training period during both the shooting and postural simulation conditions but not during the resting baseline. Interestingly, no such change in right temporal (T4) activation was noted in any of the three conditions. Although the authors did not predict any such change at T3 during the postural simulation condition, it may be that simply adopting the shooting position, which so closely mimicked actual shooting behavior, in individuals at an early stage of training elicits a similar response. Further training of longer duration may well have resulted in statistically significant differences between the cortical states achieved during these two conditions because the neural processes involved during shooting would be expected to become even more refined. In addition, exploratory analyses of the remaining sites revealed increased synchrony of alpha power at all sites except for midline frontal and parietal (Fz and Pz), whereas no such change was noted during the resting baseline condition (note: the exploratory analysis was confined to the shooting and resting tasks only). The global synchrony achieved in the event-related alpha power during the marksmanship task attests to a rather widespread change (i.e., reduction) in cortical activity and seems consistent with the phenomenological reports of well-practiced athletes that performance becomes "effortless." The time period in which such change occurs is relatively short (i.e., hours, weeks) (Etnier et al., 1996; Kerick, Douglass, & Hatfield, 2004; Landers et al., 1994), although adaptations may well continue to occur for years.

Furthermore, in a more definitive assessment of the causal link between cortical activation and target shooting performance, Landers and colleagues (1994) conducted the only study published to date in which biofeedback was used to alter brain activity in an attempt to facilitate psychomotor (e.g., archery) performance. Accordingly, 24 preelite archers underwent one of three treatment conditions: One group received of a single session of "correct" feedback to reduce left hemispheric activation; a second group received "incorrect" feedback to reduce right hemispheric activity; and a third group rested and received no feedback. Comparison of pretest and posttest performance scores revealed that only the "correct" feedback group improved target shooting accuracy after treatment, while the "incorrect" group declined in performance.

Thus it seems that the reduction in cortical activation observed in experts is, in fact, due to practice and repetition or is induced by training. Collectively, the studies described in the previous sections provide strong evidence in support of the notion that the brain (or at least the cortex) becomes more efficient, thereby reducing the possibility of interference with motor planning processes and the degradation of performance. The findings described so far are consistent with neuroimaging studies of motor skill learning involving PET (Haier et al., 1992). Essentially, Haier and colleagues also observed a gain in economy or efficient processing with practice. Convergence of different methodologies is critical for validation of the model.

Performance Variation and Cortical Arousal

An additional test for validation requires that performance variation be closely associated with cortical arousal. However, the relationship between cortical activation in the left temporal region and target shooting performance appears to be curvilinear rather than a simple linear function in which better performance is associated with greater EEG alpha synchrony (reduced activation). In one of the first investigations of cortical activation and target shooting performance, Bird (1987) conducted a case study in which an expert marksman, monitored at a single recording site (T3), executed superior shots when he exhibited less high-frequency EEG activity. Such a preliminary finding is consistent with the notion of quiescence of the left temporal region resulting in less interference with essential attentional or motor processes. Salazar and colleagues (1990) also contrasted EEG spectral content at T3 in archers during the aiming periods associated with best and worst shots. Higher amplitude of spectral power at 6, 12, and 28 Hz was noted in the left hemisphere during the period prior to worst shots. No differences in EEG spectral content between best and worst shots were noted in the right temporal region. Similarly, Landers and colleagues (1994) found heightened power at 12 Hz during worst shots in the novice archers after they had completed the instructional phase. Because the 12 Hz frequency falls within the alpha band, it would seem that such findings are more consistent with an inverted-U type of relationship versus a linear relationship between performance and left temporal activation.

Hillman and colleagues (2000) reported an interesting study in which they monitored EEG alpha and beta power in seven skilled marksmen at the left and right frontal, central, temporal, and parietal sites (F3, F4, C3, C4, T3, T4, P3, and P4), referenced to Cz, during 4 sec aiming periods prior to successfully executed shots. The observed activity was contrasted to that occurring in the period preceding the decision to abort or terminate a shot. In essence, the latter refers to an inability by the participant to achieve a state of readiness. Alpha power was typically higher at site T3 than at T4, thus replicating the temporal asymmetry observed in other studies; but the preparatory intervals that preceded the rejected shots were characterized by higher power than observed during the period prior to executed shots. The authors concluded that the decision to reject a shot appeared to be characterized by a failure to allocate the appropriate neural resources specifically associated with successful task execution. Kerick, Douglass, and Hatfield (2004) also noted a curvilinear relationship between event-related alpha power (ERAP) and pistol shooting accuracy such that higher accuracy was associated with greater ERAP up to an optimal level, beyond which further increases in power were associated with reductions in accuracy. Thus it seems that better performance is associated with elevated but limited temporal alpha power.

Although the findings of Crews and Landers (1993) presented earlier were discrepant with the specific pattern noted during target shooting, it is noteworthy that those participants who showed more alpha power (reduced activation) in the right motor cortex during the last second of preparation demonstrated better putting performance or less error. In fact, the correlation between such regional alpha power and putting performance in the 34 highly skilled golfers assessed by Crews and Landers accounted for 25% of the variance in putting accuracy. Similar to the findings of Crews and Landers (1993), a positive association between occipital alpha power and performance was also reported by Loze, Collins, and Holmes (2001) when they examined six expert air pistol shooters. Shooters were monitored for EEG at midline occipital (Oz) and left and right temporal locations (T3 and T4), referenced to linked mastoids, during a 60-shot match. The EEG alpha power recorded over three successive 2 sec epochs during the five best shots was contrasted to that during the five worst shots. The data clearly revealed a significant rise in alpha power at Oz over epochs prior to the best shots, whereas a progressive reduction in power was associated with the worst shots. Furthermore, superior performance was associated with a rise in alpha power during the last two epochs, while a reduction was associated with worst shots. The right hemisphere revealed lower levels of alpha power with no differentiation between best and worst performance. The positive linear relationship noted by the authors may have been due to superior self-regulation in such highly skilled performers compared to that of the participants in other studies. That is, the experience of the elite shooters may have largely prevented states of inattention and excessive synchrony of EEG alpha, thus precluding the detection of an inverted-U relationship.

Networking Between Cortical Association and Motor Regions

Assessment of regional cerebral cortical activity is informative in regard to the relationship between brain activity and motor performance, but additional insight can be attained through examination of functional interconnectivity or corticocortical communication between specified topographical regions. One can quantify such "networking" activity by deriving coherence estimates between selected pairs of electrodes or recording sites. In a classic investigation, Busk and Galbraith (1975) monitored EEG at occipital (Oz), motor cortex (C3 and C4), and motor planning areas (Fz) in participants before and after practice trials on a pursuit rotor task, which involves eye–hand coordination. The authors also noted that coherence between pairs of electrodes over areas known to have strong neuroanatomical connections revealed the highest estimates. Such observation provided a validation check for the interpretation of coherence estimates as indicative of corticocortical communication. In comparative control conditions, participants (1) engaged in visual tracking, without motor involvement, or (2) moved a wand around the tracking area in the absence of visual pursuit. Practice in the eye–hand coordination condition was the only intervention associated with performance improvement at posttest. Furthermore, overall coherence estimates between the recording sites were significantly reduced as a result of practice, implying greater regional autonomy or specialization as a result of training. Such a finding can also be framed within the context of efficient adaptation to imposed demand, as the change in coherence may well imply a "pruning" or refinement of neural processes with visuomotor practice (Bell & Fox, 1996). In this manner, novice performers may be heavily engaged in feature detection of the environment to guide their actions such that heightened communication between visual processing and motor planning areas would be necessitated prior to the formation of memory traces or an internal model to guide the neuromuscular apparatus. Such heightened activity not only would be more metabolically demanding (i.e., less efficient) but may well result in greater variability of "network" activity, thereby resulting in less consistency of performance.

In a recent study, Deeny and colleagues (2003) extended the work of Busk and Galbraith (1975) by assessing coherence estimates in skilled marksmen between motor planning (Fz) and association areas of the brain through additional monitoring of EEG at sites F3, F4, T3, T4, P3, Pz, and P4 as well as the motor cortex (C3, Cz, C4) and visual areas (O1 and O2). More specifically, EEG coherence was assessed during a 4 sec aiming period just prior to trigger pull in two groups of participants who differed in ability level. The superior performance group were labeled "experts" while the other group were labeled "skilled shooters." An important dimension of the study was that both groups were highly experienced (approximately 18 years of experience in each group), but the experts consistently scored higher in competition. Given that specialization of cortical function occurs as domain-specific expertise increases, experts were predicted to exhibit less corticocortical communication, especially between the cognitive and motor areas, relative to that in the skilled group. The primary analysis involved a between-group comparison of the coherence estimates between Fz and the lateral sites examined in each hemisphere. Interestingly, in terms of alpha band coherence, there were no differences between the groups at any site except at the Fz-T3 pairing, at which the experts revealed significantly lower values. The effect was also observed in the beta band (13-22 Hz) coherence (see figure 15.5). The authors interpreted the findings to mean that the experts were able to limit the communication between verbal-analytic and motor control processing. On a more global level this finding would imply that those who performed better in competition did not "overthink" during the critical aiming period.

Again, the potential importance of this refined networking in the cerebral cortex in regard to motor behavior is the reduction of potential interference from irrelevant associative, affective (e.g., limbic), and executive processes with the

executive motor loop (basal ganglia) connections to the motor cortex that largely controls corticospinal outflow and the resultant quality of the motor unit activation (Grafton, Hari, & Salenius, 2000). Excessive networking may result in undesirable alterations in the kinematic qualities of limb movement. Refinement or economy of cortical activation would more likely result in smooth, fluid, graceful, and efficient movement. Any reduction of associative networking with motor control processes would also help to reduce the complexity of motor planning and should result in greater consistency of performance.

A recent report by von Stein and Sarnthein (2000) yields the promise of greater specificity in assessment of cortical networking during psychomotor performance, as these authors provided evidence that theta band coherence (4-7 Hz), or low-frequency coherence, is indicative of long-range corticocortical communication while gamma band coherence (36-44 Hz), or high-frequency coherence, is indicative of local communication between neural generators. This would lead one to expect that novice performers may be characterized by extensive between frontotemporal or frontoparietal networking (long-range communication) due to significant reliance on frontally mediated executive control processes (Schneider & Chein, 2003). A reasonable expectation is that reductions

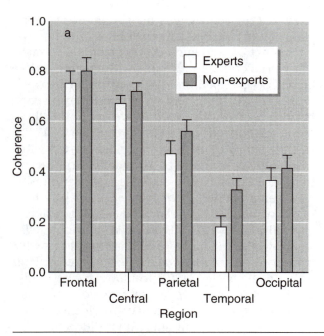
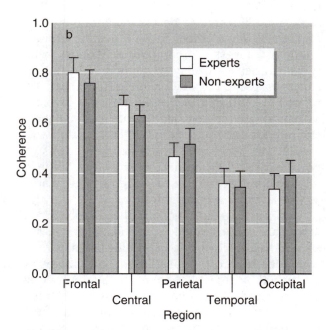

Figure 15.5   Comparative electroencephalogram coherence measures between Fz and each recording site within a hemisphere for expert and skilled marksmen. Note that the experts exhibit less coherence than the lesser-skilled group between left temporal and motor planning regions (T3 and Fz).

Reprinted, by permission, from B.D. Hatfield, A.J. Haufler, T. Hung and T.W. Spalding, 2004, "Electroencephalographic studies of skilled psychomotor performance," *Journal of Clinical Neurophysiology* 21(3): 150.

in theta band coherence would accompany skill acquisition as regional autonomy and automaticity of control processes are achieved.

Directions for Future Investigation

In addition to conceptual models of cortical function in skilled performers, a number of technical advances may help to clarify the manner in which the cerebral cortex orchestrates superior motor performance. In particular, the sport performance EEG research has typically employed few electrode sites, while dense electrode arrays consisting of 32, 64, 128, or 256 sites allow for greater spatial resolution and dipole or source localization. Such spatial resolution in accompaniment with the superior temporal resolution of EEG allows for a powerful measurement tool to assess dynamic cortical function during psychomotor preparation and performance. But such measurement sophistication needs to be applied with study designs that allow for cognitive inference (such as employed by Hatfield, Landers, & Ray, 1984—Study 2) as opposed to simple description of regional activation patterns. Furthermore, the neural structures involved in skillful motor behavior are much more extensive than considered in the sport EEG research. Although deep neural structures such as the cerebellum cannot be assessed with surface EEG, there would seem to be a need for future studies to assess the complex networking relationships between relevant cortical regions that can be assessed with EEG, such as frontal activity related to executive processes, anterior cingulate activity related to error correction and vigilance, and temporal and parietal activity associated with associative processes. Complex interactions or corticocortical communication between these regions can be captured by coherence estimates as well as nonlinear measures.

This field of research is also largely undeveloped in terms of studies in which psychological stress is applied to participants to determine the manner in which cerebral cortical processes are disrupted or perturbed by anxiety and tension. Such process-oriented studies, as opposed to outcome-oriented studies, may allow for understanding of the central neural mechanisms whereby personality and stress are related to skilled motor performance. Some investigators (Kerick, Iso-Ahola, & Hatfield, 2000; Saarela, 1999) have employed frontal EEG alpha asymmetry measures, as advanced by

Davidson (1988), to assess emotional responses from manipulation of stress states or motivational states during target shooting. However, such investigations need to be extended in various ways to examine how such states affect performance. Thus it would be informative to assess corticocortical communication patterns between frontal activation that is sensitive to the emotional state and the motor planning region (e.g., midfrontal, Fz, recording site) to determine, for example, if "excessive" networking is present during stress. Furthermore, studies are needed that incorporate multiple measures in addition to cerebral cortical assessment. For example, stress-related studies that examine cortical dynamics, EMG activity, autonomic activity, and kinematic analyses of limb movement are needed in order to determine how cognitive-motor behavior is controlled from a systems perspective. This kind of approach has been attempted by some investigators who have observed the relationship between EEG during skilled motor behavior and other aspects of performance such as the quality of limb movement (Contreras-Vidal & Buch, 2003) and concurrent eye movements or gaze behavior (Janelle et al., 2000a, 2000b). At the present time, such studies are generally lacking, but are needed to show how cortical activity covaries with other biological systems in order to understand the linkage between CNS processes and the quality of resultant motor behavior.

Finally, neuroimaging studies of motor performance may be aided by developments in behavioral genetics, and such developments also may allow predictions to be made with greater specificity. For example, the dysregulation of cortical processes with presentation of stress may be particularly problematic for carriers of the short allele of the serotonin (5-HT) transporter gene (5-HTT), as this gene variant is strongly associated with hyperactivity of the right amygdala during emotional tasks (Hariri et al., 2002). The polymorphism has been identified in the transcriptional control region of the 5-HTT gene such that a long promoter allele (L) is associated with transcriptional efficiency while the short allele (S) is associated with transcriptional deficiency and is anxiogenic. The S-type allele of the 5-HTT promoter region holds significant implications for information processing and motor control, and may provide a critical component underlying individual differences in the model presented in figure 15.1. In essence, S carriers may be considered "stress prone" while L carriers may be considered "stress regulators." A central tenet is that lack of frontal executive control over subcortical processes during stress in S carriers would result in heightened activity in emotional (limbic) structures that, in turn, would disrupt cortical association processes and lead to delayed and indecisive activation of the motor loop—the frontobasal ganglia structures that result in the execution of movement. Under high stress, such athletes may well exhibit reductions in prefrontal asymmetry, implying a lack of executive control over the frontomesolimbic circuit. The prefrontal cortex is a critical component of the motor loop. Consequently, lessened executive control will heighten activation of the limbic region (amygdala). The emotional reactivity, in turn, will result in excessive stimulation to the cortex, particularly in the left temporal and parietal regions, along with increased cortico-cortical communication between these regions and the motor planning centers. In this manner motor planning and the subsequent quality of movement may be degraded. If this is the case, then consideration of genotype and understanding of genetic influences on brain processes may provide powerful insight into why individuals differ in their emotional responses to stress. Such detailed understanding is critical for informed intervention or applied sport psychology.

Conclusions

In summary, the present review began with the theme of economy of effort as a marker of superior psychomotor performance. The study by Haufler and colleagues (2000) offered powerful evidence for this phenomenon by contrasting the EEG spectral content during rifle marksmanship in experts versus novices. In line with the position advanced by Sterman and Mann (1995), in which EEG alpha is inversely related to cognitive load, experts showed remarkably reduced cerebral cortical activation relative to the novices. Such a finding of reduced cognitive load is consistent with the decreased cerebral metabolic profiles associated with skill learning as reported by Haier and colleagues (1992) using PET. Furthermore, there seems to be a degree of specificity in that this effect is largely related to reduced activation in cortical association areas that are nonspecific to the visuospatial task demands. For example, several authors have reported relative synchrony in the left temporal area during target shooting in high-skill performers that seems logical in those who have reached the stage of automaticity. Smith,

McEvoy, and Gevins (1999) showed a similar effect during the acquisition of a video game (Space Fortress) such that EEG alpha synchrony was noted during the visual-spatial challenge while right posterior parietal activity was characterized by relative desynchrony or activation. In this regard, the participants seem to be characterized by specific allocation of neural resources to the task demands—that is, experience with the task results in an appropriate "fit" of neural resources to demand and a reduction in irrelevant processing. Such a process seems entirely consistent with (albeit much more complex than) the concept of specific adaptation to imposed demand (SAID) evidenced in other physiological systems.

Although the cortical idling hypothesis advanced by Pfurtscheller (1992) has been adopted to make sense of the EEG spectral estimates in the reported studies, we would like to acknowledge the excellent review by Shaw (1996), who described an alternative interpretation of EEG alpha synchrony as intention rather than idling. At the present stage of development in this area of research, such alternative perspectives are helpful in making sense of the data. The notion of "intention" as opposed to "idling" seems tenable if one adopts the view that alpha synchrony may be indicative of medium-range neural networking or corticocortical communication (von Stein & Sarnthein, 2000). Perhaps experiments could be devised in the future to further explain the neurophysiological basis of the observed EEG, but the more traditional hypothesis of reduced activation seems reasonable at this time.

Based on all of the facts and discussion presented in the chapter, it appears that sport psychology will derive great benefit from the cognitive neuroscience approach. This is a challenging area of research and one that calls for interdisciplinary training of future behavioral kinesiologists in the areas of neuroscience, cognition, physiology, and advanced technical tools along with expertise in signal processing. The work is difficult but may well provide answers as to "why" and "how" athletes' physical performance is influenced and altered by their mental state.

References

Attner, P. (1984, October 1). Payton vs. Harris vs. Brown. *Sporting News, 198*, 2-3.

Bear, M.F., Connors, B.W., & Paradiso, M.A. (2002). Neuroscience: Exploring the brain (2nd ed.). Baltimore, MD: Lippincott, Williams, & Wilkins.

Bell, M.A., & Fox, N.A. (1996). Crawling experience is related to changes in cortical organization during infancy: Evidence from EEG coherence. *Developmental Psychobiology, 29,* 551-561.

Beuter, A., & Duda, J.L. (1985). Analysis of the arousal/motor performance relationship in children using movement kinematics. *Journal of Sport Psychology, 7,* 229-243.

Bird, E.I. (1987). Psychophysiological processes during rifle shooting. *International Journal of Sport Psychology, 18,* 9-18.

Busk, J., & Galbraith, G.C. (1975). EEG correlates of visual-motor practice in man. *Electroencephalography and Clinical Neurophysiology, 38,* 415-422.

Cacioppo, J.T., & Tassinary, L.G. (1990). *Principles of psychophysiology: Physical, social, and inferential elements.* New York: Cambridge University Press.

Collins, D., Powell, G., & Davies, I. (1990). An electroencephalographic study of hemispheric processing patterns during karate performance. *Journal of Exercise and Sport Psychology, 12,* 223-243.

Contreras-Vidal, J.L., & Buch, E.R. (2003). Effects of Parkinson's disease on visuomotor adaptation. *Experimental Brain Research, 150,* 25-32.

Crews, D.J., & Landers, D.M. (1993). Electroencephalographic measures of attentional patterns prior to the golf putt. *Medicine and Science in Sports and Exercise, 25,* 116-126.

Daniels, J.T. (1985). A physiologist's view of running economy. *Medicine and Science in Sports and Exercise, 17,* 332-338.

Davidson, R.J. (1988). EEG measures of cerebral asymmetry: Conceptual and methodological issues. *International Journal of Neuroscience, 39,* 71-89.

Davidson, R.J., Chapman, J.P., Chapman, L.J., & Henriques, J.B. (1990). Asymmetrical brain electrical activity discriminates between psychometrically-matched verbal and special cognitive tasks. *Psychophysiology, 27,* 528-543.

Deeny, S., Hillman, C.H., Janelle, C.M., & Hatfield, B.D. (2003). Cortico-cortical communication and superior performance in skilled marksman: An EEG coherence analysis. *Journal of Exercise and Sport Psychology, 25,* 188-204.

deVries, H.A. (1968). Efficiency of electrical activity as a physiological measure of the functional state of muscle tissue. *American Journal of Physical Medicine, 47,* 10-22.

deVries, H.A., & Housh, T.J. (1994). *Physiology of exercise for physical education, athletics, and exercise science* (5th ed.). Dubuque, IA: Brown.

Elbert, T., Pantev, C., Wienbruch, C., Rockstroh, B., & Taub, E. (1995). Increased cortical representation of the fingers of the left hand in string players. *Science, 270,* 305-307.

Etnier, J.L., Whitever, S.S., Landers, D.M., Petruzzello, S.J., & Salazar, W. (1996). Changes in electroencephalographic activity associated with learning a novel motor task. *Research Quarterly for Exercise and Sport, 67,* 272-229.

Fitts, P.M., & Posner, M.I. (1967). *Human performance.* Belmont, CA: Brooks/Cole.

Galin, D., & Ornstein, R. (1972). Lateral specialization of cognitive mode: An EEG study. *Psychophysiology, 9,* 412-418.

Gallwey, T. (1974). *The inner game of tennis.* New York: Random House.

Grafton, S.T., Hari, R., & Salenius, S. (2000). The human motor system. In A. Toga & J. Mazziotta (Eds.), *Brain mapping: The systems* (pp. 331-363). San Diego: Academic Press.

Haier, R.J., Siegel, B.V., MacLachlan, A., Soderling, E., Lottenberg, S., & Buchsbaum, M.S. (1992). Regional glucose metabolic changes after learning a complex visuospatial/motor task: A positron emission tomographic study. *Brain Research, 570,* 134-143.

Hariri, A.R., Mattay, V.S., Tessitore, A., Kolachana, B., Fera, F., Goldman, D., Egan, M.F., & Weinberger, D.R. (2002). Serotonin transporter genetic variation and the response of the human amygdala. *Science, 297,* 400-403.

Hatfield, B.D., Haufler, A.J., Hung, T.M., & Spalding, T.W. (2004). Electroencephalographic studies of skilled psychomotor performance. *Journal of Clinical Neurophysiology, 21*(3), 144-156.

Hatfield, B.D., & Hillman, C.H. (2001). The psychophysiology of sport: A mechanistic understanding of the psychology of superior performance. In R.N. Singer, C.H. Hausenblas, & C.M. Janelle (Eds.), *Handbook of sport psychology* (2nd ed., pp. 362-386). New York: Wiley.

Hatfield, B.D., & Landers, D.M. (1983). Psychophysiology: A new direction for sport psychology. *Journal of Sport Psychology, 5,* 243-259.

Hatfield, B.D., Landers, D.M., & Ray, W.J. (1984). Cognitive processes during self-paced motor performance: An electroencephalographic profile of skilled marksmen. *Journal of Sport Psychology, 6,* 42-59.

Hatfield, B.D., Landers, D.M., & Ray, W.J. (1987). Cardiovascular-CNS interactions during a self-paced, intentional attentive state: Elite marksmanship performance. *Psychophysiology, 24,* 542-549.

Hatfield, B.D., Landers, D.M., Ray, W.J., & Daniels, F.S. (1982, February). An electroencephalographic study of elite rifle shooters. *American Marksman, 7,* 6-8.

Haufler, A.J., Spalding, T.W., Santa Maria, D.L., & Hatfield, B.D. (2000). Neuro-cognitive activity during a self-paced visuospatial task: Comparative EEG profiles in marksmen and novice shooters. *Biological Psychology, 53,* 131-160.

Haufler, A.J., Spalding, T.W., Santa Maria, D.L., & Hatfield, B.D. (2002). Erratum to "Neuro-cognitive activity during a self-paced visuospatial task: Comparative EEG profiles in marksmen and novice shooters." *Biological Psychology, 59,* 87-88.

Hillman, C.H., Apparies, R.J., Janelle, C.M., & Hatfield, B.D. (2000). An electrocortical comparison of executed and rejected shots in skilled marksmen. *Biological Psychology, 52,* 71-83.

Hjorth, B. (1975). An on-line transformation of EEG scalp potentials into orthogonal source derivations. *Electroencephalography and Clinical Neurophysiology, 39,* 526-530.

Hung, T., Spalding, T.W., Santa Maria, D.L., & Hatfield, B.D. (2004). Assessment of reactive motor performance with event-related brain potentials: Attention processes in elite table tennis players. *Journal of Sport and Exercise Psychology, 26*(2), 317-337.

Janelle, C.M., Hillman, C.H., Apparies, R.J., & Hatfield, B.D. (2000a). Concurrent measurement of EEG and visual indices of attention during rifle shooting: An exploratory case study. *International Journal of Sports Vision, 6,* 21-29.

Janelle, C.M., Hillman, C.H., Apparies, R.J., Murray, N.P., Meili, L., Fallon, E.A., & Hatfield, B.D. (2000b). Expertise differences in cortical activation and gaze behavior during rifle shooting. *Journal of Sport and Exercise Psychology, 22,* 167-182.

Jasper, H.H. (1958). The ten-twenty electrode system of the International Federation. *Electroencephalography and Clinical Neurophysiology, 17,* 37-46.

Kandel, E.R., & Schwartz, J.H. (1985). *Principles of neural science* (2nd ed.). New York: Elsevier.

Kerick, S.E., Douglass, L., & Hatfield, B.D. (2004). Cerebral cortical adaptations associated with visuomotor practice. *Medicine and Science in Sport and Exercise, 36,* 118-129.

Kerick, S.E., Iso-Ahola, S.E., & Hatfield, B.D. (2000). Psychological momentum in target shooting: Cortical, cognitive-affective, and behavioral responses. *Journal of Sport and Exercise Psychology, 22,* 1-20.

Kerick, S.E., McDowell, K., Hung, T., Santa Maria, D.L., Spalding, T.W., & Hatfield, B.D. (2001). The role of the left temporal region under the cognitive motor demands of shooting in skilled marksmen. *Biological Psychology, 58,* 263-277.

Kinsbourne, M. (1982). Hemispheric specialization and the growth of human understanding. *American Psychologist, 37,* 411-420.

Konttinen, N., Landers, D.M., & Lyytinen, H. (2000). Aiming routines and their electrocortical concomitants among competitive rifle shooters. *Scandinavian Journal of Medicine and Science in Sports, 10,* 169-177.

Konttinen, N., & Lyytinen, H. (1992). Physiology of preparation: Brain slow waves, heart rate, and respiration preceding triggering in rifle shooting. *International Journal of Sport Psychology, 23,* 110-127.

Konttinen, N., & Lyytinen, H. (1993a). Brain slow waves preceding time-locked visuomotor performance. *Journal of Sport Sciences, 11,* 257-266.

Konttinen, N., & Lyytinen, H. (1993b). Individual variability in brain slow wave profiles in skilled sharpshooters during the aiming period in rifle shooting. *Journal of Exercise and Sport Psychology, 15,* 275-289.

Konttinen, N., Lyytinen, H., & Era, P. (1999). Brain slow potentials and postural sway behavior during sharpshooting performance. *Journal of Motor Behavior, 31,* 11-20.

Konttinen, N., Lyytinen, H., & Konttinen, R. (1995). Brain slow potentials reflecting successful shooting performance. *Research Quarterly for Exercise and Sport, 66,* 64-72.

Konttinen, N., Lyytinen, H., & Viitasalo, J. (1998). Rifle-balancing in precision shooting: Behavioral aspects and psychophysiological implication. *Scandinavian Journal of Medicine and Science in Sports, 8,* 78-83.

Lacey, J.I. (1967). Somatic response patterning and stress: Some revisions of activation theory. In M.H. Appley & R. Trumbull (Eds.), *Psychological stress* (pp. 14-42). New York: Appleton-Century-Crofts.

Landers, D.M., Han, M.W., Salazar, W., Petruzzello, S.J., Kubitz, K.A., & Gannon, T.L. (1994). Effects of learning on electroencephalographic and electrocardiographic patterns in novice archers. *International Journal of Sport Psychology, 25,* 313-330.

Landers, D.M., Petruzzello, S.J., Salazar, W., Kubitz, K.A., Gannon, T.L., & Han, M. (1991). The influence of electrocortical biofeedback on performance in pre-elite archers. *Medicine and Science in Sports and Exercise, 23,* 123-129.

Loze, G.M., Collins, D., & Holmes, P.S. (2001). Pre-shot EEG alpha-power reactivity during expert air-pistol shooting: A comparison of best and worst shots. *Journal of Sports Sciences, 19,* 727-733.

Meichenbaum, D. (1977). *Cognitive behavior modification.* New York: Plenum Press.

Pfurtscheller, G. (1992). Event-related synchronization (ERS): An electrophysiological correlate of cortical areas at rest. *Electroencephalography and Clinical Neurophysiology, 83,* 62-69.

Pullum, B. (1977). Psychology of shooting. *Schiess-portschule Dialogues, 1,* 1-17.

Radlo, S.J., Janelle, C.M., Barba, D.A., & Frehlich, S.G. (2001). Perceptual decision making for baseball pitch recognition: Using P300 latency and amplitude to index attentional processing. *Research Quarterly for Exercise and Sport, 72,* 22-31.

Rebert, C.S., Low, D.W., & Larsen, F. (1984). Differential hemispheric activation during complex visuomotor performance: Alpha trends and theta. *Biological Psychology, 19,* 159-168.

Saarela, P.I. (1999). The effects of mental stress on cerebral hemispheric asymmetry and psychomotor performance in skilled marksmen. Unpublished doctoral dissertation, University of Maryland.

Salazar, W., Landers, D.M., Petruzzello, S.J., Han, M.W., Crews, D.J., & Kubitz, K.A. (1990). Hemispheric asymmetry, cardiac response, and performance in elite archers. *Research Quarterly for Exercise and Sport, 61,* 351-359.

Schneider, W., & Chein, J.M. (2003). Controlled and automatic processing: Behavior, theory, and biological mechanisms. *Cognitive Science, 27,* 525-559.

Schneider, W., & Shiffrin, R.M. (1977). Controlled and automatic human information processing: I. Detection, search, and attention. *Psychological Review, 84,* 1-66.

Shaw, J.C. (1996). Intention as a component of the alpha-rhythm response to mental activity. *International Journal of Psychophysiology, 24,* 7-23.

Smith, M.E., McEvoy, L.K., & Gevins, A. (1999). Neurophysiological indices of strategy development and skill acquisition. *Cognitive Brain Research, 7,* 389-404.

Sparrow, W.A. (2000). *Energetics of human activity.* Champaign, IL: Human Kinetics.

Springer, S.P., & Deutsch, G. (1998). *Left brain-right brain: Perspectives from cognitive neuroscience.* New York: Freeman.

Sterman, M.B., & Mann, C.A. (1995). Concepts and applications of EEG analysis in aviation performance evaluation. *Biological Psychology, 40,* 115-130.

von Stein, A., & Sarnthein, J. (2000). Different frequencies for different scales of cortical integration: From local gamma to long range alpha/theta synchronization. *International Journal of Psychophysiology, 38,* 301-313.

Weinberg, R.S., & Hunt, V.V. (1976). The interrelationships between anxiety, motor performance and electromyography. *Journal of Motor Behavior, 8,* 219-224.

Williams, J.M., & Krane, V. (1998). Psychological characteristics of peak performance. In J.M. Williams (Ed.), *Applied sport psychology* (pp. 158-170). Mountain View, CA: Mayfield.

The Psychophysiology of Biofeedback and Sport Performance

Dave Collins, PhD

Alan McPherson, PhD

The principle behind this book is the importance of examining the psychobiology of sport and physical activity as a means to gain understanding of the mechanisms underpinning performance or participation. Without a true understanding of the mechanisms of a particular construct (e.g., competitive anxiety) or intervention (such as meditation), we cannot be sure how best to counter the negative consequences or employ an intervention. This principle finds its best expression, or at least an attempt to best express it, in the science and art of biofeedback.

In simple terms, biofeedback consists of measuring and then providing information (feeding back) on some psychobiological index (heart rate, for example) presumed to be associated with, or causative of, good performance. And therein lies the importance—and the greatest potential weakness—of this valuable but still relatively underused tool. We are getting better and better at measuring the psychobiological index. Perhaps unsurprisingly, technical advances offer an increasing, indeed often bewildering, range of psychobiological indices to detect. We are also getting better at developing appropriate methods of feedback. As this chapter will evidence, the use of various sensory modalities to match or complement the skill being adjusted represents an exciting new direction. Biofeedback stands and falls, however, on the selection of the index. If the physical factor is truly causative of good performance, then the feedback offers a useful augmentation to any training program, or an effective way of evaluating traditional mental skills interventions, or even an intervention in itself. Even if the factor is only associated with a positive mental state or other "performance *causation* factor," then measuring the biological factor is still useful, enabling a more objective evaluation even if feedback is a bit redundant. Get things wrong, however, and the apparent objectivity and scientific rigor of the technique can lead athlete, coach, and psychologist up a cul de sac, away from genuine progress. So, is it worth the effort? The literature cited in this chapter, selected as a representation of good exemplars of the genre, may help to answer this question.

Measuring the Physiological Index

Other chapters in this text offer much more detailed consideration of various psychophysiological indices and the problems associated with their measurement and interpretation. In simple terms, the recording system usually consists of attached electrodes, some form of amplification (including preamplification for signals of smaller magnitude, such as electroencephalography [EEG]), and signal conditioning and then, for all but the simplest indices, post hoc analysis of the signal to eliminate artifact (contaminating or false signals or both) and yield the data of interest. Each of these stages carries its own special challenges and considerations, which, if not satisfactorily addressed, can severely affect the ultimate quality of the picture. So, for example, electromyographic (EMG) data depend on the selection of appropriate electrodes, the quality of skin preparation, amplification levels and filters applied, the sampling rate used by the analog–digital (A to D) converter, the methods used to eliminate artifactual signals (from other muscles, for example), and the analyses applied. Good use of biofeedback requires all these factors to be covered.

For specific use in biofeedback, however, some additional considerations come into play. By definition, rapid and real-time analysis is required so that the index can be fed back to the client. This requirement makes significant technical demands on the signal-conditioning stage, since no post hoc analysis is possible. As a result, biofeedback indices tend to be direct, using a measure that is immediately available (such as heart rate), or using electronic or rapid software manipulations to obtain a simply derived indicator such as alpha band power in the EEG spectrum. There are problems with this second approach in that, since almost all of the process is conducted within the "black box" calculation of the equipment, the exact values derived may be contaminated by artifact, or less than genuinely indicative of the concomitant psychological states claimed by the manufacturer. In short, the user needs to check the veracity and validity of the process by which the output, obviously the key focus of interest in biofeedback, is developed. For example, early versions of biofeedback machines used very gross filters to determine alpha power; filters with accuracy of ±2 Hz (Hertz or cycles per second) were not unusual—levels that, since the alpha waveband lies between 8 and 13 Hz, are inadequate. Worse still, these accuracies were obtainable only by application to the manufacturer. It was necessary to carefully read through the technical specifications for the equipment and ask some searching questions before use.

Fortunately this type of equipment is no longer available, but the point is still important. The apparent sophistication of a biofeedback unit display may also disguise some doubtful underpinning methodologies, as well as limited technology. The science of biofeedback requires a rigor equal to that for mainstream psychophysiology; users must check carefully how the equipment arrives at the numbers it provides. An example is the use of Fast Fourier Transform (FFT), a mathematical algorithm that yields the amount, or power, of each frequency in a total signal. This method, until

recently at any rate, was the method of choice for EEG investigations and applications in EEG-based psychophysiology and biofeedback. However, the specifications used for the FFT affect its accuracy or *resolution,* and critical consumers need to be fully aware of the implications of design characteristics on the resulting data. For example, running the FFT on data epochs of 2 sec results in 1 Hz accuracy. If the analysis has been used to look at blocks of 2 Hz, the potential problem should be obvious; the data may carry an error that is 50% of the dependent variable. Thus, the use of technical equipment and sophisticated analysis methods necessitates careful checking, and preferably a good understanding, of exactly what the procedures are doing.

Feedback Methods

After measurement of the index, the method of feedback is the next important issue to be addressed. Arguably, the state of the art methodology worldwide is the Wingate five-step approach (Blumenstein, Bar-Eli, & Tenenbaum, 1997), a system that both matches the underpinning principles of the biofeedback method and is a clear system for effective use with performers. Although this approach is less suitable for the newer, skill acquisition applications of biofeedback (some examples are examined later in this chapter), it is perfect for the relaxation- and concentration-based applications that have traditionally predominated. The stages of the approach are summarized in figure 16.1.

Step 1 introduces the subject to a variety of different biofeedback technologies, during which he or she learns to self-regulate psychophysiological state in both parasympathetic (calming) and sympathetic (excitation) directions. This step is carried out in a laboratory setting. From a theoretical and practical perspective, Step 1 is important since the subject becomes accustomed to the equipment and also because psychophysiological factors that may not have been previously explored or considered can be controlled.

Step 2 sees the psychologist experimenting with the various modalities, working to discover the index that best suits the subject's sport requirements and personal preferences. This stage takes into account obvious pragmatic issues; the biofeedback program must be designed with the ultimate sport performance in mind. Thus, for example, there would not be much point in teach-

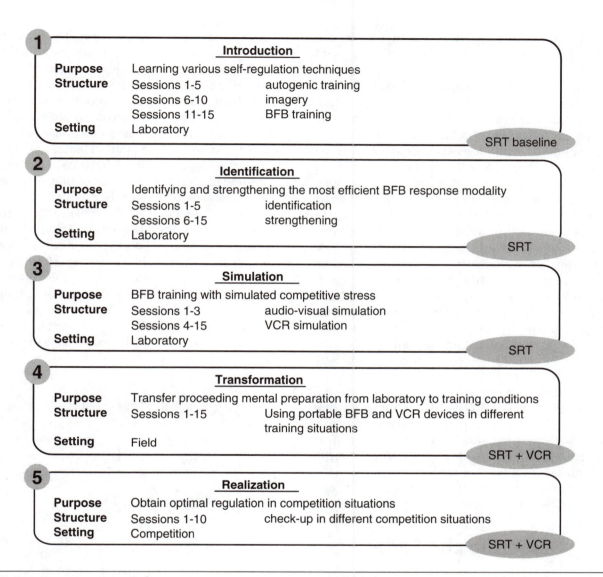

Figure 16.1 Five-step approach to mental training with biofeedback.

Reprinted, by permission, from B. Blumenstein, M. Bar-Eli, and G. Tennenbaum, 1997, "A five-step approach to mental training incorporating biofeedback," *The Sport Psychologist* 11(4): 450.

ing weightlifters a control technique associated with palmar sweating, or galvanic skin response (which is taken care of with the use of chalk and is inevitable in any case). For pistol shooters, however, the technique may be ideal. A second issue fits with our knowledge of individual differences regarding the way in which various psychological states are physically expressed (Pennebaker, 2000; Davidson, 2003) and, perhaps in association, our awareness of different states when people are under pressure (e.g., exercise; Steptoe & Vogele, 1992).

We know that for each psychological state, individuals manifest highly idiosyncratic but reasonably consistent patterns of physiologi-

cal reaction. Indeed, this individual variability is often cited as an argument against the use of generic questionnaires that utilize a "blanket" of symptoms so that all possibilities are covered. Researchers in several areas (e.g., overtraining or unexplained underperformance syndrome; Collins, 1995) now fine-tune questionnaires to best fit the individual patterning of the psychophysiological state under examination. Step 2 of the Wingate approach employs a similar method by recognizing, acknowledging, and utilizing the index that best fits the individual's own pattern. Coincidentally, since we are also somewhat differentially aware of physiological states, this also means that individuals can be steered toward an index they are already familiar with, that is, one over which they already have some level of natural control.

Step 3 is another crucial component, to be examined in more detail in the next section. Using video of real competition scenarios, the subject practices appropriate regulatory changes (relaxation or excitation) in association with the scenes. The aim is to facilitate the transfer of the subject's new skills into the competitive setting. This focus is continued in Step 4, in which the subject uses the self-regulatory skills to prepare for an event before finally developing the skills in increasingly severe competitive settings. The other important factor to acknowledge in this model is the self-regulatory tests (SRTs), which utilize VCR-presented stimuli in the later stages and are completed at each step. These tests meet the crucial need for the subject to acknowledge his or her improved skills, thus assisting the effective transfer to competition through changes in self-efficacy that keep the effort high.

This thorough approach has been developed and refined through a combination of careful theoretical consideration, empirical investigation, and practical experience. This triangulation is just what is needed, and it represents best practice in optimizing the essential mix of science and art. Readers are referred to Blumenstein, Bar-Eli, and Collins (2002) for a more thorough treatment.

Selecting the Index

So far this chapter has highlighted issues that may well be addressed through the science of biofeedback. With index selection, however, there is room for both science (against which the veracity of the index must be justified) and art, shown mainly in the creativity with which new measures, and ways of presenting them, are selected.

First, in order to exemplify this development and the application of scientific method to identify the correct index and presentation modality, I refer to the excellent study recently published by Konttinen and colleagues (2004). As part of their ongoing portfolio of work in shooting, Konttinen and colleagues used a variety of biofeedback devices with novice shooters, following many of the precepts already identified here. The study addressed a number of issues, but two are pertinent to the present discussion: first, the selection of the index, and secondly, how the information was fed back to the participants.

The study used three "causative" factors of shooting performance. Feedback about the sighting accuracy and trajectory was obtained through a laser device (a fairly standard training aid in shooting circles); since shooting uses vision, this feedback had to be provided after the fact. Feedback (this time concurrent) was also provided aurally in two conditions of stability, the steadiness of the rifle and postural balance as evaluated by a force platform. The impact of these interventions is presented in figure 16.2.

Two factors emerge. Concurrent auditory feedback was more effective than after-the-fact visual information. Secondly, the index of choice appears to be feedback on the stability of the weapon. This study offers a model for effective practice. The indices were decided on through careful consideration of literature coupled with creativity. Following selection of the indices, careful checks were conducted to establish the relative

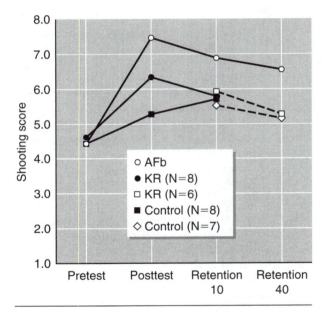

Figure 16.2 Shooting scores for auditory feedback (Afb), knowledge of results (KR), and nontraining control (Control) groups in the four tests; pretest, posttest, 10 days after the acquisition phase (Retention 10), and 40 days after the acquisition phase (Retention 40). Since some subjects were absent from Retention 40, the corresponding means are not comparable with pretest, posttest, and Retention 10 means. For KR and Control groups, the means of Retention 10 were recalculated using only those who also participated in Retention 40 (dashed lines).

Reprinted, by permission, from N. Konttinen, K. Mononen, J. Viitasalo and T. Mets, 2004, "The effects of augmented auditory feedback on psychomotor skill learning in precision shooting," *Journal of Sport & Exercise Psychology* 26(2): 311.

strengths of the different options. Of course, peer review–quality investigations are not a practical option for every biofeedback intervention. However, this study shows nicely the level of detail that needs to be considered in the design of an effective application.

Secondly, and once again through presentation of an example, we will highlight the considerable gains that sport can make by borrowing and subtly adjusting ideas developed in other fields. The exemplar relates to the use of EEG feedback, specifically the use of particular frequencies. Students at the Royal College of Music in London have recently benefited from a biofeedback program designed to elevate theta (5-8 Hz) signals over low-band alpha (8-11 Hz). As a result, clear gains in artistic aspects of performance have accrued, including creativity and "emotional conviction" (Gruzelier, 2003). These positive benefits are ascribed, both by this research and more generally by the literature, to enhanced memory retrieval processes that are associated with theta activity.

So, hopefully exploiting both the memory and emotional concomitants of this effect, we are currently testing the use of similar biofeedback techniques with subelite athletes. The recruitment of this approach is based on a conception relating to the specific competition environment—that performance losses in closed skills sports are due to inappropriate retrieval or execution of well-learned movements, incorrect emotional priming, or both. Specifically, we are interested in testing the effectiveness of this method in facilitating consistent retrieval and execution. For the present, however, consider the "acquisitive borrowing" process through which genuinely new approaches may be developed.

Weaknesses and Limitations in the Literature

For convenience and clarity, we characterize the problems and limitations in biofeedback–sport performance research in terms of the same issues discussed in the previous section: measurement problems, feedback methods, and selection of the index. Before doing so, however, and in order to outline a critical consideration on the efficacy of biofeedback as an approach, we discuss the key question that one must first address in evaluating such evidence—namely, exactly what has the study measured?

The Dependent Variable

The focus of the biofeedback intervention is a comparatively simple concern that is increasingly addressed by the majority of applications. This aspect is worth emphasizing, however, and underpins many of the points made in this chapter. Simply, the issue is this: Does the study or intervention focus on changes in the index used *or* the change in performance or behavior that the change in the index is supposed to generate? In short, can one clearly see that changes in the index *caused* the behavior (usually enhanced performance)?

As an example, consider a classic study from the literature. This often cited intervention by Peper and Schmid (1983) used a two-year longitudinal training package (an excellent and increasingly common approach) consisting of biofeedback on EMG, skin temperature, and galvanic skin response (GSR) in conjunction with progressive relaxation training, imagery, and autogenics. The subjects were elite rhythmic gymnasts, and data were subsequently (and ingeniously) collected immediately prior to performance at the Olympic event. The participants were extremely enthusiastic about the impact, reporting improvements in training and competitive performance. There are some problems, however, even with such an otherwise strong study. One is the capacity of the investigation to delineate between the impact of the various components of the intervention (between that of biofeedback and imagery, for example), or even their various interactions, in both the group and the individual. Another is the extent to which changes in each of these indices (which were reported) can be shown to be causative of changes in performance (which were also included). As a practical intervention, this project seems very effective; however, as a rigorous investigation, this work is lacking.

A study by Landers and colleagues (1991) provides an example of how to establish the link between the index and behavior. The authors used biofeedback to either increase (what they wanted to see) or decrease (for the purposes of the investigation) left hemisphere alpha (8-13 Hz) power in a group of novice archers *and* recorded the changes in shooting performance (better and worse, respectively), which were as hypothesized. This demonstration—that driving the selected index in either direction can generate commensurate change in performance—offers a powerful justification for the index–behavior link.

As a result, the investigator or practitioner can proceed, secure in the knowledge that the causative link is firmly established, at least until further research identifies an intervening variable or an even better approach.

As noted earlier, these issues are becoming less of a concern. However, answering the crucial question about biofeedback (i.e., does it work?) requires the consumer of research to pay close attention to the ways in which an investigation has proceeded.

Measurement Problems

We have already highlighted a few of the problems with measurement. In my experience, most issues come down to failure to meet technical concerns; yet again, the need for a sound appreciation of what the technology is doing *and why* is paramount.

One other common concern in the literature, however, relates to the ways in which biofeedback interventions are evaluated. Consider a typical but hypothetical study. The investigators decide to compare 15 sessions of biofeedback to an equal number of sessions of relaxation training. Interested in application, they then evaluate and compare the interventions by use of a self-reported "comfort" scale and symptoms checklist, contrasting pre- and postdata collected at a major competition. Although this study presents a number of important issues, we can single out three in particular.

Firstly, consider the earlier discussion of personal preference and differential awareness of (or susceptibility to) specific psychophysiological indices. As a consequence, the self-reported evaluation is confounded by the individuals' selection of which factor they attend to. A further complication emerges from the choice of index used as the focus for biofeedback—as a consequence, the impact of the biofeedback intervention is differential across subjects depending on the degree to which they do or do not experience that index.

Secondly, there is a possibly differential impact of the two interventions that is based solely on how systematically they address the variable of interest (cf. Tenenbaum, Corbett, & Kitsantas, 2002). When told to "relax," subjects search for methods, but in the absence of specific instructions, this process can become "hit and miss" to some extent. By contrast, biofeedback presents information about how well one is performing the promoted change (in this case, relaxing); but once again, in and of itself, it offers no guidance on how this should be accomplished. The extent to which the desired change is taught, and even whether possible strategies are presented to and discussed with the individual, are key concerns—both methodologically in terms of understanding and using the results, and practically in terms of efficacy. In short, biofeedback is an aid to learning, not a method in itself.

Finally, consider both the outcome aims and the consequent methodological decisions inherent in the design of the intervention. Why 15 sessions, for example? If people learn at different rates, then surely we should establish up front some performance criteria that must be exceeded before we accept that the athlete has effectively internalized the skill. Otherwise, we test the use of a strategy in real competition that will almost inevitably display differential levels of development across participants. A related concern is how we determine these criteria of learning success. In short, how *much* self-regulatory control must individuals demonstrate (and, of course, in what circumstances) before it is clear that they have successfully acquired the skill? Once again, and as an additional issue, this will obviously be differential across participants and further complicated by test conditions. Clearly, these points would also apply to the nonbiofeedback section of our hypothetical study. From a biofeedback perspective, however, there is still a need for careful and methodical consideration of such issues in order to further improve the theoretical and empirical underpinnings of this method (Petruzzello, Landers, & Salazar, 1991).

Issues With Feedback

In 1986, Shellenberger and Green published a comprehensive and, at its time, state of the art text on biofeedback. After critically reviewing over 300 studies, they offered a clear set of criteria for the effective employment of biofeedback—pragmatic guidelines that covered issues such as contact time, need for independent practice, motivation, and support. Given the age and comprehensiveness of this text, it is rather disappointing that many of the errors and limitations are still apparent among practitioners and in the research methodology.

Perhaps the biggest issue associated with the actual feedback process relates to the time allocated to sessions and independent practice. As with any skill acquisition process, biofeedback takes time. Failure to allow for, indeed require, subjects to complete the full schedule of practice results in "underlearned" skills that may work in the carefully controlled learning and practice environment but that collapse in the heat of competition. Improving the subject's abilities in self-regulation is an important element that can offer much toward enhancing performance (Zaichkowsky & Takenaka, 1993). Accordingly, the psychologist or coach must work hard to establish the subject's motivation and commitment to the practice regime. Since early progress is likely to be rapid (as with any skill learning process), incorporating regular "tests," as well as anticipating and preparing for the difficulties that will often occur in the later stages of the training protocol, represents good practice.

Index Selection

One of the best features of the Wingate five-step approach described earlier is the care with which the biofeedback index is chosen. The fact that this care is built into the system is one of the most positive characteristics of the approach. As already noted, the index needs to be selected against three criteria: (1) whether it fits the sport environment and its challenges, (2) how well it fits the individual's preferences and characteristics, and (3) whether it means what we think it means. If we do not assess these elements accurately, we may well lead the subject, however efficiently and effectively, to adopt irrelevant behaviors, or even worse, into habits that will damage performance.

Consequently there is a need to thoroughly explore the theoretical and empirical evidence for the use of any particular index. Indeed, as suggested earlier in the chapter, current "world's best practice" in biofeedback may well be based on procedures to establish the veracity of the index used.

Two examples may be useful here. The first relates to the still commonly held idea that static target athletes (rifle, pistol, and archery) shoot most effectively when trigger pull is completed between heartbeats, a phase termed the interbeat interval or IBI (Helin, Sihvonen, & Hänninen, 1987; Landers et al., 1980). Thus one good application of biofeedback would appear to be the encouragement of shot placement in this phase of the cardiac cycle, termed diastole. Unfortunately for this "clear evidence," however, simple checks show that this idea is far from universal. Table 16.1 reveals results from international British archers, recorded in training and competition, showing that the use of biofeedback to encourage diastole shot placement would not necessarily result, at least in the short term, in an increase in performance for some athletes.

These data simply do not support the use of biofeedback to promote shooting in diastole with all the athletes in this sample, providing evidence for the need to explore and justify the changes intended from the biofeedback intervention before it is applied.

The second example, which is more positive, relates to the application of biofeedback toward selective muscle relaxation in an athlete, changes that were identified as necessary by the athlete himself, by his coach, and by three-dimensional

Table 16.1 Shot Position Within the Cardiac Cycle During Match and Practice, Showing Good and Bad Shots

Participant	Practice		Match	
	% good shots in diastole	% bad shots in diastole	% good shots in diastole	% bad shots in diastole
Archer a	70	50	50	71
Archer b	75	75	50	100
Archer c	40	0	0	33
Archer d	100	50	100	75
Archer e	33	50	0	100
Archer f	0	60	40	0
Archer g	N/A	N/A	100	100
Archer h	N/A	N/A	60	20

N/A = values due to data lost through muscular interference.

Data from Bellamy, Collins, Holmes, & Loze, 1999.

kinematic examination of the skating action. The athlete-client, an Olympic medalist in short-track speed skating, had an excellent record at long distances. Unfortunately, however, during shorter-distance events or when he was trying to sprint as a change of pace, he had a tendency to tense up his deltoid muscles, thereby slowing his action and increasing the amount of energy required. Application of a modified version of the Wingate five-step procedure stalled at Step 3, when the athlete consistently reported feeling slower as he simulated race action in association with the targeted and biofeedback-promoted change, namely more relaxed deltoids.

The discussion and experimentation prompted by the approach soon solved this challenge, however. Data collection, following from the athlete's self-reported experience, showed an increase in latissimus dorsi activity associated with the more relaxed deltoids. In summary, this was the athlete's perceived way in which he would "relax" his shoulders. Incorporation of biofeedback on both deltoid and latissimus activity, presented to the athlete as he skated through an audio signal, resulted in lowered activity in the target sites, better acceleration, higher top speed, and a smoother action.

Taken together, these examples show the importance of carefully checking the underpinnings and the individual idiosyncrasies of any case before the biofeedback intervention is commenced. Exactly how the initial "prescription" is adjusted represents the art of the intervention, a factor that is obviously based on and follows from the science, but that is arguably equally important, at least so far as applied work is concerned.

Directions for Future Investigation

In outlining future directions, it is first necessary to stress the number of excellent applications of biofeedback apparent in the literature. Despite the challenges outlined in this chapter, carefully designed and effective interventions are commonly conducted; only a minority reveal errors and flaws that limit or counter the positive benefits claimed. Of course, the real task is to discriminate between effective and ineffective interventions. The key area, I suggest, is attention to the detail of the design. Biofeedback is, at first sight in any case, a more complex process than other more traditional and low-tech methods. Approaches such as the Wingate five-step method help to overcome the

consumer reluctance often associated with these apparent complexities. Accordingly, more careful and in-depth investigation and parameterization of the approaches will further enhance our understanding of the process and promote its use (cf. Petruzzello, Landers, & Salazar, 1991).

The next area for development is represented by the continual expansion of biofeedback approaches from their traditional role in relaxation and other aspects of parasympathetic control. Positive benefits have accrued from biofeedback on a wide variety of performance-related challenges, including strength (Lucca & Recchiuti, 1983), perceived pain following muscle endurance tasks (McGlynn, Laughlin, & Filios, 1979), and running economy (Caird, McKenzie, & Sleivert, 1999). However, many of these positive results are contested by contradictory results from other studies. Given the number of issues that must be addressed in order for biofeedback to be effective, this lack of clarity may not be surprising. If these and other supportive researchers are correct, however, there are considerable benefits available for the taking. Replications and extensions of such investigations are the key, but only when all of the considerations highlighted by this chapter and other texts are addressed in the design and are reported accurately and consistently. One important concern relates to the need for examination of effects in both laboratory and field settings (cf. the Wingate approach). There is already substantial evidence for the differences that may systematically occur between these two settings (e.g., Fahrenburg et al., 1986; Marstaller & Meischner, 1990). Ecological validity and practical applicability require that any biofeedback-generated effects be evaluated in the setting to which they are to be applied.

The third broad category relates to the optimum employment of new equipment and approaches. One of the most positive developments for biofeedback has been the ongoing improvement in technology. As equipment and software improve, both the range and potential application of new indices also increase. Consider two possible evolutions from the vast range of opportunities. One is the possibility of enhanced skill acquisition (cf. the Konttinen study cited earlier) through the use of small force transducers offering ongoing process data and immediate optimization of a technique. Information about the employment of particular muscle groups (e.g., recruitment patterns for the latissimus dorsi with use of the kayak "wing" paddle; Krueger et al., 1988) would be augmented by contingent feedback on the efficacy of the action. In similar fashion, information obtained from detailed biomechanical analysis could be operationalized through a focus on the key causative variables (e.g., velocity of javelin release; Morriss & Bartlett, 1996). Such an opportunity would considerably increase the potential contribution of biofeedback to acquisition and optimization of skill, an area that likely represents the next big expansion for biofeedback.

Another exciting technology-based advance would exploit the ever-expanding opportunities from medical imaging. It is unfortunately true that, up to now at any rate, the technology confines such work to the laboratory. Notwithstanding comments earlier in the chapter on the need for field and laboratory investigation, imaging offers a great potential to increase our understanding of the mechanisms underpinning common methodologies. When one considers the advantages of this approach for imagery, for example (cf. Paul Holmes' chapter 17 in this book), the possibilities are very exciting. An example is our expanding knowledge of the brain's ability to match observed actions with internal movement-based representations (the so-called mirror system; Gallese et al., 1996; Buccino et al., 2001). Increased mirror activity would appear to affect the vividness and controllability of the experience, since it is associated with greater understanding and expertise in the skill being observed (Glaser et al., 2003). Does this technology offer us a chance to directly improve imagery ability or efficacy, or both, through biofeedback to increase the quantity or modify the topography of this activity? Such interventions, built on the principles espoused in this chapter, would make a significant contribution.

Finally, users of biofeedback should examine the impact biofeedback has, checking that negative consequences may not be associated with its use for certain individuals. In fact, such negative impacts may accrue from biofeedback, paradoxically, as a result of its very effectiveness in promoting self-awareness and perceptions of control. For example, relaxation-induced anxiety (Borkovec & Matthews, 1988; Braith, McCullough, & Bush, 1988) has been noted in nonclinical subjects who, as their skills in relaxation improve, display unexpected greater levels of anxiety. Paralleling this research, biofeedback practitioners may usefully check that the improved self-regulatory abilities that result do not lead to the development of other concerns, quite possibly (for some susceptible individuals) due to the removal of an "excuse" for poor performance.

Conclusions

This chapter has explored and exposed just a few of the myriad of issues, applications, and challenges associated with biofeedback. Obviously a comprehensive treatment in this space would be impossible (there are books and even whole journals dedicated to this topic), but I hope such discussion can encourage wider pursuit of knowledge about and experimentation with this very useful but underrated approach.

The underlying message of this chapter for practitioners is that experimentation is the key to innovative practice and holds the potential for significant gains. Creativity can be fully exploited, with the application of imagination limited only by the need for care with regard to the scientific principles underlying the particular approach—that is, the proper use of biofeedback is art firmly based on science.

References

Bellamy, M., Collins, D., Holmes, P., & Loze, G. (1999). Shot patterns in ECG recordings for elite air-pistol shooters. *Journal of Sports Sciences, 17,* 48-49.

Blumenstein, B., Bar-Eli, M., & Collins, D. (2002). Biofeedback training in sport. In B. Blumenstein, M. Bar-Eli, & G. Tenenbaum (Eds.). *Brain and body in sport and exercise* (pp. 55-76). Chichester, UK: Wiley.

Blumenstein, B., Bar-Eli, M., & Tenenbaum, G. (1997). A five-step approach to mental training incorporating feedback. *Sport Psychologist, 11,* 440-453.

Borkovec, T.D., & Mathews, A.M. (1988). Treatment of nonphobic anxiety disorders: A comparison of nondirective, cognitive, and coping desensitization therapy. *Journal of Consulting and Clinical Psychology, 56*(6), 877-884.

Braith, J.A., McCullough, J.P., & Bush, J.P. (1988). Relaxation-induced anxiety in a sub-clinical sample of chronically anxious subjects. *Journal of Behavior Therapy and Experimental Psychiatry, 19*(3), 193-198.

Buccino, G., Binkofski, F., Fink, C.R., Fadiga, L., Fogasi, L., Gallese, V., Seltz, R.J., Zillea, K., Rizzolati, G., & Freund, H.J. (2001). Action observation activates premotor and parietal areas in a somatotopic manner: An fMRI study. *European Journal of Neuroscience, 13,* 400-404.

Caird, S.J.A., McKenzie, A., & Sleivert, G. (1999). Biofeedback and relaxation techniques improve running economy in sub-elite long distance runners. *Medicine and Science in Sports and Exercise, 31,* 717-722.

Collins, D.J. (1995). Early detection of overtraining problems in athletes. *Coaching Focus, 28,* 17-20.

Davidson, R.J. (2003). Affective neuroscience: A case for interdisciplinary research. In F. Kessel & P.L. Rosenfield (Eds.), *Expanding the boundaries of health and social science: Case studies in interdisciplinary innovation* (pp. 99-121). London: Oxford University Press.

Fahrenburg, J., Foerster, F., Schneider, H-J., & Muller, W. (1986). Predictability of individual differences in activation processes in a field setting based on laboratory measures. *Psychophysiology, 23,* 323-333.

Gallese, V., Fadiga, L., Fogassi, I., & Rizzolatti, G. (1996). Action recognition in the premotor cortex. *Brain, 119,* 593-609.

Glaser, D.E., Calvo, B., Grèzes, J., Passingham, R.E., & Haggard, P. (2003). Functional imaging of motor experience and expertise during action observation. Program No. 934.15. 2003 Abstract Viewer/Itinerary Planner. Washington, DC: Society for Neuroscience, 2003. Online.

Gruzelier, J. (2003). Optimizing performance with EEG alpha/theta biofeedback revisited. Paper presented at the annual meeting of the British Psychophysiology Society, University of Portsmouth, July.

Helin, P., Sihvonen, T., & Hanninen, O. (1987). Timing of the triggering action of shooting in relation to the cardiac cycle. *British Journal of Sports Medicine, 21*(1), 33-36.

Konttinen, N., Mononen, K., Viitasalo, J., & Mets, T. (2004). The effect of augmented auditory feedback on psychomotor skill in precision shooting. *Journal of Sport and Exercise Psychology, 26,* 306-316.

Krueger, K.M., Ruehl, M., Scheel, D., & Franz, U. (1988). Die anwendbarkeit von EMG biofeedback zur optimierung sportlicher techniken im motorischen lernprozess von ausdauersportarten am beispiel des kanurennsports. *Theorie und Praxis Leistungssport (Leipzig), 26,* 128-142.

Landers, D.M., Christina, R.W., Hatfield, B.D., Daniels, G.S., & Doyle, L.A. (1980). Moving competitive shooting into the scientist's lab. *American Rifleman, 128*(4), 36-37, 76-77.

Landers, D.M., Petruzzello, S.J., Salazar, W., Crews, D.L., Kubitz, K.A., Gannon, T.L., & Han, M. (1991). The influence of electro-cortical biofeedback on performance in pre-elite archers. *Medicine and Science in Sports and Exercise, 23,* 123-129.

Lucca, J.A., & Recchiuti, M. (1983). Effect of electromyographic biofeedback on an isometric strengthening program. *Physical Therapy, 63,* 200-203.

Marstaller, H., & Meischner, K. (1990). The predictability of psychophysical states (laboratory-field comparison). Paper presented at the 19th annual meeting of the German Psychophysiology Society (DGPA), University of Giessen, June.

McGlynn, G.H., Laughlin, N.T., & Filios, S.P. (1979). The effect of electromyographic feedback and static stretching on artificially induced muscle soreness. *American Journal of Physical Medicine, 58,* 139-148.

Morriss, C.J., & Bartlett, R.M. (1996). Biomechanical factors crucial for performance in the javelin throw. *Sports Medicine, 21,* 438-446.

Pennebaker, J.W. (2000). Psychological factors influencing the reporting of physical symptoms. In A.A. Stone & J.S. Turkkan (Eds.), *The science of self-report: Implications for research and practice* (pp. 299-315). Mahwah, NJ: Erlbaum.

Peper, E., & Schmid, A. (1983). The use of electrodermal feedback for peak performance training. *Somatics, 4,* 16-18.

Petruzzello, S.J., Landers, D.M., & Salazar, W. (1991). Biofeedback and sport/exercise performance: Applications and limitations. *Behavior Therapy, 22,* 397-392.

Shellenberger, R., & Green, J.A. (1986). *From the ghost in the box to successful biofeedback training.* Greeley, CO: Health Psychology.

Steptoe, A., & Vogele, C. (1992). Individual differences in the perception of bodily sensations: The role of trait anxiety and coping style. *Behavioural Research Therapy, 30,* 597-607.

Tenenbaum, G., Corbett, M., & Kitsantas, A. (2002). Biofeedback: Applications and methodological concerns. In B. Blumenstein, M. Bar-Eli, & G. Tenenbaum (Eds.), *Brain and body in sport and exercise* (pp. 101-122). Chichester, UK: Wiley.

Zaichkowsky, L.D., & Takenaka, K. (1993). Optimizing arousal level. In R.N. Singer, M. Murphey, & L.K. Tennant (Eds.), *Handbook of research on sport psychology* (pp. 328-264). New York: Macmillan.

The Psychophysiology of Imagery in Sport

Paul S. Holmes, PhD

All sport psychologists work, at some time, through an intervention-based approach, and the research supporting this method has traditionally focused on the processes behind techniques and their effectiveness at improving performance.

However, this has not advanced professional criteria for increasing the validity of intervention selection. Unfortunately, "without adequate theoretical explanations for the mechanisms underlying psychological processes, the reasons why the techniques succeed or fail and the influence of moderator variables on performance will not be fully understood" (Davids, 1997, p. 251). All this borne in mind, a poor understanding of the mechanisms involved is clearly an apparent weakness of the profession. Sport psychologists "know some things work, although we haven't done extensive research on why or how they work" (Landers, 1989, p. 19).

With the advent of cognitive neuroscience and neuroimaging studies it has become possible to reveal the ways in which imagery and other behaviors draw on mechanisms used in other activities, such as perception and motor control (Kosslyn, Ganis, & Thompson, 2001). Therefore, the premise of this chapter is that the findings from these types of studies can increase our understanding of the mechanisms involved in imagery and provide a more effective way forward for sport psychology.

In their simplest form, psychological intervention techniques attempt to change cognitive function, or to change conscious cognitive control over some element of somatic function. The resultant behavior is assumed to be more effective or more efficient, and since it is now almost universally accepted that cognition occurs in the brain, it is surprising that brain mechanisms and cognitive neurophysiology do not contribute more to theories in sport psychology. Where sport psychology *has* made a direct reference to brain activity, it has frequently done so in an overly simplified way.

It is intuitively appealing to think of the brain as having different specialized regions. In fact there *are* areas dedicated to certain functions, but, as has been shown in earlier chapters, most tasks require the simultaneous working of many regions of the brain. Given this integrated approach to brain functioning (cf. Keil et al., 2000), it should now be possible for some of the anatomical and functional knowledge of the brain obtained in recent years to be applied to sport. The fundamental knowledge suggests that a reconsideration of theoretical work supporting the use of psychological interventions in sport is long overdue.

The search for neural correlates of behavior and awareness may, to some, seem to place the performer within a radically reductionist and biologically mechanistic framework. This is not the case. The brain representations, or collectives of interconnected neurons, discussed here are seen *not* as static deterministic machines but as dynamic and continually fluctuating neural networks. As proposed in this chapter, only with achievement of a greater understanding of the mechanisms allowing change in these representations will sport psychologists begin to have control over the interventions they use.

Since this chapter aims to promote the physiological mechanisms of motor imagery, a modified version of the neuroscientific definition offered by

Cuthbert, Vrana, and Bradley (1991) provides a useful way forward for consideration of the process in a sporting context. Motor imagery, here, is defined as *one* of the processes through which a memory representation is accessed that is the same as, or similar to, the representation accessed for action. Since this definition makes reference to neural networks in the brain, it allows for discussion of some of the detailed systems active during action execution and imagery (and other associated techniques for representational access). Jeannerod (1997) has proposed that if "preparation [for action] and imagery represent different degrees or aspects of the same phenomenon, and if they have the same objectives, they should contain the same information" (p. 97). Cognitive neuropsychology would, therefore, seem to be an important approach for assessing the neural processes involved during imagery and promoting concern for the effectiveness of the technique in a performance setting. Imagery, if considered as an efferent process, is ideally suited for psychophysiological investigation (Cuthbert, Vrana, & Bradley, 1991). Unfortunately, however, in many sport-based studies of imagery, the physiological output has typically been seen as a concomitant of the imagery process rather than an integral component of the experience. Therefore, the Jeannerodian concept of a dynamic representation forms the main theme of this chapter, and research from fundamental cognitive neuroscience is reviewed and considered in a sporting context. Empirical data from brain imaging experiments are cited to propose that imagery and other techniques used for representation access are closely related to action, and that an increased understanding of the psychophysiology of the processes will allow for more effective and efficient control of future behavior.

Theoretical Concerns

With the exception of Lang's (1977, 1979, 1985) bioinformational theory of emotional imagery, no theories common in the sport psychology literature have been subjected to rigorous study or are based on underlying mechanisms. This must pose a question about the consistency and validity of current imagery practice. This chapter puts forward a proposal for an approach to imagery in sport that is based on fundamental cognitive neuropsychology as part of an attempt to pro-

vide a better understanding of the mechanisms involved in imagery. Through this consideration, techniques are discussed that offer a more effective exploitation of the neuroscientific theory. It will be argued that, while motor imagery may improve performance in a variety of ways, many of these ways seem to have fundamental links to the physical task itself.

Functional Equivalence

Motor imagery corresponds to a subliminal activation of the motor system that is involved not only in physical preparation and execution but also in imagined actions and similar behaviors (Jeannerod & Frak, 1999). Holmes and Collins (2001) have suggested that since imagery and motor activity are related to a shared motor representation system, consideration of the two neural processes, and the extent to which they covary (their functional equivalence), is vital if motor imagery is to be used as a successful tool in sport psychology. The authors of a number of neuroscientific experiments have interpreted their findings in support of a functional equivalence between action generation and action simulation (see meta-analysis by Grèzes & Decety, 2001). The key issue for sport psychology is that if the physical action and imagery are equivalent at a central level, then many of the procedures shown to be successful in physical practice should also be applied in mental practice as well.

Cognitive neuroscience research that supports a shared memory representation focuses on central and peripheral function during the cognitive steps to action. Specifically, the focus is on the preparation phase of intending (cf. Loze, Collins, & Shaw, 1999), planning and programming, and, in some cases, the execution phase. The ways in which the representation is active during (motor) imagery (and similar representational access techniques) and how it is shown through markers of central and peripheral activity are of particular relevance.

The concept of functional equivalence between representations for different behaviors offers a useful and parsimonious explanation for the mechanisms involved in action generation and motor imagery. However, they *will* have differences. Action generation usually produces subconsciously controlled, coordinated overt performance. Motor imagery, on the other hand, normally has full efference consciously "blocked" (see Berthoz, 1996, for a review of hierarchical gating), or suppressed, within the corticospinal flow. The result is that any overt behavior is minimal and random (cf. Lang's theory of emotional imagery, 1977, 1979). In addition, and in support of these neuronal differences, Decety and Sommerville (2003) have argued that sharedness should not mean identicality; otherwise the representation activities would completely overlap and lead to behavioral confusion. Babiloni and colleagues (2002) have shown that, in an observation condition (argued to be similar to external visual imagery), many sites showed functional equivalence. However, equivalence was negligible in parietal-occipital scalp regions, which the authors suggest could be the neural substrate to distinguish agency. Similarly, encephalography (EEG) research (Holmes, Collins, & Calmels, in press) has revealed functionally equivalent activity at all active sites across the cortex *except* at the left temporal sites during observation of rifle shooting performance compared to that during a physical shooting condition. The neuroscientific data suggest that motor imagery (and observation) conditions, while very similar to action, do not reflect behavior identical to action generation and that behavioral agency might explain this phenomenon.

In support of this view of motor imagery, some authors have found excitation of spinal motor neurons during imagery (e.g., Bonnet et al., 1997), while others have found the activity limited to cortical structures such as the motor cortex (e.g., Hashimoto & Rothwell, 1999). It is not really surprising that action generation and motor imagery show incomplete functional equivalence. Imagery is, fundamentally, about an imaginal movement without actual movement. There must, therefore, be some inhibitory processes occurring. This inhibition is a central task with neuronal activity that is likely to complicate the central functional equivalence debate. Interestingly, if the imaginal process is conscious, then the task of remaining still, as is prescribed in many sport psychology interventions, may become the primary task, with the imagined behavior being relegated to the secondary task. In this respect, functional equivalence may be severely compromised. By requiring imagers to remain still, sport psychologists may be negatively influencing the process they wish to achieve!

Under current Jeannerodian definitions, when motor preparation in the preexecution stage becomes a conscious process, it automatically becomes a motor image of the same action but still shares much of the same motor representation. The study of the neural activity involved in imagined and actual task execution provides an ideal opportunity to examine the proposition for functional equivalence. The motor imagery and motor activity profiles have been highlighted through techniques such as observing cerebral metabolism by monitoring regional cerebral blood flow (rCBF), positron emission tomography (PET), and functional magnetic resonance imaging (fMRI). While specific regions have been proposed to exclusively subserve motor preparation and execution (i.e., the primary motor cortex [PMC]), attenuated PMC activation has occasionally been observed during motor imagery conditions (e.g., Pascual-Leone et al., 1995). However, it may be that studies that have not found activity in PMC have not used imagery effectively. Decety and Grèzes (1999) have gone further, suggesting that perception of action and motor imagery of action share a similar cortical network involving the premotor cortex, supplementary motor area, inferior parietal lobule, cingulate gyrus, and cerebellum. What seems clear is that the cortical and subcortical areas, active during motor imagery, are intimately linked to those involved in at least the early stages of motor control. Such findings support the argument for a common, but not identical, neural mechanism supporting motor imagery and motor activity.

Perhaps of greater practical interest to sport psychologists is that brain activity during imagery is influenced by the nature of the imaginal task (Jeannerod & Decety, 1995). For example, attentional task requirements appear to preferentially recruit different portions of the supplementary motor area (Stephan et al., 1995). Such evidence should support a comprehensive consideration of the sport skill being imaged at any given moment in time. Sport psychologists should consider monitoring levels of conscious processing and matching attentional "switches" as the skill proceeds by making the imagery more implicit. Since attention and conscious control of action change with learning, they should also modify imagery scripts to address this issue (see Holmes & Collins, 2001, 2002 for more detail on the PETTLEP model).

It seems clear that the cortical and subcortical areas, active during motor imagery, pertain to neural networks known to be involved in at least the early stages of motor control (Decety, 1996).

One of the most compelling pieces of evidence for a common pattern of cortical activation for execution and imagination has been provided by Beisteiner and colleagues (1995). In analysis of a unilateral hand movement, direct current potential recordings showed no quantitative or qualitative difference between motor activity and motor imagery over central cortex sites. It may be logical to assume, therefore, that since motor imagery must also involve a sequential organization of action plans (Decety et al., 1990), the temporal nature of motor imagery and that of motor activity are alike. The results of Beisteiner and colleagues (1995) suggest that they must also involve the same neural substrate. Research findings in support of this claim have been provided by Decety (1996), Deeke (1996), and Fox and colleagues (1987). Sport psychologists should carefully consider all the interacting constraints that may influence the timing of the imagined behavior if they are to address temporal functional equivalence across the cortex.

The central measures have indicated a close functional equivalence between motor activity and motor imagery. A similar equivalence is also apparent between the peripheral cardiac and respiratory indices that anticipate muscular activity. This is evident in the findings of Decety and colleagues (1991), which showed that heart rate and total ventilation increased proportionally with imagined incremental workloads for treadmill and ergometer exercising. However, no overt muscle activity was discernible. Wang and Morgan's (1992) study of visual perspective effects on imagined exercise demonstrated that ventilation and effort sense were higher when an internal imagery perspective was employed. Despite observed similarities between internal and external conditions in metabolic and cardiovascular responses, they concluded that internal (motor) imagery had the closest resemblance to actual exercise. Similar results were obtained by Wuyam and colleagues (1995), who found that ventilation increased in highly trained athletes when they imagined themselves running on a treadmill. These changes were a consequence of increased respiratory frequency, which also significantly reduced end-tidal P_{CO_2}. No changes were observed in nonathletes, suggesting that the representational access in these participants was unable to activate brain regions associated with cardiorespiratory control. Representational complexity and sensory neuronal integration linked to expertise should, therefore, be a key consideration for the sport psychologist.

Influencing Physiological Change

Motor representations are constantly being reorganized and are highly sensitive to experience and learning. This is due to plasticity at the level of the synapse and cortical circuitry. There is now strong evidence that cortical-based changes result from modification to horizontal corticocortical connections. The effect of experience on the brain's plasticity is wide ranging, including increases in dendritic length, changes in spine density, synapse formation, increased glial activity, and altered metabolic activity to support structural change (Kolb & Whishaw, 1998). These physiological changes bring about the cortical reorganization responsible for modifying behavior, perceptual learning, and improved performance. But can motor imagery or other more implicit techniques replicate these changes? There does seem to be some evidence that they can. Jackson and colleagues (2003) have recently shown that learning a sequential motor task through motor imagery can produce changes in cerebral cortex (orbitofrontal cortex and cerebellum) similar to those observed after physical practice of the same task. Moreover, the authors suggest that their findings support the hypothesis that motor imagery improves performance by acting on the neural correlates for preparation and anticipation rather than the execution of movements.

If the process of imagery has the potential to access the brain in a similar way to the afferent and efferent activity involved in physical actions, then the exciting possibility exists that imagery and similar techniques such as observation can also permanently influence behavior.

Image Generation

The neurological evidence considered within the functional equivalence literature outlines some of the cortical areas of the brain involved in the imagery process. However, what is not clear is the extent to which these functionally active brain regions are involved in the generation of the image or the processing of information required to prepare and execute the predetermined goal-oriented task. There is some evidence for a distinct image generation mechanism that is required for the top-down generation of images from memory but not for bottom-up perception (see Farah, 2000b, for more detail on this issue). In reality, both tasks require a level of processing that would make it extremely difficult, with current technology, to distinguish one from the other. However, there is increasing evidence that implicates the left temporo-occipital area for image generation. It is possible that brain imaging techniques, such as fMRI, PET, and EEG, may reflect either image generation or functionally equivalent imagery of motor preparation and execution. That there is a certain amount of inseparable and fully interdependent interaction is therefore likely. If imagery is the top-down activation of a representation, it must have the associated preparation and execution plan that subserves action and perception, carrying information about color, shape, spatial location, and so on (Farah, 2000b). In visual imagery, Farah (2000a) has also proposed that imagery activates the majority of the (visual) representation independently of retinal input, with only a few neurons close to the eye being excluded. It seems likely that the "traditional" concept of the perception–cognitive distinction is more blurred than was once thought.

Kosslyn (1994) has proposed a number of sites that seem to be involved in the generation of an image. Through analysis of (rCBF), Kosslyn, Alpert, and Thompson (1993) have identified areas thought to be involved in implementing associative memory (left angular gyrus and area 19), accessing information in associative memory (left dorsolateral prefrontal cortex), shifting attention (right superior parietal lobe), the formation of the image (area 17), generation of the image and part recognition (fusiform gyrus), and encoding

spatial relations representations (right inferior parietal lobe) (see figure 17.1). It is clear that many of the regions identified are also involved in preparation for a motor act. However, it may also be the case that some of the recorded activity is specific to the imaginal process itself. Activity may be at a more conscious level than the physical motor preparation, and there may be activity associated with "blocking" any movement (see Berthoz, 1996, for a detailed review of inhibition and gating of imagined movements). What Kosslyn, Alpert, and Thompson's research suggests is that, despite the degradation in perceptual cues, the generated image is able to activate functional activity in neuronal networks for the imagined situation. It is also possible that the degraded perceptual environment frees neuronal networks normally involved with the percepts to amplify the imagery experience. These ideas remain to be tested empirically.

Imagery Modalities and Perspectives

Often in sport psychology practice, there is little consideration of the content of the imagery modality employed in relation to the preparation and execution of the desired behavior. Moreover, little attention is given to which techniques can best achieve equivalence with the physical act for different individuals.

Jeannerod (1997) defined motor imagery as a force-generating representation of the self in

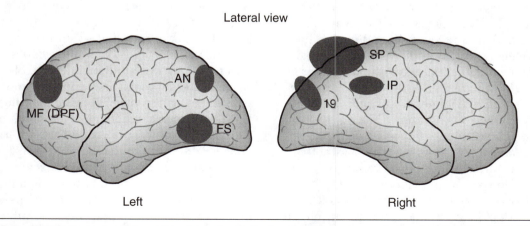

Figure 17.1 Regional cerebral blood flow foci of activity for visual imagery and visual task. MF, middle frontal area (also called the dorsolateral prefrontal cortex, DPF); AN, angular gyrus; FS, fusiform gyrus; SP, superior parietal cortex; IP, inferior parietal cortex; 19, Brodmann's area 19.

Modified from Kosslyn, Alpert, and Thompson (1993).

action from a first-person (internal) perspective with the primary representational sense being kinesthesis. Motor imagery is distinguished from visual imagery in terms of content, but may not easily be separated from it because actions take place in a spatial environment and their consequences typically involve transformations within space. Distinguishing perspectives is important for a number of reasons. Of particular importance to this chapter is the fact that neural correlates are able to distinguish the experience of agency. Farrer and Frith (2002) have demonstrated that the anterior insula is associated with primary causation of an action, whereas the inferior parietal cortex represents movements that are deemed to be the actions of others.

In many sport-based studies, the instructions provided to the participants suggest that there is normally confusion among internal visual imagery, external visual imagery, kinesthetic imagery, and stimulus and response propositions. Some authors (e.g., Collins, Smith, & Hale, 1998; Hale, 1982) have proposed that internal imagery, suggested here to be a combination of internal visual and kinesthetic perspectives, is most effective in eliciting a multimodal physiological response. However, other studies (e.g., Hardy & Callow, 1999; White & Hardy, 1995) have shown kinesthetic imagery to be equally effective with either visual perspective. Indeed, Callow and Hardy (2004) offer a useful proposition-based explanation for this finding. In a similar way to that of Jeannerod, they argue that it is difficult to separate visual images of movement from kinesthetic images irrespective of visual perspective. Based on the Hebbian theory of learning and the mechanisms of brain plasticity described earlier, the integration of the two perspectives is likely to be even stronger where the imaged skill is well learned. In a recent EEG and observation study with elite rifle shooters, we found no significant difference in functional equivalence across 11 active sites between an "internal" and an "external" visual perspective (Holmes & Calmels, in press). In a study of electromyographic (EMG) activity in rectus femoris and biceps femoris during a squatting task, Moore (2004) found that EMG activity during an external visual observation perspective condition was more temporally and spatially functionally equivalent to the physical EMG profile than during the internal condition. During the internal visual observation condition, participants reported very little change in visual array, whereas in the external observation condition they were able to see (and concurrently feel) the full movement pattern. Movements that depend heavily on form for their successful execution seem not only to benefit more from external visual imagery (see Callow & Hardy, 2004, for a review), but also to produce a more functional electromyographic response. With both central and peripheral correlates of functional equivalence discriminating visual perspective, the implications for the sport psychologist seem too important to ignore.

In a similar vein, Klatzky (1994) has suggested that "visualization" may be concomitant with, and may subjectively dominate, motor imagery. Klatzky, Lederman, and Matula's (1991) studies supporting this contention seem well founded. However, their research employs tasks that are nonsport specific and participants that are not athletic; therefore, these findings may not translate well to sporting populations. Anecdotal and empirical reports following (motor) imagery are just as frequently kinesthetic and tactile as well as visual (e.g., Callow & Hardy, 2004). Recent evidence from Naito and colleagues (2002) provides strong support for this proposal. They showed that kinesthetic sensations associated with imagined movement were internally simulated in contralateral cingulate motor areas, supplementary motor area, dorsal premotor cortex, and ipsilateral cerebellum. Given the known connections between some of these areas and those active during visual processing, it should not be surprising to find concurrent visual and kinesthetic imagery.

However, there is some recent support from sporting populations for Klatzky's argument for visual dominance. Smith and Holmes (2004) showed that for high-performing golfers, an internal visual perspective was the most effective mode of imagery compared to auditory imagery or a written imagery script. Concurrent kinesthesia was reported by all the groups, and internal visual imagery was suggested to be most effective at representational access. Since there was no external visual imagery condition, it is not possible to make a visual perspective comparison. However, a certain amount of caution should be exercised here. It is possible that, where visual imagery does predominate in the verbal account of an imagined action, it is the conscious descriptor of the more complex, implicit, functional kinesthetic representation. The conscious account of motor processing may be less subjectively accessible to some individuals. This behavior may also be mediated by skill level. If motor imagery is consciously accessible, then it is likely to always involve a large visual element that accompanies the spatially directed goal. Whether this is true for nonconscious motor imagery remains to be investigated. While more research is certainly required to consider Klatzky's proposal, there is some evidence that visual modalities in imagery and observation seem to be most effective.

Electromyographic activity has not always been associated with imagery (Yue & Cole, 1992). The reason may be that inhibition of movement is better in certain participants or conditions or that the preparatory fibers involved are deeper and of the slow tonic type so that usual surface EMG techniques are unlikely to record this activity. It is also likely that the instructions provided to the client will have an effect on muscular activity (Jeannerod, 1997). As discussed earlier, requiring an athlete to remain still during an imagery session could not only alter the attentional focus, but also reduce the efferent activity in the muscle. Neither of these would seem to be an efficient use of imagery.

There is clearly substantial evidence for the existence of neurophysiological and behavioral equivalence between motor preparation and execution and motor imagery. From a psychological perspective, Lang (1985) has proposed a conceptual network containing three basic levels: a semantic code, stimulus information, and efferent code. The contention is that the three are synonymous with Jeannerod's concept of the brain representation. Once the memory is stored, abstract information in the semantic code is available to the image that is accessed through three propositional routes: the stimulus, response, and meaning propositions. Furthermore, Lang's theory proposes that an image is accompanied by a physiological response appropriate to the imagined scenario. When appropriate response propositions are processed, through a response emphasis in the imagery modality, there is an associated change in somatovisceral arousal. The psychophysiological response is similar to that observed in the overt behavior, although usually at a lower amplitude, and is modified through conscious inhibition, probably at the cerebellar level (Decety et al., 1990; Hecker & Kaczor, 1988). While Lang made no direct comment on the congruence of the response proposition behavior with the actual behavior, he stated that greater similarities resulted if a response emphasis was encouraged. Furthermore, congruence was considered with respect to the relevance and meaning the image had for the performer. The key factor, however, was Lang's contention that the greater

the conceptual match between the memory and the motor image, the more strengthening of the memory trace would take place. Thus, Lang provided a psychophysiological theory to support the neurophysiological argument for functional equivalence.

Memory representations of psychophysiological events figure importantly in cognition (Lang, 1985). Although the observed imagery-induced neurological patterning is not identical to that of motor preparation and execution, motor imagery that most closely approximates motor preparation and execution in psychoneurophysiological correlates should be most effective in facilitating future performance. Sport psychologists with concern for the validity of their imagery intervention *must* consider the functional equivalence of the imagery techniques to the overt performance if they are to advance their client's performance.

In sport psychology, imagery techniques involving the use of mental practice in preparation for competition are perceived to be key skills linked to successful performance (e.g., Murphy, 1994; Vealey, 1994). Support for the view that imaging goal-directed movement can have beneficial effects on performance is well documented. Our understanding of the neural mechanisms involved in motor imagery, and, critically, their influence on sport performance, is still severely limited. Many athletes have a limited understanding of how best to utilize imagery (Hall, Rogers, & Barr, 1990). It seems likely that the lack of understanding about the use of imagery reflects the lack of consensus evident among sport psychologists about underlying psychological processes. Cuthbert, Vrana, and Bradley (1991) have suggested that cultural definitions emphasize a visual and pictorial mode for images. This bias systematically reinforces the use of generic stimulus propositions rather than more individualized response propositions. The lack of agreement over the mechanisms involved in mediating performance change achieved by imagery use may be a consequence of the limited scope of much of the research in the area (Goginsky & Collins, 1996).

In light of these views, an attempt to identify mechanisms and structures underpinning the role of imagery in the acquisition and performance of skilled sport behavior would seem important. A review of the sport psychology literature would suggest that imagery's effectiveness in improving performance is based on multiple influences. However, in cases in which imagery has been shown to enhance performance, there are fundamental links between the nature of the imagery undertaken and the physical properties of the task. For example, the inclusion of perceptual information from different modalities involved in the actual performance of the skill has been suggested to enhance the vividness of the image and to increase central and behavioral functional equivalence (Holmes & Collins, 2001, 2002). It is likely that this is the result of perceptual information stimulating parts of neural networks associated with the task and increasing the excitation of the neurons involved. The increased afference associated with the motor task is also likely to include force information, which has been shown to be critical in determining the timing of actions (Decety, Jeannerod, & Prablanc, 1989).

Neuroscientific Implications for Imagery Use by Sport Performers

As identified earlier, it is plausible that elite athletes perceive less information in a conscious analytical manner (although it depends on specific task constraints) when performing well. Explicit motor imagery "scripts" encourage rehearsal of information through a more conscious process as a result of their language-based nature. This creates a conscious visual experience. Certain types of propositional scripts and imagery perspectives may serve to accentuate the effect. A further problem has been raised by Weeks and colleagues (2001). They examined rCBF changes with externally instructed movements compared to internally generated, self-paced movements. They found that the supplementary motor area (SMA) and premotor areas were not activated during the externally instructed condition. The tradition of delivering verbal scripts to athletes must now be seen as questionable from a functional equivalence perspective.

If the specific task constraints applicable to the desired behavior are a main concern with the use of imagery, then matching the conscious and subconscious attentional processes involved also appears important (see the task element of the PETTLEP model of Holmes & Collins, 2001, 2002). Athletes are rarely able to give comprehensive verbal accounts of good performance in visuomotor terms. This is often in contrast to

accounts of poor performances, which typically include detailed technical and analytical descriptions. However, written or verbal imagery scripts seem to direct attention, consciously, to task-relevant cues in a manner dissimilar to that evident during actual performance. The challenge to sport psychologists is to find ways in which athletes can mentally practice in a realistic manner that encourages attentionally appropriate rehearsal.

One method of attempting to achieve closer conscious functional equivalence may be for athletes to use observation-based techniques in addition to imagery. In this case, the percepts are provided and the athlete is not required to generate the image. This more bottom-up approach certainly would seem to have the potential to address the consciousness concerns. It is equivalent, in terms of corticospinal facilitation, to imagery (Clark, Tremblay, & Ste-Marie, 2003), and there is some evidence that action observation can prime subsequent execution (Castiello et al., 2002). Even observation of still photographs that imply motion (for example of an athlete running) are able to activate the inferior temporal sulcus, which is known to be involved in the analysis of human motion (e.g., Kourtzi & Kanwisher, 2000).

However, as with the imagery research, an understanding of the neurological basis of the processes of observation is important. The neurological foundations seem to lie within "mirror neurons." These neurons were first discovered in the ventral premotor cortex of the macaque monkey via single-neuron recording (Rizzolatti et al., 1998). The neurons fired when the monkey executed a goal-directed hand movement and also when it observed this same action executed by another monkey or by a human (Gallese et al., 1996). These results offer the exciting possibility of an observation–execution matching system that maps the observed action onto an internal motor representation of the observed action (Iacoboni et al., 1999; Rizzolatti, Fogassi, & Gallese, 2001), as well as providing a neuroscientific mechanism to explain the use of observation in sport.

Indirect Evidence for the Mirror Neuron System

The existence of an observation–execution matching system or a mirror system in humans may not be as clear as has been reported. Three different research groups (Babiloni et al., 2002; Grèzes & Decety, 2001; Rizzolatti et al., 1996) have shown that the brain areas involved during action observation did not overlap those identified during the execution of the same action. However, as we have already discussed, sharedness should not mean identicality. The incomplete mapping of activity, during observation, may be part of the determination of agency.

The EEG research (e.g., Cochin et al., 1998; Gastaut & Bert, 1954) also provides indirect evidence for mirror neuron activity. However, in these studies, participants were tested only under observation conditions. The central alpha or "mu" rhythm was desynchronized during action observation, in a similar way to actual movement. However, a claim cannot be made for direct evidence for the existence of the mirror system, since the cortical areas must be shown to be active during both execution and observation of an action before the imagery can be considered to have mirror properties (Rizzolatti, Fogassi, & Gallese, 2001).

Brain imaging studies have also shown indirect evidence for mirror neuron activity (Decety et al., 1997; Grèzes, Costes, & Decety, 1998). Unfortunately, participants observed only hand or arm actions. The involvement of just these motor system areas during action observation is not synonymous with the possession of mirror properties by these areas (Rizzolatti, Craighero, & Fadiga, 2002; Rizzolatti, Fogassi, & Gallese, 2001).

Direct Evidence for the Mirror Neuron System

There are an increasing number of studies providing direct evidence for the existence of an observation–execution matching system in humans. Fadiga and colleagues (1995) found that the muscular response pattern generated by a transcranial magnetic stimulus (TMS) during an observation sequence was the same as that recorded while the participants actually executed the observed action. Cochin and colleagues (1999), Hari and colleagues (1998), Iacoboni and colleagues (1999), and Nishitani and Hari (2000) have confirmed the findings of Fadiga and coworkers using a variety of brain analysis techniques (EEG, TMS, and fMRI). In these studies, participants were directly assessed as they performed hand movements in an observation condition and an action condition.

Weaknesses and Limitations in the Literature

With the exception of the work conducted by Iacoboni and colleagues (1999), the studies discussed have involved object-oriented actions and have used motor acts limited to the actions of reaching, grasping, and eating. The participants in these studies have been nonhuman primates (i.e., the macaque monkey) or healthy volunteers with no previous history of neurological or visual disorders. The analysis techniques used in most studies have been single-cell recordings for monkeys and fMRI or PET for humans. While these techniques show excellent spatial resolution, they also provide relatively poor temporal information (Pfurtscheller & Lopes da Silva, 1999; Servos, 2000), which is a significant concern for fast sport behavior.

These issues raise several concerns regarding the ability of the mirror neuron system to be responsive to types of movement other than those from the hand, foot, and mouth. For example, to what extent is the system reactive to whole-body movements or actions performed by oneself in contrast to those of others? Research from therapeutic settings and sport psychology (see Dowrick, 1999; McCullagh & Weiss, 2001, for reviews) showed that watching oneself was preferred to watching someone else (e.g., Knoblich & Flach, 2001; Starek & McCullagh, 1999). However, whether this translates to more functionally equivalent mirror neuron activity remains to be tested and would have important implications for learning and teaching in sport psychology. Since the extent of task complexity in the work reviewed here has been relatively small (i.e., reaching, grasping, and eating), the activity of the mirror system during observation of more complex sport behavior would provide a valuable addition to the scientific knowledge in this area.

Directions for Future Investigation

To assess the aspects of mirror neuron activity effectively in sport settings, a technique is required that allows effective temporal resolution of the brain activity. EEG addresses this methodological concern and allows for analysis during preparation and execution of movement and recovery from the same movement (Stancak et al., 2000). It has also been shown to be effective in the observation of an action (e.g., Cochin et al., 1999). The technique will also allow for analysis of neuronal synchronization and desynchronization in functionally relevant brain areas. This being the case, it is likely that different neuronal activity should be observed in experts in motor functions compared to novices. Again, this postulate remains to be tested.

It seems that functional equivalence (meaning in this case the extent to which *observation* correlates share neural mechanisms with the physical task) may not be as clear as has been reported. Decety and his coworkers (1997) showed that during action observation, different patterns of brain activity were elicited. The varying patterns were dependent upon the nature of the required executive processing (modified by the instructions given during the observation) and on the nature of the extrinsic properties of the action (whether they were meaningless or meaningful). The observation of meaningful, familiar actions involved the left hemisphere and, more specifically, the areas that coincide with the ventral visual pathway. In contrast, the observation of meaningless, unfamiliar actions engaged the right hemisphere and the areas associated with the dorsal visual pathway (Jeannerod, 1999). Observation of an action with the aim of a later imitation involved the SMA, the ventral premotor cortex, and the dorsolateral prefrontal cortex. The observation of an action with the aim of a later recognition activated the temporal lobe and specifically the parahippocampal gyrus (Decety et al., 1997). It seems clear that observational functional equivalence, and hence motor representation access, can be significantly influenced by task requirements. This equivalence remains to be tested in a sporting context.

Conclusions

An increasing body of literature supports a central, peripheral, and behavioral functional equivalence between action and imagery and between action and observation. This chapter has reviewed some of the research that makes a strong case for sport psychologists to adopt a more neuroscientific approach to their research and practice and to use the psychophysiological data to inform their use of imagery and other interventions.

References

Babiloni, C., Babiloni, F., Carducci, F., Cincotti, F., Cocozza, G., Del Percio, C., Moretti, D.V., & Maria Rossini, P. (2002). Human cortical electroencephalography (EEG) rhythms during the observation of simple aimless movements: A high resolution EEG study. *Neuroimage, 17,* 559-572.

Beisteiner, R., Höllinger, P., Lindinger, G., Lang, W., & Berthoz, A. (1995). Mental representations of movements. Brain potentials associated with imagination of hand movements. *Electroencephalography and Clinical Neurophysiology, 96,* 183-193.

Berthoz, A. (1996). The role of inhibition in the hierarchical gating of executed and imagined movements. *Cognitive Brain Research, 3,* 101-113.

Bonnet, M., Decety, J., Jeannerod, M., & Requin, J. (1997). Mental stimulation of an action modulates the excitability of spinal reflex pathways in man. *Brain Research and Cognitive Brain Research, 5,* 221-228.

Callow, N., & Hardy, L. (2004). The relationship between the use of kinaesthetic imagery and different visual imagery perspectives. *Journal of Sport Sciences, 22,* 167-177.

Castiello, U., Lusher, D., Mari, M., Edwards, M.G., & Humphreys, G.W. (2002). Observing a human robotic hand grasping an object: Differential motor priming effects. In W. Prinz & B. Hommel (Eds.), *Attention and performance XIX* (pp. 314-334). Cambridge, MA: MIT Press.

Clark, S., Tremblay, F., & Ste-Marie, D. (2003). Differential modulation of corticospinal excitability during observation, mental imagery and imitation of hand actions. *Neuropsychologica, 42,* 105-112.

Cochin, S., Bathelemy, C., Lejeune, B., Roux, S., & Martineau, J. (1998). Perception of motion and qEEG activity in human adults. *Electroencephalography and Clinical Neurophysiology, 107,* 287-295.

Cochin, S., Bathelemy, C., Roux, S., & Martineau, J. (1999). Observation and execution of movement: Similarities demonstrated by quantified electroencephalography. *European Journal of Neurosciences, 11,* 1839-1842.

Collins, D.J., Smith, D., & Hale, B.D. (1998). Imagery perspectives and karate performance. *Journal of Sport Sciences, 16*(1), 103-104.

Cuthbert, B.N., Vrana, S.R., & Bradley, M.M. (1991). Imagery: Function and physiology. In *Advances in psychophysiology, 4* (pp. 1-42). New York: Jessica Kingsley.

Davids, K. (1997). Do psychological strategies for performance enhancement actually work? In T. Reilly & M. Orme (Eds.), *The clinical pharmacology of sport and exercise.* Amsterdam: Elsevier Science B.V.

Decety, J. (1996). The neurological basis of motor imagery. *Behavioral Brain Research, 77,* 45-52.

Decety, J., & Grèzes, J. (1999). Neural mechanisms subserving the perception of human actions. *Trends in Cognitive Sciences, 3,* 172-178.

Decety, J., Grèzes, J., Costes, N., Perani, D., Jeannerod, M., Procyk, E., Grassi, F., & Fazio, F. (1997). Brain activity during observation of actions: Influence of action content and subject's strategy. *Brain, 120,* 1763-1777.

Decety, J., Jeannerod, M., Germain, M., & Pastène, J. (1991). Vegetative response during imagined movement is proportional to mental effort. *Behavioral Brain Research, 42,* 1-5.

Decety, J., Jeannerod, M., & Prablanc, C. (1989). The timing of mentally represented actions. *Behavioral Brain Research, 34,* 35-42.

Decety, J., Sjöholm, H., Ryding, E., Stenberg, G., & Ingvar, D. (1990). The cerebellum participates in mental activity: Tomographic measurements of regional cerebral blood flow. *Brain Research, 535,* 313-317.

Decety, J., & Sommerville, J.A. (2003). Shared representations between self and other: A social cognitive neuroscience view. *Trends in Cognitive Sciences, 7,* 527-533.

Deeke, L. (1996). Planning, preparation, execution, and imagery of volitional action. *Cognitive Brain Research, 3,* 59-64.

Dowrick, P.W. (1999). A review of self-modeling and related interventions. *Applied and Preventive Psychology, 8,* 23-39.

Fadiga, L., Fogassi, L., Pavesi, G., & Rizzolatti, G. (1995). Motor facilitation during action observation: A magnetic stimulation study. *Journal of Neurophysiology, 73,* 2608-2611.

Farah, M.J. (2000a). *The cognitive neuroscience of vision.* Malden, MA: Blackwell.

Farah, M.J. (2000b). The neural bases of mental imagery. In M.S. Gazzaniga (Ed.), *The new cognitive neurosciences* (2nd ed.). Cambridge, MA: MIT Press.

Farrer, C., & Frith, C.D. (2002). Experiencing oneself vs another person as being the cause of an action: The neural correlates of the experience of agency. *Neuroimage, 15,* 596-603.

Fox, P.T., Pardo, J.V., Peterson, S.E., & Raichle, M.E. (1987). Supplementary motor and premotor responses to actual and imagined hand movements with positron emission tomography. *Society for Neuroscience Abstracts, 13,* 1433.

Gallese, V., Fadiga, L., Fogassi, L., & Rizzolatti, G. (1996). Action recognition in the premotor cortex. *Brain, 119,* 593-609.

Gastaut, H.J., & Bert, J. (1954). EEG changes during cinematographic presentation. *Electroencephalography and Clinical Neurophysiology, 6,* 433-444.

Goginsky, A.M., & Collins, D. (1996). Research design and mental practice. *Journal of Sports Sciences, 14,* 381-392.

Grèzes, J., Costes, N., & Decety, J. (1998). Top-down effect of strategy on the perception of human biological motion: A PET investigation. *Cognitive Neuropsychology, 15,* 553-582.

Grèzes, J., & Decety, J. (2001). Functional anatomy of execution, mental simulation, observation, and verb generation of actions: A meta-analysis. *Human Brain Mapping, 12,* 1-19.

Hale, B.D. (1982). The effects of internal and external imagery on muscular and ocular concomitants. *Journal of Sport Psychology, 4,* 379-387.

Hall, C.R., Rogers, W.M., & Barr, K.A. (1990). The use of imagery by athletes in selected sports. *Sport Psychologist, 4,* 1-10.

Hardy, L., & Callow, N. (1999). Efficacy of external and internal visual imagery perspectives for the enhancement of performance on tasks in which form is important. *Journal of Sport and Exercise Psychology, 21*(2), 95-112.

Hari, R., Forss, N., Avikainen, S., Kirveskari, E., Salenius, S., & Rizzolatti, G. (1998). Activation of human primary motor cortex during action observation: A neuromagnetic study. *Proceedings of the National Academy of Sciences, 95,* 15061-15065.

Hashimoto, R., & Rothwell, J.C. (1999). Dynamic changes in corticospinal excitability during motor imagery. *Experimental Brain Research, 125,* 75-81.

Hecker, J.E., & Kaczor, L.M. (1988). Application of imagery theory to sport psychology: Some preliminary findings. *Journal of Sport and Exercise Psychology, 10,* 363-373.

Holmes, P.S., & Collins, D.J. (2001). The PETTLEP approach to motor imagery: A functional equivalence model for sport psychologists. *Journal of Applied Sport Psychology, 13*(1), 60-83.

Holmes, P.S., & Collins, D.J. (2002). The problem of motor imagery: A functional equivalence solution. In I. Cockerill (Ed.), *Solutions in sport psychology* (pp. 120-140). London: Thomson Learning.

Holmes, P.S., & Calmels, C. (in press). Electroencephalographic functional equivalence during observation of action. *Journal of Sports Sciences.*

Iacoboni, M., Woods, R.P., Brass, M., Bekkering, H., & Mazziotta, J.C. (1999). Cortical mechanisms of human imitation. *Science, 286,* 2526-2528.

Jackson, P.L., Lafleur, M.L., Malouin, F., Richards, C.L., & Doyon, J. (2003). Functional cerebral reorganization following motor sequence learning through mental practice with motor imagery. *Neuroimage, 20,* 1171-1180.

Jeannerod, M. (1997). *The cognitive neuroscience of action.* Oxford, UK: Blackwell.

Jeannerod, M. (1999). The 25th Bartlett lecture. To act or not to act: Perspectives on the representation of actions. *Quarterly Journal of Experimental Psychology, 52A,* 1-29.

Jeannerod, M., & Decety, J. (1995). Mental motor imagery: A window into the representational stages of action. *Current Opinion in Neurobiology, 5,* 727-732.

Jeannerod, M., & Frak, V. (1999). Mental imaging of motor activity in humans. *Current Opinion in Neurobiology, 9,* 735-739.

Keil, D., Holmes, P., Bennett, S., Davids, K., & Smith, N. (2000). Theory and practice in sport psychology and motor behaviour needs to be constrained by integrative modelling of brain and behaviour. *Journal of Sports Sciences, 18,* 433-443.

Klatzky, R.L. (1994). On the relation between motor imagery and visual imagery. *Behavioural and Brain Sciences, 17*(2), 212-213.

Klatzky, R., Lederman, S.J., & Matula, D.E. (1991). Imagined haptic exploration in judgements of object properties. *Journal of Experimental Psychology: Learning, Memory and Cognition, 17,* 314-322.

Knoblich, G., & Flach, R. (2001). Predicting the effects of actions: Interactions of perception and action. *Psychological Science, 12,* 467-472.

Kolb, B., & Whishaw, I.Q. (1998). Brain plasticity and behaviour. *Annual Reviews in Psychology, 49,* 43-64.

Kosslyn, S. (1994). *Image and brain: The resolution of the imagery debate.* Cambridge, MA: MIT Press.

Kosslyn, S.M., Alpert, N.M., & Thompson, W.L. (1993). Visual mental imagery and visual perception: PET studies. In *Functional MRI of the brain: A workshop presented by the Society of Magnetic Resonance in Medicine and the Society for Magnetic Resonance Imaging* (pp. 183-190). Arlington, VA.: Society of Magnetic Resonance in Medicine.

Kosslyn, S.M., Ganis, G., & Thompson, W.L. (2001). Neural foundations of imagery. *Nature Reviews: Neuroscience, 2,* 635-642.

Kourtzi, Z., & Kanwisher, N. (2000). Activation in human MT/MST for static images with implied motion. *Journal of Cognitive Neuroscience, 12,* 48-55.

Landers, D.M. (1989). *New York Times,* September 11, p. 19.

Lang, P.J. (1977). Imagery in therapy: An information processing analysis of fear. *Behavior Therapy, 8,* 862-886.

Lang, P.J. (1979). A bio-informational theory of emotional imagery. *Psychophysiology, 17,* 495-512.

Lang, P.J. (1985). Cognition in emotion: Concept and action. In C. Izard, J. Kagan, & R. Zajonc (Eds.), *Emotion, cognitions and behavior* (pp. 192-225). New York: Cambridge University Press.

Loze, G.M., Collins, D.J., & Shaw, J.C. (1999). EEG alpha rhythm, intention and oculomotor control. *International Journal of Psychophysiology, 33,* 163-167.

McCullagh, P., & Weiss, M.R. (2001). Modeling: Considerations for motor skill performance and psychological responses. In R.N. Singer, H.A. Hausenblas, & C.M.

Janelle (Eds.), *Handbook of research on sport psychology* (pp. 205-238). New York: Wiley.

Moore, E. (2004). Electromyographic functional equivalence during internal and external observation of movement. Unpublished master's thesis, Manchester Metropolitan University, UK.

Murphy, S.M. (1994). Imagery interventions in sport. *Medicine and Science in Sports and Exercise, 26*(4), 486-494.

Naito, E., Kochiyama, T., Kitada, R., Nakamura, M., Yonekura, Y., & Sadato, N. (2002). Internally simulated movement sensations during motor imagery activate cortical motor areas and the cerebellum. *Journal of Neurosciences, 22,* 3683-3691.

Nishitani, N., & Hari, R. (2000). Temporal dynamics of cortical representation for action. *Proceedings of the National Academy of Sciences, 97,* 913-918.

Pascual-Leone, A., Dang, N., Cohen, L.G., Brasil-Neto, J., Cammarota, A., & Hallett, M. (1995). Modulation of motor responses evoked by transcranial magnetic stimulation during the acquisition of new fine motor skills. *Journal of Neurophysiology, 74,* 1037-1045.

Pfurtscheller, G., & Lopes da Silva, F.H. (1999). Event-Related Desynchronization. *Handbook of electroencephalography and clinical neurophysiology,* revised series, vol. 6. Amsterdam: Elsevier.

Rizzolatti, G., Carmada, R., Fogassi, L., Gentilucci, M., Luppino, G., & Matelli, M. (1988). Functional organization of inferior area 6 in the macaque monkey: II. Area F5 and the control of distal movements. *Experimental Brain Research, 71,* 491-507.

Rizzolatti, G., Craighero, L., & Fadiga, L. (2002). The mirror system in humans. In M.I. Stamenov & V. Gallese (Eds.), *Mirror neurons and the evolution of brain and language* (pp. 37-63). Amsterdam: John Benjamins.

Rizzolatti, G., Fadiga, L., Matelli, M., Bettinardi, V., Paulesu, E., Perani, D., & Fazio, F. (1996). Localization of grasp representations in humans by PET: I. Observation versus execution. *Experimental Brain Research, 111,* 246-252.

Rizzolatti, G., Fogassi, L., & Gallese, V. (2001). Neurophysiological mechanisms underlying the understanding and imitation of action. *Nature Reviews: Neuroscience, 2,* 661-670.

Servos, P. (2000). Functional neuroimaging of mental chronometry. *Brain and Cognition, 42,* 72-74.

Smith, D.K., & Holmes, P.S. (2004). The effect of imagery modality on golf putting performance. *Journal of Sport and Exercise Psychology, 26,* 385-395.

Stancak, A., Feige, B., Lucking, C.H., & Kristeva-Feige, R. (2000). Oscillatory cortical activity and movement-related potentials in proximal and distal movements. *Clinical Neurophysiology, 111,* 636-650.

Starek, J., & McCullagh, P. (1999). The effect of self-modeling on the performance of beginning swimmers. *The Sport Psychologist, 13,* 269-287.

Stephan, K.M., Fink, G.R., Passingham, R.E., Silbersweig, D., Ceballos-Baumann, A.O., Frith, C.D., & Frackowiak, R.S.J. (1995). Functional anatomy of the mental representation of upper extremity movements in healthy subjects. *Journal of Neurophysiology, 73,* 373-386.

Vealey, R.S. (1994). Current status and prominent issues in sport psychology interventions. *Medicine and Science in Sports and Exercise, 26*(4), 495-502.

Wang, Y., & Morgan, W.P. (1992). The effect of imagery perspectives on the psychophysiological responses to imagined exercise. *Behavioral Brain Research, 52,* 167-174.

Weeks, R.A., Honda, M., Catalan, M.-J., & Hallett, M. (2001). Comparison of auditory, somatosensory, and visually instructed and internally generated finger movements: A PET study. *Neuroimage, 14,* 219-230.

White, A., & Hardy, L. (1995). Use of different imagery perspectives on the learning and performance of different motor skills. *British Journal of Psychology, 86,* 169-180.

Wuyam, B., Moosavi, S.H., Decety, J., Adams, L., Lansing, R.W., & Guz, A. (1995). Imagination of dynamic exercise produced ventilatory responses which were more apparent in competitive sportsmen. *Journal of Physiology, 482*(3), 713-724.

Yue, G., & Cole, K.J. (1992). Strength increases from the motor program: Comparison of training with maximal voluntary and imagined muscle contractions. *Journal of Neurophysiology, 67,* 1114-1123.

Epilogue: Future Challenges in Understanding Human Behavior

Edmund O. Acevedo, PhD

Panteleimon Ekkekakis, PhD, FACSM

The challenge set forth in this text was to present literature demonstrating the unique and significant contributions that an integrated psychobiological approach makes in the study of physical activity. Implicit in meeting this aim was the purpose of setting the stage for initiating further study. Here we provide a short summary of the breadth of knowledge presented in the text with a focus on directions for future investigations into the psychobiology of physical activity.

It is clear that the behavior of physical activity is under continuous control of the central nervous system. From control of overt movement to the mechanisms responsible for adapting to the metabolic stress of the activity, the central nervous system (CNS) is the primary coordinator of the intricate relationships among all the systems of the body during physical activity. Furthermore, the central autonomic system also affects the emotional context of the overt behavior. Part I introduces the text and provides a brief background to the area of psychobiology of physical activity. In addition, it provides clear evidence in support of the neuroanatomical basis for subjective physical awareness and the effects of physical activity, in particular aerobic fitness training, on the neuroanatomy of the brain and its function. Part II of this text explicitly presents the evidence supporting the beneficial relationship between physical activity and cognition, with a focus on the mechanisms responsible for this adaptation. Part III begins with theoretical explanations for the relationship of physical activity to affect; it progresses with chapters that provide supporting evidence from literature examining neural and neurotransmitter mechanisms that help explain the "pleasure" and "displeasure" of physical activity. The psychobi-

ology of physical activity is integrated within our understanding of psychosomatic health in part IV. From a public health perspective, this section is likely the most intriguing. Pain perception, stress reactivity, and the health implications of the study of psychoneuroimmunology present a plethora of questions—the answers to which may potentially have a great impact on human health. Finally, part V provides examples of systematic investigations that have applied a psychobiological perspective to research on human performance. Several groups of researchers have participated in years of investigation and established an in-depth understanding of the psychobiological nature of human performance, as well as the potential application of this knowledge.

Integrated throughout the text are several themes or emerging trends that will likely direct future investigations into the psychobiology of physical activity. Highlighting these themes and trends provides a basis from which researchers can continue to contribute to the body of knowledge and depth of understanding. The first theme focuses on the impact that new discovery has had on our understanding of human movement. The second theme provides a clear representation of the struggle to propose and develop integrated theory. And the third theme is the continual effort to enhance the scientific rigor of methodologies utilized and the development of more sophisticated conceptual integration.

A central theme, and in part the rationale for the importance of publishing this inaugural text, is the presentation of discoveries that can potentially have great impact on our understanding of how and why humans move. The work summarized in chapters 2 and 3 by Craig and Williamson, respectively, identifying specific areas of the CNS and brain that are responsible for voluntary movement, is a clear demonstration of relatively recent discovery and presents compelling discussion for further inquiry. Exciting discovery is further exemplified by the mechanism-driven investigation summarized in the psychoneuroendocrine approach discussed by Meeusen (chapter 9) and Hand and colleagues (chapter 13), and the examination of neurogenesis and learning presented by van Praag (chapter 5). Discovery is also blossoming from efforts to answer questions that have been lingering in the literature for some time. Underscoring these discoveries are the chapters by Sothmann (chapter 10), addressing stress reactivity; the chapter by Hong and Mills (chapter 12), addressing psychoneuroimmunology; and the chapter by Kramer and Hillman (chapter 4), addressing cognitive adaptations to physical activity.

The second theme, referring to the integration of theory to study the psychobiology of physical activity, has led to systematic inquiry and substantive knowledge development. Cabanac in chapter 6 provides an integrated theory for explaining affective responses to physical activity. Similarly, Petruzzello and colleagues (chapter 8) utilize the framework proposed by Davidson (1993) to predict and explain the meaning of electroencephalographic (EEG) asymmetry and exercise-induced changes. Whereas Hatfield and colleagues (chapter 15) use a model focused on efficiency to explain EEG activity and movements that require a high level of skill. Furthermore, Boutcher and Hamer (chapter 11) propose an integrated model for addressing stress reactivity; and the chapters authored by Ekkekakis and Acevedo (chapter 7), Cook (chapter 14), Holmes (17), and Collins and McPherson (chapter 16) each focus on theories or models that can guide future investigation.

The third theme represents an ongoing struggle of all science to raise the scientific standard of investigation. In this text that is exemplified by methodological advancements, including electrophysiological techniques, brain imaging techniques, biochemical assays, and microdialysis. However, one could argue that the scientific standard of investigation has also been elevated by conceptual refinement of research approaches and methodologies. Conceptual advances are presented, for example, by Boutcher in his examination of moderating variables and in the chapter by Kramer and Hillman in their proposal of a selective benefit hypothesis.

Although this text offers a substantial amount of content in support of the psychobiological nature of physical activity, it is even more evident that this text sets the stage for further investigation with the likelihood of developing a greater understanding of human behavior in the context of physical activity and mental and physical health. The authors of the chapters in the text have provided an excellent basis for future investigation.

Theory-driven, mechanistic investigation that utilizes multiple appropriate measures while controlling for potential confounding effects is considered common protocol for scientific investigation. However, the psychobiology of physical activity presents several distinct characteristics for consideration that are highlighted in the recommendations for future research offered by the authors in this text.

In chapter 8, Petruzzello and colleagues call for an enhancement in our understanding of physical activity behavior beyond subjective experience and physiological response, independently. Clearly this calls for theory-driven investigation, preferably addressing and contributing to existing theory, into mechanisms that explain the psychobiological nature of physical activity. An intuitive point of entry into this area of investigation is the CNS, although this system maintains substantial challenges. For example, the research conducted with animals documenting changes in the CNS may not parallel the changes that occur in humans. In addition, Hand, Phillips, and Wilson in chapter 13 specify differences between animal species that must be considered; and, in work with animals, workload is often not quantified. The less invasive techniques used with humans (EEG, PET, SPECT, and fMRI) also have limitations, including the indirect assessment of neuronal activity that implies changes in local metabolism, blood flow, and blood oxygenation with no assessment of the biochemical basis for a response, along with the technological challenges intrinsic to the cumbersome equipment and the limited ability to gather data during and in response to exercise. Thus, the investigator is directed toward utilizing the most current, reliable, and valid techniques possible and interpreting data from within the boundaries of these limitations. In addition, future investigation into the CNS and physical activity should consider combining methodologies to support the examination of a proposed mechanism. Hatfield and colleagues (chapter 15) further propose that investigation of central neural processing efficiency and the interactions between neural structures, in particular in response to a perturbation (i.e., stress), may shed light on the adaptive mechanisms that enhance neural function. Finally, those examining the CNS adaptations would be remiss if they did not address the reciprocal impact of other biological systems.

The challenges inherent in examining human psychobiological adaptations are often exacerbated within the physical activity paradigm. This is highlighted in the chapter by Ekkekakis and Acevedo (chapter 7), which provides evidence supporting the notion that the psychobiological affective response to exercise intensity seems to interact specifically with metabolic demands (the shift to anaerobiosis). Incidentally, stress hormones including the catecholamines (end products of the sympathoadrenal axis) and cortisol (an end product of the hypothalamic adrenocortical axis) respond in a nonlinear manner to exercise intensity and duration (indicating a threshold response). These psychobiological markers of stress beckon in-depth investigation. A provocative arena that seems to have been ignored is the possibility of perceptual or cognitive thresholds that may have psychobiological implications. Furthermore, physiological stressors such as dehydration, hypoglycemia, heat, and cold are fertile areas for investigation. A noteworthy consideration in this area of research that facilitates our understanding of psychobiological responses is to identify exercise and recovery response relative to resting baseline measures.

Sothmann (chapter 10) states that the idiosyncratic adaptations of specific populations are of further interest when one is identifying potential cardiovascular health benefits of exercise. For example, old, young, male, female, fit, unfit, trained, and untrained—all are distinctions that may affect psychobiological adaptations. In addition, Boutcher and Hamer (chapter 11) provide very specific considerations for the future examination of cardiovascular reactivity. These include a call for investigation of individuals who display exaggerated reactivity (i.e., hot reactors, hypertensive individuals, and coronary artery disease-prone individuals) with a focus on the somewhat neglected area of vascular reactivity. This area of investigation would also benefit from a systematic examination of the mechanisms accounting for the stress reactivity adaptations in response to chronic versus acute exercise. Interestingly, the results from the stress reactivity literature might

become more consistent should examination of perceived stressor controllability and stressor novelty be extended into stress reactivity experimental paradigms.

The authors in the section on psychosomatic health present several intriguing issues for further investigation. Included are

1. the interesting ramifications of the cross-stressor adaptation and the mechanisms that might explain this beneficial adaptation;
2. the cyclical psychobiological pattern of pain perception and muscular contraction;
3. the role of the CNS in the stress response; and
4. the interactions among social cognition, neural activation, and the immune system during and in response to physical activity.

Hand and colleagues (chapter 13) state that "in contrast to other stressors, exercise can provide a therapeutic modality for many mental and physical ailments," thus providing a tremendously interesting and important area for investigation. The level of critical importance has been supported with documentation by the World Health Organization (2003) of 1.9 million deaths and 19 million disability-adjusted life-year losses attributed annually to physical inactivity. Furthermore, according to the United States Department of Health and Human Services (2000), despite public health campaigns the proportion of the population reporting physical activity remains dismal. The argument proposed, and supported by the evidence presented in this text, is that a psychobiological approach to understanding the behavior of physical activity can enhance our understanding of the health benefits associated with physical activity, exercise motivation, and human performance.

The 1990s congressional declaration of the "Decade of the Brain" preceded the publication of most of the literature cited in this text. It is clear that much attention has been directed to the examination of the function of the brain. However, as Meeusen has stated (chapter 9), "When we examine the literature and we determine that results are totally contradictory or inconsistent, it is likely due to the fact that we are only at the beginning of the 'age of the brain.'" As inquiry continues, an optimal view of the generous contributions of the authors of this text is that the content presented here will serve as fodder for further thought and inquiry, providing greater understanding of the psychobiological nature of physical activity.

References

Davidson, R.J. (1993). Parsing affective space: Perspectives from neuropsychology and psychophysiology. *Neuropsychology, 7,* 464-475.

United States Department of Health and Human Services. (2000). *Healthy people 2010* (2nd ed., vol. 2). Washington, DC: U.S. Government Printing Office.

World Health Organization. (2003). *Annual global move for health initiative: A concept paper.* Geneva: Author.

Index

Note: Page numbers followed by an italicized *f* or *t* denote a figure or table.

About the Editors

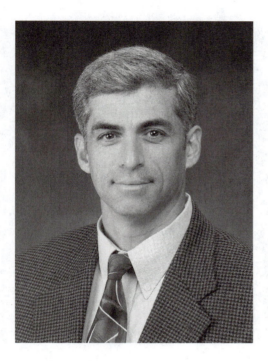

Edmund O. Acevedo, PhD, is an associate professor in the Department of Health, Exercise Science, and Recreation Management at the University of Mississippi and serves as director of the Applied Physiology Laboratory. For 20 years he has conducted research in the area of psychobiology of physical activity with a focus on the psychobiology of stress during physical activity. He has published in numerous journals and books and has made scientific presentations throughout the world.

Dr. Acevedo is a fellow of the American College of Sports Medicine and a certified exercise specialist. He has served as a reviewer for nine different journals in exercise and sport psychology, psychobiology, and exercise physiology. He is a member of the American Physiological Society, American Psychological Association, North American Society for the Psychology of Sport and Physical Activity, and Sigma Xi, the Scientific Research Society. In addition, he is a certified consultant of the Association for the Advancement of Applied Sport Psychology and has consulted with athletes and coaches at the professional, collegiate, and youth sport levels.

Panteleimon Ekkekakis, PhD, is an assistant professor of exercise and sport psychology at the Department of Health and Human Performance at Iowa State University. His research focuses on the affective responses that accompany acute exercise of different intensities, their underlying psychobiological mechanisms, and their implications for exercise adherence over the long haul. His publications span the areas of theoretical and affective psychology, psychometrics, psychophysiology, exercise science, preventive and behavioral medicine, and obesity.

Dr. Ekkekakis is a regular reviewer for many scientific journals, is a psychology section editor for *Research Quarterly for Exercise and Sport*, and serves on the editorial board of *Psychology of Sport and Exercise*. He is a fellow of the American College of Sports Medicine and a member of the North American Society for the Psychology of Sport and Physical Activity.